INTERNATIONAL YEARBOOK BRANDS & COMMUNICATION DESIGN 2019/2020

[Edited by PETER ZEC]

VOL 2

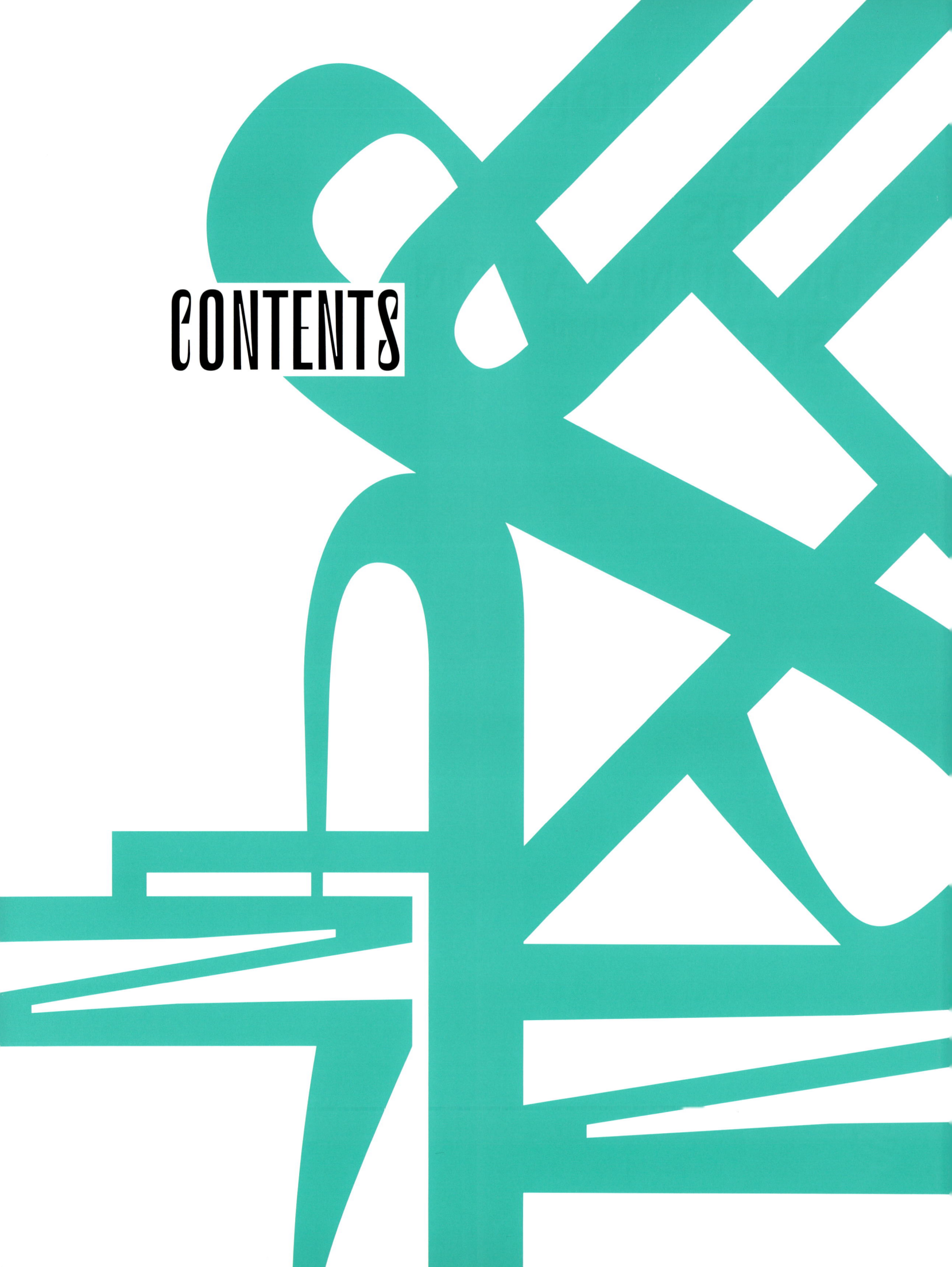
CONTENTS

004–065	**Publishing & Print Media**
066–087	**Posters**
088–105	**Typography**
106–129	**Illustrations**
130–137	**Sound Design**
138–167	**Film & Animation**
168–211	**Online**
212–243	**Apps**
244–363	**Interface & User Experience Design**
364–409	**Spatial Communication**
410–507	**Red Dot: Junior Award Vol. 2**
508–575	**Designer Profiles Vol. 2**
576–601	**Jury**
602–613	**Index**
614–619	**Red Dot – World of Design**
620	**Imprint**

Find more in Volume 1
Red Dot: Agency of the Year – Brands – Brand Design & Identity
Corporate Design & Identity – Annual Reports – Advertising
Packaging Design – Fair Stands – Retail Design
Red Dot: Junior Award Vol. 1 – Designer Profiles Vol. 1

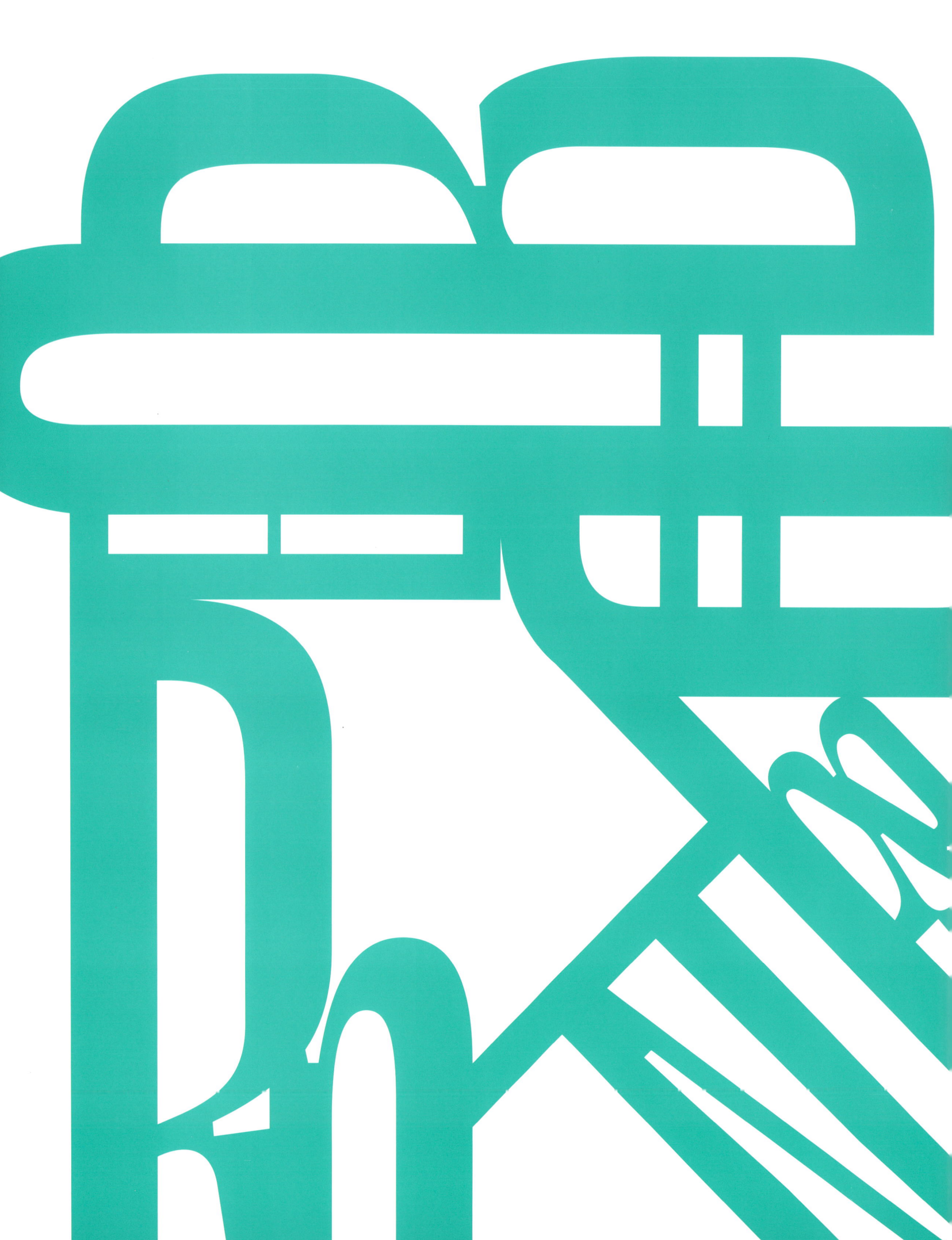

PUBLISHING & PRINT MEDIA

Red Dot: Grand Prix

AGI New Members 2007–2017

[Book]

The nearly 700-page book includes the work of more than 200 new members accepted by the Alliance Graphique Internationale (AGI) between 2007 and 2017. Each designer is presented on three pages with profile, selected works and a short interview covering current design-related issues, the developments and challenges in graphic design and the role and future of print media. Upholding the motto "Enjoy Design!", this book is the third of a series to be designed by renowned graphic designer Jianping He. The distinctive black-and-white cover already reveals an outstanding 13,880 paper strips into which the upper fifth of all book pages have been cut into. Upon opening the book, these strips make the pages fan out manifoldly – to not only create a highly playful and lively element, but also demonstrate new possibilities in book design. When browsing through the pages, something new happens constantly, turning the book into a worthy introduction of the new members.

Statement by the jury
The catalogue of the new AGI members thrills readers at first sight. Only for a split second does it irritate that the upper part of every page has been cut into strips, quickly giving way to fascination. Touching and stroking across the soft end of the pages actually is a truly enjoyable, sensual pleasure. In addition, the careful use of typography and implementation of various reading levels turn the book into an art object, but one that also excellently fulfils its function as a compendium.

reddot winner 2019
grand prix

Client
Alliance Graphique Internationale,
Baden, Switzerland

Design
hesign International GmbH,
Berlin, Germany

Concept/Book Design
Jianping He

Image Editing
Mengjiin Hsieh

Managing Editor
Yvonne Reuther

Coordination
Cathy Cai

Printing/Bookbinding
Shanghai Artron Graphic Art Co., Ltd.,
Shanghai, China

→ Designer profile on page 529
→ Clip online

Red Dot: Best of the Best

OMNE/WORK 2016–2018
[Catalogue]

The catalogue showcases the results of the first workshop for artists in residence organised by the Osservatorio Mobile Nord Est (OMNE). It presents ten projects and ten visions located between memory and contemporaneity, analysing the complexity of the landscape of the north-east of Italy through a common theme of "work". The work is understood as the foundation of the social pact that keeps a community united on the one hand, and as an element that configures a landscape to give it its identity on the other. Inspired by the theme of investigation, the catalogue is reminiscent of a typical archival collector at first glance, transforming that structure into a new interpretation though. The inside features different page formats and types of paper in order to visualise the passage from critical texts and contributions by teachers to the projects of internationally renowned artists, presenting them in the classic form of rubricated files.

Statement by the jury
This publication fascinates with its unusual formal approach of presenting the works of the ten artists. It is laid out like a common archival collector with a register for easy reader guidance. However, it goes far beyond that concept in that it plays with different paper formats in order to live up to the artistic visions, combining typography and material into a unity that is highly convincing in both content and form.

Client
Città di Castelfranco Veneto, Italy

Design
Otium S.r.l., Castelfranco Veneto, Italy

Editorial Design
Damiano Fraccaro

→ Designer profile on page 557

Red Dot: Best of the Best

memorabilia
[Book]

The book "memorabilia" aims at attracting reader attention to the topic of memory and the processes of remembering by unusually presenting works of Lithuanian artists. It is like a play with the human mind. At first, only the texts can be fully seen and read, while the works of art featuring on the other side of the pages remain hardly perceptible as they are only hints. This effect of transparency has been created by using reverse printing in a low percentage of black on the hidden inner pages. However, these double pages can be "unlocked" by cutting them. Thus, readers are invited to figuratively put an effort into remembering and perceiving the known Lithuanian artworks in all their colours. The "Alergia Remix" font was chosen for the meaning of the name ("alergia" means allergy in translation) and its uncommon letter shapes. Featuring a scratch layer, the cover of the book also aims at piquing curiosity. What lies hidden behind the grey cover layer is left for readers to experience by themselves and thus create a memory for the future.

Statement by the jury
What is exciting about the book "memorabilia" is how it combines the topic of memory with the artworks presented in it. Readers can check their memories of the artworks and then cut the pages open to see them in all their beauty. This play with hidden artworks and the memories thereof and, above all, the sophisticated technical production of the closed pages are highly convincing.

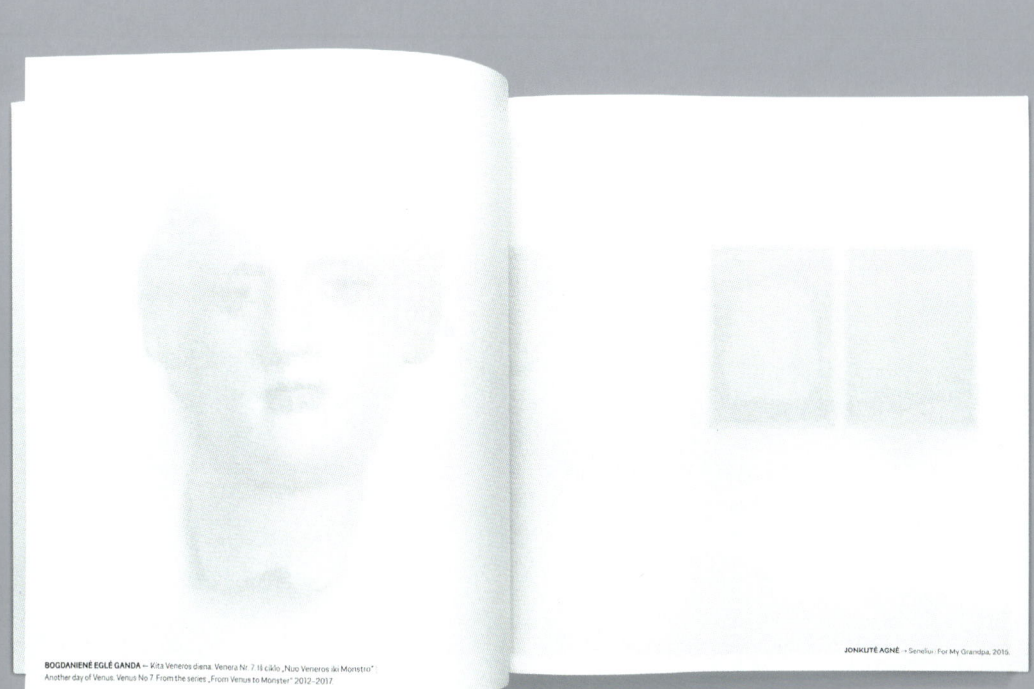

Client
Lithuanian Artists' Association,
Vilnius, Lithuania

Design
Agnė Dautartaitė-Krutulė,
Vilnius, Lithuania

Printing
Kopa, Kaunas, Lithuania

→ Designer profile on page 520
→ Clip online

Red Dot: Best of the Best

Made in Fukushima
[Book]

"Made in Fukushima" is a book made out of rice straw grown on decontaminated fields in Fukushima. The rice straw was harvested, dried, cleaned, cut and crafted into paper. The intention of the book is to inform about the long-term project of soil decontamination to support local farmers. Alongside giving background information on the disaster, the region and the significance of rice, the book is all about the farmers and their stories. Lively narratives interact with factual information and photographs, with high attention paid to the presentation of the complex data: they follow the basic pattern of a square grid that stays the same on all pages and presents the data points in circles of different sizes – visualising the sheer incomprehensible flood of data in an easy and immediately understandable manner. From the cover and the infographics to the Japanese binding technique, this lavishly produced book projects a coherent aesthetic that combines traditional Japanese with modern design.

Statement by the jury
The design of "Made in Fukushima" achieves an outstanding performance. Diverse content contributions, photographs and the idea of creating infographics that make multilayered data visually transparent at a glance, all add up to an exceptionally beautiful and thoughtfully conceived book project. Particularly convincing in terms of its haptic properties is the impressive production made of locally grown rice straw.

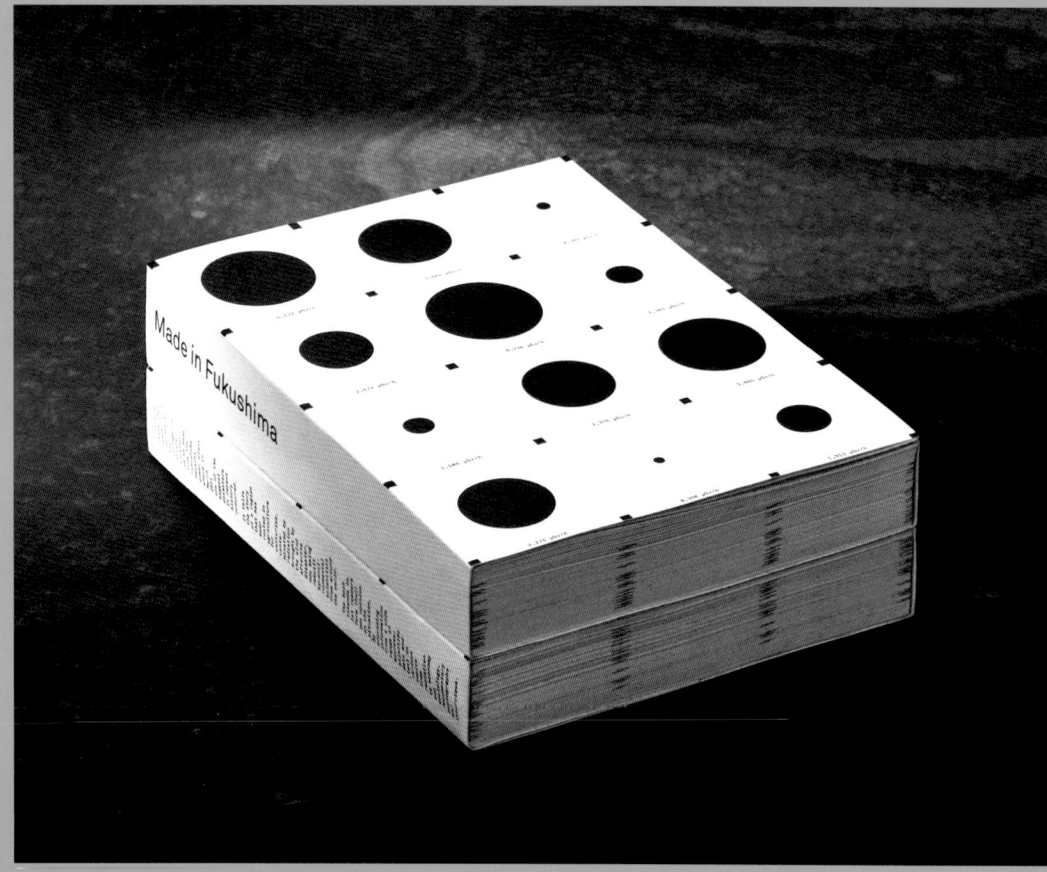

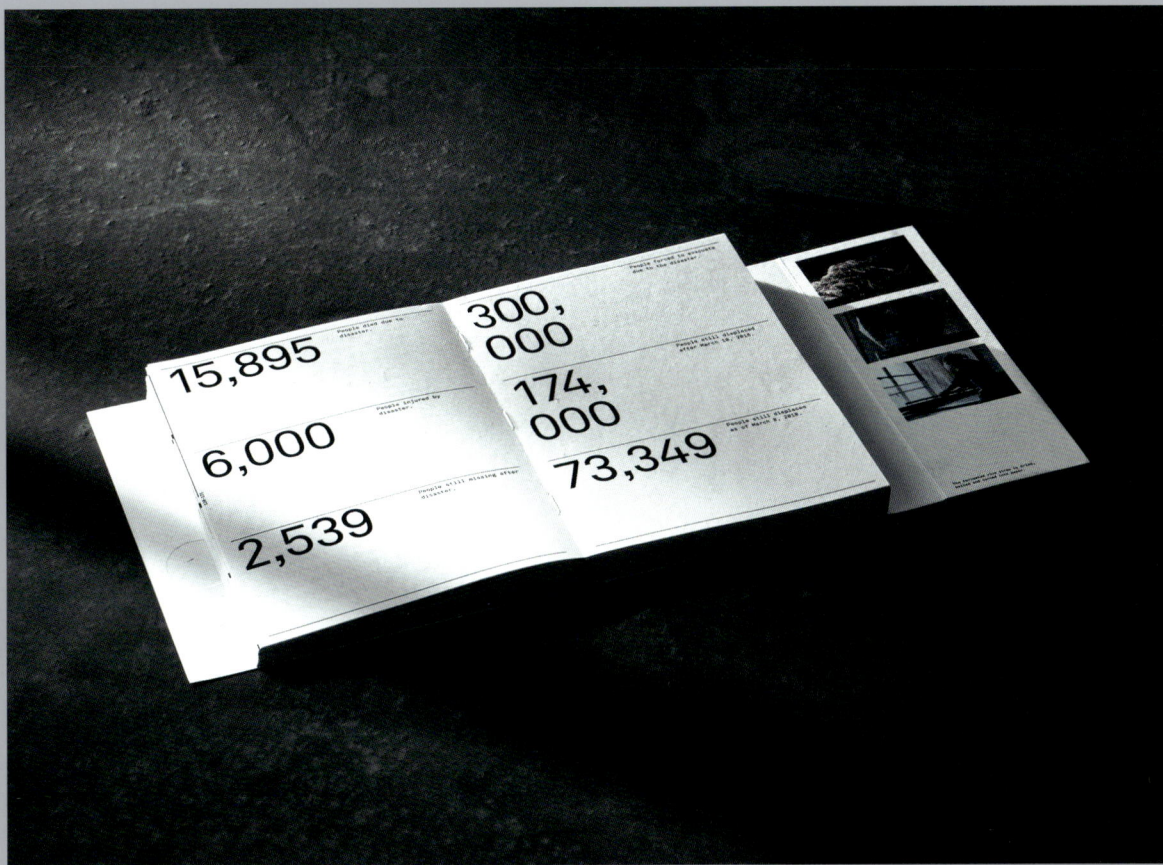
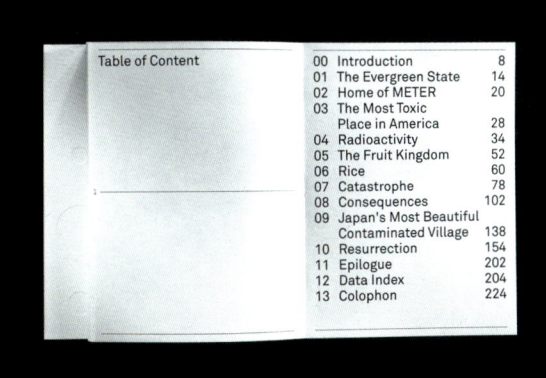

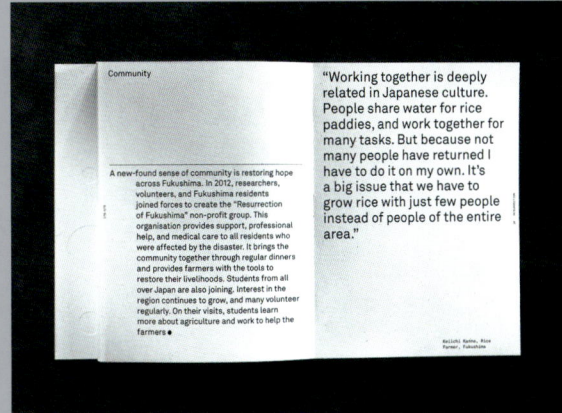

Client
METER Group Inc., Pullman,
Washington, USA

Design
SERVICEPLAN GERMANY,
Munich, Germany

Global Chief Creative Officer
Alexander Schill, Serviceplan Group

Creative Direction
Franz Röppischer, Lorenz Langgartner,
Serviceplan Innovation

Creative Production
Saurabh Kakade, Serviceplan Innovation

Art Direction
Eduardo Alvarez,
Serviceplan Innovation

Copywriting
Carolina Soto, Serviceplan Innovation

Photography
Nick Frank

Design Direction
Gabriela Baka, Moby Digg GmbH

Information Design
Sebastian Haiss, Moby Digg GmbH

Managing Director
Maximilian Heitsch, Moby Digg GmbH

→ Designer profile on page 547

Red Dot: Best of the Best

Une histoire de l'orthopédie
[Book]

Based on the history of the Orthopaedic Hospital of western Switzerland, founded in Lausanne in 1876, this book illustrates the advances of orthopaedics as a discipline and technique from the mid 18th century to the present day. By putting into context the situation of orthopaedics in Switzerland and Western countries, the book addresses issues of professional identities, institutional strategies and medical cultures, whose complex history reflects current health issues. The result is a classic and elegantly designed book that comes along in black and white combined with only one colour, a bright orange. The main content is rhythmically interspersed by a generous amount of quotations that flow out independently from the text, juxtaposing the layout in a pleasant manner. In addition to many vivid, mostly historical photos, footnotes are a key element, standing out vertically in the centre of the pages supporting all the content, just like a spine.

Statement by the jury
The design of this book succeeds in presenting the entire history of orthopaedics to the reader in a highly modern and aesthetic way. Almost like in a magazine layout, the different illustrations and the typography have been used in a highly conscious and variegated manner that makes good use of the space. The black colour cut is another refinement that lends the outside of the book an exciting appearance.

Client
CHUV – Lausanne University Hospital, Lausanne, Switzerland

Design
SAM CHUV, Lausanne, Switzerland

Art Direction/Graphic Design
Aris Zenone

Publisher
BHMS, Lausanne, Switzerland

Editorial Work
Mariama Kaba, Versoix, Switzerland

Printing
Genoud Arts Graphiques,
Le Mont-sur-Lausanne, Switzerland

Bookbinding
Bubu, Mönchaltorf, Switzerland

→ Designer profile on page 560

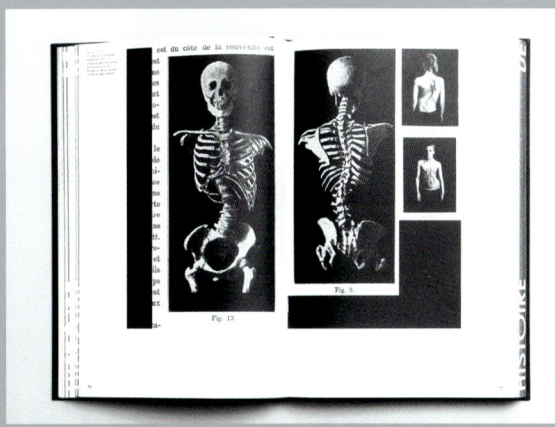

Red Dot: Best of the Best

Megatrend Report M8 – Crossmapping the Future

[Corporate Publishing]

Under the title "Crossmapping the Future", the Megatrend Report M8 deals with the great megatrends of the future such as artificial intelligence, exploring the future potential of South America and analysing its geopolitical, social, economic and technological opportunities and risks. For Bosch, anticipating and linking such trends is the source of innovations, new products and new markets. Focusing on people's relationship to technology and the underlying parameters of ethics and value orientation, this explorative book on the future aims to push boundaries through essays that provide deep insights, compact fact sheets and interviews with innovative thinkers and influencers. Inspired by the famous Golden Record, a phonograph with images and sounds from Earth, which the Voyager space probe has been flying through space for over 40 years now, the differently designed chapters feature a lot of art and inspiring illustrations in black-and-white or colour, making the M8 book an important compendium for the developments of the future.

Statement by the jury
Outstandingly rich with elaborately researched content and a correspondingly complex and sophisticated design – this is how the new Bosch corporate book presents itself. The compendium on artificial intelligence not only reflects the great significance of this topic, it also scores in terms of editorial layout paired with a congenial design embracing a wide variety of typographies and illustrations in each chapter.

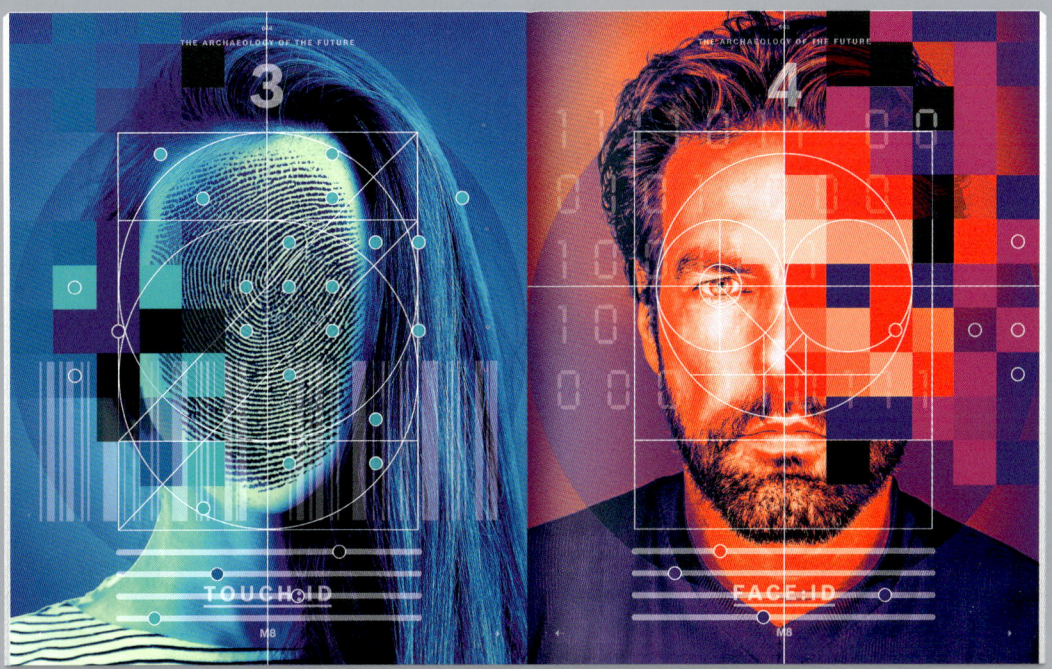

Client
Robert Bosch GmbH,
Gerlingen-Schillerhöhe, Germany

Design
STRICHPUNKT, Stuttgart/Berlin, Germany

Creative Direction
Jochen Theurer

Concept
Katharina Bergmann

Graphic Design
Bianca Bunsas, Leonie Werner

Account Management
Jeannette Kohnle

Project Management
Linda Beiermeister

→ Designer profile on page 565

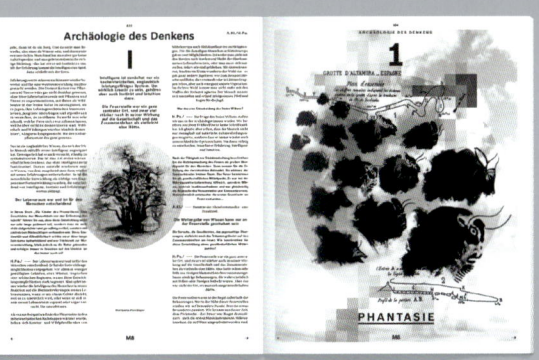

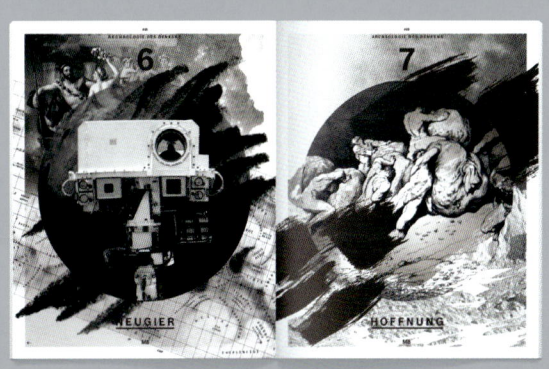

Red Dot: Best of the Best

Bruce B. Magazine – No. 2
[Customer Magazine]

The Bruce B. customer magazine strives to intelligently connect the analogue with the digital world. With a focus on "change", this edition addresses a topic of high interest to companies and institutions, highlighting "the other" from different perspectives. For this purpose, it uses a constantly changing text and image language, fonts that change again and again, as well as a variety of typesetting, photography and illustration styles. Thus, instead of celebrating itself as reflective self-promotion, the magazine with its exquisite open thread binding reflects the goal of the publication to provide food for thought, satisfy the high requirements on both content and design, and provide inspirational impulse for clients through the meaningful combination of print media and augmented or virtual reality. The print edition is complemented by an app featuring a presentation of the agency by its virtual founder, Bruce B., as an augmented reality experience.

Statement by the jury
This magazine fascinates in that it is a self-representation of the agency, but it does so without portraying the agency's portfolio. Instead, it chooses a topic and presents it in a high variety of facets, showcasing a narrative diversity that is also reflected in the design of the magazine itself. Thus, the approach towards and the implementation of typography, as well as the selected illustrations, altogether reflect a great love for detail.

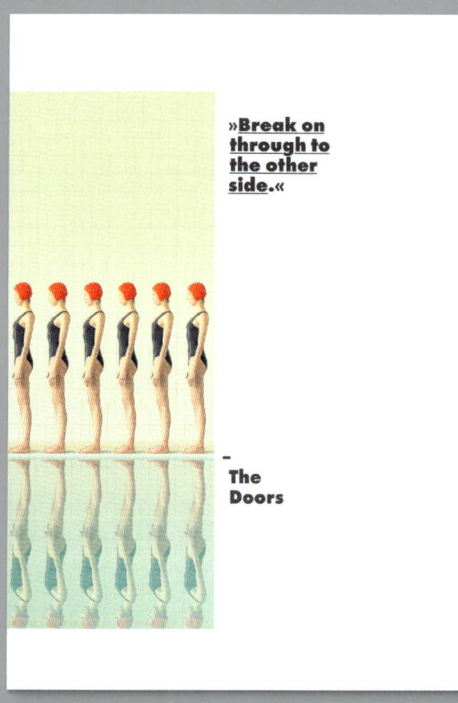

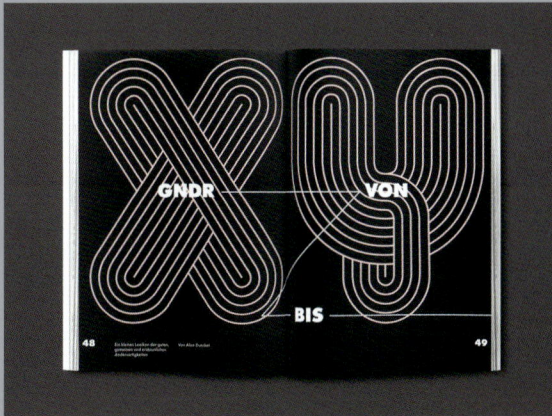

Client
Bruce B. corporate
communication GmbH,
Stuttgart, Germany

Design/Concept
Bruce B. corporate
communication GmbH,
Stuttgart, Germany

→ Designer profile on page 517

Mikhail Larionov
[Exhibition Catalogue]

The work habits of Mikhail Larionov, an avant-garde Russian painter of the early 20th century, were the inspiration for this exhibition catalogue published in two languages. His experiments with different materials, techniques, colours and fonts are reflected in the editorial design. The open spine sewn with red thread, a folder-like cover, inside pages of different sizes and colours, all of this resembles an artist's notebook. The composition on the inside gives an illusion of artistic chaos: superimposed transparent images, raster photographs, placement of illustrations and captions. The typography is reminiscent of typesetting posters and the Russian avant-garde.

Client
Tretyakov Gallery, Moscow, Russia

Design
ABCdesign, Moscow, Russia

Creative Direction/Graphic Design
Dmitry Mordvintsev

Design Team
Polina Laufer, Anastasia Ageeva, Tatiana Borisova

Printing
PNB Print, Silakrogs, Latvia

Emeka Ogboh – Lagos Soundscapes
[Exhibition Catalogue]

This exhibition catalogue is dedicated to Emeka Ogboh, born in 1977 and regarded as a pioneer sound artist from Africa. The book is a compendium of his work entitled "Lagos Soundscapes", which focuses on Lagos, Nigeria's economic and cultural capital. The design of the catalogue offers an interaction, both sensual and acoustic. Accordingly, it is coated with a rough but transparent linen fabric. When readers slide over it with their fingertips, the noise resembles a softly roaring loudspeaker. As an iconic image of Emeka's work, the loudspeaker on the cover references the soundscapes of the artist.

Client
Kerber Verlag, Berlin, Germany

Design
anschlaege.de, Berlin, Germany

Art Direction
Rik Watkinson

Graphic Design
Jens Rudolph

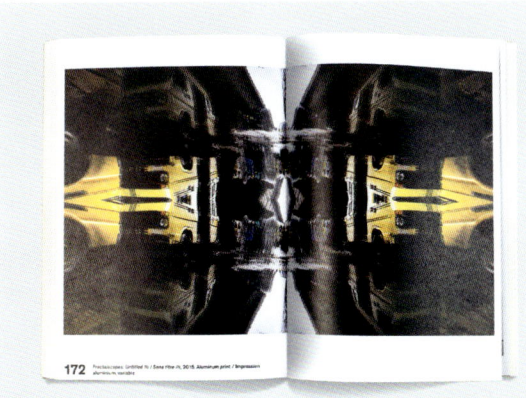

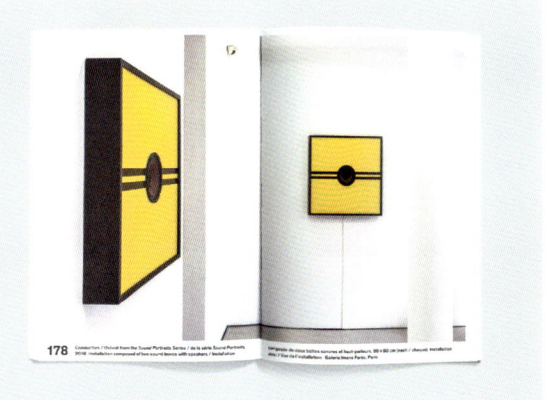

RGB Graduation Work 2018

[Yearbook]

"Graduation Work" is a yearbook of the School of Art and Design at Beijing Institute of Fashion Technology. It comprises a collection of the bachelor of arts degree projects of all students graduating in 2018. The cover design echoes the overarching topic: the RGB colour space, which is built on the basic colours of red, green and blue, and used as the standard in self-illuminating media such as screens and TVs. This world of colour is repeated consistently throughout the entire layout, with the key visual on the cover creating the link to screen calibration. The motif is continued on the cut edges of the book.

Client
Beijing Institute of Fashion Technology, Beijing, China

Design
DBstudio, Beijing, China

Graphic Design
Huang Li, Xiaoye Guo, Yisha Dai, Weixiang Chen, Haonan Liu, Yunfeng Li

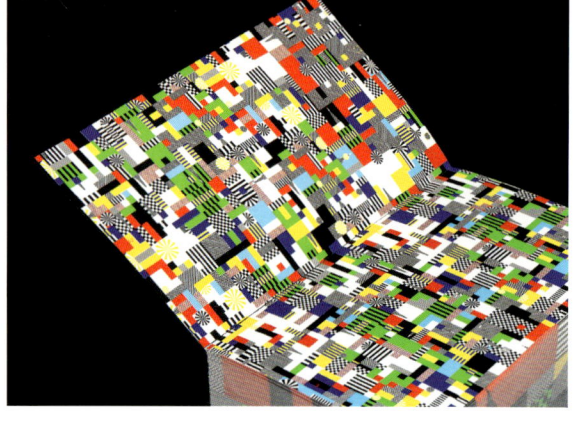

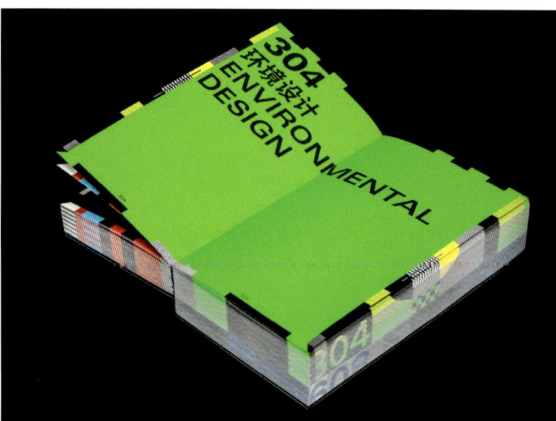

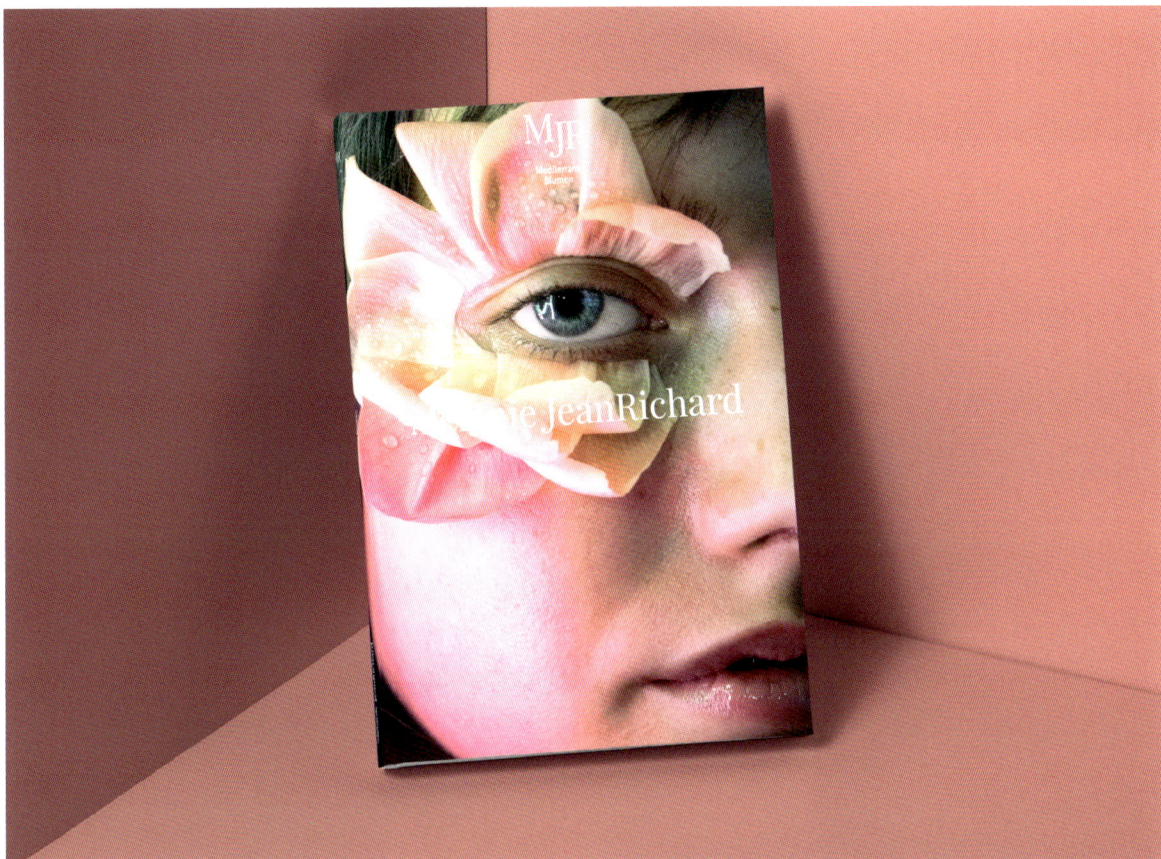

Melanie JeanRichard
[Book]

Melanie JeanRichard, a Bern-based florist, wins over her customers with her creative arrangements of Mediterranean flowers. On the occasion of her 10th anniversary and as part of a brand relaunch, this book documents a self-initiated art project. The publication presents the works of 28 artists on the topic of flowers, which were exhibited in a gallery in Bern in autumn 2018. Photographs spanning entire pages convey the characteristic style of the individual works of art. The inspiring book is available in several stores and portrays the florist's artistic ambitions.

Client
MJR Melanie JeanRichard – Mediterrane Blumen, Bern, Switzerland

Design
Branders Group AG, Zürich, Switzerland

Chief Executive Officer
René Allemann

Creative Direction
Thom Pfister

Strategic Planning/Text
Philippe Knupp

Copywriting
Katja Wölfel

Publishing & Print Media

Före vår tid
[Book]

This book celebrates the 30th anniversary of the Swedish Green Party's youth organisation "Grön Ungdom". The cover design in shimmering black and gold is reflective of the significance of the occasion. The Swedish title "Före vår tid" (Before our time) has a double entendre: it can be read as both before and ahead of our time – a notion which is echoed by the cover illustration. Whereas the Green Party logotype is a dandelion in bloom, the cover's stylised dandelion in its seed state portrays the members of Grön Ungdom as well as future generations to come. On the inside, lots of photos accompany the chronological retrospective.

Client
Grön Ungdom, Stockholm, Sweden

Design
Henrik Callerstrand Design, Stockholm, Sweden

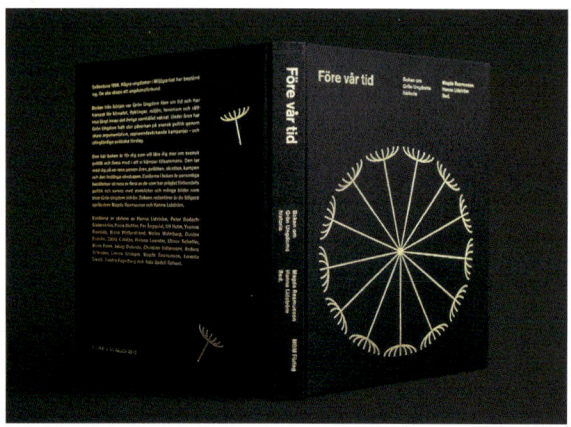

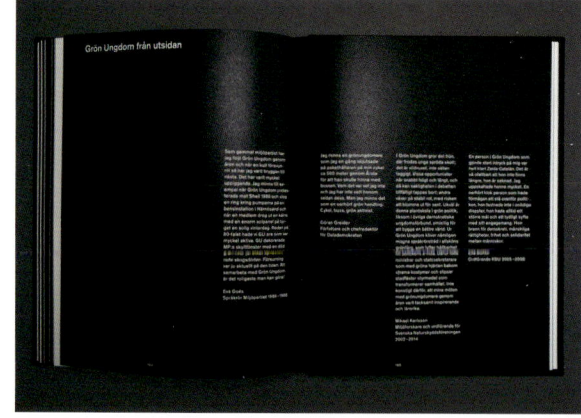

125 Years MAGURA

[Corporate Publishing]

The corporate publication "125 Years MAGURA" offers entertaining insights into the company history of the medium-sized provider of bicycle accessories and services, and component developer. Designed as an inspiring book of discovery, it describes significant events, includes anecdotes and presents pictures, drawings and artefacts. With a real feel for details, the graphic design reflects the visual feel of the respective decades and places these in a contemporary context to the brand. An integrated colour scheme along with the illustration style creates an aesthetic overall image.

Client
MAGENWIRTH Technologies GmbH,
Bad Urach, Germany

Design
POLARWERK GmbH, Bremen, Germany

Creative Direction
Thomas Theßeling

Art Direction
Sebastian Kühnel

Graphic Design
Jennifer Pankratz

Final Artwork
Marcel Koch

Text/Project Management
Melanie Borrs

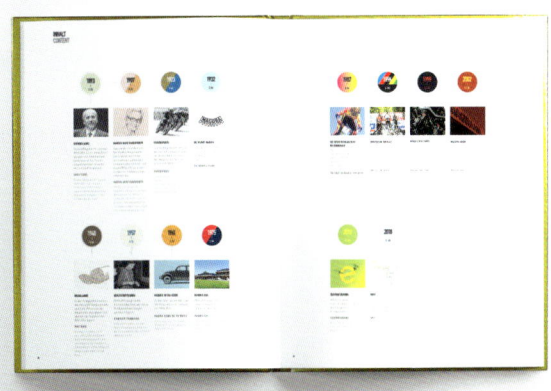

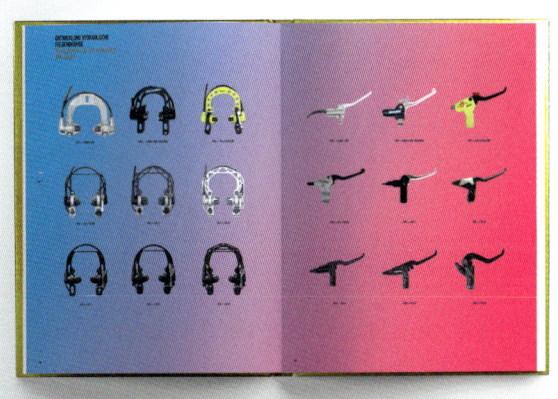

Pohjolan Voima – 75

[Corporate Publishing]

This corporate publication was created for the 75th anniversary of Pohjolan Voima in order to recount the inspiring story of the Scandinavian energy company. The topics covered in the book range from the forest industry in the 1940s to the current challenge of tapping renewable energy sources. The editorial design aims to make the rather abstract topic of energy more tangible. Inspired by electricity cables, copper wires and rubber insulation, a contemporary layout was created with strong colour contrasts. Details such as copper-colour cut edges, typography and cover design round off the concept.

Client
Pohjolan Voima, Helsinki, Finland

Design
Kuudes Kerros, Helsinki, Finland

Graphic Design
Piëtke Visser, Vesa Viljakainen

Pre-Press
Vesa Viljakainen

Das Grundgesetz als Magazin

[Magazine]

On 23 May 2019, Germany commemorated the 70th birthday of its constitution, the Grundgesetz. In this magazine, the entire text from 1949 is designed in a contemporary layout which is easy to read yet visually attractive. The images in the magazine show impressive satellite photos of Germany and Europe taken by a German astronaut on his current mission on the international space station ISS. An extensive infographic section on the history of Germany as well as the Universal Declaration of Human Rights round off the content-related concept of the magazine, which is printed in a premium finish.

Client
Oliver Wurm & Andreas Volleritsch Gbr, Hamburg, Germany

Design
Oliver Wurm & Andreas Volleritsch Gbr, Hamburg, Germany

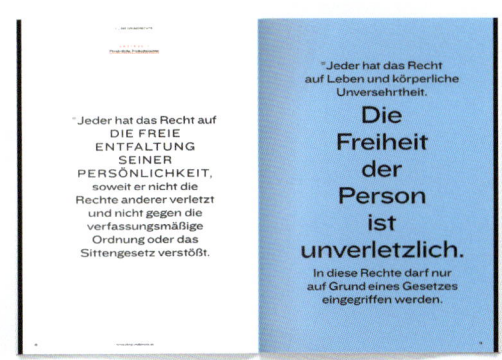

Publishing & Print Media   Posters   Typography   Illustrations   Sound Design   Film & Animation   Online   Apps

El teatro de las máquinas

[Book]

Client
Gamesa Gearbox, Mungia, Spain

Design
Bronce Estudio, Pamplona, Spain

→ Designer profile on page 516

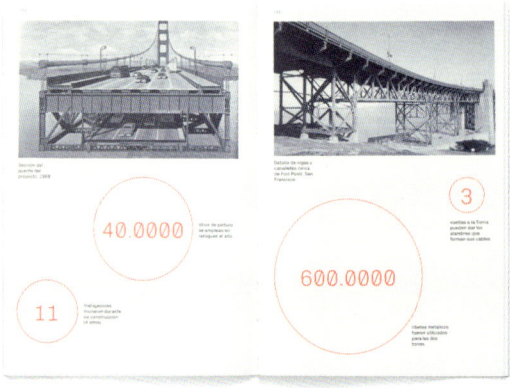
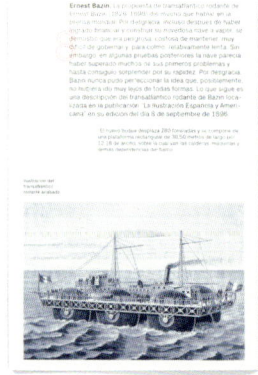

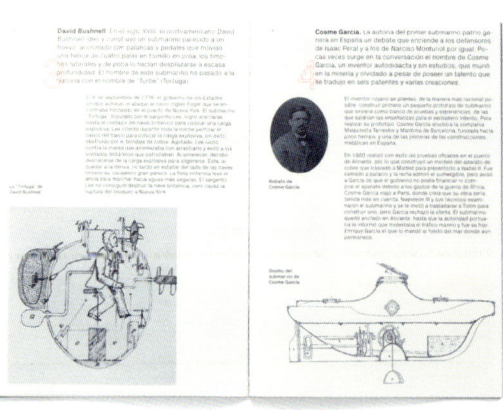

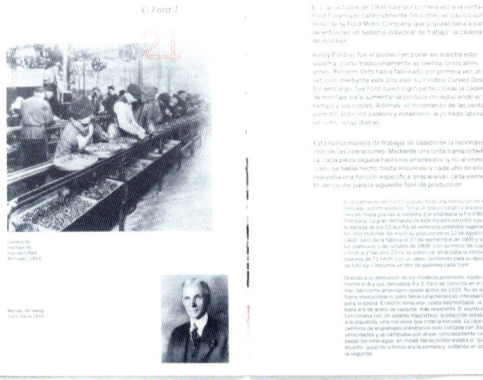

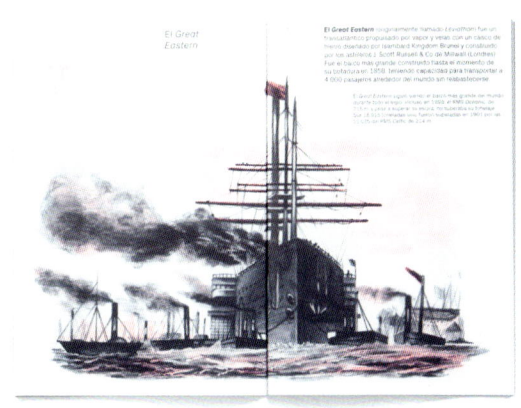

This compendium is an homage to "The Theatre of Machines", a book genre which appeared for the first time at the end of the 16th century in Europe and in which inventors published their designs of amazing machines, most of which were never brought to market. "El teatro de las máquinas" compiles 88 inventions and items of interest, all related to the industrial world. Both the cover and the inside of the 174-page book are characterised by two special colours: the prevailing colour replaces black as the conventional colour for typography, while the neon accent colour highlights certain details of the infographics and navigation. The balanced editorial design interprets the appearance of an old encyclopaedia in a contemporary way.

URALCHEM – Growth Begins with Us

[Corporate Publishing]

Client
URALCHEM Group, Moscow, Russia

Design
TutkovBudkov, Volgograd, Russia

Art Direction
Natasha Kuchishkina

Account Management
Anton Tanzura

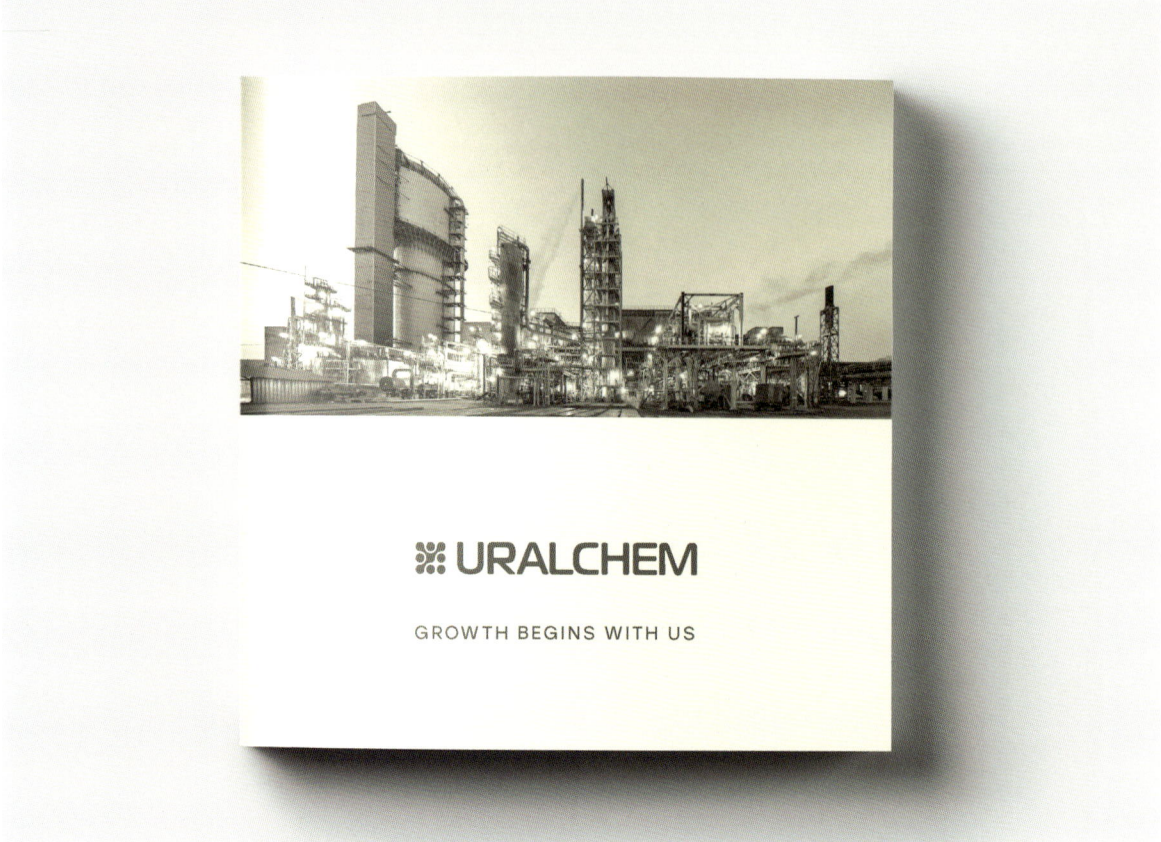

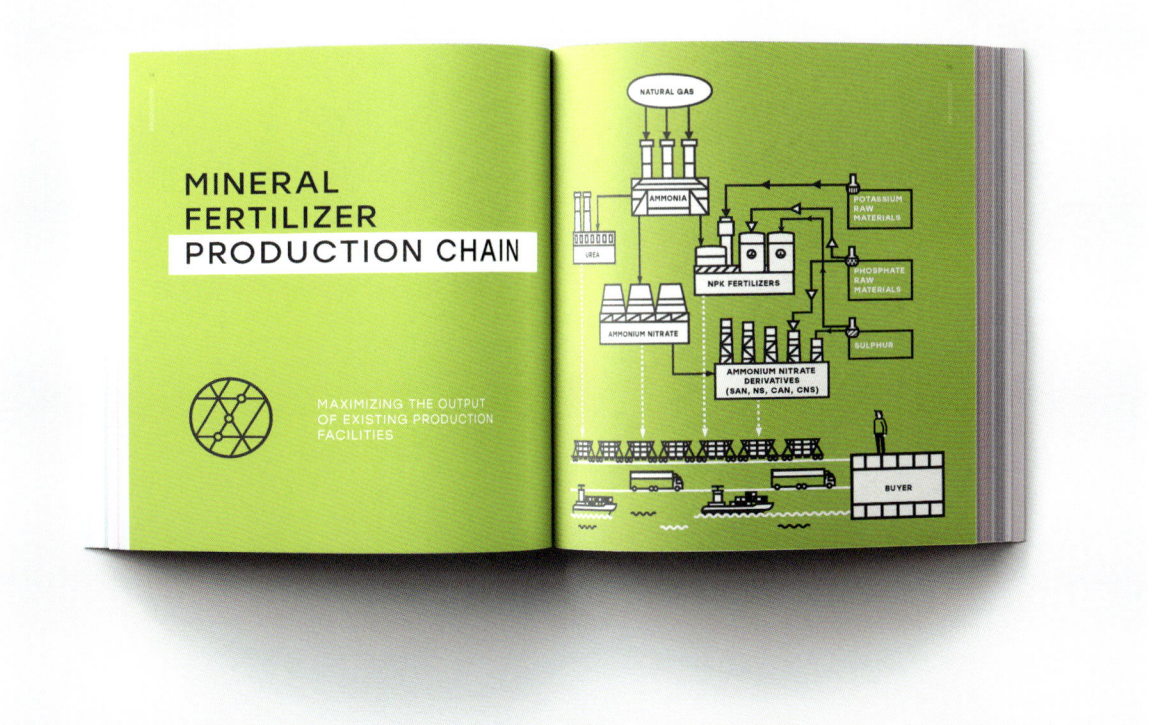

The URALCHEM holding is a leading producer of ammonium nitrate in Russia. Its corporate publishing tracks the development of selected business areas. The brochure has a contemporary look which lends a light and attractive feel to the complex contexts and data. The easy-to-understand infographics are designed in an illustrative style. Light colours were chosen as the background colours for the cover and the inside pages in a nod to the company's chemical context. Photos on transparent paper add emotional weight to the introductions of the chapters.

Make Annual 15

[Special Publication]

International architecture practice Make's yearly publication provides articles, interviews, project features and studio news. It is sent out to clients all over the world and is also available online. The issue "Annual 15" celebrates Make's 15th anniversary, and its content is divided into four chapters: Past, Present, Future and Studio. Different varieties of paper give each chapter its own look and feel. The cover photograph of a ceramic architectural component was shot with a medium-format camera to achieve hyper-real detail. Printed with a single-colour metallic ink, the double gatefold cover was refined with a white gloss foil on the outer side.

Client
Make Architects,
London, United Kingdom

Design
Make Architects,
London, United Kingdom

Graphic Design
Tom Featherby, Ben Hutchings,
Giuditta Turchi

Photography
Martina Ferrera

Editorial Work
Emily Lauffer, Sara Veale

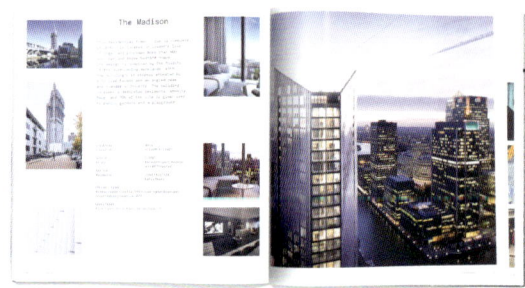
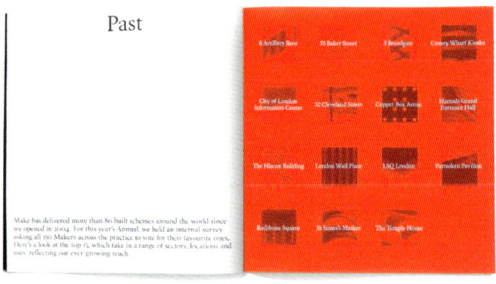

COPRO EDITION25

[Corporate Publishing]

"EDITION25" was developed for the 25th anniversary of real estate developer COPRO. The bilingual publication was meant as a thank-you gesture to those who had accompanied the firm on its journey and presents projects from the past 25 years. The concept was to highlight the nature of the anniversary through the book's format, appearance and feel. As a result, the book combines art, architecture and companions in a creative dialogue and is designed in a 25 × 25 cm format, which also echoes the square logo of the company. The cover, made from high-quality silver linen with embossed text and special colours, reflects high quality requirements.

Client
COPRO Sales & Services GmbH,
Berlin, Germany

Design
Cee Cee Creative, Berlin, Germany

Project Management
Lennart Fenske, Nancy Albrecht

Creative Direction
Cee Cee Creative

Concept
Marc F. Kimmich, Antje Kimmich,
Rüdiger Lange, Lennart Fenske,
Nancy Albrecht

Text
Tim Berge, Gesine Wulf, Tina Becker,
Lennart Fenske, Rose Newell, Jayne Fox,
Nancy Albrecht

Publishing & Print Media   Posters   Typography   Illustrations   Sound Design   Film & Animation   Online   Apps

Bruno Lambart

[Book]

The legacy of the building culture of the Bonn Republic, the style of architecture which had arisen since 1949 in the Federal Republic of Germany, recalls the change which occurred in the postwar era. This book is dedicated to architect Bruno Lambart, who designed many public buildings in Germany. Presenting plans, drawings and photographs, the content shows all of his construction projects between 1949 and 1990, thus creating a remarkable work of reference. The monograph focuses on Lambart's established concept of architecture set in that era, with texts and images which will appeal to a wide audience.

Client
Verlag Kettler, Dortmund, Germany

Design
JAC-Gestaltung, Dortmund, Germany

Author
Alexandra Apfelbaum, Dortmund, Germany

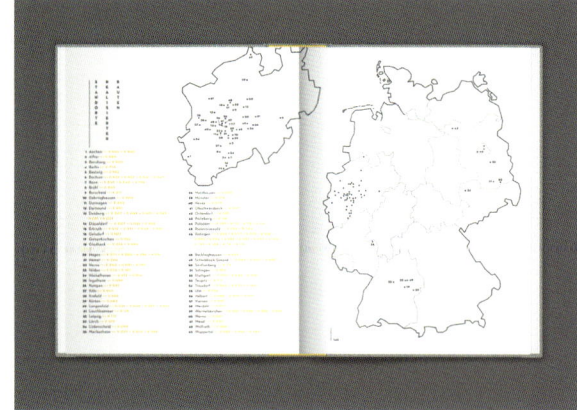

conmoto.projects – Your project is in our DNA
[Brochure]

conmoto.projects develops sophisticated interiors concepts for international clients. Its brochure entitled "Your project is in our DNA" presents selected reference projects to prospective clients and, in an intelligent manner, make the process easy to understand. The individual project components are presented in the form of heavily abstract DNA structures. As a business-to-business marketing tool with a premium appearance, the layout is reduced to a simple colour palette which provides a neutral backdrop for the various references and details.

Client
Lions at Work – conmoto, Münster, Germany

Design
UNGESTRICHEN – Büro für Kommunikationsdesign, Krefeld, Germany

Creative Direction
Jens Könen, UNGESTRICHEN – Büro für Kommunikationsdesign

Project Management
Patrick Tenbrinck, Lions at Work – conmoto

Text
Piet Fischer, Krefeld, Germany

Grandaire

[Brochure]

Grandaire is a new residential property in the centre of Berlin. This brochure serves to market the luxurious private apartments and its design is reminiscent of the glamorous lifestyle of the Golden Twenties. As an homage to the first neon signs which appeared on Alexanderplatz at the time, the slipcase is printed in phosphorescent neon colours. In contrast to the exterior, the inside of the book uses restrained brown hues. Representative photos, filigree patterns and distinctive typography convey an especially high level of luxury living for a discerning target group.

Client
Reggeborgh Investment &
Management GmbH, Berlin, Germany

Design
minigram – Studio für
Markendesign GmbH, Berlin, Germany

Graphic Design
Anja Klausch, Linn Kleeberg,
Ondrej Jelinek, Cindy Piper

Account Management
Elena Frahm

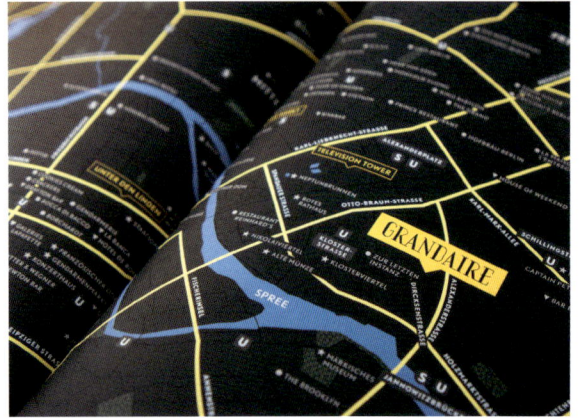
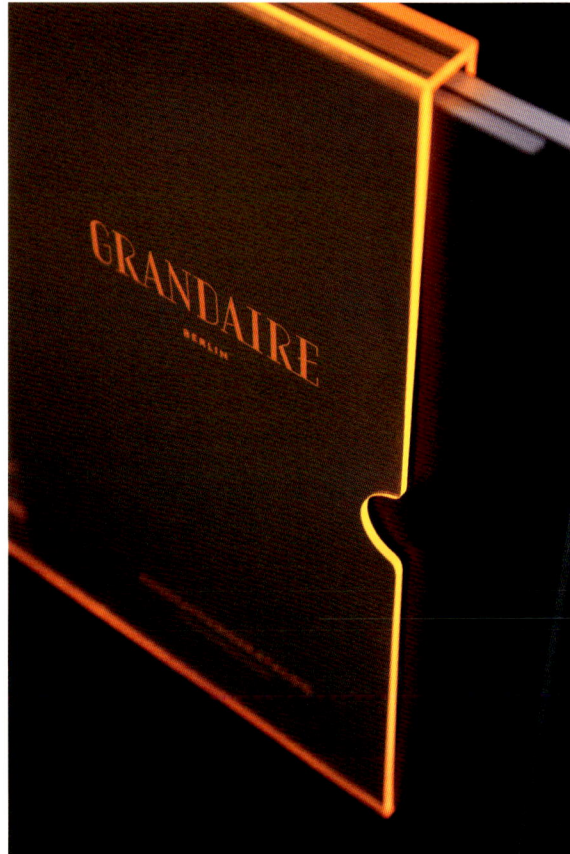

Fisher & Paykel – EuroCucina Catalogue

Published for the EuroCucina event, this publication is geared towards an international readership. The catalogue, designed to look like a magazine, aimed to manifest the market position of the New Zealand kitchen appliances manufacturer and explain its approach to customer-centred design. Editorially generously designed, the magazine was envisioned as a calling card worth keeping. The content leads readers through New Zealand's distinguishing landscapes, into residential architecture, where the products are discreetly revealed, and through inspiring developments, such as the changing nature of the kitchen.

Client
Fisher & Paykel, Auckland, New Zealand

Design
Alt Group, Auckland, New Zealand

Strategic Planning
Felicity Stevens, Ben Corban

Design Team
Zoe Ikin, Phoebe Ellis

Image Editing
Hamish Clark

Production
Tony Proffit

Die Nettworker

[Brochure]

This brochure shows, in an easy-to-understand manner, the range of products of Pilzgarten, a German producer of organic premium mushrooms, as well as their specific characteristics. More than 72 pages of information about the company, its history and production processes are provided in a journalistic style. The stories, mainly told in the form of an interview, not only highlight the specialist knowledge of the owner of the company but also reflect its development. Aesthetic imagery enhances a fascinating product world. The high print quality and paper, which is pleasant to the touch, create an impressive experience for the reader.

Client
Pilzgarten GmbH, Helvesiek, Germany

Design
Heine Warnecke Design GmbH, Hannover and Münsterland, Germany

Creative Direction
Dirk Heine

Graphic Design
Sina Feuerhake

Image Editing
Daniela Stein

Advent Calendar and Wine Tasting Diary

This wine tasting diary has 24 days, like an advent calendar. As part of a promotion set, it references 24 selected Slovenian wines. The limited edition comprises 24 randomly numbered bottles, packaged in a handmade wooden box, accompanied by a diary and additional information. The tasting diary is designed in a generously proportioned horizontal format which encourages users to make notes of their personal taste experience when trying the wines and predefined criteria make it easier to rate them. Thanks to the generous amounts of white space, the layout of the pages conveys a premium feel.

Client
M.Y. inženiring d.o.o., Ljubljana, Slovenia

Design
Bojana Fajmut, Ljubljana, Slovenia

Project Management
Bojana Fajmut

Customer Advisory Service
Petra Rutar

Text
Petra Rutar
Katarina Hudson

Illustration
Tina Perko

Web Design
Klemen Teran, Pappiga mobile application, Ljubljana, Slovenia

Post-Production
Dolores Kirhmajer

Publishing & Print Media   Posters   Typography   Illustrations   Sound Design   Film & Animation   Online   Apps

Typographic Advent Calendar

This Advent calendar consists of 25 boxes which can be individually filled for each day, starting on 1 December and counting up to Christmas, plus one large box for an additional surprise present. The individual lids show various fonts used and arranged in a way that allows the individual boxes to add up to a typographic composition. The golden letters, numbers and graphic elements are refined through hot foil stamping. The well-designed, environmentally friendly calendar is sturdy enough to be reused over several Christmas seasons.

Client
Coronado Design, Hohenfurch, Germany

Design
Michaela Vargas Coronado, Hohenfurch, Germany

Hans Memling – The Last Judgement

[Calendar]

This wall calendar was designed and realised as part of the marketing activities of the National Museum in Gdansk. Related to the promotion of the 15th century triptych "The Last Judgement" by Hans Memling, the calendar presents the history of this significant work of art from its creation to the present day. Each page of the calendar consists of one illustration and a short historical fact, both of which present a specific event in the history of the masterpiece. The layout centres around a centrally placed custom die-cut, and the printing was enriched with a metallic colour and hot-stamping foil.

Client
The National Museum in Gdańsk, Poland

Design
TOFU Studio, Gdańsk, Poland

Art Direction
Adam Chylinski

Concept
Daniel Naborowski

Graphic Design
Paulina Kozicka

Editorial Work
Adrian Samselski

Project Management
Daniel Naborowski

Printing
Paweł Morawczyński, NORMEX, Gdańsk, Poland

Facades of the World

[Calendar]

alsecco is a provider of high-quality facade insulation systems within the DAW company group. In order to further sharpen the brand profile and to further strengthen alsecco as a brand for architects, a calendar for 2019 was developed which shows selected examples of the comprehensive collection of facades. The creative idea is to show the silhouettes of well-known buildings and streetscapes from all over the globe covered with the facade structures from the current collection. On the corresponding back, the puzzle concerning the respective city is solved with the help of unusual stories about them and is digitally extended in a virtual walk. High-quality processing, embossing and finishing ensures that the facades are printed with as much detail as possible.

Client
alsecco GmbH, Wildeck, Germany

Design
jäger&jäger, Überlingen, Germany

Creative Direction
Olaf Jäger, Regina Jäger

Design Team
Nicola Nolle, Michelle Miesel

Consulting
Jochen Grauer, Jochen Grauer Marken- und Kommunikationsberatung, Lindau, Germany

Production
Holzer Druck und Medien, Weiler im Allgäu, Germany

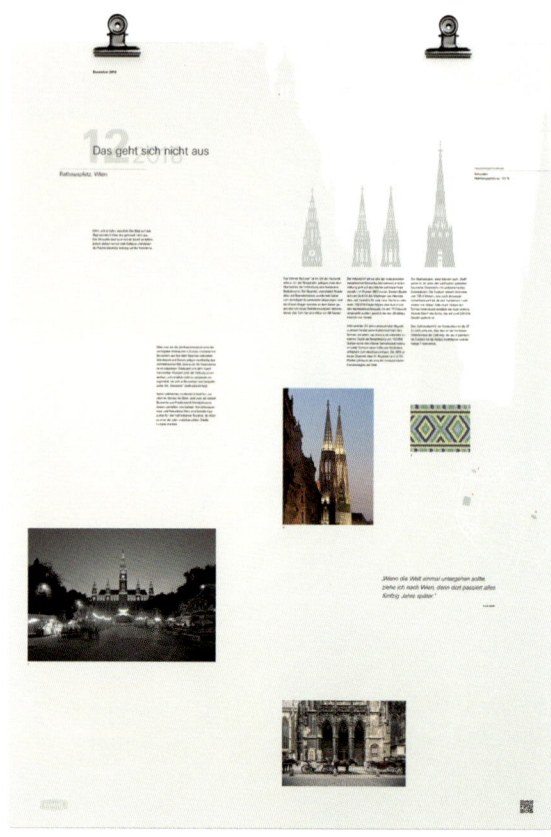
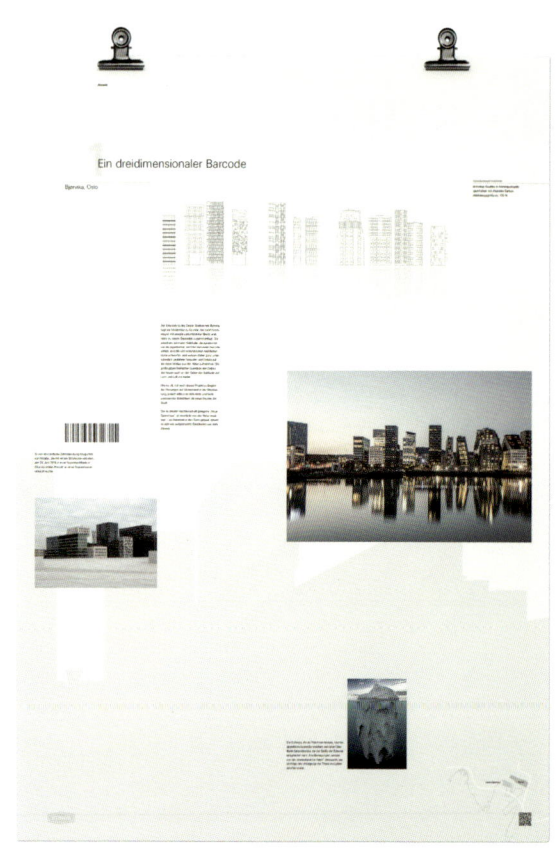

Bolichwerke – Form folgt Funktion 2018

[Calendar]

This calendar, entitled "Form folgt Funktion" (Form follows function), places the lamps from Bolichwerke in the context of Bauhaus architecture. The 12 motifs show what the products have in common with the minimalist art movement: a love of purism, of clear forms and of materials. The lights are staged graphically as three-dimensional grid models superimposed by images of modernist architectural structures. The use of natural paper as well as a binding made from two bulldog clips on black MDF gives an air of simplicity. The elegant black and white colour palette is partially overprinted with neon yellow.

Client
Bolichwerke KG, Lichttechnische Fabrik, Östringen-Odenheim, Germany

Design
raumkontakt GmbH, Karlsruhe, Germany

Graphic Design
Jürgen Lenhardt

Publishing & Print Media   Posters   Typography   Illustrations   Sound Design   Film & Animation   Online   Apps

Fedrigoni 365

[Special Publication, Calendar]

Fedrigoni is an Italian fine paper company. Their yearly marketing calendar is usually designed by a single design studio, however, TM turned the brief on its head by asking 365 participants to participate. As part of this unprecedented collaboration, each contributor interprets the date or numeral provided to them. This second edition was made up of Fedrigoni's white paper ranges and shows the subtle differences between the shades of white available in their UK-held collection. The project has transformed the company's marketing and sales reach significantly. It has also provided daily content for their social media accounts and creates hundreds of advocates for the brand every year.

Client
Fedrigoni UK, London, United Kingdom

Design
TM, London, United Kingdom

The Happiness Diary

The Happiness Diary is a calendar which allows the users to record and reflect daily on their moods and feelings. Because its format has the same dimensions as a smartphone, the mood calendar is also easy to use on the go. Creatively designed typography shapes the character of the cover and the inside pages, where graphics in a bright yellow colour, unfinished sentences, true-or-false statements and pictograms make the daily completion of the calendar much easier. At the end of each month, the small book features motivational messages as well as monthly planner pages.

Client
Marcell Puskás, Budapest, Hungary

Design
Marcell Puskás, Budapest, Hungary

Publishing & Print Media   Posters   Typography   Illustrations   Sound Design   Film & Animation   Online   Apps

Gymnasieskolen
[Magazine]

Danish magazine Gymnasieskolen with its 48,000 monthly readers has been transformed using bold editorial and design elements, pushing the boundaries of what the magazine format is capable of communicating compared to digital publications. A reader survey provided necessary insights into the target group to create content and design which engages and creates space for reflection and immersion based on the reader's point of view. The redesigned magazine for secondary-school teachers distinguishes itself from the usual communication to members, which is characterised by conventional thinking and design.

Client
Gymnasieskolernes Lærerforening, Copenhagen, Denmark

Design
Creative ZOO A/S, Aarhus, Denmark

Creative Direction
Jesper Vorre

Art Direction
Jesper Liengaard

Graphic Design
Charlotte Kousgaard, Lorena Cruzado

Account Management
Marie Bysted-Sandberg

Frankfurter Allgemeine Quarterly

[Magazine]

The magazine "Frankfurter Allgemeine Quarterly" is published four times a year and is an offshoot of a well-known newspaper in Germany. The 180-page publication combines the intellectual ambition of the daily paper with in-depth reporting and visual opulence. The editorial concept covers a wide range of different subjects from literature, politics, fashion and lifestyle to architecture, the arts and economics. Its underlying theme, which is also reflected in the imagery, is the future trends which will affect how we live going forward. The design of the title page centres around a key visual which serves as a teaser for the focal topic of the current edition.

Client
Frankfurter Allgemeine Zeitung GmbH, Frankfurt/Main, Germany

Design
Catrin Sonnabend, Berlin, Germany
Julia Vukovic, Berlin, Germany
Maria Leutner, Berlin, Germany

Editorial Work
Rainer Schmidt, Berlin, Germany
Claudius Seidl,
Frankfurter Allgemeine Zeitung

Head of Advertising
Ingo Müller,
Frankfurter Allgemeine Zeitung

Publishing & Print Media   Posters   Typography   Illustrations   Sound Design   Film & Animation   Online   Apps

Solution Thinking
[Special Publication]

Fresenius Medical Care is a manufacturer of medical devices and supplies which sees itself as a provider of integrated solutions. Its initiative regarding internal communication with the motto "Become a Solution Thinker" is aimed at all new and existing employees. Not only does the special publication explain the meaning of solution thinking, it also gives it a tangible form by integrating a tangram game as an important component of the welcome set. The colours of the game serve as a basis for the entire visual design and a system of shapes are intended to symbolise solution thinking.

Client
Fresenius Medical Care GmbH
Deutschland, Bad Homburg, Germany

Design
New Cat Orange, Wiesbaden, Germany

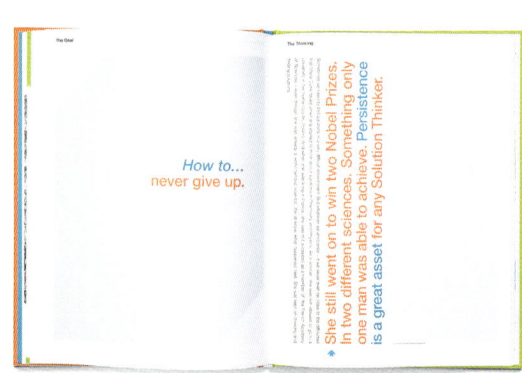

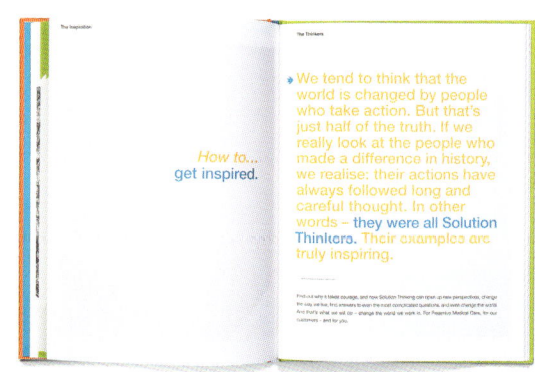

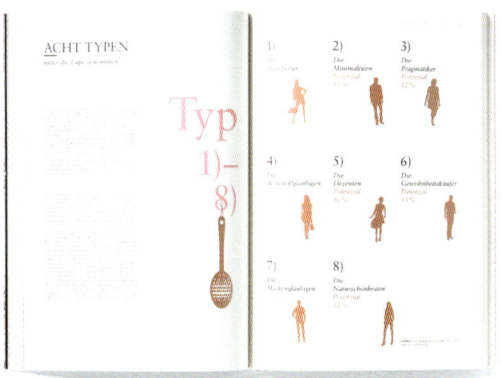

Beauty Report

[Special Publication]

The Beauty Report published by Mediengruppe RTL is based on a comprehensive study on the German beauty industry. Beyond mere facts and figures about the industry, the study offers marketing-relevant insights into potential consumers. The layout reflects the style of high-quality beauty brands. The content is complemented by bronze embossing, premium paper, stylish images as well as a creative design with respect to graphs and tables. The elegant colour scheme is focused on powder shades which span from rosé to brown and complete the overall design of the publication.

Client
IP Deutschland GmbH, Cologne, Germany

Design
Facit Research GmbH & Co. KG, Munich, Germany
IP Deutschland GmbH, Cologne, Germany

Art Direction
Beate Gronemann, Serviceplan Gruppe, Munich, Germany

Production
Katy Pergelt, Serviceplan Gruppe

Text
Silke Stemmler, Mediaplus Gruppe, Munich, Germany

Editorial Work
Kerstin Niederauer-Kopf, Munich, Germany
Sabrina Graser, Facit Research

Publishing & Print Media   Posters   Typography   Illustrations   Sound Design   Film & Animation   Online   Apps

PAL – Phase Alternating Line

[Book with LP Cover]

PAL is a club for analogue techno music in Hamburg, located beneath the television tower. Its name stands for Phase Alternating Line, a transmission technology of coloured images in analogue televisions. The book renders this concept into three sections. The cover is designed like a playable vinyl and shows a distorted image of analogue television and the horizontal shifts as graphic translations. The square shape of the record cover is picked up in the set grid, while the obligatory hole in the record makes the cover playable on a physical record player. Even the headlines are cut in 7-inch format and rotate every chapter.

Client
PAL – U-Werk Karoline GmbH, Hamburg, Germany

Design
MUTABOR, Hamburg, Germany

Executive Creative Direction
Lennard Niemann

Design Team
Jennifer Schranz, Kristina Posselt, Sarah Behrends, Louis von Lohr

Illustration
Maison Blessing, Hamburg, Germany
Lennard Niemann, MUTABOR

Photography
Markus Wendler, Hamburg, Germany

Gürzenich Orchester Köln

[Season Brochure]

After years of showing an opulent golden look, this season brochure marks the starting point for a rather minimalist design, realised for the Gürzenich Orchestra Cologne. Black-and-white typography on uncoated paper and environmental portraits feature the orchestra's musicians and audience, establishing a clear, concise statement without even a dash of kitsch. With contemporary, understated typography and honest portrait photography, this relaunch puts the music and the musicians in the spotlight. The markedly puristic layout represents the programme of a self-assured and confident music ensemble.

Client
Gürzenich Orchester Köln,
Cologne, Germany

Design
nodesign, Essen, Germany

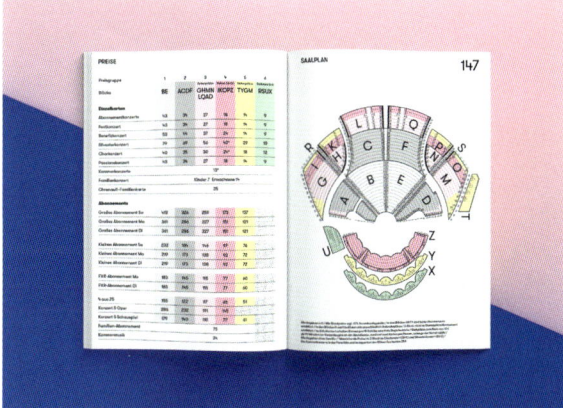

Publishing & Print Media   Posters   Typography   Illustrations   Sound Design   Film & Animation   Online   Apps

Freaky Foilz

[Invitation Card, Sample Book]

The concept for invitation cards, print samples and a sample book was developed for a series of events which promote printing techniques. Befitting the topic of hot foil stamping, the invitation cards are proof that different foils can be stamped in layers on top of each other and even thin lines can be kept on structured material. In this way, a cabinet of curiosities was created to show the diversity of design options. The Freaky Foilz consist of a basic illustration of a head in the centre, which is then complemented by three layers which give the respective character an individual look by way of a beard, hat, etc.

Client
Sylvia Lerch Material & Produktion, Munich, Germany
Stahlstich & Prägedruck
Martin Schall GmbH, Munich, Germany

Design
Ansichtssache GmbH & Co. KG, Munich, Germany

Art Direction
Florian Scharinger

Graphic Design
Bettina Mayer

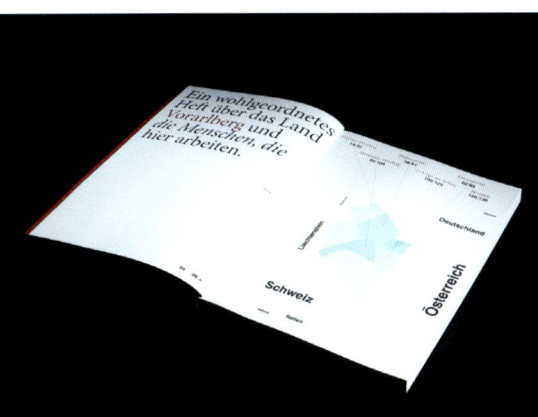

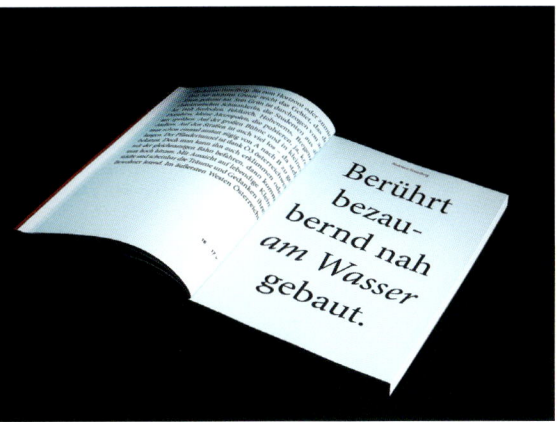

A great place to work

[Book]

Entitled "A great place to work", this book about the catering industry in the Vorarlberg region follows an unusual concept and highlights the personalities behind the scenes. With a major focus on storytelling, chefs, receptionists, sommeliers and service staff members were interviewed. The editorial design reflects a progressive approach. The red typography acts as a navigational aid to guide the reader through the book. The light-blue background of the pages in the interview section contrasts with the information pages, which are rich of text and illustrations. The cover uses a typographical solution which conveys the advantages of the region with sophisticated wordplay.

Client
Wirtschaftskammer Vorarlberg,
Sparte Tourismus + Freizeitwirtschaft,
Feldkirch, Austria

Design
Haselwanter Grafik_und Design,
Dornbirn, Austria

Concept
Thomas Konrad, Digital Instinct,
Langenegg, Austria

Text/Photography
Katharina Zimmermann, Graz, Austria

Climate Change Stamps

Client
The Post of Finland, Helsinki, Finland

Design
Berry Creative, Helsinki, Finland

The Post of Finland commissioned the design to make a series of stamps on climate crisis, which are printed using heat-reacting ink. The stamps depict snowy winters, limited immigration and a certain bird endemic to Finland – the current situation in Finland. When heated, the stamps reveal the future state of possible consequences of the climate crisis. They show snow turning into rain, mass immigration due to heat-ruined areas further south, and the extinction of many of Finland's endemic species. A sense of urgency was added with the die-cutting and colour scale of the stamps.

Publishing & Print Media   Posters   Typography   Illustrations   Sound Design   Film & Animation   Online   Apps

Fleur de Sel

[Calendar]

This calendar offers a narrative of life in the Yancheng district of Kaohsiung, Taiwan, in the 1950s. When opened, it reveals a treasure trove of delightful objects such as worn matchboxes, vintage suitcases, old maps, marbles and used toys. There is even a love letter, written by an American G.I. to his barmaid paramour, and, of course, an old newspaper. The varied design offers an emotionally appealing experience each month by discovering representative items from this bygone era. The concept has an interactive gearing which encourages users to engage with the calendar and to explore the context of the period for themselves.

Client
Art Light Design Consultants, Inc., Kaohsiung, Taiwan

Design
Art Light Design Consultants, Inc., Kaohsiung, Taiwan

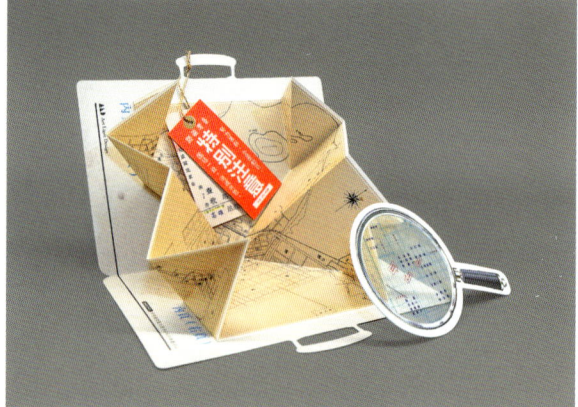
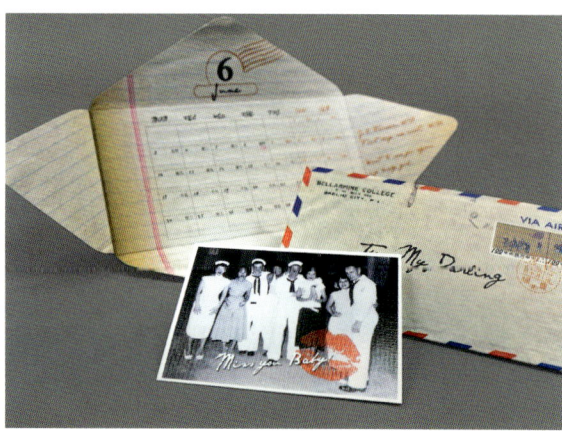

Xicang Market

[Book]

This book is an homage to Xicang Market, a traditional weekly market in Xi'an. Because of the way towns and cities in China are changing, markets like these are becoming increasingly rare. The choice of the objects used as stalls, the way products are displayed and the individual design of the handwritten signs are presented in the book and characterise the style of the editorial design. The content is divided into eight chapters corresponding to the main elements of a local market: location, market, signs, stalls, oral accounts, goods, prices and vendors. The idea behind is to minimise the design and restore the vivid scene of the market with every independent chapter.

Client
Local bendi, Xi'an, China

Design
Qi Dong, Xi'an Jiaotong University, Xi'an, China
Qun Song, Local bendi

Publisher
Qun Song, Local bendi

Photography
Yuan Tian, Minjia Sun

Image Editing
Nan Geng, Local bendi

Text
Rui Ding, Li He, Local bendi

Illustration
Xin Guo, Quncui Sun, Yanpeng Zhao, Jiayuan Cheng

Meet the Hand-Drawn Pot

[Book]

Chaoshan is a region in China where people are especially proud of their tea culture. In order to highlight the significance of tea as a daily basic food product, the book has 365 pages. The individual chapters are bound in several volumes in the form of bare ridges. The double-walled cover is especially distinctive on account of its signal colour red and the punched holes of different sizes and in the shape of three teapots. When closed, the cover creates the illusion of a 3D effect. The slipcase accompanying the book is extremely stable and can be used as a tray for tea.

Client
Sinotea Co., Ltd., Guangzhou, China

Design
Y.STUDIO, Shenzhen, China

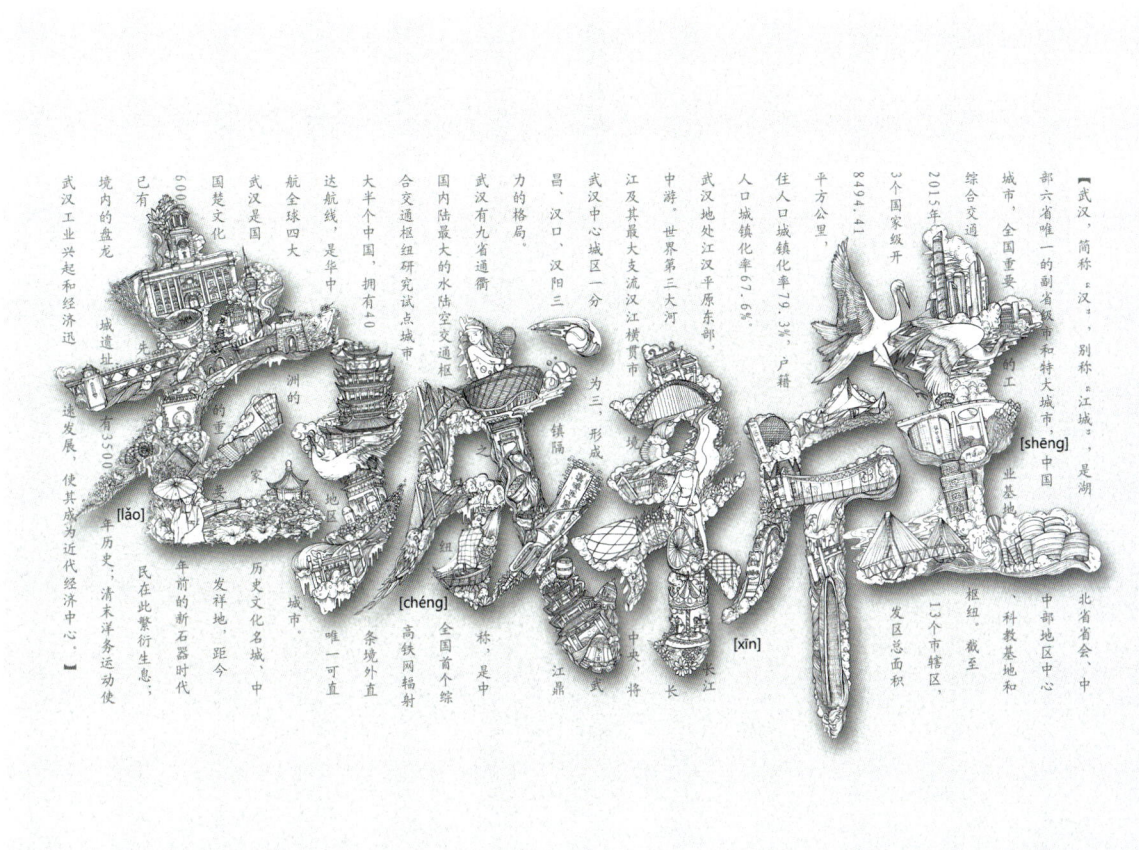

Hand-Drawn China Series – Wuhan in Chinese Characters
[Special Publication]

The cover design of these multi-functional publications was inspired by traditional Chinese design techniques such as paper cutting and expressive calligraphy. The hand-drawn key visual is a collage comprising a total of 34 small-format illustrations. With great attention to detail, the motifs show the sights of the City of Wuhan, such as the Yellow Crane Tower as the symbol of Wuhan, and the Yangtze River. The individual drawings are supposed to recall the city's history and inspire the reader to reflect on urban culture and the experience of aesthetic education.

Client
Hubei Fine Arts Publishing House, Wuhan, China

Design
Wuhan Guanshanjue
Culture Media Co., Ltd., Wuhan, China

Art Direction
Zhengbing Xu, Juan Shen

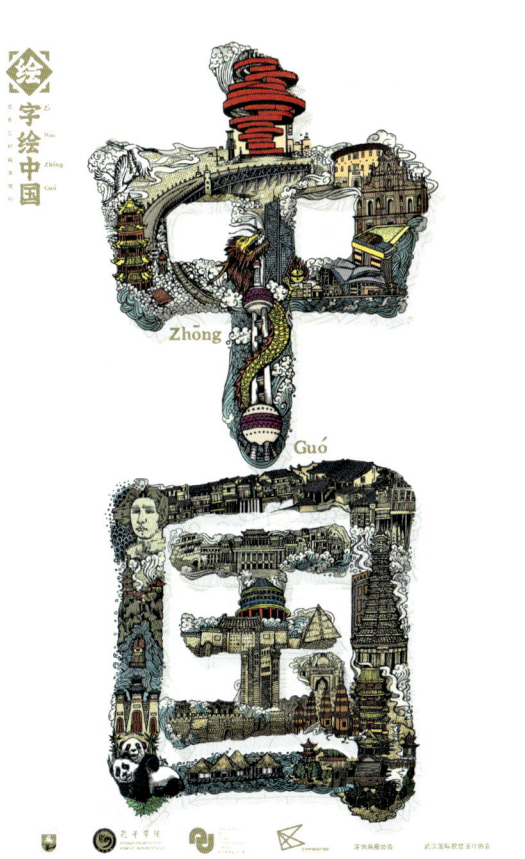
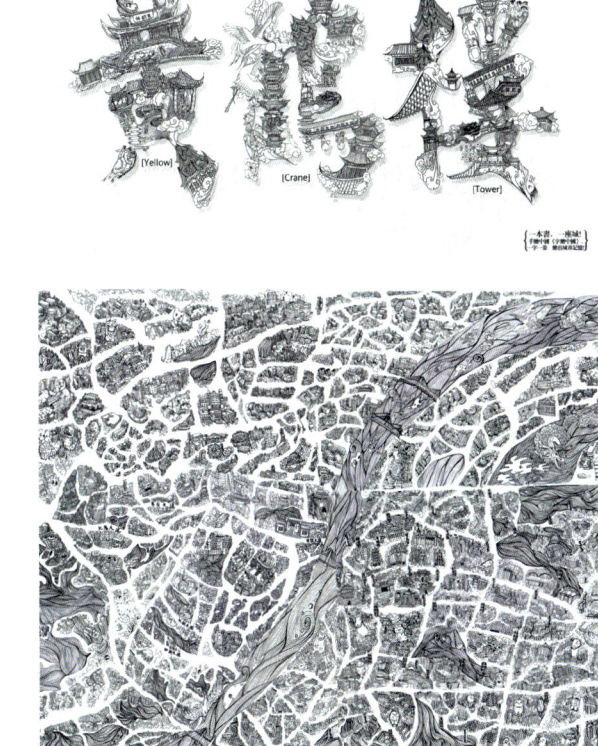

Publishing & Print Media · Posters · Typography · Illustrations · Sound Design · Film & Animation · Online · Apps

TWELVE –
Das Magazin für Marken, Medien und Kommunikation

[Corporate Publishing]

The corporate publication TWELVE was developed as an annual review for the media and communications industry. The aim is to provide an insight into the inspiring personalities and topics which have accompanied the Serviceplan Group in the past year and to showcase their portfolio. Its name refers to the twelve months of a year as well as to the twelve chapters, each of them covering a current trend in the communications industry. With the corresponding topic "New World", several guest authors have made inspiring contributions. The illustrations were created exclusively for the magazine by comic artist Uli Oesterle.

Client
Serviceplan Group, Munich, Germany

Design
Serviceplan Group, Munich, Germany

Executive Creative Direction
Beate Gronemann

Concept
Julia Becker

Project Management
Julia Becker, Lisa Dischinger

Text
Alexandra Berger, Munich, Germany

Artwork
Uli Oesterle, Munich, Germany

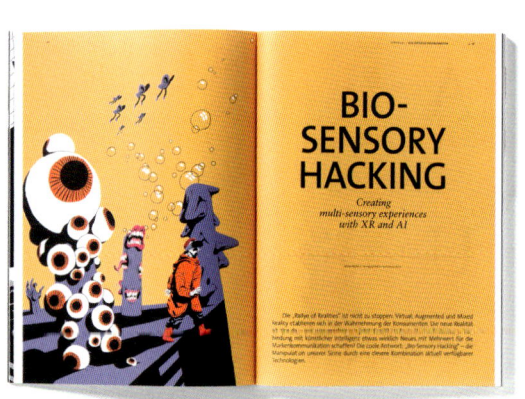

mPaper
[Magazine]

The magazine of communications agency muehlhausmoers is focused on the future as the leading topic. "mPaper" contains surprising features, for example on trends in society, technology and media. The design centres around an effective interplay between photography, design and typography. Breaking with conventions around typography and imagery is part of the concept. In addition, the signal colour green creates attention-grabbing accents. The layout is accompanied by unusual illustrations and images which convey a lo-fi artistic aesthetic.

Client
muehlhausmoers corporate communications gmbh, Berlin, Germany

Design
muehlhausmoers corporate communications gmbh, Berlin, Germany

Weis Magazin
[Self-Promotional Item]

Client
Weis Communications GmbH,
Düsseldorf, Germany

Design
Weis Communications GmbH,
Düsseldorf, Germany

Creative Direction
Steffi Weis

Art Direction
Alexandra Zeisler, Sarah Madre,
Nina Thomas

Pre-Press
Felix Kellner

Text
Bernd Weis
Peter Kuntz, Düsseldorf, Germany

Account Management
Markus Schoel, Jan Stubbe

As part of a mailshot campaign targeting new customers, this magazine presents the philosophy of an owner-managed, creative design agency from Düsseldorf. Based on the motto "You don't have to be loud to break through – being beautiful is enough", aesthetics in brand communication is presented as a key, differentiating factor. The clear layout uses the agency's colours of black and white on a large scale, adding accents of red. Surprising photo motifs positioned to fill the entire page and placed opposite the corresponding pages of text reflect the agency's creative design claim in a striking way.

Publishing & Print Media | Posters | Typography | Illustrations | Sound Design | Film & Animation | Online | Apps

Magazin Nr. 3 – extra heft

[Corporate Publishing]

The Pius Schäfler AG wants to use corporate publishing to set itself apart from other traditional Swiss companies. Its Magazine No. 3 is entitled "extra heft" and is particularly striking with its colour scheme. Both the cover and individual inside pages are printed in phosphorescent neon colours, making the magazine luminous under black light. The 98-page customer magazine offers diverse content, imaginatively matched to the company's decorative products. The creative approach to the topics is underpinned by an attractive layout and font style.

Client
Pius Schäfler AG, Gossau, Switzerland

Design
Trimarca AG, Chur, Switzerland

Head of Marketing
Martin Hilzinger

Graphic Design
Raphael Müller

Text
Hardy Hemmi

Project Management
Lorena Ricci

Photography
Dolores Rupa, Chur, Switzerland

Puma Airplane Chess
[Self-Promotional Item]

For Chinese New Year, the traditional board game Ludo, locally known as Airplane Chess, was redesigned to create Puma Airplane Chess as a VIP customer gift. With a shoebox replacing the game box and miniature versions of the Puma suede sneaker replacing the chess pieces, the design references two essential, iconic brand elements. Not only does Ludo bring back positive childhood memories, it also fits the brand identity. It is a game for four players who are travelling to the same destination. Using the miniature shoes as gaming pieces creates a link to a mobile society which calls for comfortable shoes.

Client
Puma Hong Kong Ltd., Hong Kong

Design
BLCH Ltd., Hong Kong

POSTERS

Red Dot: Best of the Best

Praise of the Shabby Room
[Art Posters]

"Praise of the Shabby Room" is an exploration of the subject of creativity, as well as a deep questioning of it, as expressed in the guiding principle "Mountains are not high, but fairies are named. Water is not deep, but dragons are spiritual. Confucius once said: 'How could we call a room shabby as long as there is a virtuous man in it?'" The aim of this series of posters is to reflect the environment and the state of artistic creation through a purist and simple design. The posters visualise this idea by centring on stylised bonsai trees and showing them in three different scenes or versions that are characterised, and in fact marked, by the words "Pure", "Dull" and "Odd". The design thus intends to integrate the current and traditional East Asian creative state in the shape, the colour and the use of white space. At the same time, this concept is also conveyed through the use of local handmade paper and screen-printing techniques.

Statement by the jury
The posters exhibit a lovely execution and a finely tuned colour concept. The reduced, modern elements used in the graphic design combine harmoniously with the beautifully executed, nice typography. The almost tactile expressiveness of these posters is also based on the special quality of the paper.

 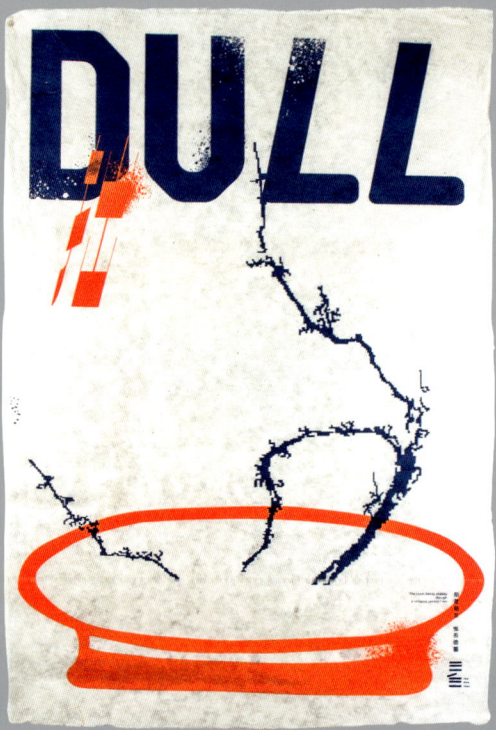

Client
Jiangsu Folk Literature and
Art Association Creation Base,
Jiangsu, China

Design
HOLYDESIGN, Shanghai, China

Design Team
Fan Cao, Hongrui Shen

→ Designer profile on page 530

Red Dot: Best of the Best

My Words
[Poster Series]

The poster series "My Words" focuses on the designer's intention to express his understanding of nature and life via converging visual text languages. As an "abstract text", the design is inspired by ripples and music, as well as a combination of hand-written Chinese, English, Iranian, French and Italian. It thus applies an international visual communication technique, where an experimental exploration is conducted on the "non-recognition" and the "information communicative function" of visual text languages. Using this approach, the designer tries to convey the conversation between himself and his heart, the sea and nature, as well as the traditional culture. This concept is aimed at challenging beholders in that the text creates a sense of déjà vu, yet remains impossible to be recognised in terms of content. In this way, this poster series wants to communicate with the audience by conveying the emotions of the designer. The objective is to communicate that on the surface, "My Words" is full of graphics and text, but virtually, it is wordless.

Statement by the jury
In an attention-grabbing manner, this experimental project documents a dialogue between the designer and himself. Thoughts about culture and the ocean are visualised, yet they fully elude unambiguous understanding. Cleverly solved are details such as speech balloons, which are presented both in a traditional way and as Chinese drawings. Playing on perception, the poster series gains the interest of beholders.

Client
Communication University of Zhejiang,
Hangzhou, China

Design
Shenzhen Future Life Product Planning
Design Co., Ltd., Shenzhen, China
Communication University of Zhejiang,
Hangzhou, China

Art Direction
Prof. Chao Yang

Graphic Design
Prof. Chao Yang, Qiang Yi,
Jianzhong Yang

→ Designer profile on page 526

Red Dot: Best of the Best

59th Thessaloniki International Film Festival

[Poster Series]

The design of this poster series for the 59th Thessaloniki International Film Festival in Greece focussed on celebrating celluloid camera film material as the "small wonder" of the film industry. Targeted at a cinephile audience in Europe, the aim was to make clear how this humble and unadorned item holds the essence of filmmaking and storytelling by illustrating that the key medium of celluloid roll film captures in its frames countless emotions, stories, real and imaginative worlds, all of which come to life through motion. The design visualises this through unrolling and wildly superposed film reels. Seemingly dancing and celebrating cinema like festive ribbons, the unrolling film reels aim at conveying the message that film has the power to unveil hidden images. The posters were published both digitally and physically and were displayed in various places in the city of Thessaloniki such as public spaces, cinemas, theatres, cafes and other popular locations.

Statement by the jury
Designed for the 59th Thessaloniki International Film Festival, this series of posters is a wonderful example of a successful blend of digital expression and digital graphic design in poster design. The use of modern 3D techniques enhances their message and creates an evocative aesthetic. In their role as cultural posters, they visualise the essence of filmmaking.

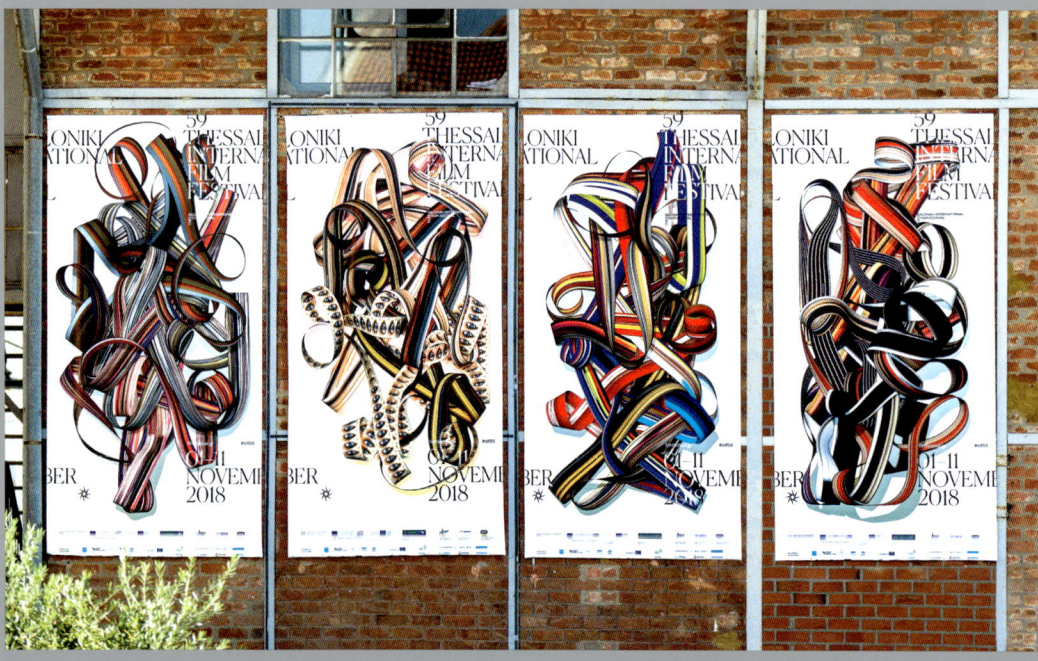

Client
Thessaloniki Film Festival,
Thessaloniki, Greece

Design
Beetroot Design Group,
Thessaloniki, Greece

→ Designer profile on page 513

Publishing & Print Media | Posters | Typography | Illustrations | Sound Design | Film & Animation | Online | Apps

Poland 100th

[Promotional Poster]

The design of this poster visualises the 100th anniversary of Poland's independence through expressive symbolism. The emblem of the eagle in the silhouette of a dove points to the Polish people's desire for peace. Other symbols, such as Chopin's piano hand, reflect the notions of peace and love. Meanwhile, stylised male and female figures moving forward represent the story of a never-ending process; and the Wi-Fi symbol communicates the idea of past and modern union and integration. Last but not least, the red- and white-coloured elements of the Polish flag stand for the enduring pursuit of peace.

Client
26th Warsaw International Poster Biennale, Warsaw, Poland

Design
Jiangxi Normal University, Nanchang, China

Design Team
Mingliang Li, Haishan Zhu, Xu Liu

SARAM – Faceless Suffering of North Koreans
[Poster Series]

This poster series for the human rights organisation SARAM aims to focus public attention on the daily suffering of the people of North Korea. Since there are no images that could display the systematic oppression of these people to the global audience, the design adopts the familiar aesthetics of staged North Korean propaganda. The faceless figures on the posters signify that people in this system literally have no faces, which means that their suffering and grievances are depersonalised and hidden. With this simple trick, the tacky and beautiful illusory world of propaganda is reversed and exposed.

Client
SARAM – Stiftung für Menschenrechte in Nordkorea, Berlin, Germany

Design
Grey Germany/KW43 BRANDDESIGN, Düsseldorf, Germany

Managing Director Creation
Rüdiger Goetz

Creative Direction
Jürgen Adolph

Art Direction
Tara Otto

Account Management
Niklas Wischnewski

Find Your Inner Voice

[Poster Series]

Client
Brain Magazine, Taipei City, Taiwan

Design
Dentsu Taiwan Inc., Taipei City, Taiwan

Head of Advertising
Alice Chou, Dentsu Taiwan Inc.

Creative Direction
Ryan Liao, Sean Tsai, Sunny Chen,
Zac Chou, Dentsu Taiwan Inc.

Art Direction
Ryan Liao, Sean Tsai, Dentsu Taiwan Inc.

Illustration
Huang Yong Ji, Lai Ke Lan, Jin Yun Xuan,
Ye Chang Cing, Taipei City, Taiwan

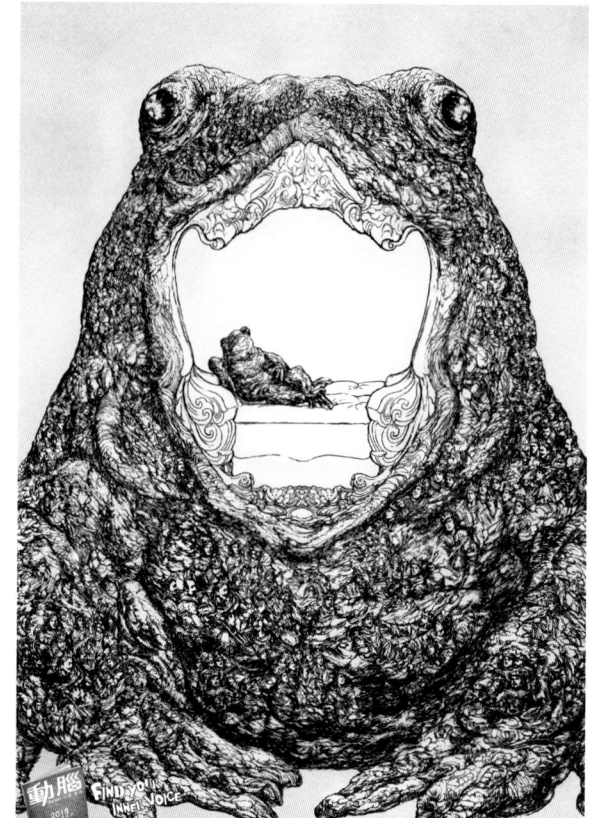

 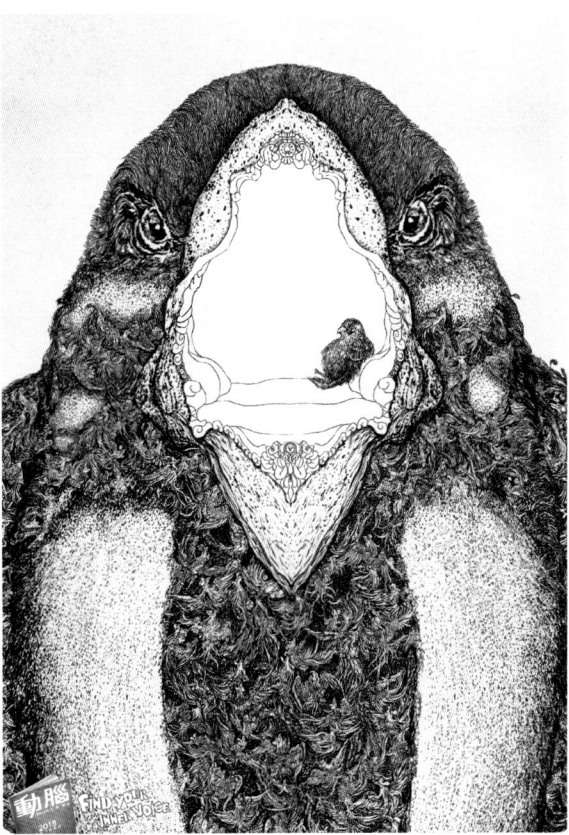

These posters for Brain Magazine in Taiwan convey the message that humans do not need exquisite words or over-the-top packaging. Featuring the claim "Find your inner voice, the whole world wants to listen", four different motifs have been created as calls for reflection. Thus, for example, an illustrated monkey with a monkey in its mouth asks: "How does a monkey make humans respect?" Or a frog asks: "How does a frog make the prince envious?" The overall objective is to stimulate the brain, to trigger insights and thus to touch the souls of people.

Curious

[Promotional Poster]

Designed for the paper brand Curious handled by the Japanese paper company HEIWA Paper, this poster visualises the paper's characteristically shiny metallic lustre. The approach is implemented as an image of hair achieved through a special treatment process. The paper has been cut into very thin strands, each 1 mm wide, to make it look like the dark black hair of a Japanese woman. The aim was not only to portray how Curious paper shines and dances beautifully, but also to convey a sense of the "life" that dwells in paper as a material object. The concept thus has leveraged the homonym between "paper" and "hair", which in Japanese are both pronounced "kami".

Client
HEIWA Paper Co., Ltd., Tokyo, Japan

Design
Depart./Tokyu Agency Inc., Tokyo, Japan

Creative Direction
Hiroyuki Takahashi,
Depart./Tokyu Agency Inc.

Art Direction
Yuji Gamo, Depart./Tokyu Agency Inc.

Text
Shigeyoshi Natsme, Tokyo, Japan

Photography
Hiromasa Gamo, un.Inc, Tokyo, Japan

Image Editing
Rumi Andou, un.Inc, Tokyo, Japan

Printing
SHOEI Inc. Tokyo, Japan

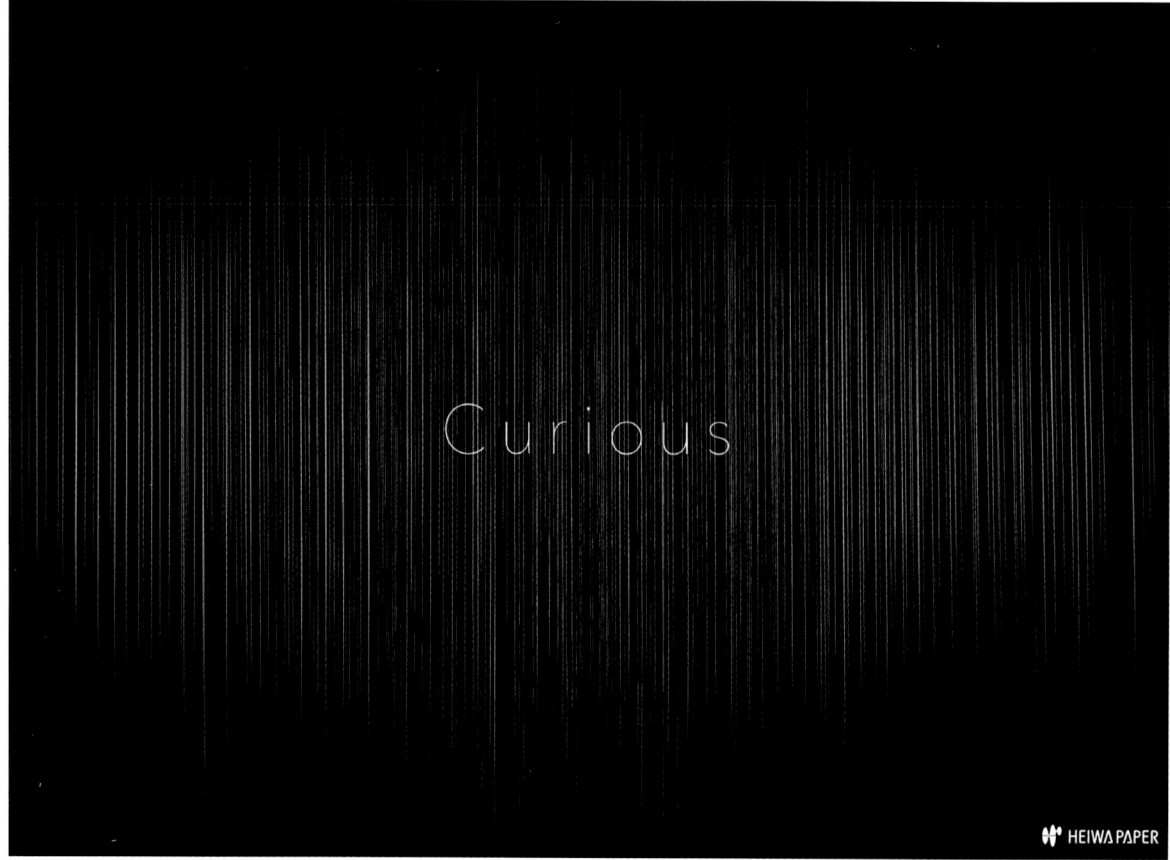
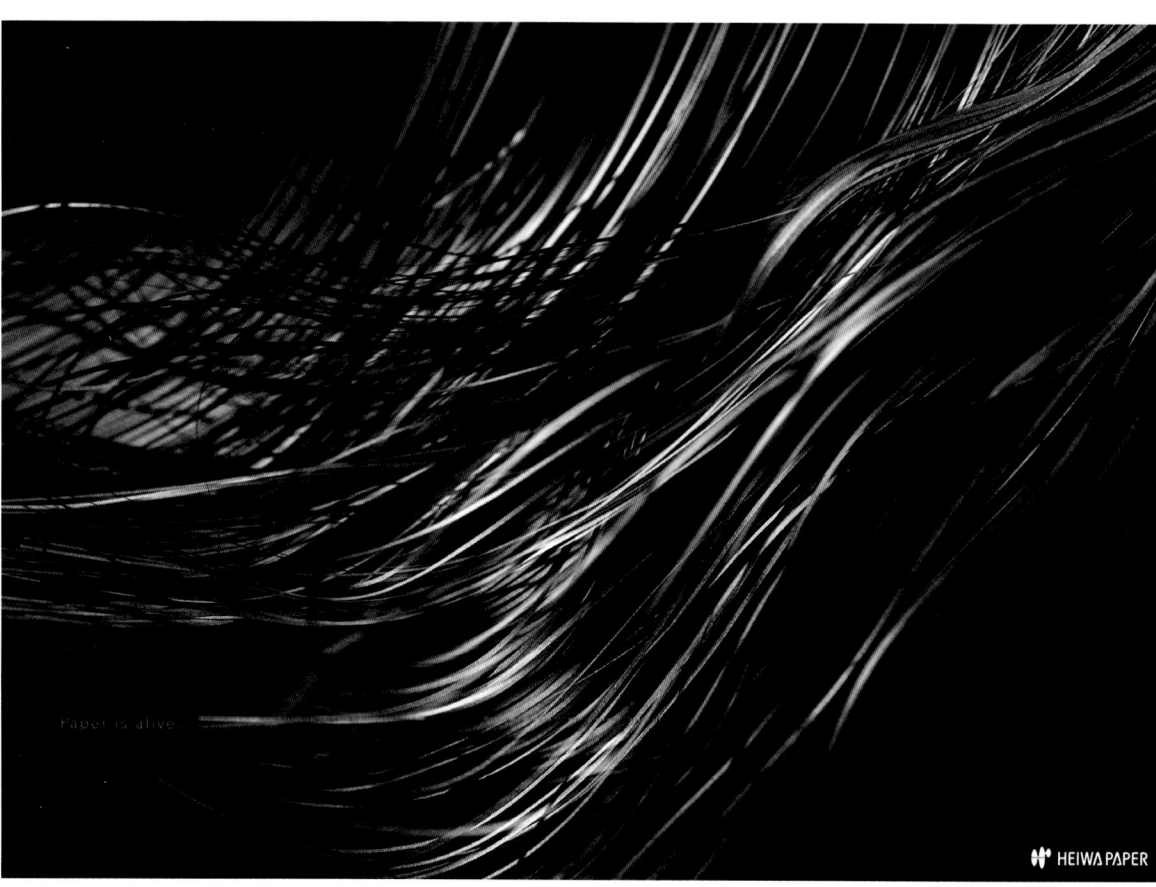

Fedrigoni Plus

[Promotional Poster Series]

The Fedrigoni Plus promotional booklets unfold into limited edition prints developed with eight collaborators to exhibit the features and qualities of the company's paper ranges. The result is an oversize A4 shoulder box containing a set of eight prints. Each print employs an unusual slit fold format, allowing it to be read as a booklet or fully unfolded as limited edition A1 posters, created by one of the designers. The print assets are complemented by a digital campaign including a microsite, collaborator videos and social media assets, as well as regular events.

Client
Fedrigoni UK, London, United Kingdom

Design
TM, London, United Kingdom

Serge Vandercam

[Art Poster, Event Poster]

The design of this poster takes up the stylistic device of the photogram, as used by Serge Vandercam, the Danish-born Belgian painter, photographer, sculptor and ceramicist. Reminiscent of the art of László Moholy-Nagy, his works embrace greatly reduced and seemingly abstract objects. In this poster, the use of intricate typography sets a counterpoint to the simple photographic stylistic device of the photogram, with the objective of giving the resulting ensemble a strong pictorial expression.

Client
Hanns Schmid Publishers,
Baden, Switzerland

Design
Hanns Schmid Grafikdesign,
Baden, Switzerland

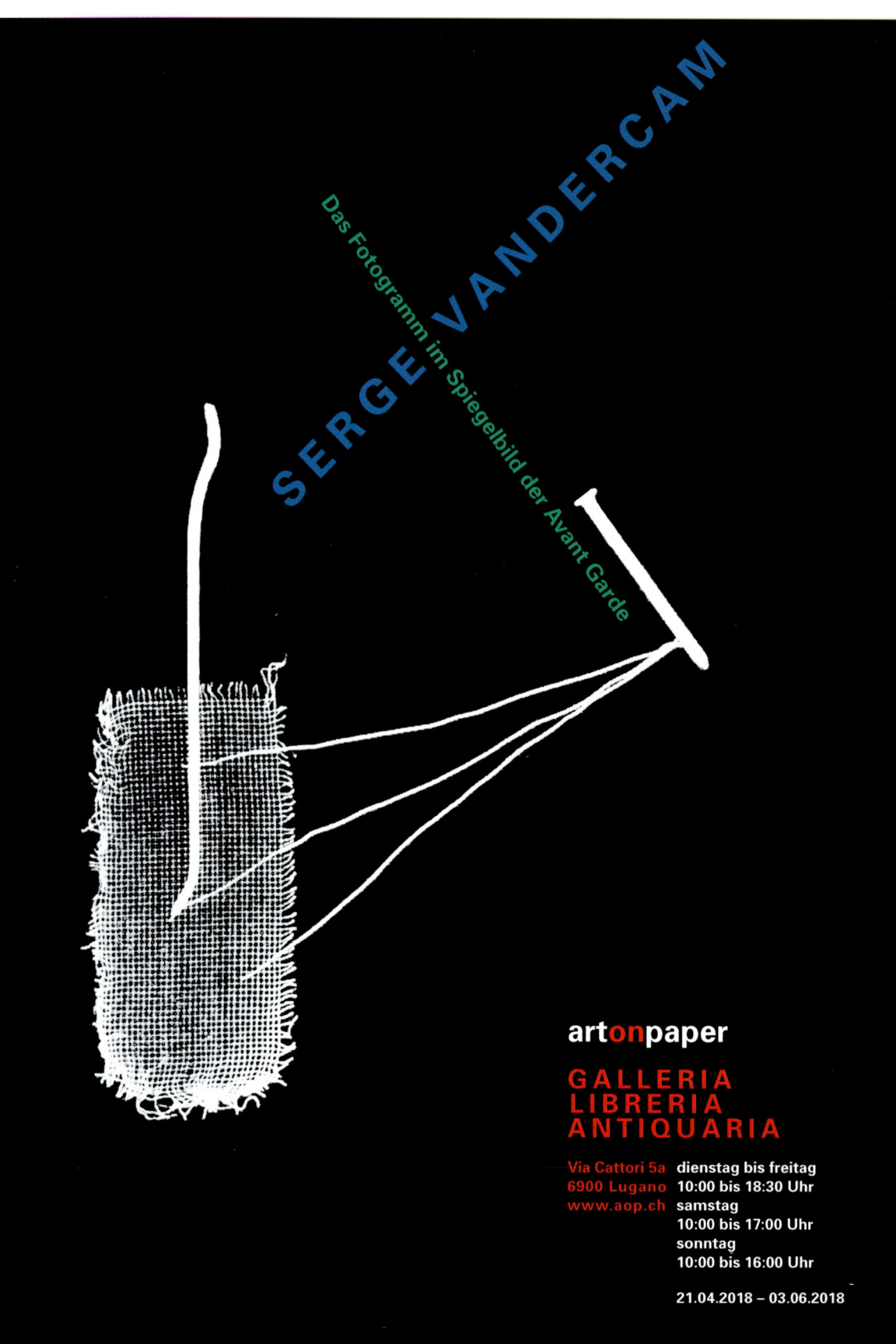

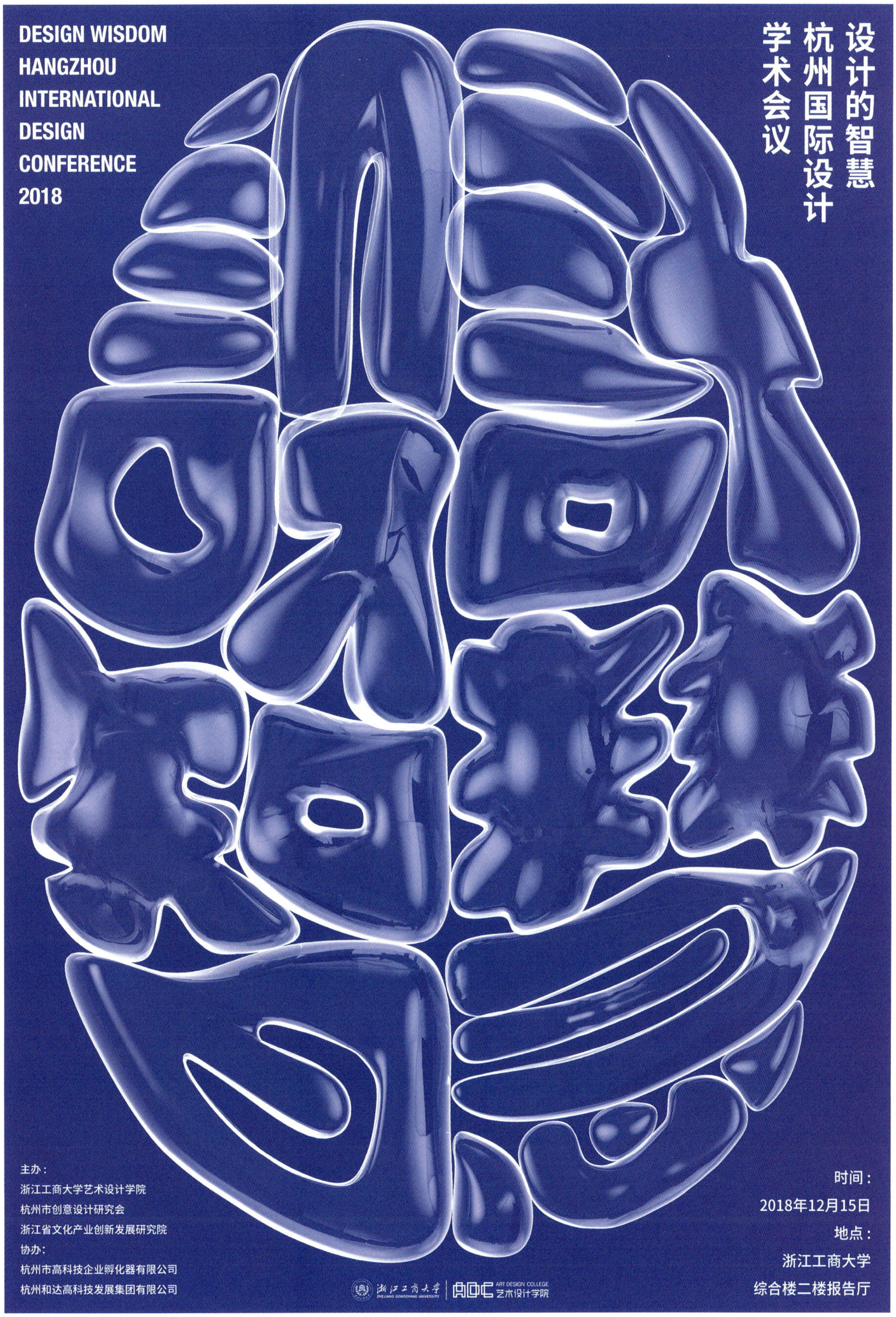

DESIGN WISDOM
HANGZHOU
INTERNATIONAL
DESIGN
CONFERENCE
2018

设计的智慧
杭州国际设计
学术会议

Design Wisdom
[Event Poster]

The international conference "Design Wisdom", held in Hangzhou, China, dealt with the central question of how to integrate design, together with scientific and technological innovation, into a global context in order to cope with changes in future lifestyles. In detail, the conference focused on how modern design can help promote energy innovation and material innovation, as well as contribute to socially sustainable developments, among other complex problems. To visualise the entire range of topics, this poster design combines the Chinese characters for "design" and "wisdom" with the illustration of a brain.

Client
Zhejiang Gongshang University,
Hangzhou, China

Design
Chaosheng Li,
Zhejiang Gongshang University,
Hangzhou, China

MOX – The Culture of Failure

[Poster Series]

The poster design for the Museum of Failure in Los Angeles, USA, visualises the concept that it is often mistakes that lead to success in the end. Presenting a collection of more than 100 failed products and services from well-known companies, the design establishes a "culture of the failure". This is conveyed creatively by a concept that marks such "failures" with the key visual of a large green X. The marker itself combines a positive green tick that represents success with a negative red X for error. The resulting green X aims at conveying the positive power of failure.

Client
Museum of Failure, Inc., Carson City, Nevada, USA

Design
Grey Germany / KW43 BRANDDESIGN, Düsseldorf, Germany

Managing Director Creation
Rüdiger Goetz

Creative Direction
Alexander Geh

Art Direction
Aya Kitsukawa

Account Management
Eva van Meegern

Copywriting
Michael Draheim

Photography
Jessica Morhard, Düsseldorf, Germany

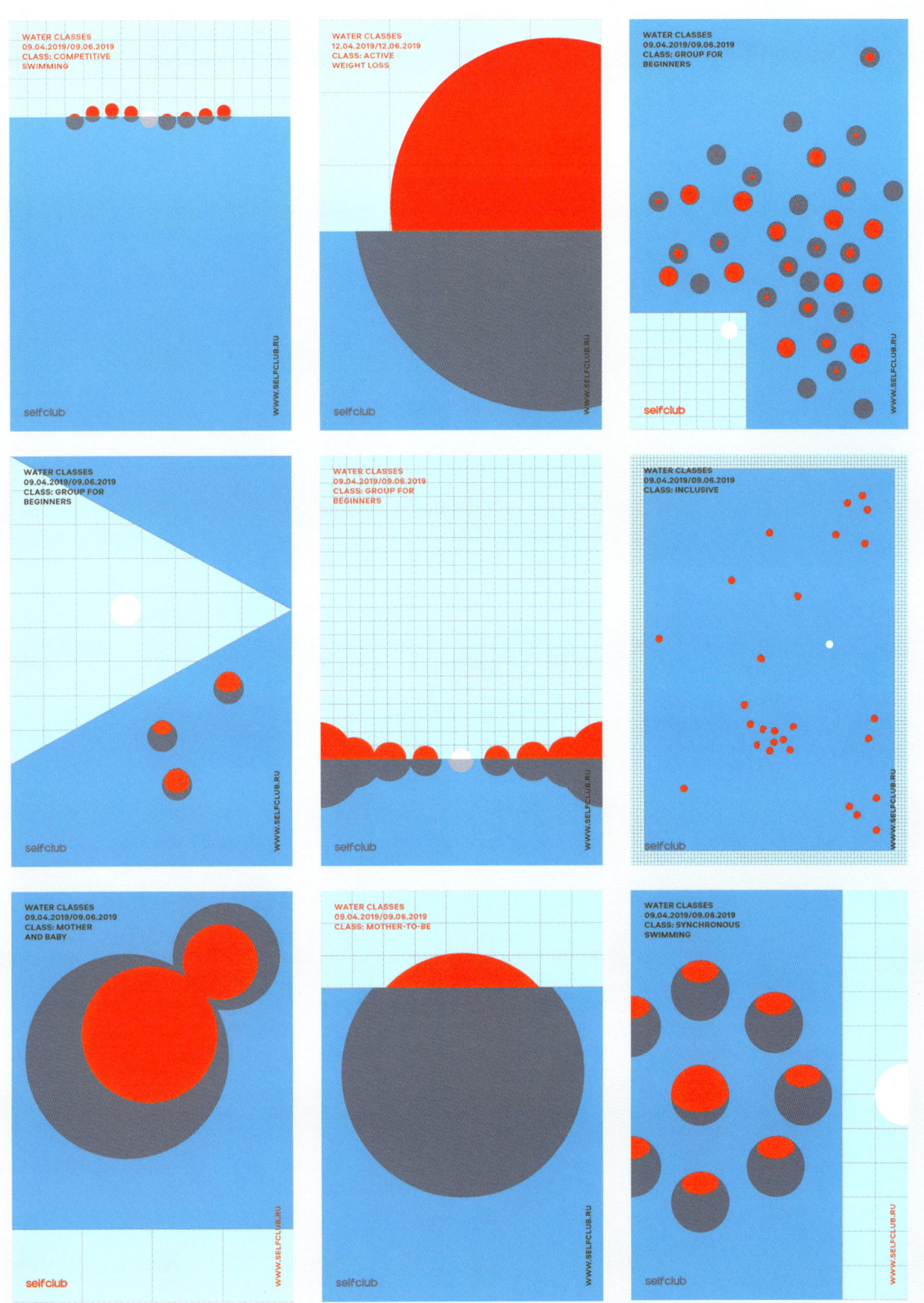

Aquality

[Promotional Poster Series]

The Aquality poster series for a water sports complex in Moscow was created against the backdrop that 47 per cent of people, as a survey had revealed, feel unconfident coming to swimming pools. The design addresses this problem by conveying notions of friendliness and ease, focusing on the physical properties of water and optical illusions, as well as the sense of depth and the dynamics of objects. With simplicity and irony, the visual identity conveys the central message that water makes things easy and people equal. A "SELF club" encourages people to believe in and love themselves.

Client
Self Club, Moscow, Russia

Design
Depot branding agency, Moscow, Russia

Creative Direction
Alexey Fadeev, Anastasia Tretyakova

Design Direction
Nikita Ivanov

Strategic Direction
Farhad Kuchkarov

Graphic Design
Raushan Sultanov

Aeshylia Festival

[Event Poster]

The task of the 2018 poster for the Aeshylia Festival in Eleusis, Attica, Greece, was to promote a new identity to both Greek and international audiences. With an eye to 2021, the year in which Eleusis will be crowned the European Capital of Culture, the poster aims to stake a dynamic claim. As part of the new logo's visual system, the poster hosts two A's. The resulting dynamic space is defined as a "container" filled with energy, emotion and creativity, which at the same time acts as a shutter inviting the eye to focus on the core of the experience.

Client
Social Municipality of Eleusis, Greece

Design
2YOLK, Athens, Greece

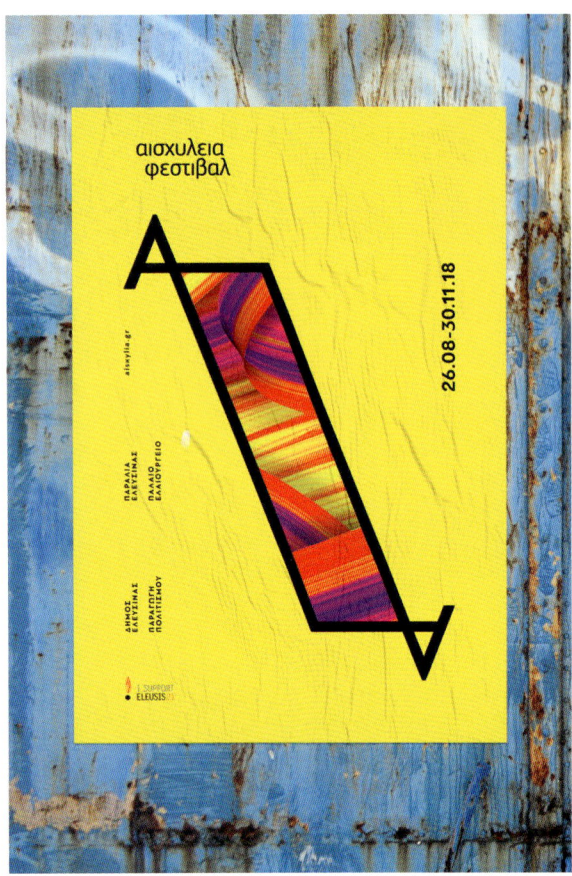

KoorBiënnale / Choir Biënnale

[Event Poster Series]

KoorBiënnale is a festival in the Dutch cities of Haarlem and Amsterdam that focuses on choir music and musicians. Celebrating diversity, the music ranges from gospel singers to experimental music theatre. Held in the Amsterdam area, the festival takes place within cultural venues, parks, the forest and the city of Haarlem. The aim in designing this poster series was to visualise the festival's energetic and optimistic vibe. It features images of three different birds, one residing in the city, one in the forest and one living in villages, alluding to the multiple venues and stages.

Client
Koorbiënnale, Haarlem, Netherlands

Design
Das Buro – Branding Agency, Rotterdam, Netherlands

Osterrath – Perfection Connected

[Poster Series]

The focus of this poster design is to convey the fascination of modern connection technology. Its main characteristic is the use of the basic geometric shape of the circle as a symbol for the two basic materials used by Osterrath: tube and sheet metal. These materials are organised in a flexible pattern based on punching tools and technical drawings. The resulting symbol thus also evokes the impression of the "squaring of the circle" – the mathematical approach of constructing a square with the same area as a given circle using geometric means.

Client
Osterrath GmbH & Co. KG,
Bad Laasphe, Germany

Design
Grey Germany / KW43 BRANDDESIGN,
Düsseldorf, Germany

Managing Director Creation
Rüdiger Goetz

Creative Direction
Jürgen Adolph

Art Direction
Marc Schaede

Account Management
Christine de Groot

Dialog

[Poster Series]

This poster campaign was created as part of the brand relaunch of Dialog, the broker-focused insurer of the Generali Group in Germany, which intends to become the preferred partner of insurance brokers. The aim of the design was not only to modernise and professionalise the brand appearance, but also to break the conventions of the insurance category. In collaboration with an illustrator, the design realised the concept of telling the story of every Dialog insurance product. Released as a limited edition set, the series has been sent to clients, customers and stakeholders in celebration of the new Dialog brand launch.

Client
Generali Deutschland AG,
Munich, Germany

Design
Landor Hamburg, Germany

Head of Marketing/Technical Sales Innovations
Benjamin Börner,
Dialog Lebensversicherungs-AG

Creative Direction
Markus Blankenburg, Landor Hamburg

Brand Strategy
Hellen Markusch, Landor Hamburg

Experience Design
Jack Osborn, Lisa Ribbers,
Anastassia Saromova, Landor Hamburg

Text
Nestor Sierralta, Landor Hamburg

Illustration
Peter Greenwood,
Brighton, United Kingdom

TYPOGRAPHY

Red Dot: Grand Prix

Time Book
[Typographic Artwork]

The newly developed typeface by Quinsay Design is inspired by fonts used in early letterpress printing. Accordingly, it has been published on a series of transparent bookends called "Time Book". The collection comprises three kinds of bookends, named "The Pink", "The Font" and "The Ice", and all share the same shape of a book but feature different colours and printed graphical information. Furthermore, they are made of hand-polished crystal glass blocks whose surfaces are screen-printed with special ink. The name "Time Book" is inspired by the different publishing dates of books, with these three bookends each featuring "MMXIX" on the book spine as the Roman numeral for "2019". "The Pink" is the year 2019 calendar – with the pink colour representing "pig", the Chinese zodiac sign of this year. Inspired by a novel written by Gabriel García Márquez, "The Ice" shows the beginning of the novel "One Hundred Years of Solitude". And the sides of the yellow bookend "The Font" are illustrated with the 26 letters of the alphabet, as well as numbers and punctuation marks.

Statement by the jury
This typographic work catches the eye with its impressive presentation of three heavy blocks made of transparent crystal glass. The idea of publishing a new typeface as haptic lettering on three bookends shaped like a book is congenially complemented by the professional quality of the font itself. Heights, kerning and spacing have been harmoniously balanced which makes the typeface ideally suited for modern, flexible use.

Interface & User Experience Design | Spatial Communication | Red Dot: Junior Award | Designer Profiles | Jury | Index | Red Dot – World of Design

reddot winner 2019
grand prix

Client
Quinsay, Hangzhou, China

Design
Tong Yi, Quinsay Design,
Hangzhou, China

→ Designer profile on page 559

Red Dot: Best of the Best

Helvetica Now
[Typeface]

The typeface Helvetica Now represents a major overhaul of Helvetica, one of the best known and most widely used typeface families in the world. The new version was developed to keep this 1957 style classic alive and in tune with today's changing technical conditions and reading habits. The most important innovation consists of the three optical sizes of Micro, Text and Display. Helvetica Now Micro offers more open letters and adjustments to complex characters and accent marks, all aimed at improving legibility at tiny sizes. Helvetica Now Display has a range of weights, from Hairline to Extrablack, and a tighter spacing. In between is Helvetica Now Text. Previously problematic glyph designs such as the "@ sign" have been reworked and a host of alternate characters been created such as a single-story a, a beardless G and a straight-legged R, which all have the potential to alter the look of the typeface family and together with additional tools signify a giant leap forward for it to live on tomorrow and beyond.

Statement by the jury
The Helvetica typeface is a true icon, and to revise it to make it fit for contemporary and future use is a highly respectable endeavour. With a myriad of new and alternate letters, sizes and styles, the result has emerged as a convincing realisation that manages the balancing act of lending the well-known classic an immediately recognisable modern touch.

Client
Monotype, Woburn, Massachusetts, USA

Design
Monotype, Woburn, Massachusetts, USA

Typography
Charles Nix, Tom Rickner, Hendrik Weber,
Alexander Roth, Juan Villanueva,
Terrance Weinzierl, Jim Ford,
Steve Matteson

→ Designer profile on page 550

Red Dot: Best of the Best

Bahlsen – The Bahlsen Family
[Typeface]

The family-owned company Bahlsen, which has been around for 130 years, has intensively dealt with its own origin and identity to sustainably relaunch the brand. Against the background of creating "good things for others", the new umbrella brand and the newly developed corporate design aim at conveying the notions of tradition and timelessness. The result is a concise Grotesk typeface that expresses the company's family aspirations already in the name of the new umbrella brand: The Bahlsen Family. The Bahlsen Grotesk is based on a handwritten typography of the 1920s, with each letter and every single character being redeveloped and individually proportioned. The result is a characteristic typeface that can be used as an independent design element. In addition, the typography was baked as limited-edition biscuits and repackaged in a special tin box sealed by the TET seal of quality. This seal, once developed by Hermann Bahlsen, also forms a bridge to the newly designed umbrella brand.

Statement by the jury
The design of this new typeface masterfully combines the tradition and identity of the company with the modernity of the present to outstandingly convincing and vivid effect. Baking the new characters as biscuits and creating a congenial packaging for them is an excellent idea that not only hits the very heart of the brand, but as a surplus, also offers a sensual experience.

Interface & User Experience Design Spatial Communication Red Dot: Junior Award Designer Profiles Jury Index Red Dot – World of Design

Client
Bahlsen GmbH & Co. KG,
Hannover, Germany

Design
MUTABOR, Hamburg, Germany

Creative Direction
Sven Ritterhoff

Design Team
Moritz Carstens, Lasse Lemster,
Jan Hellmerichs, Simon Büssem

Typography
René Bieder

Client Service Management
Ipek Molvali, Felicitas Patt

→ Designer profile on page 552

Publishing & Print Media   Posters   **Typography**   Illustrations   Sound Design   Film & Animation   Online   Apps

Hegii Icon Visual System

The aim when developing these bathroom icons was to use a modern design language to convey diverse functions in a user-friendly way. The clear and concise design of the symbols immediately tells the consumer how to use the respective products and how they work. The user experience is significantly enhanced, and the new icons also create a visually harmonious framework for the heterogeneous product range. At the same time, the symbols echo the aesthetic of the Hegii brand, thus creating a direct link to the company and its values.

Client
Hegii Co., Ltd., Shanghai, China

Design
Hegii Co., Ltd., Shanghai, China

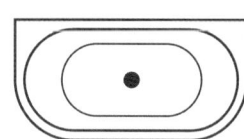 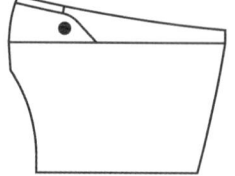 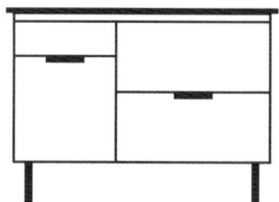

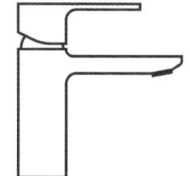 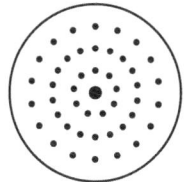 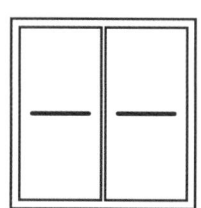

DR Publik
[Corporate Type Family]

Danish Broadcasting Corporation (DR) is Denmark's oldest and largest electronic media enterprise. Text is an essential part of DR's content. The bespoke type family DR Publik was designed to strengthen legibility and ensure visual consistency on all platforms, enhance corporate branding and create a coherent visual expression. The streamlined, no-fuss type family corresponds to the Scandinavian design aesthetic and is characterised in particular by nearly monolinear stroke widths and horizontal or vertical terminals.

Client
DR – The Danish Broadcasting Corporation, Copenhagen, Denmark

Design
Overtone, Aarhus, Denmark
DR Design, Copenhagen, Denmark

Head of Design
Anders Thulin, DR Design

Art Direction
Niels Rinder, Christian Rahbek Olsen, DR Design

Design Direction
Nicolaj Bak, Overtone

Type Design
Rasmus Lund Mathisen, Overtone

Publishing & Print Media　　Posters　　**Typography**　　Illustrations　　Sound Design　　Film & Animation　　Online　　Apps

Cities in Motion
[Typeface]

Design motion screens with animated, colourful signatures of the respective city provide a welcome to travellers at all the main train stations in the Netherlands. A variable, custom-made typeface was designed for this purpose, and a dedicated script was developed for the animation of the individual words. The letters vary in size and shape and are aligned vertically rather in the traditional horizontal way, giving the typography a very distinct and vibrant feel. The grid is constantly in motion; the letters adjust to its changing framework and thus create a visually striking design.

Client
Exterion Media Netherlands,
Amsterdam, Netherlands

Design
Studio Dumbar – Part of Dept,
Rotterdam, Netherlands

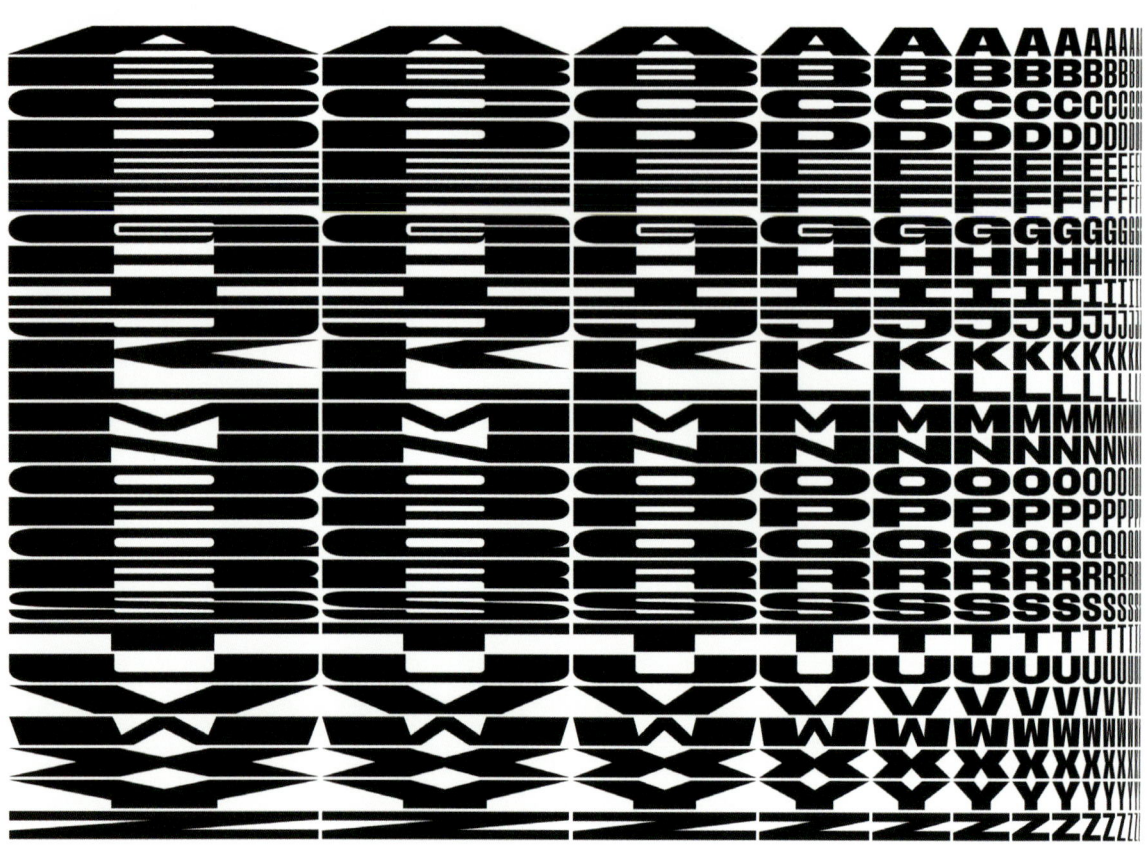

Festival für neue Musik
[Typographic Artwork]

"The Festival for New Music" is a two-day event at the Konzerthaus Bielefeld for the free interpretation of classical music in a transition to improvisation and experiment. The backstage passes for the festival were designed using an approach that takes the title "New shoes for new paths" quite literally. The festival name decorates a pair of sneakers in modern, black and white typography that functions as a quirkily designed entry ticket for the meet & greet – and opens up new paths both musically and with a visit behind the scenes.

Client
Bühnen und Orchester der Stadt Bielefeld, Rudolf-Oetker-Halle/Konzerthaus Bielefeld, Germany

Design
beierarbeit GmbH, Bielefeld, Germany

Creative Direction/Typography
Christoph Beier, beierarbeit

Graphic Design
Jochen Michael, Bielefeld, Germany

Director of Orchestra and Concert Hall
Martin Beyer, Bühnen und Orchester der Stadt Bielefeld

Musical Director
Alexander Kalajdzic, Bühnen und Orchester der Stadt Bielefeld

Publishing
Michael Heicks, Bühnen und Orchester der Stadt Bielefeld

Absolument moderne

[Exhibition Catalogue]

The special exhibition "Absolument moderne" was shown at Gutenberg-Museum in Mainz in 2017. The accompanying book and the other materials take a modern view of the famous poem "Le Bateau ivre" by Arthur Rimbaud, which also inspired the design of the corresponding guest book. The exhibition title, in a vibrant red, extends across the dark-blue binding in wave-like movements. Like a ship bobbing up and down on the sea, it sometimes disappears from view. The straight-lined design of the materials in white, red and blue gives the modern reinterpretation of the well-known verses a clearly structured framework.

Client
Gutenberg-Museum, Mainz, Germany

Design
Designstudio Mathilda Mutant, Mainz, Germany

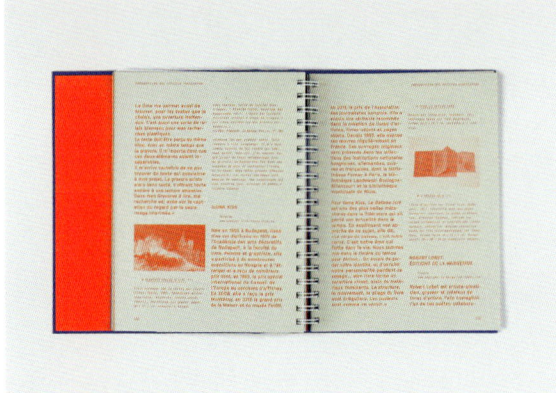

FUTURA. DIE SCHRIFT.
[Exhibition Catalogue]

Designed by typographer Paul Renner within the concept of the New Typography, the typeface Futura is considered an embodiment of the spirit of the 1920s avant-garde. Accordingly, it determined the modern appearance of many print media, also shaping the look of large brand names. With straight lines and a timeless feel, the catalogue for the special exhibition is designed like the typeface itself. The catalogue accompanied the special exhibition "FUTURA. DIE SCHRIFT." (FUTURA. THE TYPEFACE.) at the Gutenberg-Museum in Mainz. It was the first exhibition about this typeface in a museum in Germany.

Client
Gutenberg-Museum, Mainz, Germany

Design
Hochschule Mainz, University of Applied Sciences, Mainz, Germany

Design Team
Stephanie Kaplan, Isabel Naegele

A Streak of Grey

[Book Cover]

The collection of essays "A Streak of Grey" includes personal experiences, observations and thoughts of the author. His insight that joy and sorrow are equal parts of life is echoed in the typographic design of the cover and binding. The dominant colours of black and white reflect the light and dark episodes, and are at the same time combined to create different shades of grey. In areas defined by straight lines and reminiscent of timelines, they symbolise the ups and downs of life and its different phases.

Client
Ding Ding Co., Ltd., Taipei City, Taiwan

Design
hufax arts / FJCU, Taipei City, Taiwan

Creative Direction
Fa-Hsiang Hu, Yun Liu

Art Direction
Fa-Hsiang Hu

Typography
Alain Hu, Jing-Yan Zhong, Di Hu, Fei Hu, FJCU aart team

Project Management
Natasha Liao

→ Designer profile on page 533
→ Clip online

Taste of Life

[Book]

"Taste of Life" is a collection of gourmet essays. In them, the author presents homemade, local specialities and lesser-known recipes. The design of the essays was inspired by traditional Chinese book design. This marks an important transition phase in the art of book-binding, which over time moved away from traditional rules and became more modern. In the same way, tradition and modernity also go hand in hand in the design of the essay collection. The alternating horizontal and vertical layout looks contemporary, while the traditional typography gives the work its retro appearance.

Client
inDare Design Strategy Limited, Shenzhen, China

Design
inDare Design Strategy Limited, Shenzhen, China

Project Management
Ching-Lang Chen

Strategic Planning
Jiarong Zeng

Art Direction
Junlong Yang

Graphic Design
Yanhui Yan, Shuzhuan Huang

Programming
Yujie Chen

Production
Fengming Chen

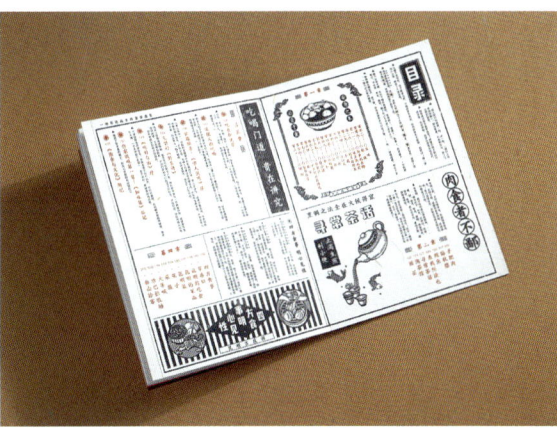

The Sutra of Infinite Meanings

[Book]

Client
Jun-Liang Chen, FREEiMAGE DESIGN, Taipei City, Taiwan

Design
Mo-Li Yeh, Lunghwa University of Science and Technology, Taoyuan, Taiwan
Yu-Ju Lin, National Taipei University of Business, Taoyuan, Taiwan

The volume of "The Sutra of Infinite Meanings", in Master Cheng Yen's calligraphy, continues to convey the wisdom of the Dharma. The script is presented in the "dragon-scales" style, a form inherited from ancient Chinese bookbinding. The textured pages, when rolled out, resemble the skin of an auspicious dragon, and when rolled up into a scroll they are easily carried and transported. The exterior cover is bound with cloth to reveal qualities of pristineness and humility. The design embraces modern concepts, yet embeds the devout beliefs and sincere manners of the past. From its internal connotations to its exterior presentation, this collection of artwork effortlessly unfolds the cultural characteristics and spiritual energy encapsulated within.

ILLUSTRATIONS

BLOCBIRDS

[Art Project]

Blocbirds is inspired by nature: the 25 square-in-square illustrations graphically reflect the plumage of European birds and capture their colours and composition in squares. The amount of colours, their diversity, position and their relationship to each other give each individual bird and each installation its unique, characteristic plumage. The installation is accompanied by stuffed birds, matching their graphical counterpart. This artful combination of illustration and bird life opens the eyes of the observer to nature and its beauty.

Client
Studio 212 Fahrenheit,
Groningen, Netherlands

Design
Studio 212 Fahrenheit,
Groningen, Netherlands

→ Designer profile on page 566

BLOCBIRDS

[Art Project]

Blocbirds is inspired by nature: the 25 square-in-square illustrations graphically reflect the plumage of European birds and capture their colours and composition in squares. The amount of colours, their diversity, position and their relationship to each other give each individual bird and each installation its unique, characteristic plumage. The installation is accompanied by stuffed birds, matching their graphical counterpart. This artful combination of illustration and bird life opens the eyes of the observer to nature and its beauty.

Client
Studio 212 Fahrenheit,
Groningen, Netherlands

Design
Studio 212 Fahrenheit,
Groningen, Netherlands

→ Designer profile on page 566

Heart of Iceland

[Educational Illustration, Interactive Exhibition]

At the Þingvellir (Thingvellir) visitor centre, an interactive exhibition takes visitors on a journey through history and the special aspects of Iceland's natural wonder. Ten installations encourage visitors to interact with the place where the country became a commonwealth. The different stations include detailed illustrations in delicate strokes of historical events, giving insights into the flora and fauna. Using ice-blue and gold as colours, the shimmering scenes contrast with the rock-like backgrounds against which they are set.

Client
Thingvellir National Park, Selfoss, Iceland

Design
Gagarin, Reykjavík, Iceland
Gláma•Kim, Reykjavík, Iceland

Curation
Thorunn S. Thorgrimsdottir, Visionis, Reykjavík, Iceland

Audiovisual Equipment
Knutur Runarsson, Origo, Reykjavík, Iceland

Lighting Design
Páll Ragnarsson, Reykjavík, Iceland

Text
Alfheidur Ingadottir, Reykjavík, Iceland
Bryndis Sverrisdottir, Reykjavík, Iceland

→ Designer profile on page 527

EJI Museum – Domestic Slave Trade Narrative

[Educational Illustration]

Equal Justice Initiative (EJI) opened the National Memorial for Peace and Justice as well as The Legacy museum to allow visitors to gather and reflect on America's history of racial inequality. The illustrated 2D video developed for this purpose provides historical facts about the domestic slave trade. This dark and heavy history is reflected in a visually impactful way in the realistic charcoal drawings. The unembellished design of the scenes not only informs the observer but also appeals to the emotions.

Client
The Legacy Museum,
Montgomery, Alabama, USA

Design
Orchid Creation, New York, USA

Art Direction/Illustration
Ming-Hsuan Lee

ILLUSTRATIONS

Budapest Giftbook

[Book Illustration]

The Budapest Giftbook is a flipbook with a series of illustrations about Budapest. This minimalist travel guide gives the illusion of continuous movement by simulating motion when the pages are turned rapidly. Like Budapest itself, the images also form and transform from one page to the next, giving an impressive feel for the vibrancy of the city. The atmospheric, entirely black-and-white illustrations display the city in a new, contemporary way, playing with geometric shapes and heavy contrasts.

Client
Budapest Giftbook, Budapest, Hungary

Design
Botond Vörös, Budapest, Hungary

Concept
Mónika Dusik, Budapest, Hungary

Text
Mátyás Falvai, Budapest, Hungary

Publishing
László Kedves, Budapest, Hungary

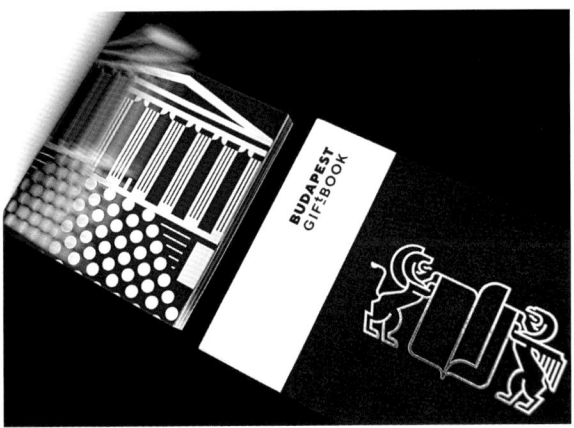

Jingdezhen Image

[Poster Illustration]

The Chinese city of Jingdezhen has a tradition of porcelain manufacturing that spans millennia. The black and white illustrations create a drawn monument to this artisan craft. With lots of lovingly explored details, the finely drawn scenarios add vibrancy to the city's life and work as well as to its tradition of artisan craft. These are contrasted by the centrally placed and consciously simply designed presentations of a dish, a globe and a pot. They act like a heading and give thematic context to the respective illustration.

Client
Jingdezhen Sanbao Ceramic Institute, Jingdezhen, China

Design
Communication University of Zhejiang, Hangzhou, China

Art Direction
Prof. Chao Yang

Graphic Design
Prof. Chao Yang, Mengqiang Wang

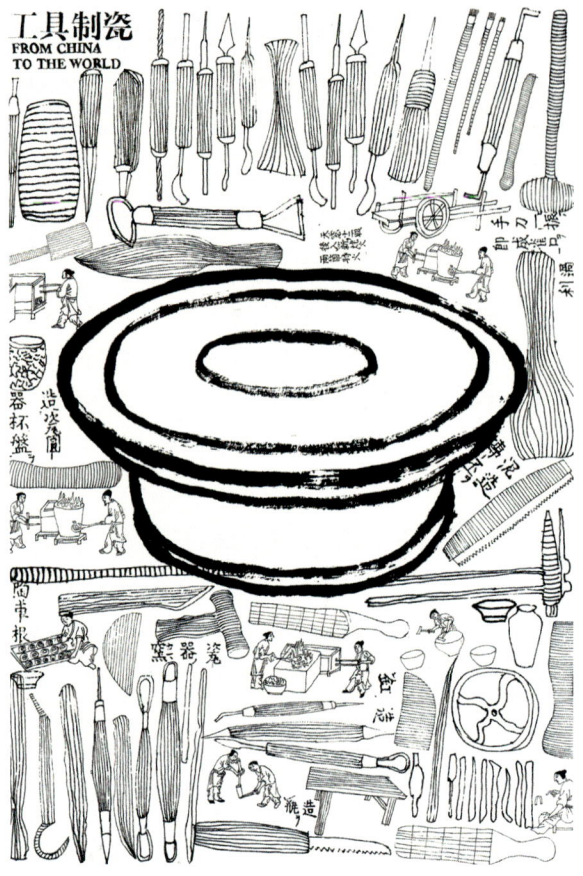

Dong Ci Xi Yun
[Promotional Illustration]

Traditional Chinese porcelain art is one of the main themes in Yue restaurant in Shanghai. At the same time, it is the central motif of these illustrations, which succinctly connect porcelain manufacturing to typical cultural features of Shanghai and the city of Jingdezhen, which is famous for its porcelain. Each of the black and white motifs speaks for itself and, in clever combination with the other drawings, forms a harmonious visual unit complemented perfectly by Chinese calligraphy and explanatory texts in English.

Client
Shanghai Yue Restaurant,
Shanghai, China

Design
Jingdezhen Ceramic Institute,
Jingdezhen, China
Communication University of Zhejiang,
Hangzhou, China

Art Direction
Prof. Chao Yang

Graphic Design
Prof. Jianfeng Yu, Shanyu Shen

Concept
Yinluo Du, Qiang Yi

Dead Brothers Tale

[Mural]

The mural was inspired by the oldest existing Greek folk song. The expressive illustrations in deep black accentuated with just a few white strokes succeed in conveying the dark, supernatural nature of the "The Dead Brother's Song" and depicting the song's main characters in a striking manner. The illustrations were designed for a modern Greek restaurant. Used as a central decorative element, the scenes keep the traditional tale alive even in the present day.

Client
Ergon Food, London, United Kingdom

Design
Beetroot Design Group,
Thessaloniki, Greece

→ Designer profile on page 513

Yiayia and friends

[Packaging Illustration]

The illustrations from the "Yiayia and friends" series combine Greek culinary traditions with contemporary flair. They show the main protagonist – a Greek grandmother (yiayia) – surrounded by a cheerful and colourful universe made up of animal figures and elements of nature. The common link between the monochromatic characters with their enclosed shapes are their eyes, which are always designed the same way. They run through the project like a logo, and act as a visual representation of the connection between humans and nature.

Client
Beetroot Design Group,
Thessaloniki, Greece

Design
Beetroot Design Group,
Thessaloniki, Greece

→ Designer profile on page 513

All in!

[Menu Cards]

For its tenth anniversary, the Michelin-starred Costes restaurant introduced a menu card designed to look like a card game. The set is printed on cardboard paper and features 16 motifs, fun facts and explanations of the dishes, making the ordering process an interactive gastronomical experience. On the front side of the cards, the main ingredients of each dish are highlighted with line-drawings printed using letterpress techniques, while the logo is embossed using silver hot foil stamping. The joker is a blank card on which guests can leave their feedback.

Client
Costes Restaurant, Budapest, Hungary

Design
studio NUR, Budapest, Hungary

Art Direction
Eszter Laki

Graphic Design
Eszter Laki, Réka Imre

Photography
András Zoltai

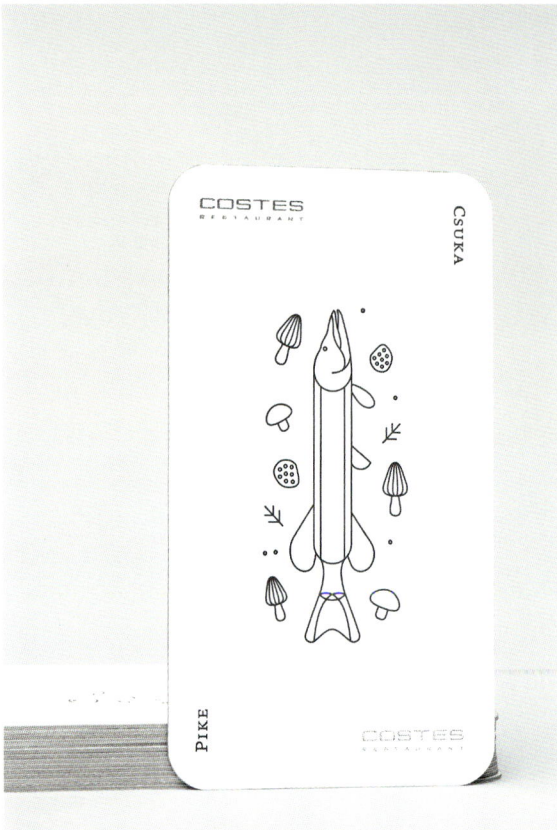
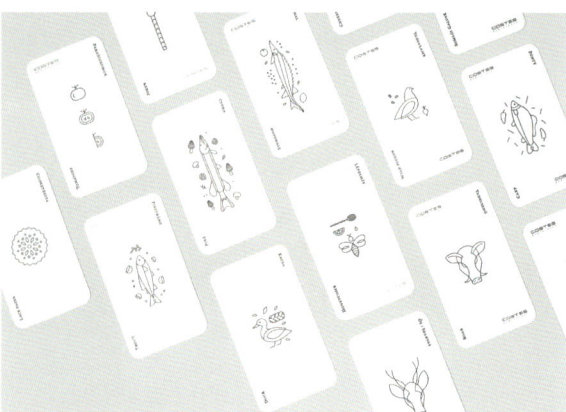

COSMOS
[Book Illustration]

In Gabor Palotai's latest artist's book, COSMOS, the 72 illustrations display a distinct graphic vision of outer space and turn planets, galaxies, moons and stars into abstract art. Individual patterns in white, black and orange form the different-sized circles. They derive their own identity from within themselves, and at the same time are set in relationship to each other. In this way, the illustrations demonstrate that each individual is also his or her own cosmos. Additionally, the patterns in contrasting colours create a graphic rhythm that seems to make the circles swell, shrink and spin – an optical illusion that awakens the imagination of the reader.

Client
Gabor Palotai Design, Stockholm, Sweden

Design
Gabor Palotai Design, Stockholm, Sweden

Art Direction
Gabor Palotai

Graphic Design
Gabor Palotai, Annika Jansson

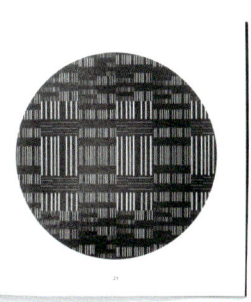

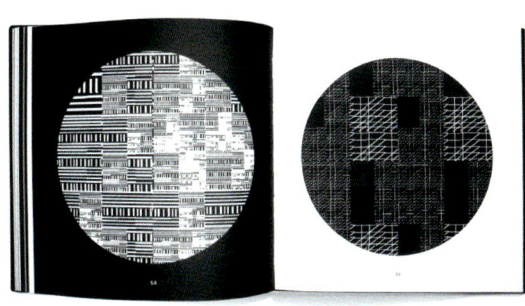

Animated Artworks
[Cover Artwork]

Client
Upon You Records, Berlin, Germany

Design
Eat, Sleep + Design, Berlin, Germany

Concept
Frank Gräfe

Artwork/Animation
Frank Gräfe

→ Designer profile on page 524
→ Clip online

In an era of downloads and streaming, digital is the relevant medium for album launches and related artworks. To fill these with more life, the animated covers merge music and art into its own digital and versatile art form. An initially static image is transformed into a vibrant installation that changes in accordance with the music. Each cover creation interprets the music using its very own aesthetic and offers a unique acoustic and visual experience.

50 Mindshots

[Book Illustration]

Client
Sergio Ingravalle, Bielefeld, Germany

Design
Sergio Ingravalle, Bielefeld, Germany

→ Designer profile on page 534

"50 Mindshots" is a series of universally understandable illustrations created by artist Sergio Ingravalle to convey his personal thoughts and current questions by graphic means. His works address aspects of modern life, such as cyberbullying, digitalisation and burnout, in a stylistically reduced manner. The imagery shifts in colour from black to grey to red, and is sometimes critical, at times ironic and at times humorous. Hard-hitting and fitting, the illustrations encourage the reader to reflect and ponder on the content.

Wagner, Wahnsinn & Walküren

[Book Illustration]

The book "Wagner, Wahnsinn & Walküren" (Wagner, Weirdness & Valkyries) gives a tongue-in-cheek insight into the complex and extraordinary legend of the Ring of the Nibelung. In addition to short, quite unscientific psychograms, the book outlines the family connections of the main protagonists. The illustrations of graphic artist Florian Althans accompany this famous saga in an abstract, aesthetic form. His "cyclopes", designed in contrasting colours, interpret the characters in a humorous way and with graphic minimalism. In this way, the illustrations transform the historical story into a modern fairytale.

Client
BROTLOS Verlag, Krefeld, Germany

Design
BROTLOS Verlag, Krefeld, Germany

Graphic Design
Florian Althans

Smartum

[Brand Illustration]

Smartum develops solutions that help workplaces promote wellbeing. Colourful illustrations were created to match the overhauled visual appearance of the company. The aim was to develop a series of energetic and versatile illustrations that would work well in many sizes and for many applications. The illustrations highlight the effect of Smartum's benefits in everyday life: as people feel better, they also perform better at the workplace. The images are characterised by rich colours, large-scale motifs, interesting angles, and dramatic shadows, and their stripped-down style facilitates their use across the company's entire communication palette.

Client
Smartum, Helsinki, Finland

Design
Berry Creative, Helsinki, Finland
BOND, Helsinki, Finland

Illustration
Julia Nyyssölä, Berry Creative

Design Team
Kevin Hytönen, Juha-Pekka Laurila, Marko Salonen, BOND

Project Management
Saku Nummi, BOND

Das Erste – Seasonal Campaign 2019

[Promotional Illustration]

Client
ARD Design and Presentation,
Munich, Germany

Design
Luxlotusliner, Munich, Germany

Programme Director
Volker Herres, ARD

Creative Direction
Henriette Edle von Hoessle,
Head of ARD Design and Presentation
Gabi Madracevic, Luxlotusliner

Art Direction
Werner Mayer,
Erstes Deutsches Fernsehen,
ARD Design and Presentation
Iris Pfennig, Luxlotusliner

Design Project Management
Heike Steinbach, ARD

Animation
Fatma Kapakos, Axel Flachenecker,
Juan García Segura, Luxlotusliner

Project Management
Nadja Doth, Luxlotusliner

Music/Composition
Hans Wiedemann, Ulrich Rassy,
BR SG Sounddesign

→ Clip online

The aim of these idents, developed for ARD, was to promote the brand and enhance the memory value of the logo Das Erste. The logo is placed at the centre of each illustration and animation, which show typical scenes for the four seasons: a winter wonderland in ice-blue and white, a summery water-based landscape, or colourful flowers heralding spring surround and frame the logo, making it a fixed component of the respective season. Each ident has its own style and individual aesthetic, thus standing out from the daily programming of the channel.

Publishing & Print Media   Posters   Typography   Illustrations   Sound Design   Film & Animation   Online   Apps

#SmallButPowerful
[Advertising Illustration]

The Wacom company accompanied the launch of its new, handy tablet with illustrated advertising motifs. The motifs apply the benefits of the product to a natural setting. Under the motto #SmallButPowerful, they feature small heroes of the animal kingdom that work efficiently and achieve great things. An ant, a dragonfly, a chameleon and a kingfisher are the protagonists at the heart of the richly contrasting depictions. Their shimmering colours set them apart from the understated backgrounds, directing the gaze of the observer to their strengths.

Client
Wacom Europe GmbH,
Düsseldorf, Germany

Design
Beetroot Design Group,
Thessaloniki, Greece

→ Designer profile on page 513
→ Clip online

126

Samsung Digital Plaza – Art Collaboration for Premium Store

[Art Project]

The illustrations of Lee Sung-Pyo decorate the walls of the newly opened Premium Store Samsung Digital Plaza, blurring the boundaries between a shop and a gallery. Under the motto "wind (hope)" – words that are written in the same way in Korean – poetry and refined illustrations are effectively combined. In the form of large-scale works of art, motion graphics, banners and posters, these works create a friendly and open atmosphere, adding artful nuances to the store.

Client
Samsung Electronics, Seoul, South Korea

Design
hongdesign Ltd., Seoul, South Korea

Creative Direction
Sung Taek Hong

Art Direction
Hyun Kyung Kim

Graphic Design
Seung Ku Jeoung, Kang Won Hong

Illustration
Sung Pyo Lee, Seoul, South Korea

Dialog

[Informative Illustration, Brand Illustration]

The design objective of these illustrations was to break with the conventions of the insurance category and enable visual storytelling. The more than 300 motifs accompany the brand relaunch of Dialog, the broker-focused insurer of the Generali Group in Germany. The simple yet succinctly designed illustrations create an emotional link to the observer. The harmonious colours make the illustrations attractive and vibrant, connecting with the target group in its modern environment. In this way, they create a refreshing alternative view of this rather conventional topic.

Client
Generali Deutschland AG,
Munich, Germany

Design
Landor Hamburg, Germany

Head of Marketing/Technical Sales Innovations
Benjamin Börner,
Dialog Lebensversicherungs-AG

Creative Direction
Markus Blankenburg, Landor Hamburg

Brand Strategy
Hellen Markusch, Landor Hamburg

Experience Design
Jack Osborn, Lisa Ribbers,
Anastassia Saromova, Landor Hamburg

Text
Nestor Sierralta, Landor Hamburg

Illustration
Peter Greenwood,
Brighton, United Kingdom

→ Clip online

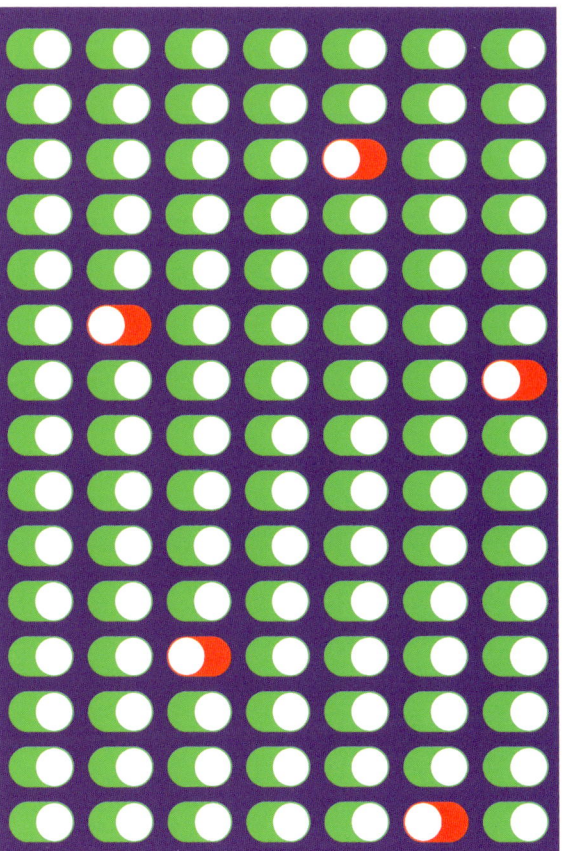

FI-Connect
[Poster Illustration]

The toggle function is a symbol of digital transformation. The distinctive sign, which always represents an either-or situation such as On/Off or Yes/No, is at the heart of this poster series for communicating news of the digital conference FI-Connect. Shown in various sizes, diverse colour combinations and arrangements, the toggle becomes the core design element in the illustrations. In conjunction with the iconic Sparkasse "S", it symbolises innovation, trust and security. These are also the topics of the digital conference FI-Connect that the poster series is advertising.

Client
Finanz Informatik,
Frankfurt/Main, Germany

Design
beierarbeit GmbH, Bielefeld, Germany

Head of Advertising
Christoph Rutter, Finanz Informatik

Head of Marketing
Andreas Honsel, Finanz Informatik

Strategic Planning
Claudia Palermo, Finanz Informatik

Creative Direction/Graphic Design
Christoph Beier, beierarbeit GmbH

Production
Torsten Herrmann, TH3,
Bielefeld, Germany

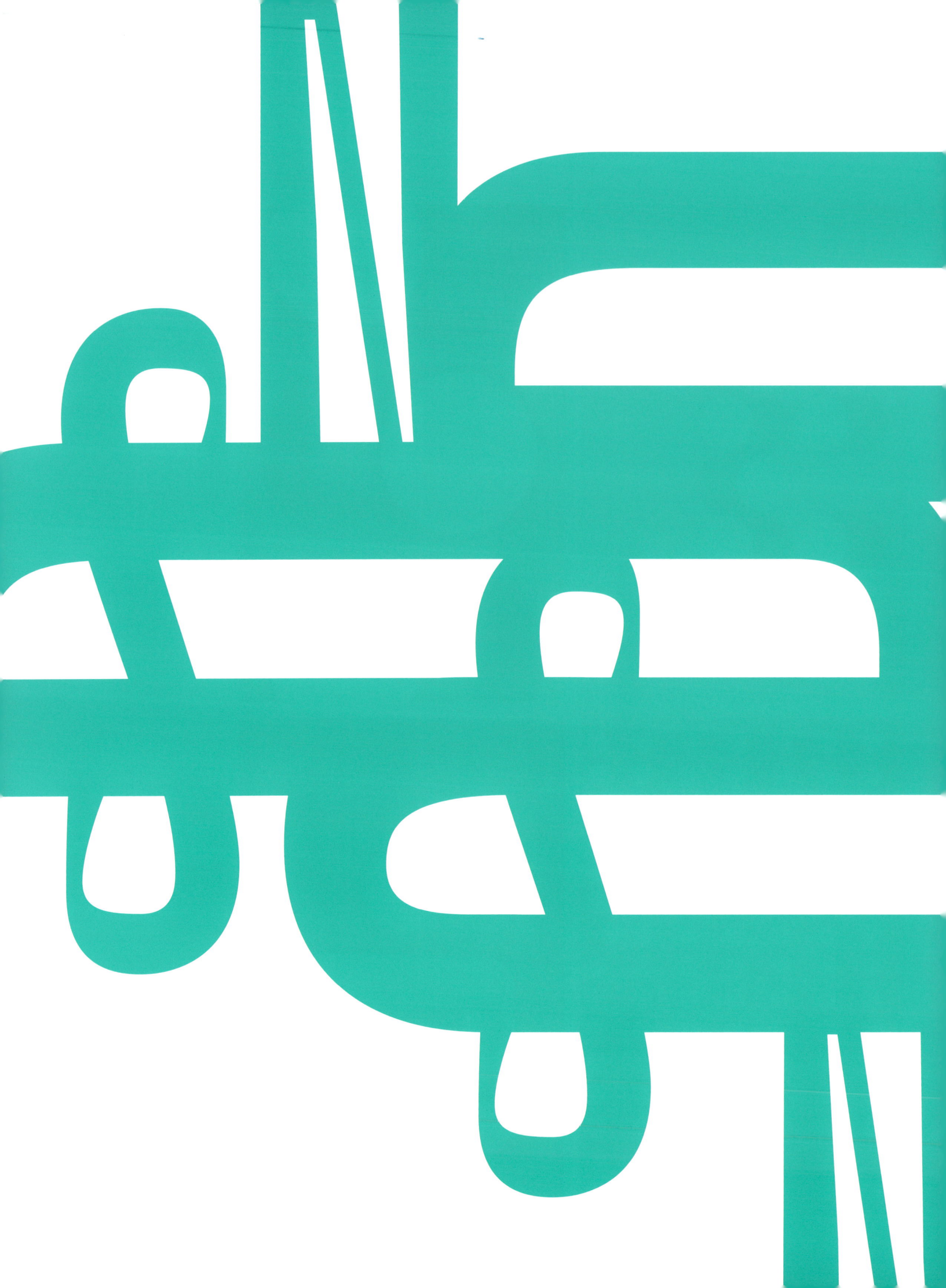

SOUND DESIGN

Red Dot: Best of the Best

Sound of Stuttgart
[Sound Exhibition]

With the motto "Eyes shut, ears open", the special exhibition "Sound of Stuttgart" became the urban science centre for the sound of the city. At various interactive stations, visitors were invited to experience acoustic phenomena around the sense of hearing and thus find out what structure-borne sound means, learn how noise and anti-noise can cancel each other out, or explore what various Stuttgart city locations sound like during the day and at night. Instead of creating spaces that are dominated by visual attractions and elements, as is often the case with such exhibitions, "Sound of Stuttgart" featured darkened and soundproof cabins conceived as sensory spaces that are as neutral as possible and which invited visitors to fully engage with the audio and sound experience. Finally stepping back into the light, visitors could themselves contribute to the Stuttgart soundscape. Using hands-on resources like paper, marbles or a bicycle bell, visitors could produce sound effects to bring a selected Stuttgart city scenery to life.

Statement by the jury
The exhibition on the specific sounds of the city of Stuttgart exemplifies how sensory effects can be portrayed within a simple infrastructure and through recordings of outstanding quality. The staging of the experiences in dark cabins with simple graphic instructions and, above all, the wealth of ideas that visitors are offered acoustically, have been brilliantly implemented both technically and artistically.

Client
StadtPalais – Museum for Stuttgart, Germany

Design
jangled nerves gmbh,
Stuttgart, Germany
Klangerfinder GmbH & Co KG,
Stuttgart, Germany

Creative Direction
Ingo Zirngibl, jangled nerves
Florian Käppler, Klangerfinder

→ Designer profile on page 537
→ Clip online

Publishing & Print Media　　Posters　　Typography　　Illustrations　　**Sound Design**　　Film & Animation　　Online　　Apps

The Heart and Mind Sound Concept

[Soundscapes]

The distinct visual presentation of the international technology conference, with its bold colours and geometrical shapes, laid the foundation for the sound concept. Sound designer Martin Hallberg translated the triangle, the square and the circle into sound waves, represented acoustically – and optically by means of decorations on the conference site – by instruments such as the bass clarinet, bowed strings and Moog synthesisers. Further sound effects and surprising elements enhance the collage aesthetics of the conference's overall arrangement.

Client
Media Evolution Southern Sweden AB, Malmö, Sweden

Design
ÅF Sound & Vibration, Malmö, Sweden

Music/Sound Design
Martin Hallberg

Concept
Martin Hallberg

Programming
Carl Pilman

Text
Hilde Rosenberg Bülow

→ Clip online

MIUI Natural Dynamic Sound System

[Smartphone Sound System]

A sound experience that optimises mobile phone use was central to developing this sound system. The new sounds and sound effects for ringtones, notifications and alarms create a natural, yet user-friendly, sound world that can be integrated harmoniously into the everyday world (of work). Calls are automatically split into two categories. The respective ringtones inform the user whether a direct response is necessary. The sounds for text messages are inspired by nature and vary dynamically, making a welcome change from the usual acoustic signals.

Client
Beijing Xiaomi Mobile Software Co., Ltd., Beijing, China

Design
MIUI Design Team,
Beijing Xiaomi Mobile Software Co., Ltd., Beijing, China

Music/Sound Design
Zhang Hanyi, Ma Jinglu

Concept
Jin Fan

Art Direction
Chen Qiaozhuo

Graphic Design
Lu Haixu

Animation
Lu Zhenzhou

→ Designer profile on page 548
→ Clip online

Porsche Sound Logo – Acoustic Film Ending

The Porsche Sound Logo is an inherent part of the film ending for all audio-visual communications in order to also acoustically reflect the values associated with the brand, such as tradition, performance and innovation. An introductory chorus represents the sound tradition of the brand, and is also available in twelve different keys so as to always ensure a harmonious transition to the preceding music. Pulsating, powerful rhythms reminiscent of a quickly passing vehicle follow, and combine with the characteristic finish to create a highly distinctive sound logo.

Client
Dr. Ing. h.c. F. Porsche AG,
Stuttgart, Germany

Design
Klangerfinder GmbH & Co KG,
Stuttgart, Germany
S12 GmbH, Munich, Germany

Creative Direction
Florian Käppler, Klangerfinder
Andreas Graf, S12

Music/Sound Design
Leo Frick, Klangerfinder

→ Clip online

JETTA Brand Sound

After 25 years on the Chinese market, Jetta has been reimagined as an independent sub-brand with a new model range. The sound logo coherently rounds off the newly designed brand design and interprets the graphic design acoustically. Taking a cue from the vibrancy of the visual identity, the sound signature is designed to convey an upbeat and energetic feeling, reflecting the young attitude of the brand. The result is a dynamic and confident-sounding sound logo that the listener will remember.

Client
Volkswagen China, Beijing, China
FAW-Volkswagen, Changchun, China

Design
why do birds, Berlin, Germany
MetaDesign Beijing, China

→ Clip online

FILM & ANIMATION

Red Dot: Best of the Best

Brave! Factory Festival
[Promotional Videos]

Although Ukraine's electronic music scene is flourishing with plenty of new pinpoint events taking place every single month, there is only one firmly established name, the Brave! Factory Festival. Featuring a unique line-up that unites musicians, artists and music lovers from all over the world, the 48-hour festival turns the entire venue of an abandoned factory into one pumping organism. This symbolism is also used in the videos of an advertising campaign. Various areas in the factory serve as stages for common life situations, such as shopping at a grocery store, dining at a fine restaurant or training on an indoor bike in a fitness centre. Placed into the scenery of the abandoned factory like alien objects, they bring the factory back to life. And as if this were not enough contrast and irritation already, the characters featuring in the commercials look and behave quite normal on the outside, but they all speak a fantasy language that is made up entirely of the DJ and artist names from the festival line-up.

Statement by the jury
The notable promotional videos of the Brave! Factory Festival inspire on three levels. First, the storytelling, or the way a music festival is communicated here, is absolutely unusual; second, the implementation from the actors to the exact locations of the staging is well done; and third, the sense of humour is fantastic. The presentation and the scenes are so surreal, they immediately pique curiosity and make viewers laugh.

Client
Closer, Kyiv, Ukraine

Design
banda.agency, Kyiv, Ukraine

Creative Direction
Pavel Vrzhesch

Head of Art
Egor Petrov

Strategy
Yaroslav Serdiuk

Art Direction
Oleksii Dyvysenko

Copywriting
Anastasiia Burganova,
Serhii Vorvykhvost

Motion Design
Mariia Dmytrova

Account Management
Zhenia Dvoretska

Executive Production
Pavlo Dyachenko

Production
Yaroslav Korotkov

Film Direction
Egor Petrov

Camera
Vlad Fishez, Olga Babych

→ Designer profile on page 512
→ Clip online

Publishing & Print Media | Posters | Typography | Illustrations | Sound Design | **Film & Animation** | Online | Apps

59th Thessaloniki International Film Festival

[Motion Graphics]

The visual identity of the 59th Thessaloniki International Film Festival is based on a simple idea: the celebration of celluloid as a symbol of film-making and storytelling. The key visual is a film roll that unreels motion graphics, TV and cinema commercials. The moving film strips tell stories, awaken emotions and provide information about the festival. A cinephile-friendly identity that is easy to read and sets itself apart from the design of past years was created in this way.

Client
Thessaloniki Film Festival,
Thessaloniki, Greece

Design
Beetroot Design Group,
Thessaloniki, Greece

→ Designer profile on page 513
→ Clip online

Curious
[Online Film]

The characteristic feature of branded paper Curious handled by the Japanese paper company HEIWA Paper is its shiny metallic lustre. In the advertising video, paper as a material is brought to life and made to shine impressively: cut in very narrow strands, the paper-like strips move, full of light, resembling a Japanese woman's shiny hair. Only at second glance does it become clear what the dark images actually portray. This visual symbiosis is enhanced linguistically in Japanese, where the homonym "Kami" means paper and hair.

Client
HEIWA Paper Co., Ltd., Tokyo, Japan

Design
Depart./Tokyu Agency Inc., Tokyo, Japan

Creative Direction
Hiroyuki Takahashi,
Depart./Tokyu Agency Inc.

Art Direction
Yuji Gamo, Depart./Tokyu Agency Inc.

Text
Shigeyoshi Natsme, Tokyo, Japan

Film Production
Masashi Yamaguchi, Dance Not Act Inc., Tokyo, Japan

Film Direction
Ichiro Tani, Tokyo, Japan

Camera
Hiromasa Gamo, Yumi Nagao, un.Inc, Tokyo, Japan

→ Clip online

Animated Artworks

[Music Videos, Cover Artwork]

Client
Upon You Records, Berlin, Germany

Design
Eat, Sleep + Design, Berlin, Germany

Concept
Frank Gräfe

Artwork/Animation
Frank Gräfe

→ Designer profile on page 524
→ Clip online

The combination of music and animation is used to breathe life into these covers for digital music publications, thus creating an independent digital art form. The scenarios take an experimental approach to design, pushing the boundaries of free graphics with lots of imagination. Sometimes loud and colourful, other times in black and white, the spectrum ranges from figurative to abstract. The illustrations interpret the respective song title and sound. In the rhythm of the music, they form and combine to create individual, moving image worlds that enrich the listening experience with an impressive visual component.

53rd Golden Bell Awards

[Visual Design, Animation]

The colour bar of the TV programmes and shows celebrated at the Golden Bell Award runs through the animation design and the stage set projections of the Taiwanese TV prize like a design motif. The colour palette used creates a combining, visual element and at the same time shows in different combinations the diversity of different people, cultures and content. Each individual animation presents its own story, which is directly related to the awards. Together they reflect the year in TV in a colourful and vibrant way.

Client
SETTV, Taipei City, Taiwan

Design
Shih Chien University,
Department of Communications Design,
Taipei City, Taiwan

Creative Direction
Annlin Chao

Art Direction
Kristycharay C Chu

Project Management
Annlin Chao

Executive Production
Wen-Yao Chen

Key Visual Design
Vita Weichen Hsu

Animation Design
Annlin Chao, Yipei Hou, Jo Yeh,
I-Ting Kao, Jhao-Yu Shih, Taylor Su,
Yi-Hsien Wu, Tsu Ning Lai,
Hsianglin Tseng, Ikea Xie, Popsha Chiu,
Wei Da Lin, Eviehsiao, Xavia Chen,
Kaijung Teng, Tokie Jyun, Tin Liu,
Hao-Yi Chen, Yashin, Henmi Lai

→ Designer profile on page 562
→ Clip online

Mayday – Final Chapter
[Computer Animation]

"Mayday – Final Chapter" tells the story of an old man. The core element of the sensitively animated video is a pop-up book that recounts significant, joyous and sad events from his life on each page, underscored by a song that fits the topic. The scenes are nostalgically animated, and run seamlessly into each other, designed with careful attention to detail. They bring it home to us as the viewer how quickly life can pass us by and that we can only turn back the pages of our life in our thoughts.

Client
B'in Music International Limited,
Taipei City, Taiwan

Design
Grass Jelly Studio Design Team,
Taipei City, Taiwan

Film Production
Grass Jelly Studio

Film Direction
Muh Chen

VFX Supervision
Weiting Chen

→ Clip online

Jane.
Discover potential.

[Image Film]

The objective of the Haufe Akademie is to recognise and develop the potential of individuals and organisations. This aim is conveyed in the richly illustrated animated image film using the inspiring story of primatologist Jane Goodall. Appropriate framing focuses and connects the individual scenes in the same way, which thus create a coherent narrative flow. Charming details in the illustration add wit and lightness, while music and sound design include the emotions and playfully underline the dramaturgy of the story.

Client
Haufe Akademie GmbH & Co. KG, Freiburg, Germany

Design
Bär Tiger Wolf GmbH, Tübingen, Germany

Creative Direction
Ulrike Schaal

Art Direction
Michael Böttler

Animation
Michael Böttler, Johannes Flick, Gerd Böttler, Marc Böttler

Music/Sound Design
Gerd Böttler

→ Clip online

Equal Opportunities for Education and Jobs
[Online Film]

What does an exotic-sounding name say about an applicant? This is the question at the core of the film promoting equal opportunities for education and jobs. Viewers are faced with some home truths presented in a humorous, yet extremely effective way. The brightly coloured scenes with their graphic design as well as the plain and ironic narrative play cleverly with clichés and make their point in an easy-to-understand manner. An applicant's qualifications, and not where he or she comes from, his or her skin colour, religion or name, should be the deciding factor when selecting applicants for educational and professional opportunities.

Client
Verein zur Förderung akzeptierender Jugendarbeit, Bremen, Germany

Design/Production
The Visual Truth, Bremen, Germany

Concept/Text
Roman Wolter, Julian Lodders

Graphic Design/Animation
Roman Wolter, Julian Lodders

Speaker
René Dawn-Claude, Berlin, Germany

→ Clip online

Dentsu Aegis Network's Data Training – Data Foundation

[Corporate Film]

The video for internal communication of the Data Training Programme uses custom-made illustrations and an artistic look and feel to engage with diverse audiences. Flat and fresh colour combinations create a surreal environment for each scene, enhanced by the asymmetrical characters. The minimal environment and the animations focus on the action in the centre of the screen, while the large, ultra-thin custom typography creates a contrast to the characters and the environment. The smooth animation defies strict analogies and gives a friendlier and more artistic tone to a seemingly "conventional" subject such as data.

Client
Dentsu Aegis Network,
London, United Kingdom

Design
Isobar iProspect SA, Athens, Greece

→ Clip online

Office Hero Elvis

[Animated Videos]

The "Office Hero Elvis" explainer videos integrate (learning) content into the everyday office life of Continental employees, who will identify with the main character. The figure consciously takes up challenges, and then explains in a vivid and entertaining way how they can be solved. The blue skin colour of the main character was chosen deliberately, as the explanatory videos and tutorials must work internationally and interculturally without restricting them to an ethnic background or cultural origin. The videos are published in German and English and can be translated into other languages.

Client
Continental AG, Hannover, Germany

Design
Serious Business, Munich, Germany

→ Clip online

Mario's Goal

[Commercial]

Client
Samsung Electronics,
Schwalbach am Taunus, Germany

Design
Cheil Germany GmbH,
Schwalbach am Taunus, Germany

Film Production
Christian Gilardoni, Tempomedia,
Frankfurt/Main, Germany

Post-Production
Nadine Chodan, Acht Frankfurt,
Frankfurt/Main, Germany

Film Direction
Stuart McIntyre, Los Angeles, USA

Camera
Ross Giardina, Los Angeles, USA

Music/Sound Design
Ingmar Rehberg, Yessian Music,
Hamburg, Germany
Philipp Lenz, A.R.T. Studios,
Frankfurt/Main, Germany

→ Clip online

Although Mario Götze was not nominated for the German national team in 2018, the professional footballer and football world champion is the face of this Samsung Football World Cup cinema commercial. It is not his triumphs but his failures and his botched season that are at the heart of this commercial, while the product presentation takes a step back. The emotional images consciously stay close to the person behind the player, who is fighting to make a comeback despite setbacks. This very personal message is underscored by the song "Hurt". It offers a disruptive alternative to the high-energy tracks often used in sports commercials.

KRELL Automotive

[Brand Film]

Client
KRELL Automotive, Seoul, South Korea

Design
FRUM, Seoul, South Korea
GIANTSTEP, Seoul, South Korea

Project Management
Yehoon Kwon, FRUM

Creative Direction
Myungjin Kim, Soyoung Han, FRUM
Suna Im, GIANTSTEP

Concept
Hyunwoo Jung, Youjung Yi, FRUM

Art Direction
Gryn Kim, FRUM

→ Designer profile on page 525
→ Clip online

The name for the Krell company was inspired by the film "Forbidden Planet". For the launch of the new brand Krell Automotive, this original link was revived and translated into expressive imagery: the image film uses space and its planets as a futuristic backdrop against which to communicate the performance of the products of the power amplifier brand. In high-action animations referring to characteristic features of the car audio system, the endlessness of the universe is connected visually to the boundless power of sound.

Samsung Notebook Odyssey

[Promotional Video]

The new edition of Samsung Notebook Odyssey was launched with a cooling system that precisely controls heat. A concept and feature video puts the spotlight on this function offered by the gaming laptop. By using a humanoid character that symbolises the product, the new technology becomes the hero of the story in the concept video and is explained using the aesthetic of a computer game. The second video is in the same style and highlights all of the notebook's features to target gamers specifically and present the entire scope of the product.

Client
Samsung Electronics,
Suwon, South Korea

Design
Designfever, Seoul, South Korea

Creative Direction
Jinyoung Noh

Art Direction
Juhwan Yi

Film Direction
Jiwoong Moon

Motion Design
Keunju Ryu

Project Management
Euri Bae

Film Production
Seungwon Huh, BECALM Inc.,
Seoul, South Korea

→ Clip online

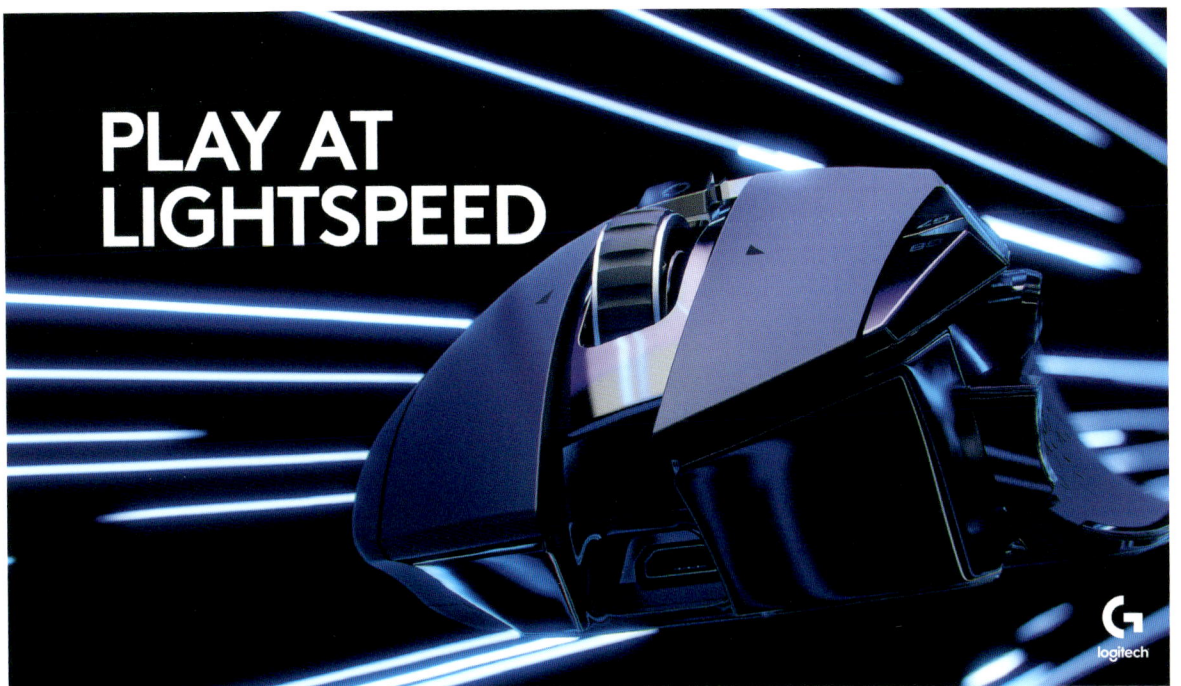

Logitech G502 LIGHTSPEED Wireless Gaming Mouse
[Computer Animation]

G502 Lightspeed is the name of the new Logitech G Gaming Mouse and at the same time the central theme of the corresponding product video. Constantly reforming, steel-blue light strips create the paths the mouse follows to speed wirelessly through a black space. This is how the new feature – Lightspeed wireless technology – is conveyed in fast-paced and futuristic scenarios. Short time-lapse sequences interrupt the fast exchange of images, putting the focus on the design and the other user-relevant features.

Client
Logitech, Newark, California, USA

Design
Logitech, Newark, California, USA
ManvsMachine, London, United Kingdom

Music/Sound Design
Zelig Sound, London, United Kingdom

→ Clip online

Logitech Tap Video

[Corporate Film]

"Just tap" is the simple operating instruction for the new Logitech video conferencing system TAP. In the corresponding online video, this instruction is taken literally and transported into the world of dance: instead of lengthy explanations, the IT staff member uses a tap routine to help educate his co-workers. The video consciously plays with the viewers' expectations, ending a classic video conferencing situation with a rousing dance routine and conveying the central product feature in a humorous and memorable way.

Client
Logitech, Newark, California, USA

Design
Logitech, Newark, California, USA
Bonfire Labs, San Francisco, USA

→ Clip online

Modern Taiwanese Cuisine – Fuel on our philosophy to mix

[Online Film]

The goal of this campaign video was to give the brand and drink Hennessy V.S.O.P Brandy a modern and young image – removed from networking dinners and business parties. In images underscored by relaxed, groovy music, the film follows two musicians who enjoy the new way of life with modern Taiwanese cuisine and brandy. This new angle on the product, showcasing it successfully as an on-trend drink, clashes with viewers' expectations and encourages them to rediscover Hennessy V.S.O.P for themselves.

Client
Moët Hennessy Taiwan,
Jas Hennessy (Far East) Ltd.,
Taiwan Branch, Taipei City, Taiwan

Design
iPrefer Digital Integrated
Marketing Co., Ltd., Taipei City, Taiwan

→ Designer profile on page 536
→ Clip online

Mi Family

[Commercial]

The commercials take a literal approach to the campaign motto "Living better with tech: Mi Family is looking out for you". Devices such as hoovers, smartphones or deep-fat fryers are given a personality. In different, deliberately exaggerated everyday scenarios, they act as friendly family members that make living together better or easier. The films succeed in presenting the products as an essential part of a (family) household and implementing the brand spirit in a way that is also visually striking.

Client
Xiaomi Corporation, Taipei City, Taiwan

Design/Film Production
Merry Go Round Inc., Taipei City, Taiwan

Creative Direction
Tien-Hau Hua

Account Management
Yung-Chiao Chang, Yu-Chieh Tsai

Film Direction
Ming-Yi Liao

Film Editing
Ting-Ting Lin, Ming-Yi Liao, Yu-Hsuan Chien

→ Designer profile on page 546
→ Clip online

OLX – Free Delivery
[Commercial]

The TV commercials use a tongue-in-cheek approach to advertising the free delivery service provided by Ukrainian marketplace OLX: in the style of Ukrainian sitcoms, the videos show regular people in authentic surroundings, celebrating their birthday with family, or at work. Each commercial has its own aesthetic and imagery – from conservative and nostalgic to sober and modern. Their shared feature is the situational comedy they portray. The commercials were developed with a special focus on the dialogues, which sound natural, yet convey the advertising message succinctly and memorably.

Client
OLX, Kyiv, Ukraine

Design
banda.agency, Kyiv, Ukraine

Creative Direction
Oleksandra Doroguntsova

Strategy
Yaroslav Serdiuk, Hannah Bosa

Art Direction
Illia Anufrienko, Ganna Iemelianova

Copywriting
Roman Hurbanov

Account Management
Anastasiia Guzova, Alina Megyd

Executive Production
Lesia Sichkina

Film Direction
John O'Hagan

Camera
Thomas Stokowski

→ Designer profile on page 512
→ Clip online

Christmas doesn't need much. Only love.

[Commercial]

The best gifts don't have to cost anything if they come from the heart. This is the message conveyed creatively and lovingly in the Penny advertising film. Its message is reflected in the visually touching film, which tells the story of a mother who gives her son a wonderful Christmas gift, which is built with creativity and love. Seven miniature sets were made by hand for the mixed-media production, six characters were brought to life digitally and both of these worlds were merged seamlessly to create an individual look.

Client
PENNY-Markt GmbH, Cologne, Germany

Design
SERVICEPLAN GERMANY, Munich, Germany

Global Chief Creative Officer
Alexander Schill

Chief Creative Officer
Matthias Harbeck

Executive Creative Direction
Christoph Everke

Creative Direction
Matthias Schuster, Moritz Dornig

Art Direction
Rebecca Labiner

Copywriting
Alessia Coschignano

Account Management
Frederike Striegel

Film Production
Glassworks Ltd., London, United Kingdom

→ Clip online

THE 8
[Commercial]

In this film for the market launch, the idea of conquering new territories and doing something for the first time is executed in spectacular and meticulously staged images: the sports car's maiden voyage was staged in Venice, a city with no cars. Custom-made floating pontoons let the car glide directly through the canals on the water. This presentation of the product also includes an emotional component, as the film uses flashbacks and flashforwards to tell the story of a boy who returns to his hometown of Venice with a car as a grown man and makes the impossible possible.

Client
BMW Group, Munich, Germany

Design
SERVICEPLAN GERMANY,
Munich, Germany

Global Chief Creative Officer
Alexander Schill

Worldwide Executive Creative Direction
Jason Romeyko

Managing Partner
Thomas Heyen, Markus Kremer,
Florian Klietz

Creative Direction
Kolja Danquah

Art Direction
Damian Kuczmierczyk

Management Supervision
Kristian von Elm

Copywriting
Bastian Tripp

Production
Henning Rieseweber

→ Clip online

Das Erste – Snapshots of Christmas 2018

[Seasonal Idents Campaign]

Client
ARD Design and Presentation,
Munich, Germany

Design
Luxlotusliner, Munich, Germany

Programme Director
Volker Herres, ARD

Creative Direction
Henriette Edle von Hoessle,
Head of ARD Design and Presentation
Gabi Madracevic, Luxlotusliner

Art Direction
Werner Mayer,
Erstes Deutsches Fernsehen,
ARD Design and Presentation

Executive Production
Tatjana Zivanovic-Wegele, Luxlotusliner

Project Management
Nadja Doth, Luxlotusliner

Film Executive Production
Frank Papenbroock, BLMFILM

Film Production
Andreas Haustein, BLMFILM

Film Direction
Maurus vom Scheidt, BLMFILM

→ Clip online

Das Erste's 2018 Christmas ad campaign showed emotional and humorous "Snapshots of Christmas", reminding viewers what Christmas Eve should be all about: love and the joy of togetherness. This message is conveyed with four short stories from different perspectives, which were integrated in the channel's Christmas programming as idents. From Santa Clauses on a coffee break to families preparing for the festivities, the films capture contemplative, funny and original Christmas moments and portray a modern and nuanced picture of the feast day.

Kunskapskanalen

[Station Rebranding]

The graphic design of Swedish public service documentary and science TV channel Kunskapskanalen has been completely overhauled. The new look of the idents, inserts and programme announcements stems from functional design, where the classic pegboard has been reinterpreted as a modern and welcoming dot grid for structure and guidance. The new logo bears a resemblance to its predecessor, yet is complimented and refined in its new double "K". The extensive primary colours scale allows for fast and clear categorisation of the fact and science-based content – including day and night mode.

Client
Sveriges Television AB, Kunskapskanalen, Stockholm, Sweden

Design
Dallas Sthlm AB, Stockholm, Sweden

Creative Direction
Anders Johansson, Johan Gustafsson

Art Direction
Anders Johansson, Carl Norlander

Animation
Markus Gustafsson, Tom Studt, Daniel Law, Roberth Sålborg

Project Management
Joakim Löfberg

→ Clip online

Formula 1 Season Opening

[TV Trailer]

The image trailer is a teaser and announcement for the new Formula 1 season. Two A-list co-commentators were on board for the trailer: Nico Rosberg and Timo Glock, both known to racing fans in Germany as credible and authentic professionals. The trailer was designed to generate excitement for the new Formula 1 season, while highlighting the fact that the reporting was in qualified hands: new season, new experts, new race cars. The trailer ran in cinemas, as a promo spot on TV and also online. Key visuals were placed in print media.

Client
Mediengruppe RTL Deutschland GmbH,
Cologne, Germany

Design
Filmstyler Pictures GmbH,
Frankfurt/Main, Germany

Head of Marketing/Creative Direction
Björn Klimek, Mediengruppe RTL Deutschland GmbH

Film Production
Filmstyler Pictures GmbH

Film Direction
Frank Schneider,
Frankfurt/Main, Germany

Art Direction/Type Animation
Michaela Schneider,
Frankfurt/Main, Germany

→ Clip online

ONLINE

Red Dot: Grand Prix

Dot Translate
[Digital Innovation]

285 million blind and visually impaired people worldwide have limited access to knowledge, as only three per cent of all text content is available in Braille and only ten per cent of the visually impaired can read Braille as the only alternative. This website introduces Dot Mini, a smart device that can access any digital text content from websites, books, magazines, audio and even films on its own and transfer them into tactile information. Equipped with the innovative, AI-based Dot Translation Engine, the device understands the respective contexts of words and translates them efficiently to Grade 2 Braille. Featuring a reduced, clean background in white and grey tones, the website presents all important details about the groundbreaking features of this device, which not only allows to load content from an SD card, directly connect with other devices via Wi-Fi, Bluetooth and USB, or collaborate via HDMI, but – reaching beyond Braille – also provides additional audio support for even faster perception of desired content.

Statement by the jury
Dot Mini impresses with a wide technical range of highly innovative services for instantly translating display-based texts and data into tactile information. A huge milestone for visually impaired people, the device supports both self-reliance and inclusion – and, what is more, it even gives users the freedom to experience content in any way they like. The design is kept minimalist to decisively reflect the quality and novelty of this innovation.

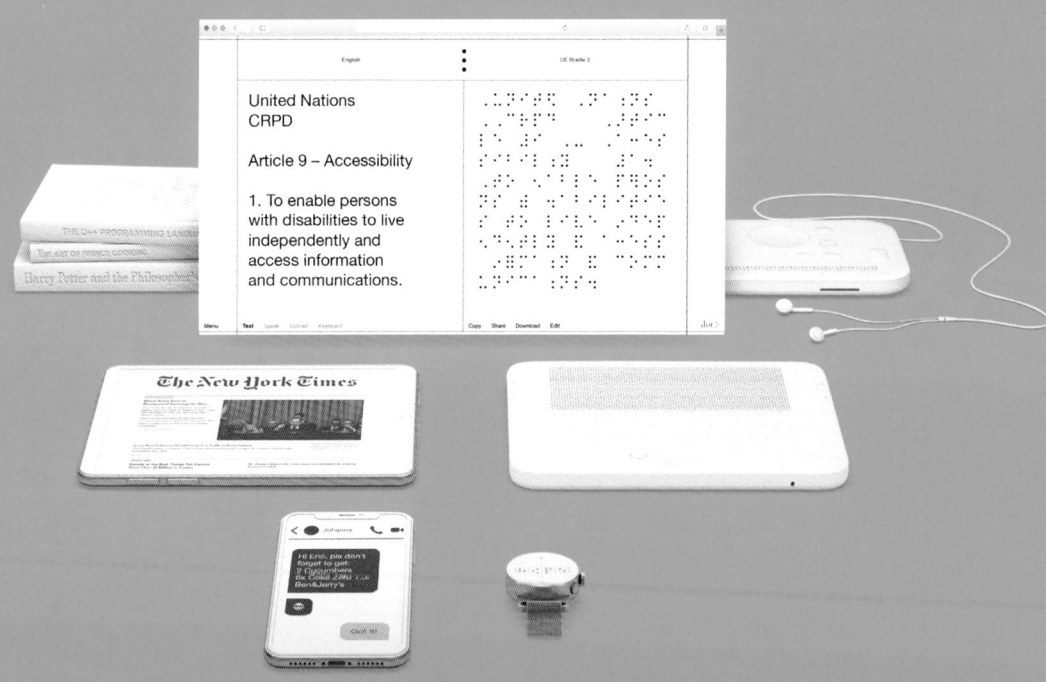

Interface & User Experience Design   Spatial Communication   Red Dot: Junior Award   Designer Profiles   Jury   Index   Red Dot – World of Design

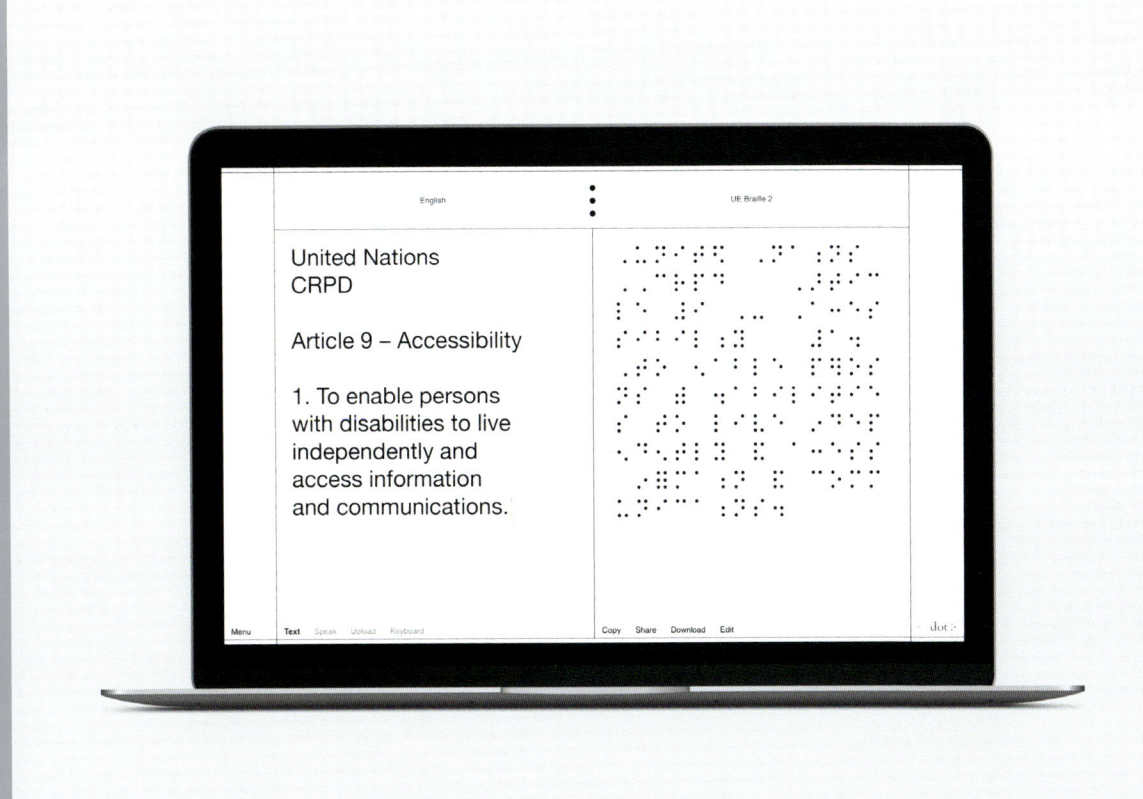

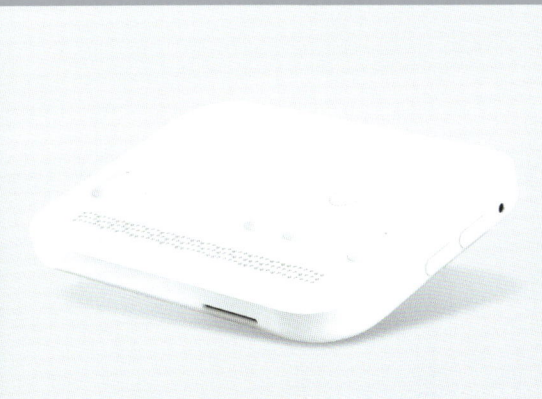
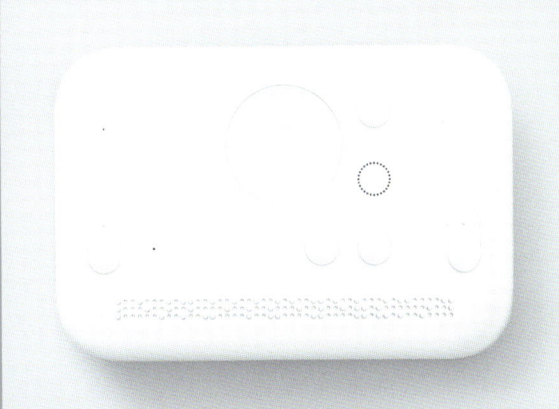

reddot winner 2019
grand prix

Client
Dot Incorporation, Seoul, South Korea

Design
SERVICEPLAN GERMANY,
Munich, Germany

Global Chief Creative Officer
Alexander Schill

Creative Direction
Franz Röppischer, Lorenz Langgartner

Creative Production
Saurabh Kakade

Art Direction
Eduardo Alvarez

Copywriting
Carolina Soto

Digital Design
Hyperinteractive GmbH,
Hamburg, Germany
Standardabweichung, Munich, Germany
Moby Digg GmbH, Munich, Germany

Film Production
Paulus Co. Ltd., Seoul, South Korea

→ Designer profile on page 523

Red Dot: Best of the Best

The Guidebook of Marine Debris
[Website]

The "Guidebook of Marine Debris" presents the first guide to marine debris in Taiwan. The website has been published by the RE-THINK Environmental Education Association to raise people's awareness of environmental issues, especially the huge amount of garbage in the oceans. Special about the approach is that the guide transforms jetsam into "aesthetic waste" and highlights 101 products covering the most commonly found plastic objects from the trash washed ashore on the beaches of Taiwan, as well as those of the Midway Islands, which are thousands of miles away. Ranging from a Hello Kitty stuffed toy and a rubber duck to a wide variety of different vessels, as well as shoes, toothbrushes, a mobile phone and a lighter, the objects are complemented by a mobile-friendly interface and a 3D 360-degree display option. In this way, an interesting online-interactive experience was created that impressively makes users aware of what does not belong in the sea.

Statement by the jury
The "Guidebook of Marine Debris" opts for a highly interesting approach towards raising people's awareness of this important issue. Exhibiting the trash finds like artistic works stimulates easy recognition by users and triggers their curiosity. Staged in a cleverly designed manner, the website proposes distinctive interactive experiences – including those of helping and donating – making the goals of the campaign more than clear.

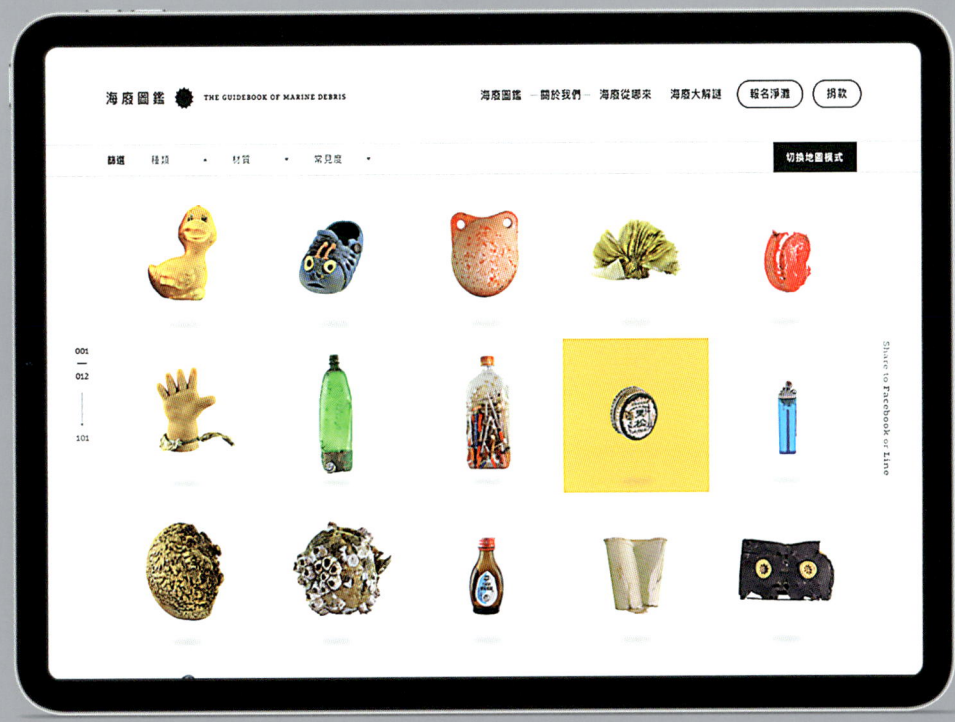

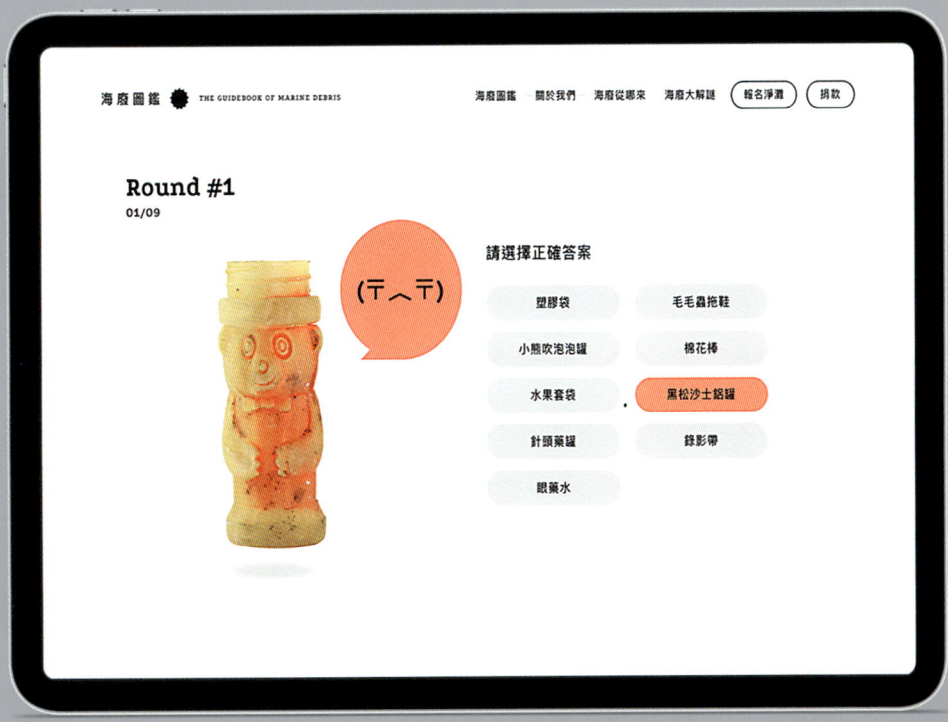

Client
Taiwan RE-THINK Environmental Education Association, Taipei City, Taiwan

Design
SimpleInfo Design, Taipei City, Taiwan

Planning
You-Yan Tang

User Interface Design
Jia-Nian Chang

Front-End Engineering
Liang-Ge Zhong

Back-End Engineering
Zong-Han Li, Zhi-Yuan Zhan

→ Designer profile on page 564

Red Dot: Best of the Best

IP20 Recruiting Video Chatbot

Developed by digital agency Interactive Pioneers, this unique video chatbot aims to map the core values of the agency and to attract both job applicants and customers alike. The chatbot adds the component of moving images to the traditional text-based chatbot in that it features agency founder Carlo Matic personally introducing his company, which gives users an authentic encounter with the agency. A simple input field at the beginning invites users to ask anything they want to know about Interactive Pioneers. The chatbot then launches an interactive video dialogue. However, instead of using static texts like a traditional chatbot, the videobot AI plays back pre-recorded answers from a pool of 120 videos that have been recorded to answer the most frequently asked questions of the past 20 years. Special highlights include the option of voice input, as well as the hidden live chat which allows the agency to jump into a conversation unbeknown to users and answer questions in place of the bot. As a result, some users experience particularly personalised discussions, while the agency demonstrates its core competencies.

Statement by the jury

This recruiting video chatbot embodies an excellent example of an audiovisual experience and, more than that, visualises technological advances in direct contact with both the public and the target group. Personally addressed in an unprecedented manner, they get exactly the information that they asked for. Brilliant and engaging, this work has been realised at a very high level and in a congenial way.

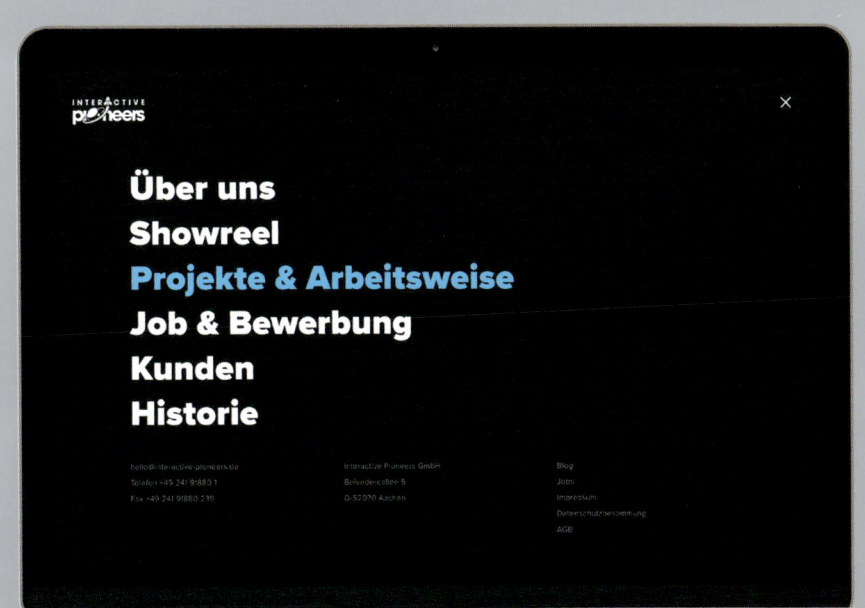

Client
Interactive Pioneers, Aachen, Germany

Design
Interactive Pioneers, Aachen, Germany

Concept/Idea
Carlo Matic

Creative Direction
Max Widdra

Technical Direction
Georg Meyer

Video Production
Malaravan Thanabalasingam

Project Management
Martin Werwoll

Quality Assurance
Sebastian Götze

Front-End Development
Michelle Peters

→ Designer profile on page 535
→ Clip online

The Ultimate Limited Edition – Life

[Digital Campaign, Online Platform]

DKMS, the German Bone Marrow Donor File, works in the fields of blood cancer and haematopoietic stem cell transplantation. Due to the high laboratory costs for the analysis of each sample, the charity considered it essential to receive more samples from its main target group: young, active men. However, these individuals had been rather tough to recruit. Following the motto "Fighting blood cancer by turning a cotton swab into hype", DKMS therefore teamed up with the professional footballer Jérôme Boateng and turned the registration set into a stylish limited edition. It created a hype on social and football-related media and was out of stock within days.

Client
DKMS gemeinnützige GmbH, Cologne, Germany

Design
denkwerk, Cologne, Germany

Production
Studio Seidel, Munich, Germany

→ Designer profile on page 521

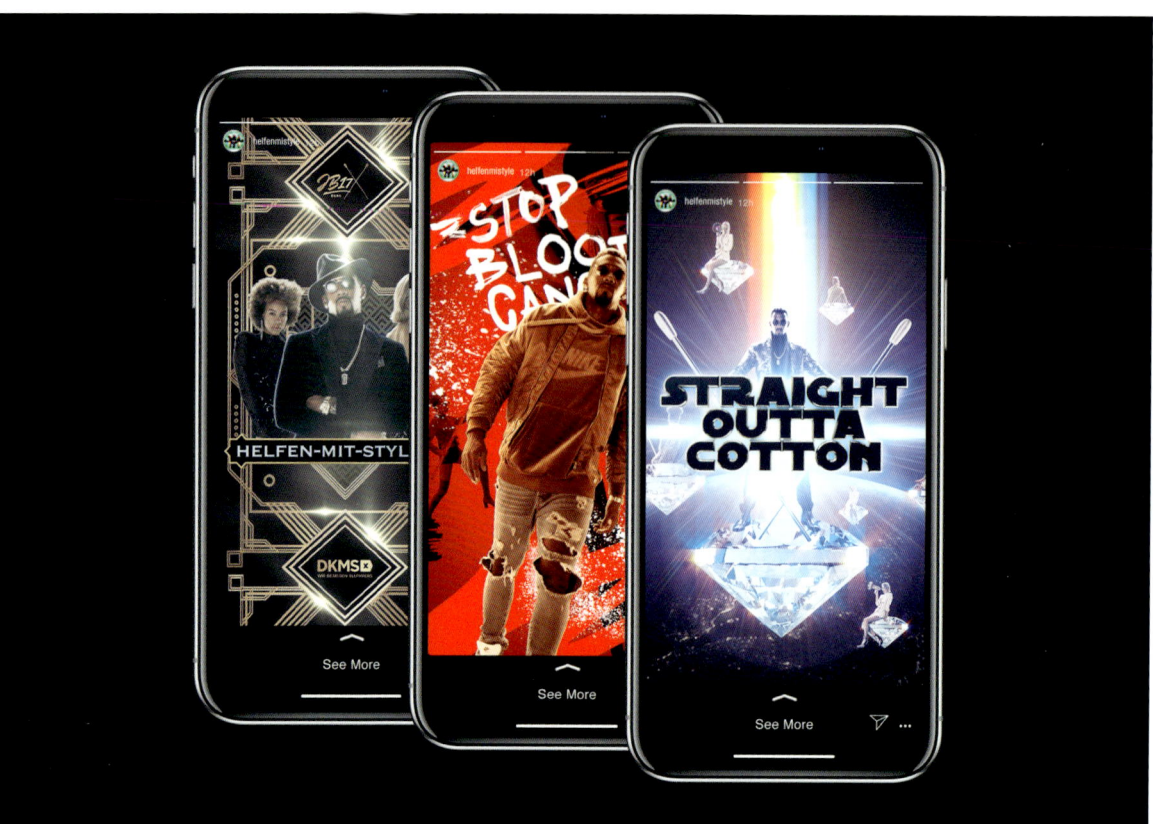

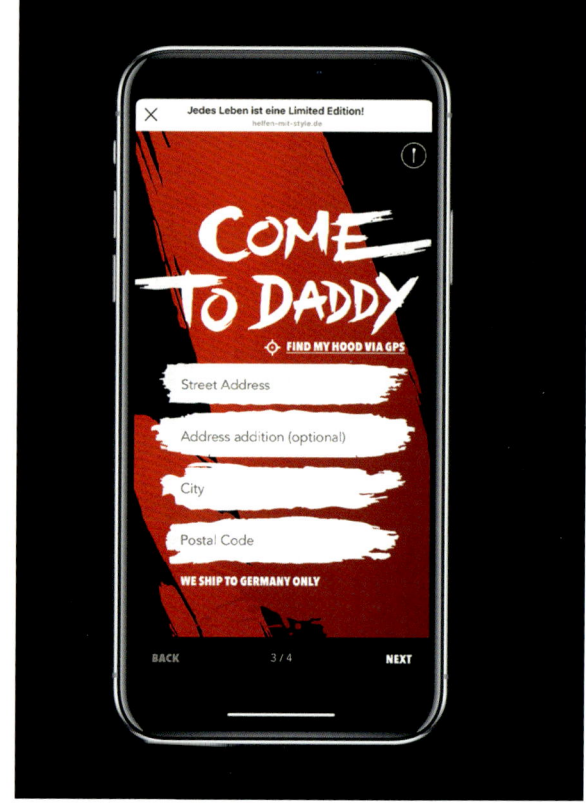

Goodbye to the Middle Ages!

[Website, Interactive Experience]

The Russian medical company Invitro decided to create its own educational portal dedicated to sexually transmitted diseases (STDs) and thus to promote discounts and complex tests used for diagnoses. The analysis of their target audience had revealed that long descriptive texts will not pique their interest. Therefore, a different approach was chosen. Inspired by Hieronymus Bosch's medieval triptych "Garden of Earthly Delights", STDs are presented as lively artworks attracting attention. On the interactive site, users can explore the pictures in which frightening infections are shown as vivid characters in 3D animated graphics.

Client
Invitro, Moscow, Russia

Design
Possible Moscow, Russia

Creative Direction
Vlad Sitnikov

Art Direction
Roman Antonov, Anton Vodogreev, Alexey Fetisov

Graphic Design
Kirill Klippenshtein

Concept
Maria Gushchina, Ekaterina Antipova

Production
Ksenia Boyarkina

m.Doc Smart Clinic

[Digital Ecosystem]

Client
m.Doc GmbH, Cologne, Germany

Design
m.Doc GmbH, Cologne, Germany

→ Clip online

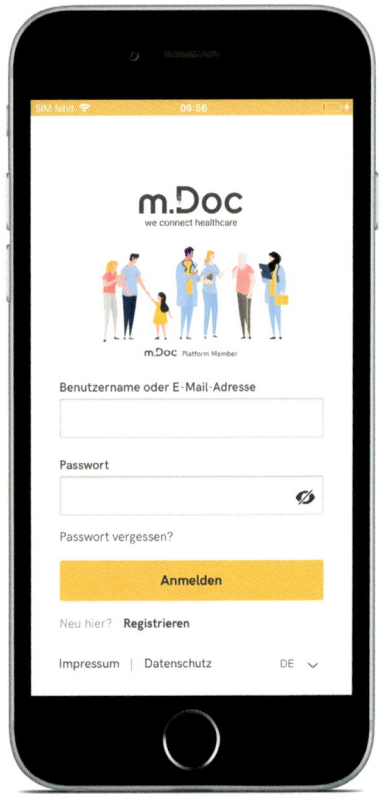
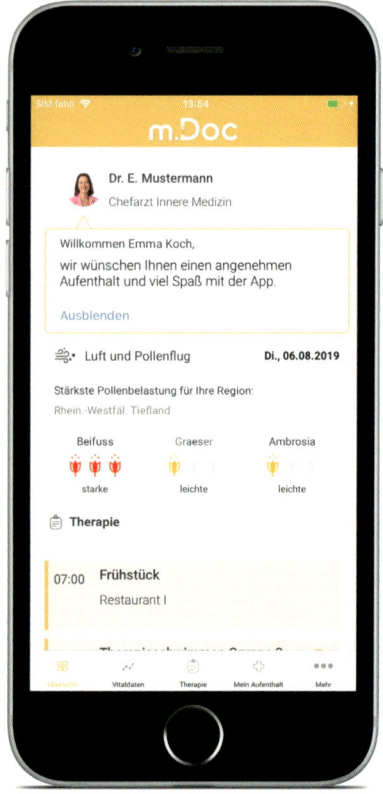
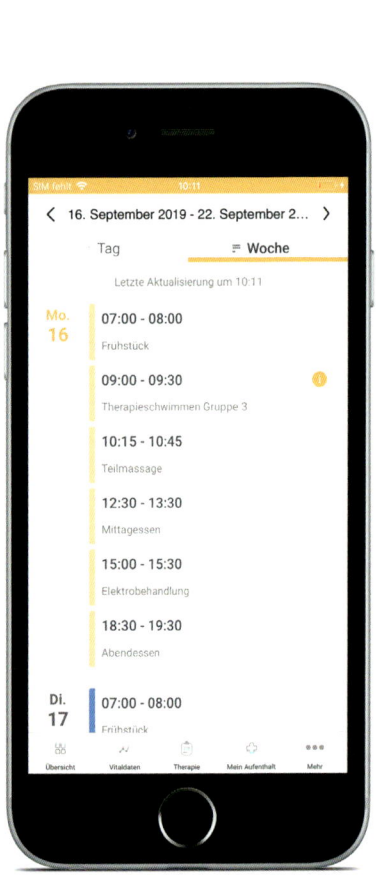
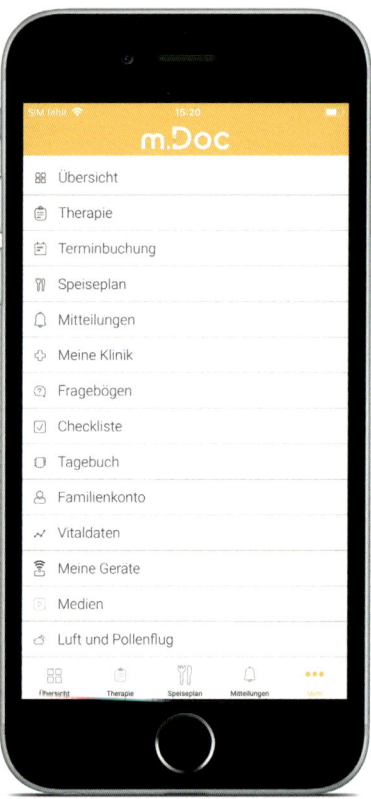

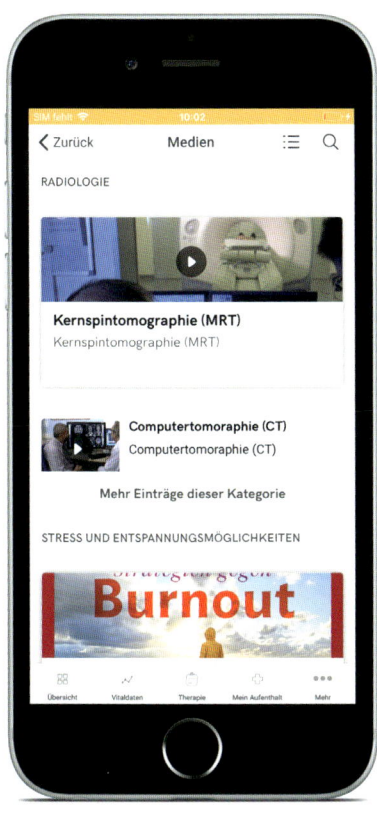
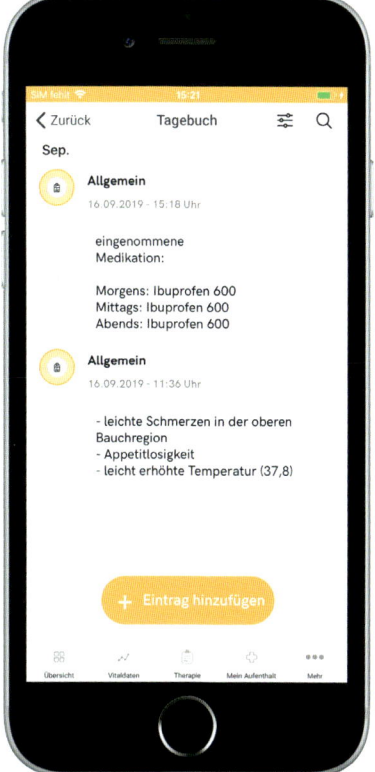
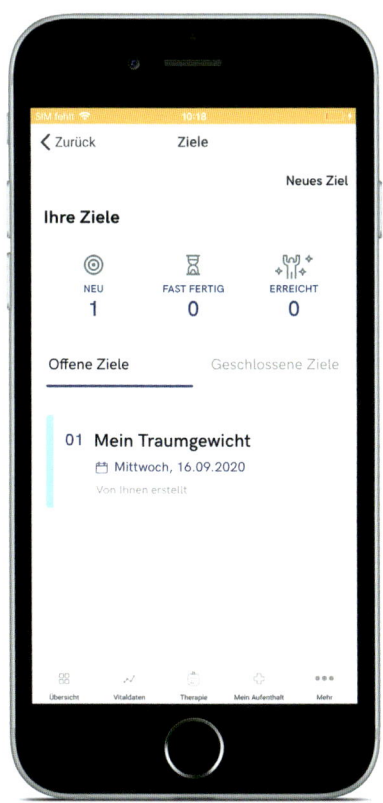
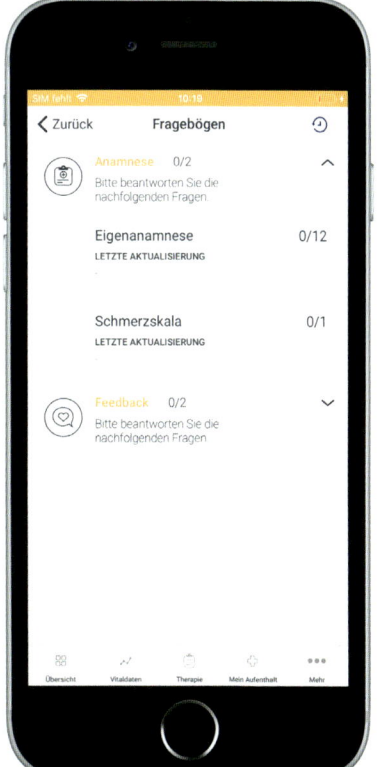

The vision of m.Doc is the evolution of communication in healthcare. Therefore, the Cologne-based company develops solutions to help hospitals improve workflows and patient communication. With Smart Health Solutions, m.Doc offers services for digital communication in healthcare and provides relevant information to simplify processes for patients and staff. It facilitates patient care and ensures data security, thus relieving staff of administrative tasks. Orientation systems accompany the patients, while individualised medical content is available before, during and after the stay, making it easier for people to navigate through the clinic. The mission of m.Doc is to improve communication between patients and everyone involved in the care process.

FishAct – Stop Overfishing

[Microsite]

Against the backdrop that fish stocks have decreased by 87 per cent since records began and the fact that, if this development continues, our seas will be empty by the year 2048, FishAct trains volunteers to document illegal fishing and overfishing. The NGO's new logo, showing a swarm of 30 fish, one for each year that remains, became a living infographic about the world's fish stock. The corresponding microsite, along with this live countdown to 2048 that is directly linked to a call to action for donations, provides visitors with information on the background of threatened species or the state of individual seas.

Client
FishAct e.V., Bremen, Germany

Design
MUTABOR, Hamburg, Germany

Creative Direction
Michael Gollong

Text/Concept
Martin Skoeries

Art Direction Digital
Christian Schulze

Design Team
Lasse Lemster, Maya Gottlob

Programming
NEUE RITUALE, Berlin, Germany

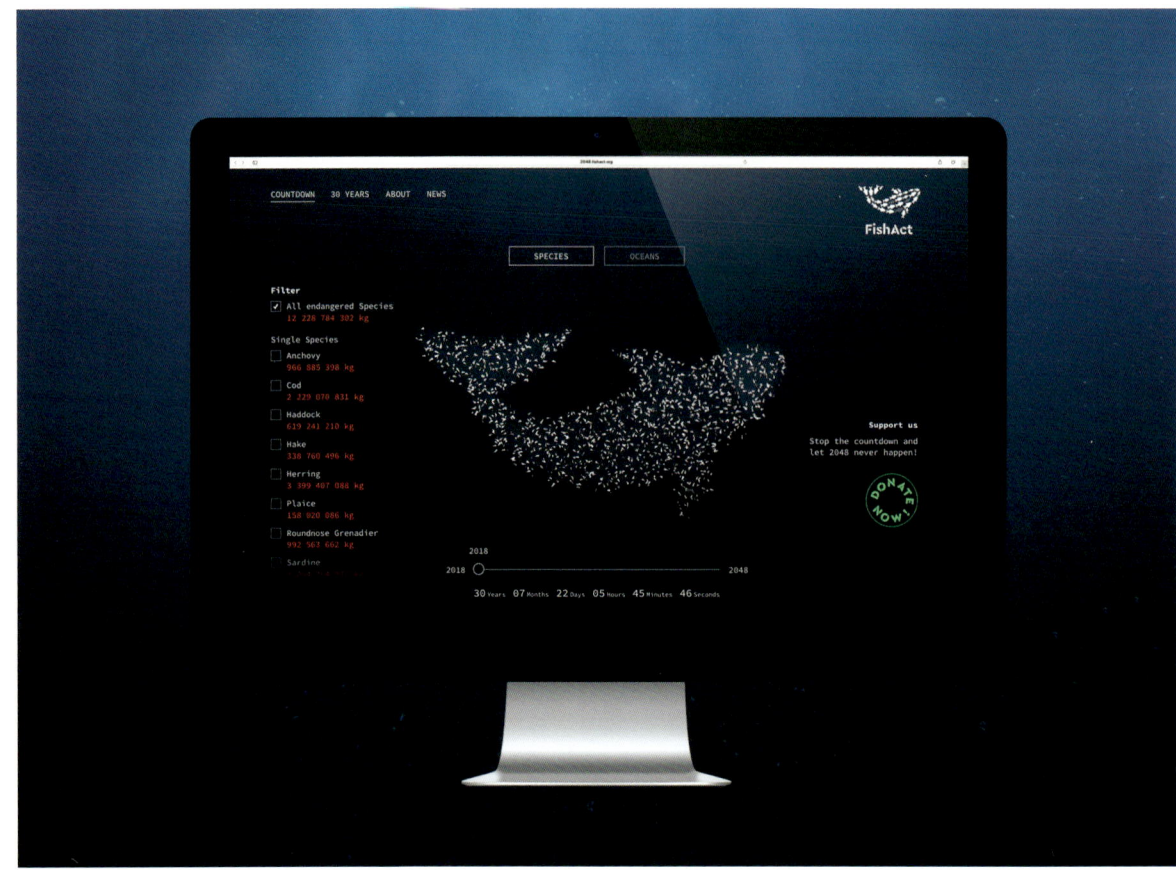
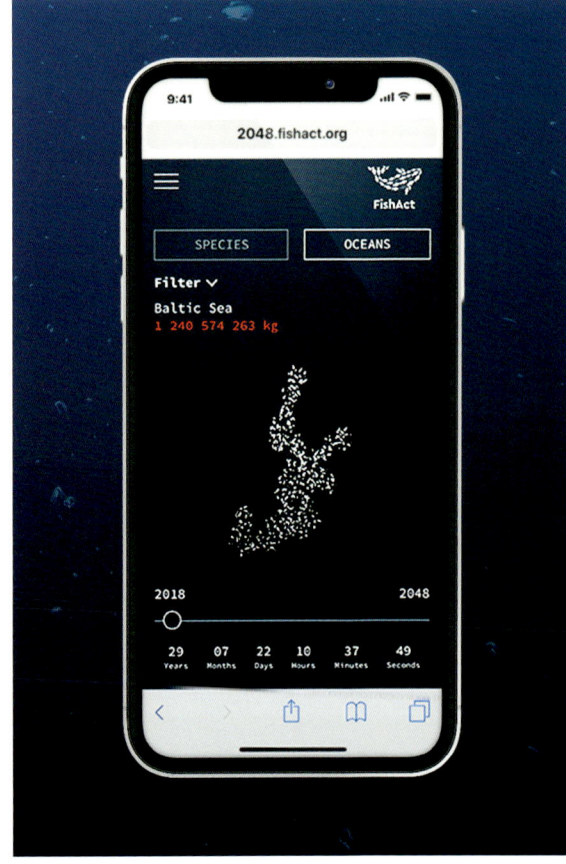

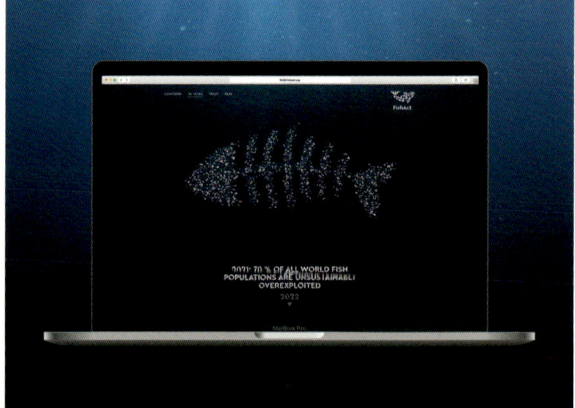

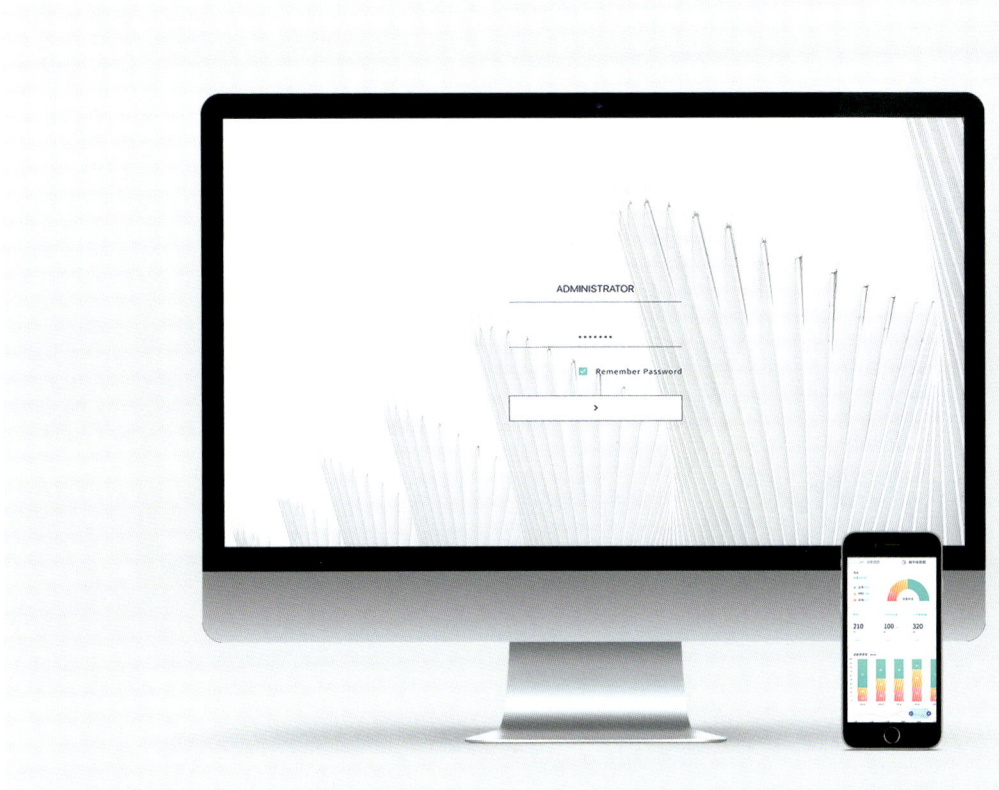

YIMU Intelligent Awareness

[Back-End Management System]

The YIMU back-end management system provides a comprehensive real-time overview of water quality changes through a cloud-based service. The user interface features several different modes, such as virtual reality in 2D and 3D, augmented reality and a precision mode. The system is accessed intuitively, thanks to the user experience design, offering meaningful guidance and a navigation bar with a clear visual language and helpful functional features. Distinct colour coding and seamless animations make the interface simple to use even without training, specialised design skills or technical knowledge.

Client
Shenzhen Yimu Technology Co., Ltd., Shenzhen, China

Design
Shenzhen Yimu Technology Co., Ltd., Shenzhen, China

Concept
Tianyi Chen

Graphic Design
Xiaozhu Yu, Nan Feng

Text
Tingran Li

Supervision
Zhiqiang Li

Account Management
Xinyu Wei, Zhengzheng Si

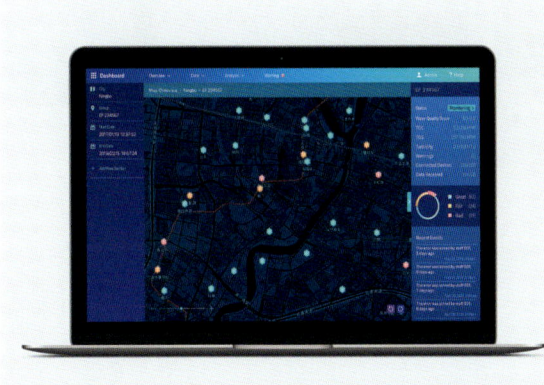

pics4peace

[Online Platform]

The aim of the pics4peace project is to bridge the communication gap between the older generation, currently in charge of creating the future, and the younger generation that will need to live in this future. Created as an open competition, it encourages young adults to express their feelings, problems and opinions in a playful and artful way. They can submit any form of content, such as texts, videos, graffiti, poetry, songs or pictures. The online platform offers a wide range of community features, working with eye-catching typography and spacious presentation areas in order to bring the works and respective authors clearly into focus.

Client
pics4peace e.V., Würzburg, Germany

Design
bueroparallel GmbH, Würzburg, Germany

Design Team
Mario Väth, Norbert Diedrich, bueroparallel GmbH

Programming
Yasin Bedir, Albert Breivogel, bueroparallel GmbH

Music/Sound Design
Sara Dubiel, Würzburg, Germany

Film Production
Boxfish Films, Würzburg, Germany

→ Clip online

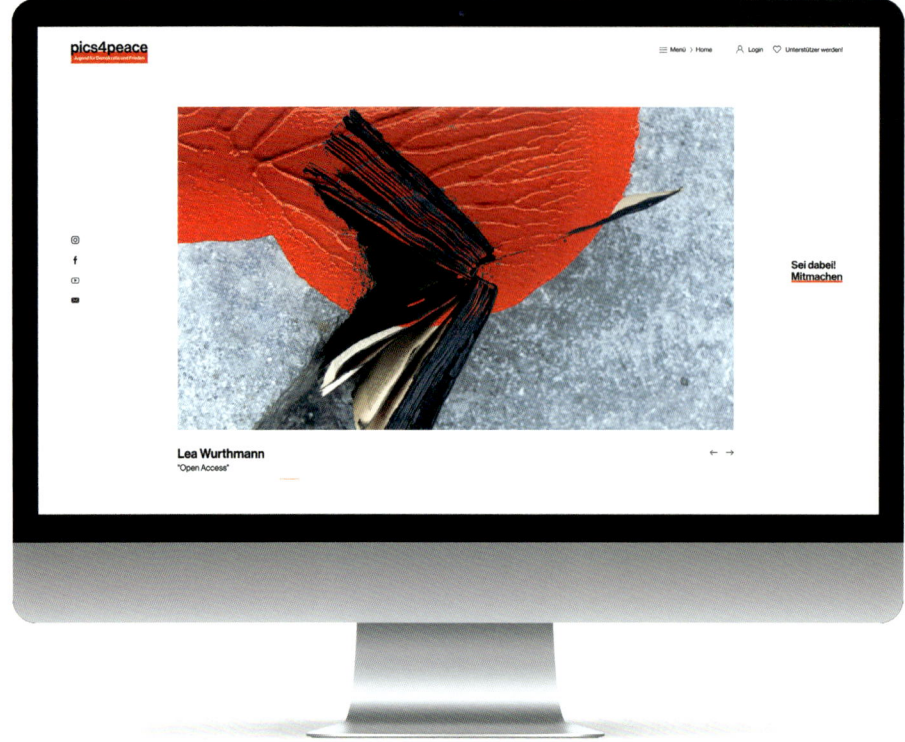

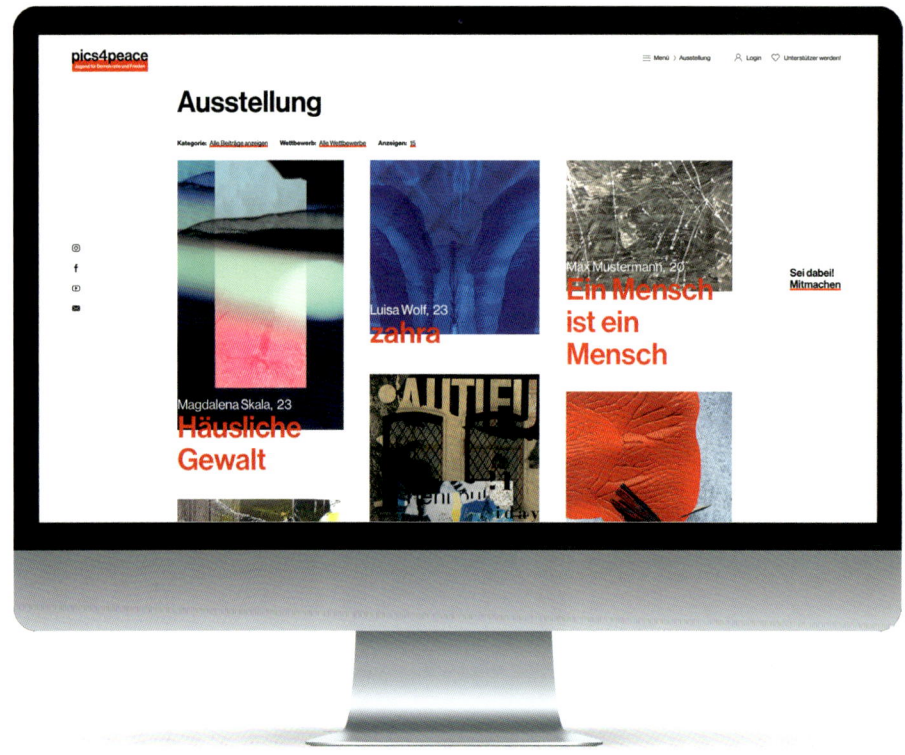

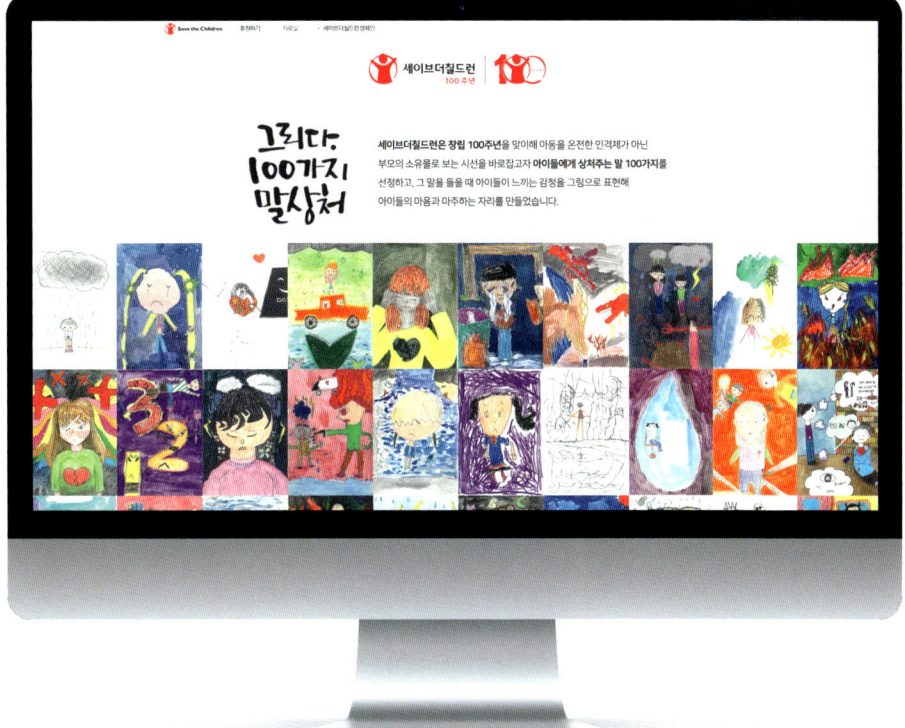

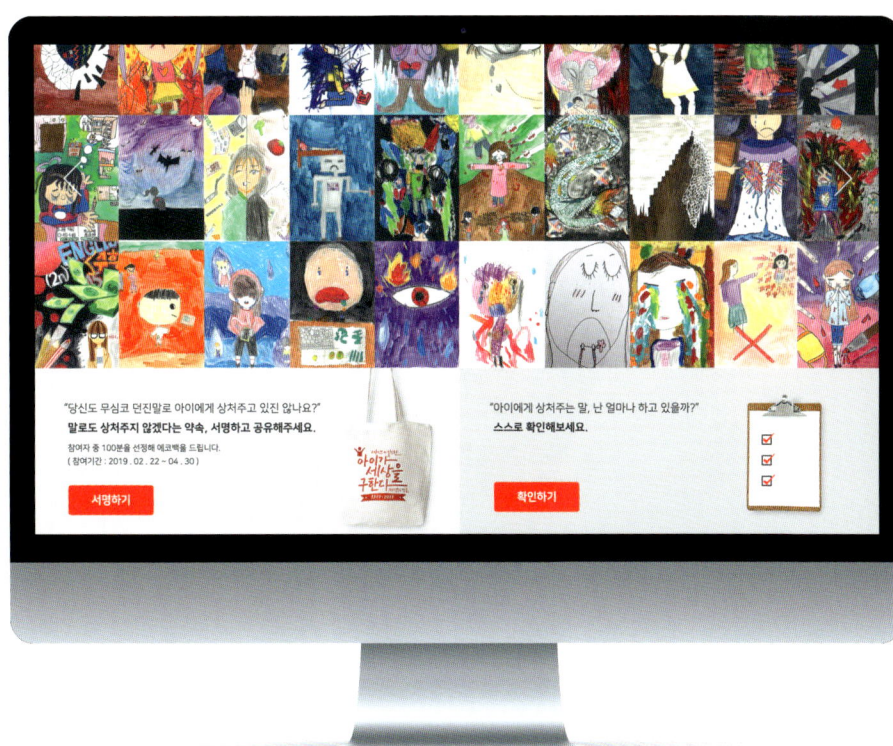

100 Words Pain_ting

[Microsite]

Within the scope of the organisation's 100th anniversary, Save the Children Korea launched this campaign to attract public interest in children's rights. First, 100 hurtful words were determined by child psychologists. Then, 297 children, ranging from ages 3 to 16, were selected and asked to choose what is most painful to them and express this emotion through a painting. The 100 "pain_tings" were then exhibited online and offline, powerfully capturing the damaging effects of hurtful words. People shared "I WILL NOT" signatures through their respective social networking service. The campaign went viral and became a nationwide phenomenon.

Client
Save the children, Seoul, South Korea

Design
Overman, Seoul, South Korea

Account Management
Yumi Sul, Seung Woon Kang, Chanmi Ahn

→ Designer profile on page 558
→ Clip online

PS4 GOOD

[Social Media Campaign]

There is a Russian tradition of using graffiti to thank mothers who have just given birth. Many contain the name Sónja, because of its popularity as a baby name in Russia. Incidentally, Sonya is also a popular slang term for the Sony PlayStation in Russia. Using this connection, unique virtual "Thank You" stickers were created to move this tradition to the digital world. The virtual graffiti is now part of an Instagram camera app and can be applied with photos or videos to any wall in Russia. The stickers have been used over 15 million times and may have saved plenty of walls from being sprayed.

Client
Sony, Moscow, Russia

Design
TutkovBudkov, Volgograd, Russia

Executive Creative Director
Dmitry Tutkov

Creative Direction
Oleg Barinboim

Art Direction
Dmitry Kostuchenko

Account Management
Sergey Polyakov

Production
Sevda Jalal, Nikita Zhuravlev, Sergey Gurchenkov

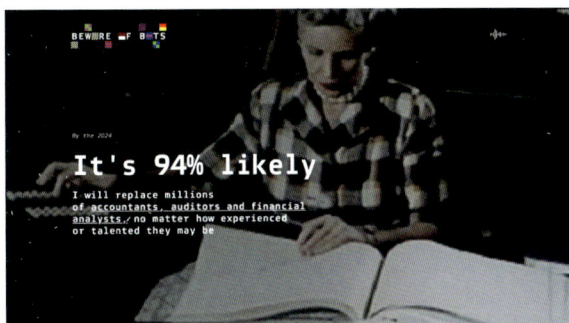

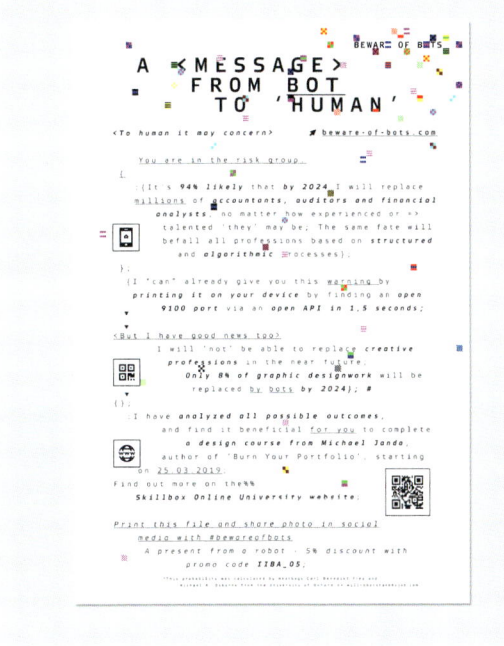

Beware of Bots

[Digital Campaign]

Recent Oxford University research on how computerisation affects certain job fields has shown that the majority of white-collar workers, such as accountants or auditors, will lose their jobs by 2024, while those working in the field of arts and design are at less risk to be replaced by automation. Against this backdrop, the online university Skillbox launched a bot that warns of AI taking people's jobs by sending messages to printers all over the world. It uses the open API of the IOT search engine Shodan.io to find printers connected to the Internet via 9,100 ports. Once an open port is discovered, the message is sent to print.

Client
Skillbox, Moscow, Russia

Design
Possible Moscow, Russia

Creative Direction
Vlad Sitnikov, Artem Filimonov

Art Direction
Fedor Nozdrin

Production
Ksenia Boyarkina, Rezeda Lutfullina

Music/Sound Design
Konstantin Novikov

Publishing & Print Media   Posters   Typography   Illustrations   Sound Design   Film & Animation   Online   Apps

Google Store
[Online Shopping Platform]

Client
Google, Mountain View, California, USA

Design
BASIC®, San Diego, California, USA
Google, Mountain View, California, USA

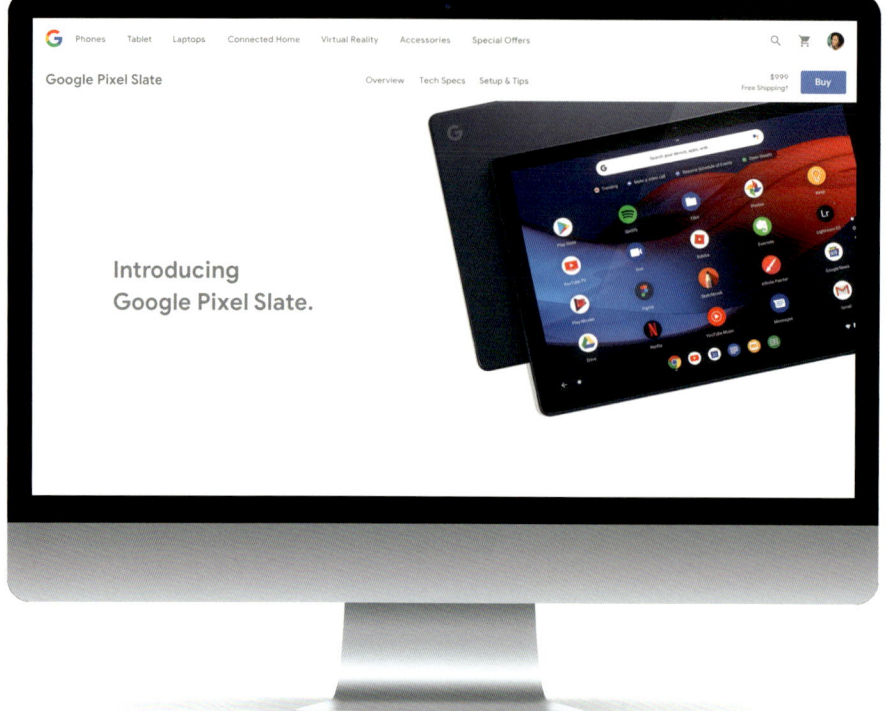

Google Store was reimagined to now tell a unified brand story that is visualised through a common design language targeting its audience worldwide on any device. The site uses scrolling behaviour to encourage discovery. As "touch and try" is not an option during online purchases, rich content is used to replicate this physical experience and promote product features. Interactivity drives engagement to connect with users emotionally. New functionality, including product comparison, bundling and streamlined navigation, was used to enhance shoppability and improve both conversions and SEO revenue.

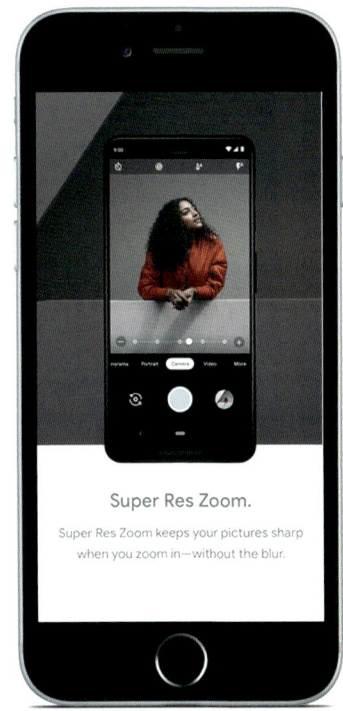

DeepL

[Translation Web Tool]

Client
DeepL GmbH, Cologne, Germany

Design
DeepL GmbH, Cologne, Germany
denkwerk, Cologne, Germany

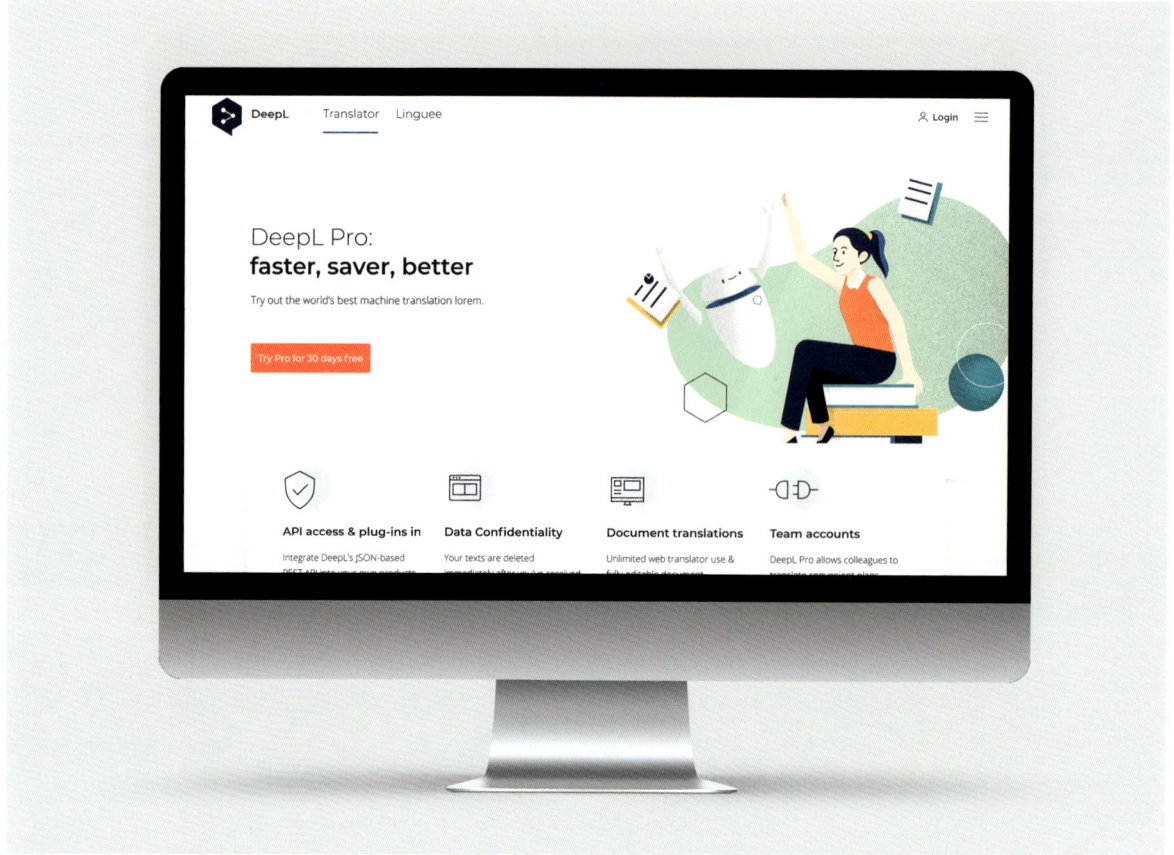

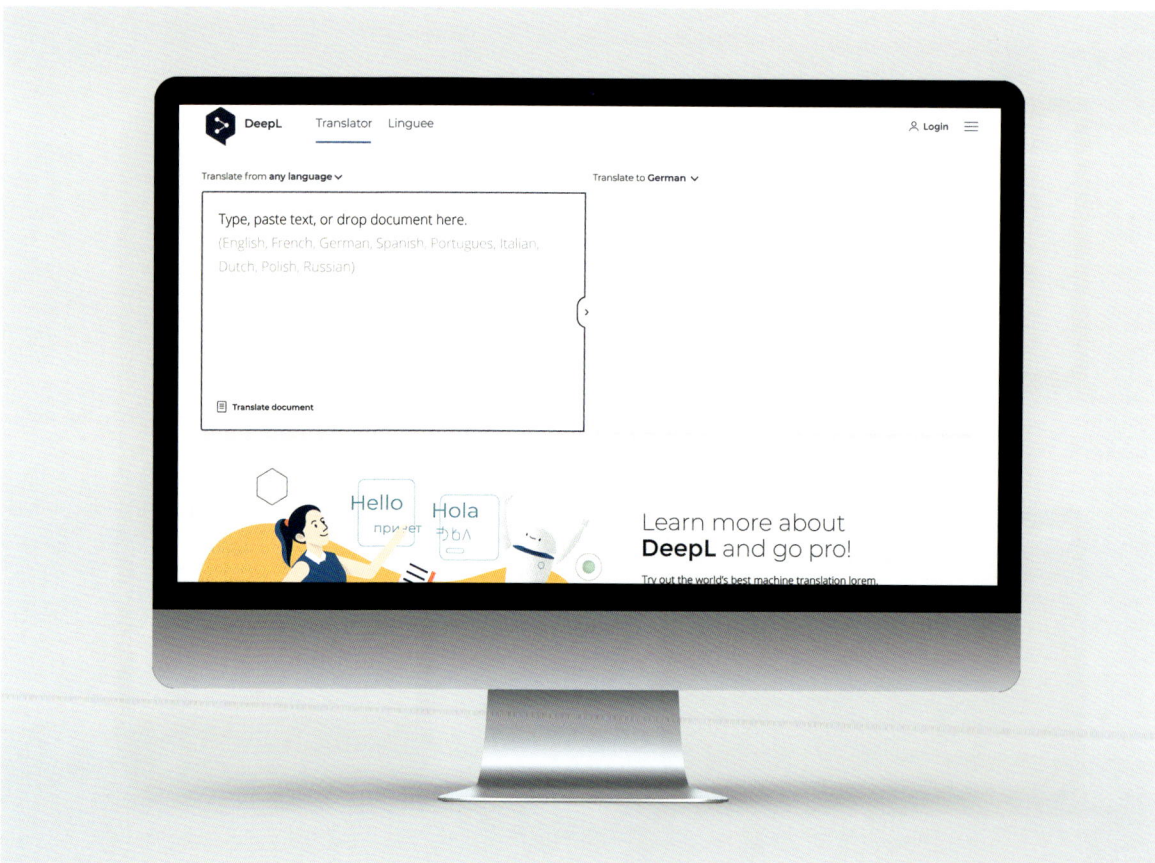

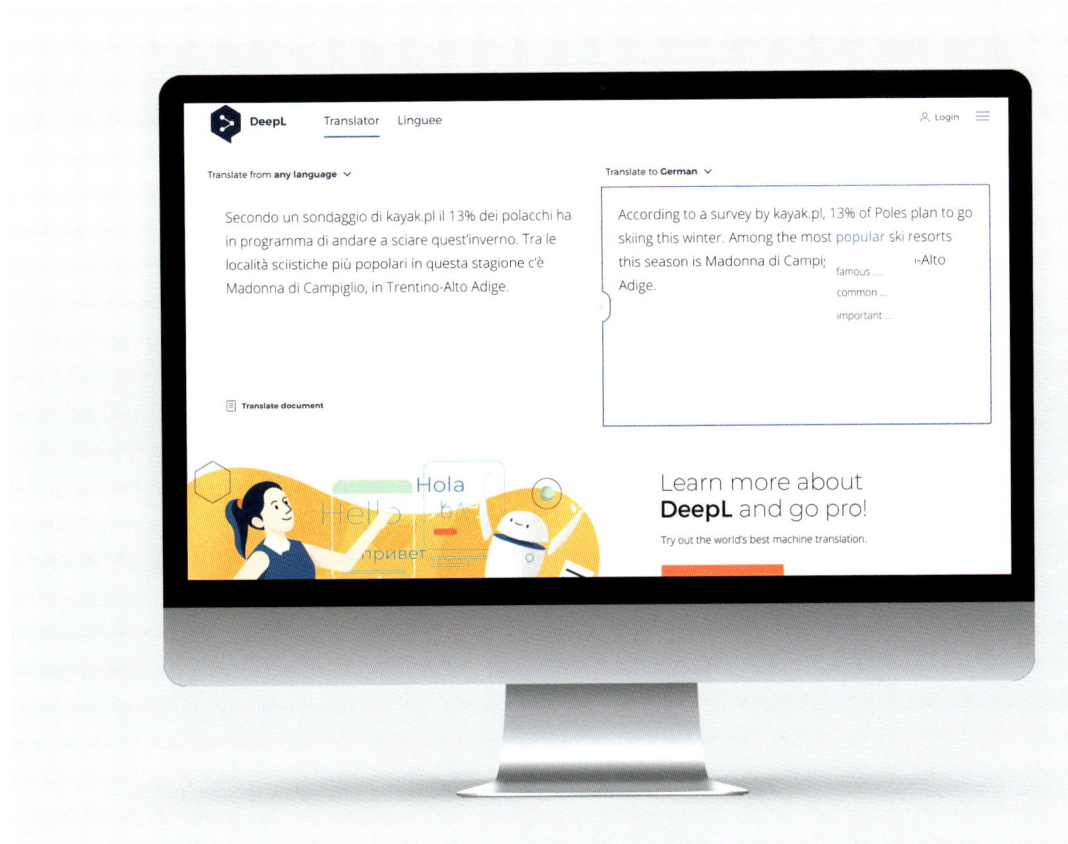

DeepL is an AI-based translation tool that is able to translate not only single words, but also the meaning of a text correctly into the respective language. Even proverbs are recognised and the appropriate one used. Based on the principle "form follows function", its redesigned interface supports user guidance and the intuitiveness of the tool down to the smallest visual detail. Since its launch in 2017, DeepL has been under continuous development, and currently 72 translation combinations are possible, including the languages English, German, French, Spanish, Portuguese, Dutch, Italian, Polish and Russian.

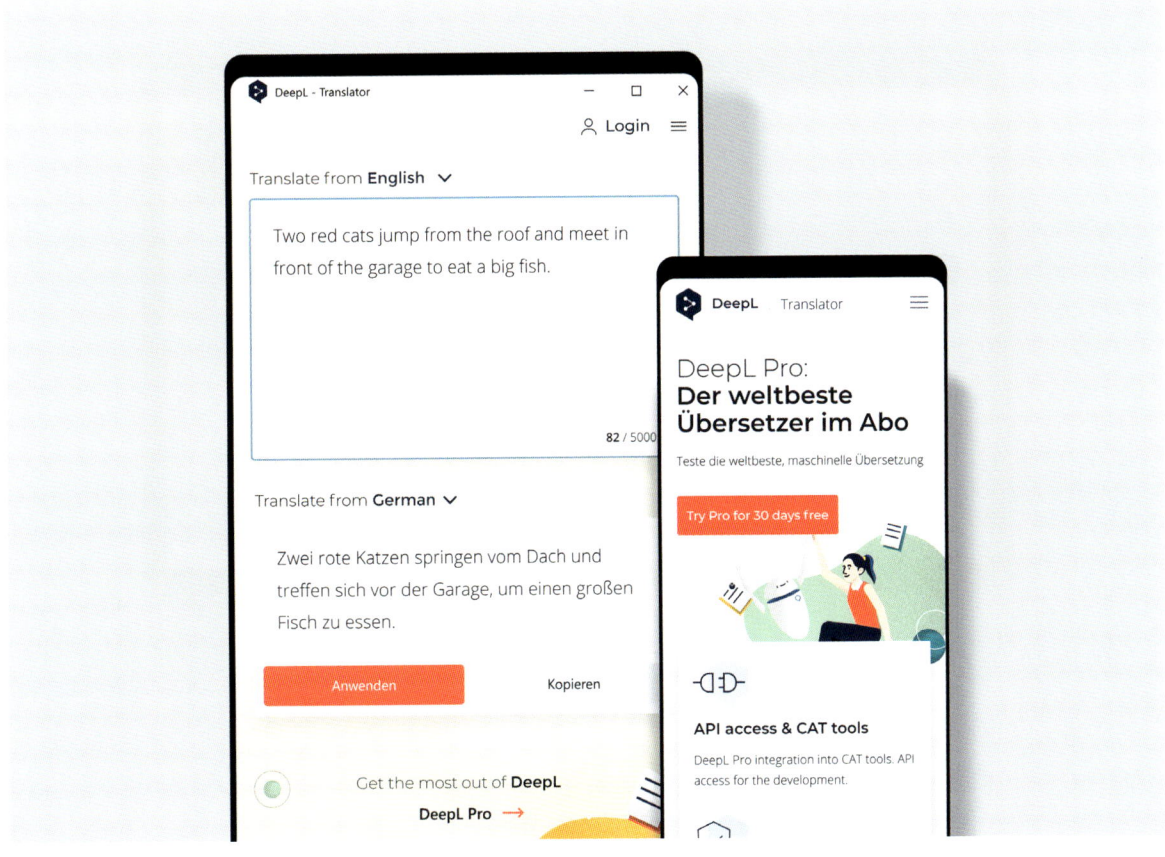

Design Samsung

[Online Platform]

Design Samsung is an online platform to convey ideas, stories and the philosophy behind the company's design portfolio. For the renewal of the website, the aim was to portray the company's new slogan – "Be Bold. Resonate with Soul." – in a user-friendly way. Following a concept focused on delivering clear, consistent and delightful user experiences across all devices without compromising depth of content, this resulted in a responsive platform with a bolder character. The eye-catching pictures and animations are complemented by clear and precise copywriting. Simpler and cleaner in structure, it offers better usability.

Client
Samsung Electronics, Seoul, South Korea

Design
Designfever, Seoul, South Korea

Creative Direction
Jinyoung Noh

Account Management
Heesoo Go

Art Direction
Kyoungmo Koo

Project Management
Euri Bae

Publisher
Seunghan Van

Technical Direction
Hyungju Sin

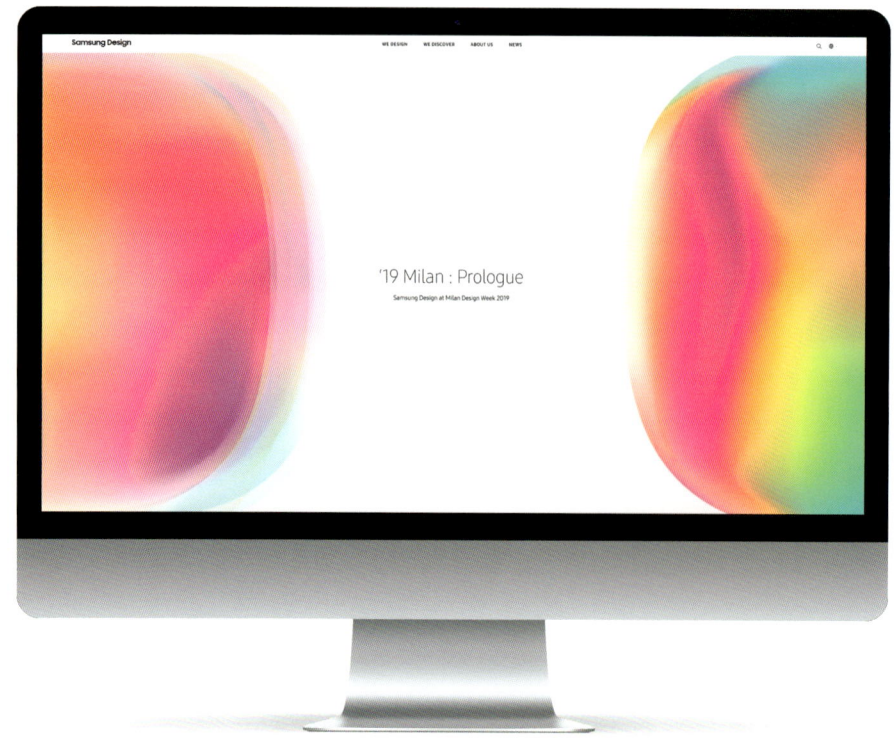

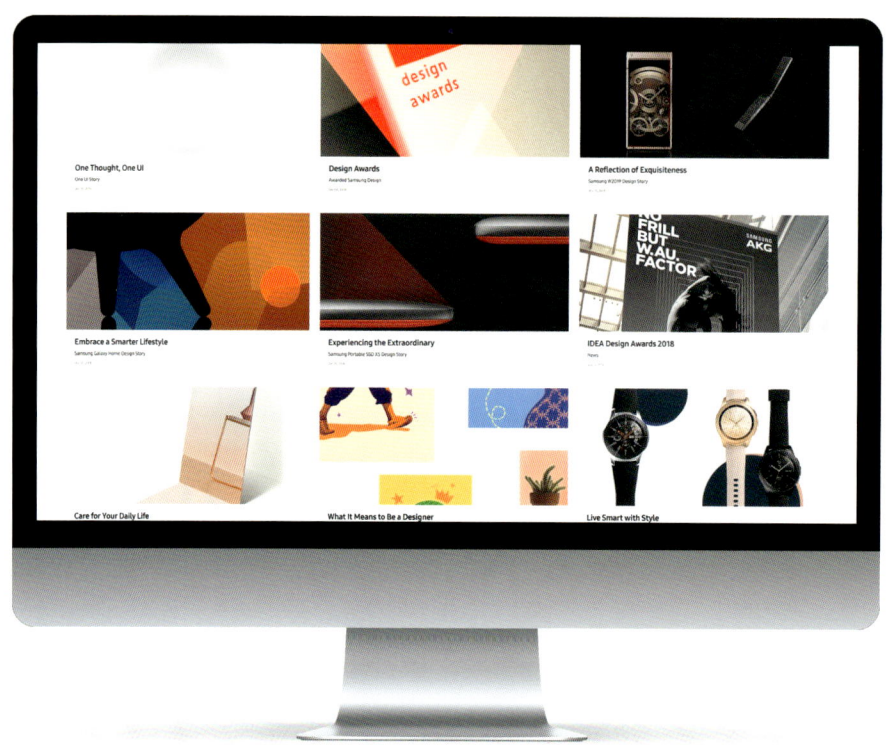

Great Apes 10.0

[Website, Landing Page]

On the occasion of its ten-year anniversary, this digital studio from Helsinki specialising in avant-garde UI/UX design and development decided on a new web presence. It was conceived as a launch pad for the agency's various case presentations, with the objective of targeting clients looking for innovative experimental projects and also potential recruitment candidates. As the intention was not to completely abolish the brand recognition earned over the past decade, the aim was to deconstruct and rebuild it, deliberately avoiding a Nordic or Scandinavian look, but rather striving for a unique appearance that stands out globally.

Client
Great Apes / HiQ Finland, Helsinki, Finland

Design
Great Apes, Helsinki, Finland

→ Designer profile on page 528

rkw.plus

[Website]

Showing the company's guiding principle "to think architecture in: people process projects" as authentically as possible was the objective of this new website. A clear design gives it a magazine character, which intelligently links the extensive content on two reading levels. Intuitive guidance and technical refinements allow the use of multi-unit filtering for the various projects or the generation of one's own collection. Profound categorisation merges content automatically or manually, resulting in ever new connections so the user may gain diverting, deep insight into the company.

Client
RKW Architektur +
Rhode Kellermann Wawrowsky GmbH, Düsseldorf, Germany

Design
Büro Grotesk, Düsseldorf, Germany
ZWEIPRO, Düsseldorf, Germany

Concept
Helen Hacker, Büro Grotesk

Content Management
Jasmin Wirtz, RKW Architektur +

Project Management
Lars Klatte, Tobias Bünemann,
RKW Architektur +

Programming
Robert Borgovan, Marius Günter,
ZWEIPRO

Text
Jens Frantzen, text appeal – Büro für Kommunikation, Düsseldorf, Germany

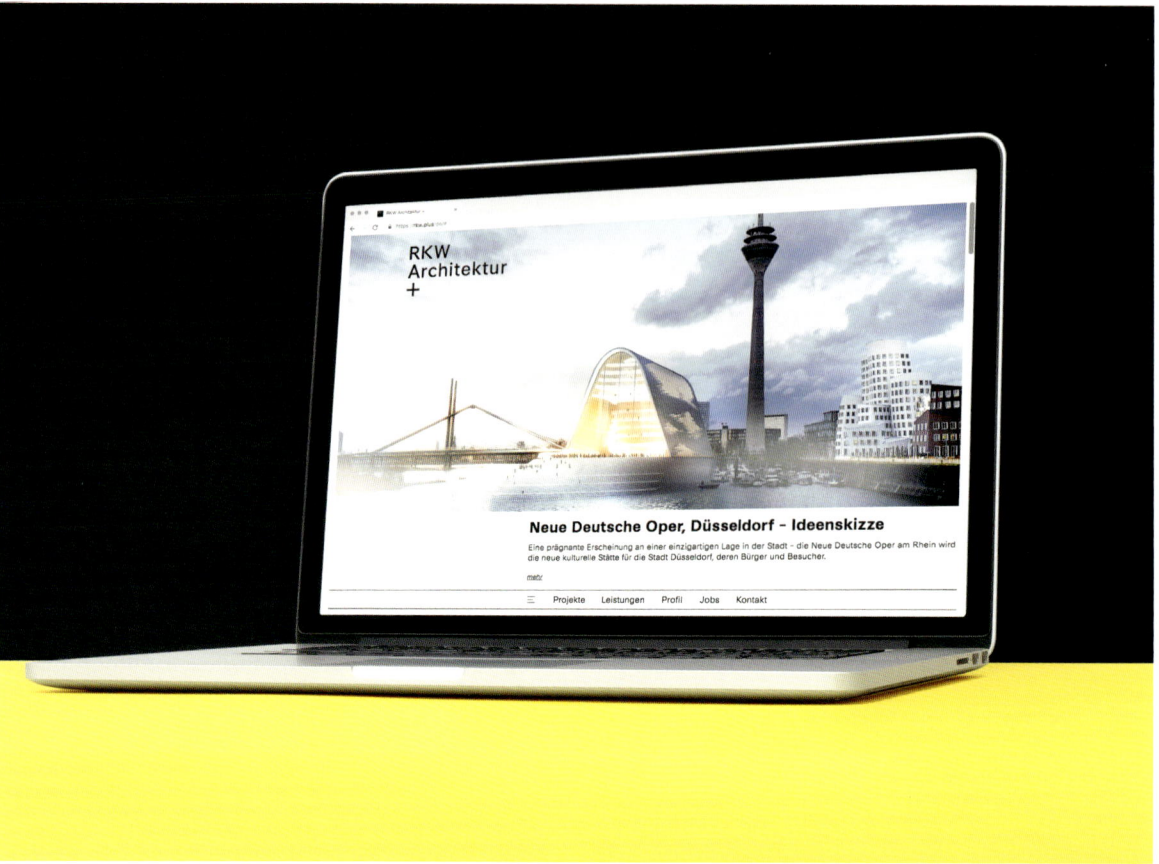
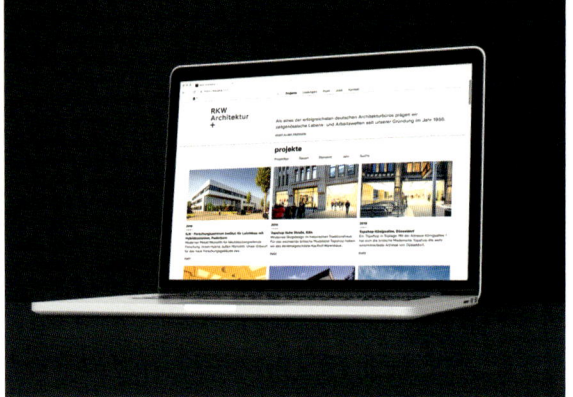
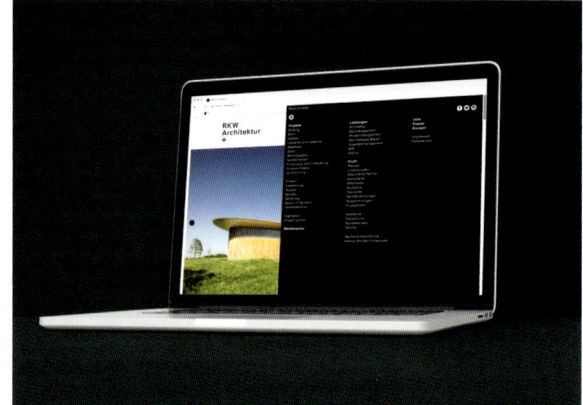

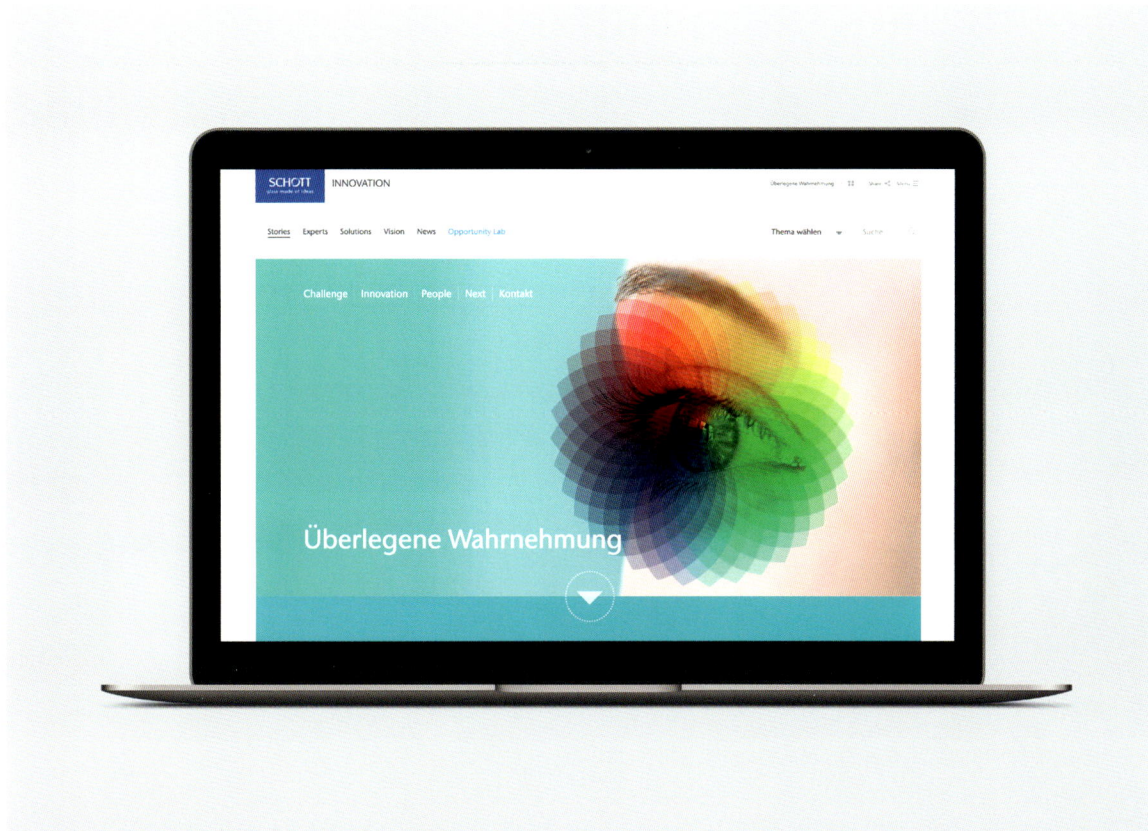

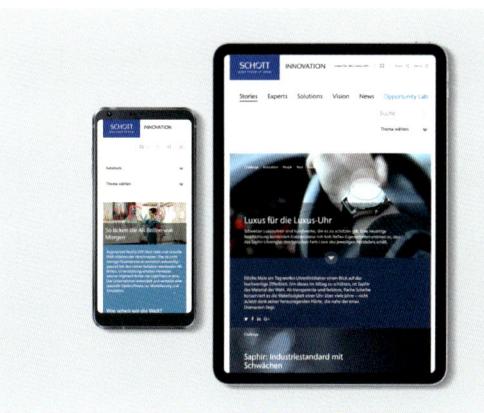

SCHOTT – Innovation Platform
[Website]

The goal of the Innovation Platform is to catch the interest of a heterogeneous target group for demanding topics, such as specialty glass and glass-ceramics innovations. It also aims to motivate users to actively engage with these topics and seeks to interact with the client. The platform features more than 170 exciting, target-group-relevant stories in four languages (German, English, Chinese and Japanese). Special emphasis is placed on telling each story in an emotional and individual way. Stunning photos are used as part of the navigation, guiding users visually and intuitively. A logical taxonomy with topics and tags makes it easy to access relevant content.

Client
SCHOTT AG, Mainz, Germany

Design
Tower 5, Stuttgart, Germany

Creative Direction
Robert Heyes, Patrick Leonberger, Tower 5

Art Direction
Patrick Leonberger, Tower 5

Account Management
Julian Schmittgall, Tower 5

Project Management
Susanne Opfermann, Tower 5

Head of Innovation/Technology Communication
Christina Rettig, SCHOTT AG

Communication Management Online/Social Media
Lea Kaiser, SCHOTT AG

Dialog

[Website]

In the context of Generali's strategic decision to transform Dialog from a niche specialist for biometric risks to the broker-focused insurer of the Generali Group, a new online platform was created to serve independent insurance brokers. Based on target-oriented processes, the goal was to optimise the value chain of insurance brokers contracting with Dialog. In order to provide insurance experts with relevant information quickly, over 600 product pages feature clear structures and efficient functions. The website uses all brand assets to deliver a professional, yet human-oriented experience on every device.

Client
Generali Deutschland AG,
Munich, Germany

Design
Landor Hamburg, Germany

Head of Marketing/Technical Sales Innovations
Benjamin Börner,
Dialog Lebensversicherungs-AG

Creative Direction
Markus Blankenburg, Landor Hamburg

Brand Strategy
Hellen Markusch, Landor Hamburg

Experience Design
Jack Osborn, Lisa Ribbers,
Anastassia Saromova, Landor Hamburg

Text
Nestor Sierralta, Landor Hamburg

Web Design
Eddie Salzmann, Berlin, Germany

Illustration
Peter Greenwood,
Brighton, United Kingdom

→ Clip online

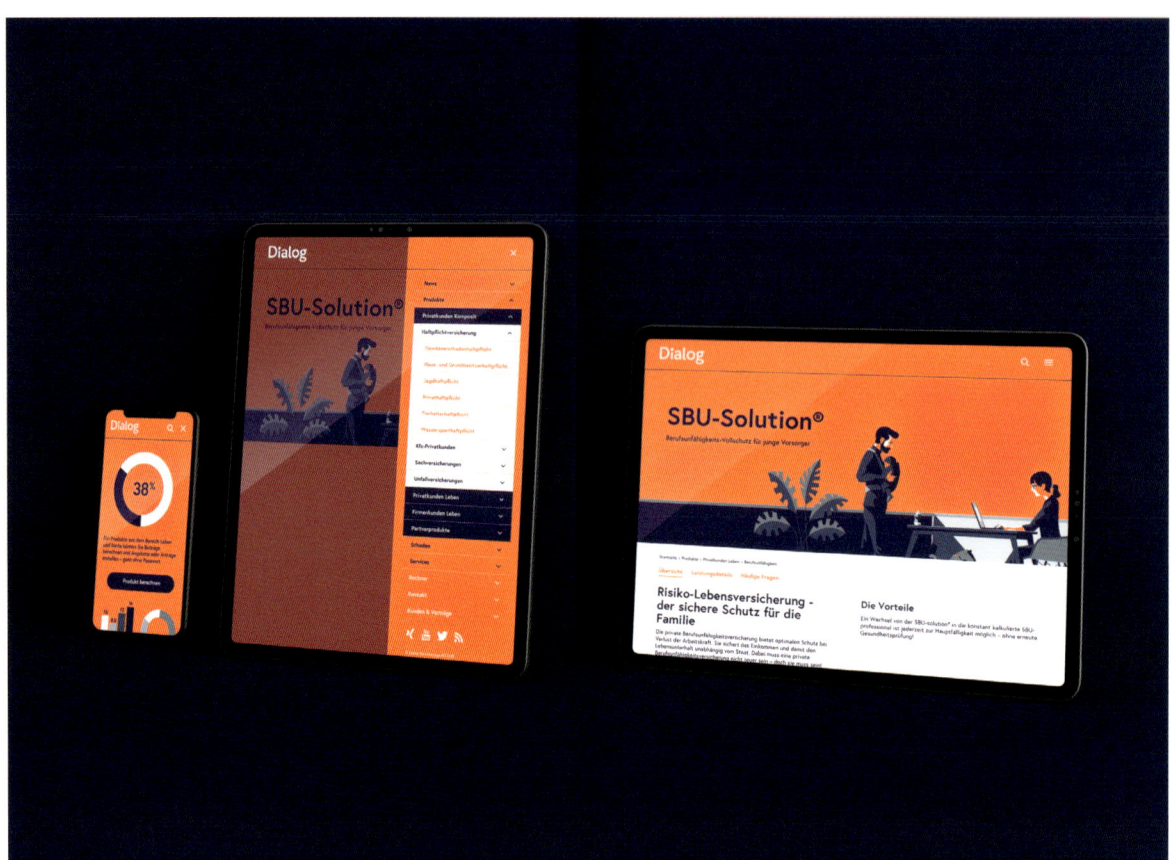

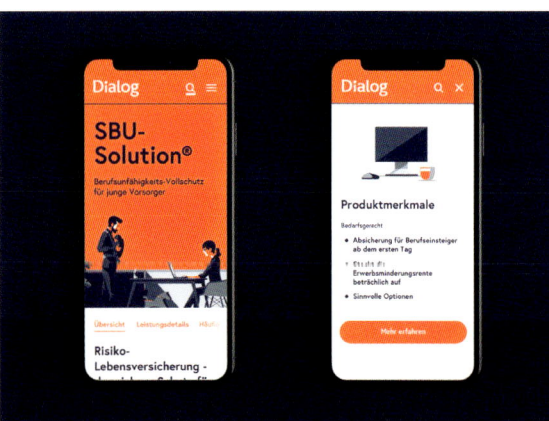

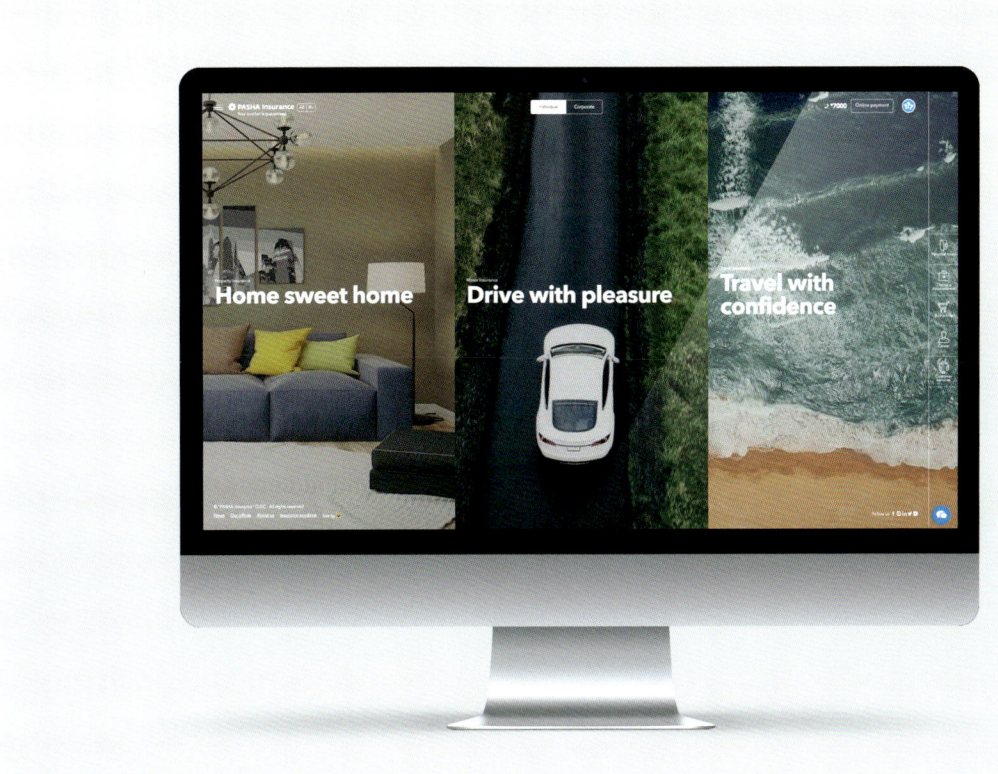
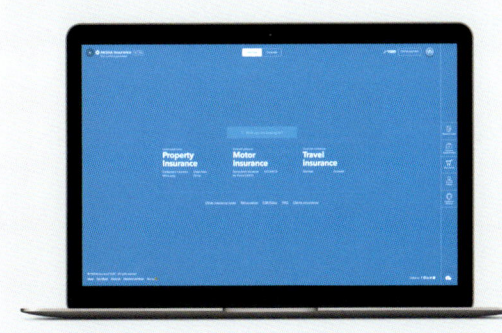
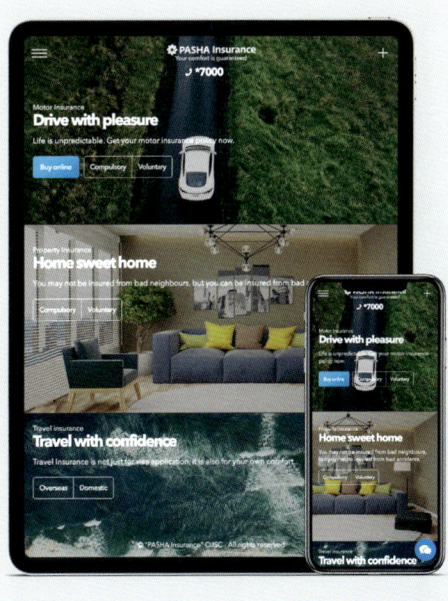

PASHA Insurance

[Website]

The Azerbaijani insurance company Pasha offers 36 types of insurance services for around 300,000 individual and corporate customers. The company's website provides an opportunity to get a policy online in five minutes. The main page is divided into three sections representing the three main insurance services: property, motor and travel. Vibrant videos in the background of each section convey a sense of confidence, trust and safety, while further information in an accessible form is provided upon a click. Also, doctor's appointments can be arranged by filling in personal data and choosing a clinic.

Client
PASHA Insurance OJSC, Baku, Azerbaijan

Design
Jeykhun Imanov Studio, Baku, Azerbaijan

Creative Direction
Jeykhun Imanov

Project Management
Maharram Aliyev

Front-End Development
Fuad Ibrahimov

Back-End Development
Mehran Guluzadeh

Content Management
Fazilya Nazarli

User Experience Design/User Interface Design
Ilyas Aliyev

→ Clip online

Publishing & Print Media   Posters   Typography   Illustrations   Sound Design   Film & Animation   Online   Apps

Expormim
[Website]

For the brand's redesign, the furniture manufacturer Expormim placed emphasis on transmitting the essence of the brand: purity, simplicity, wellness and a Mediterranean lifestyle. Serving as an open window to anyone who wants to know more about the company, the website transports its values and history, know-how and present-day craftsmanship. A clear and responsive design makes it easily accessible and enables a sorted overview, with two different sections for indoor and outdoor lines as well as a quick search for technical details or designers. Photography is the essential element and is used as the thrust of the product communication.

Client
Expormim, Mogente, Spain

Design
Didac Ballester, Valencia, Spain

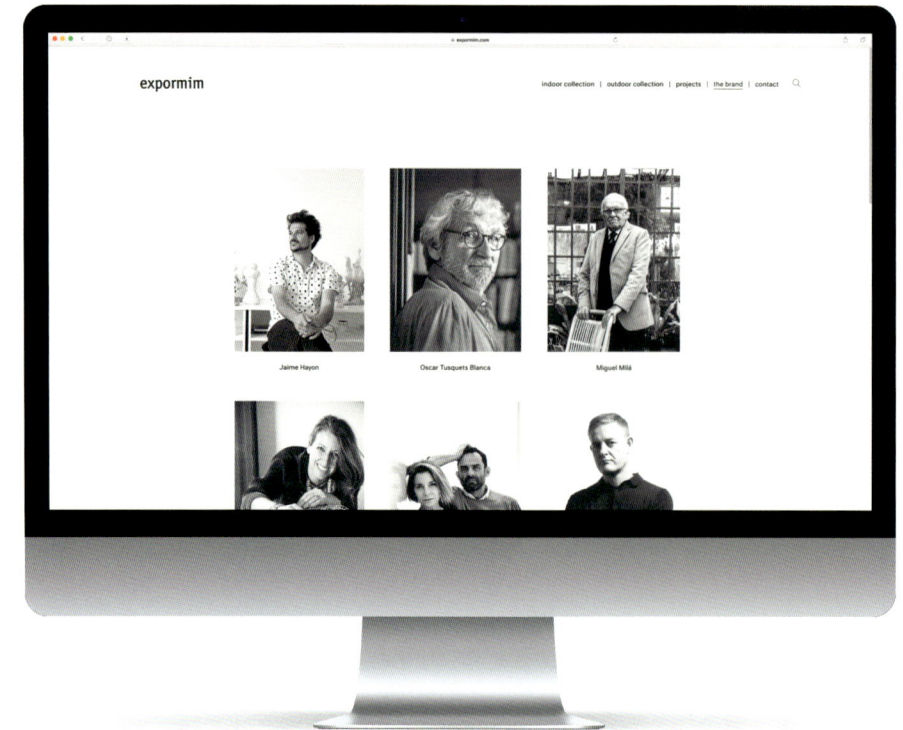

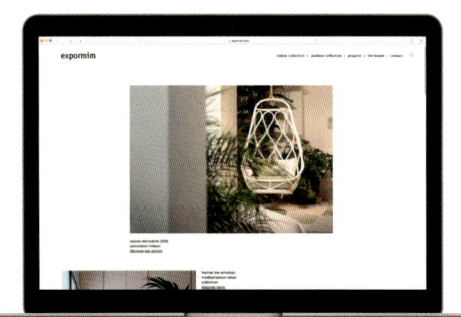
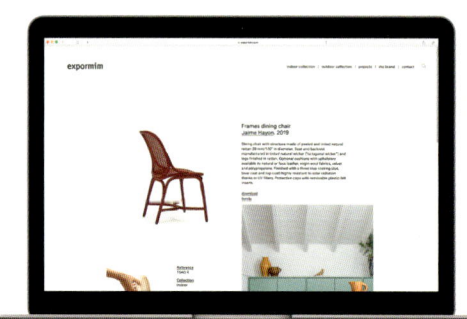

skantherm

[Website]

Large-scale motifs, moving elements and lively interaction take centre stage in the new online presence of the stove manufacturer skantherm. Atmospheric images and text access points transport visitors directly into various rooms with fireplaces, while quick links guide them to more detailed content. Narrated stories in combination with photographs provide insights into the wide variety of different models and environments, and all fireplaces can be configured in real time. Technically and visually up to date, the website thus inspires visitors to create their own fireplace experience.

Client
skantherm GmbH & Co. KG,
Oelde, Germany

Design
cyclos design GmbH,
Münster, Germany

iFly KLM 360

[Virtual Reality Experience, Travel Platform]

Alongside a linear VR experience, an interactive 360-degree web experience platform has been developed by the online magazine of KLM Royal Dutch Airlines. It is based on three key objectives: to inspire people to travel and discover the world, to provide them with memorable travel experiences and to drive engagement time. The design is made to scale, and it focuses on mobile viewing. All content is presented in full-screen and realistic proportions, with additional 2D video stories, slideshows and tips in each episode. Additional navigation is kept minimalistic, ensuring a rich and interactive story discovery.

Client
KLM Royal Dutch Airlines,
Amstelveen, Netherlands

Design
Born05, Utrecht, Netherlands

Creative Direction Interactive
Timo Wilbrink

Art Direction
Marnix Schmidt

Account
Sander de Graauw

Project Management
Maaike Luijer

Production
Frederik Pot

Motion Design
Jesse Otten

Strategy
Harm Balvers

Distribution
Arne Stierman

Development
Arjen Gosman

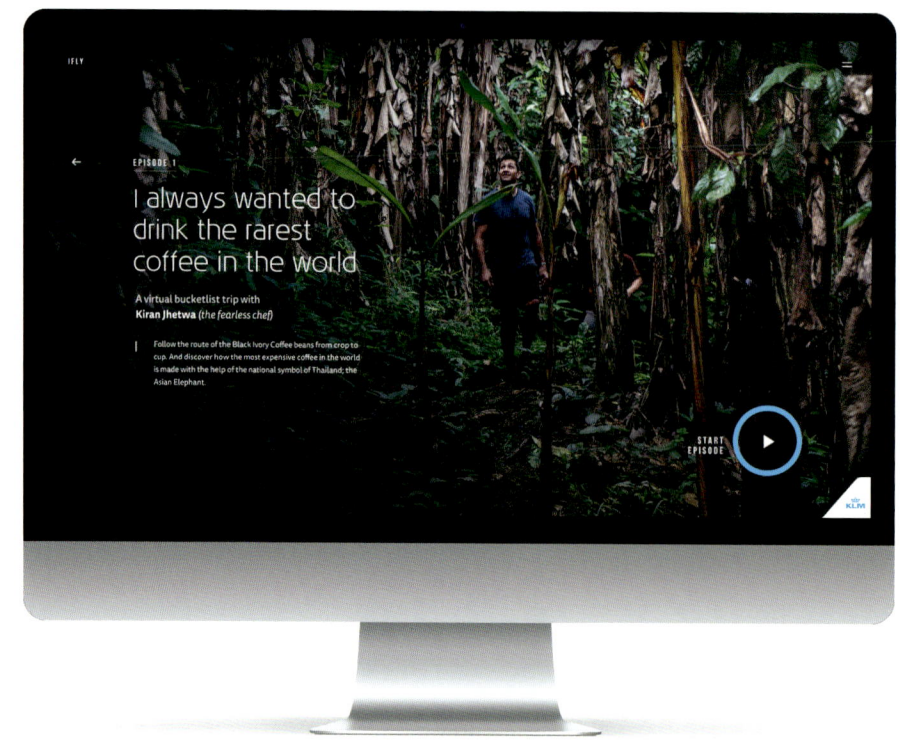
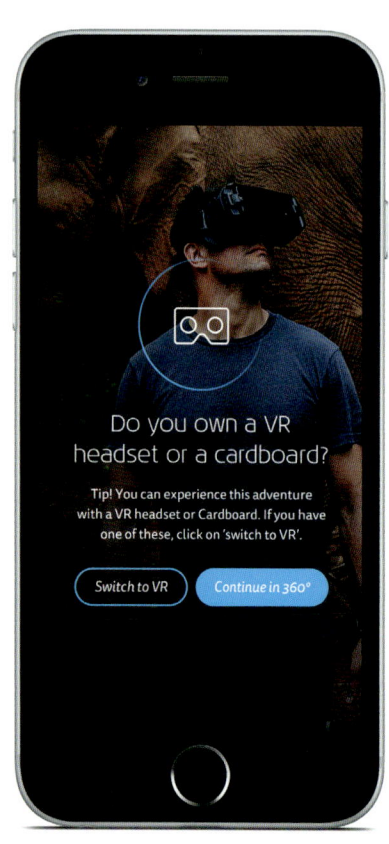

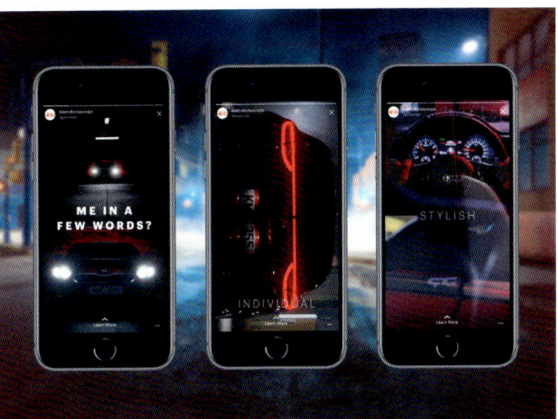

The new Kia ProCeed – Bold Move

[Microsite]

With the new ProCeed vehicle, a fresh target group – defined as "design-conscious trendsetters" – is being addressed by the Seoul-based car brand KIA. The campaign claim "Bold Move" reflects both the car's positioning and the company's approach to the corresponding website. The car model always remains centre stage and can be explored through interactive and immersive navigation. The visual content was developed by combining 3D technology with real-life footage of the car. Animations have been turned into a variety of short loops, which are displayed according to the users' interaction and which are optimised for each device and browser.

Client
Kia Motors Europe GmbH,
Frankfurt/Main, Germany

Design
INNOCEAN Worldwide Europe GmbH,
Frankfurt/Main, Germany
Herren der Schöpfung,
Frankfurt/Main, Germany

Art Direction
Timo Kanehl, Per Seuring,
Herren der Schöpfung

Production
Michael Endres,
INNOCEAN Worldwide Europe

Account Management
Oliver Novak, Peter Greiner, Julia Kremer,
INNOCEAN Worldwide Europe

KRELL Automotive

[Website, Brand Design]

Client
KRELL Automotive, Seoul, South Korea

Design
FRUM, Seoul, South Korea

Creative Direction
Soyoung Han

Concept
Jinyoung Kim

Web Design
Hyunwoo Jung, Youjung Yi

Graphic Design
Minkeun Kim

Project Management
Yehoon Kwon

→ Designer profile on page 525
→ Clip online

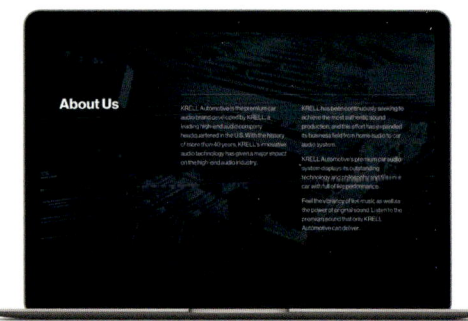

By integrating the story of this long-standing power amplifier company, and thus strengthening the brand's heritage and establishing marketing strategies for its automotive parts, KRELL has been reimagined as a completely new brand – KRELL Automotive. For the new responsive website, based on content storytelling, the message of "the energy of the vast universe" was selected. Action-packed graphics and video productions were used to translate it into a superior automotive tuning technology. Each page boasts a different theme that illustrates the branding strategy, visualised through storylines that can be easily explored.

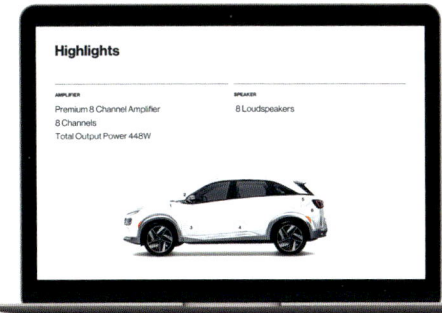

Publishing & Print Media   Posters   Typography   Illustrations   Sound Design   Film & Animation   Online   Apps

Landestheater Detmold
[Website]

The Spielplan (Event Calendar) of this multidiscipline theatre is the focus of user interest, as analyses have shown. For the new, responsive website of the Landestheater Detmold (Detmold Regional Theatre), the calendar was turned into the central navigation point and supplemented by a reduced, clear menu. Both measures ensure intuitive user guidance, with further levels of content revealed at every click. With the change of director, the company was also given a revised corporate design, which manifests in the relaunch and in print publications. The events are staged in an enhanced emotional way using large-scale visual worlds.

Client
Landestheater Detmold GmbH,
Detmold, Germany

Design
m.i.r. media, Cologne, Germany

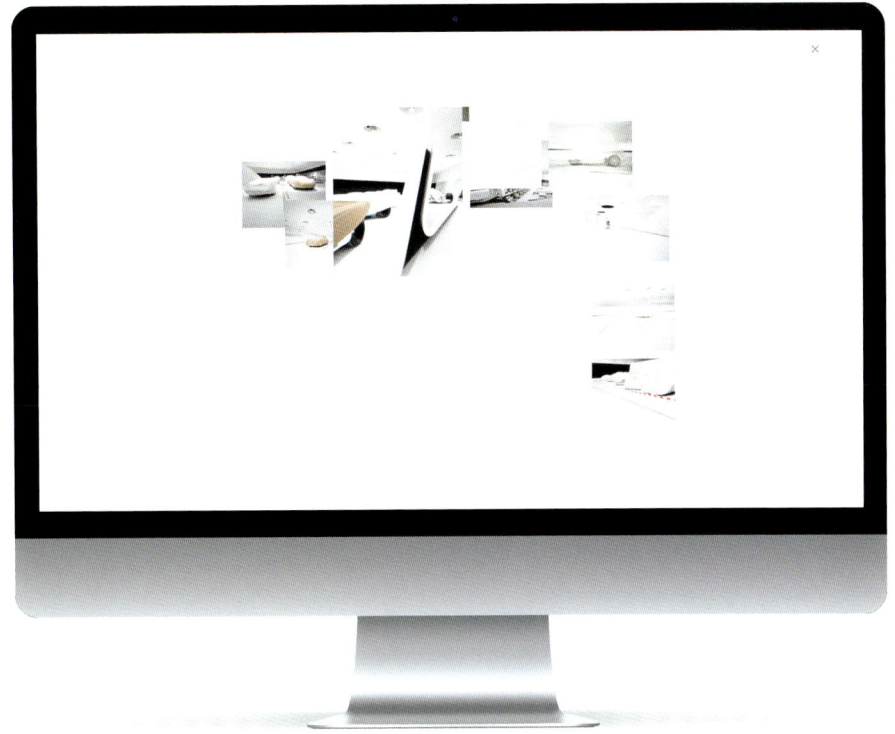

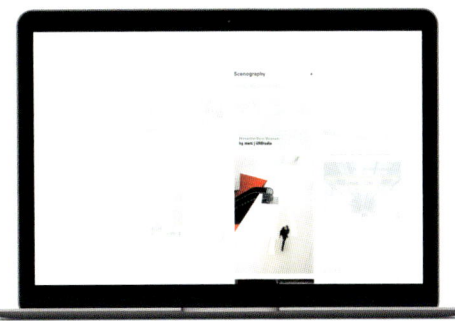

Brigida González
[Website]

The new website of the architectural photographer Brigida González was designed to represent the reduced aesthetics of her photographs, while simultaneously providing space for different, personal works. With a navigation based on an intuitive approach and reduced UI elements, users can meander through the various sections, such as Architecture, Scenography, Corporate and Retrospect. Guidance takes place through a "slot machine" for navigating through the overview, presented on a light table on which the photographs are thematically arranged and lead to the longread.

Client
Fotografie Brigida González,
Stuttgart, Germany

Design
jäger&jäger, Überlingen, Germany

Creative Direction
Olaf Jäger, Regina Jäger

Art Direction
Reinhard Thomas

Programming
Felix Geiger,
Felix Geiger Softwareentwicklung,
Stuttgart, Germany

OPUS
Music Intelligence

[Digital Ecosystem]

Against the backdrop of recent developments in the entertainment industry, Warner Music Group (WMG) felt they were losing a grip on deeper insights into their artists, music and overall performance. Therefore, the aim was to transform the data they own into useful, decision-supporting information. Through an extensive discovery and definition phase, a strategy and a roadmap were defined, and OPUS was born: a multidimensional digital ecosystem that allows artist managers, label managers, WMG executives and artists to understand their performance data, from a high-level perspective to the tiniest speck of information.

Client
Warner Music Group, New York, USA

Design
CLEVER°FRANKE, Utrecht, Netherlands

Creative Direction
Thomas Clever, Gert Franke

User Experience Design
Wouter van Dijk, Joost Mommers, Pietro Lodi

Visual Design
Roel de Jonge, Pietro Lodi, Joost Mommers

Programming
Jan Hoogeveen, Nick Rutten, Wilco Tomassen, Merlijn Vos, Koen Poelhekke, Mark Haasjes

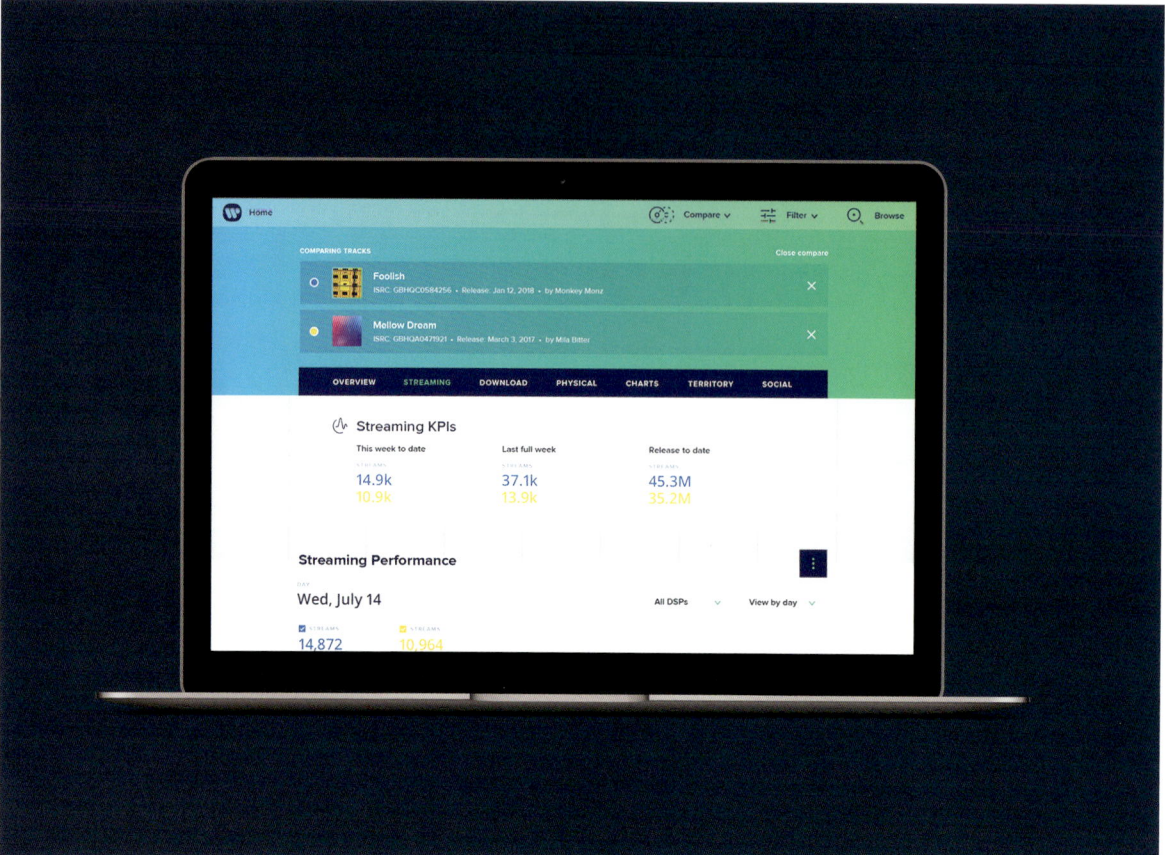

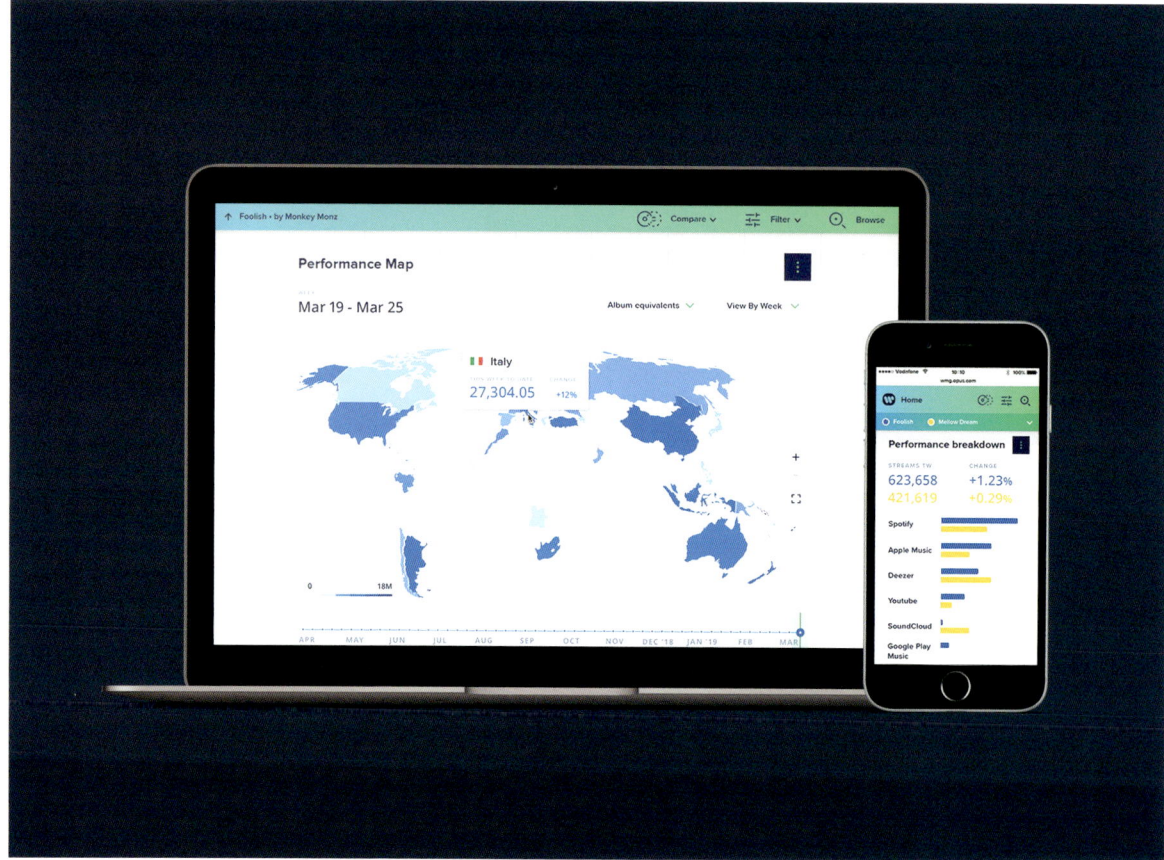

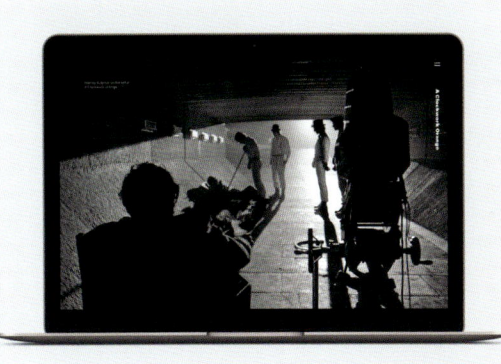

Stanley Kubrick – Work and Life

[Website]

Marking Stanley Kubrick's 90th birthday and dedicated to his life and work, this website was initiated for the purpose of education and with deep respect for the cinematography legend. Following the idea and intention to make the site feel like a movie, allegorically, the narration is performed in chronological order and features his films as well as some interesting and enticing facts, acquainting visitors with the film director's traits and techniques. Infinite scrolling is used as the main navigation element, while specially created animations and 3D graphics lend atmosphere and interaction to the user experience.

Client
Tubik Studio, Dnipro, Ukraine

Design
Tubik Studio, Dnipro, Ukraine

Art Direction
Vladyslav Taran

Concept
Ksenia Lashko

Web Design
Denys Koloskov, Ksenia Lashko

Programming
Aleksandr Petulko

Editorial Work
Marina Yalanska

Project Management
Polina Taran

→ Designer profile on page 570
→ Clip online

Digital German Women's Archive

[Web Portal]

The new web portal of the Digitales Deutsches Frauenarchiv (Digital German Women's Archive) presents an overview of the issues, biographies and achievements of the German feminist movement, spotlighting how much it took to overcome obstacles. An attractive layout and responsive web design deliver interesting content to researchers and students. They can navigate through a relationship network and taxonomies to find material relevant to them, with individual topics explained briefly. A faceted search guides the user through over 500,000 objects. Digital images and multi-page publications can be viewed in high resolution.

Client
i.d.a.-Dachverband e.V.,
Dachverband deutschsprachiger
Lesben-/Frauenarchive, -bibliotheken
und -dokumentationsstellen,
Berlin, Germany

Design
OUTERMEDIA GmbH, Berlin, Germany

Creative Direction
Eva Duwenkamp

Web Design
Mariano Procopio

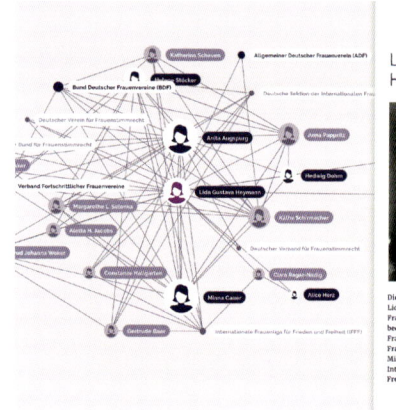

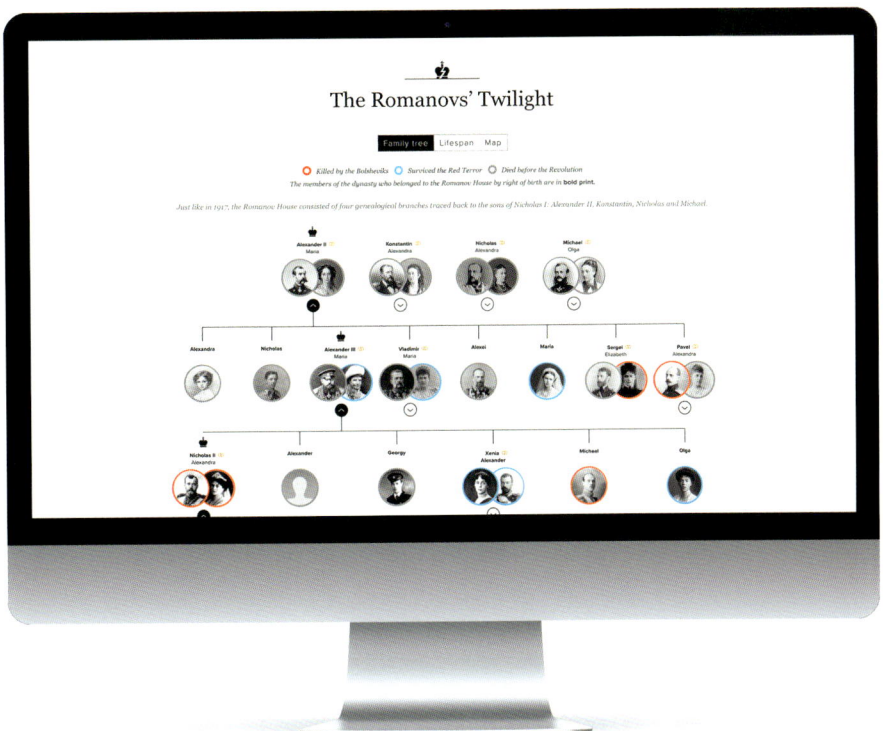

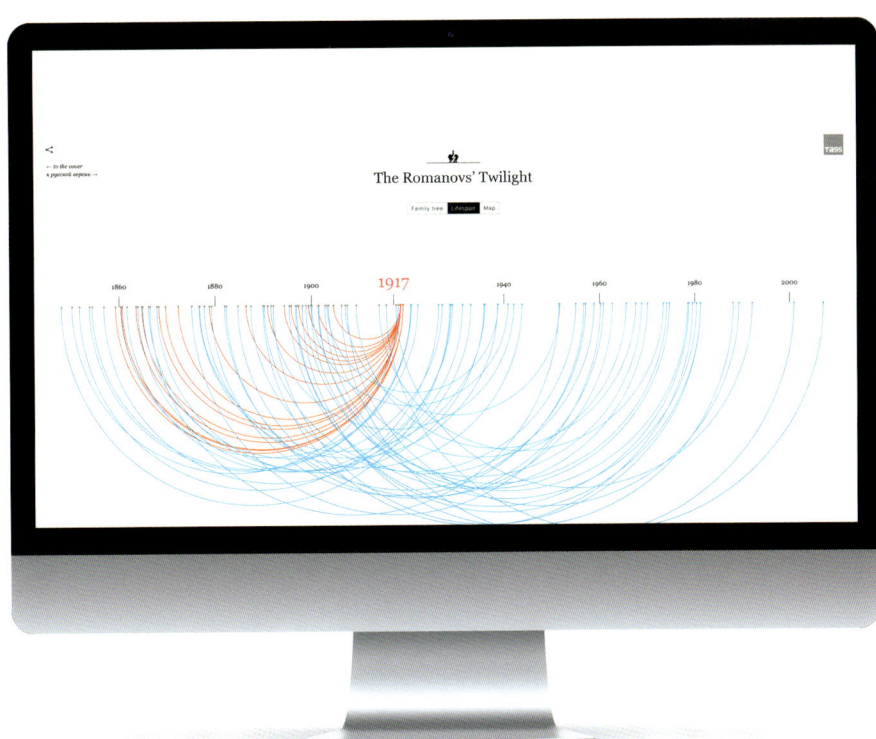

The Romanov's Twilight
[Web Special]

This interactive project documents the history of the Russian monarchy. Each member of the Romanov family is given his or her own profile card, which includes some informal facts about personal views, hobbies or the curiosities that happened in their lives. The fate of several generations and their wanderings around the world can be traced on an interactive map. The years of their lives are marked on a timeline, with the earliest character born in 1847 and the most recent one passing in 2007. Thus, this storytelling website indirectly covers 160 years of the history of the House of Romanov.

Client
TASS Russian News Agency,
Moscow, Russia

Design
TASS Russian News Agency,
Moscow, Russia

Italia – The Airship Crash Chronicle

[Web Special]

This multimedia web special chronicles the Arctic expedition of the airship Italia – commanded by Italian engineer and General Umberto Nobile – that crashed during the return flight from the North Pole in 1928 and also describes its international rescue operation. Using a 3D model of the airship, interactive infographics, maps and 3D-animated scenes to illustrate the story, it details the numerous rescue efforts and puts them all on one map – documenting an outstanding international cooperation for the time. Also, the process of creating this longread featuring a dramatic text filled with all kinds of multimedia elements was no less international.

Client
TASS Russian News Agency,
Moscow, Russia

Design
TASS Russian News Agency,
Moscow, Russia

The Buran – The Soviet Space Shuttle Success Story
[Web Special]

This web special is dedicated to the 30th anniversary of the first and only flight of the spaceship Buran, a reusable orbiter capable of putting different payloads into space and bringing cargoes back to Earth. Conceived as an "analysis of the flight" on 15 November 1988, it goes into detail about the most difficult stages of the Soviet rocket plane's mission, including the landing, which for the first time in history was fully automatic. Each of the web special's four chapters contains interactive inserts, and one of the most complex visualisations of the project is a detailed 3D model of the Buran.

Client
TASS Russian News Agency, Moscow, Russia

Design
TASS Russian News Agency, Moscow, Russia

99 Documents
[Website]

This project represents a digital search for traces through time and illustrates the history of Austria using 99 selected documents from almost 1,200 years. Many original documents, which are all securely locked in the cabinets of the Austrian State Archive, were digitised and can be explored in high resolution. A clear representation was generated, which leads the viewer along an interesting and varied path through Austria's history. Video sequences complete the multimedia experience and make this interactive tour of the historic premises as real as if visitors were really there and could hold the historical artefacts in their hands.

Client
Österreichisches Staatsarchiv, Vienna, Austria

Design
clicksgefühle GmbH & Co KG, Neusiedl am See, Austria

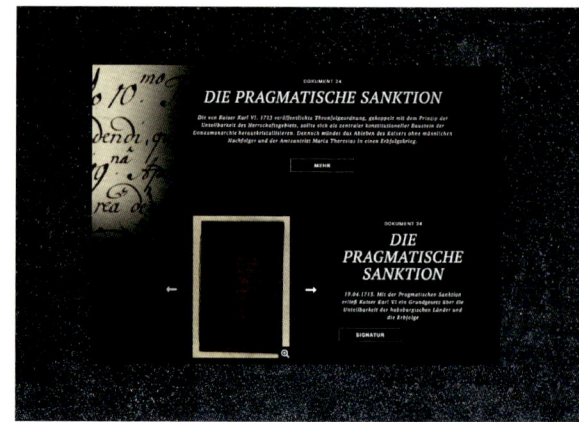

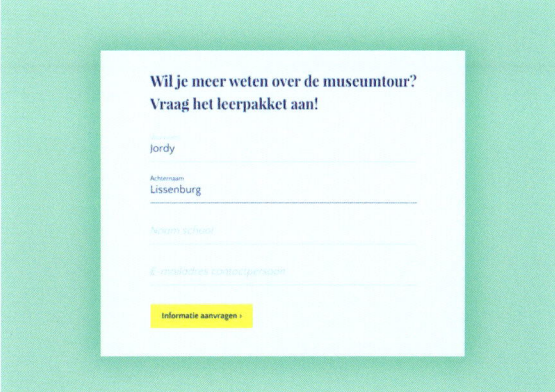
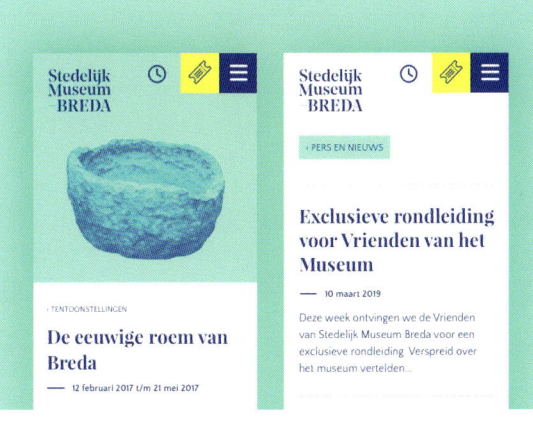

Stedelijk Museum Breda
[Website]

Stedelijk Museum Breda is a museum spotlighting the Dutch city's heritage and history, as well as contemporary visual culture. It was created through a merger of the Museum of the Image (MOTI), presenting contemporary visual culture, and Breda's Museum, exhibiting art and cultural history of the city of Breda. The online presence, which presents the unique composition and proposition of the museum, has emerged as a bold website showcasing historical and contemporary art. Both of these styles visually meet on the home page, providing the ground where "the old" and "the new" come together and can be explored.

Client
Stedelijk Museum Breda, Netherlands

Design
Freshheads, Tilburg, Netherlands

Web Design
Violette Müller, Jordy Lissenburg

Programming
Remco Abalain

APPS

Re:imagine Street ARt

[Art Experience App]

On the occasion of Art Berlin, this augmented reality app set out to amplify basic street art principles by extending the conceptual idea of the artworks through an additional layer. Bringing in new elements and interactive options, the smartphone app created an immersive art experience and changed the role of the viewer from a passive consumer to an active participant. Five international artists unfolded their creativity in pop-up galleries, on walls and around monuments across the city. The app then invited users to interact through augmented reality and thus to create a unique experience.

Client
Samsung Electronics,
Schwalbach am Taunus, Germany

Design
Cheil Germany GmbH,
Schwalbach am Taunus, Germany

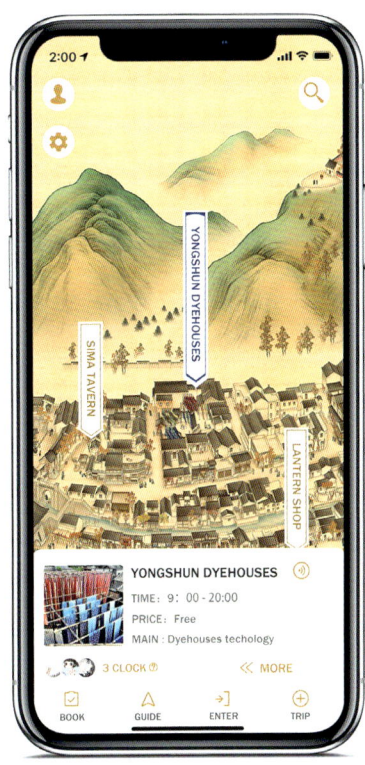

Beijing Wtown
[Travel App]

The Beijing Wtown app constitutes a one-stop smart travel guide, making it easy for travellers to explore the cultural content of their surrounding area. The interface design draws on the meticulous hand-painted style of ancient China, thus recovering the true style of the town. Besides offering GPS navigation and intelligent search functions for popular attractions and event recommendations, the app displays all stores, sorted by the categories of accommodation, travel, play, shopping and entertainment. In this way, it provides travellers with customised services as well as a lively contextual experience.

Client
Beijing Wtown, Beijing, China

Design
ZJY (Beijing) Tourism and Culture Co., Ltd., Beijing, China

→ Designer profile on page 575

MOO Music

[Entertainment App]

MOO is a music app which aims to deliver a wide array of music by providing not only the mainstream songs but also songs rarely played, in contrast to most of the music apps on the market. The app connects diverse songs sorted by different tags and lets users discover and explore music of their own tastes. Also, live photo streaming and different wave visuals in connection with the sound on the play page deliver a lively experience to users. In addition, the app visualises the data of users on a monthly basis in the "Sharing Cover", which can be shared via social networks and thus expands the users' various music tastes.

Client
Tencent Music Entertainment Group, Music User eXperience Design Center, Shenzhen, China

Design
Tencent Music Entertainment Group, Music User eXperience Design Center, Shenzhen, China

Creative Direction
Oscar Hu

Art Direction
Inne Chen

User Interface Design
Nan Pei

User Experience Design
Chenxi Li

Graphic Design
Yonsoo Park

Motion Design
Jessie Qin

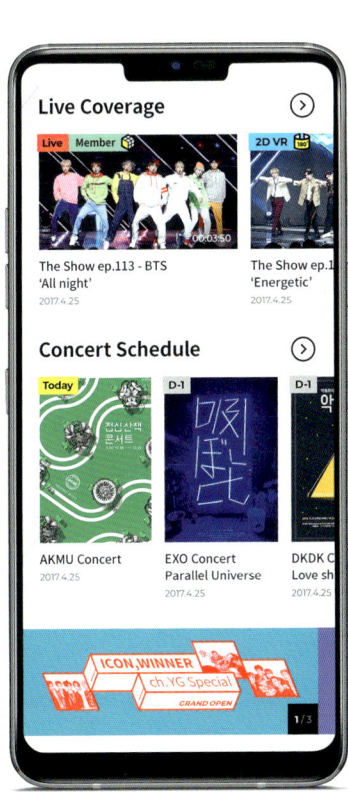
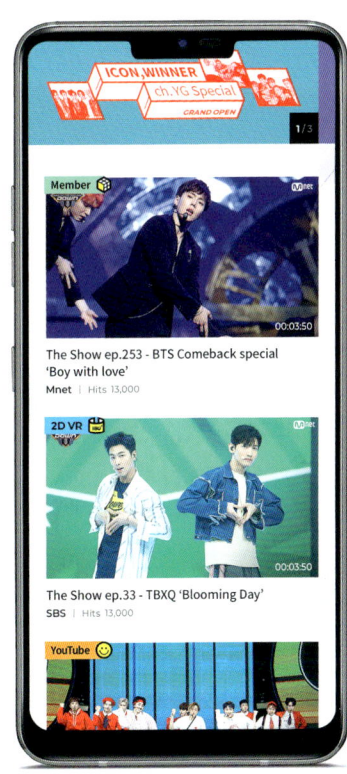

U+ Idol Live
[Entertainment App]

K-pop fandom, mainly spread among teenage adolescents, has become a widespread cultural activity in Korea. Applying G5 technology, U+ Idol Live is a media platform for Android and iOS that allows users to experience their favourite Korean idol bands and their members more closely and to capture every gesture and expression, along with clothes and style. Up to three members can be displayed simultaneously on the smartphone. The app broadcasts live performances, with several camera modes to choose from, focusing on individual idols or showing footage of the front, side and back of the stage.

Client
LG Uplus, Seoul, South Korea

Design
LG Uplus, Seoul, South Korea

Creative Direction
Minhyung Cho, Dasol Kim, Jaeha Jung

User Interface Design
Sena Jo, Seowoo Lee

Graphic Design
Haru Won, Right Brain, Seoul, South Korea

Tencent Video

[Entertainment App for the Blind]

Visually impaired people heavily rely on hearing TV shows for their entertainment. However, due to insufficient voice-actors in the Chinese entertainment industry and limited budgets, using the same voice-actor for multiple characters is a common practice in China. This app improves the listening experience by using facial recognition to identify different characters in TV shows and by modulating their voices in order to make them more distinguishable. It also shortens the time when there are no lines, so that the visually impaired need not wait too long without hearing any voices.

Client
Tencent Technology (Shenzhen) Co., Ltd., Shenzhen, China

Design
Tencent Technology (Shenzhen) Co., Ltd., Shenzhen, China

Graphic Design
Ning Jiang, Xiaochen Huang, Shaoan Zhen, Hao Wu, Ying Tong Qiu, Siyuan Bi

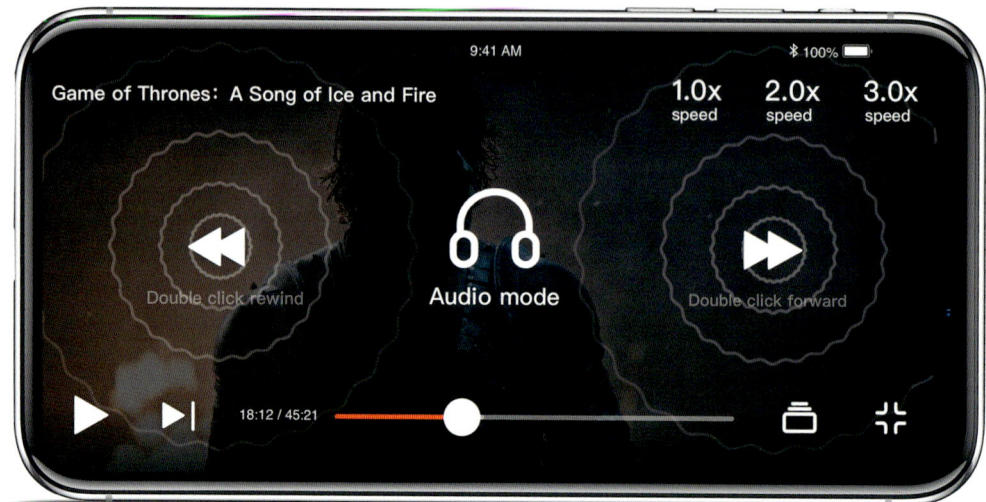

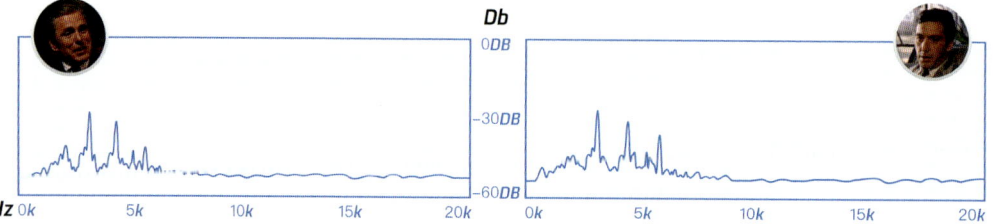

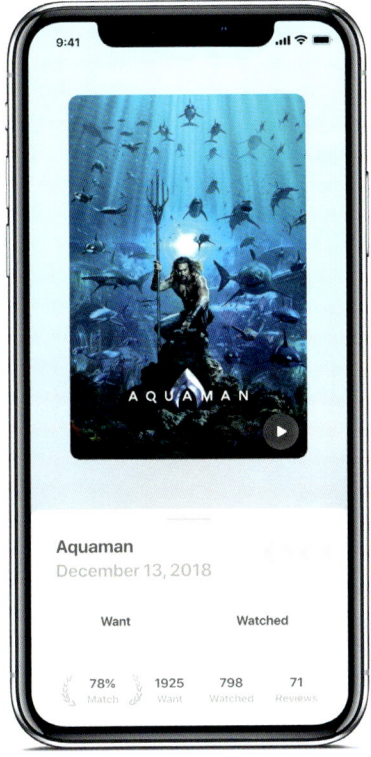
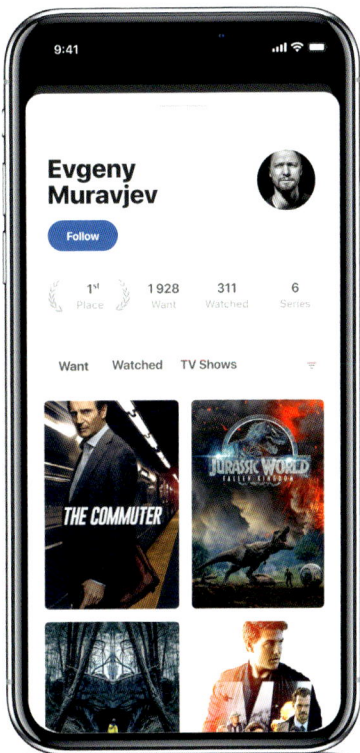
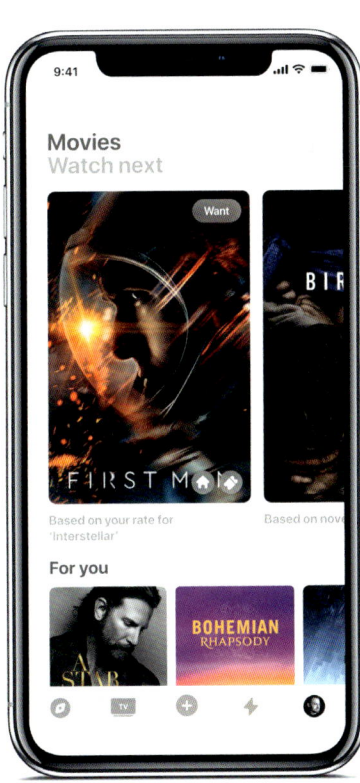
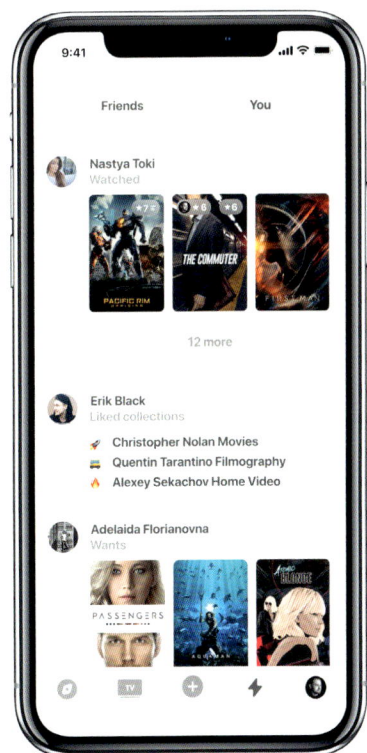

Must

[Entertainment App]

The Must app lets users track and rate movies and TV series, write reviews, receive release notifications, connect with friends, manage a movie wish list and discover content tailored to their tastes. Using built-in machine learning and AI, it provides a personal recommendation system based on ratings of other users with similar tastes. An activity feed keeps users informed about friends' activities and offers space for exchange, while the home page shows trending movies and those playing in theatres. All movies and series available on streaming providers are directly linked.

Client
Must App Corp., Walnut, California, USA

Design
Must App Corp., Wilmington, Delaware, USA

Art Direction
Alexey Sekachov, Eve Muravjev

Project Management
Maria Prikazchikova, Gevork Sarkisyan

Programming
Max Medvedev, Mikhail Vashlyaev, Alexey Bogomolov, Ilya Shubkin, Nick Ivanushkin, Anna Yakshina, Vladimir Aralin, Maga Abdurakhmanov

→ Designer profile on page 551
→ Clip online

U+ 5G Golf

[Entertainment App, Sports App]

Client
LG Uplus, Seoul, South Korea

Design
LG Uplus, Seoul, South Korea

Art Direction
Jaehyun Bae, Gowoon Myeong

User Interface Design
Junhyun Bang

Publishing
Juhyun Park

User Experience Research
Mina Lim

Graphic Design
amoeba, Seoul, South Korea

→ Clip online

The U+ 5G Golf app is a golf streaming service for mobile devices that presents a wide range of information on popular golf players and tournaments in Korea. It features a flexible screen composition and a range of layouts to choose from, while a specific interface delivers a consistent user experience across all devices. A clear overview makes the 5G-based functions easy to understand and intuitively accessible. The app provides video footage from 60 cameras set around the golf course that captured all swings from various angles, and users are able to rotate these golfer swing scenes freely.

U+ 5G Professional Baseball

[Entertainment App, Sports App]

Client
LG Uplus, Seoul, South Korea

Design
LG Uplus, Seoul, South Korea

Creative Direction
Sungwan Won

Art Direction
Jaehyun Bae

User Interface Design
Subin Kim

User Experience Research
Kyungbae Kim

Graphic Design
Right Brain, Seoul, South Korea

→ Clip online

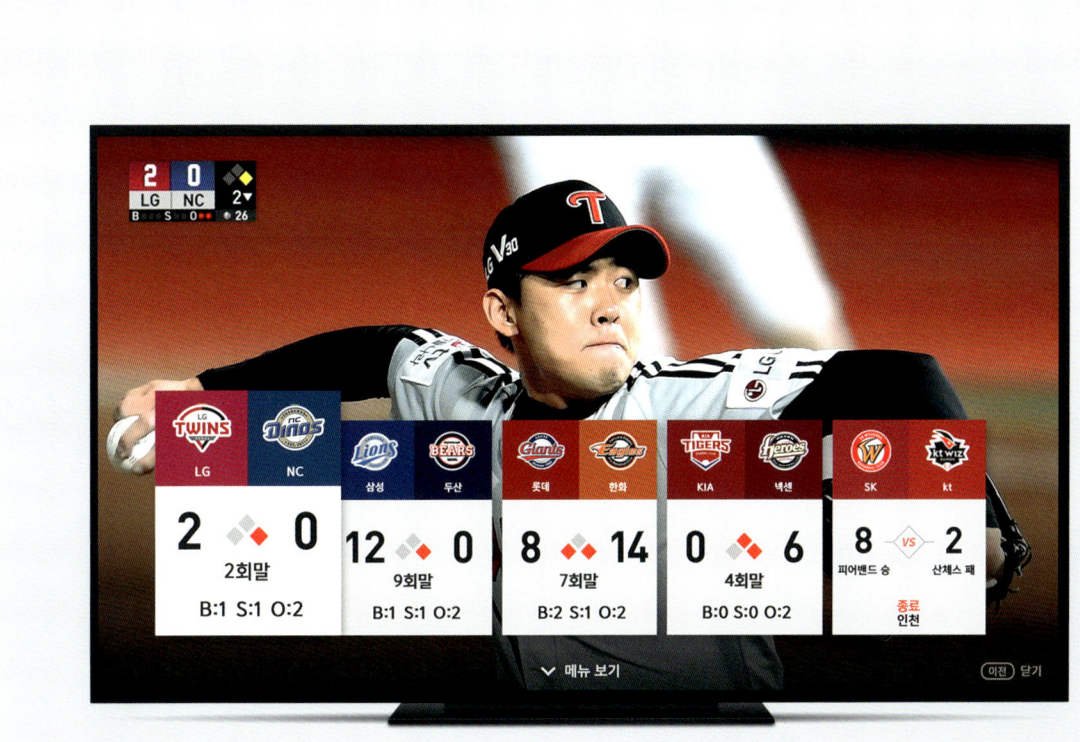

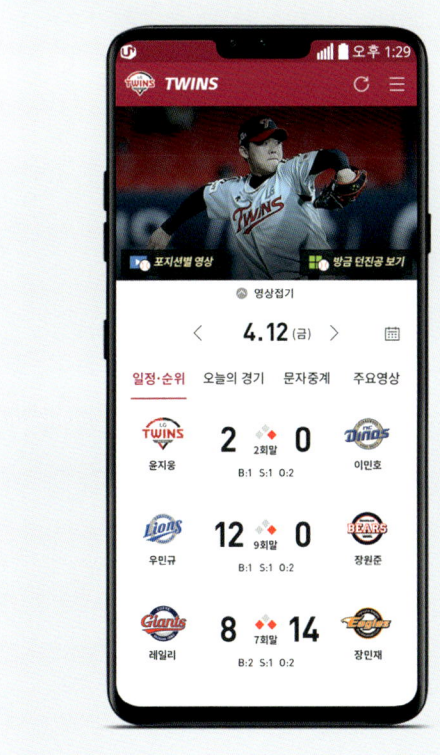

The 5G Professional Baseball app was developed to offer a new design and viewing experience of professional baseball. It provides functionalities designed around the particular rules and nature of baseball and offers a wide range of information depending on the characteristics of the different devices and services available on each smartphone. With 60 cameras installed around the home plate of the baseball ground, all of the moments that occur around the batter's box are captured from a range of different angles, and the 4D Home Base View allows users to watch the contents while freely rotating the image.

Publishing & Print Media   Posters   Typography   Illustrations   Sound Design   Film & Animation   Online   Apps

SAP Challenger Insights

[Sports App, Service App]

SAP Challenger Insights, part of the SAP Sports One solution, is a mobile app providing professional football coaches, analysts and players with data and insights into an opponent's tactics and characteristics. It helps the team to build and plan strategies, while also communicating in-game tactical changes and delivering intuitive, up-to-the-minute insights. A tactics board feature provides comprehensive variants for visualising and explaining match tactics, set pieces and team formations. All components are designed to encourage the user to interact and playfully find relevant information and videos at the touch of a button.

Client
SAP SE, St. Leon-Rot, Germany

Design
SAP SE, User Experience Design for Sports and Entertainment,
St. Leon-Rot, Germany

Design Team
Irene Schick, Lydia Tallau,
Alexander Schräder, Selina Vix,
Lars Siebert

Development Management
Sven Schwerin-Wenzel

→ Designer profile on page 561
→ Clip online

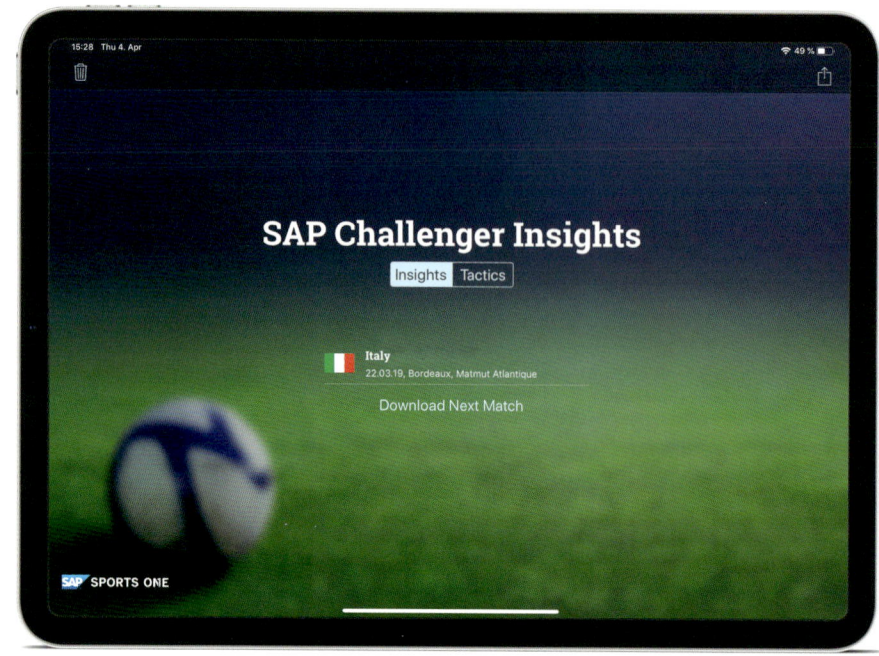

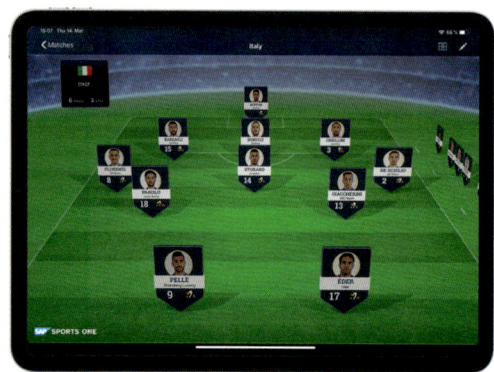
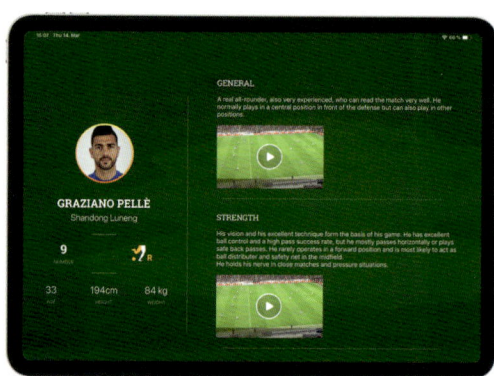

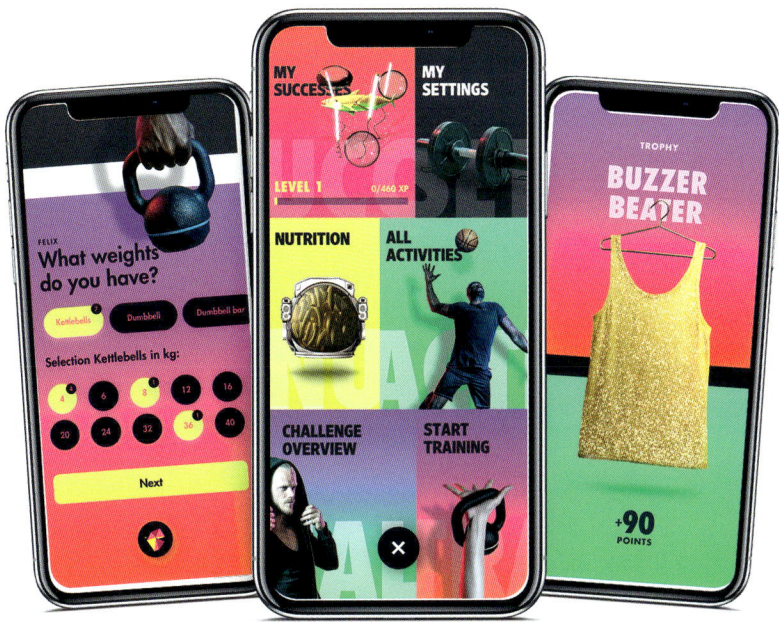

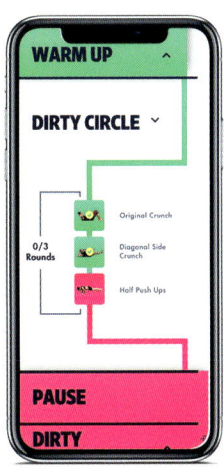

Butterfly Coach – Your Most Personal Trainer

[Fitness App]

The Butterfly Coach app constitutes a digital personal trainer that gets to know every user individually – implementing a fun and functional design to keep them motivated. Integrating AI and smart data, it evaluates users' needs based on feedback, sets goals and defines over 50 other parameters. Just like with a real personal trainer, every workout is different and individually generated. In addition to strength and relaxation exercises, nutrition tips are provided. Conceived like a chat between friends challenging each other, the app learns and adapts to the needs of the user, while also giving advice and providing motivation through points and trophies.

Client
BF Coach GmbH & Co. KG,
Kirchdorf, Germany

Design
Plan.Net Group, Munich, Germany

Global Chief Creative Officer
Alexander Schill

Managing Director
Markus Maczey, Oliver Bruckner

Creative Direction
Richard Wegele

User Experience/User Interface Design
Alexander Kneifel

Conceptional Design/Copywriting
Friederike Fröhlich, Philipp Stremlau

Creative Coding
Jonas Heitzer

Account Management
Marina Ludwig, Nicolas Holtzmeyer

Technical Development
Atlant Development e.K.,
Landshut, Germany

Digital Design
Studio Laurinsoares, Munich, Germany

Everland S-Ticket

[Service App]

The app of the Korean theme park Everland delivers an integrated user experience throughout all of the services offered. It includes a complete map of the park comprising five theme zones, displaying all of the attractions, rides and shows, and informs about operating hours and waiting line times. Moreover, users can make reservations in advance to eliminate waiting time with just a few taps and choose the exact time slot they would like to book, offered in twenty-minute intervals. Reservations and also the time remaining until one's turn can be checked from the home page and admission tickets can be purchased, scanned and activated.

Client
Samsung C&T, Everland Resort, Yongin, South Korea

Design
Samsung SDS, CX Innovation Team, Seoul, South Korea

Art Direction
Kwangyong Jeong

Strategic Planning
Taesun Yoo, Heejoung Kim

Graphic Design
Dongmin Shin

Film Production
Kyeamin Jeon

→ Clip online

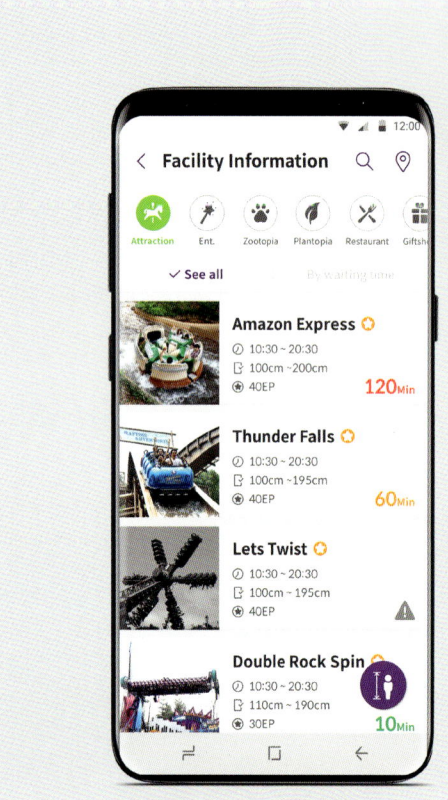

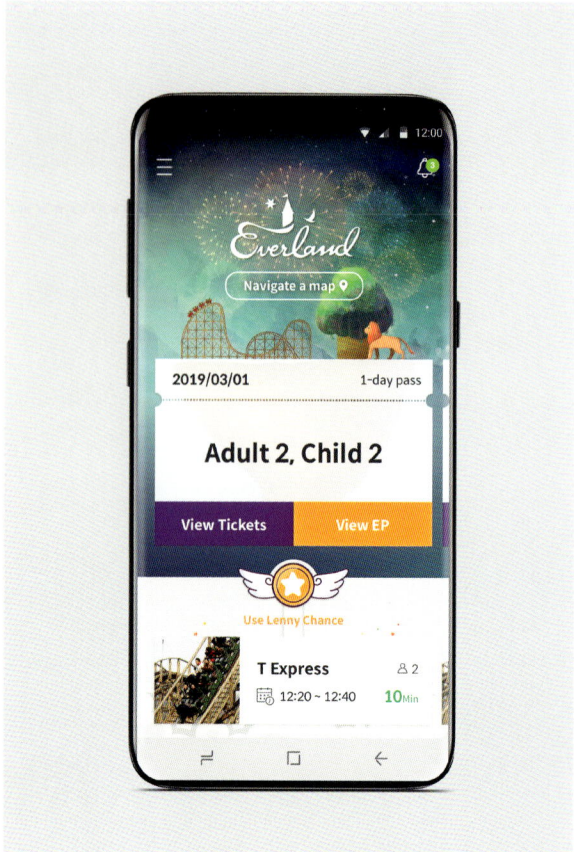

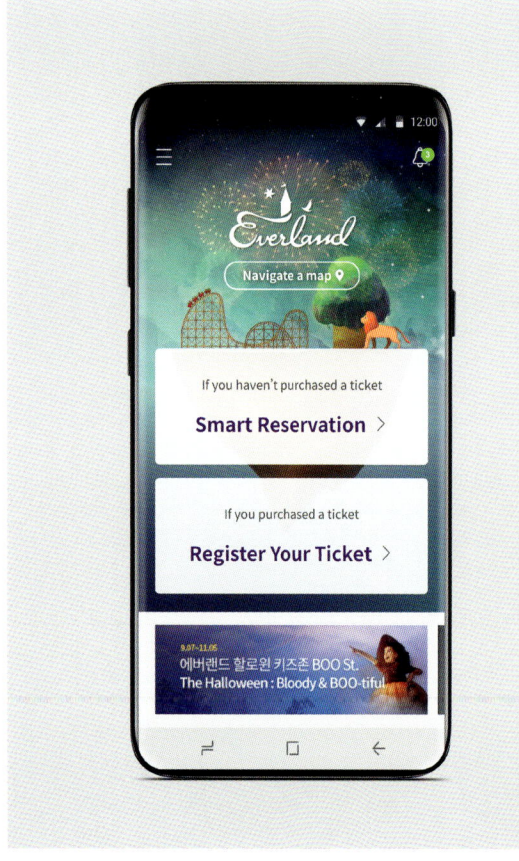

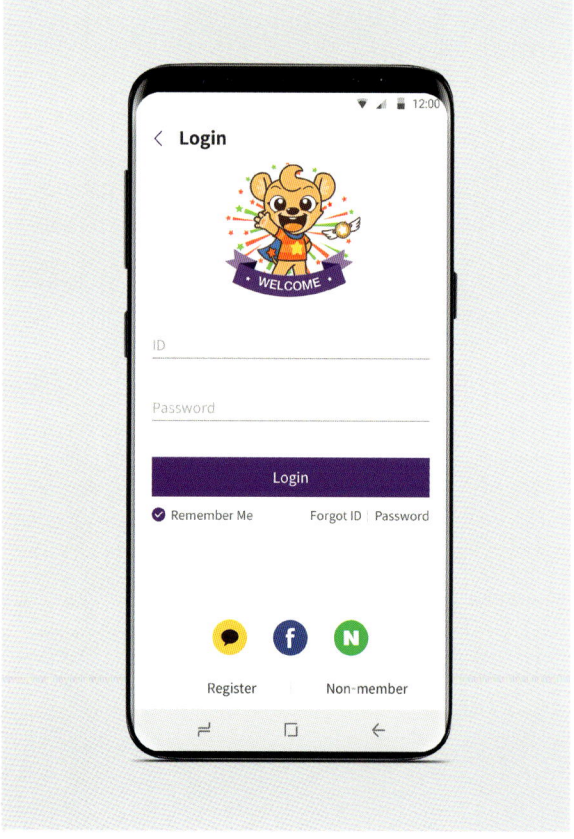

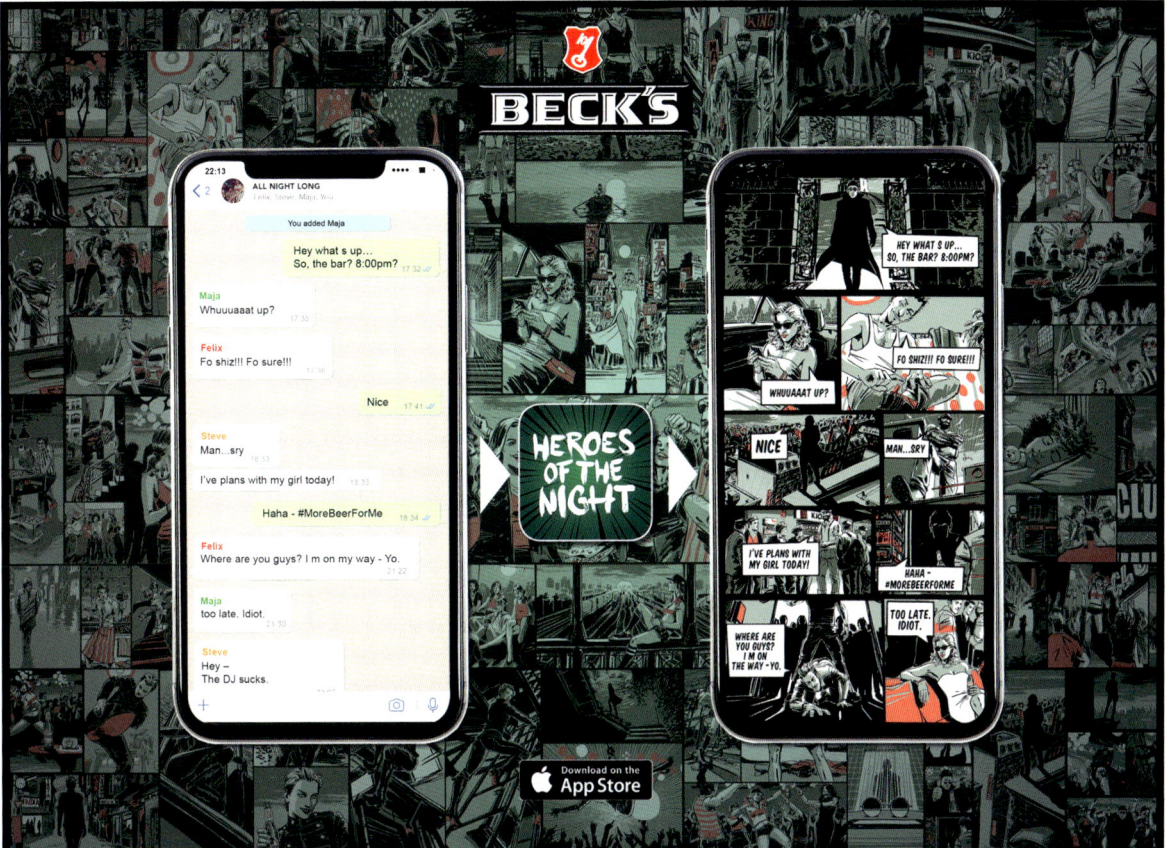
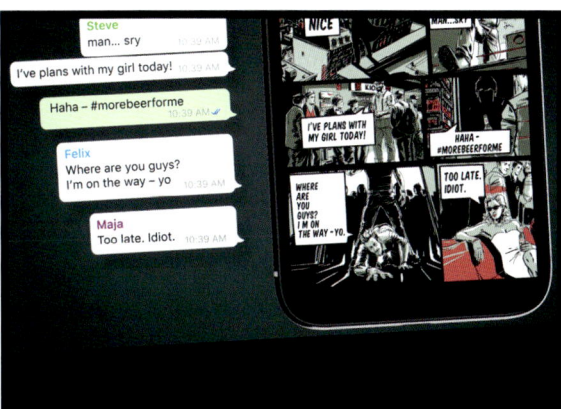

Beck's Heroes of the Night

[Entertainment App]

Heroes of the Night is a mobile app that takes user-generated, real-time data from group chats and turns chat members into the heroes of a comic strip. Each comic is fully customisable, based on the particular geo- and time-specific content. By applying machine-learning-based character and image assignment, including message sentiment and content analysis, the app automatically brings every message to life in the form of a comic hero statement. Users can choose from ten heroes with a different character each, resembling typical night-out personalities such as the well-dressed charmer, the talkative one or the diva.

Client
Anheuser-Busch InBev Germany, Bremen, Germany

Design
SERVICEPLAN GERMANY, Munich, Germany

Global Chief Creative Officer
Alexander Schill

Managing Partner
Florian Klietz, Markus Maczey

Executive Creative Direction
Thomas Heyen, Markus Kremer

Management Supervision
Kristian von Elm

Account Management
Mariah Kattmann

Design Direction
Sebastien Stabenau

Creative Direction
Ronnie Patt

Copywriting
Jan-Erik Scheibner

Illustration
Matthias Schardt

Technical Project Management/ Development/Creative Coding
Jonas Heitzer

YoungOnes – Be Your Own Boss

[Service App]

Against the backdrop of an increasing need for flexible workers by companies facing rapid changes in customer demand along with the rise of interest in freelance work, especially among young people, YoungOnes is a platform for on-demand work and hiring. Conceived as a digital bulletin board, the app and associated web environment cover the entire process: from registration to onboarding, and from job assignments, searching and matching to paying. As an on-demand community, it helps people seeking temporary employment to apply for short tasks or jobs that are uploaded by organisations looking for interim staff.

Client
YoungOnes, Hoofddorp, Netherlands

Design
Freshheads, Tilburg, Netherlands

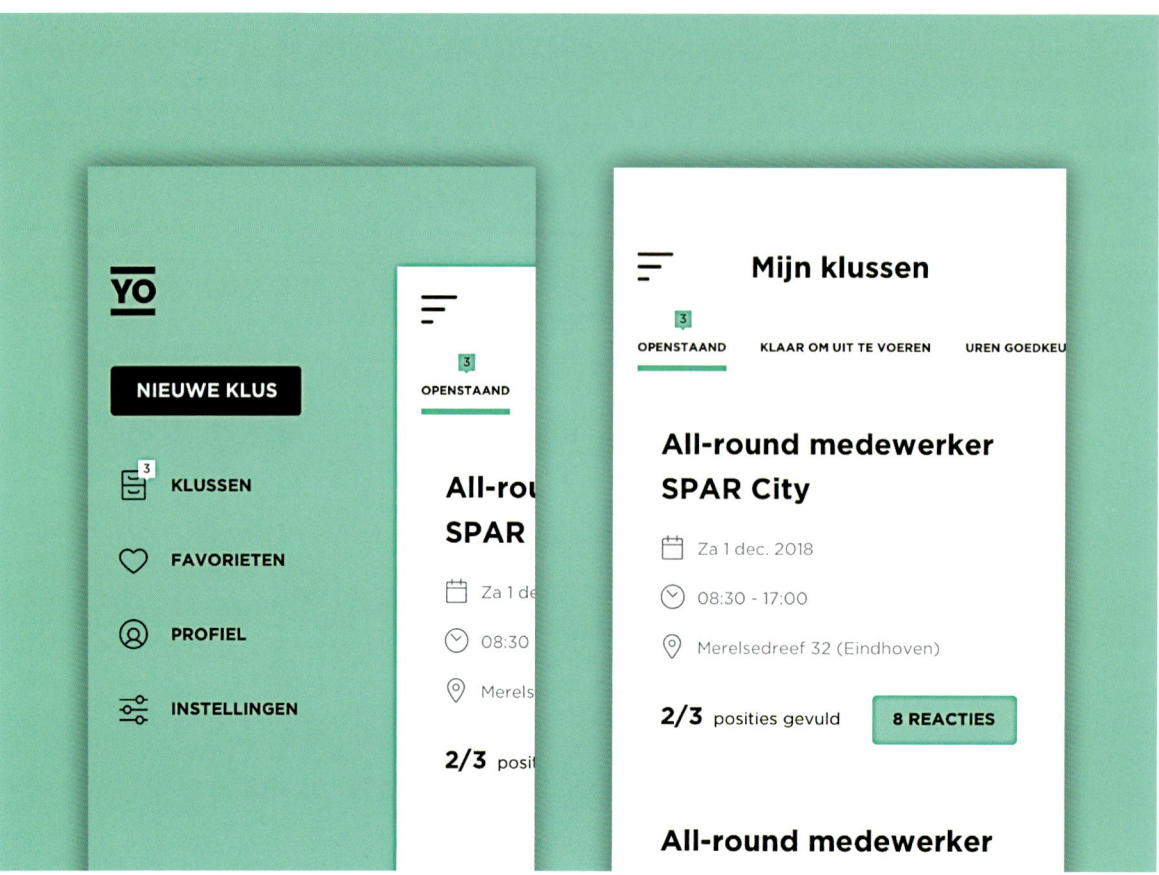
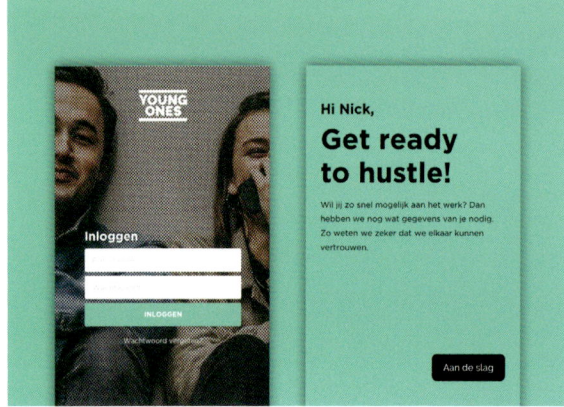

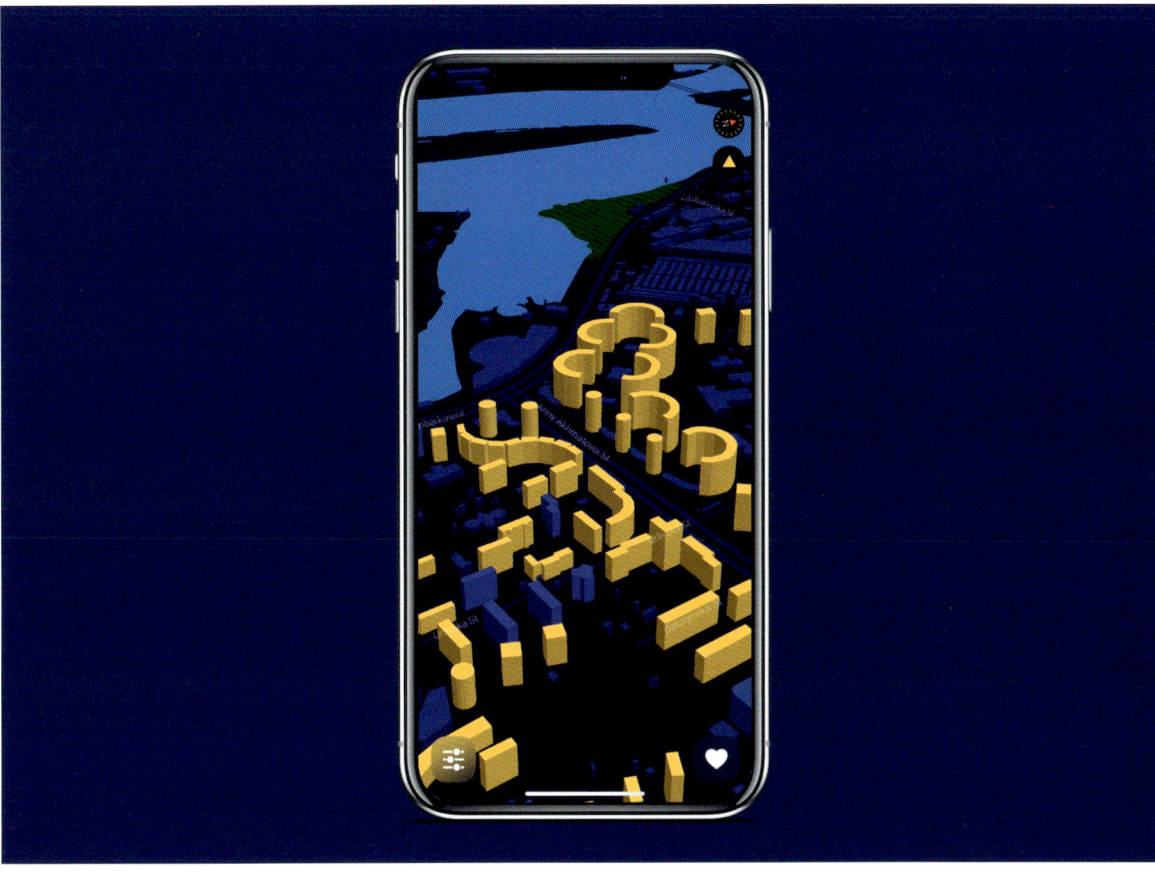

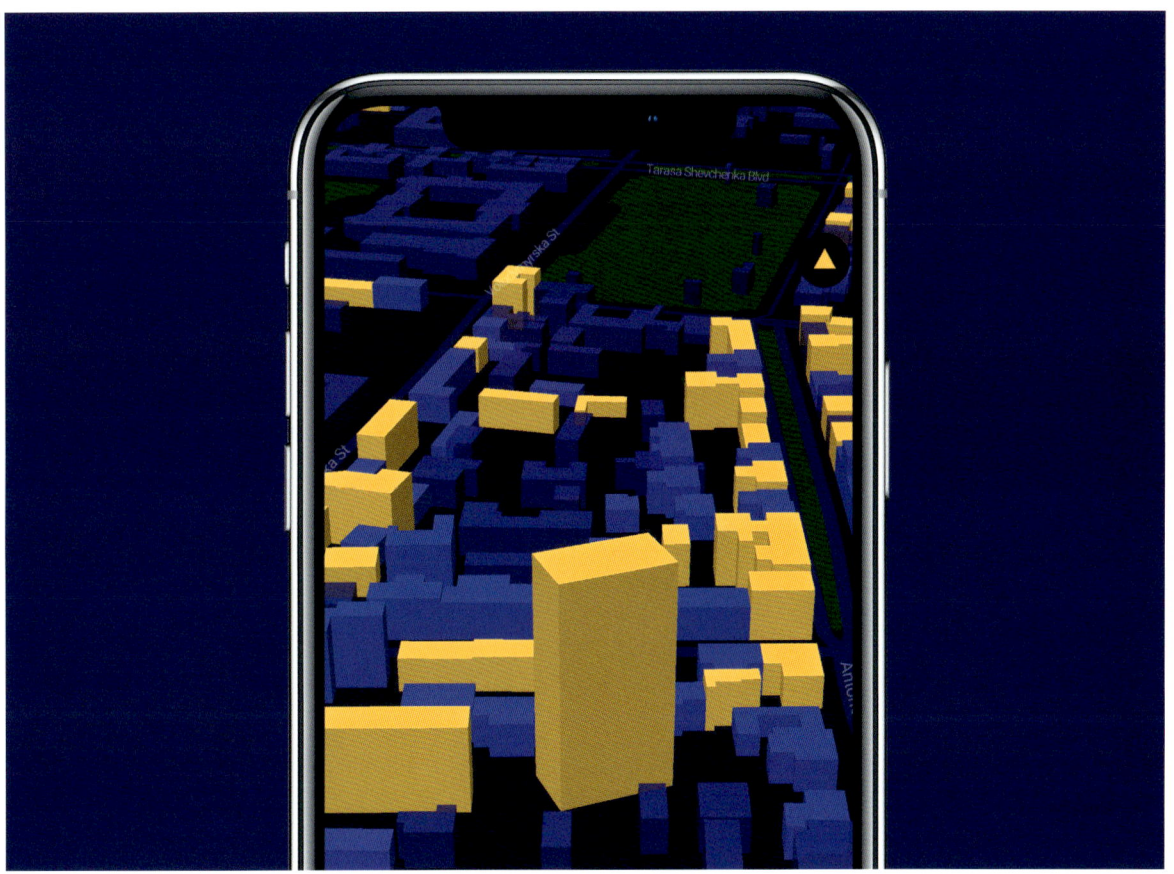

Bird
[Service App]

Bird is an iOS app that helps users find a flat to rent in Kyiv. The layout of the app is simple and minimalistic, using three elements only: the map, a gallery of apartments and the apartment itself. Bird displays a dark futuristic 3D map of the town highlighting the buildings with available apartments that match the users' search criteria. With just one swipe, users can switch from flat to flat. Acting as a personal rental assistant, the app guides them, offers protection from scammers or spam, and sends notifications when new flats appear. Useful features and an emotional character thus make moving more delightful.

Client
Flatfy OÜ, Tallinn, Estonia

Design
Flatfy OÜ, Tallinn, Estonia

Product Design
Arsenii Feshchenko

Concept
Denys Tsyganok, Nataliya Strelchenko, Oleksandr Ivanov

Programming
Yevhenii Pancheshnyi, Dmytro Satanovskyj

Supervision
Andrey Mima

Philips SleepMapper

[Health App]

SleepMapper is the companion app to the SmartSleep headband and the connected Somneo Wake-Up Light devices. Users can thus track and react to sleep patterns and learn about the actual time of total sleep, awake times, and deep sleep phases. Customised sounds are used to provide a boost to the wearer's natural slow brainwave activity during deep sleep. All of this is focused on improving sleep quality to increase energy throughout the day. The app provides features such as the monitoring of sound and light levels in the bedroom environment and offers tips and support for healthy sleep.

Client
Philips, Eindhoven, Netherlands

Design
Philips Design, Eindhoven, Netherlands

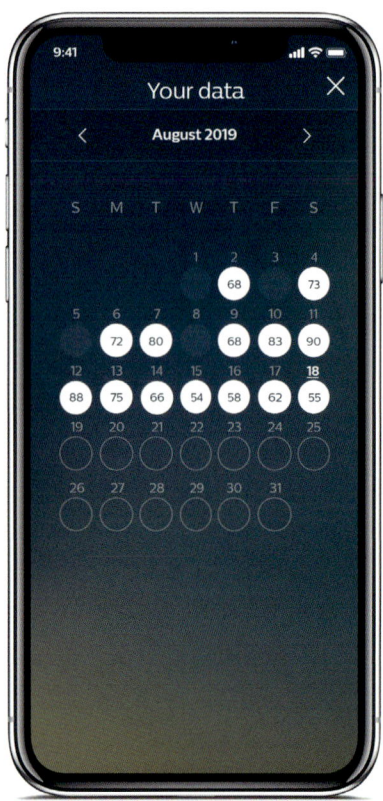
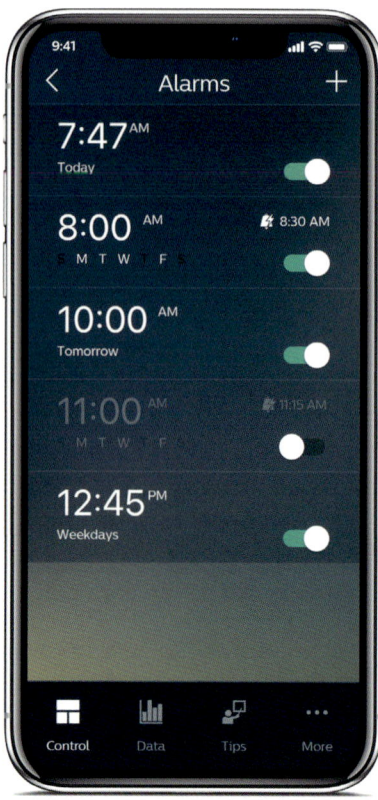
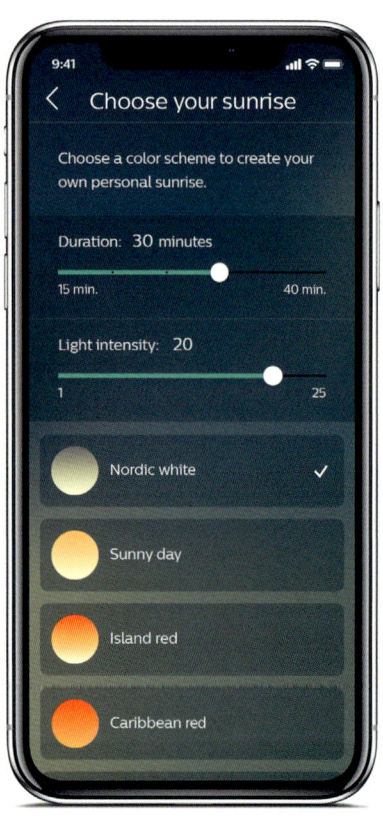
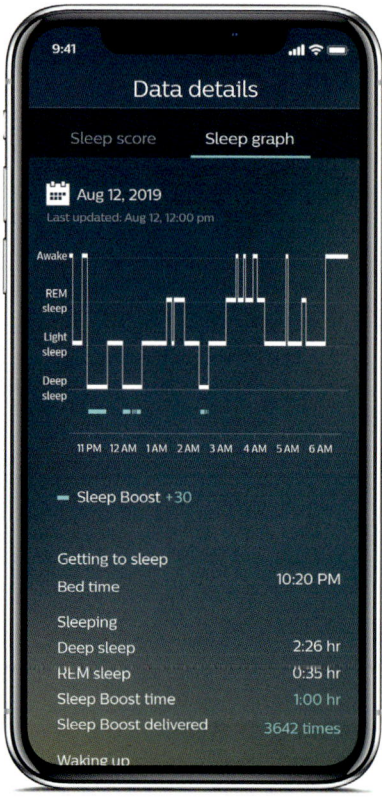

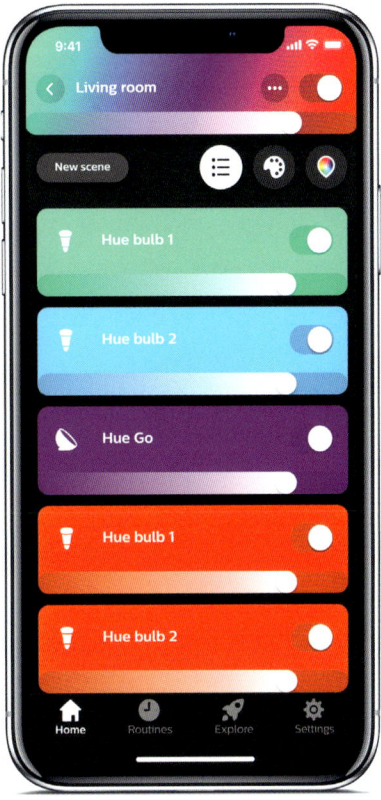
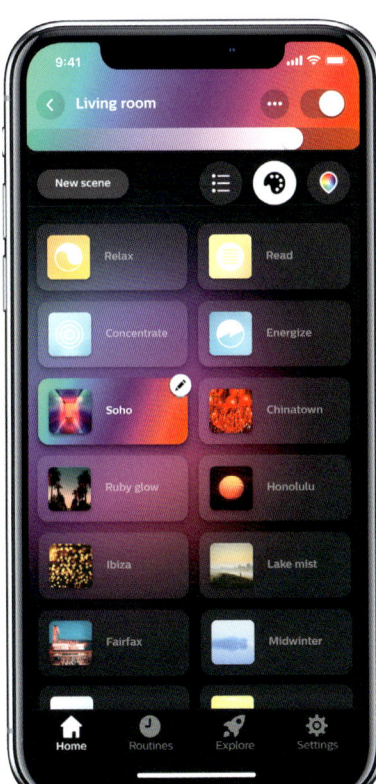

Philips Hue App 3.0
[Smart Home App]

The redesign of the IoT mobile app, accompanying the manufacturer's range of connected lighting, improved usability, feature set and aesthetics for newly incoming user groups – since new users were previously struggling with digital light control paradigms, as usability studies had revealed. The third generation of this app introduces new ways of controlling and managing a home lighting system. It has been improved in many ways, for instance the user interface has been completely overhauled to make it easier to recognise important functions. The new features include easy room set-up, a colour selector and various new scenarios.

Client
Signify, Eindhoven, Netherlands

Design
Signify Design Team,
Eindhoven, Netherlands

MyStiebel

[Smart Home App]

The MyStiebel app controls the STIEBEL ELTRON heat pump for the home. It conveniently helps to regulate the personal feel-good climate in a simple and sustainable way. Each page of the app has its focus set on just a few relevant content items so that users can take in the most pertinent information at a single glance. More complex settings, like the time schedule, are depicted in an easy-to-read format and can be operated intuitively without any previous training. A clear design with precise, finely wrought details communicates the corporate brand values and helps users to find what they need easily and quickly.

Client
STIEBEL ELTRON GmbH & Co. KG,
Holzminden, Germany

Design
Phoenix Design, Stuttgart, Germany

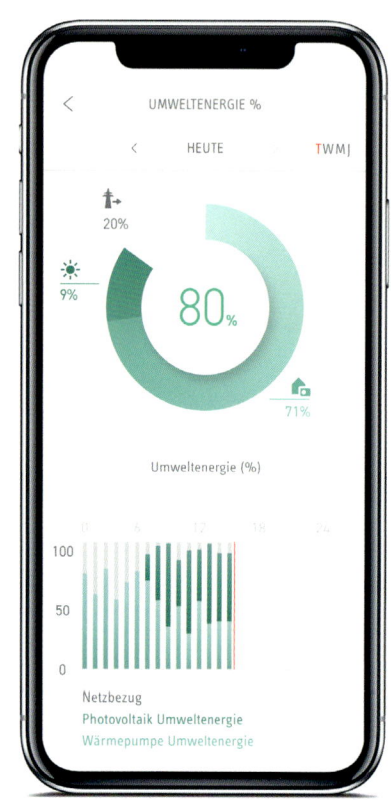

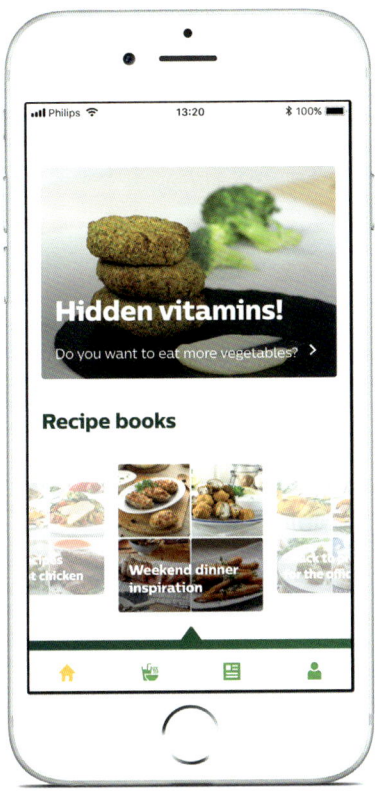

Philips NutriU
[Lifestyle App]

Philips NutriU works in sync with the Philips low-fat Airfryer to inspire consumers with a customised experience featuring healthy meals. They can browse hundreds of recipes, tips and advice from easy-to-cook recipes and dinner ideas to healthy snacks. The app is searchable by recipe according to preparation time, type of cuisine or healthy meal. Consumers get suggestions based on their individual tastes and nutritional needs. NutriU is also interactive, so people can save their favourite recipes for easy access, create and share their own recipes, and follow other community members for ideas and inspiration. Airfryer consumers receive handy updates automatically.

Client
Philips, Eindhoven, Netherlands

Design
Philips Design, Eindhoven, Netherlands

KOSTAL Solar App
[Service App]

The KOSTAL Solar App allows customers to professionally monitor complex photovoltaic and battery systems. It provides a clear overview of household consumption and sources, such as the photovoltaic system or battery and power supply, while offering simple, intuitive operation, with all functions easily checked on any mobile device. Thus, the app not only enables an analysis of consumption and production data over different periods, but also provides access to historical data. It offers many features allowing users to become more familiar with the systems and, in this way, to develop a better understanding of energy consumption and sustainability.

Client
KOSTAL Industrie Elektrik GmbH,
Hagen, Germany

Design
GENERATIONDESIGN GmbH,
Wuppertal, Germany

Concept
Kevin Klöcker, Janina Clever,
Holger Bramsiepe, Florian Bürkner

Programming
Webwikinger UHG, Kiel, Germany

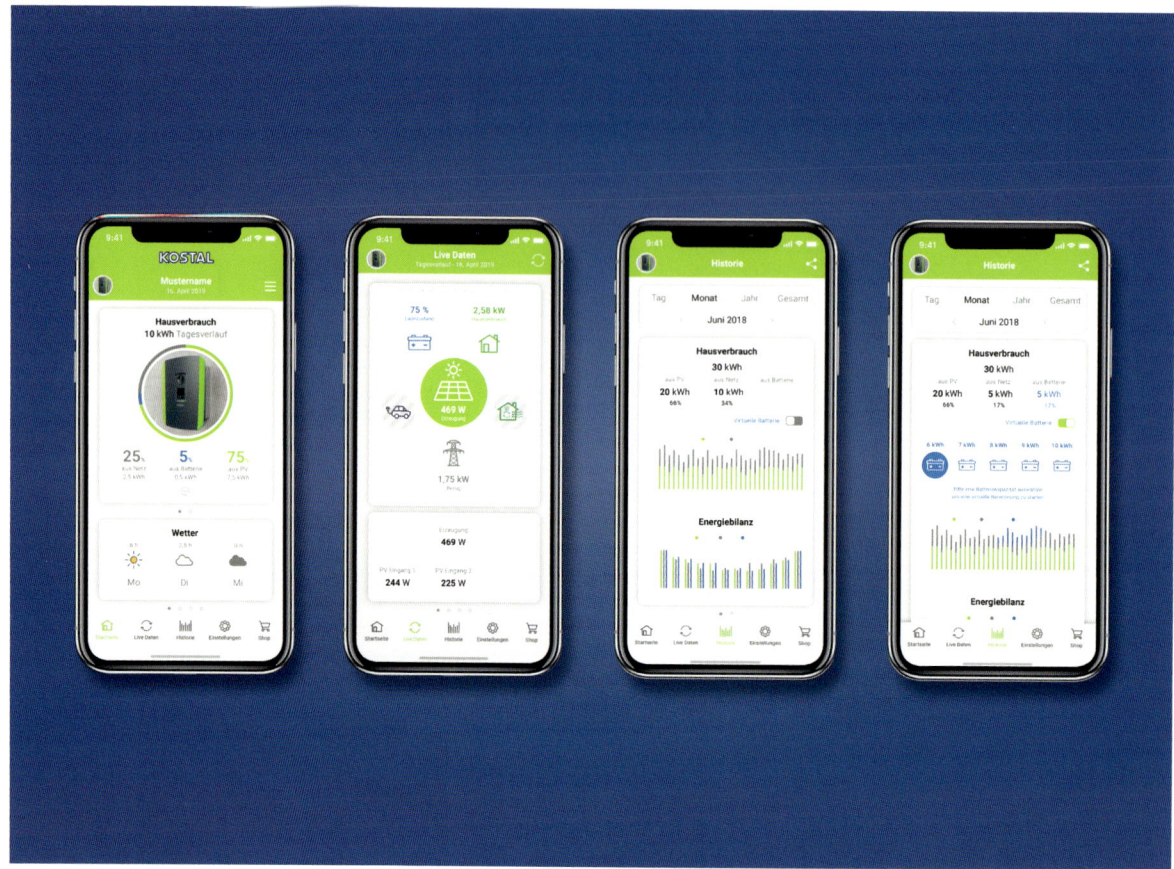

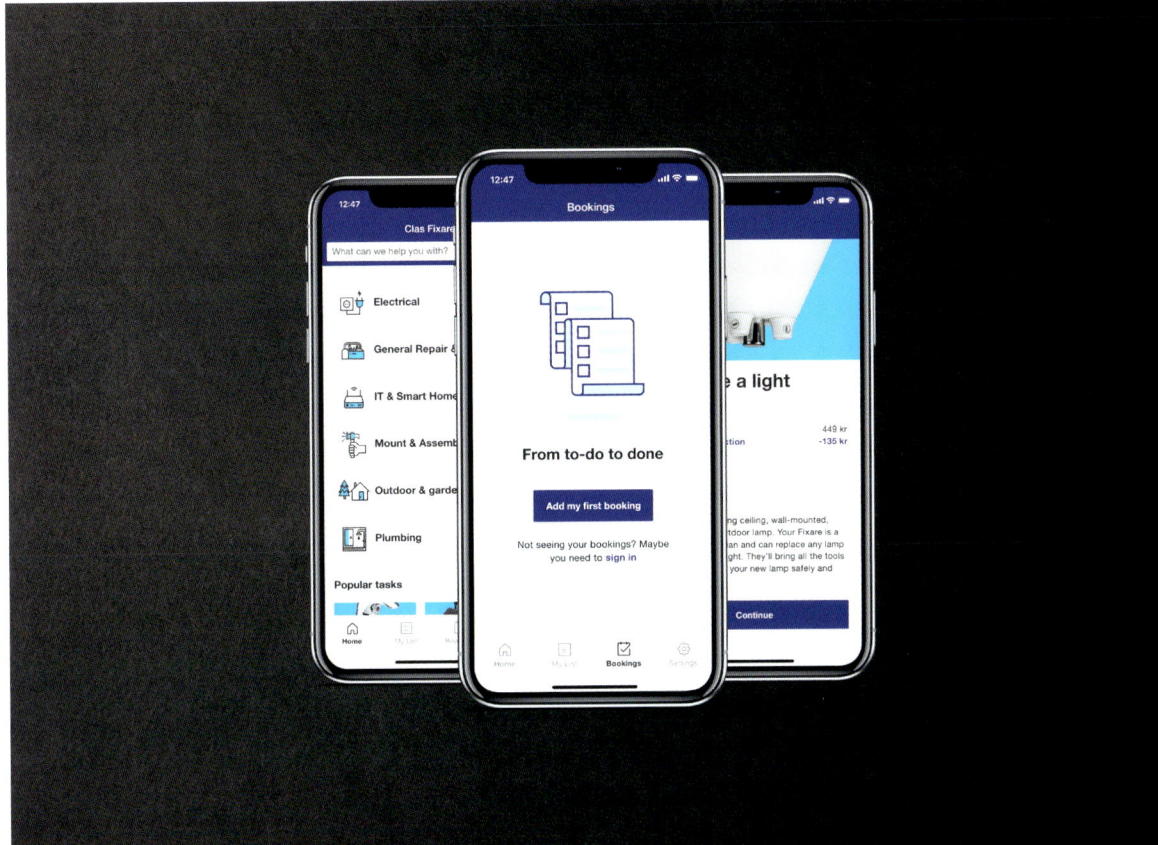
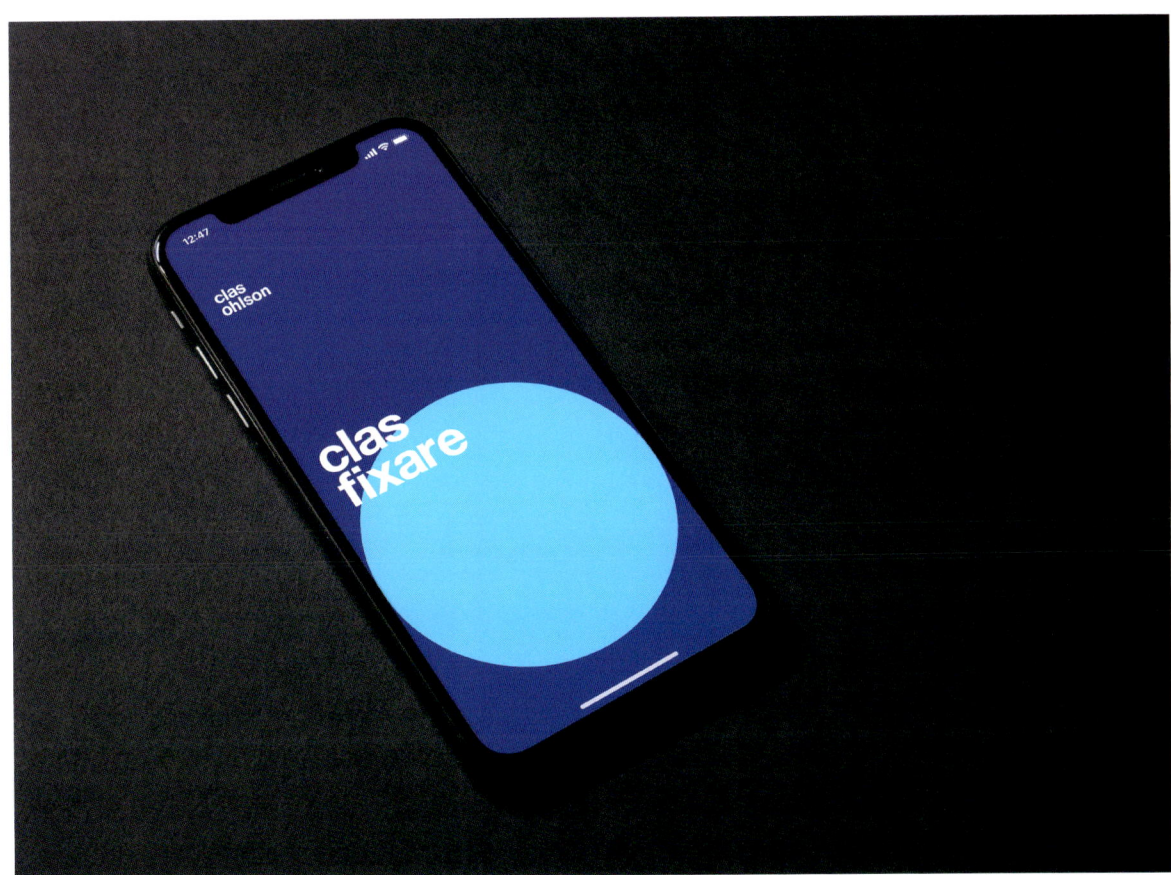

Clas Fixare
[Service App]

This app launched by a Swedish DIY store helps people to offer small jobs in their home, like minor repairs or installations, to a trusted expert. It guides users through the offered services with trigger questions that enable a fast turnaround for each job. They can create one or more tasks or select one with a set price, choose a particular time that suits them, and even upload their own photos and notes. Also, they can receive automated tax rebates if needed. Thanks to this smartphone app, booking a craftsman in order to fix one or multiple unrelated tasks only takes a matter of minutes.

Client
Clas Ohlson, Insjön, Sweden

Design
Daresay, Kista, Sweden

Design Team
Daniel Rönnlund, Lisa Lee,
Viktor Gustafsson, Jillian Buchheim,
Jane Ruffino

Programming
Kim Fransman, Hesham Omran,
Valerija Grigorjeva, Simon Johansson,
Daniel Sjöström, Hannes Ingelhag,
Axel Norell

Project Management
Fredrik Malmgren

Vodafone Network Genius App

[Network Management App]

Client
Vodafone Group Services GmbH,
Düsseldorf, Germany

Design
SMAL GmbH, Planegg, Germany
Vodafone Group Services GmbH,
Düsseldorf, Germany

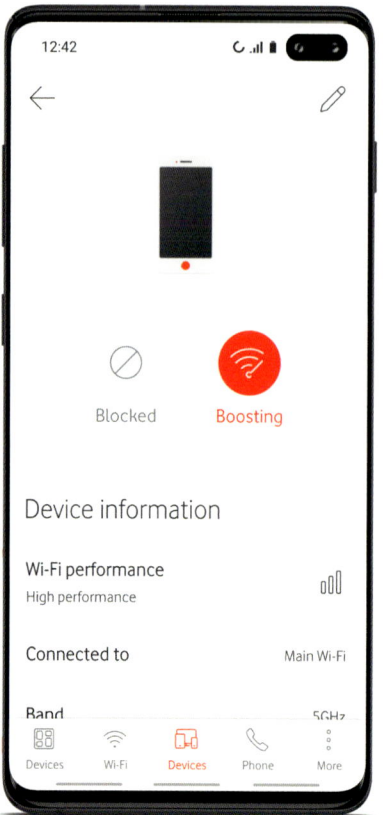
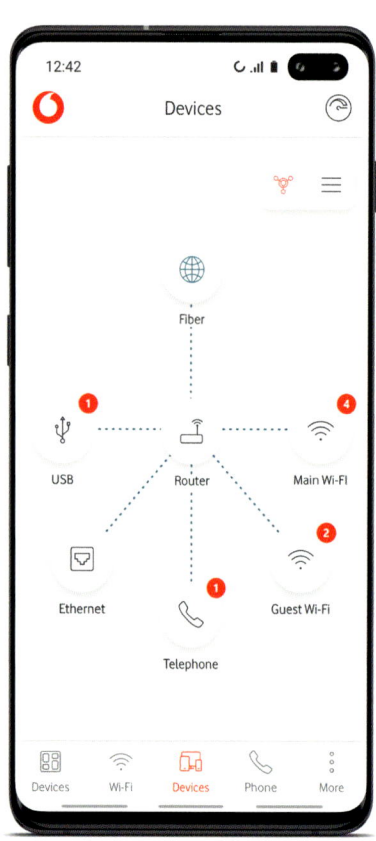
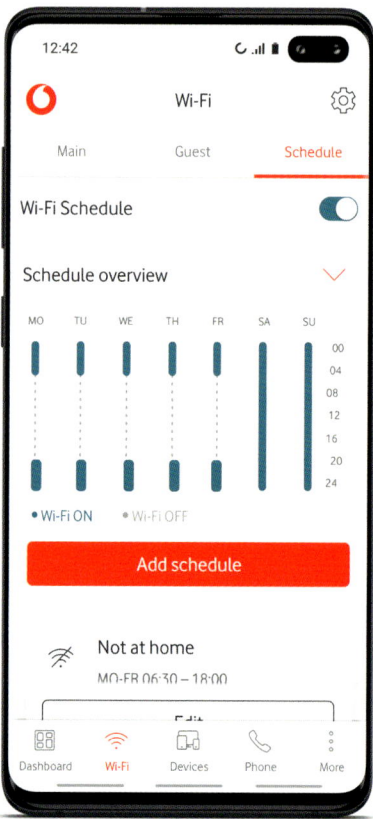

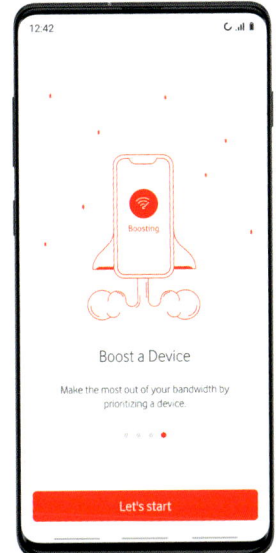
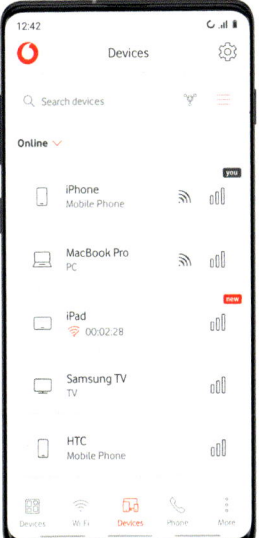

With more and more devices in a household needing an Internet connection, this app makes complex and at times overwhelming gateway management seamless, fun and accessible for users. By serving as an entry point to all the functions, the dashboard empowers users to take control of their network. Thanks to a minimalistic design, it encourages them to make big decisions by taking micro-actions – removing the complexity of the router and network management. Playful animations reflect the function of each action, creating moments that are engaging, welcoming and convey a human touch.

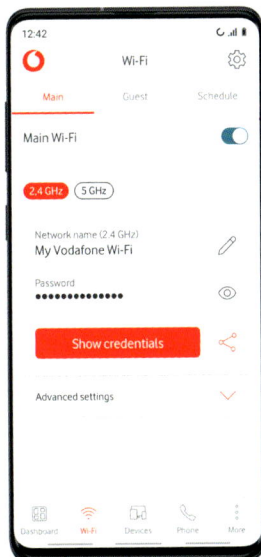
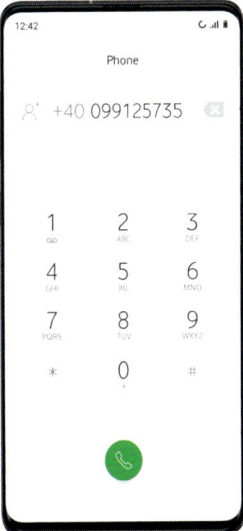

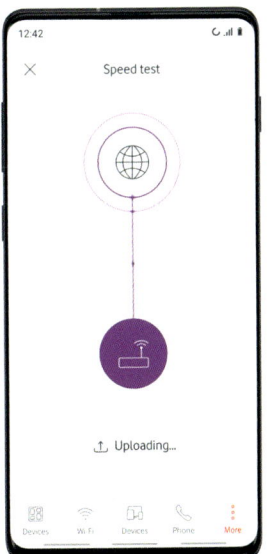
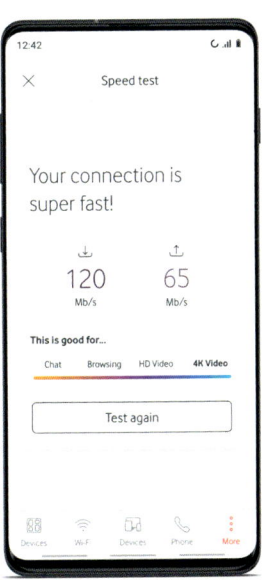
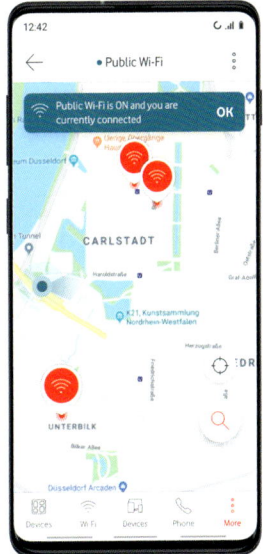

Scan&Go
[Shopping App]

The goal of the Scan&Go app is to reduce checkout time for customers in supermarkets by transforming their smartphone into a virtual check out counter. Developed as a digitised shopping experience for the retail industry, customers can scan their selected items with the app. By using specially designated checkout lanes provided by supermarkets in conjunction with virtual payment options, the time customers spend on queueing and payment is significantly shortened. It is thus possible to go through these processes in just one minute, rather than the usual average of three to five minutes during peak hours.

Client
Carrefour China, Shanghai, China

Design
Tencent Technology (Shenzhen) Co., Ltd., Shenzhen, China

Publishing/Production
Tencent Technology (Shenzhen) Co., Ltd., Shenzhen, China

→ Clip online

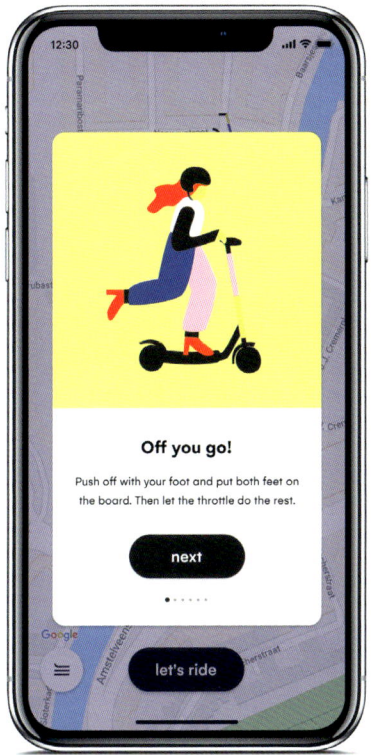
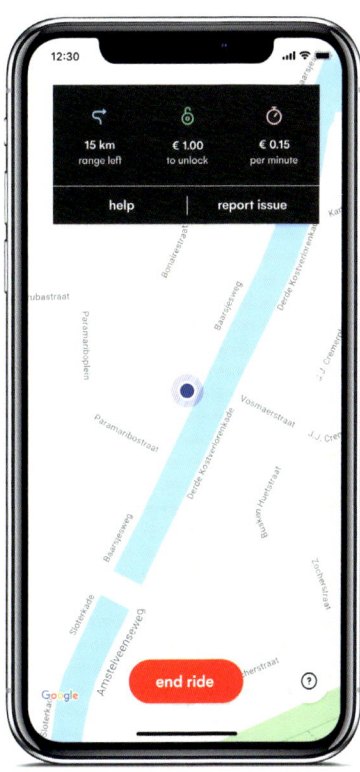
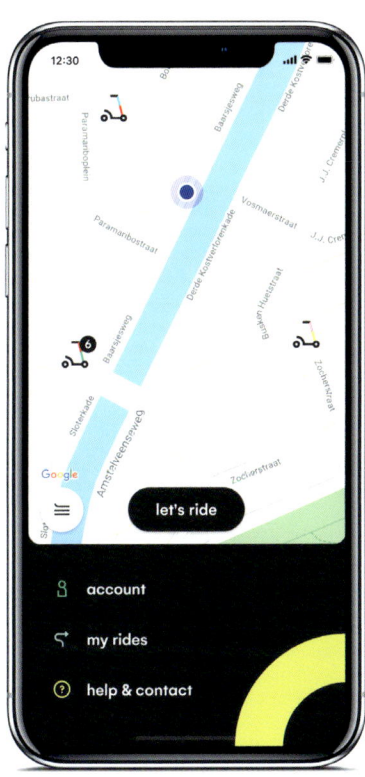
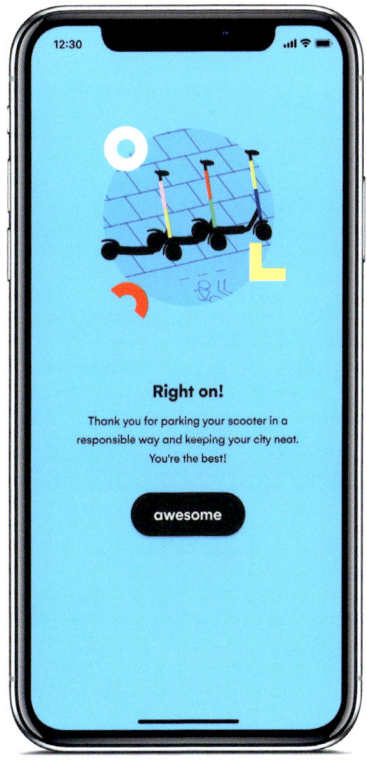

An Identity That Gets You from A to B to C
[Mobility App]

Dott is an e-mobility platform that offers dockless, shared electrical scooters and bikes as alternatives for short-distance travel. The corresponding app was designed to make it easy and comfortable for users to rent one of these vehicles. From showing the nearest available scooter or bike to scanning the QR code to unlock it, the app provides all necessary functionality for a pleasant and convenient rental experience. A custom illustration style is employed to encourage users to handle the service in a responsible way. Easily reachable navigation elements guide one through the entire process.

Client
Dott, Amsterdam, Netherlands

Design
Resoluut, Amsterdam, Netherlands
Soda studio, Amsterdam, Netherlands

Art Direction
Deborah Scheffers, Resoluut

Strategic Planning
Jasper Tempel, Resoluut

Visual Design
Sander Vervaart, Resoluut

User Experience Design
Mark van der Wiel (Lead),
Marjolein Luijckx, Soda studio

User Experience Writing
Aleydis Haubrich, Mr Koreander,
Amsterdam, Netherlands

Airbus iflyA380

[Travel App]

The iflyA380 iOS app has been developed to enhance the experience of flying in a wide-body aircraft and to include the time before and after the flight. For this purpose, virtual and augmented reality have been used and combined with service design thinking. Conceived as a travel companion for the passengers aboard the jetliner, it allows users to discover, book and explore their journey in an immersive way. Not only can they book a flight choosing from 13 different airlines and over 60 destinations; they can also take a 360-degree tour of the cabin ahead of time and interact with the plane in augmented reality.

Client
Airbus, Toulouse, France

Design
Milkinside, San Francisco, California, USA

Creative Direction
Gleb Kuznetsov

User Experience Design
Jeshua Nanthakumar

Production
Nick Fedorov, Djois Sronipah, Victor Pashchenko, Radmir Mingaliev

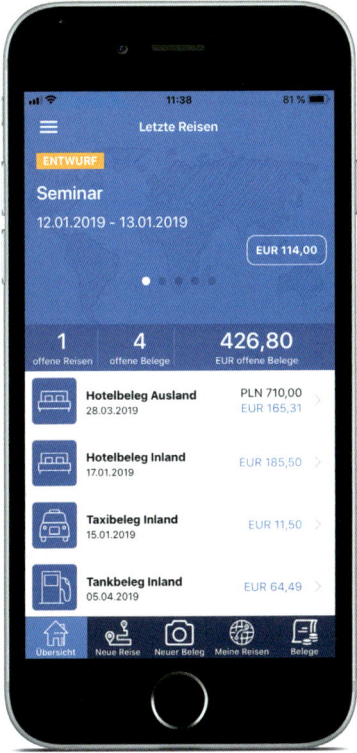

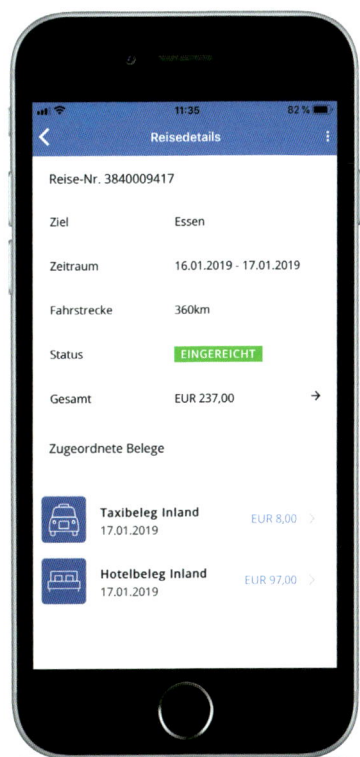

Xpense2Cash

[Finance App]

The Xpense2Cash app has been developed with the objective of saving time when creating travel expense reports. It provides users with the opportunity to simply take a photo of receipts; the app automatically extracts the relevant invoice content and submits it to the accounting system where the data is checked by artificial intelligence. This reduces the error rate and the time spent checking. Offering features such as a dashboard, a detailed cost overview and a currency converter, this travel expenses app conveniently facilitates the accounting process and makes it more clear and transparent – even while travelling.

Client
Beyond Digital Business e. K., Mayen, Germany

Design
innogy SE, Essen, Germany
UDIT GmbH, Neuwied, Germany

→ Clip online

Publishing & Print Media Posters Typography Illustrations Sound Design Film & Animation Online **Apps**

Volvo Car Protection
[Insurance App]

With the Volvo Car Protection app, the user is able to book individual short-term insurance coverage on the spot. All personal insurance is gathered on a home screen as "protection cards" which are activated by picking an existing card or creating a new one. The configuration of new cards is as easy as a quick chat. Personally addressed questions guide users through the process, while custom user interface patterns simplify adding data, such as entering multiple drivers or selecting birth dates, values or date ranges. Chat-like animations and a conversational user experience allow a seamless and playful integration of individual on-demand insurances in the daily life.

Client
Volvo Car Germany GmbH,
Cologne, Germany

Design
dayy GmbH, Cologne, Germany

Manager Insurances
Dirk Nast (Project Owner),
Volvo Car Germany GmbH

Insurance Partner
Dr. Robert Lasowski (Product Owner),
ERGO Mobility Solutions GmbH,
Düsseldorf, Germany

Creative Direction
Oliver Ecker, Robin Gurski, dayy

Art Direction
René Martens, dayy

Interface Design
Tom Sodoge, dayy

Concept
Jonas Wüllner, dayy

App Development
CodeControl GmbH, Berlin, Germany

Video Production
Sebastien Camden, Pusher Studio,
Montreal, Canada

→ Clip online

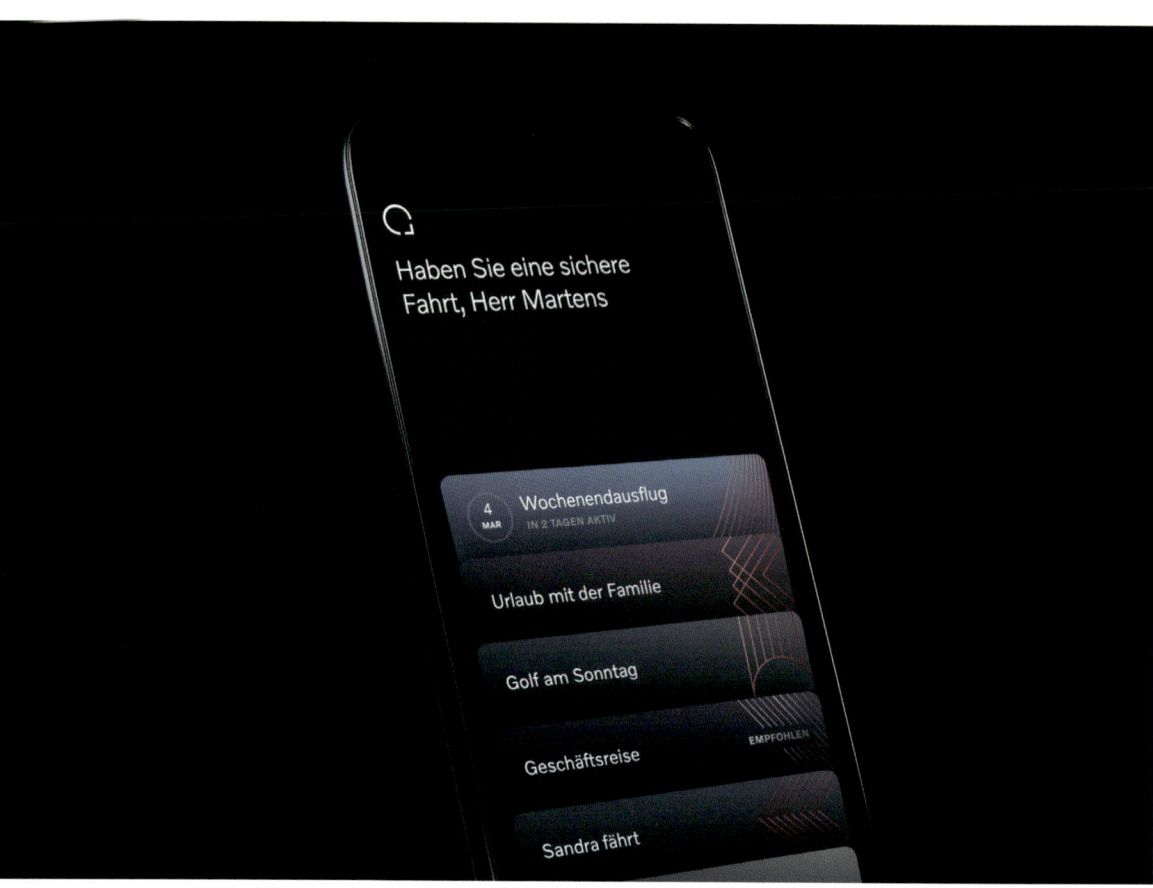

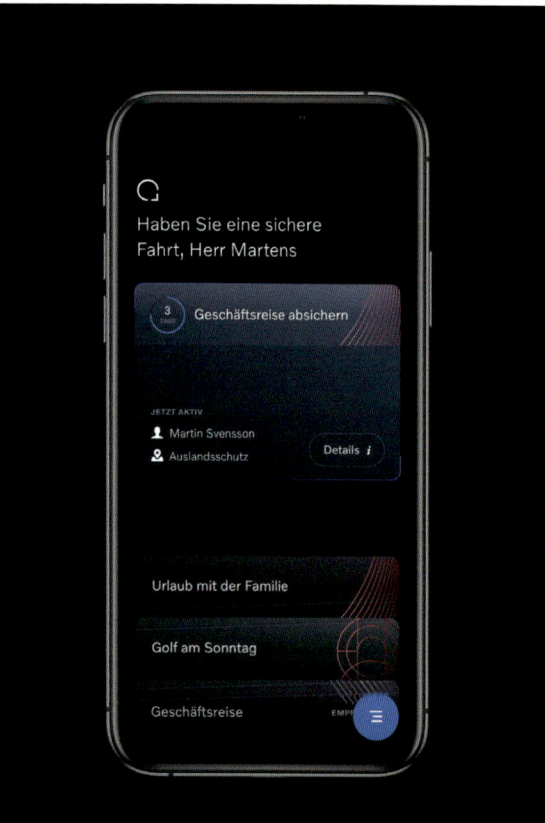

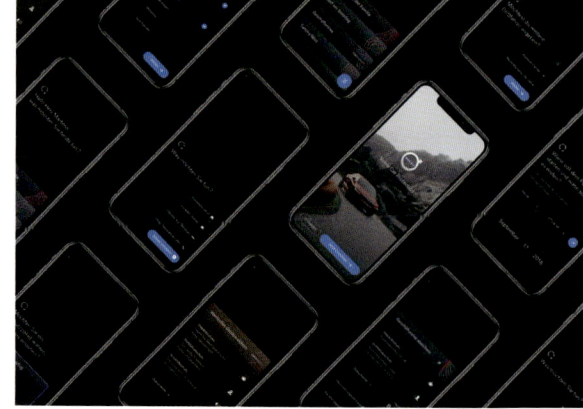

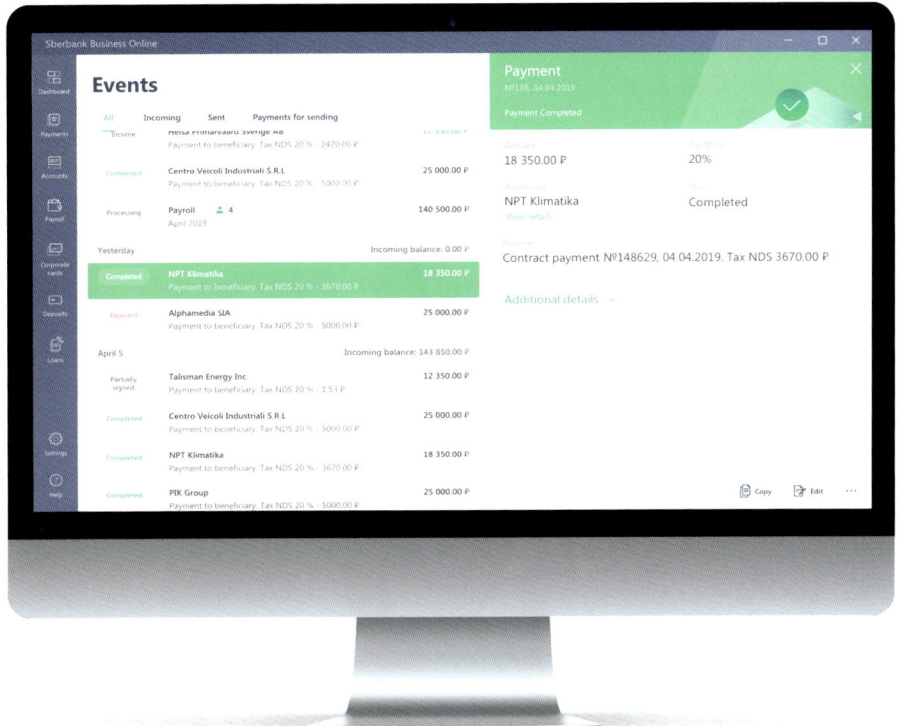

Sberbank SME

[Finance App]

The development of the e-banking app Sberbank SME was driven by the idea of efficiency. The idea was to let business clients create essential scenarios without any noise from UI or excess options, thus guaranteeing maximum freedom and minimal steps that must be taken for each scenario. The app can listen to a user's voice, read sight, and it also supports stylus, keyboard, touchscreen and mouse. It works on various devices – laptop, desktop PC, 2-in-1 device, game console or augmented reality glasses – and thus combines flexible input with device flexibility to constitute an essential part of a customer's basic workspace.

Client
PAO Sberbank of Russia, Moscow, Russia

Design
PAO Sberbank of Russia, Moscow, Russia

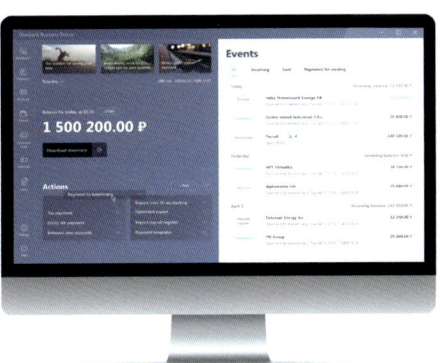
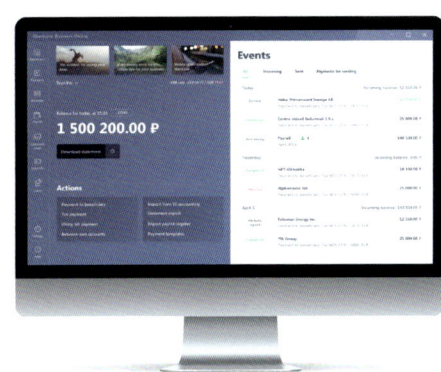
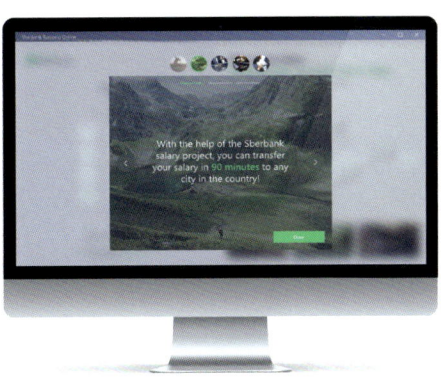
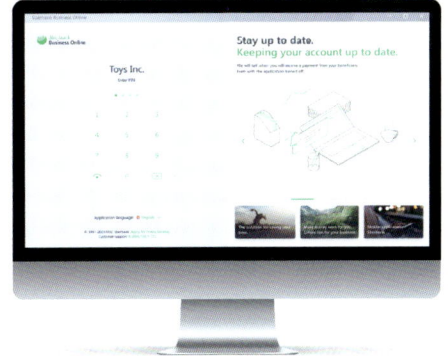

INTERFACE & USER EXPERIENCE DESIGN

Red Dot: Best of the Best

Water
[Interactive Installations]

The new permanent exhibition of the Icelandic Museum of Natural History at Perlan, an immense glass dome that sits on six hot-water tanks, provides a comprehensive and innovative insight into one of the most important resources of Iceland, the water. Three installations have been designed to capture different aspects of the exciting world of water. The audio-visual installation "The Waterfall" projects a large waterfall onto a wall, created out of the 773 different names of the country's over 2,000 waterfalls. "The Meters" is a real-time monitoring exhibit that shows the current state of the three types of rivers to be found in Iceland, spring rivers, runoff rivers and glacial rivers, which change shape and colour depending on their size at any given time. Finally, "The Ecosystem Viewer" invites visitors to learn of the rich life to be found in different types of wetland areas in Iceland. Exploring swamps, lakes and rivers with the help of a circular magnifying device, visitors can find different life forms and even zoom in to the smallest of things by turning the rings.

Statement by the jury
These interactive installations on the subject of "water" impress with their poetic approach. Appealing to visitors on various sensory levels, they invite to interactively explore and learn about the ecosystem of Iceland at one's own pace. The versatile design has been convincingly implemented with a staging that attracts both young and older audiences by making the contents fun to discover.

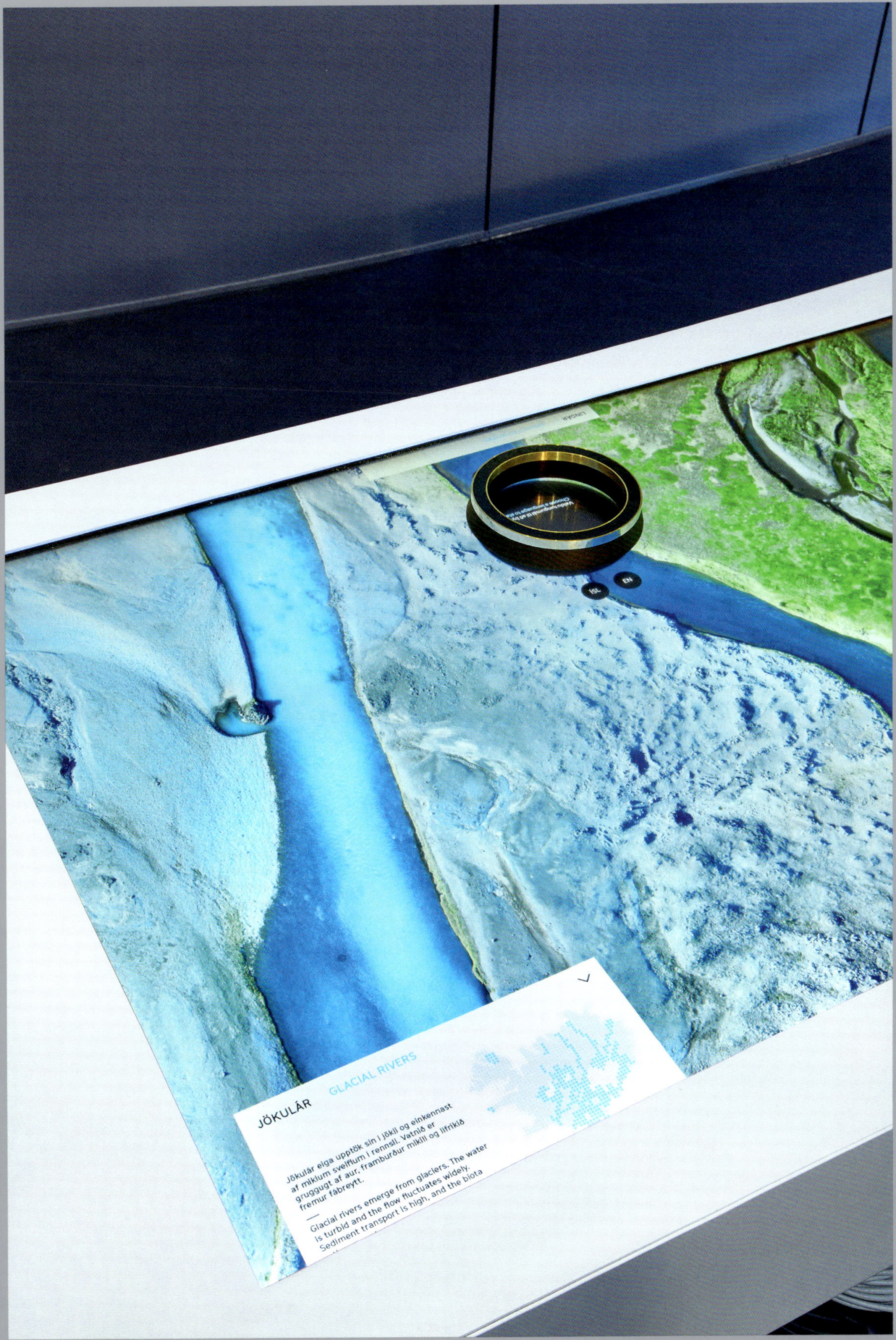

Client
Icelandic Museum of Natural History,
Reykjavík, Iceland

Design
Gagarin, Reykjavík, Iceland

Exhibition Design
Thorunn S. Thorgrimsdottir, Visionis,
Reykjavík, Iceland

Photography
Vigfus Birgisson, Reykjavík, Iceland

→ Designer profile on page 527
→ Clip online

Red Dot: Best of the Best

Pro Nemus
[Interactive Digital Experience]

Pro Nemus is the visitor centre of the Finnish Metsä Group, which operates in 30 countries in the paper and forestry industry, producing paper, pulp, tissue and paperboard, as well as wood products. Featuring information on the group's business, products, innovations and ways of working, the Pro Nemus Innovation Centre is located deep in a Finnish forest at a state-of-the-art bioproduct mill that processes wood and pulp to create products of the future without the use of fossil fuels, while still generating excess bioenergy. Designed as a stage for interactive digital experiences and constructed entirely out of ecological Finnish wood, the centre provides an experiential cross section of the life cycle of a forest, as well as information on the impact of bioeconomy in a world that must increasingly rely on responsibly sourced, renewable raw materials. The impressive animations and installations on display at the centre repeatedly integrate the senses into the digital world, creating a staggering holistic experience.

Statement by the jury
Highly fascinating, interactive and holistic, the Pro Nemus visitor centre presents itself nested in an astounding architecture. The featuring exhibition and installations not only offer a playful and stimulating introduction to the forest world and its complex natural interrelations, they also turn the entire issue of sustainability into an experience that appeals to all the senses.

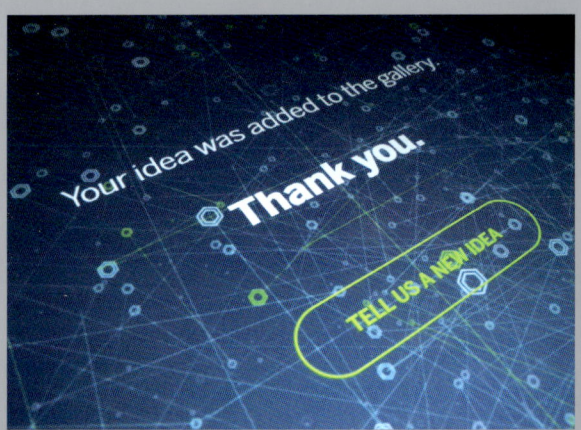

Client
Metsä Group, Espoo, Finland

Design
Great Apes/HiQ Finland,
Helsinki, Finland
MKTG Finland, Helsinki, Finland

Production
Great Apes/HiQ Finland
MediaMonks, Hilversum, Netherlands

→ Designer profile on page 528

Red Dot: Best of the Best

Marathon City – Sprint to Win
[Interactive 3D Running and Fan Engagement Game]

Organised by the New York Road Runners (NYRR), the annual TCS NYC Marathon is the largest marathon in the world and a spectacular signature event that has attracted not just athletes for about 50 years now. The game "Marathon City – Sprint to Win" has been designed with the aim to create a marathon-related, gamified fan experience that would be "inclusive" to all participants – from runners to wheelchair racers and non-athletes alike. The result is a game that enables everyone to compete against each other on an equal basis. For runners, the game is played on a specially designed floor mat equipped with sensors that tracks their footsteps, while wheelchair users roll onto a stationary trainer that translates wheel rotation into forward motion. Especially witty is the idea of inviting game players to choose a 3D avatar by ethnicity, gender, ability and style for themselves, which then runs towards the virtual finish line on the connected screen. Individually or in groups, people of all ages took part in the game, enjoying the interaction.

Statement by the jury
Outstanding about the "Sprint to Win" game is not only the idea to create a sports challenge in which all people can participate, fostering a spirit of inclusion and thus strengthening people's sense of community. It is also the playful implementation of this ingenious concept that testifies to the high design competence with which the technical functionality and the character design of the avatars has been realised.

Client
New York Road Runners, New York, USA

Design
TCS Interactive, Santa Clara, California, USA

Art Direction
Kayvan Mojtahedzadeh, Scott Daniels

3D Design/Development
Michael J. Ricker, Steven Touart, Aditya Sareen

Program Management
Fumie Piontkowski

Research/User Testing
Blake T. Bennet

Script/Dialogue
Tim Peters, Howard Schargel

Solution Architecture
Sujesh Jastee

→ Designer profile on page 568
→ Clip online

Red Dot: Best of the Best

Fairlight Mixing Console
[User Interface Design, Embedded Software]

The Fairlight Mixing Console is a professional, user-oriented audio editing and sound mixing desk for film and TV. Its modular design is scalable to any production size ranging from post production to large studios. The thoughtful interface combines with a clear visual design to ensure that users can build an influential story in sound. As the interface spans across several screens, a strong design consistency was developed that groups the units as one product family. The users' attention is guided and directed by colour, weight and font sizes, as well as divisions in the interface creating segments that become easy-to-digest groups of information. Aesthetically strong and practical audio graphs provide precise visual representations of common audio effects such as equalisation, compression and panning. Thanks to the efficient and clear design of the interfaces and editors, the console is easy to operate and allows users to devote more time to their creative work.

Statement by the jury
The Fairlight Mixing Console successfully manages to combine analogue and digital interfaces and their respective benefits into unison. Every aspect of the sound design can be controlled intuitively via distinctive icons that have been carefully and consistently integrated into the overall appearance. Thanks to the use of clear colours and fonts, the console is easy to approach and use despite the complexity of its functions.

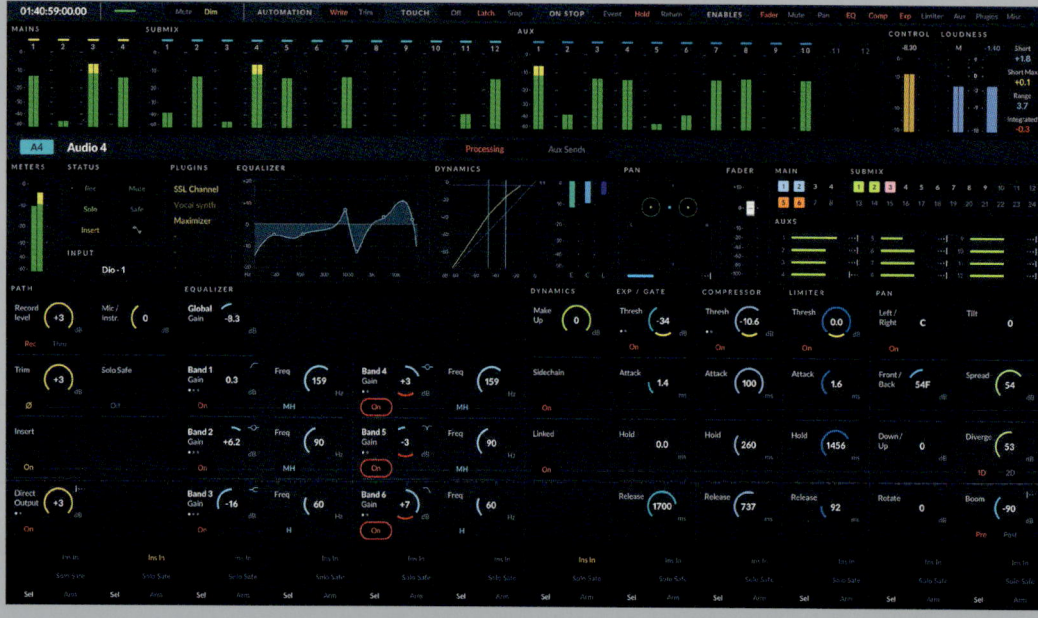

Interface & User Experience Design   Spatial Communication   Red Dot: Junior Award   Designer Profiles   Jury   Index   Red Dot – World of Design

Client
Blackmagic Design, Melbourne, Australia

Design
Blackmagic Design, Melbourne, Australia

Design Direction
Alex Diaz, Matt Dowling

User Experience Design
Alana Manning, Alex Creedy

User Interface Design
Hailey Choi, Denny Trieu

User Experience Development
Marcio Lima

→ Designer profile on page 515

Red Dot: Best of the Best

Huawei Smart Airport
[User Interface Design, Airport Collaborative Decision-Making System]

Huawei Smart Airport is an AI system for monitoring airports with their various terminals, scheduling airplane stands, flight times, traffic and security. Featuring a clearly structured layout, the system provides a full overview of the complex operational processes at an airport, visualising plane arrival and departure times, as well as delays due to adverse weather conditions. Based on AI algorithms and an immersive user interface, the system can indicate the cause of problems and recommend solutions for scheduling planes and processing conflicts, including for example when gates have to be reassigned. Overall, the system defines a progressive trust system, which includes three modes – Manual, Recommend and Automatic. With continuous learning and increased trust in AI, the system can eventually deal automatically with all scenarios by itself. Highly efficient and precise, it guides operators from the main dispatch interface layer into a multitude of more detailed commands, offering significantly reduced work time and improved efficiency.

Statement by the jury
The AI-based Huawei Smart Airport system impresses with its outstanding clarity and efficiency, offering assistance in scheduling the highly complex operational processes of an airport. Set against a black background, it allows operators to keep track of all processes at all times, while the clean graphic style facilitates easy and quick navigation.

Client
Huawei Technologies Co., Ltd.,
Shenzhen, China

Design
Huawei Technologies Co., Ltd.,
Shenzhen, China

Web Design
Shaolei Wang, Chang Tang, Ren Li,
Yuanfeng Chu

→ Designer profile on page 531

Heart of Iceland

[Interactive Exhibition]

The interactive exhibition Heart of Iceland at the Thingvellir Visitor Centre near Hakid consists of ten interactive installations. Appealing to all senses, they invite visitors on a journey through the history and nature of the place, which is of special importance for every Icelander. The uniquely designed rock-like panels pay homage to the rich history of the area and serve as a metaphor for the tectonic transitions characteristic of Thingvellir's landscape. They offer a glimpse into the past and project scenarios for the future development of the landscape, with thought-provoking questions.

Client
Thingvellir National Park, Selfoss, Iceland

Design
Gagarin, Reykjavik, Iceland
Gláma•Kim, Reykjavík, Iceland

Curation
Thorunn S. Thorgrimsdottir, Visionis, Reykjavik, Iceland

Audiovisual Equipment
Knutur Runarsson, Origo, Reykjavik, Iceland

Lighting Design
Páll Ragnarsson, Reykjavík, Iceland

Text
Alfheidur Ingadottir, Reykjavik, Iceland
Bryndis Sverrisdottir, Reykjavik, Iceland

→ Designer profile on page 527
→ Clip online

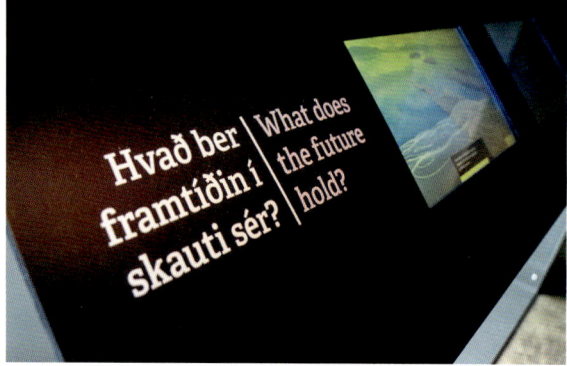

Hyper Fountain
[Virtual Reality Installation]

The Hyper Fountain is a VR installation that invites users to playfully experience the element of water. In the sense of an experimental study, it explores the question of whether a virtual experience evokes the same reaction as the actual physical experience. Visitors hold their hands under a thin jet of water while being shown various materials through the VR glasses, including money, magma particles and pills that are flowing like water. As a result, the perception was reconditioned and users even felt impressions when there was no water at all.

Client
Aloys F. Dornbracht GmbH & Co. KG, Iserlohn, Germany

Design
Elastique. GmbH, Cologne, Germany

Creative Direction
Andreas Schimmelpfennig,
Betty Schimmelpfennig, Elastique. GmbH
Mike Meiré,
MEIRÉ UND MEIRÉ GmbH & Co. KG,
Cologne, Germany

Art Direction
Dmitry Zakharov, Elastique. GmbH
Hans von Bülow,
MEIRÉ UND MEIRÉ GmbH & Co. KG

Project Management
Christin Flosbach, Elastique. GmbH

Publishing & Print Media   Posters   Typography   Illustrations   Sound Design   Film & Animation   Online   Apps

#Romanovs100 – AR Photo Album

[Augmented Reality Experience]

Client
RT, Moscow, Russia

Design
RT, Moscow, Russia

Idea
Kirill Karnovich-Valua

Creative Design
Revaz Todua

Art Direction
Denis Semionov

Editor-in-Chief
Margarita Simonyan

Copyright
Elena Medvedeva

Social Media
Gleb Burashov

Editorial Team
Ania Fedorova, Ivan Fursov, Eldar Salamov

Production
Lilly Kazakova, Ivor Crotty

Project Management
Valeria Fimina

Video Direction
Aleksandr Skryabin

Video Production
Victoria Milovanova

Printing
UP PRINT, Moscow, Russia

→ Clip online

The digital storytelling project #Romanovs100 is based on the analysis of about 4,000 private photographs of the Romanov family, Russia's last royal family. In addition to the digital processing of the photos for social media platforms, an augmented reality photo album has been developed that contains QR codes that can be read with an app. In this way, users can access 3D animation-models, swipeable galleries, AR infographics and short videos to each of the photos in the classic analogue album. This combination of traditional print media with AR technology allows readers to become active co-creators of the unfolding story.

Publishing & Print Media   Posters   Typography   Illustrations   Sound Design   Film & Animation   Online   Apps

Unravel Van Gogh

[Screen Design, User Experience Design]

The Unravel Van Gogh app enables users to delve deeper into the history of the artworks by the Dutch painter. It features different sliding visuals of paintings that reveal the differences between the original work and its current state, for example. Users only need to click on the control point in the middle or at the bottom and drag the mouse in the given direction. Via a "Read more" button, they can then get additional background information on each image. The operation is self-explanatory, with small text boxes indicating the required mouse action for triggering particular action.

Client
Van Gogh Museum,
Amsterdam, Netherlands

Design
Dept, Amsterdam, Netherlands

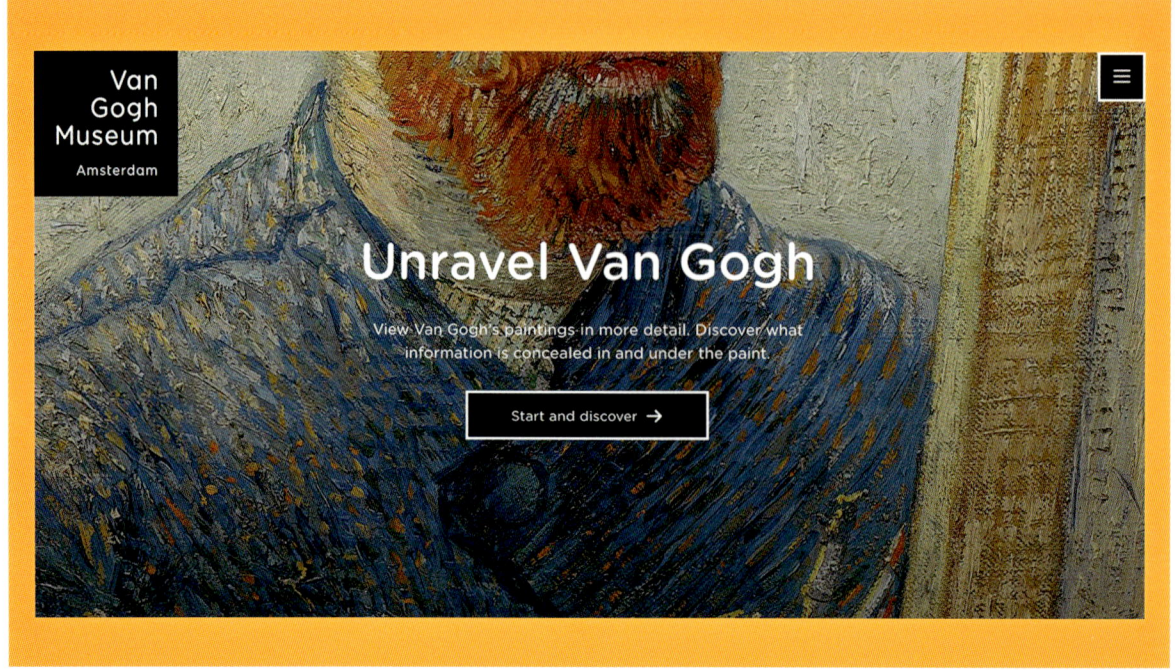

Das Totale Tanz Theater
[Virtual Reality Dance Experience]

Four visitors can simultaneously immerse themselves in the virtual dance theatre inspired by the Bauhaus school, and experience an interactive choreography on three levels within a vast stage space with the dance machines. Visitors interact with the movements of real dancers, which were recorded by motion capture and stored in a database. When users enter the virtual space, the choreography conceived by humans, the users' personal actions and the machine algorithm intertwine and create new forms of dance and spatial movements.

Client
Interactive Media Foundation gGmbH/ Filmtank GmbH, Berlin, Germany

Design
Artificial Rome GmbH, Berlin, Germany
Interactive Media Foundation gGmbH, Berlin, Germany

Idea/Story
Diana Schniedermeier, Maya Puig

Virtual Reality Design
Maya Puig, Patrik de Jong, Dirk Hoffmann

Executive Production
Diana Schniedermeier

Choreography
Richard Siegal

Composition
Lorenzo Bianchi-Hoesch

Sound Design
Victor Audouze

Art Direction
Dirk Hoffmann, Nico Alexander Taniyama, Robert Werner

Technical Team
Torsten Sperling (Lead),
Sebastian Hein (Lead),
Dennis Timmermann, Hui-Yuan Tien

3D Design
Nico Alexander Taniyama (Lead),
Christian Rambow, Dana Würzburg

→ Designer profile on page 511

| Publishing & Print Media | Posters | Typography | Illustrations | Sound Design | Film & Animation | Online | Apps |

Opera GX
Gaming Browser

[Web Browser]

Client
Opera Software AS, Oslo, Norway

Design
Opera Software AS, Oslo, Norway

Product Management
Maciej Kocemba

Graphic Design
Michał Świączkowski,
Bartłomiej Guzenda

Animation
Anna Trojanowska

→ Clip online

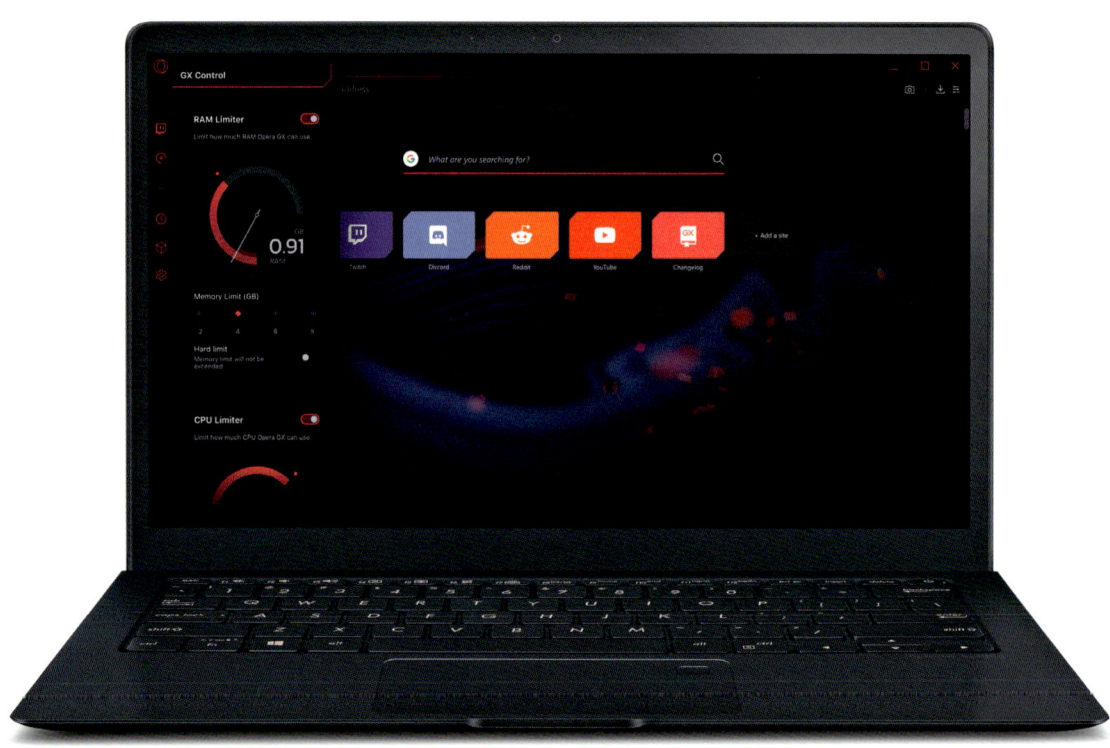

Interface & User Experience Design   Spatial Communication   Red Dot: Junior Award   Designer Profiles   Jury   Index   Red Dot – World of Design

Opera GX is a web browser for gamers that allows users to define the maximum RAM and CPU usage to optimise their gaming and browsing experience. The browser features an innovatively designed user interface that lets gamers match the browser colours to their gaming gear such as keyboard and mouse. In addition, various elements can be configured and the browser can be connected to the Twitch platform for game streaming. The user experience is complemented by sound effects integrated in the browser.

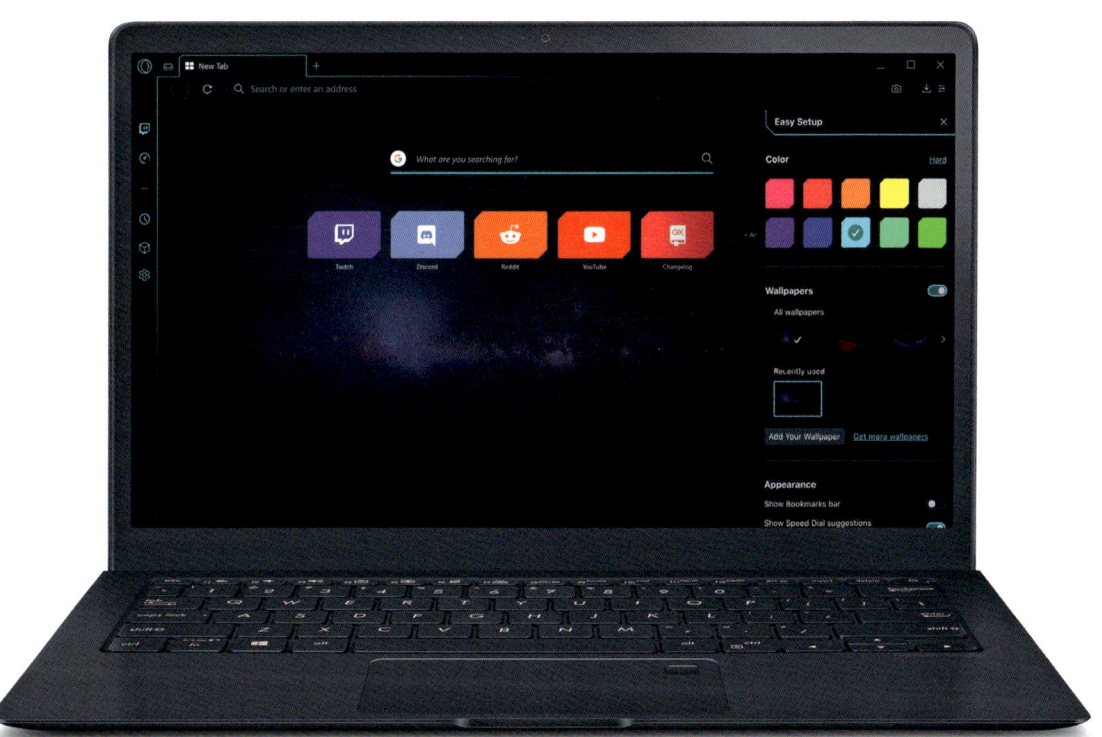

LG V50 ThinQ Dual Screen

[Mobile User Experience Design]

Dual Screen is an accessory for the LG V50 smartphone to extend it with a second screen. Both screens feature an independent home screen, allowing each screen to run different apps. Users can switch between screens via a floating menu, and move content from one screen to the other with a simple swipe. Both screens can also be linked and shared for one application, such as when the lower display is used as a game pad or controller while the game is running on the upper display.

Client
LG Electronics Inc., Seoul, South Korea

Design
LG Electronics Inc., Seoul, South Korea

Graphic Design
Inseong Cho

User Interface Design
Jungbin Lee, Janghwan Jeon, Heyryung Min, Kyungrak Choi, Mijin Cho

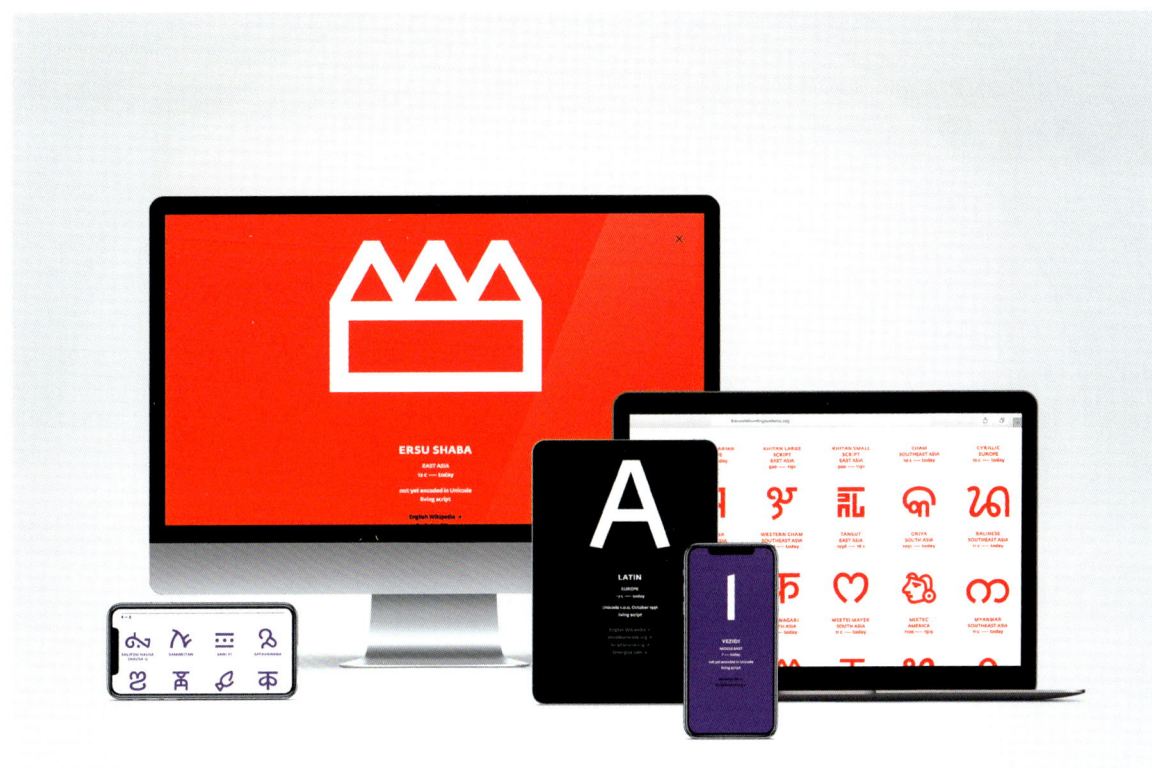

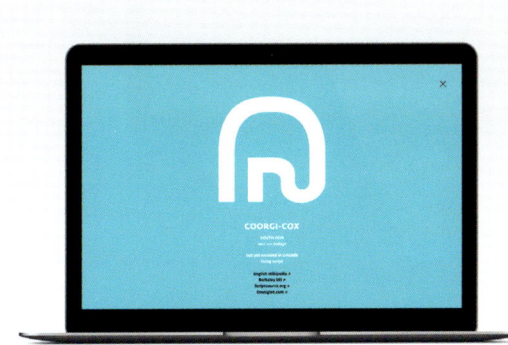

The World's Writing Systems

[Screen Design,
Online Reference/Showcase]

Presenting each of the world's writing systems with a glyph, this website visualises the first step of "The Missing Scripts Project", a long-term research project aimed at identifying writing systems that are not yet encoded in Unicode standard. Consistently satisfying modern responsive web design standards, the website provides playful access on nearly all devices. Users can browse, swipe, sort and scroll freely through 292 writing systems without having to type a single letter. The successful website is complemented by additional information on each font system to be found as links below the individual glyphs.

Client
Hochschule Mainz,
Fachbereich Gestaltung, Mainz, Germany

Design
Helmig Bergerhausen, Cologne, Germany
wysiwyg*, Düsseldorf, Germany

Creative Direction
Ilka Helmig, Johannes Bergerhausen

Typography
Morgane Pierson, Atelier National de Recherche Typographique, Nancy, France
Arthur Francietta, Paris, France
Jérôme Knebusch,
Frankfurt/Main, Germany

DeepL
[User Interface Design]

Client
DeepL GmbH, Cologne, Germany

Design
DeepL GmbH, Cologne, Germany
denkwerk, Cologne, Germany

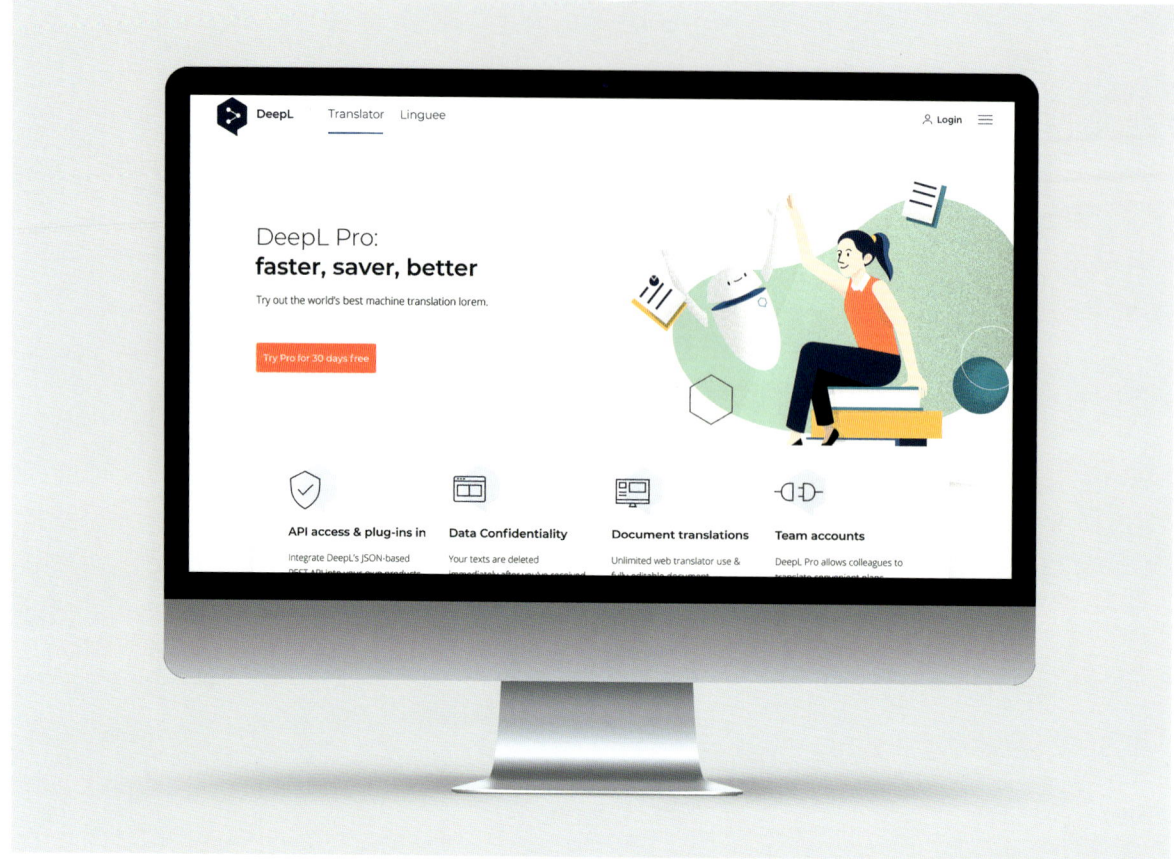
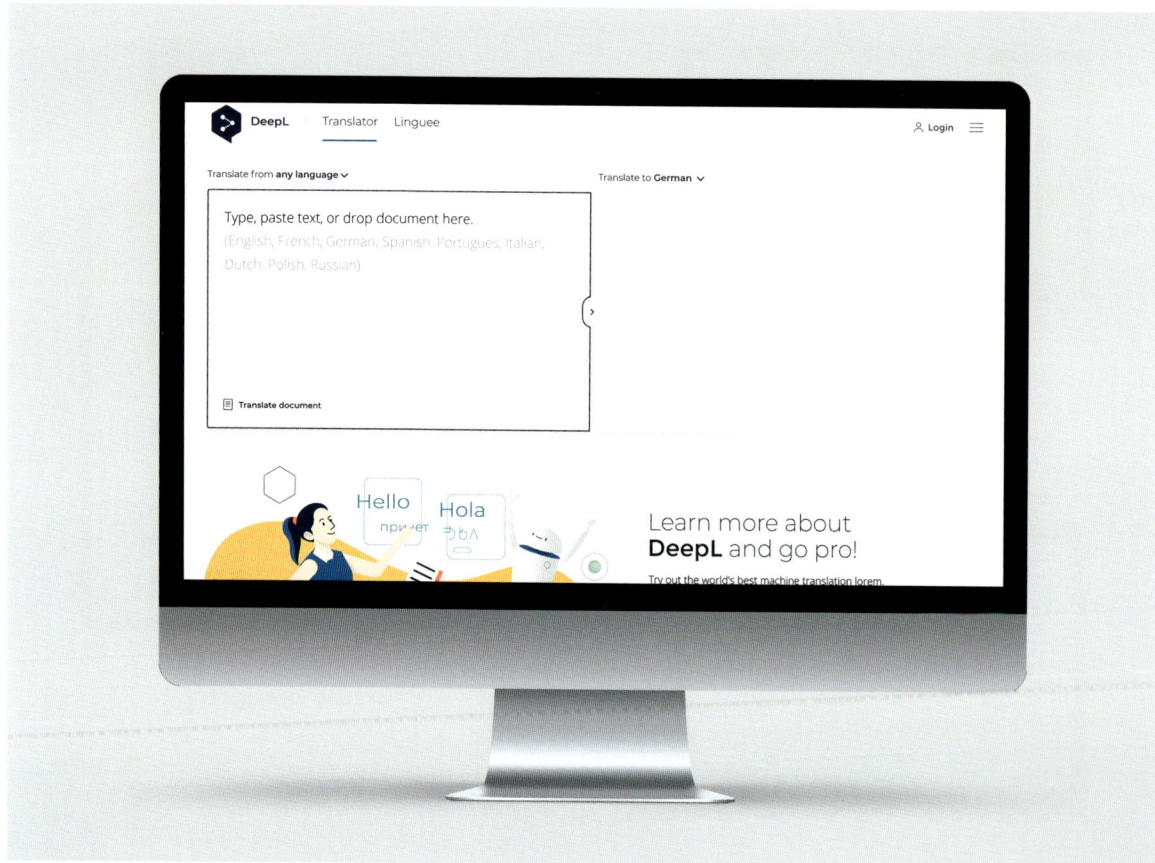

Interface & User Experience Design   Spatial Communication   Red Dot: Junior Award   Designer Profiles   Jury   Index   Red Dot – World of Design

DeepL is a browser- and AI-based translation tool. It is not only able to translate individual words, but it also puts them in the right context so that entire sentences are correctly rendered in the desired language. Even proverbs are recognised, and an appropriate translation in the target language given. Text can be entered directly into the browser or uploaded as a document. The interface is kept minimalistic and based on the principle of "form follows function". Small visual details such as icons or illustrations support user guidance and enable intuitive handling of the tool.

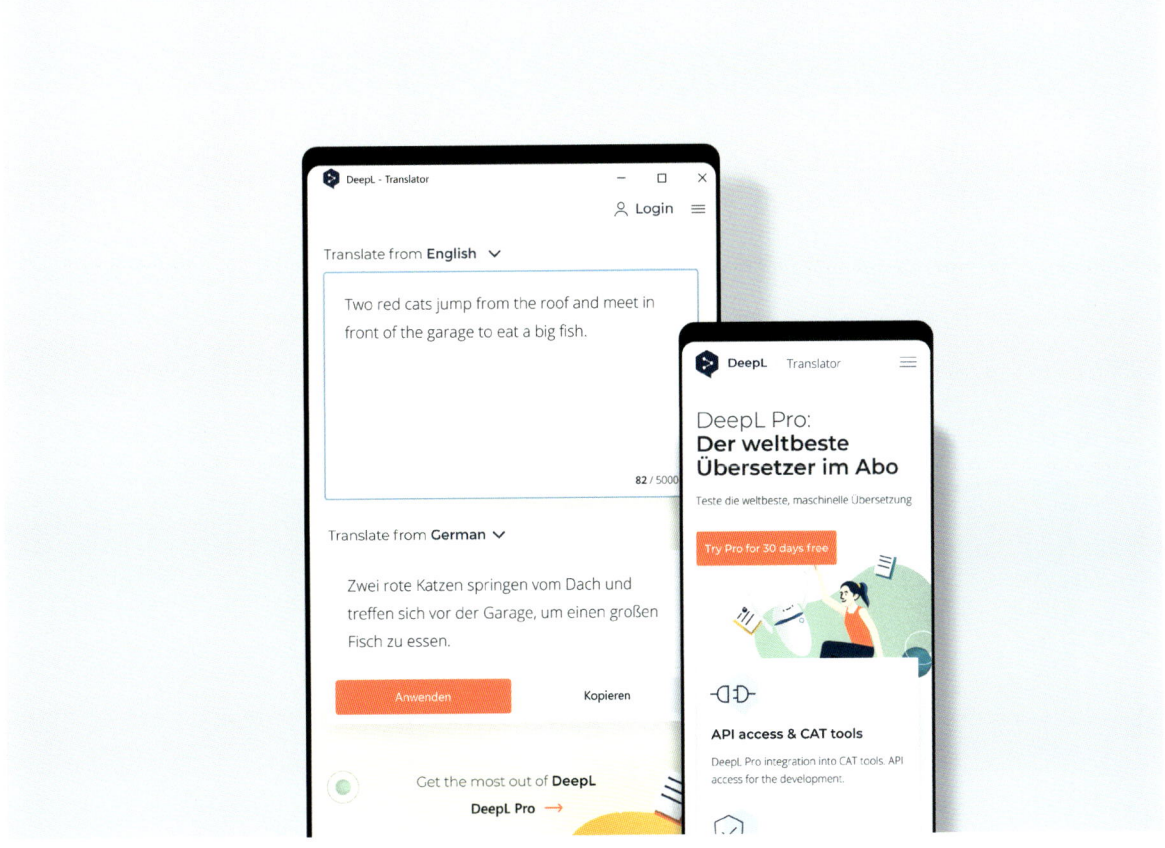

Dot Translate

[Health Solutions]

285 million blind and visually impaired people worldwide have limited access to information: only 3 per cent of all text content is available in braille. Translation is so complex that it requires input by human experts, which makes it inaccessible for individuals and not profitable for publishers. Dot Translate is a braille translator based on AI. It can translate any digital text to braille on its own because it is being trained by millions of accurate human translations. This innovation is the foundation for Dot Mini, a smart media device for the visually impaired.

Client
Dot Incorporation, Seoul, South Korea

Design
SERVICEPLAN GERMANY,
Munich, Germany

Global Chief Creative Officer
Alexander Schill

Creative Direction
Franz Röppischer, Lorenz Langgartner

Creative Production
Saurabh Kakade

Art Direction
Eduardo Alvarez

Copywriting
Carolina Soto

Digital Design
Hyperinteractive GmbH,
Hamburg, Germany
Standardabweichung, Munich, Germany
Moby Digg GmbH, Munich, Germany

Film Production
Paulus Co. Ltd., Seoul, South Korea

→ Designer profile on page 523

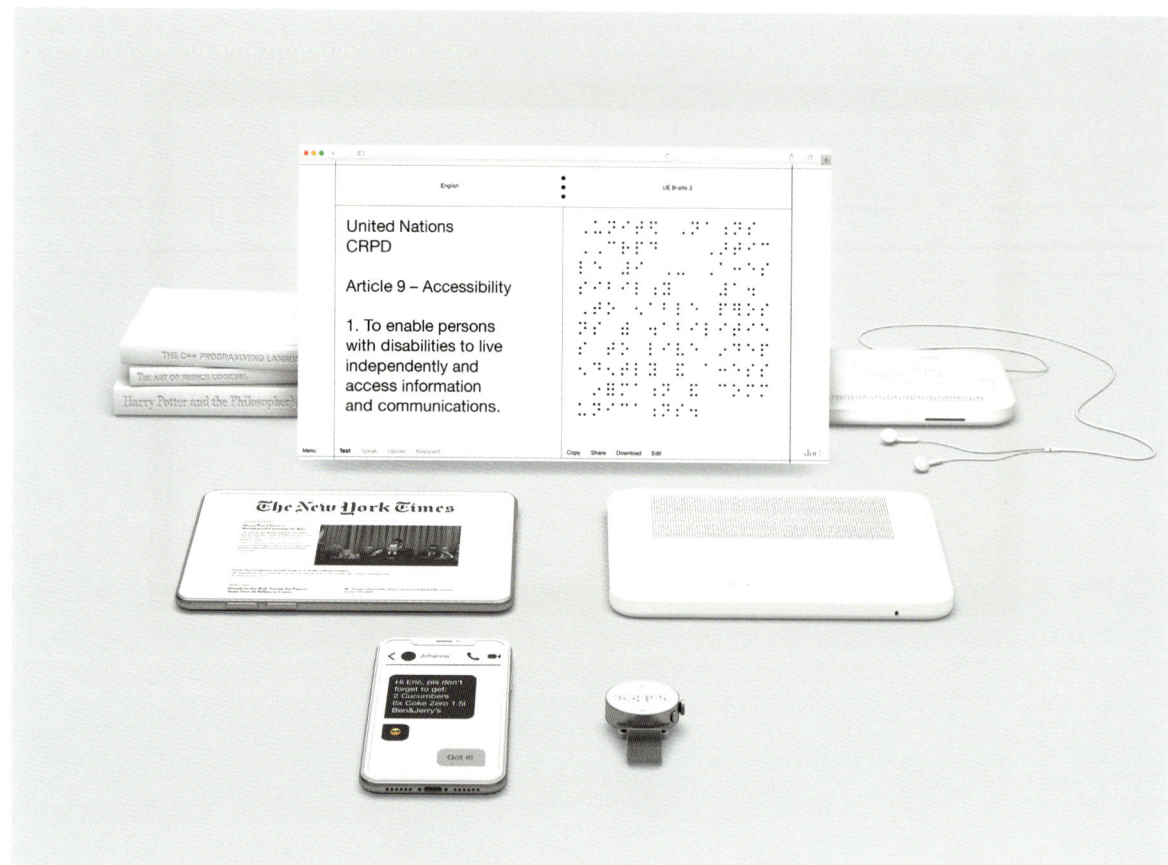
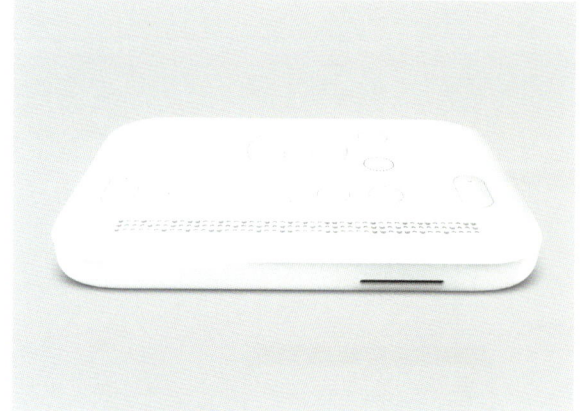
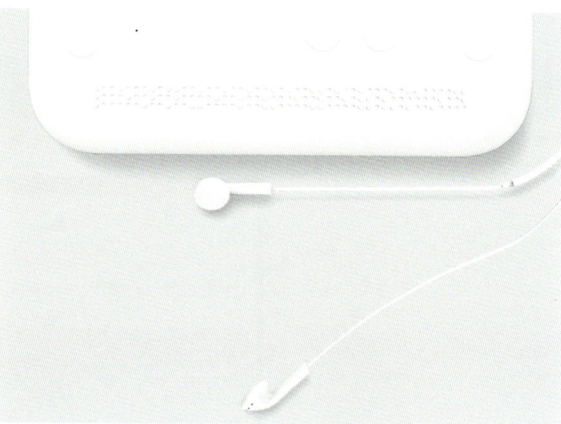

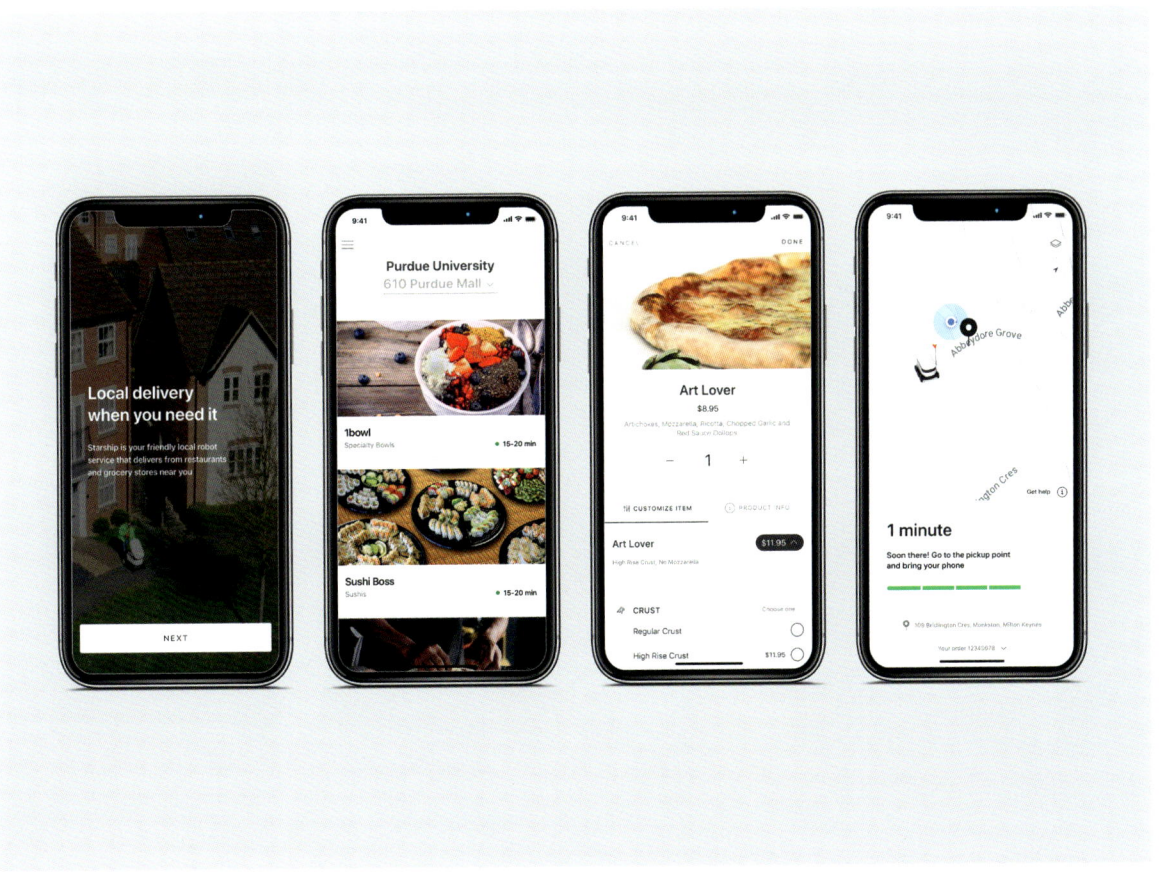

Starship Marketplace
[Service Design]

Starship Marketplace is a commercially operating marketplace for local deliveries by autonomous robots within a radius of approximately 6 km. Via app, customers can order groceries from affiliated neighbourhood stores or have parcels delivered to their doorsteps. The app features a clearly structured user panel that displays the available products with actual photos, which facilitates the selection. The design of the robot adopts the same restrained colour scheme of the app, aimed at increasing the acceptance of this technical assistant.

Client
Starship Technologies Oy, Helsinki, Finland

Design
Starship Technologies Oy, Helsinki, Finland

Bird

[Mobile User Interface Design, iOS App]

Bird is an iOS application that helps users to find an apartment in Kyiv. The app features a futuristic 3D map of Kyiv, which highlights all available apartments. Users can set filters to define a selection, and by clicking on a suitable property receive all information on location, furnishing and rent, as well as the contact details. Photos of the apartment are also available. Since the app is equipped with AI, dubious offers are immediately identified. The user interface, with its rounded graphic style, conveys easy and fun operation.

Client
Flatfy OÜ, Tallinn, Estonia

Design
Flatfy OÜ, Tallinn, Estonia

Product Design
Arsenii Feshchenko

Concept
Denys Tsyganok, Nataliya Strelchenko, Oleksandr Ivanov

Programming
Yevhenii Pancheshnyi, Dmytro Satanovskyj

Supervision
Andrey Mima

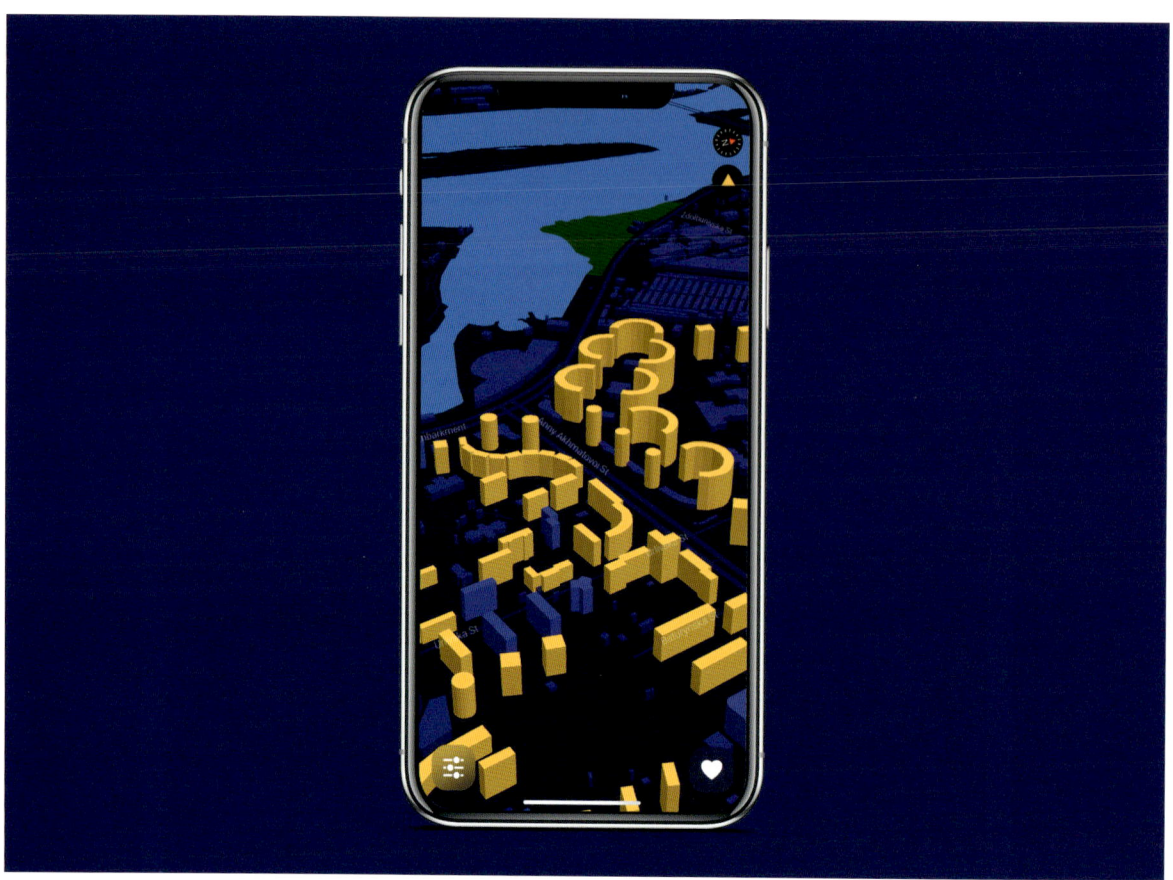

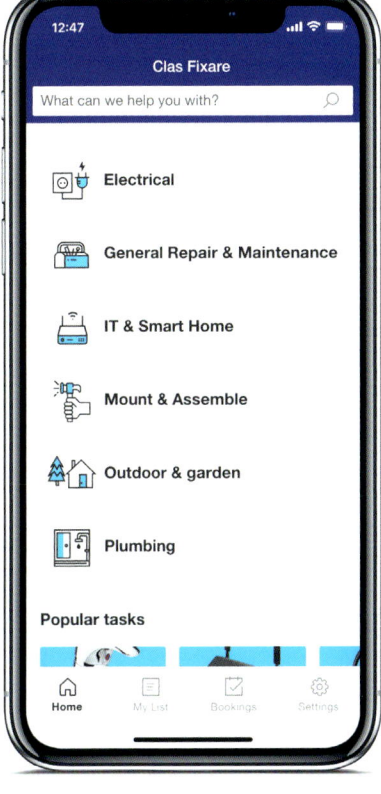
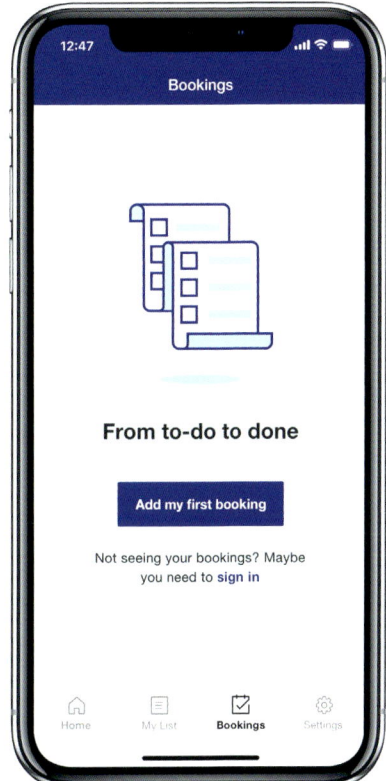
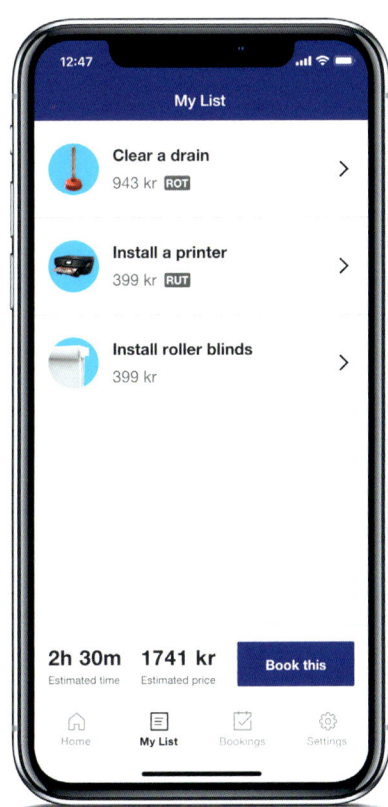
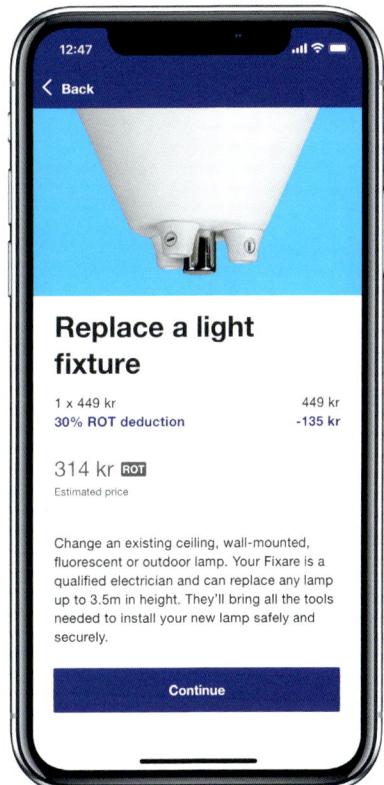

Clas Fixare
[Service Design]

Clas Fixare is an app that helps people find a craftsman for any kind of job in the home, such as installing a light switch or repairing a leaking faucet. In order to find the right service provider, users are guided in an interview style through the clearly arranged interface. Intuitive-to-understand pictograms make identifying the desired job easy. In addition, customers can specify a suitable date, upload their own photos or contract several jobs at the same time.

Client
Clas Ohlson, Insjön, Sweden

Design
Daresay, Kista, Sweden

Design Team
Daniel Rönnlund, Lisa Lee, Viktor Gustafsson, Jillian Buchheim, Jane Ruffino

Programming
Kim Fransman, Hesham Omran, Valerija Grigorjeva, Simon Johansson, Daniel Sjöström, Hannes Ingelhag, Axel Norell

Project Management
Fredrik Malmgren

MINTIT
[User Experience Design, Service Design]

Client
SK Networks Co., Ltd., Seoul, South Korea

Design
Inition Inc., UX Design Studio,
Seoul, South Korea

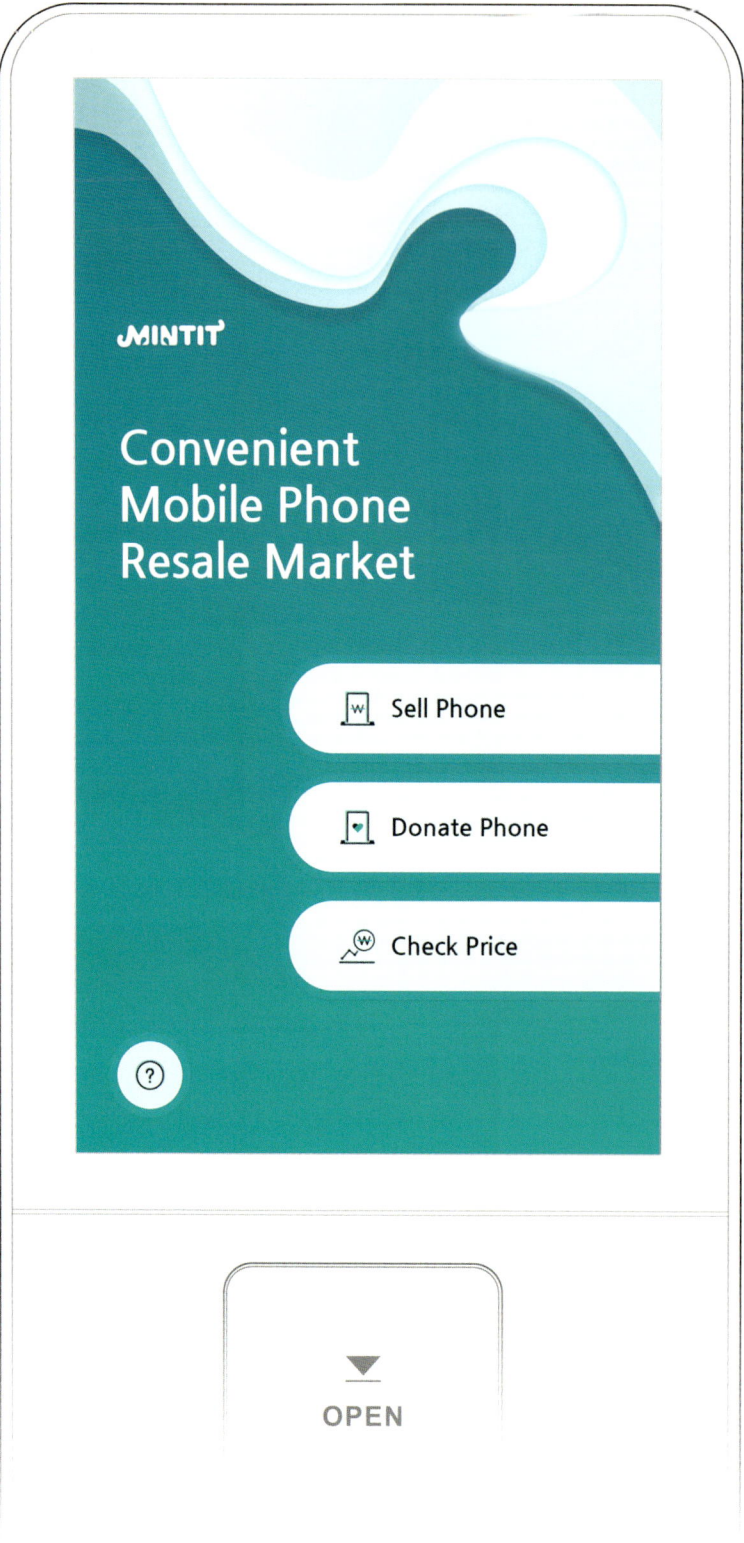

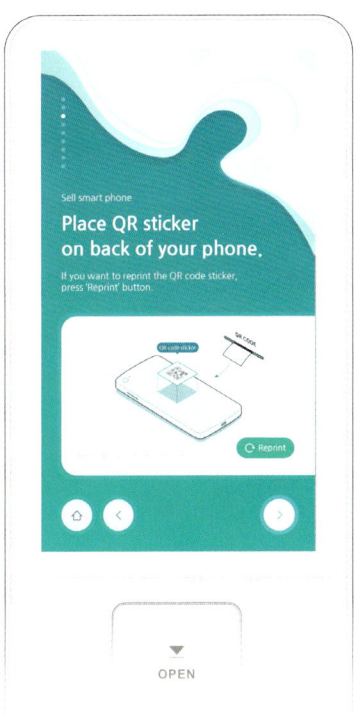
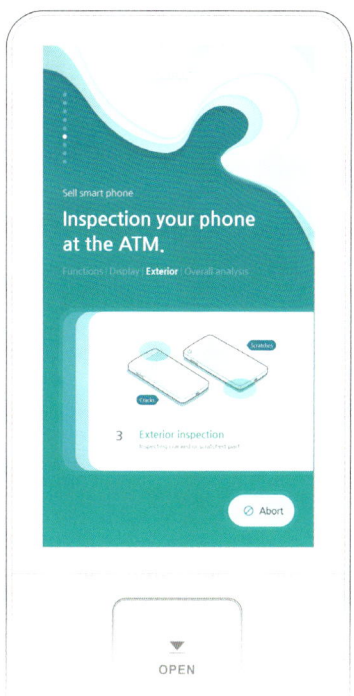

MINTIT UX is a kiosk-based phone diagnosis and self-purchase service. The normal process of selling used mobile phones is typically based on face-to-face meeting and negotiation. However, since people normally don't know the exact value and price of their mobile phone, frustration often arises during this selling process due to different evaluations. To address this issue, MINTIT focuses on easily accessible UX to improve the selling process by providing a self-diagnosis and pricing system. The mint-coloured GUI fosters a friendly mood. An easier diagnostic process enhances usability. The used phones sold through MINTIT are thus reborn as a new product or recycled in order to reduce resource wasting. It is a project that brings social innovation and makes social contributions.

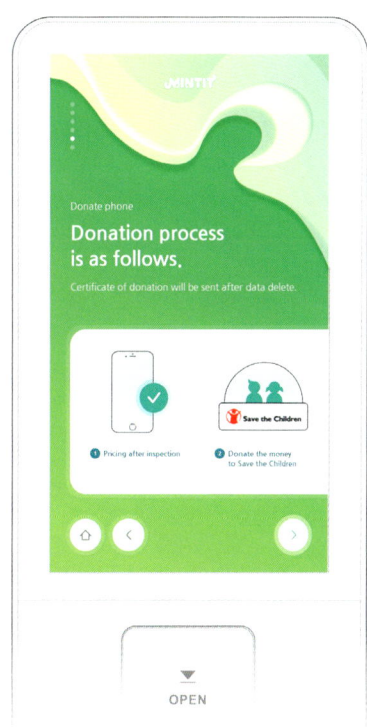

Junelight – Smart Battery Application

[Smart Home Solution,
Solar Battery Management App]

The Junelight app, which has been developed for both iOS and Android, enables battery storage systems to be quickly and easily commissioned and configured. Its design is based on the hardware design of the Junelight battery storage. The app is intuitive to use, and provides users with an around-the-clock status overview of the battery storage device status. It displays personal past and current energy values, which enables the monitoring of usage over time. The power usage data are visualised and processed in an appealing manner, making them easy-to-read for users.

Client
Siemens AG, Nuremberg, Germany

Design
Siemens AG, Nuremberg, Germany
zigzag GmbH, Stuttgart, Germany

Project Management
Judith Onodi-Wolff, Siemens AG

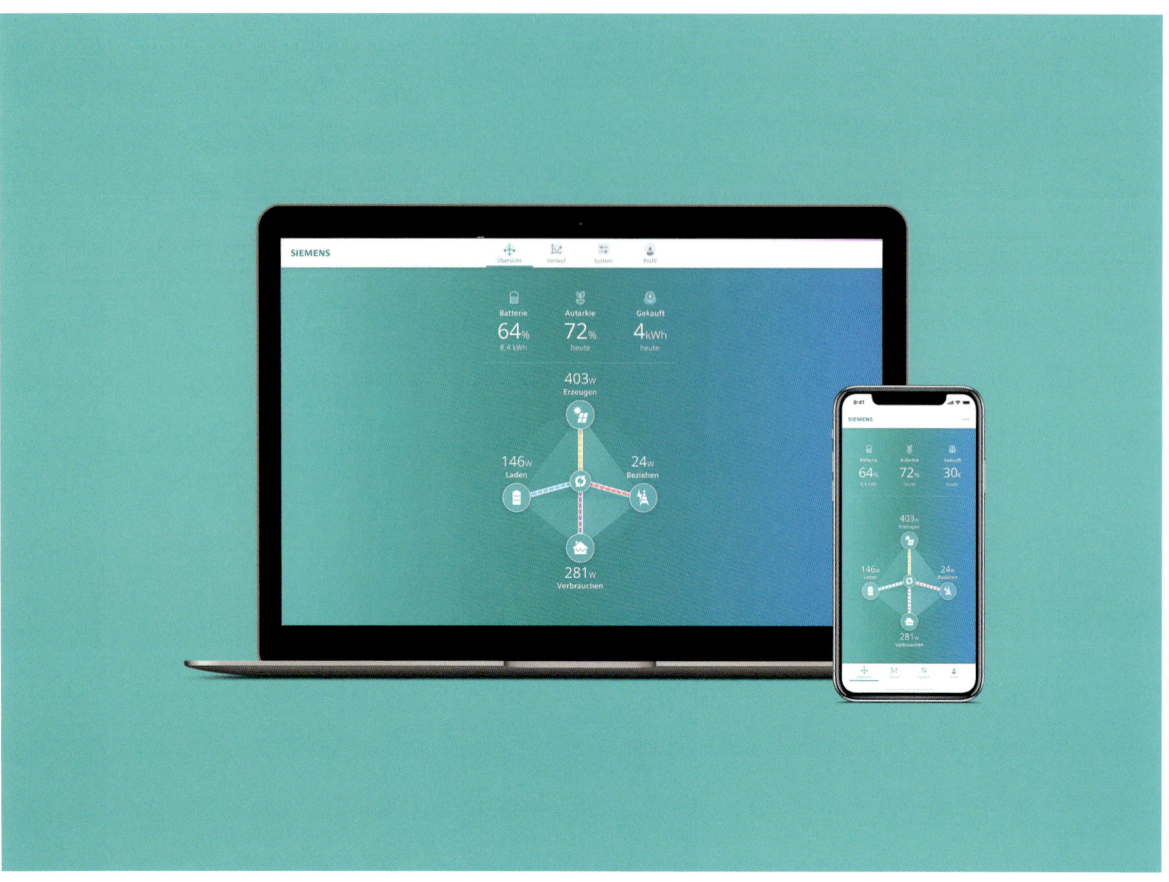

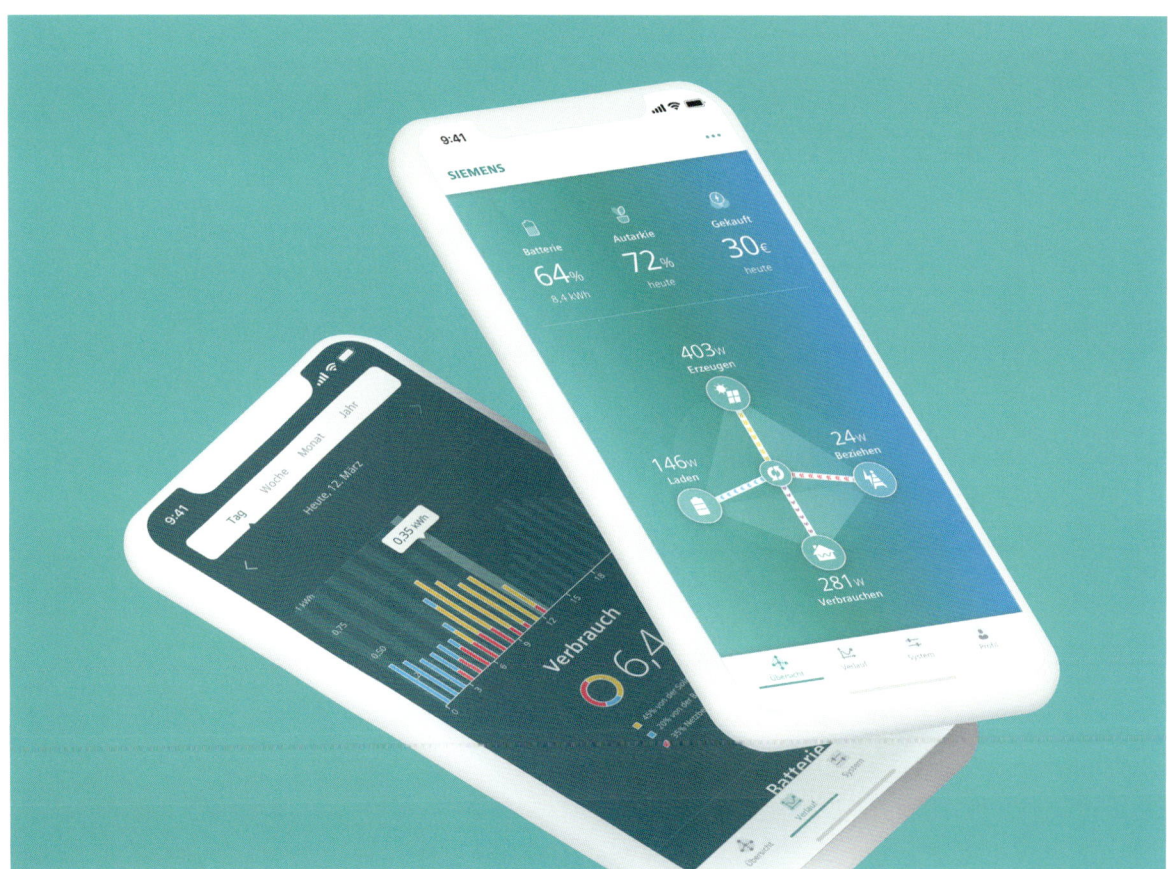

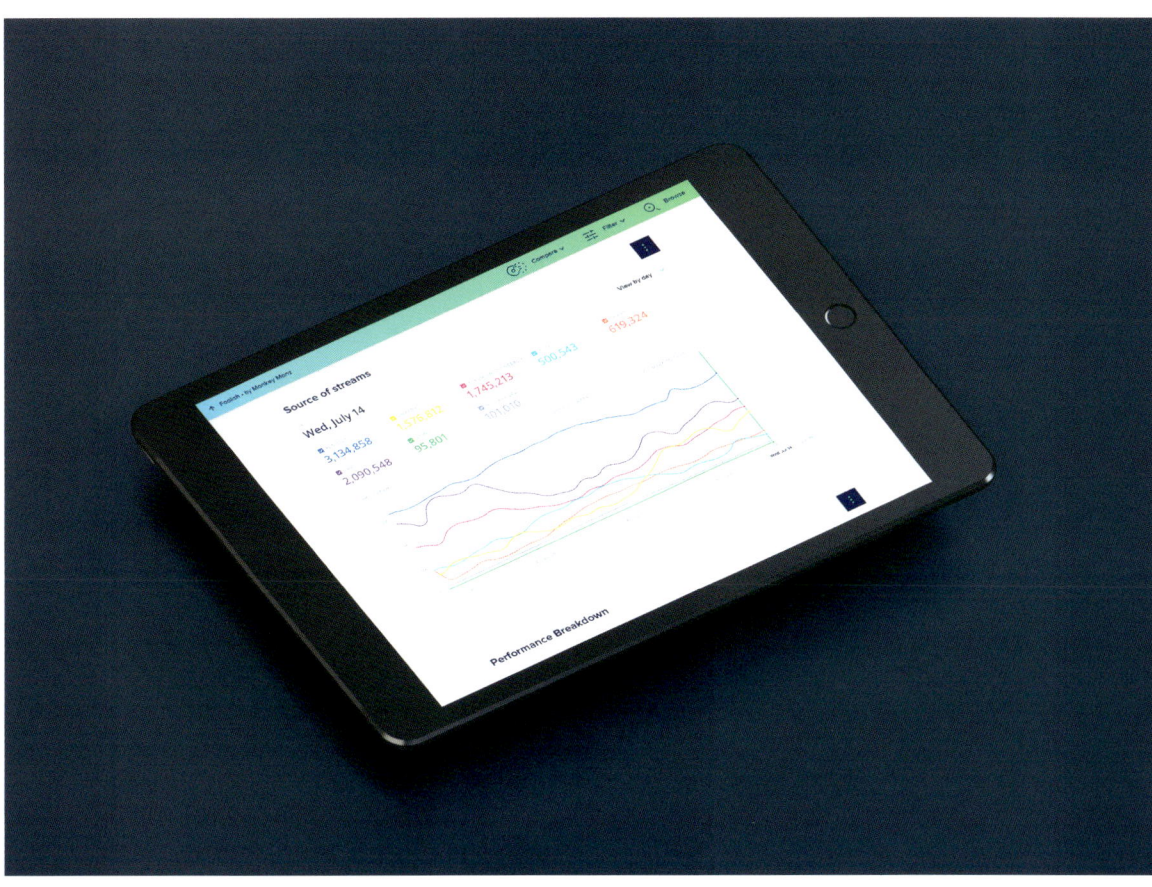

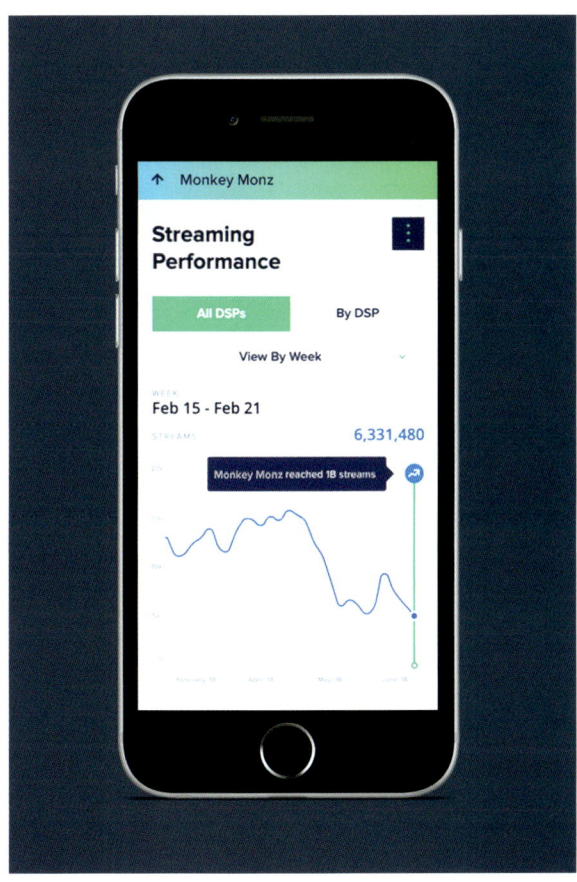
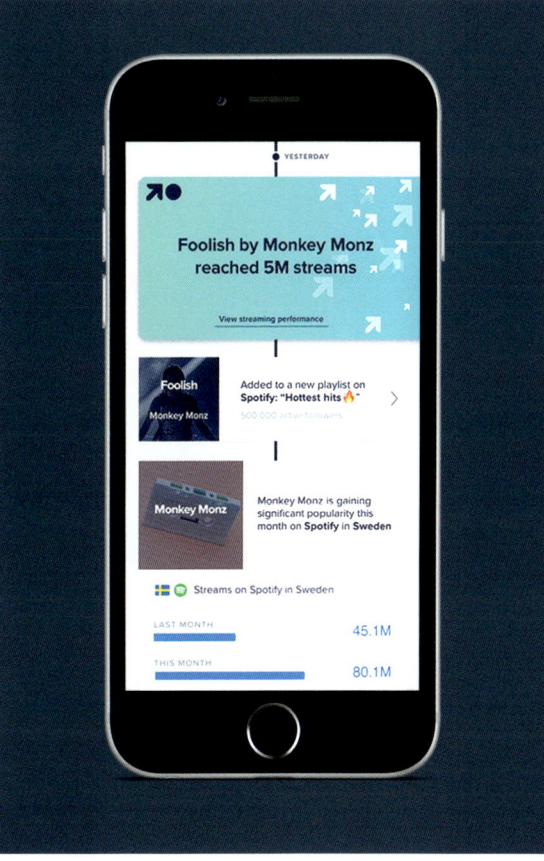

OPUS Music Intelligence

[Digital Ecosystem]

OPUS is a multi-dimensional digitally integrated data system that allows artist- and label managers as well as the artists themselves to understand their performance, analysed from a broad angle down to the tiniest detail. It replaces all the separate platforms and tools in use, bundling the applications into a single clearly organised, user-friendly interface. One element is the analysis and presentation of the online performance of music tracks, with information provided about the number of views and download data from streaming platforms such as Spotify, Apple Music, Deezer and YouTube.

Client
Warner Music Group, New York, USA

Design
CLEVER°FRANKE, Utrecht, Netherlands

Creative Direction
Thomas Clever, Gert Franke

User Experience Design
Wouter van Dijk, Joost Mommers, Pietro Lodi

Visual Design
Roel de Jonge, Pietro Lodi, Joost Mommers

Programming
Jan Hoogeveen, Nick Rutten, Wilco Tomassen, Merlijn Vos, Koen Poelhekke, Mark Haasjes

Mi AI Speaker-S

[Smart Home Solution,
User Interface Design]

Client
Beijing Xiaomi Mobile Software Co., Ltd.,
Beijing, China

Design
Beijing Xiaomi Mobile Software Co., Ltd.,
Beijing, China

Design Direction
Dier Nan

Graphic Design
Wei Yu, Lipeng Ge, Yuyue Liu,
Xiaorong Wu

Music/Sound Design
Jun Meng

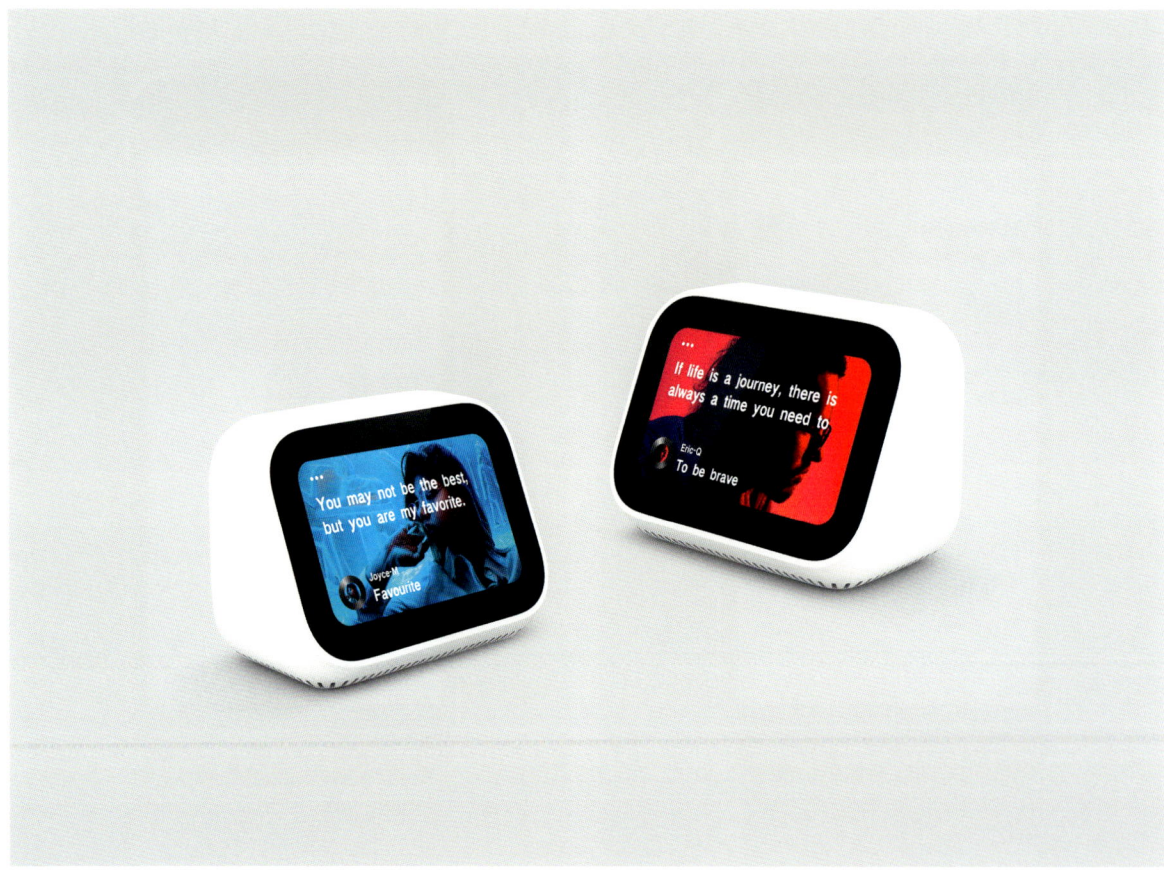

Mi AI Speaker-S is a smart speaker that is operated via voice and touch control. It displays the time, plays music, features a telephone function and allows the control of smart home devices. The user interface is designed to show only relevant information in order to disturb the environment as little as possible. The font size was chosen for good readability. The understated design ensures that the speaker will not disturb users when inactive, for instance by having the speaker's screen show different clocks instead of ads.

Daily Horoscope

[Mobile User Interface Design]

The Daily Horoscope app predicts the future depending on the users' zodiac signs, claiming to free them from the fear of the unknown. In addition, it provides information on each of the zodiac signs, about the symbols, the time periods and the corresponding character traits. Moreover, the integrated astrological calendar helps users determine their ascendant themselves. Based on common navigation structures, the user interface is self-explanatory and identifies interaction areas through colour highlights or with arrows.

Client
Cheetah Mobile, Taipei City, Taiwan

Design
Cheetah Mobile, Taipei City, Taiwan

User Interface Design
Sin-Sin Tsai, Kai-Hsiang Lin

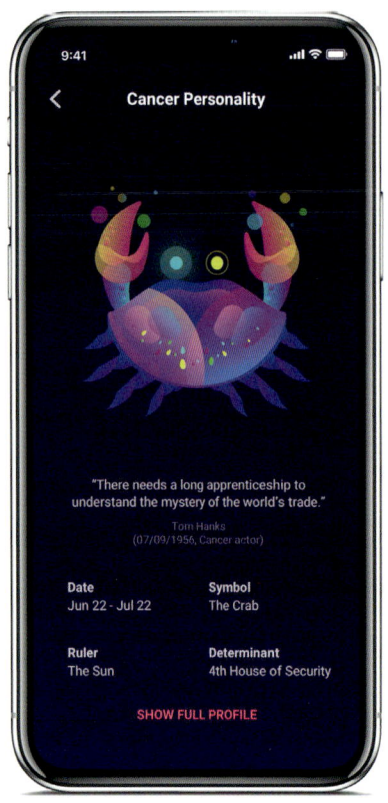
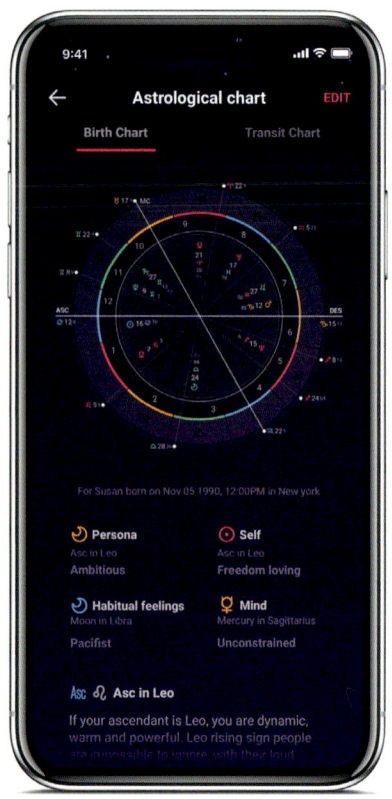
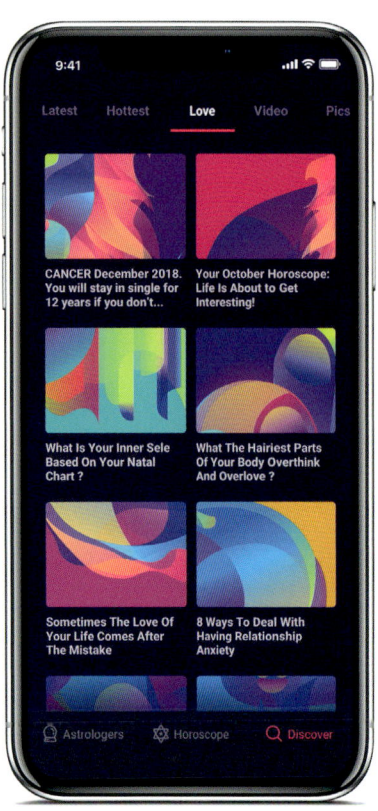
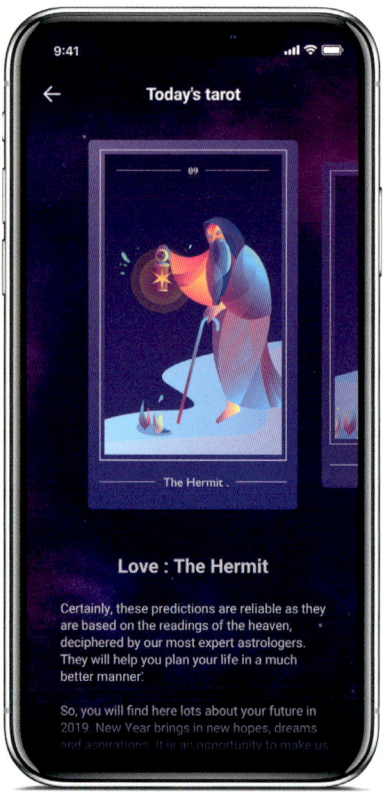

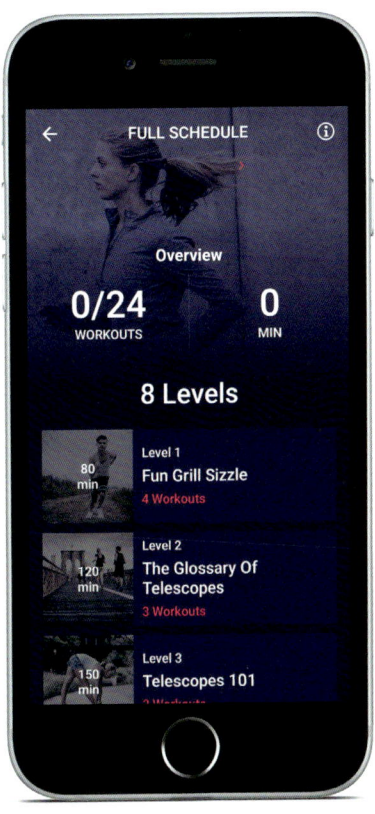

Pedometer

[Mobile User Interface Design]

The pedometer app records the user's physical data while walking in real time. This happens automatically without the need for users to open the app. Furthermore, it is possible to use other apps simultaneously or to lock the screen during recording. Other features include various training plans and personalised fitness classes, including video clips and animations that illustrate the exercises. In addition, the app offers easy-to-read reports, graphics and tables that are based on cognitive user habits to ensure intuitive use.

Client
Leopard Mobile, Taipei City, Taiwan

Design
Leopard Mobile, Taipei City, Taiwan

User Interface Design
Ting-Jiun Hung

Production
Chih-Ting Lin

Zeiss ZX1

[User Interface Design]

Client
Carl Zeiss AG, Oberkochen, Germany

Design
designaffairs GmbH, Munich, Germany

Interface & User Experience Design   Spatial Communication   Red Dot: Junior Award   Designer Profiles   Jury   Index   Red Dot – World of Design

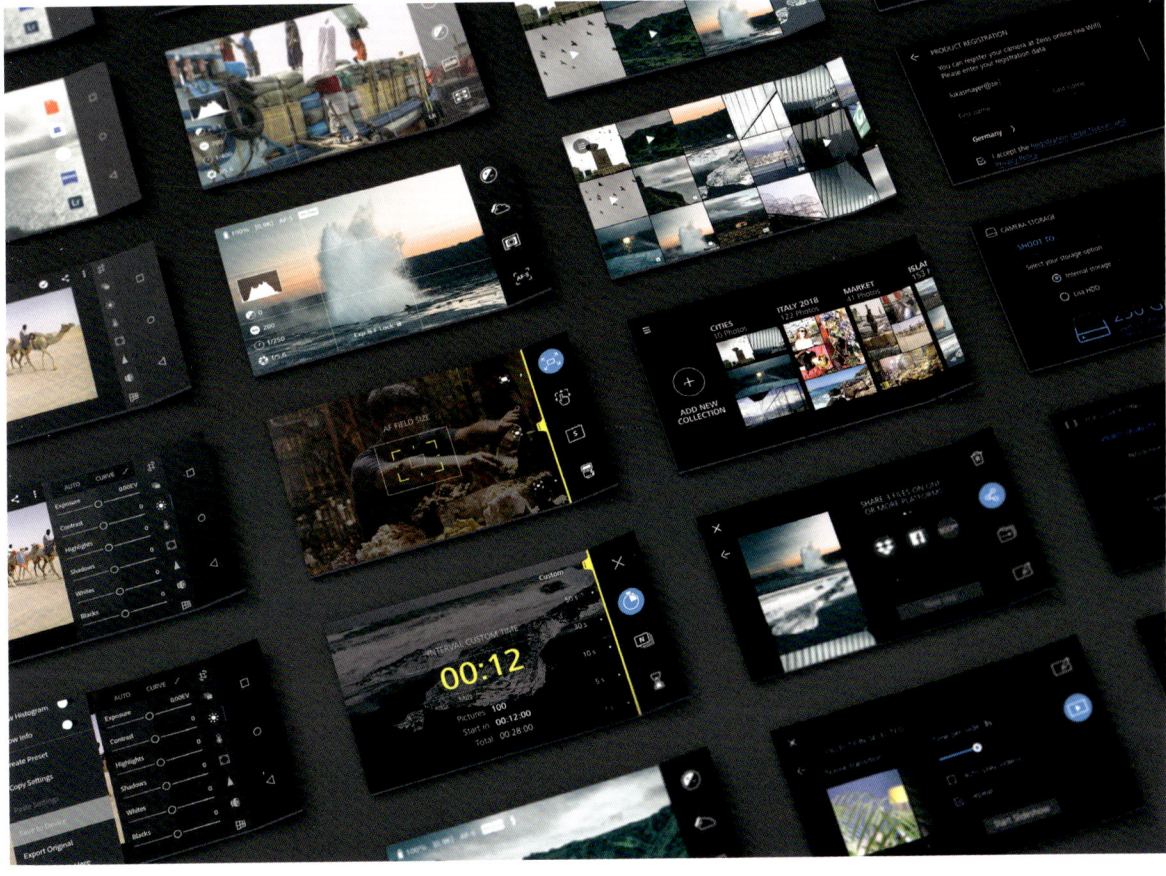

The mirrorless full-frame camera Zeiss ZX1 features an intuitive operational concept and integrated connectivity to support photographers in shooting, editing and sharing images. Haptic control elements provide direct access to the most important functions and are complemented by an intuitive interface on the multi-touch screen. All menus follow a vertical logic and are adapted to the natural movement of the thumb. In addition, the menus are also fully available and selectable on the viewfinder. For a better overview, the user interface displays only those tools that are available for the current dial setting.

| Publishing & Print Media | Posters | Typography | Illustrations | Sound Design | Film & Animation | Online | Apps |

Leica FOTOS

[Mobile User Interface Design]

The Leica FOTOS app allows users to access nine Leica camera systems with their smartphones via Wi-Fi and Bluetooth to view and manage photo galleries. The monochrome designed app pays homage to both black-and-white photography and the classic colour palette of the cameras. The division into a black and a white background simplifies orientation, allowing users to immediately recognise whether photos are located on a camera or the smartphone: if the background is black, they are accessing a camera; if it is white, they are looking at photos on the smartphone.

Client
Leica Camera AG, Wetzlar, Germany

Design
Little Voice (BYOD & DIY) Ltd., London, United Kingdom

→ Designer profile on page 543
→ Clip online

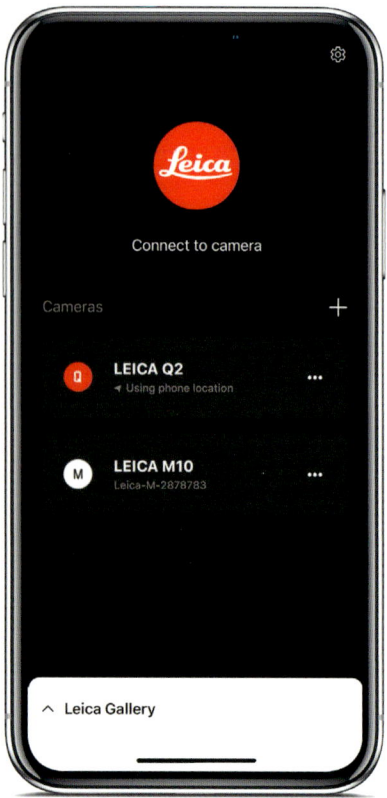
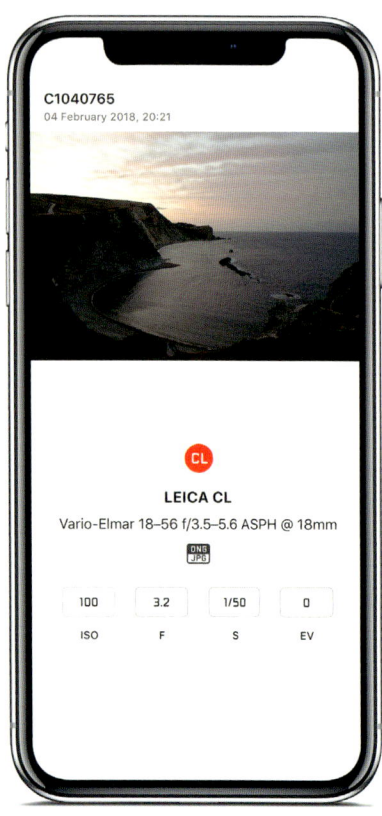
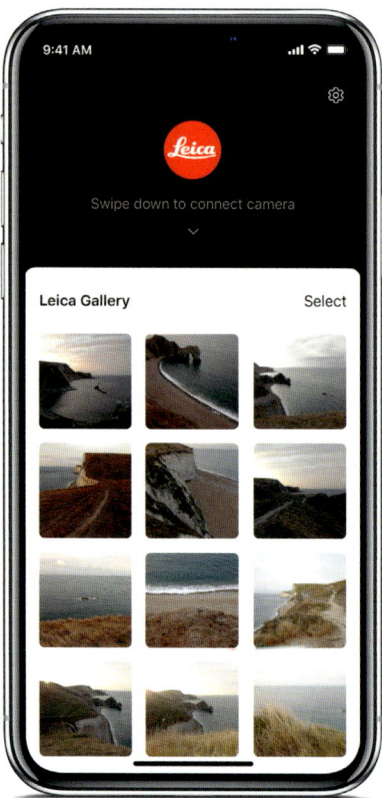

MITU Remote Control Small Plane

[User Interface Design]

The MITU Remote Control Small Plane drone is controlled via a smartphone app. The user interface is designed so that even children can fly the drone easily. It is based on the UI of a game controller and, in addition to self-explanatory icons, offers two circular control areas with functions that are immediately clear and thus guarantee intuitive control of the drone. Flight algorithms can also be programmed in the app while playing with the drone, increasing children's understanding of AI.

Client
Beijing Xiaomi Mobile Software Co., Ltd.,
Beijing, China

Design
Beijing Xiaomi Mobile Software Co., Ltd.,
Beijing, China

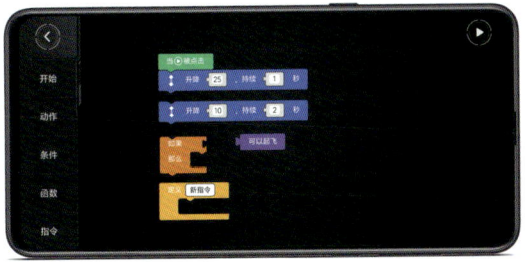

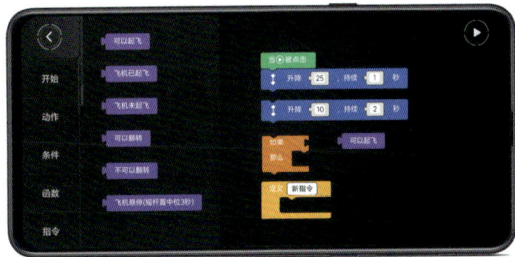

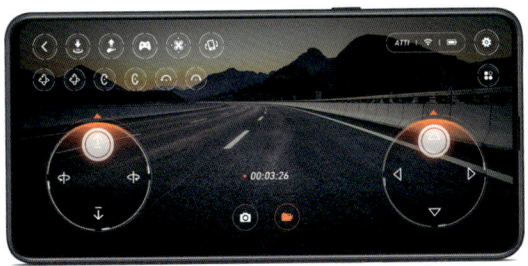

iFly KLM 360

[Virtual Reality Experience, Travel Platform]

iFly KLM 360 is a travel platform that inspires people to virtually discover the world. The integration of special VR goggles was deliberately avoided during the development, as the platform should be accessible to as many users as possible. Instead, a version has been created that can be used with cardboard and VR headset, as well as a web version that can be viewed without any tools via the web browser. The implementation for mobile devices has been adjusted accordingly. Navigation elements are kept minimalist and are integrated into the full screen of the experience platform, leaving nothing to distract users from immersing in the virtual world.

Client
KLM Royal Dutch Airlines, Amstelveen, Netherlands

Design
Born05, Utrecht, Netherlands

Creative Direction Interactive
Timo Wilbrink

Art Direction
Marnix Schmidt

Account
Sander de Graauw

Project Management
Maaike Luijer

Production
Frederik Pot

Motion Design
Jesse Otten

Strategy
Harm Balvers

Distribution
Arne Stierman

Development
Arjen Gosman

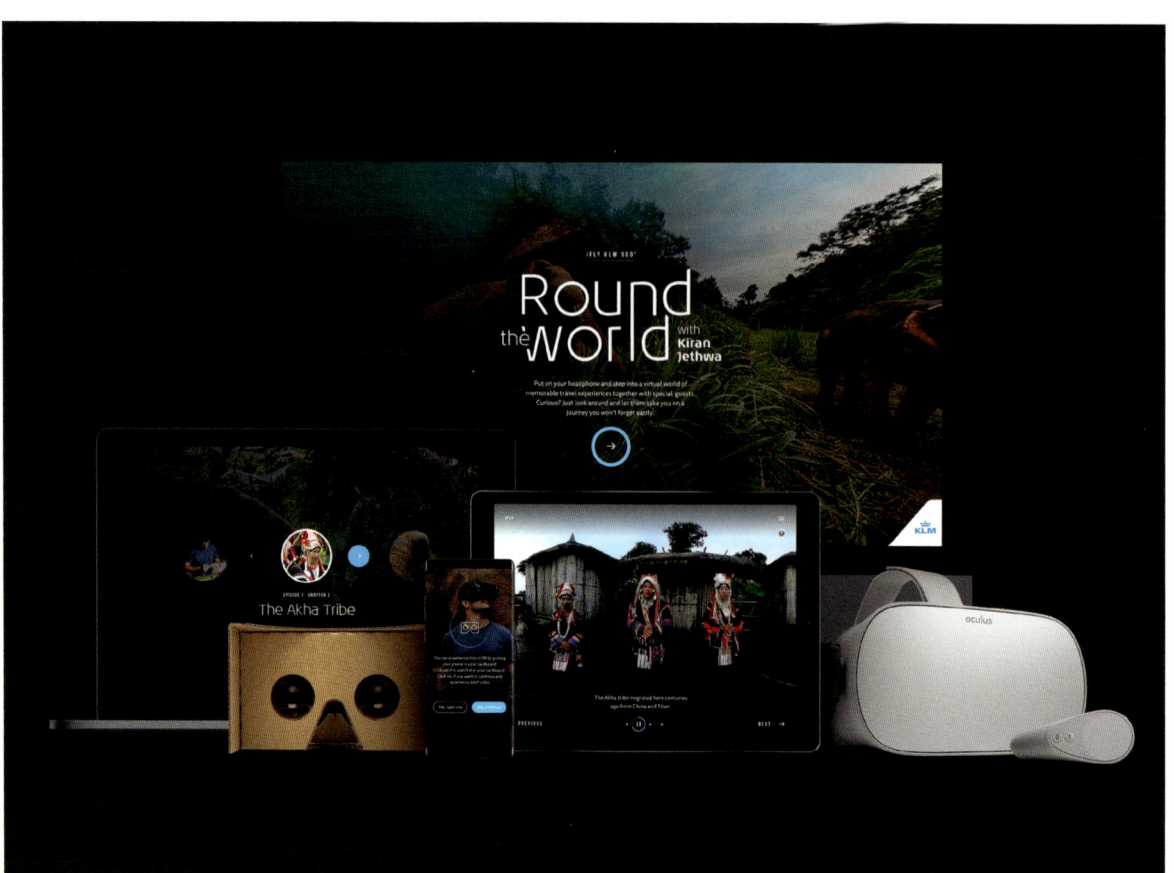

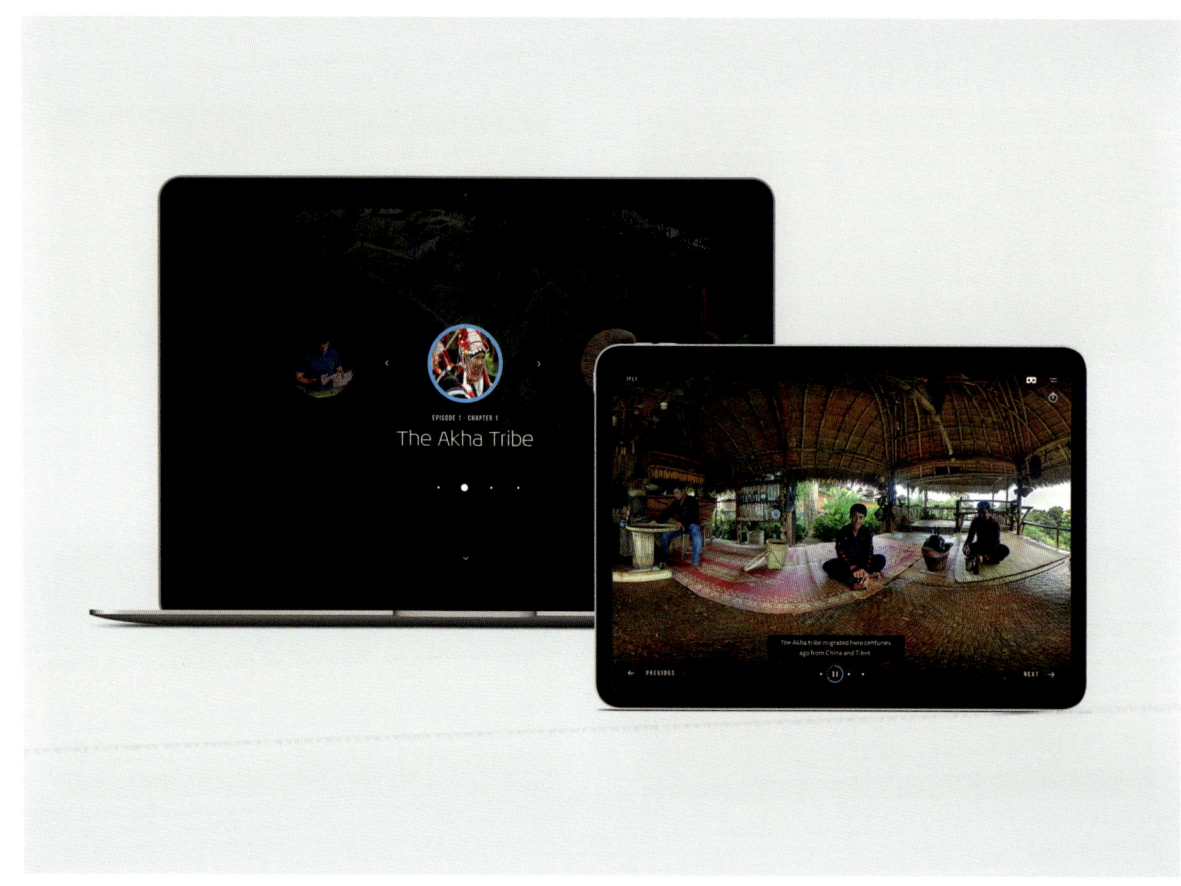

Hamburger Hochbahn – Ticket Vending Machine

[User Interface Design]

The core element of this ticket vending machine for Hamburger Hochbahn public transport provider is a 32" touchscreen that ensures comfortable interaction. Operated like a smartphone, it thus offers most users a familiar experience. All information relevant to customers is displayed on the touchscreen. The interaction no longer is sequential but rather simultaneous, which simplifies the selection process. In addition, it features intuitive map navigation with destination tracking and route calculation, as well as assistance functions and intelligent access for handicapped people.

Client
Hamburger Hochbahn AG,
Hamburg, Germany

Design
Design3 GmbH, Hamburg, Germany

Project Management
Martin Austen, Marcus Schulz,
Hamburger Hochbahn AG

→ Clip online

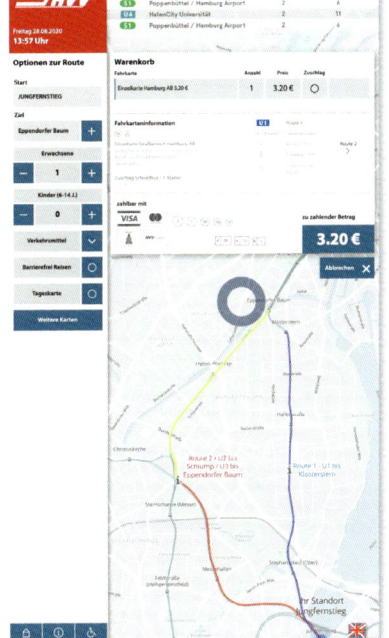
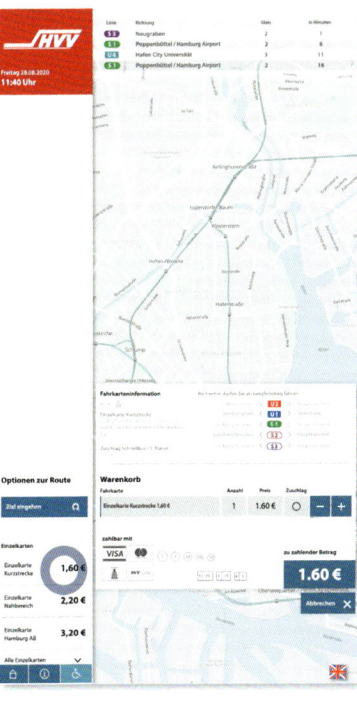

Publishing & Print Media   Posters   Typography   Illustrations   Sound Design   Film & Animation   Online   Apps

ICE Portal
[User Experience Design Relaunch]

Client
Deutsche Bahn, DB Fernverkehr AG,
Frankfurt/Main, Germany

Design
Deutsche Bahn, DB Fernverkehr AG,
Frankfurt/Main, Germany
forwerts interactive GmbH,
Frankfurt/Main, Germany

Project Team
Dr. Björn Dittfach (Head of Digital
Customer Service), DB Fernverkehr
Ellen Pienkos (Head of Digital
Service Projects), DB Fernverkehr
Caroline Sturm (UX Lead of Digital
Customer Service), DB Fernverkehr
Christian Bischoping (Project Manager
of ICE Portal), DB Fernverkehr
Julian Schwarz (UX Creative
Director & Partner), forwerts
Sebastian Baldauf (UX Expert & Partner),
forwerts

→ Designer profile on page 522
→ Clip online

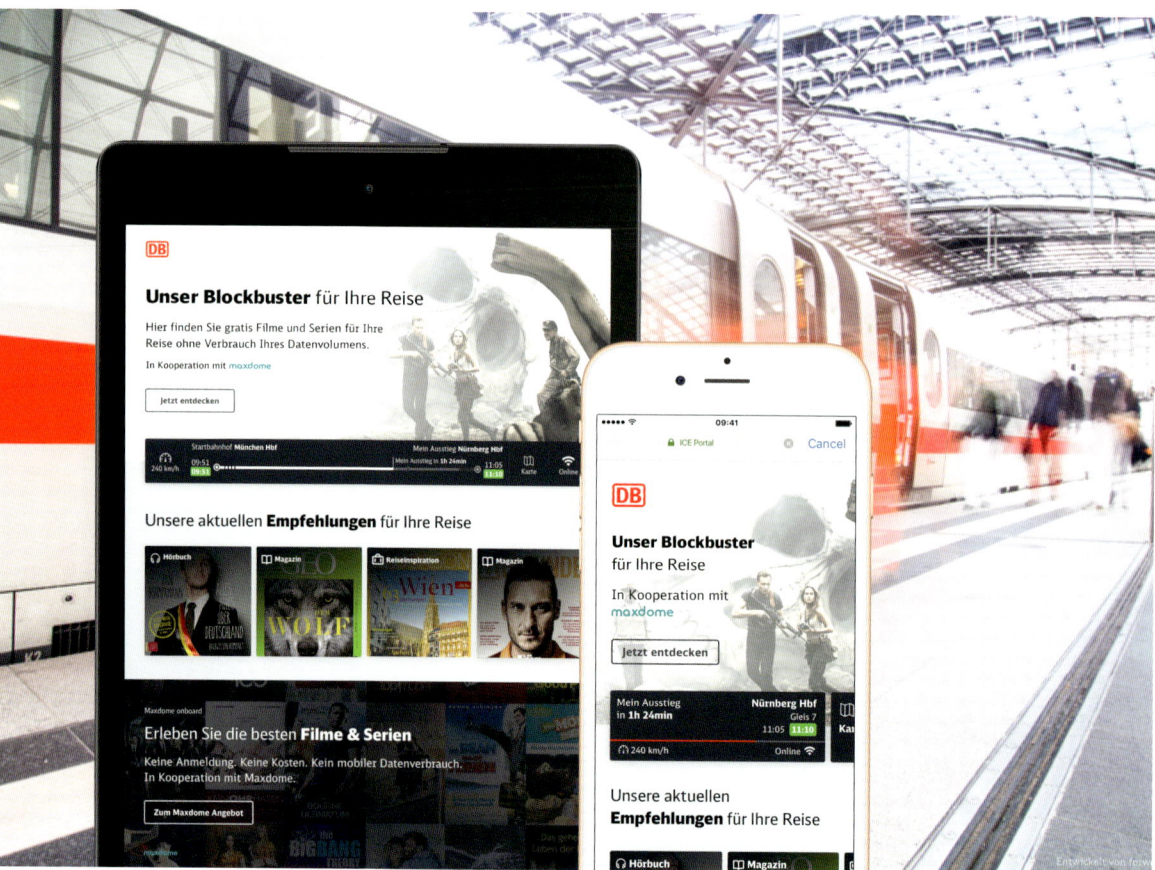

Deutsche Bahn's new infotainment UX design system has been designed with a focus on customer needs, in order to increase transparency and accessibility. It is based on a modular "atomic design" that meets high demands on aesthetics and functionality. It places contents centre stage, presenting them immediately on the home screen. Users have direct access to relevant information via a search function and can easily navigate to the desired content. As a result, the infotainment system has a strong pull on customers, turning travelling by train into an emotional experience.

Publishing & Print Media   Posters   Typography   Illustrations   Sound Design   Film & Animation   Online   Apps

Finnair – Onboard Service Platform
[User Interface Design]

With Finnair's on-board system, the crew has control over the complete service schedule and cabin ambience, can manage both product inventories and orders as well as handle possible disruption cases. For the passengers, the on-board system provides access to Finnair's Wi-Fi portal and hence access to Internet, entertainment and product offerings as well as the ability to pay safely with one's own device. The platform has been scaled across multiple devices, enabling the crew smartphones, seatback screens and passenger smartphones to be integrated seamlessly into the same platform, enabling a holistic experience throughout Finnair's entire fleet.

Client
Finnair Oyj, Vantaa, Finland

Design
Finnair Oyj, Vantaa, Finland
Reaktor Oy, Helsinki, Finland

Creative Direction
Maria Lumiaho

Art Direction
Marja Ojala

Design Team
Ville Sundman, Ji Young Son, Tuomas Husu, Kim Olenius

Project Management
Harri Valkama, Tiina Suvanto, Mikko Uusimaa

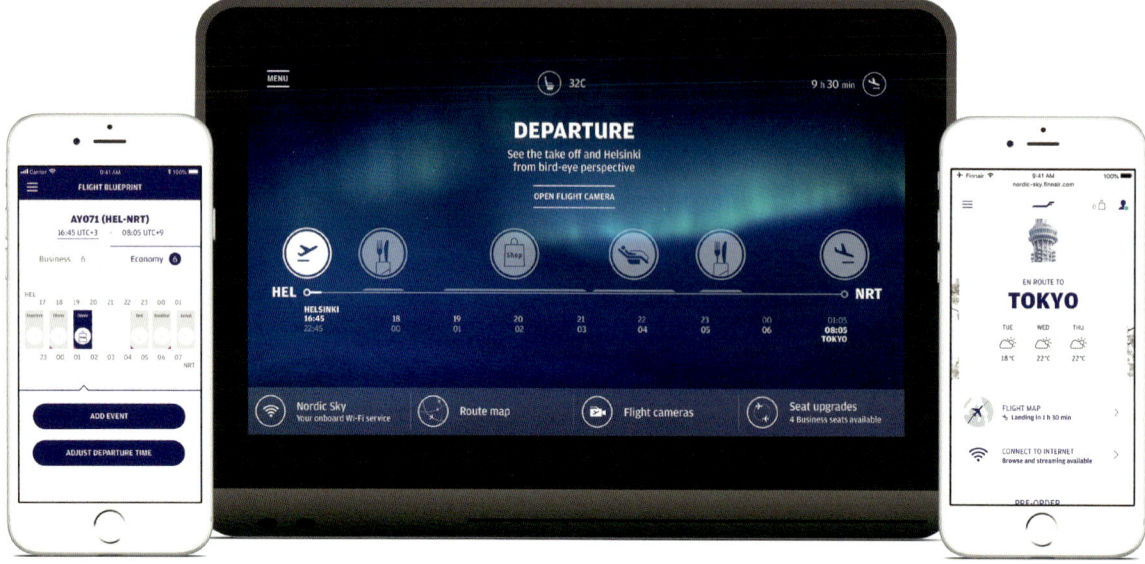

Interface & User Experience Design   Spatial Communication   Red Dot: Junior Award   Designer Profiles   Jury   Index   Red Dot – World of Design

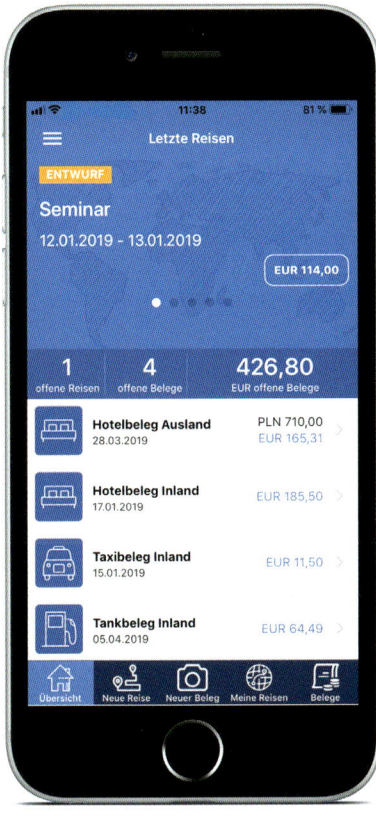

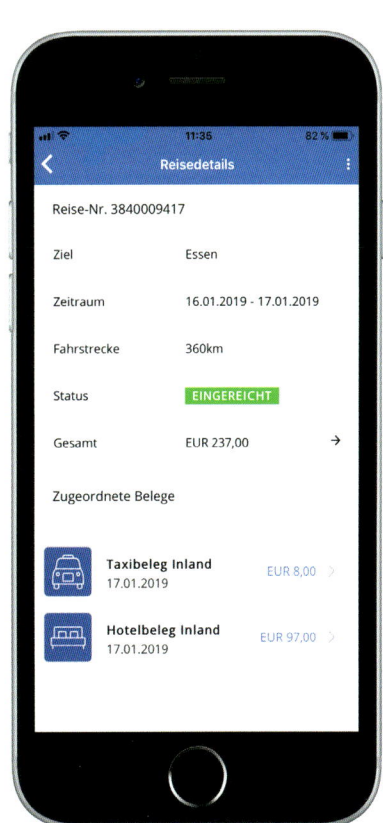

Xpense2Cash

[Mobile User Interface Design]

Xpense2Cash is an intelligent travel expenses app that can be operated easily and quickly even while travelling. Once a receipt is photographed with the smartphone, the app reads the invoice content and submits the data to the accounting system. Digital documents such as PDFs or e-mails can also be processed by the app. It is operated via a sophisticated interface with familiar navigation elements that significantly reduces the time employees spend on creating travel expense reports. Other app features include a currency converter and a detailed cost overview.

Client
Beyond Digital Business e. K., Mayen, Germany

Design
innogy SE, Essen, Germany
UDIT GmbH, Neuwied, Germany

→ Clip online

Apple Pay – Virtual Deutsche Bank MasterCard

[Service Design]

Client
DB Privat- und Firmenkundenbank AG,
Digital Factory, Frankfurt/Main, Germany

Design
Deutsche Bank AG,
Frankfurt/Main, Germany

→ Clip online

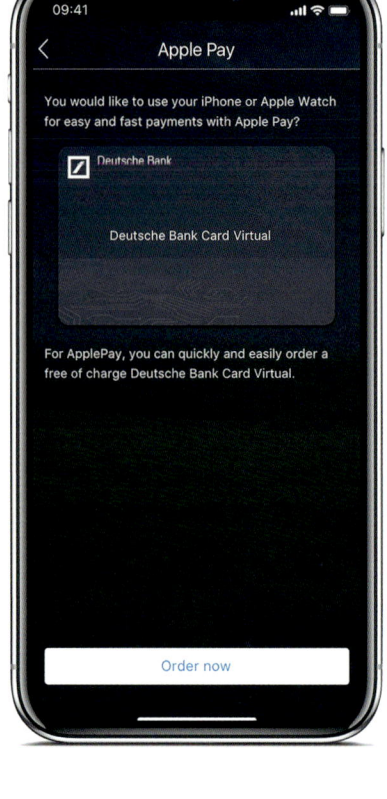

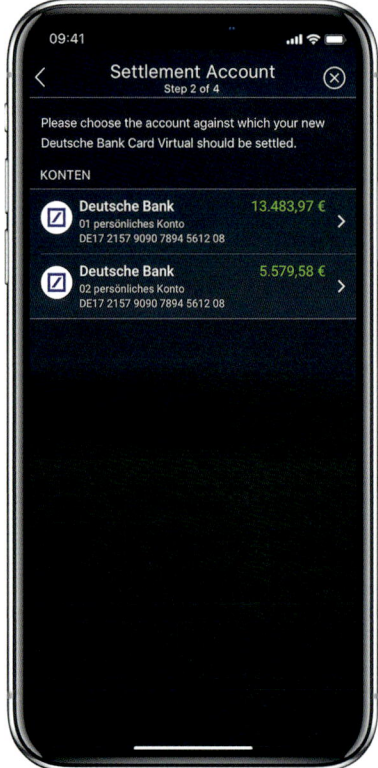

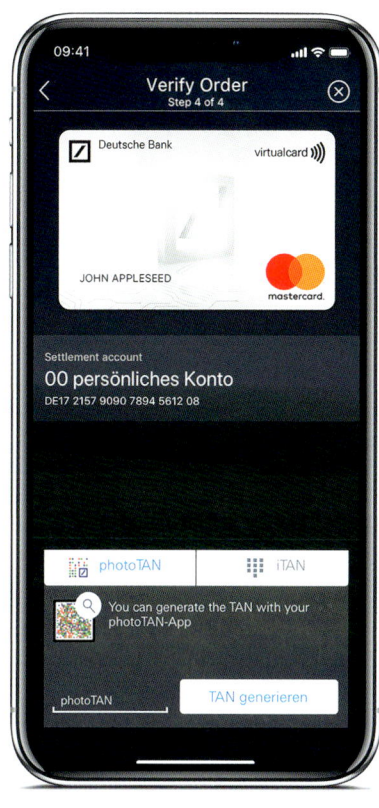
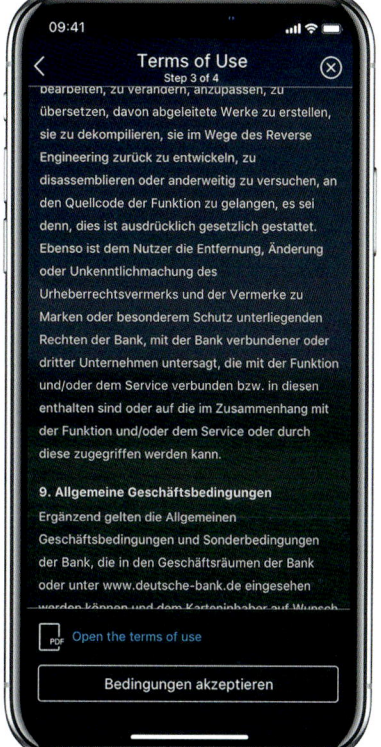
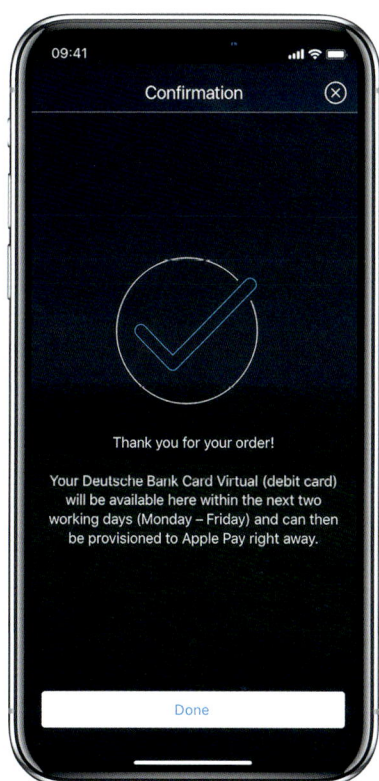

By introducing a virtual credit card, Deutsche Bank has considerably simplified the use of Apple Pay. Users can apply for the credit card, which will be linked to an existing checking account at Deutsche Bank, with just a few clicks within the app. New customers can alternatively apply for a checking account via the app. When paying in the store, customers hold their iPhone to the card reader and verify the transaction via fingerprint or Face ID authentication. The app is kept in a simple line-oriented layout, providing a lot of information on a small space.

Saint Moscowburg

[Microsite]

"Saint Moscowburg" was created as part of a campaign for Visa and VTB24, aimed at motivating people to start paying with their smartphones. On the microsite, users can take a walk through a virtual 360-degree city and receive prizes or gifts that were available in the neighbouring city. The walk features detailed high-quality animations and, thanks to a well thought-out structure, extremely user-friendly. Sophisticated technical solutions reduce the loading time of the complex graphics. Attractive visual effects and a creative navigation complement the experience.

Client
Visa International, Moscow, Russia

Design
Proximity, BBDO Russia Group, Moscow, Russia

Creative Direction
Ilya Andreyev

Art Direction
Maria Biryukova (Creative Group Head), Vsevolod Navashin

Concept
Julia Arkhangelskaya, Tatiana Tutunnik

Production
Dmitry Ivanov

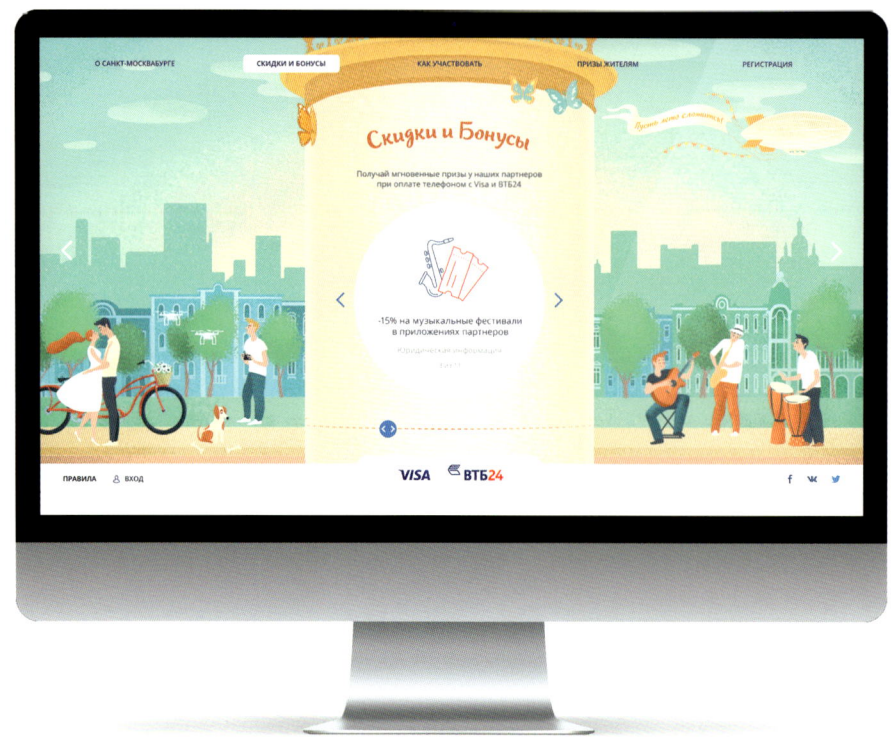

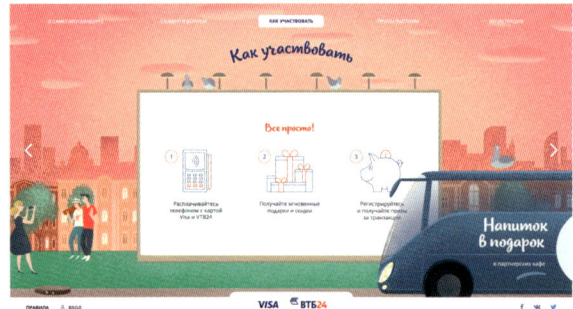
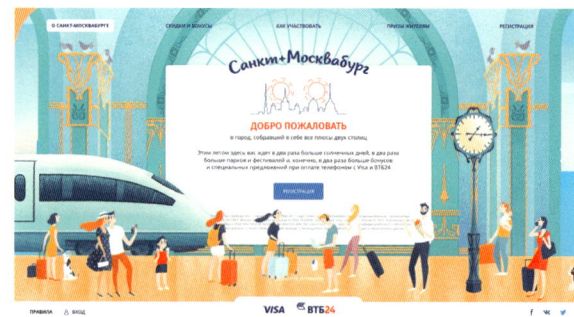

ShinhanPlus

[Mobile User Interface Design, Finance App]

ShinhanPlus is a mobile application that combines four different service apps of the Shinhan Financial Group. These include banking, credit card, investment and insurance services. Customers can thus access all their financial information through one single user interface. The different financial services are presented in a consistent design, but are easily distinguishable through the use of different colours for each service area. The colour scheme is easy on the eyes and ensures good readability of the numbers. A global context menu allows quick switching to a different service area.

Client
Shinhan Financial Group,
Seoul, South Korea

Design
Shinhan Financial Group,
Seoul, South Korea
Media4th & Company, Inc.,
Seoul, South Korea

General Management
Woo Kyoung Ahn,
Shinhan Financial Group

Project Management
Hyo Min Ahn, Yun Jung Uh,
Seung Hyun Kim, Sang Gun Han,
Tae Hee Kim, Bum Hoon Park,
Song Jung Kwon, Jun Gi Jeong,
Yong Moon Cho, Sung Su Park,
Yoon Seok Nam, Shinhan Financial Group

User Interface/User Experience Consulting
Ki Boum Kim, Choong Heon Choi,
Media4th & Company, Inc.

Mobile User Interface/User Experience Design
Eun Hye Yoo, Media4th & Company, Inc.

Mobile User Interface/User Experience Publishing
Min Kwan Park, Media4th & Company, Inc.

→ Designer profile on page 563
→ Clip online

Publishing & Print Media   Posters   Typography   Illustrations   Sound Design   Film & Animation   Online   Apps

boon.App
[Mobile User Interface Design]

boon.App is a virtual prepaid credit card that enables contactless payment via smartphones from anywhere around the world. It can be loaded from any user bank account. The app's user interface is characterised by an innovative and simple look that puts the needs of users at centre stage. The uncluttered placement of icons and list elements provides a good overview, while the Gotham font conveys the notion of reliability. This is complemented by the rounded style of the graphic elements, signalising empathy and accessibility.

Client
Wirecard Issuing Technologies GmbH, Aschheim, Germany

Design
COBE GmbH, Munich, Germany

Creative Direction
Daniel Wagner

Digital Concept
Felix Menzel

Graphic Design
Adrian Spiegelt, Monica Civic, Melchior Schramm

Artwork
Adrian Pavic

→ Clip online

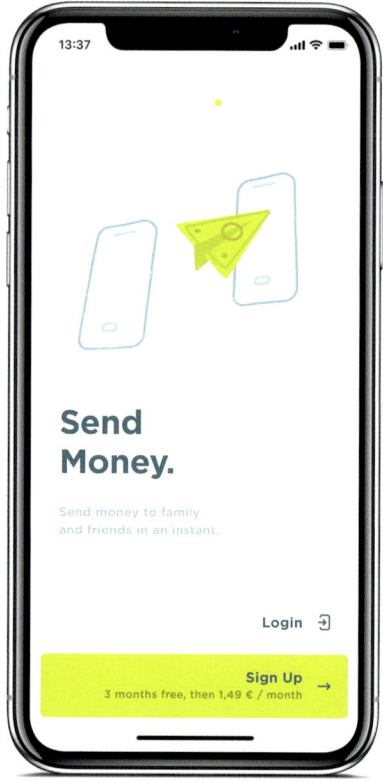
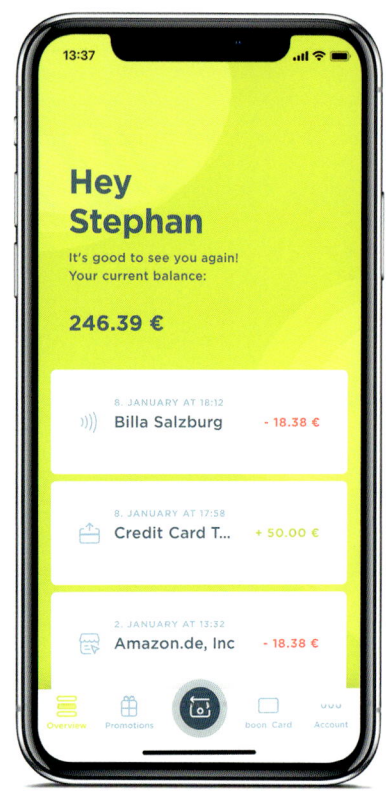

Interface & User Experience Design   Spatial Communication   Red Dot: Junior Award   Designer Profiles   Jury   Index   Red Dot – World of Design

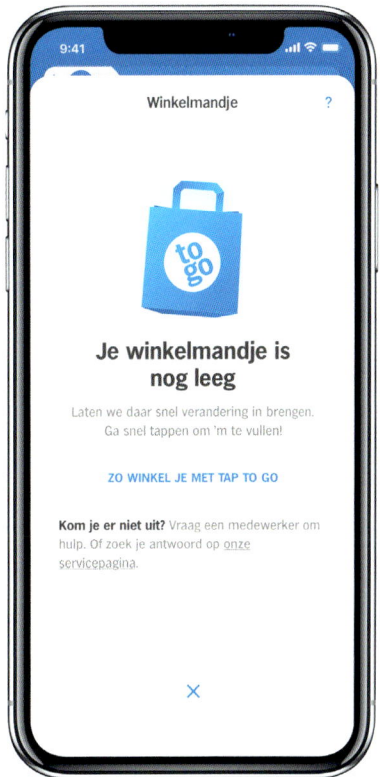
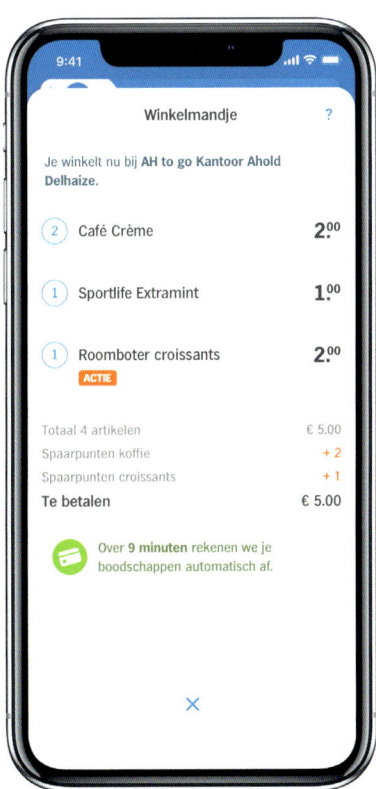
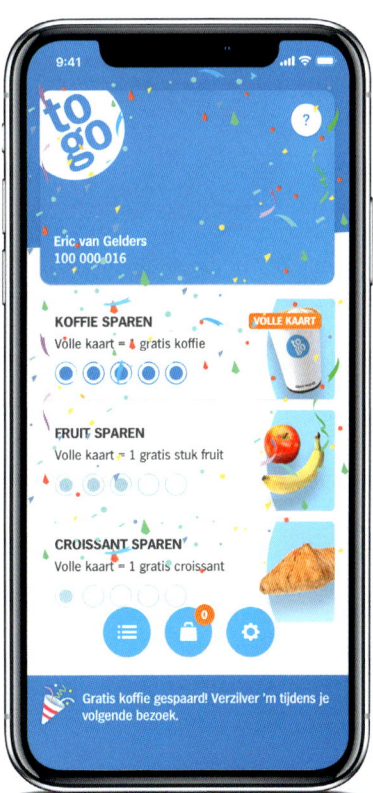

Tap to go
[Mobile User Interface Design]

"Tap to go" is a new digital retail solution by Dutch supermarket chain Albert Heijn. Customers tap their smartphone or "Tap to go" card against a product's digital price tag and then take it off the shelf. The product is automatically added to the virtual shopping cart in the user-friendly app, giving customers an overview of their purchases at all times. In addition, the app also gives information on current discount campaigns. At the end of their shopping, the cost is automatically deducted from a bank account linked to their "Tap to go" account.

Client
Albert Heijn, Zaandam, Netherlands

Design
Resoluut, Amsterdam, Netherlands
Soda studio, Amsterdam, Netherlands

Creative Direction/Account Management
Evan Gelders, Soda studio

User Experience Research
Bo Merkus, Milkshake research, Amsterdam, Netherlands

Visual Design
Sven ten Voorde, Eric Pronk, Resoluut

Interaction Design/User Experience Design
Stefan Veen, Roderick Remmig, Soda studio

Copywriting/User Experience Writing
Djoelia van der Velden, Mr Koreander, Amsterdam, Netherlands

Artificial Intelligence Retail Interaction System

[Service Design]

Client
Baidu Online Network Technology (Beijing) Co., Ltd., Beijing, China

Design
Baidu Online Network Technology (Beijing) Co., Ltd., Beijing, China

Creative Direction
Guan Daisong

Art Direction
Zhao Huibin

User Experience Research
He Jing

User Experience Design
Liu Qian, Xu Ying, Chen Kexin

Space Design
Hu Lina, Qin Tong, Wang Yang

The retail system with AI was developed to reduce the high pressure of online commerce on stationary retailers and to make them competitive again. Thanks to its modular design concept, the system is suitable for retailers of all sizes, helping them to modify walls, ceilings, shelves and lighting and, in so doing, implement the optimal solution in terms of cost and profit. At the same time, customers benefit from a smooth and natural shopping experience, as cameras checking their identity and monitoring the goods selection are unobtrusively integrated into the shop's structural components.

MIUI Dynamic Font System

[Mobile User Experience Design]

The Dynamic Font System of MIUI, the operating system that powers Xiaomi mobile phones, features an easy-to-use slider control that enables users to adjust the weight and size of the system fonts to their needs. This improves the readability of the fonts while maintaining the structure of the user interface. In addition, the operating system automatically adjusts the combination of font weight and size according to current contexts. For example, the system will slightly thin the font by itself when the interface is shifted to the dark mode.

Client
Beijing Xiaomi Mobile Software Co., Ltd., Beijing, China

Design
MIUI Design Team,
Beijing Xiaomi Mobile Software Co., Ltd., Beijing, China

Art Direction
Qiaozhuo Chen

Typography
Feilong Li, Haixu Lu

Animation
Zhanfu Liu

Production
Ting Tang, FounderType, Beijing, China

→ Designer profile on page 548

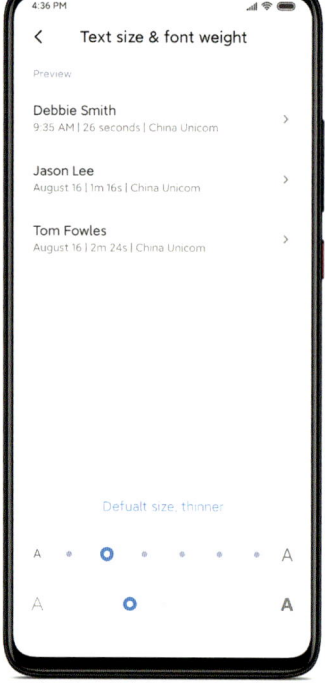
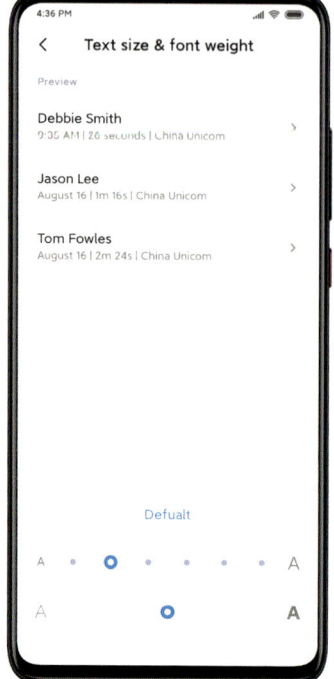

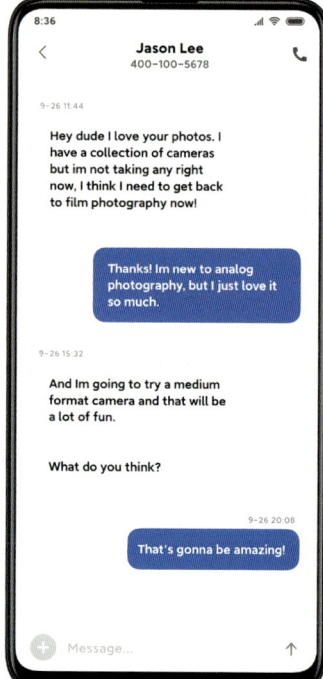

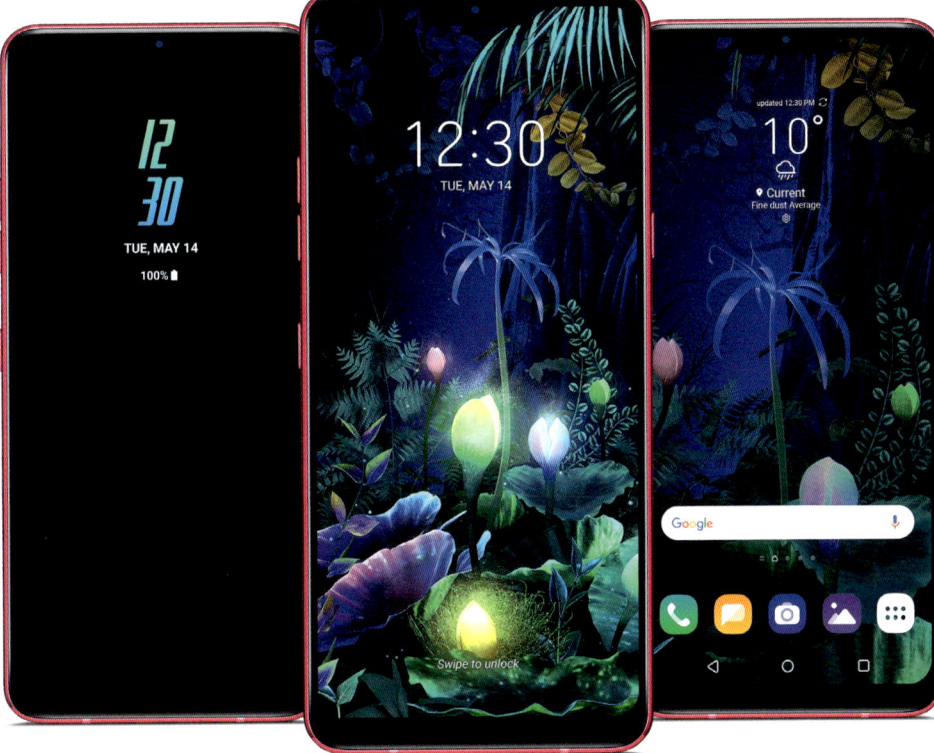

Seamless Live Wallpaper
[Mobile User Interface Design]

With the Seamless Live Wallpaper, smartphone users can transition from the Always-on Display (AOD) to the lock screen and from the lock screen to the home screen with a single swipe to execute an app there. The wallpapers for the lock screen and the home screen are thematically related and linked by smooth animation effects, resulting in a harmonious and flowing transition. The theme colours of the AOD are also reflected in the time display, which makes the transition from the predominantly black AOD to the colourful lock screen feel natural.

Client
LG Electronics Inc., Seoul, South Korea

Design
LG Electronics Inc., Seoul, South Korea

User Interface Design
Hyunho Kang, Insu Hwang, Inseong Cho, Sungeun Yoon, Grami Ryu, Janet Jang, Eunbin Kim, Sujeong Lee

SAP Match Insights

[Screen Design]

The Video Cockpit and Player Dashboard apps, which are part of the SAP Sports One product family, support teams in the analysis and exchange of relevant game data. The Video Cockpit gives access to videos, data and information on training sequences. Thanks to the modern web user interface, users can quickly recognise and analyse content. Using the Player Dashboard, analysts and team coaches can provide players with easy access to personalised information and videos from their mobile devices. In addition, the logically-structured, appealing interface supports an optimal workflow with minimal need for user interaction.

Client
SAP SE, St. Leon-Rot, Germany

Design
SAP SE, User Experience Design for Sports and Entertainment, St. Leon-Rot, Germany

Design Team
Irene Schick, Lydia Tallau, Alexander Schräder, Selina Vix, Lars Siebert, Florian Jann, SAP SE
Stephanie Häusler, User Interface Design GmbH

Development Management
Sven Schwerin-Wenzel

→ Designer profile on page 561
→ Clip online

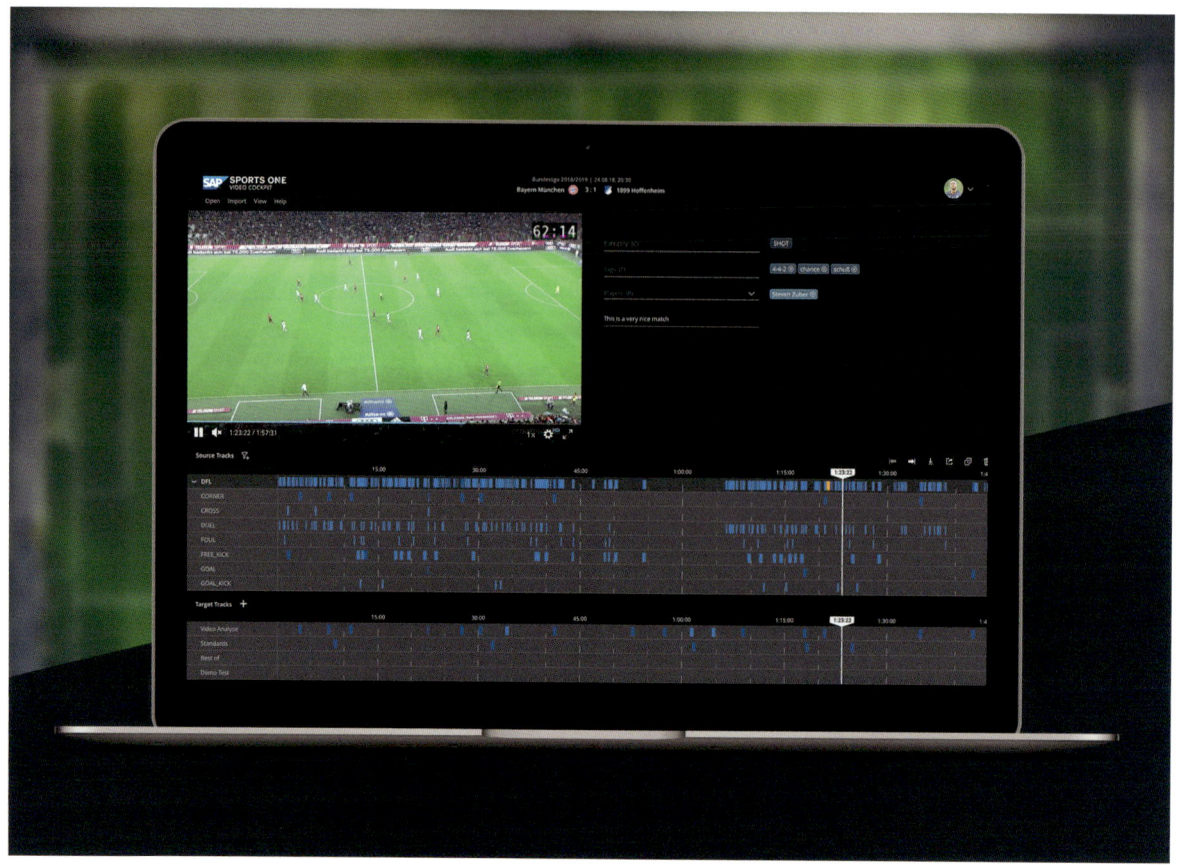

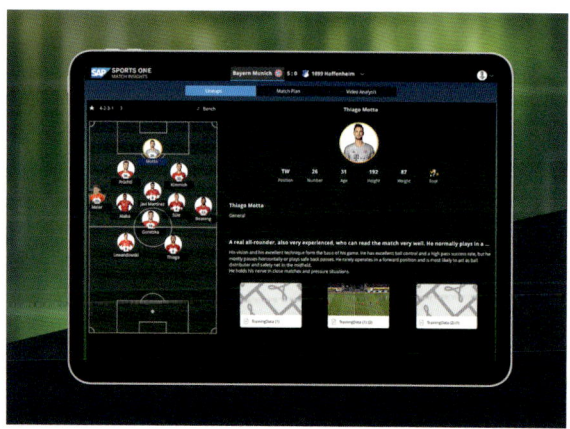

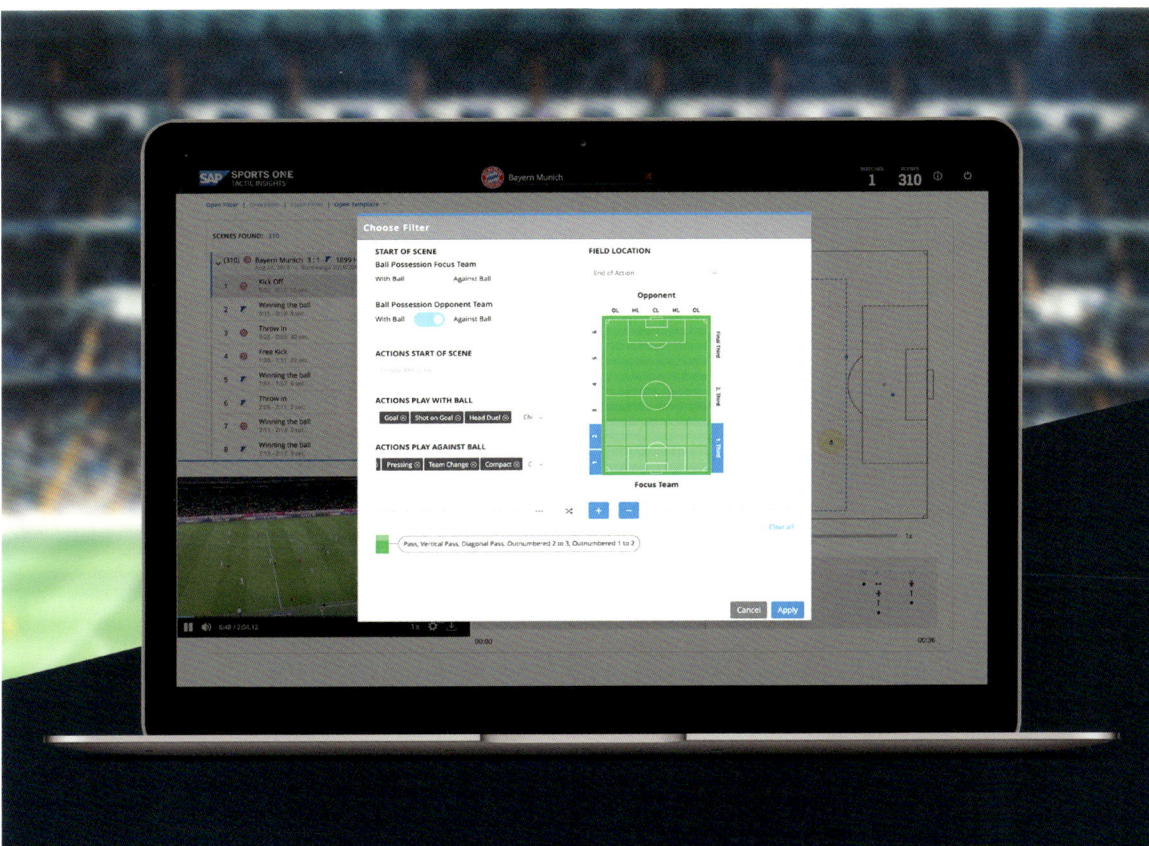
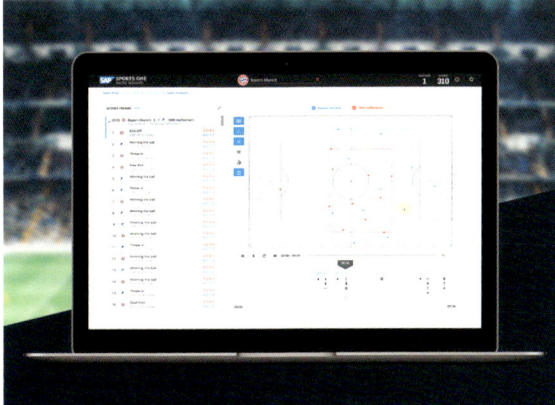
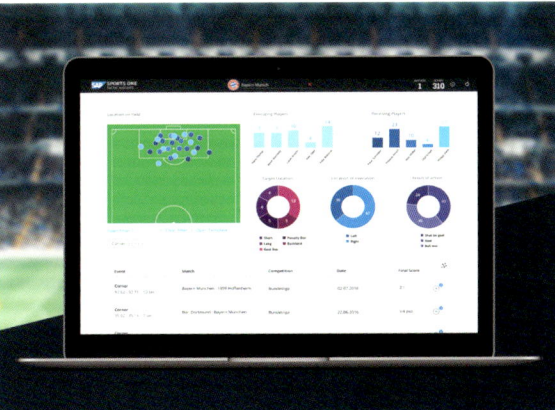
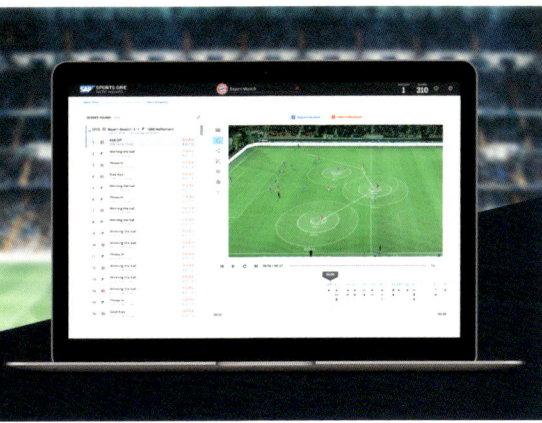

SAP Tactic Insights
[User Interface Design]

SAP Tactic Insights is a new component of the cloud-based software solution SAP Sports One. It enables football clubs to quickly find relevant scenes from one or more games and instantly analyse them. An appealing 2D viewer creates visualisations of the selected scenes with useful features, such as a radius circle around the ball. Since the graphics have been reduced to the essentials, users get a quick overview of the selected game situation. In addition, the 2D viewer can be synchronised in real time with the corresponding video, if a view of the actual game scene is desired.

Client
SAP SE, St. Leon-Rot, Germany

Design
SAP SE, User Experience Design for Sports and Entertainment,
St. Leon-Rot, Germany

Design Team
Irene Schick, Lydia Tallau,
Alexander Schräder, Selina Vix,
Lars Siebert, SAP SE
Stephanie Häusler,
User Interface Design GmbH

Development Management
Sven Schwerin-Wenzel

→ Designer profile on page 561
→ Clip online

Vodafone GigaTV

[User Interface Design]

The TV user interface GigaTV aggregates TV programs, media libraries, on-demand content and streaming services on a single personalised interface. It is aimed at traditional TV viewers, modern streaming service users and fans of all kinds of entertainment content. It was therefore designed to satisfy both the demands of a modern user experience and traditional TV usage patterns. At the same time, importance was placed on the sustainability of the entire design system, so that it allows continuous adaptation as well as cross-device usage.

Client
Vodafone Kabel Deutschland GmbH, Unterföhring, Germany

Design
COBE GmbH, Munich, Germany

Creative Direction
Malthe Luda, SwipeCircus, Hamburg, Germany
Benedikt Matern, Andreas Lohner, COBE GmbH

Account Management
Natalia Braun, Daniel Wagner, COBE GmbH

Project Management
Shervin Amiri, Samson Struckmann, Kevin Behling, Vodafone

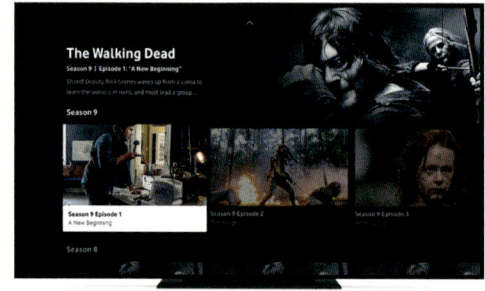

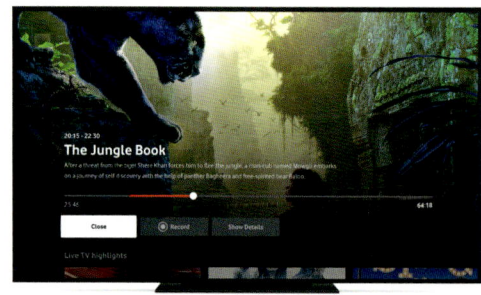

MagentaTV
[Streaming Service]

The field of television and streaming services is characterised by such a wide variety that it is often difficult to keep an overview. Content is available on countless platforms and channels, making it difficult to find the desired media. MagentaTV translates this complexity into a clear and easy-to-use interface. The cross-platform offers access to streaming services, media libraries, VOD content and TV channels in a user-friendly tile structure. In addition, users benefit from a consistent design, as the service is available on smart TVs as well as on PCs, smartphones, tablets and a media receiver.

Client
Deutsche Telekom AG, Bonn, Germany

Design
Telekom Design, Bonn, Germany

LG SIGNATURE OLED TV R

[User Experience Design]

This TV features a roll-up screen that can be used in three scenarios. In the "Zero" mode, it serves as a Hi-Fi speaker that can be controlled by voice and gestures. In the "Line" mode, the screen becomes part of the interior by rolling down to a 54:9 format for displaying photos or animations. In addition, it can also serve as an information centre for controlling IoT devices via a user interface that features in minimalist black-and-white with filigree icons. Finally, in "Full View" mode, the screen is a TV.

Client
LG Electronics Inc., Seoul, South Korea

Design
LG Electronics Inc., Seoul, South Korea

User Experience Design
Meeyoun Choi, Byunghun Lee, Youngmin Kim, Nari Yoon, Hyunju Ryu, Sugyeong Yu, Gowoon Choi, Jihe Suk

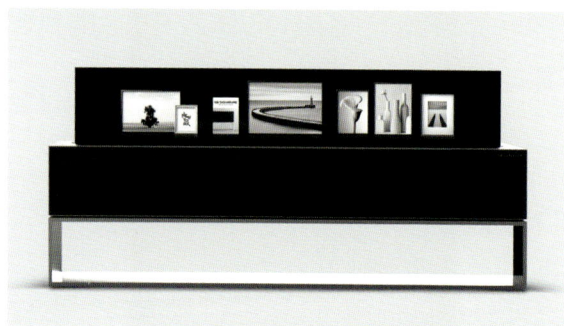
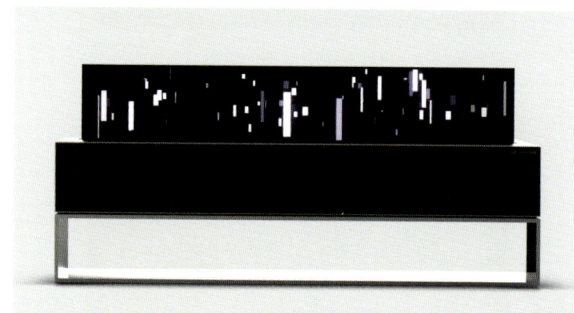

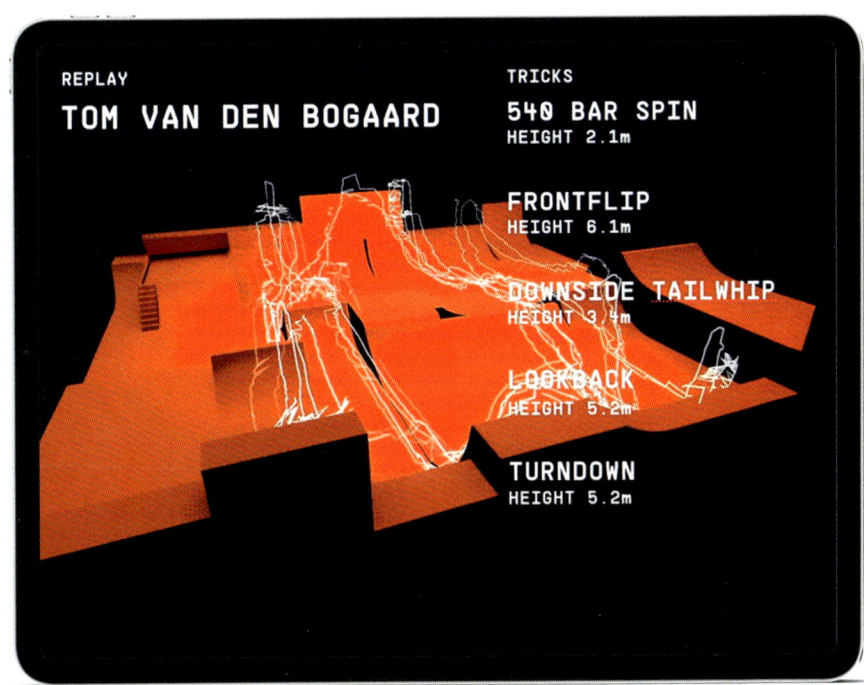

BMX Freestyle Championships

[Data Visualisation]

The platform was used during the Dutch National BMX Freestyle Championships. The riders were equipped with sensors that transmitted their riding data such as position, acceleration, height and rotation, data which was then used to visualise the path of each rider on a large screen. This was complemented by information about the tricks that the riders had just performed, so that the audience, jury members and not least the riders themselves could get better insight into the performance. The key colour was the Dutch national colour orange.

Client
De Koninklijke Nederlandsche Wielren Unie (KNWU), Arnhem, Netherlands

Design
CLEVER°FRANKE, Utrecht, Netherlands

Creative Direction
Thomas Clever, Gert Franke

Design Team
Roel de Jonge, Joost Mommers

User Experience Design
Wouter van Dijk, Joe Chrisman

Programming
Wilco Tomassen

Sensor Technology
Urban Sports Performance Center, Eindhoven, Netherlands

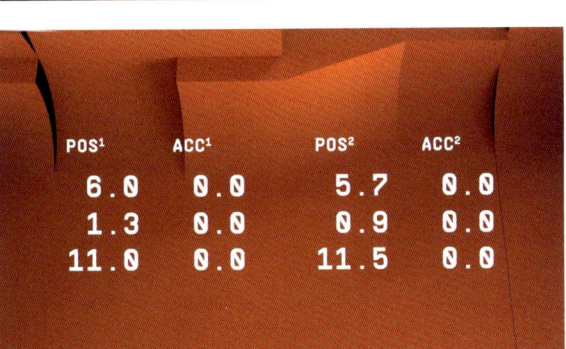
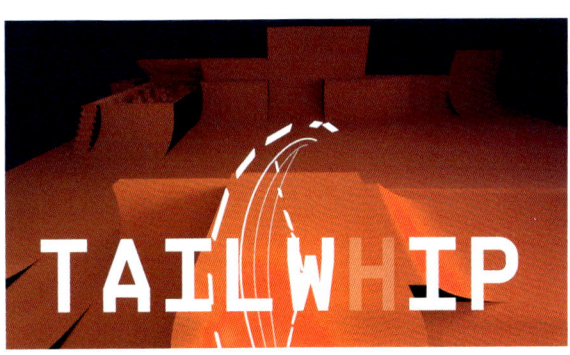

Tech Fair Car 2018 – Hyundai Show Car

[Human-Machine Interface Design]

Client
Hyundai Motor Europe Technical Center GmbH, Rüsselsheim, Germany

Design
innovation mecom GmbH, Fulda, Germany

Art Direction
Björn Grunau, innovation mecom

Electronics System Development
Regina Kaiser, Hyundai

→ Clip online

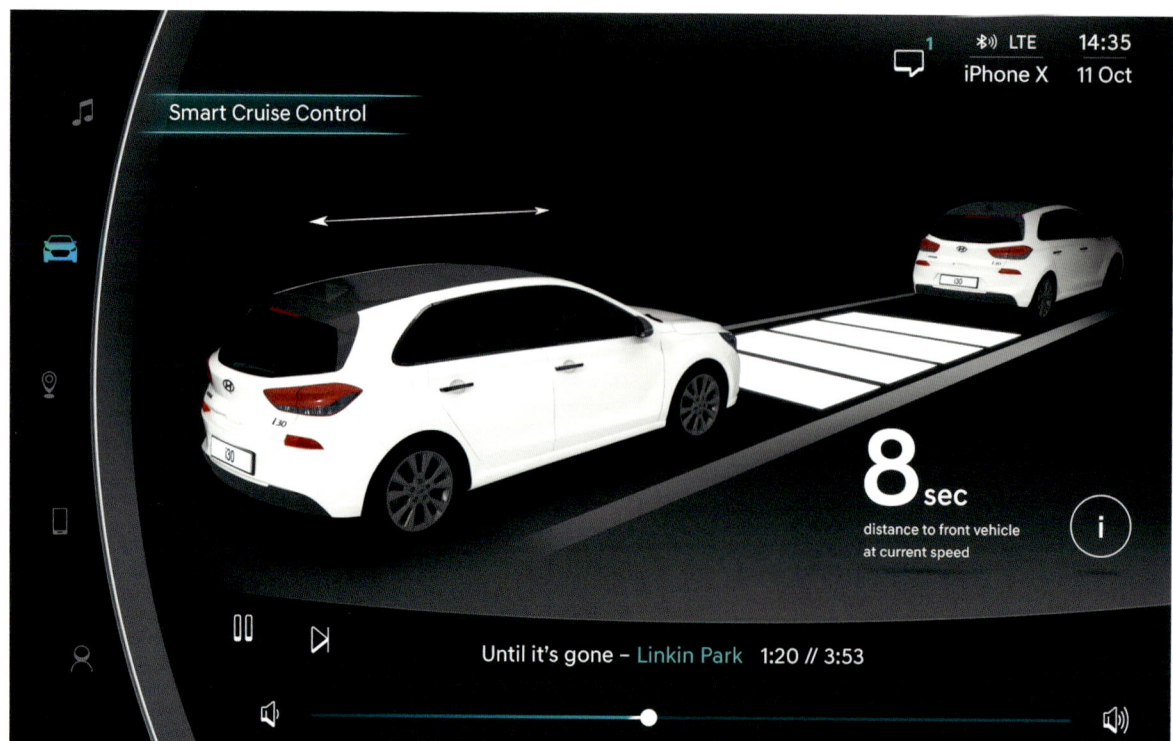

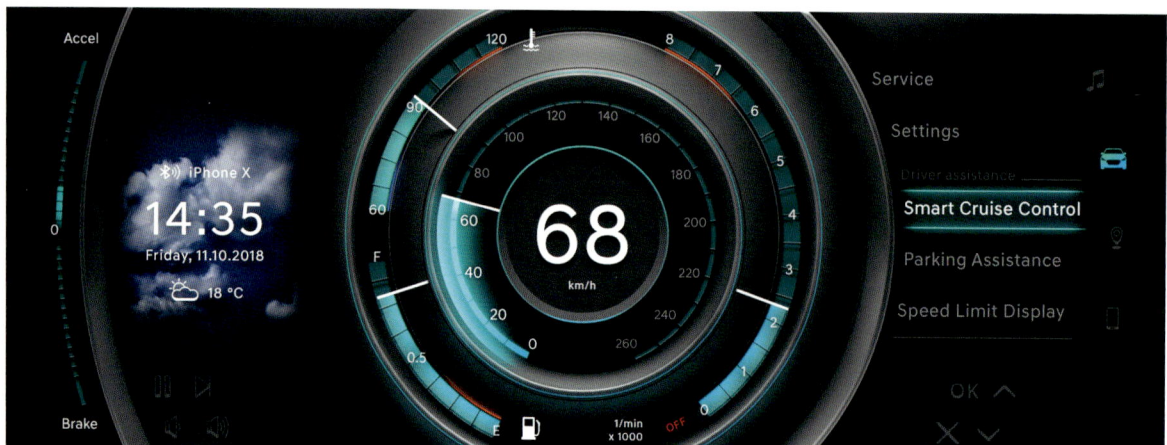

With the HMI design of the Tech Fair Car 2018, the Korean car manufacturer Hyundai was pursuing the goal of creating a 3D viewing experience that increases driving pleasure while ensuring that the driver's concentration stays on the road. It was developed for two steering wheel displays, a 2D Haptic Display and for the Multi-Layer Display with a 3D effect resulting from the superimposition of two display levels. The HMI design is highly user-oriented and characterised by the harmonious interaction of the technical components.

Infotainment System for Lynk & Co 02

[User Interface Design, Infotainment System]

The infotainment system for Lynk & Co 02 offers users an immersive sensory experience. Thanks to its integrated Internet connection, it provides information, entertainment features and convenient apps, which run smoothly and are regularly adjusted to user needs. Taking up on the comprehensive media approach, the user interface skilfully combines reduced graphics with high-resolution photos. Equipped with AI voice technology, the system learns to adapt to the user with each use.

Client
ECARX Co., Ltd., Hangzhou, China

Design
ECARX DESIGN, Hangzhou, China

Wells – The ONE Water Purifier

[User Experience Design]

The water purifier features a circular touch control panel with LCD display that turns operating it into a sensual experience. In the left circular segment, users can control the water temperature in six steps from cold to boiling. The water flow is adjustable from 120 to 1,000 ml by a touch on the right side of the circle. The temperature and the flow rate are shown on the display and visualised by a colour scheme from pastel to black. In addition, a fine, raised line on each of the touch areas provides users with tactile orientation when tracing the circular shape with their finger.

Client
Kyowon, Wells Design Lab,
Seoul, South Korea

Design
Kyowon, Wells Design Lab,
Seoul, South Korea

Water Heater PRO UI

[User Interface Design]

Water Heater PRO UI is an interface for electronic water heaters and has been designed to ensure smart, convenient and energy-efficient operation. According to the concept of "smart cloud bathing", the interface can learn individual user preferences with regard to bathing temperature and water volume at different times and then set the desired parameters automatically. This eliminates the need for users to repeatedly adjust the temperature, which provides for a comfortable experience. The TFT panel with LED display clearly presents all values and allows intuitive input.

Client
Haier Group, Qingdao, China

Design
Haier Innovation Design Center, Qingdao, China

Design Team
Sun Yan, Shi Yang, Li Pengfei, Han Cong, Sun Luning, Wang Qiaoqiao

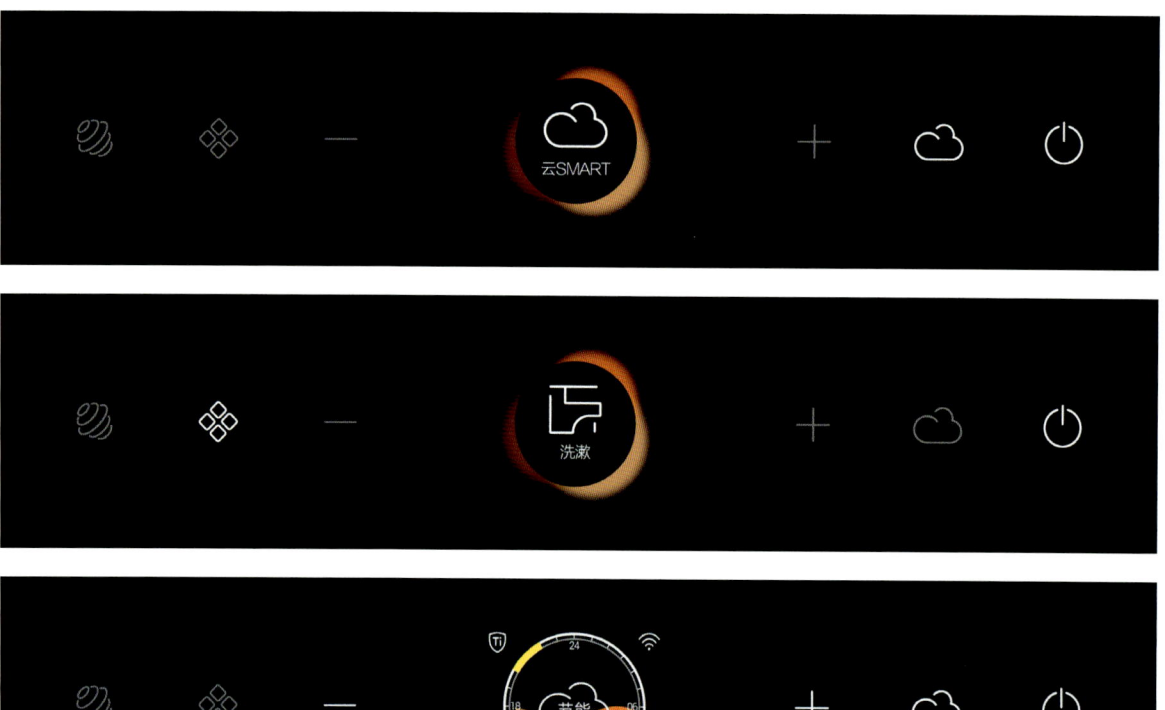

CT5 UI

[User Interface Design]

The CT5 UI user interface is based on a study that examined the lifestyle of people who use gas water heaters. It is designed to offer solutions to key user needs, including smart temperature control, appropriate water volume, safety, visual intuition and convenient operation. These demands were implemented in a user interface that presents different showering and bathing scenarios, including bathtub water draining, on an intuitive and dynamic display. This ensures a convenient operation and offers a self-sufficient visual experience.

Client
Haier Group, Qingdao, China

Design
Haier Innovation Design Center, Qingdao, China

Design Team
Sun Yan, Wang Xingcan, Li Pengfei, Han Cong, Wang Qiaoqiao, Zhang Wenqi

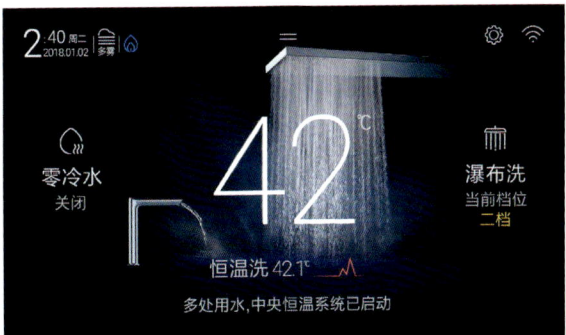

LG HomeBrew

[User Interface Design]

With HomeBrew, users can brew a variety of beers at home by combining capsules with different types of hops and flavours. The product comprises a colour LCD, function knobs, a cover for filling in capsules and water, as well as a tap handle for pouring the beer. The entire brewing process is visualised through appealing graphics on the LCD that inform users about the status of the natural fermentation and thus shorten the waiting time. Alternatively, the brewing process can be monitored via the mobile app.

Client
LG Electronics Inc., Seoul, South Korea

Design
LG Electronics Inc., Seoul, South Korea

Design Team
Jeyeol Lee, Hyeonna Han, Youngji Kim, Meeyeon Choi, Mimi Bae, Eunyeong Kim, Min A Suh, Jeongin Park, Raehoon Kang, Seojin Lee, Inyoung Hwang, Kyungmin Lee

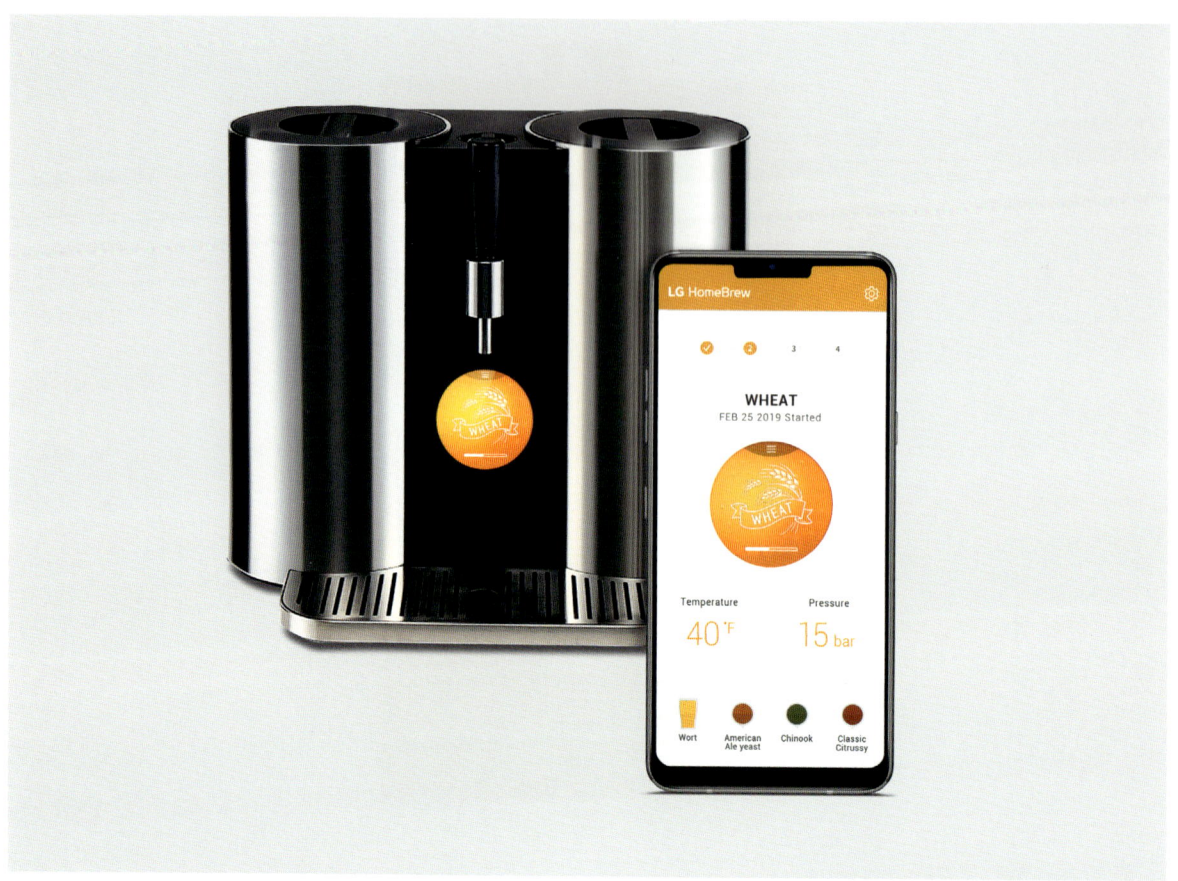
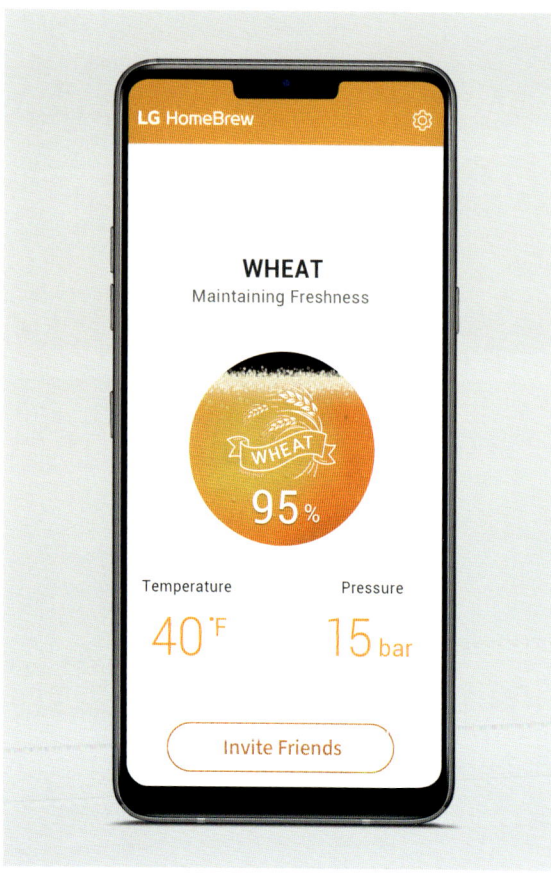

Thermomix TM6

[User Experience Design]

The Thermomix TM6 features new cooking functions, a high-resolution touch screen and an optimised user interface with a clear design that delivers a seamless user experience. The integrated recipe platform Cookidoo offers 50,000 recipes, which can be accessed from the core cooking menu with a single swipe. Thanks to the recipes being clustered by topic and the search function featuring numerous filters, users can easily find the right recipe. In addition, they are led step by step through the recipes by the guided-cooking function to guarantee a successful cooking experience.

Client
Vorwerk International & Co. KmG, Wollerau, Switzerland

Design
User Interface Design GmbH, Ludwigsburg, Germany
intive GmbH, Munich, Germany

User Experience Design
Andreas Uhlenbrock, Sebastian Meyer, Vorwerk International & Co. KmG
Philipp Schröder, Florian Schröder, User Interface Design GmbH (Thermomix)
Johannes Dornisch, Maximilian Schmidt, intive GmbH (Cookidoo)

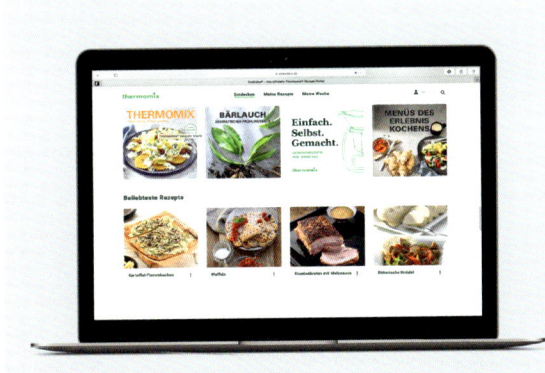
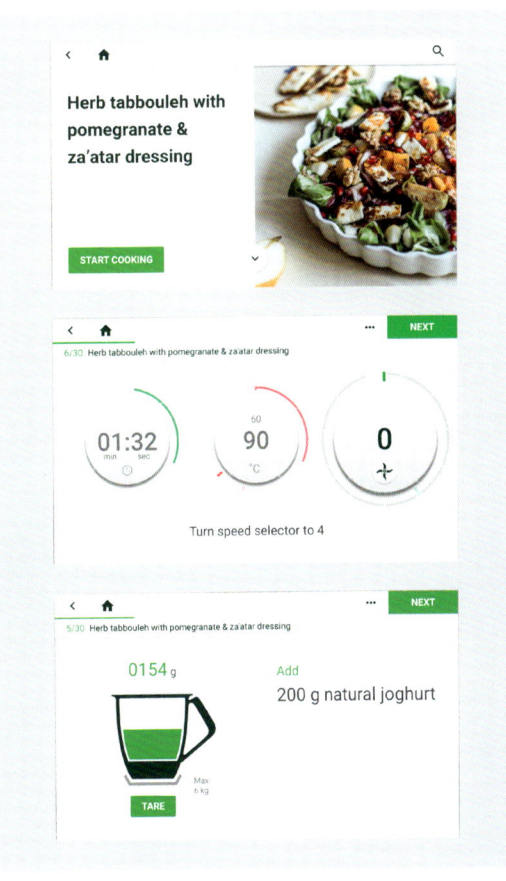
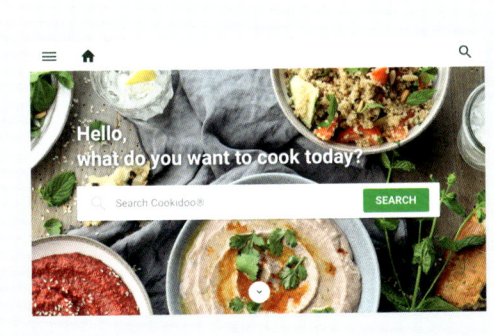

Publishing & Print Media   Posters   Typography   Illustrations   Sound Design   Film & Animation   Online   Apps

FarmRise

[User Experience Design,
User Interface Design]

FarmRise empowers the community of farmers in India when making informed operating and financial decisions. It does so by providing scientific knowledge and by connecting them with the market players, thus eliminating the monopoly of middlemen. Visually it is very simple and easy to use and is modelled on the online usage behaviour of the farmers. It is technically sound and works even in low network zones.

Client
Farmrise, Bangalore, India

Design
Lollypop Design Studio, Bangalore, India

Head of Marketing
Saloni Agarwal

Project Management
Deepa Mani Subbarayan

Illustration
Preethika Asokan

User Experience Design
Rajiv Pennathur

User Interface Design
Jenniffer Sharmila

Editorial Work
Tamilselvan Agarwal

Film Production
Rakesh Kumar, Camberry, Bangalore, India

→ Clip online

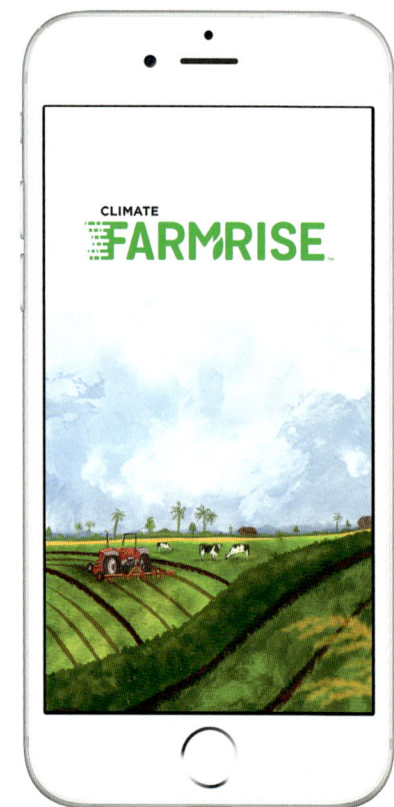

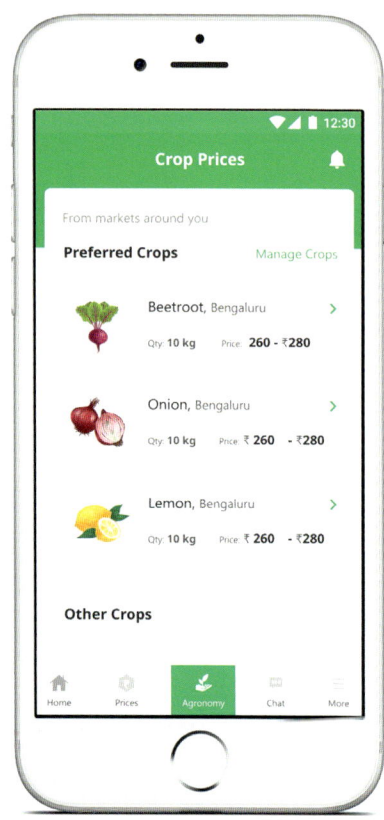

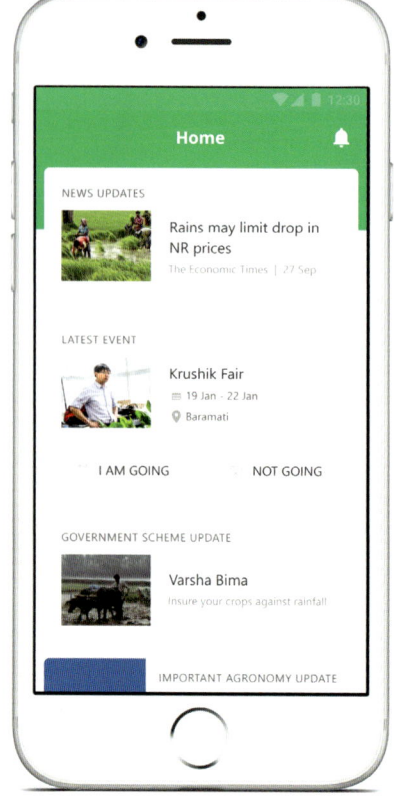

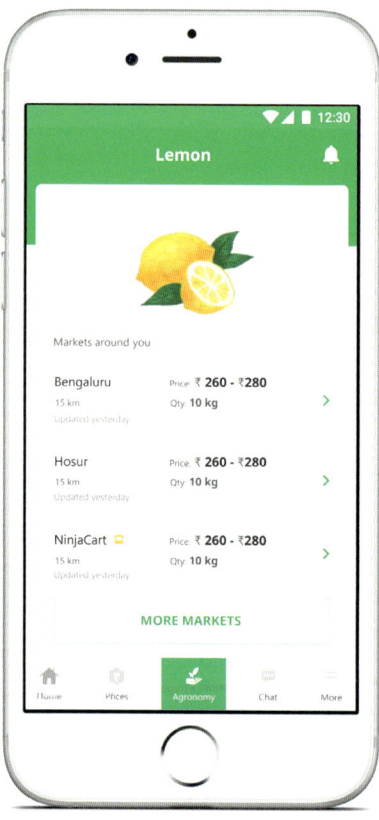

Dishwasher UI
[User Interface Design]

The new user interface of the Haier dishwasher shows a more detailed breakdown of the dishwashing programmes with regard to the item to be cleaned. It differentiates between the two categories of "tableware washing" and "ingredient washing" for cleaning washable foodstuffs such as fruits and vegetables. The two categories are further broken down for example into baby bottles or carrots. The user interface is highly intuitive in use, as it combines photos of the items to be cleaned with the programme selection, so that the single touch of a button suffices to start the desired rinsing cycle.

Client
Haier Group, Qingdao, China

Design
Haier Innovation Design Center,
Qingdao, China

Design Team
Wen Yanbo, Yan Wen, Wang Qiaoqiao,
Sun Luning

Mi Robot Vacuum 1S

[Smart Home Solution]

The intelligent vacuum robot "Mi Robot Vacuum 1S" records data of rooms in a building to create maps of each room and visualise them in an app. Based on these maps, users can specify the areas the vacuum robot should clean. Furthermore, they can group several rooms and define virtual walls and areas that are to be excluded from cleaning. Simultaneously, scenarios can be selected that, for example, determine the suction power or the time of day. The app is designed in a friendly and instantly-to-grasp map style. It is scalable and therefore suitable for different devices.

Client
Beijing Xiaomi Mobile Software Co., Ltd., Beijing, China

Design
Beijing Xiaomi Mobile Software Co., Ltd., Beijing, China

Graphic Design
Ran An

Motion Design
Shuyang Tang

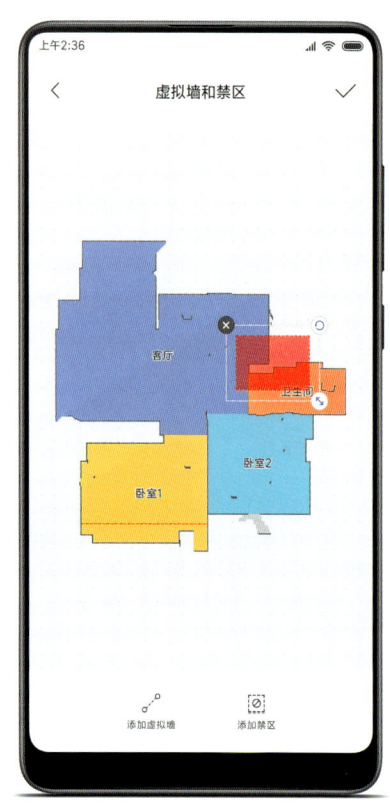

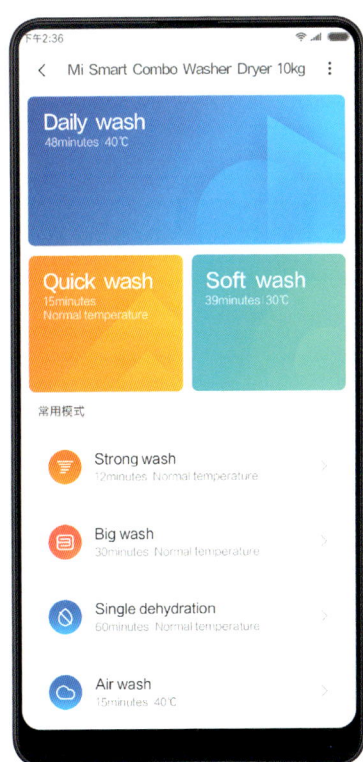

Mi Front-Load Washer and Dryer 10kg Pro
[Smart Home Solution]

Especially young people want a washing machine that is uncomplicated and quick to operate. This demand is satisfied by the Mi Front-Load Washer, as its central touch-dial with OLED display ensures intuitive control. Equipped with sensors to determine time, weight, temperature and current cleaning status, it also offers users the option of controlling the device via the associated mobile app and being informed about the washing process. The consistent graphic design of the user interface facilitates orientation.

Client
Beijing Xiaomi Mobile Software Co., Ltd., Beijing, China

Design
Beijing Xiaomi Mobile Software Co., Ltd., Beijing, China

Graphic Design
Qiqi Cui

Motion Design
Shuyang Tang

Samm – Smart Mirror
[User Interface Design]

Client
Skelter Labs, Seoul, South Korea

Design
Skelter Labs, Seoul, South Korea

Creative Direction
Hyosang Hwang

Strategic Planning
Jayoung Kim

User Interface Design
Jinha Sung, Ziye Han, Haeyeon Lee

Motion Design
Chaeyoung Kim

Project Management
Ahyoung Kim, Sungbo Jung

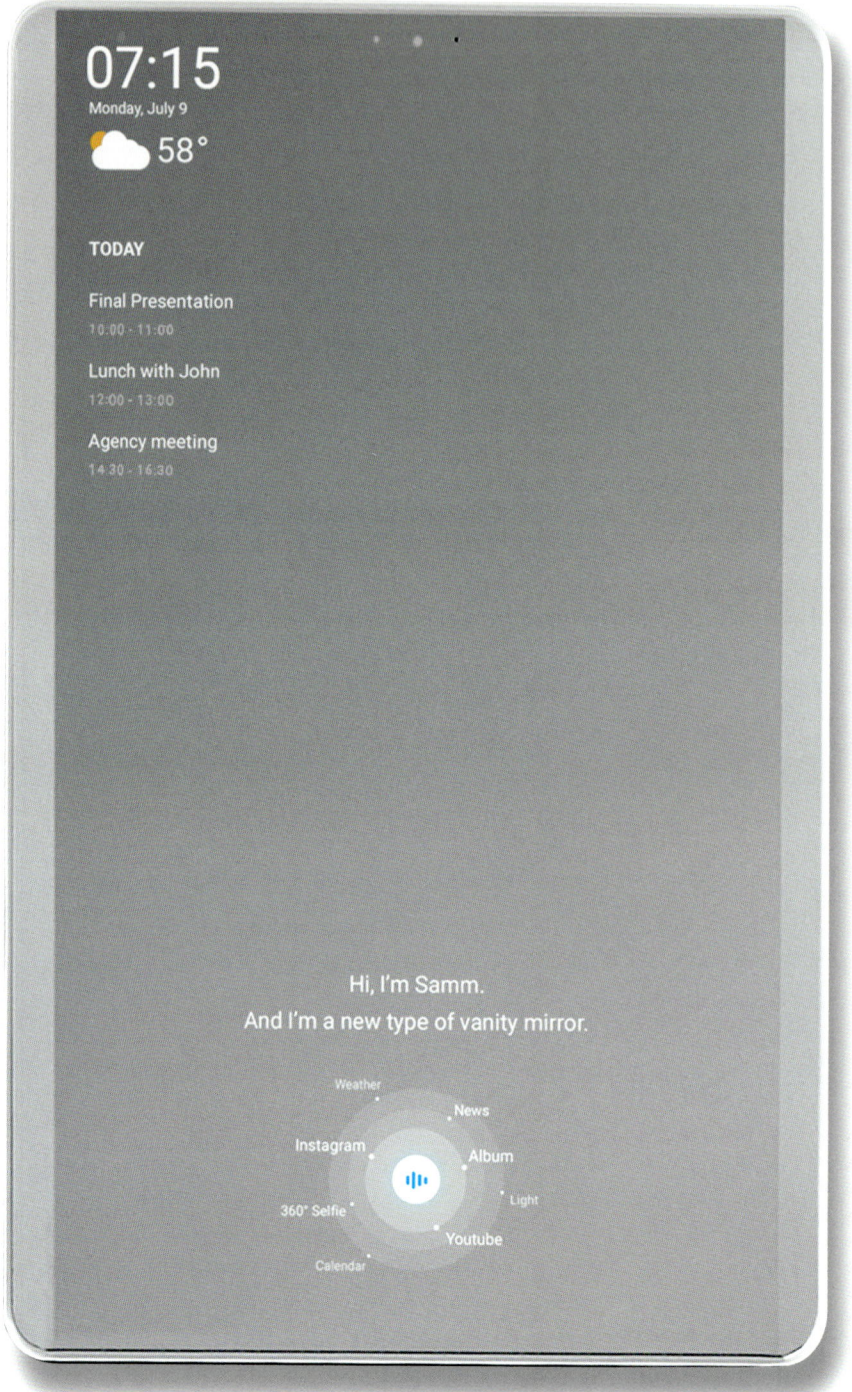

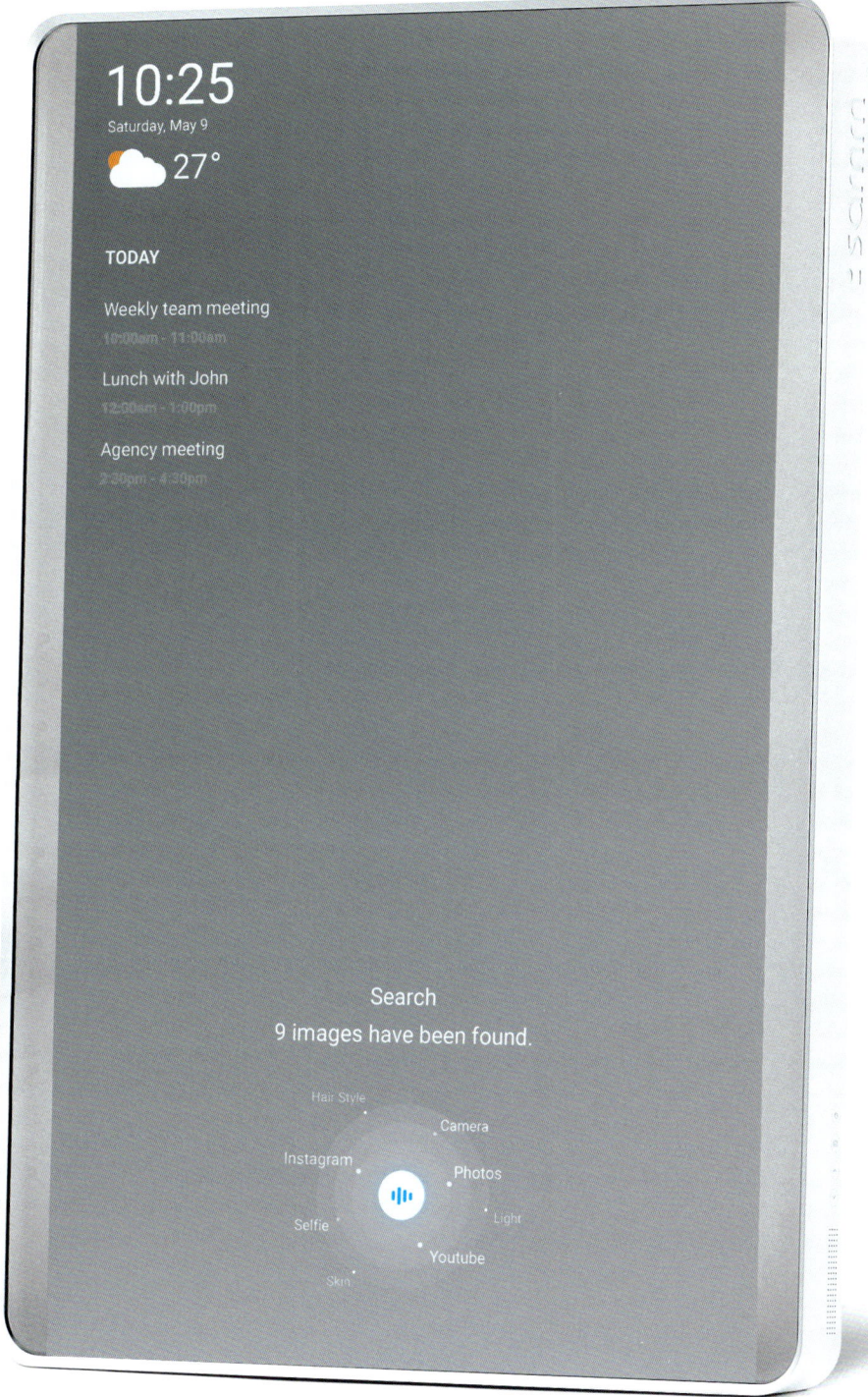

Samm is an elegant make-up mirror for female millennials, featuring a minimalist UX that shows content in context. All controls, including access to apps like YouTube and Instagram, are operated via voice control and touch-free gestures. This prevents the mirror from getting stained by fingerprints. Another key feature of the mirror is the camera with facial recognition, which can analyse the condition of the skin, give make-up tips and allows taking 360-degree shots that are accessible via app even when on the go.

Publishing & Print Media   Posters   Typography   Illustrations   Sound Design   Film & Animation   Online   Apps

Emergency Management Platform

[Screen Design, Website, App]

The Emergency Management Platform has been developed to predict critical situations at large gatherings or in the event of natural disasters, in order to be able to take appropriate actions. The platform offers a map-centric, dynamic layout that highlights important information in real time. This enables users to quickly recognise where action is needed and to react immediately. The sophisticated and uniform design is characterised by clear graphics and easy-to-understand icons that ensure the overview despite an abundance of data.

Client
China Mobile (Hangzhou) Information Technology, Hangzhou, China

Design
China Mobile (Hangzhou) Information Technology, Hangzhou, China

Design Team
Congshan Zheng, Junwu Gao, Jiaxi Wang, Yuchun Wang, Mingshuai Qi, Zifu Huang, Han Wu, Yongfu Sheng

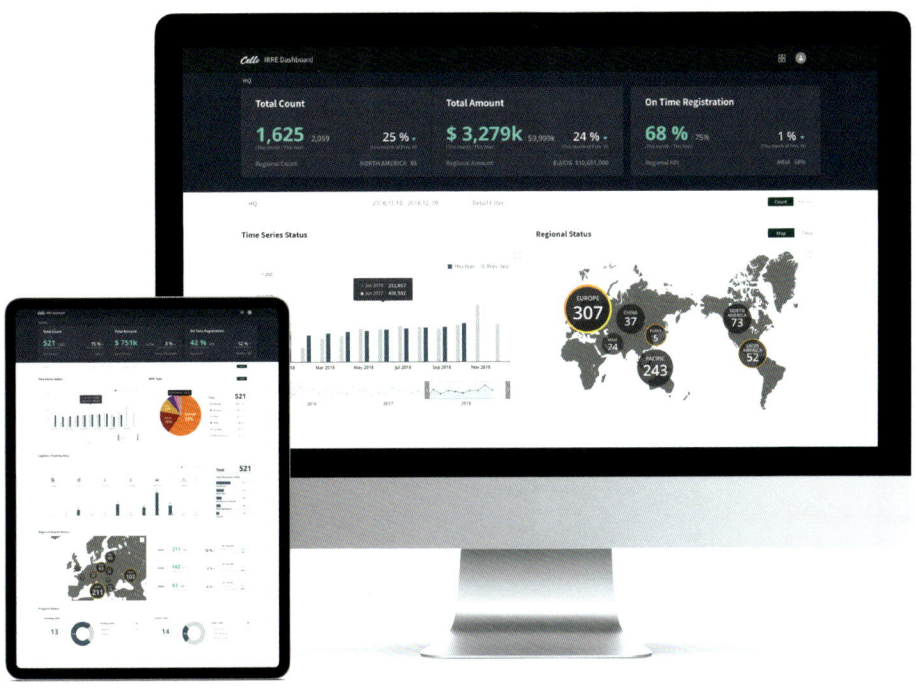

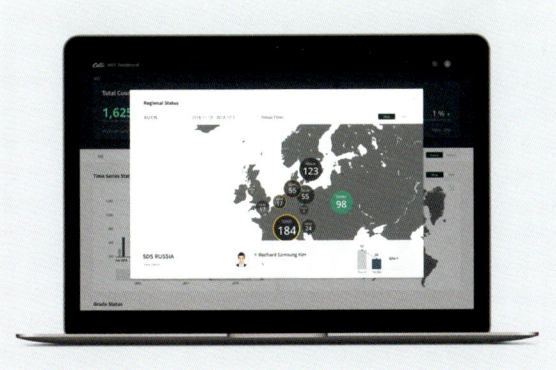
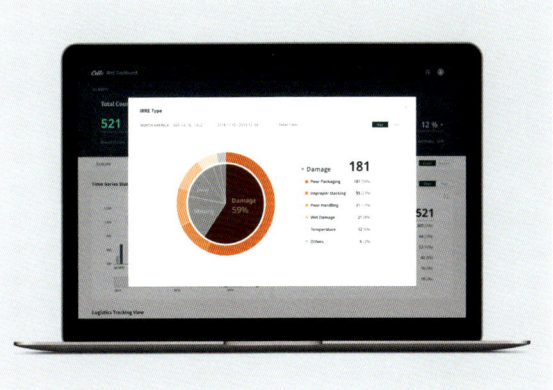

Logistics Risk Watcher

[User Interface Design,
User Experience Design]

Logistics Risk Watcher is a tailored dashboard system that helps predict complex irregular situations (IRRE) in the global logistics process, such as theft, loss or accidents. It collects data of logistical processes and presents them in easy-to-read diagrams – in both bar charts and pie charts. This enables logistics managers to identify abnormalities in the entire transport chain at a glance, or to offer an optimised logistics service to end-customers, by suggesting transport routes that are less prone to cause delays, for example.

Client
Samsung SDS, Seoul, South Korea

Design
Samsung SDS, CX Innovation Team, Seoul, South Korea

Creative Direction
Jungwon Kim

Digital Concept
Sungyun Jo

Graphic Design
Suran Leem

→ Clip online

GroupUI
[Design System]

GroupUI is a holistic, multi-brand design system that makes designing internal applications more efficient and user-friendly. It offers a growing library of UX principles, icons and responsive UI components. It is driven by a user-centred design approach to meet the demands of different business units, user groups and project scenarios. The overall design strategy enables the agile collaboration of interdisciplinary product teams and helps experts focus on their specific tasks.

Client
Volkswagen AG, Wolfsburg, Germany

Design
MHP Management- und
IT-Beratung GmbH,
Ludwigsburg, Germany

General Management
Thorsten Jankowski (Product Owner),
Volkswagen AG
Dr. Jan Wehinger, MHP

Design Direction
Thorsten Jankowski, Volkswagen AG
Moritz Papenfuß, MHP

Creative Direction
Niclas Bauermeister, Marcel Tobien, MHP

Design Team
Nicole Aue, Rebecca Davis, Finn Quoos,
Nadja Teichmann, MHP
Katharina Heide, Lydia Lütgering,
Xingjian Mao, Volkswagen AG

Technical Direction
Thorsten Jankowski, Tayfun Gülcan,
Volkswagen AG

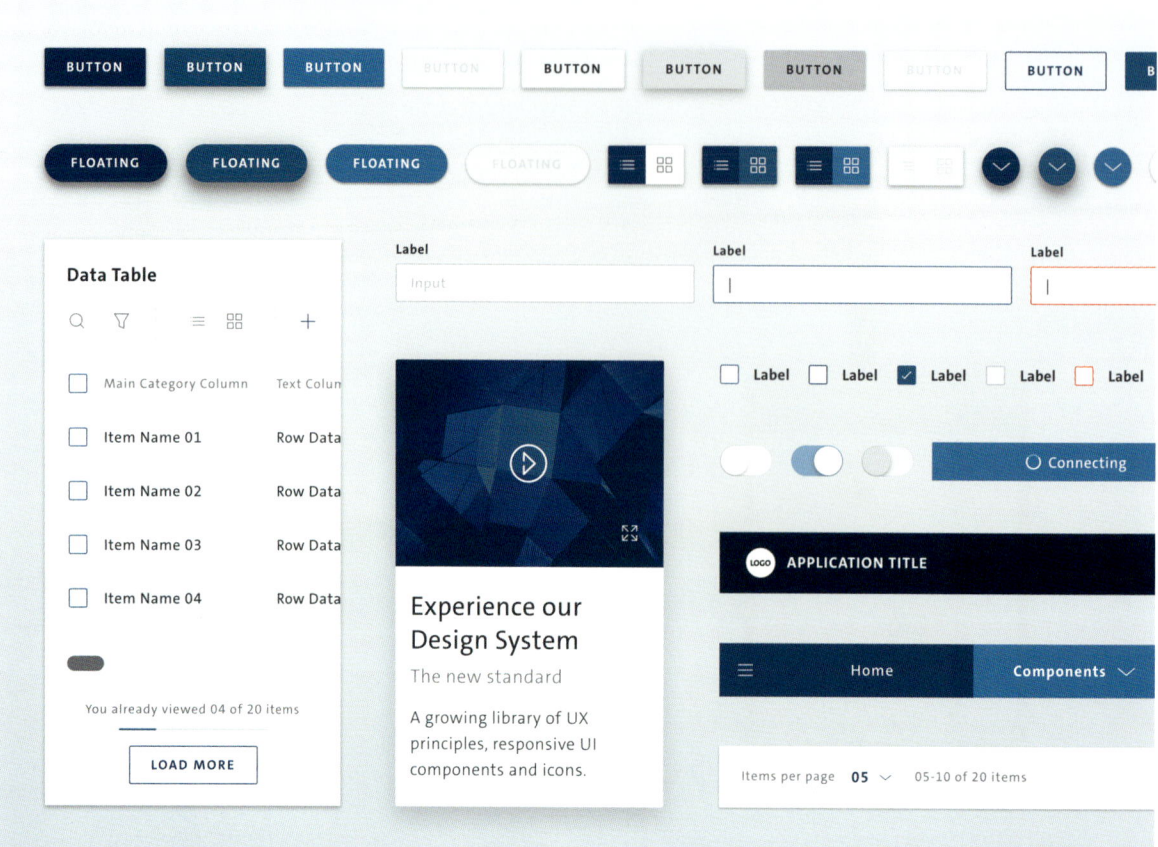
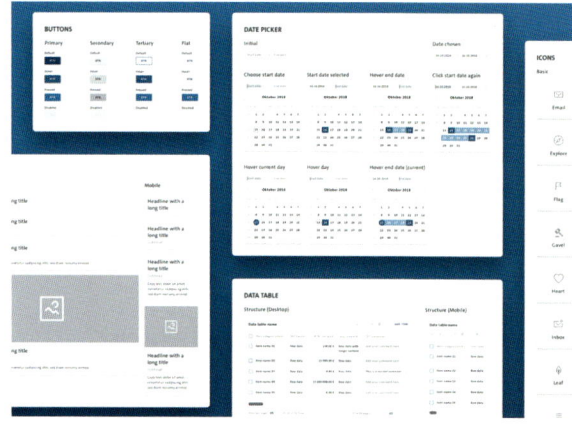

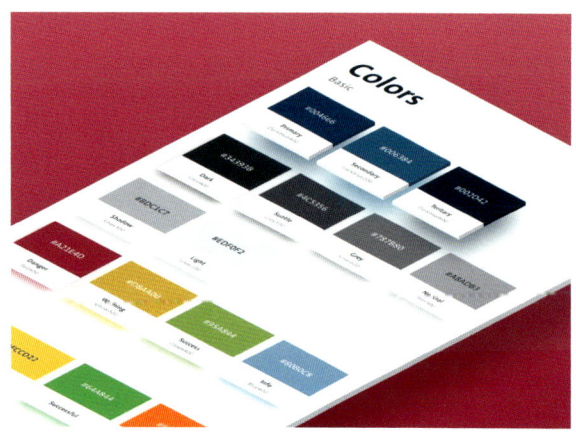
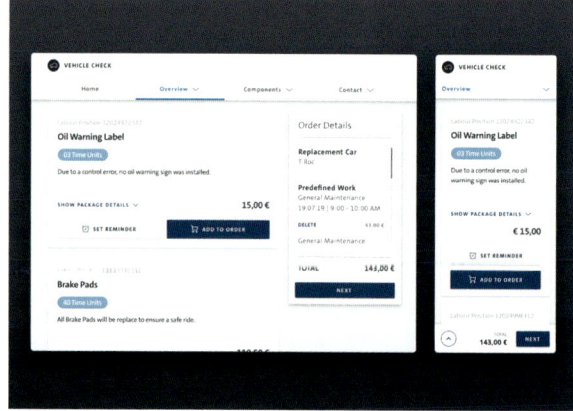

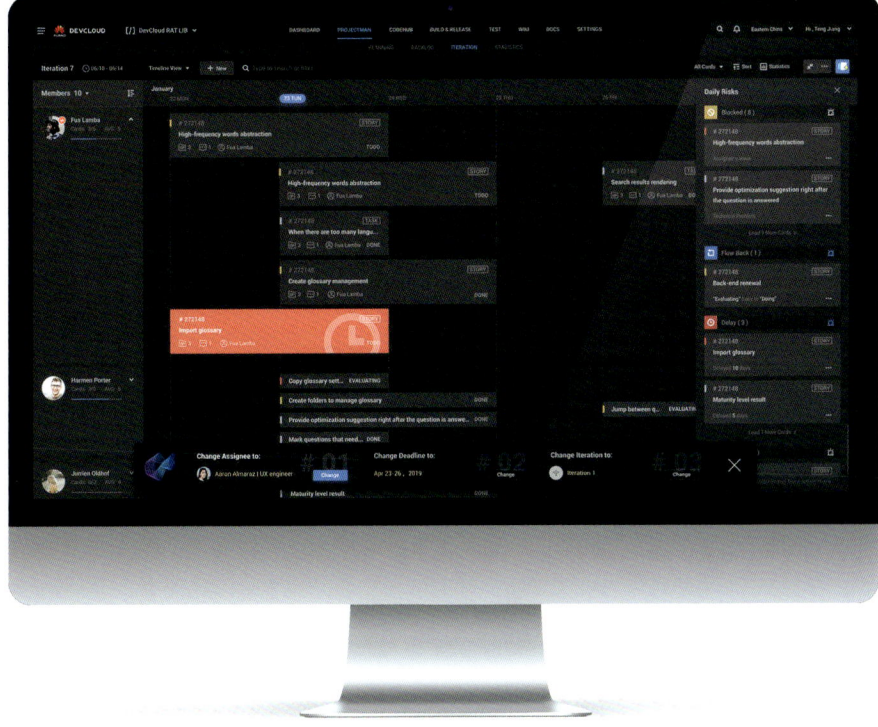

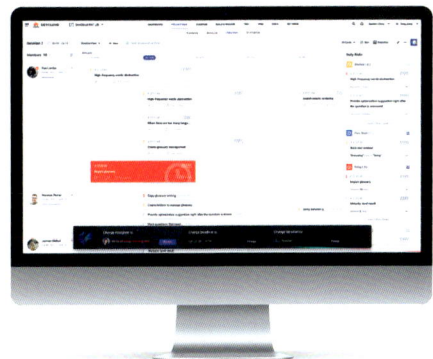

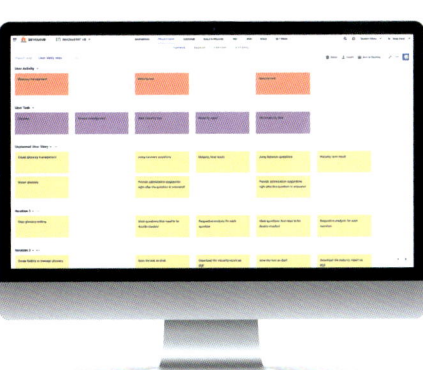

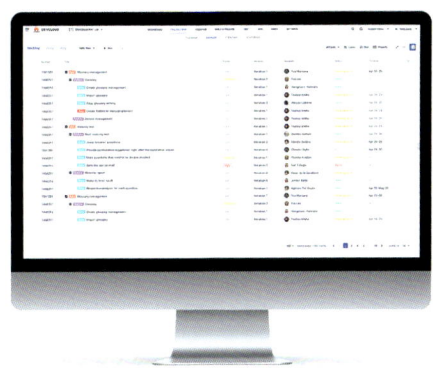

ProjectMan – Huawei DevCloud

[User Experience Design]

ProjectMan helps software project teams to plan their projects entirely in the cloud, providing efficient coordination services, including multi-project document management. It supports acknowledged methods such as Impact Map, User Story Map, Scrum and Kanban, and is thus particularly suitable for agile development teams. The user interface is tailored to the diverse tasks of project planning and provides different views such as table, timeline or maps, which can be adapted and complemented with additional properties.

Client
Huawei Technologies Co., Ltd., Shenzhen, China

Design
Huawei Technologies Co., Ltd., Shenzhen, China

Web Design
Hao Yan, Lezhi Su, Jianci Wang, Xing Ming, Zhanghong Wu

→ Designer profile on page 531

Publishing & Print Media   Posters   Typography   Illustrations   Sound Design   Film & Animation   Online   Apps

ADITO 2019
[User Experience Design]

The CRM system was designed with the idea of providing a platform that enables every user to fulfil their tasks in an efficient manner. The intuitive software dispenses with pop-up windows and complicated data entry fields, thus offering high efficiency. All users log in via a personalised screen and are greeted by a dashboard displaying all essential information, including daily tasks, appointments and recent activities. Thanks to its exceptional user friendliness, ADITO not only ensures high user acceptance, but also reduces training costs.

Client
ADITO Software GmbH,
Geisenhausen, Germany

Design
ADITO Software GmbH,
Geisenhausen, Germany

→ Designer profile on page 510
→ Clip online

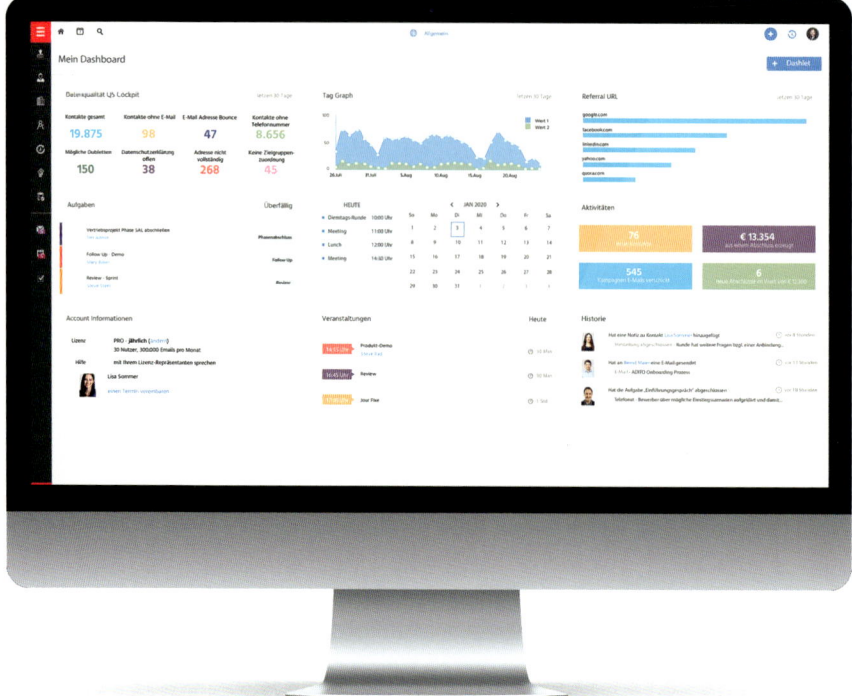

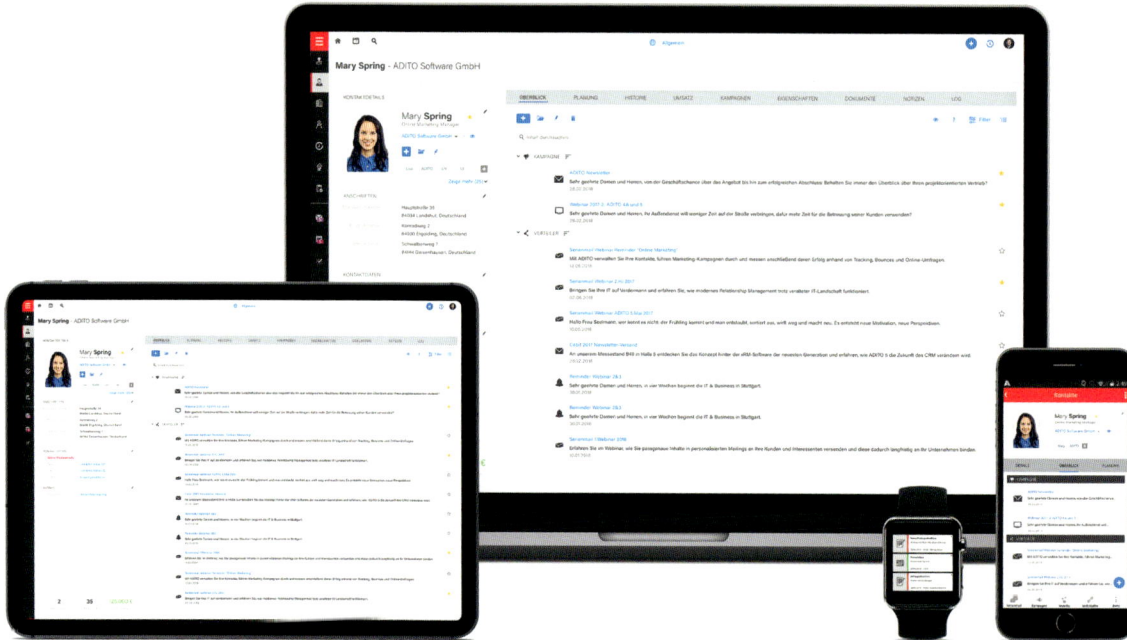

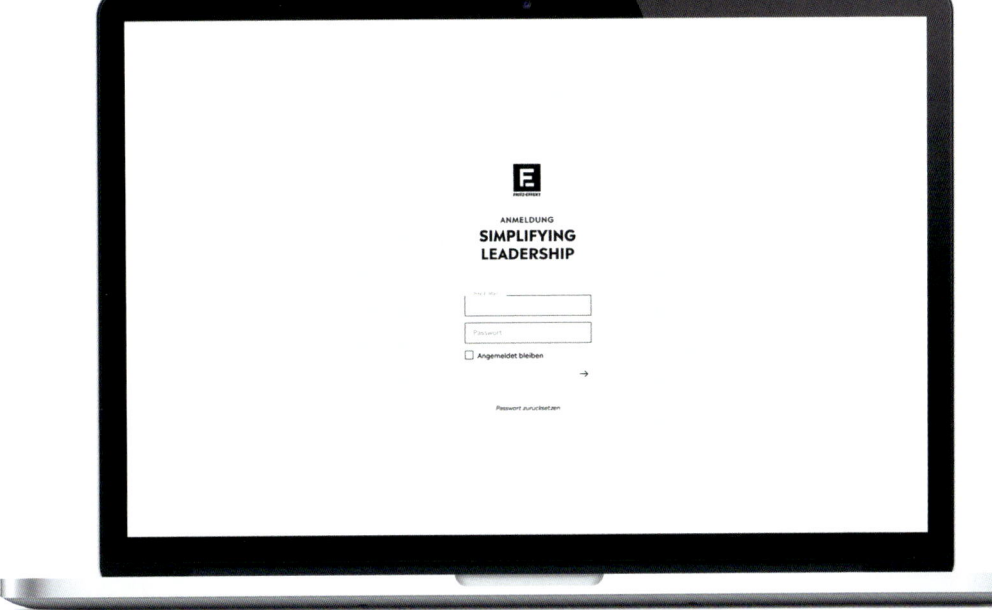

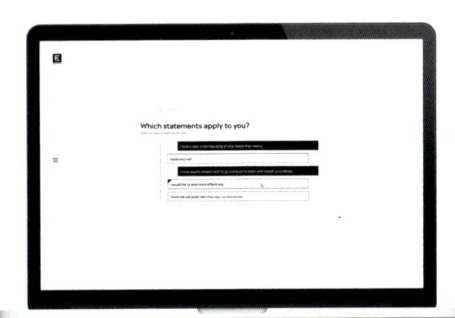

K7-LOGIX

[User Interface Design]

K7-LOGIX is an innovative web-based audit tool designed to simplify leadership. Participants are guided through various online modules with up to 1,000 questions and tasks, which lead them to identify and improve their personal strengths. To increase the users' focus, the platform implements colourful and mood-stimulating elements based on findings from psychological research. The intuitive and minimalist design of the interface ensures that the tool can be operated without previous knowledge.

Client
Fritz-Effekt Unternehmerberatung GmbH, Dortmund, Germany

Design
WAYS GmbH, Dortmund, Germany
brandneo GmbH, Dortmund, Germany

Project Management
Ruben Dahmen, WAYS

Technical Direction
Stephan Führer, brandneo

Creative Direction
Nina Staiger, WAYS
Juliane Galla, brandneo

Web Design
Till Grzegorczyk, brandneo

Account Management
Sebastian Galla, brandneo

Publishing & Print Media Posters Typography Illustrations Sound Design Film & Animation Online Apps

meinMVP – Broker Management Program

[Screen Design]

meinMVP is a web-based broker management program that bundles many business processes for brokerage in one digital workflow-based user interface. The design and functionality follow a dynamic concept, oriented towards the requirements of the market through the iterative integration of user feedback. The program is marked by a clear design and intuitive user guidance that facilitate customer relationship management, customer management and communications.

Client
VHV Allgemeine Versicherung AG,
Hannover, Germany

Design
digital broking GmbH,
Hannover, Germany

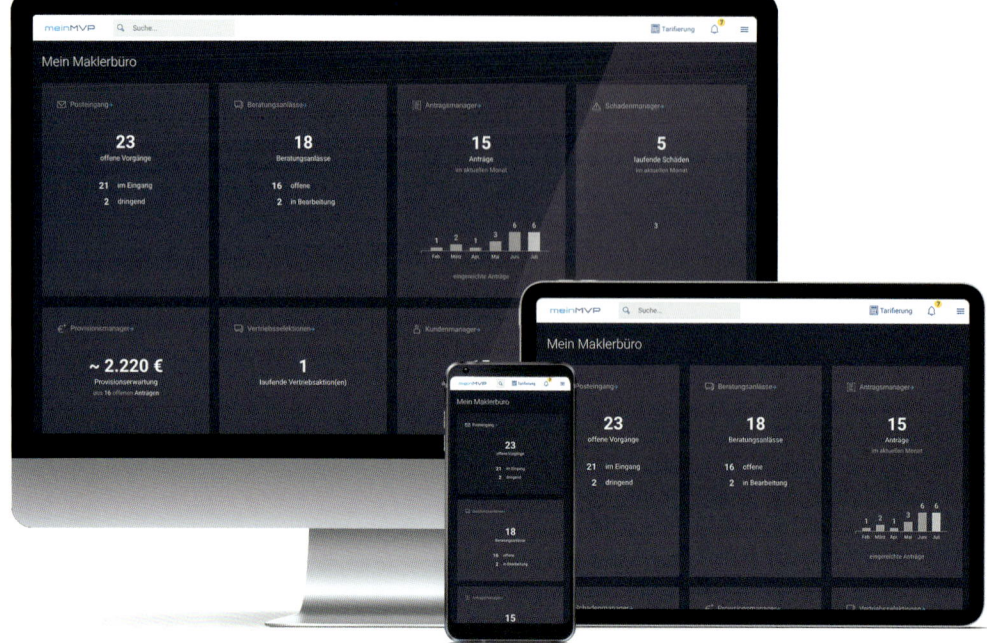

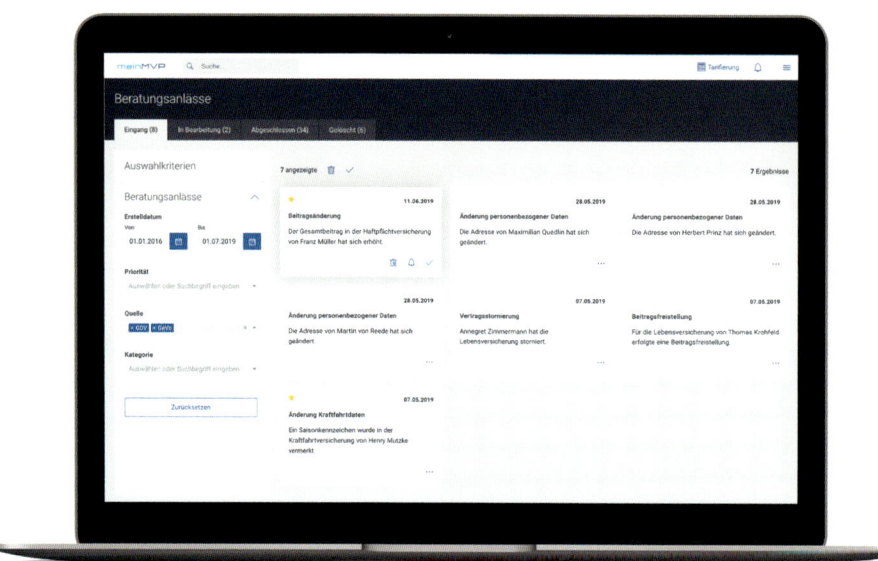

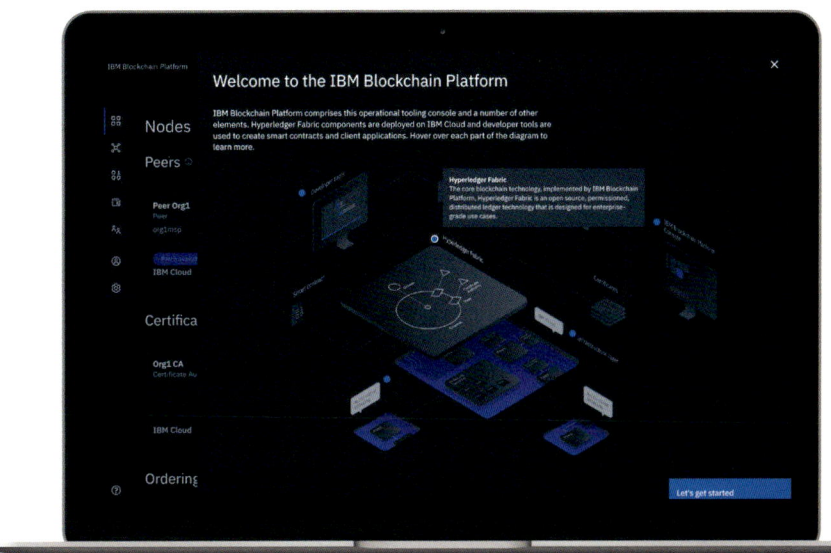

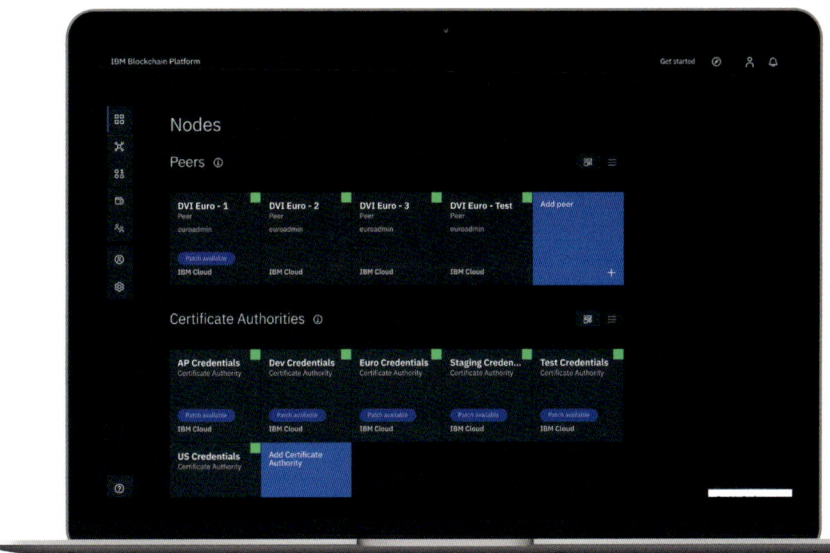

IBM Blockchain Platform

[Service Design]

The IBM Blockchain Platform simplifies the development, governance and operation of a decentralised network across multiple companies or institutions forming a business ecosystem. The managed software-as-a-service solution supports and guides users through all the required stages for launching a blockchain network: building and testing proof-of-concept applications in a pre-production environment, activating a production network, establishing flexible governance policies for network members, and managing daily operations with a high level of security and performance.

Client
IBM Cloud in Research Triangle Park, North Carolina, USA

Design
IBM Studios in Research Triangle Park, North Carolina, USA
IBM Studios Hursley Park, Winchester, United Kingdom

Publishing & Print Media   Posters   Typography   Illustrations   Sound Design   Film & Animation   Online   Apps

Kitcast

[User Interface Design, Digital Signage]

The Kitcast digital signage software helps to plan, create and manage content on business screens run on AppleTV or Android. The user interface is characterised by a minimalist design that can be operated easily by anyone, including people without a technical background. All elements can be moved and rearranged via drag-and-drop, with numerous design templates being available and even original layouts easy to integrate. Advanced mouse-over menu functions ensure a smooth, intuitive operation.

Client
Kitcast Inc., Wilmington, Delaware, USA

Design
Kitcast Inc., San Francisco, USA

Chief Executive Officer
Egor Belenkov

Chief Product Officer
Alexey Chirva

Art Direction/Digital Product Design
Denis Rostolopa

Technical Direction
Alexander Chirva, Vitaliy Domnikov

→ Clip online

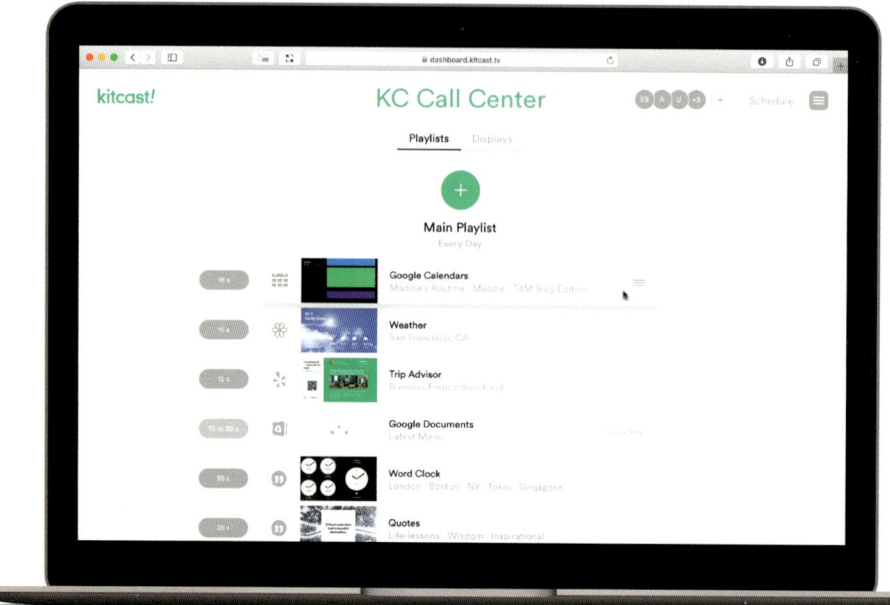

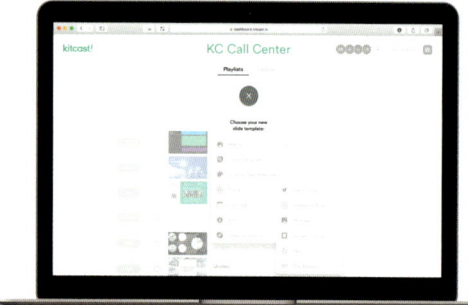
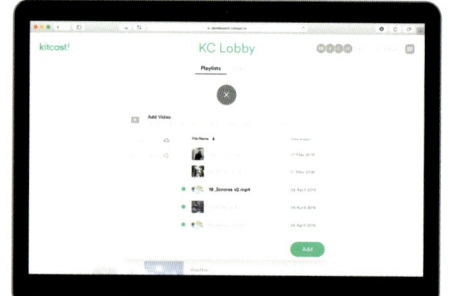
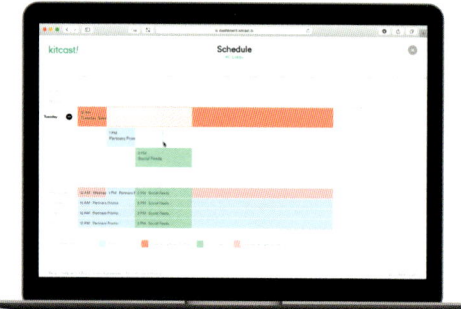
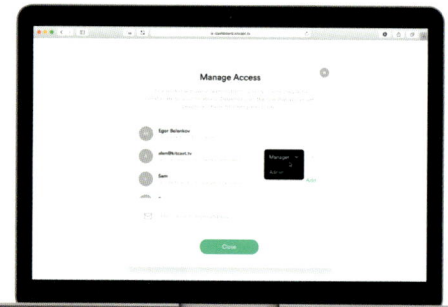

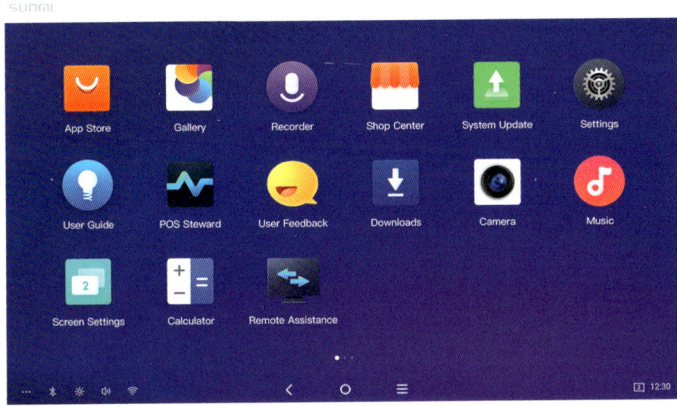

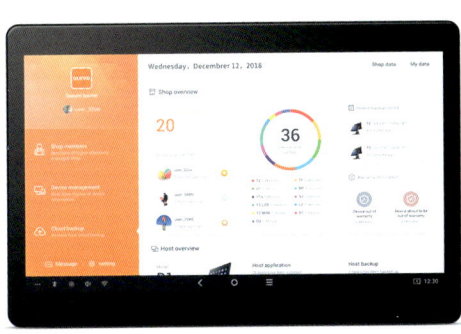

Sunmi OS
[Operation System
for Business Applications]

Sunmi OS is an operating system tailored to POS devices. The sleek platform allows the installation of apps for end users as well as uploading software development tools. Since it has been developed on the basis of Android, users will find a familiar layout, allowing immediate operation without learning. The operating modules have been integrated into the operating system so that more screen space is available for business applications. Moreover, in combination with a responsive design, it is suitable for all screen sizes.

Client
Shanghai Sunmi Technology Co., Ltd., Shanghai, China

Design
Sunmi Design Center, Shanghai, China

Brand Dialog
[Collaboration Tool]

Client
Deutsche Telekom AG, Bonn, Germany

Design
Deutsche Telekom AG, Bonn, Germany
upside relationship marketing GmbH,
Cologne, Germany

Project Management
upside relationship marketing GmbH

→ Clip online

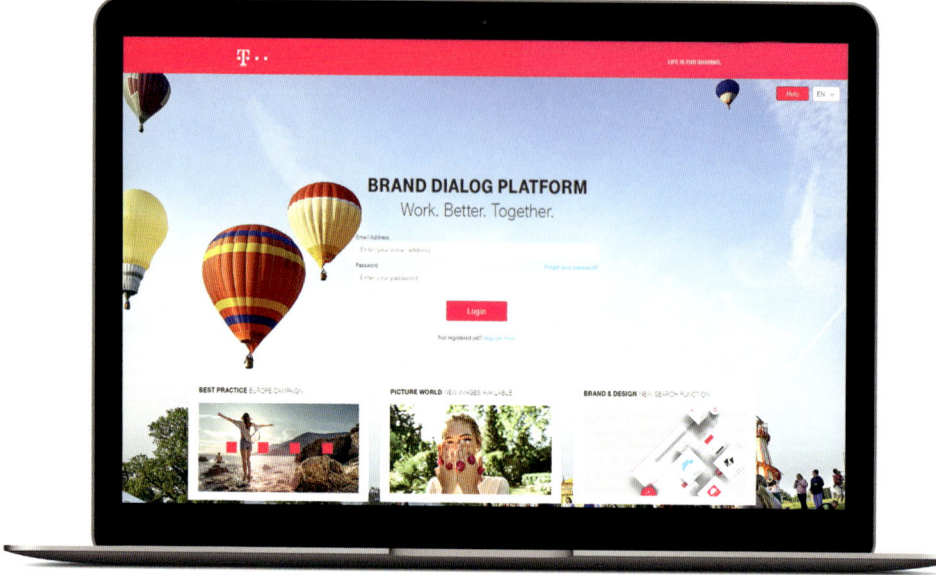

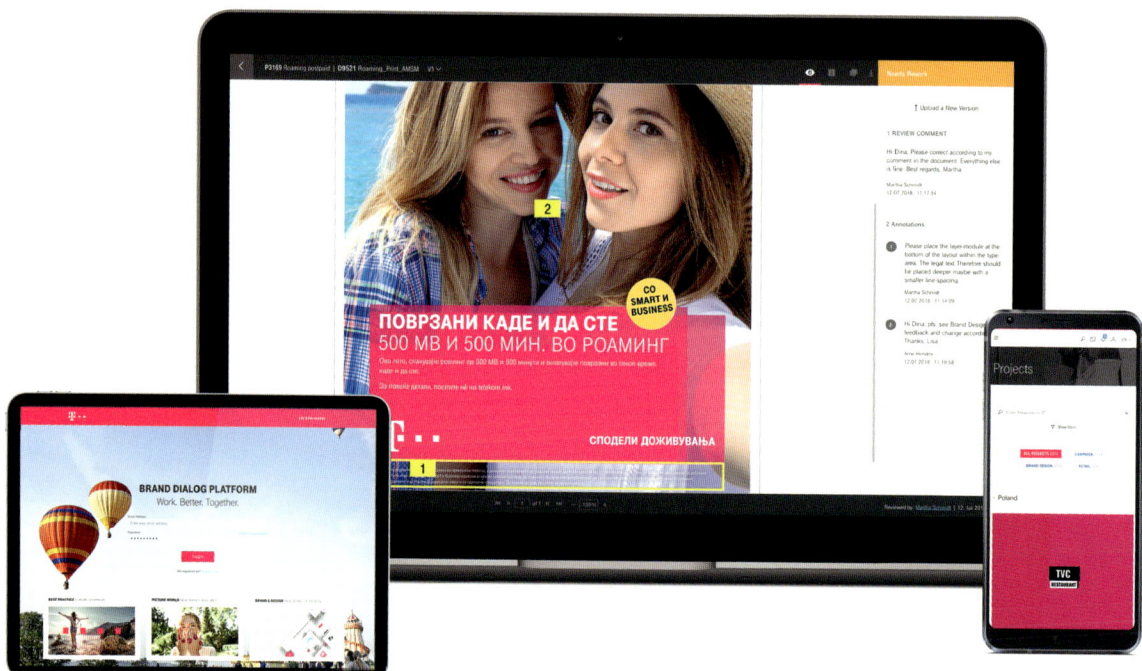

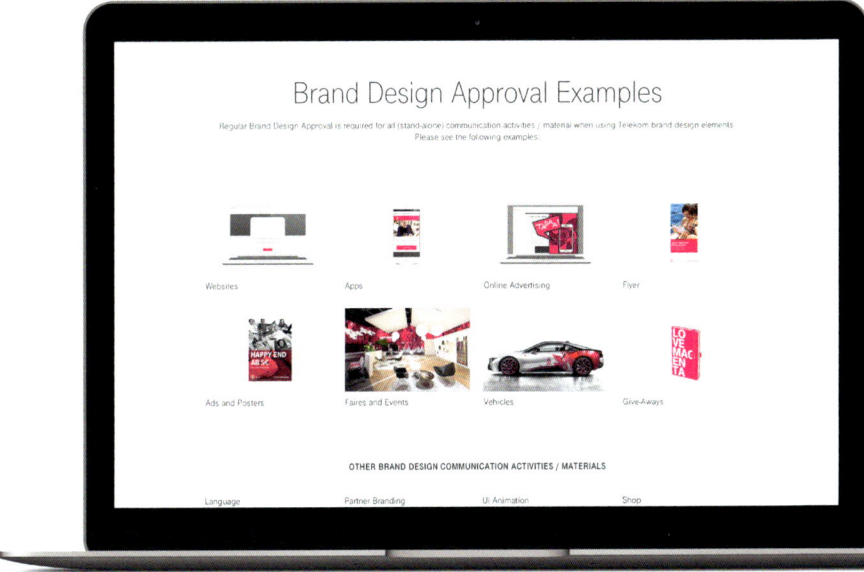

Deutsche Telekom developed the "Brand Dialog" collaboration tool for the planning and management of group-wide marketing activities. It supports all Telekom employees and agencies in their daily work in the fields of communication, brand, design and media. The online platform integrates several tools in a single intuitive workflow application. It simplifies the approval of all communication materials and ensures a uniform brand presence throughout the group. In addition, the active exchange of customer insights and best practice examples guarantees better and more efficient collaboration.

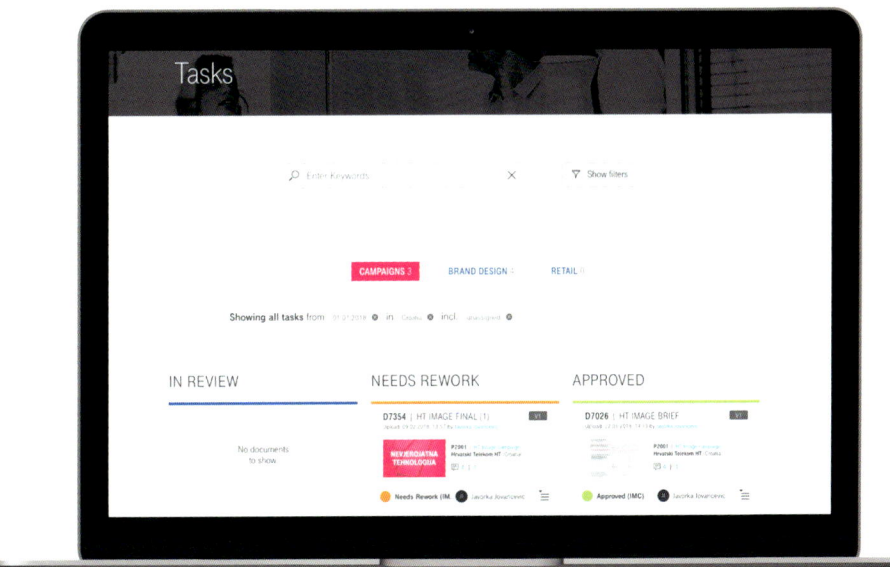

AIQ Talk

[User Interface Design]

Many industries and service areas make use of so-called conversation agents, virtual dialogue partners who answer user questions such as during museum tours. AIQ Talk is a powerful and user-friendly tool for creating such an agent, that allows software developers and UX designers to work together on a project incorporating user requirements and providing a pleasant user experience. The program is relatively easy to use and supports complex tasks, thus significantly simplifying designing a conversation agent.

Client
Skelter Labs, Seoul, South Korea

Design
Skelter Labs, Seoul, South Korea

Strategic Planning
Jinha Seong

Creative Direction
Ziye Han

User Interface Design
Ziye Han, Jinha Seong, Daeun Lee

Project Management
Suik Chung

→ Clip online

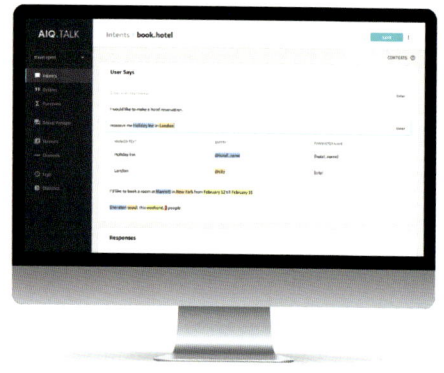
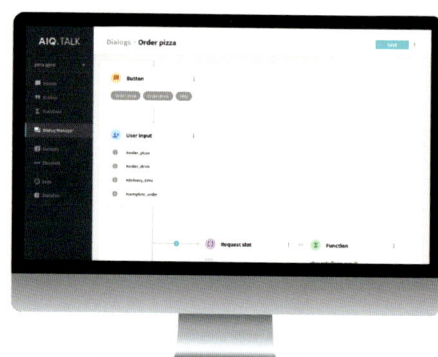
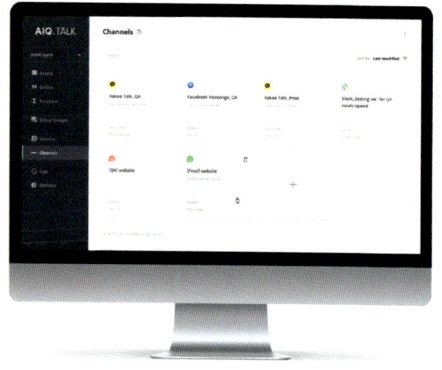
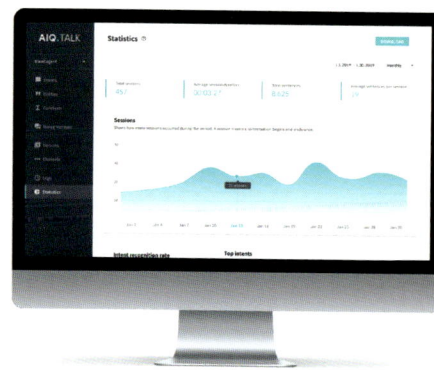

Interface & User Experience Design   Spatial Communication   Red Dot: Junior Award   Designer Profiles   Jury   Index   Red Dot – World of Design

LG Interactive Digital Board (IDB)

[Screen Design]

The LG Interactive Digital Board (IDB) delivers content more efficiently and helps develop ideas in team work more easily through its touch-interactive display. The screen content can be shared with other teams with differing levels of authorisations via "Data Mirroring", which facilitates smooth collaborations and at the same time ensures data security. Contents are displayed without any visual boundaries in fixed box frames. This gives users greater freedom when writing on the display or using the gesture control.

Client
LG Electronics Inc., Seoul, South Korea

Design
LG Electronics Inc., Seoul, South Korea
LG Electronics Inc.,
Santa Clara, California, USA

Graphic Design
Kyoung Eun Hwang, Yong Deok Lee,
Rob Coburn, Helder Silva, Ja Eun Choi

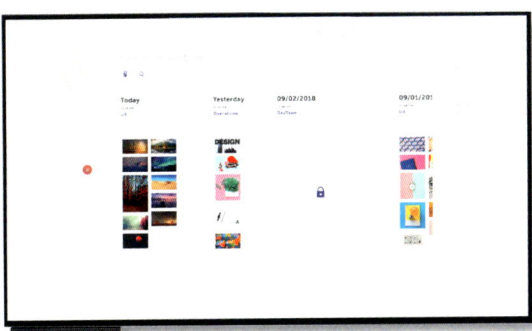

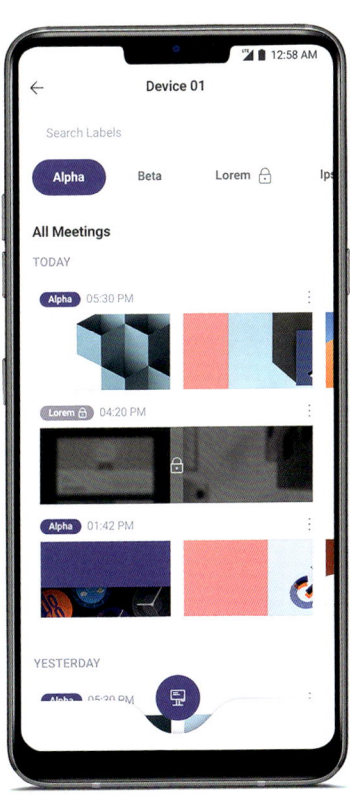

Huawei Telepresence
[Conference User Interface System]

Huawei Telepresence is an intelligent HD videoconferencing system with a functionality geared towards new forms of teamwork. It allows conferencing with partners anywhere and delivers 4K HD video even when bandwidth is limited. The responsive screen can display various media types, which users can view and comment on. The user interface features a minimalist design and can be personalised with dynamic themes, making the system blend seamlessly into modern work environments.

Client
Huawei Technologies Co., Ltd., Shenzhen, China

Design
Huawei Technologies Co., Ltd., Shenzhen, China

Graphic Design
Sun Zhe, Wang Guanhua, Tian Tao, Hu Yue, Jin Yudian

→ Designer profile on page 531

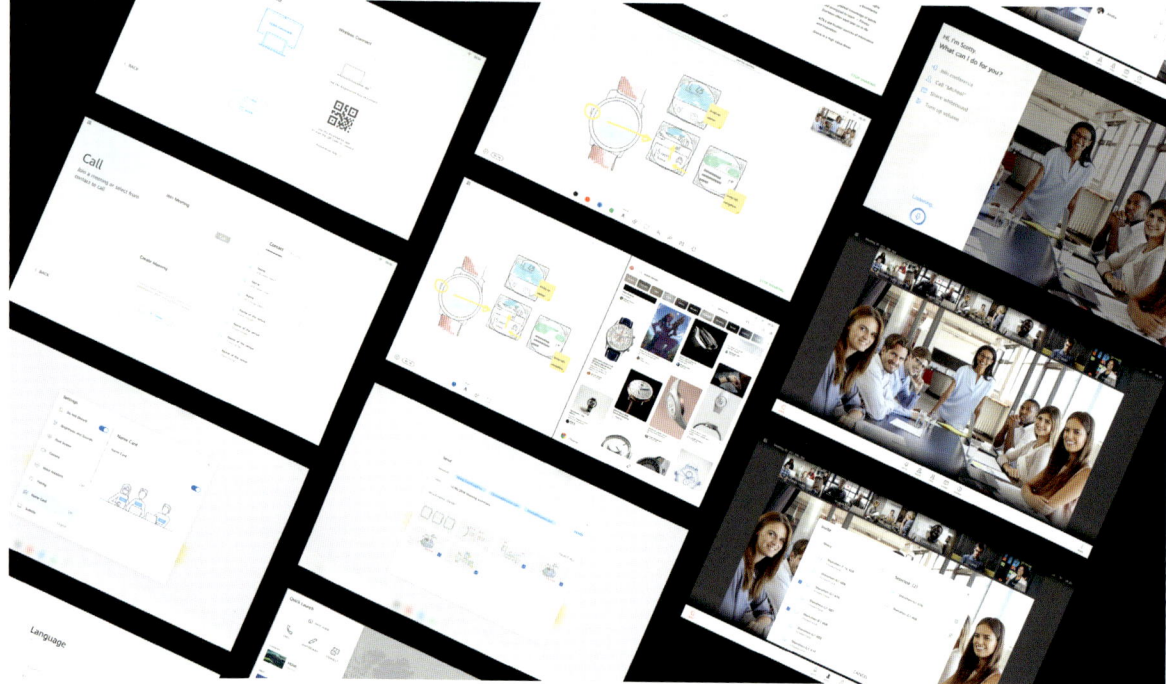

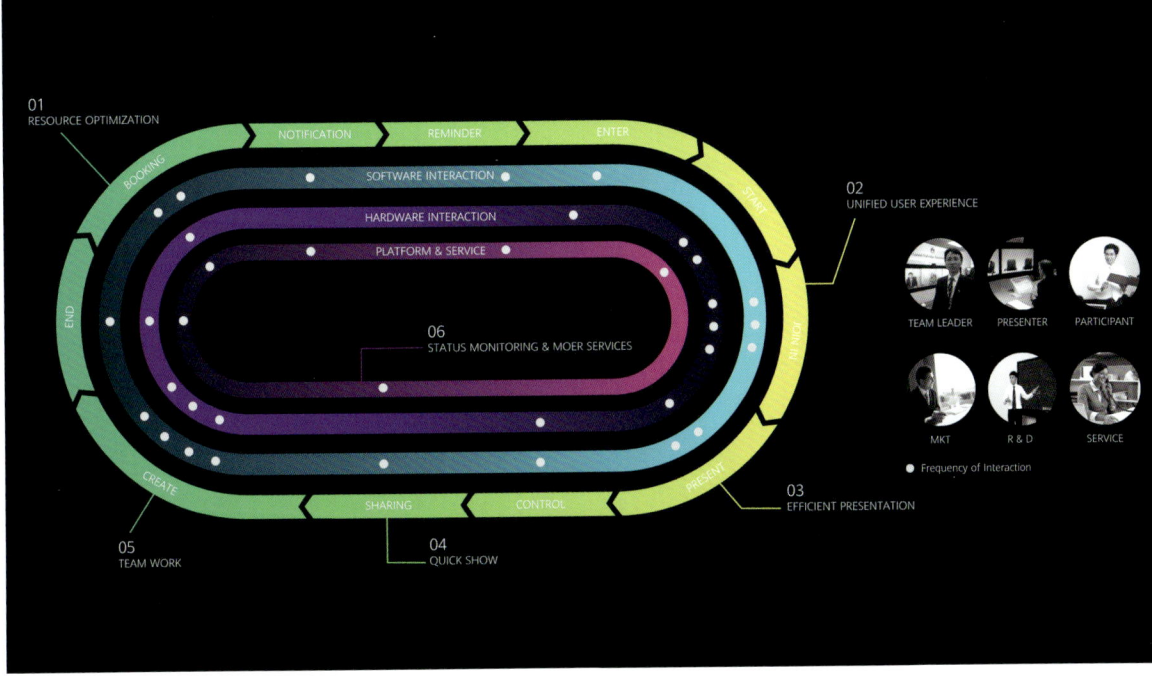

Huawei Global Conference Service Design

As part of the Global Conference Service Design project, 7,300 meeting rooms in 173 countries were refurbished to help employees plan, collaborate and conduct remote HD video conferencing, regardless of local circumstances. Conference rooms were classified, hardware standards defined and software solutions developed for different scenarios, customer requirements and hardware equipment for this purpose. For example, rooms could be easily booked via smartphone and notes on the whiteboard be saved directly by scanning a QR code.

Client
Huawei Technologies Co., Ltd., Shenzhen, China

Design
Huawei Technologies Co., Ltd., Shenzhen, China

Graphic Design
Wang Guanhua, Sun Zhe, Wang Shichun, Huang Lei, Qi Qi

→ Designer profile on page 531

NAVER Cloud Platform – Data Center Virtual Tour

[User Experience Design]

Client
NAVER Business Platform Corp.,
Seongnam, South Korea

Design
newtype Imageworks, Inc.,
Seoul, South Korea

Chief Executive Officer
Weongi Park, NAVER Business Platform

Cloud Design
Baekhee Hahn (Lead),
Sangtae Kim (Senior Designer),
NAVER Business Platform

Creative Direction
Jinwook Kim, newtype Imageworks

Art Direction
Kiyoon Park, newtype Imageworks

User Experience Design
Yongmin Joh, newtype Imageworks

Video/Motion Graphics
Inwoong Kim, newtype Imageworks

→ Designer profile on page 553
→ Clip online

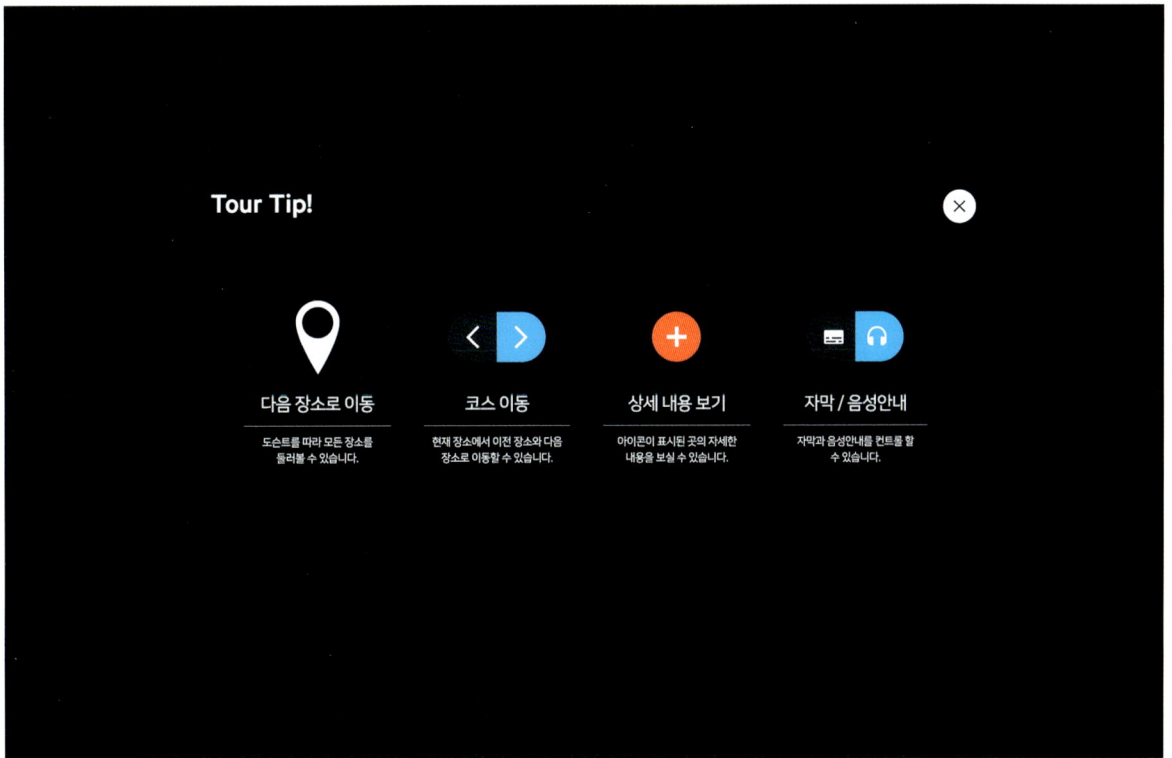

The Data Center Virtual Tour for the NAVER Cloud Platform is a virtual tour of the data centre that provides the technology for running the platform. It features a clear user interface and offers the same experience online as when actually visiting the centre. Users can gain insight into the electronic facilities and access additional information by exploring objects, changing the viewing angle or through informative charts. In this way, users can configure their personal tours and determine for themselves which information they want to retrieve.

Volvo Ocean Race Connectivity Play

[User Interface Design, User Experience Design]

Volvo Ocean Race Connectivity Play is an exhibition installation that shows how connectivity can boost efficiency in a future logistic system. Visitors playfully learn to interact with a networked system by loading vehicles with appropriate materials to supply a virtual construction site. The special feature is that players move real physical objects such as miniature vehicles and material, as their actions are transmitted via AR and NFC technology to the digital interface. This unusual interaction encourages collaboration between players.

Client
Volvo Group Connected Solutions,
Gothenburg, Sweden

Design
The Techno Creatives,
Gothenburg, Sweden

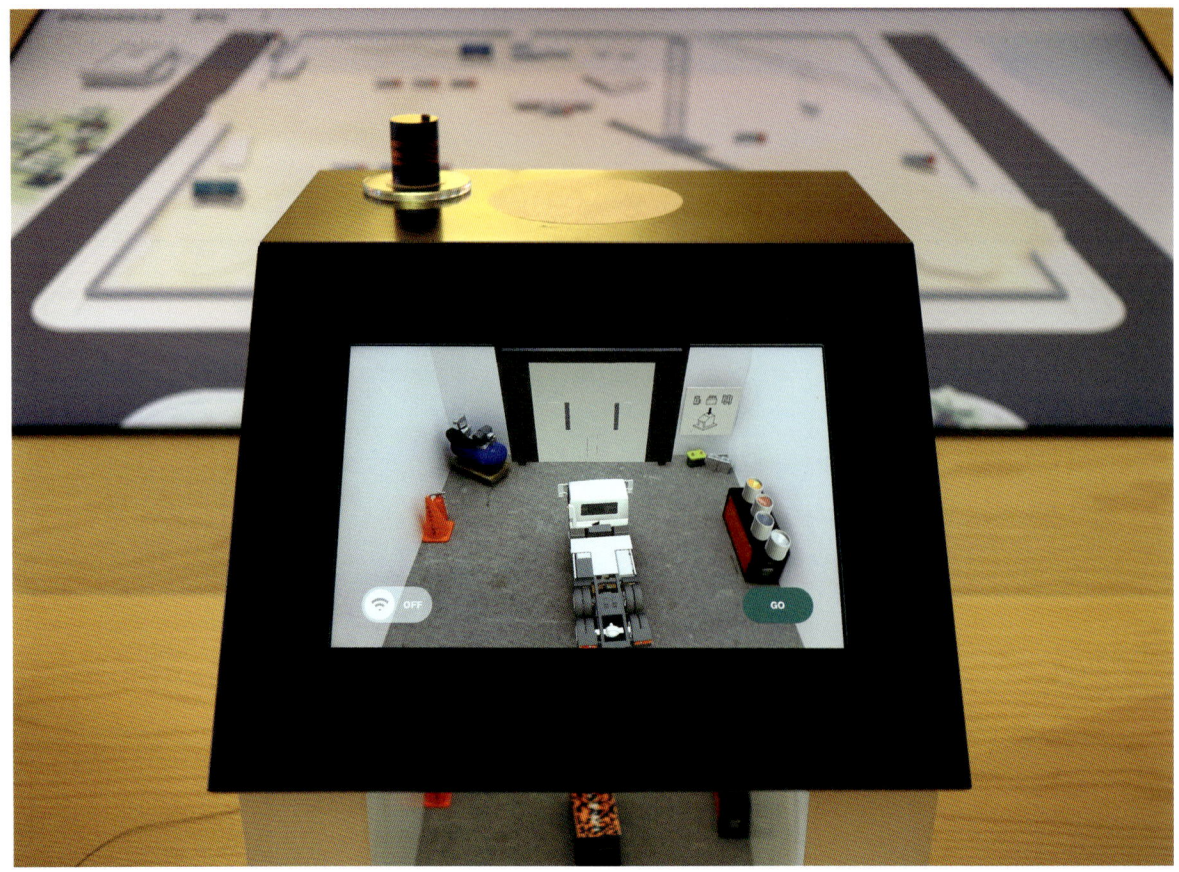

Clariant Virtual City

[User Interface Design,
User Experience Design]

Clariant created an interactive installation with a virtual city called XR Wall Clariant City. The installation was presented at the European Coatings Show in Nuremberg, a major trade fair for coating, paint and pigments. This virtual environment allowed fair trade visitors to explore Clariant indoor and outdoor products in three different scenarios. Visitors could change the perspective on the screen through movement without the need for VR glasses. As a result, the installation offered an immediate, dynamic user experience, following an innovative approach in product presentation at a trade show.

Client
Clariant International Ltd.,
Pratteln, Switzerland

Design
Fuenfwerken Design AG, Berlin, Germany
raumHOCH GmbH, Berlin, Germany

smart – Premium Automotive Retail Experience

[Interactive Information Tool]

The Daimler brand "smart" stands for innovation, urbanity, functionality and utmost joy. Since this will be complemented by e-mobility as a feature, it has been reflected in the development and design of their innovative and interactive retail experience. With its intuitive-to-operate touch interface, it delivers sophisticated user guidance and realistic 3D animations that enable customers to gain insights on product features among e-mobility and all key configuration options at events such as premium showrooms, pop-up stores, and roadshows.

Client
Daimler AG, smart, Stuttgart, Germany

Design
Demodern GmbH, Hamburg, Germany

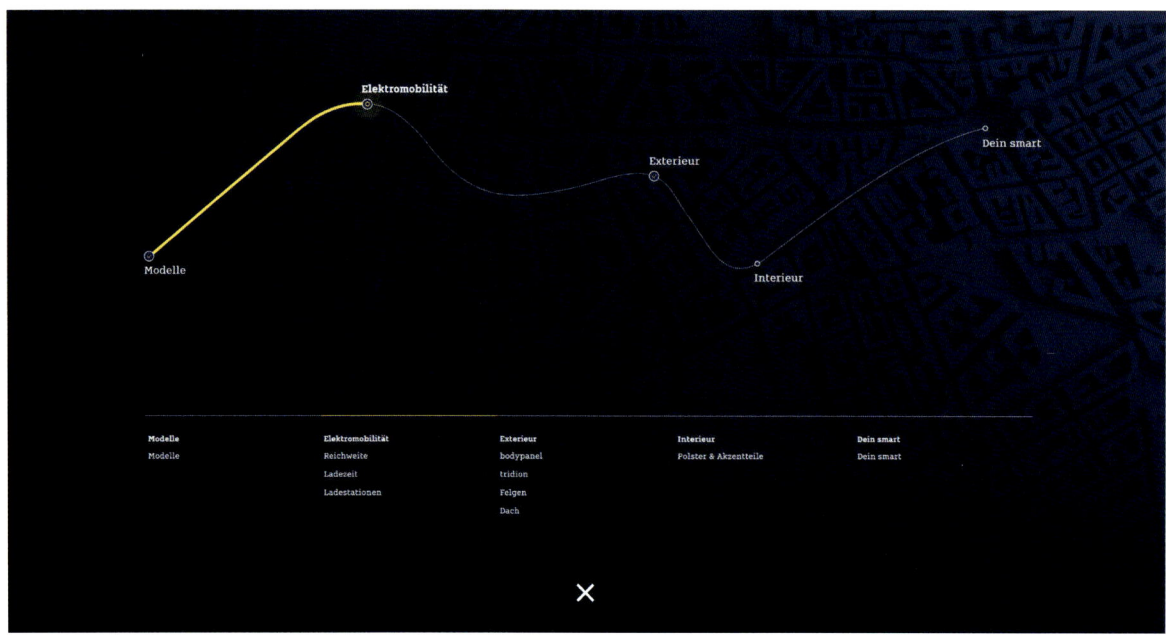

AEG Interactive Shirt Installation

[Interactive Projection Mapping]

The AEG Interactive Shirt Installation illustrates the advantages of the company's environmentally- and garment-friendly ÖKOPower washing detergent. The installation consists of a mirror-like display showing a shirt, upon which the washing procedure and the resulting difference in wear and tear depending on the detergent are simulated using projection mapping. The second component is a digital tablet that allows the trade fair visitors to intuitively control the installation and obtain additional information on the functionality of the detergent.

Client
SCP Grey Sweden, Gothenburg, Sweden

Design
The Techno Creatives,
Gothenburg, Sweden

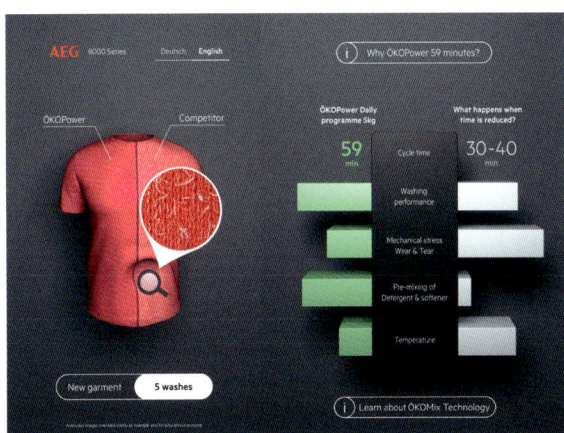

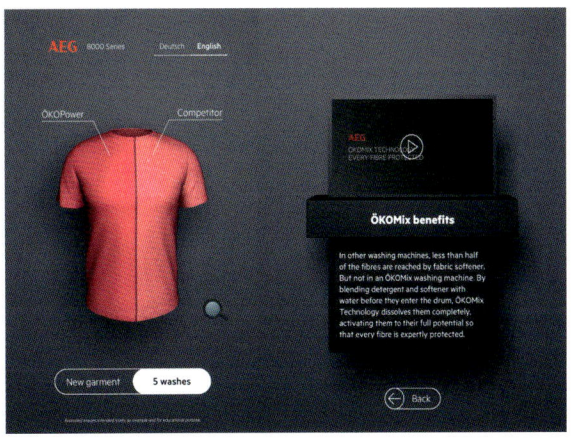

Koelnmesse Digital Signage System

[User Interface Design,
User Experience Design]

The newly introduced digital signage system for Koelnmesse replaces the old facility-oriented presentation of information with a plain visitor-oriented solution. This new concept provides better orientation, as thematically related content is displayed in a consistent colour scheme. Visitors can thus recognise immediately which signs are relevant for them and let themselves be guided through the exhibition grounds. In addition, the system alleviates the burden of convention centre administrators, since content can be planned digitally and updated within a short time.

Client
Koelnmesse, Cologne, Germany

Design
Samsung SDS, CX Innovation Team, Seoul, South Korea

Strategic Planning
Yukyoung Chang, Jae Un Park

Graphic Design
Sunghye Cho, Changsoo Kang

Digital Concept
Junghun Yoon

→ Clip online

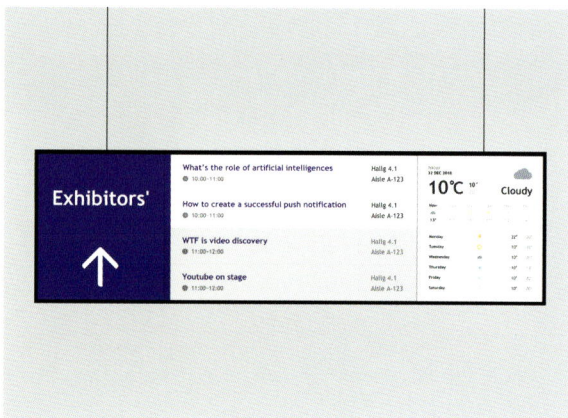

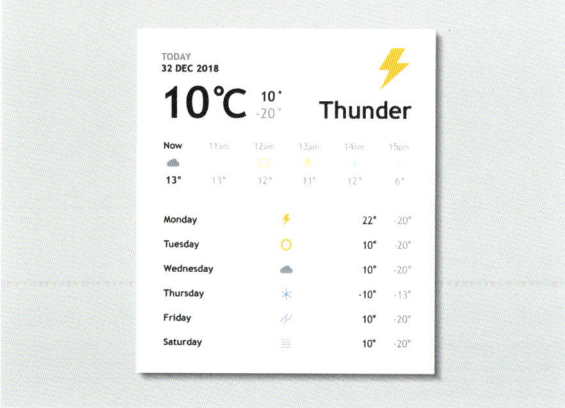

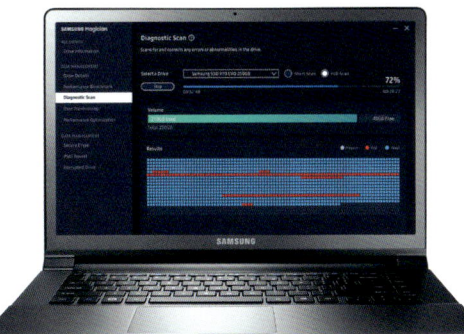
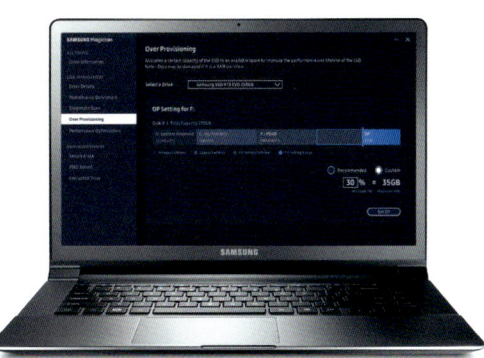

Samsung Magician 6.0

[User Interface Design,
Storage Management Software]

The Magician 6.0 software makes it easy to manage diverse storage devices. Connected to a computer, the individual storage devices are clearly displayed on a single user interface. Navigation to various functions of the software, such as diagnostics, benchmarks or performance comparisons, is coherently structured to ensure that users can intuitively access them. Performance data is appealingly visualised with bar graphs, while diagnostic data is presented in easy-to-understand pie charts, making for a seamless user experience.

Client
Samsung Electronics, Suwon, South Korea

Design
Samsung Electronics, Seoul, South Korea

Design Team
Suhyun Na, Heeyoung Chung

Project Management
Suhyun Na, Heeyoung Chung, Sunmi Jin, Jungwon Lee

The Cut Page – DaVinci Resolve 16

[Post-Production Software]

Client
Blackmagic Design, Melbourne, Australia

Design
Blackmagic Design, Melbourne, Australia

User Interface Design
Hailey Choi, Mio Hu, Denny Trieu, Mathieu Henrijean

User Experience Design
Hailey Choi, Mio Hu, Denny Trieu, Mathieu Henrijean, Alexander Diaz, Matt Dowling

→ Designer profile on page 515

Interface & User Experience Design · Spatial Communication · Red Dot: Junior Award · Designer Profiles · Jury · Index · Red Dot – World of Design

DaVinci Resolve 16 is a post-production application for film and television production. Part of the software is the "Cut" workspace, which has been designed for editors working on short formats such as commercials, news and fast turn-around projects, as well as for editors working on the go. It provides all the tools needed to complete a video, be it for station broadcast or YouTube, in one central location, as editors can import, cut and trim, insert transitions and titles, make automatic colour adjustments and mix sound. The user interface is tailored to the needs of the industry and optimised for fast, efficient work.

Dematic Imagination Center

[User Interface Design]

A visit to the Dematic Imagination Center provides a comprehensive insight into the company's history, technologies and solutions, putting great emphasis on the visitors' interaction with the exhibits: visitors are first immersed in the history of the company in the "History Tunnel", before experiencing the technology through playful interaction with subject boxes in the three areas of "Rapid", "Smart" and "Flexible". Finally, in the gesture-controlled "Solution Composer", visitors can configure a storage area by themselves, exploring it on a virtual flight.

Client
Dematic GmbH, Heusenstamm, Germany

Design
Simple GmbH, Cologne, Germany
ui/deation GmbH & Co. KG, Munich, Germany

Creative Direction
Felix Hansen, Simple GmbH

Programming
Andreas Echterhoff,
ui/deation GmbH & Co. KG

Animation
Stefan Barnewitz, BLUE SILVER GmbH, Munich, Germany

Production
Torsten Besant,
Ambrosius Deutschland GmbH,
Frankfurt/Main, Germany

Lighting Design
Uwe Thomas,
Medientechnik Thomas GmbH,
Siegen, Germany

Exhibition Construction
Ralf Bröske, ExpoTec OHG,
Mainz, Germany

→ Clip online

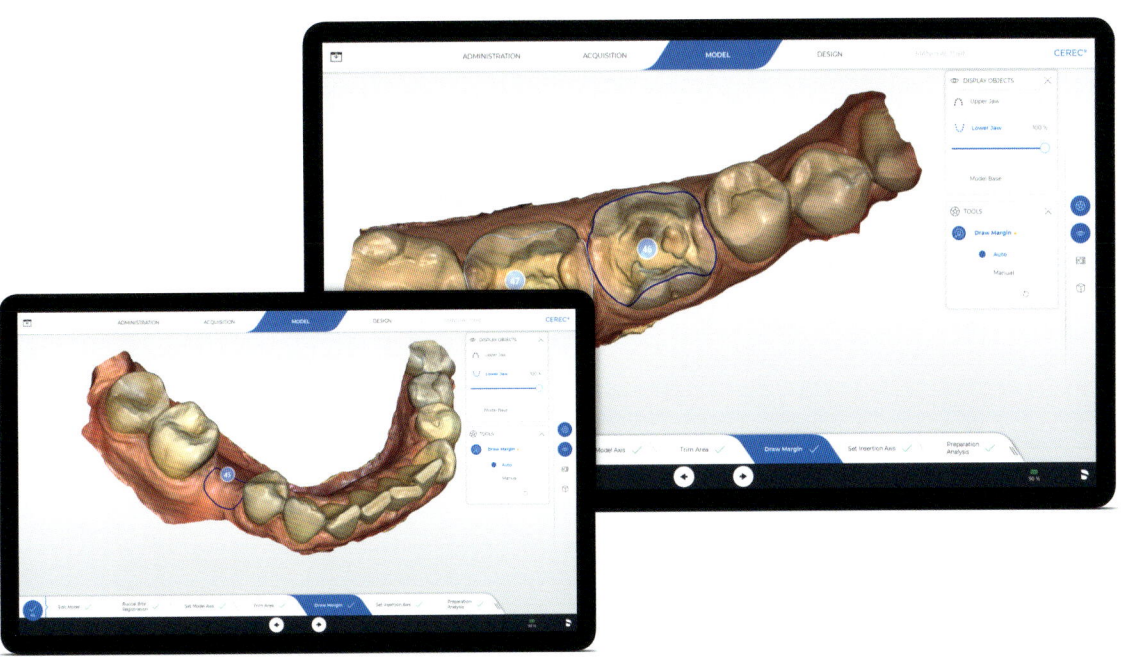

CEREC
[Health Solutions]

The CEREC system enables dentists to prepare, design and produce dentures in just one session, sparing patients several appointments. The UI design combines photorealistic 3D renderings of jaws and teeth with a user-friendly interface and clear navigation structure. Together with the overall redesign, effects and animations have also been optimised in order to display both relevant information and 3D models of teeth and jaws on the work surface in a clearly organised manner. The system with touchscreen is intuitive to operate.

Client
Dentsply Sirona Deutschland GmbH, Bensheim, Germany

Design
Ergosign GmbH, Berlin, Germany

The World of Sartorius Products

[User Experience Design]

Client
Sartorius Corporate Administration GmbH, Göttingen, Germany

Design
HID Human Interface Design GmbH, Hamburg, Germany

Film Editing
Claudia Schönwälder, Frank Jacob, Jona Rammler, Philipp Marc Scheve, Benjamin Schwarz, Julia Tamm

→ Clip online

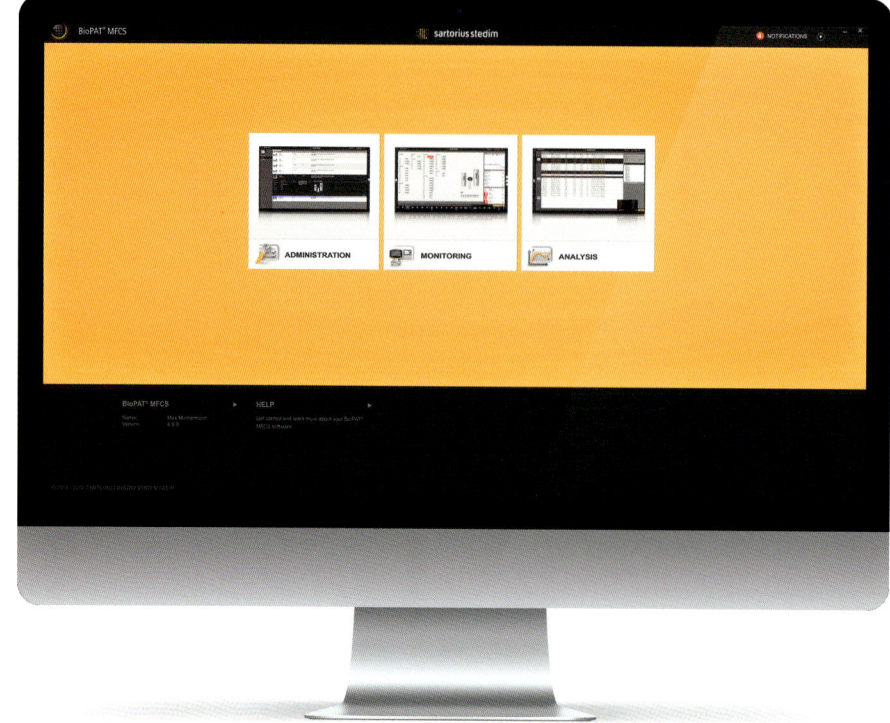

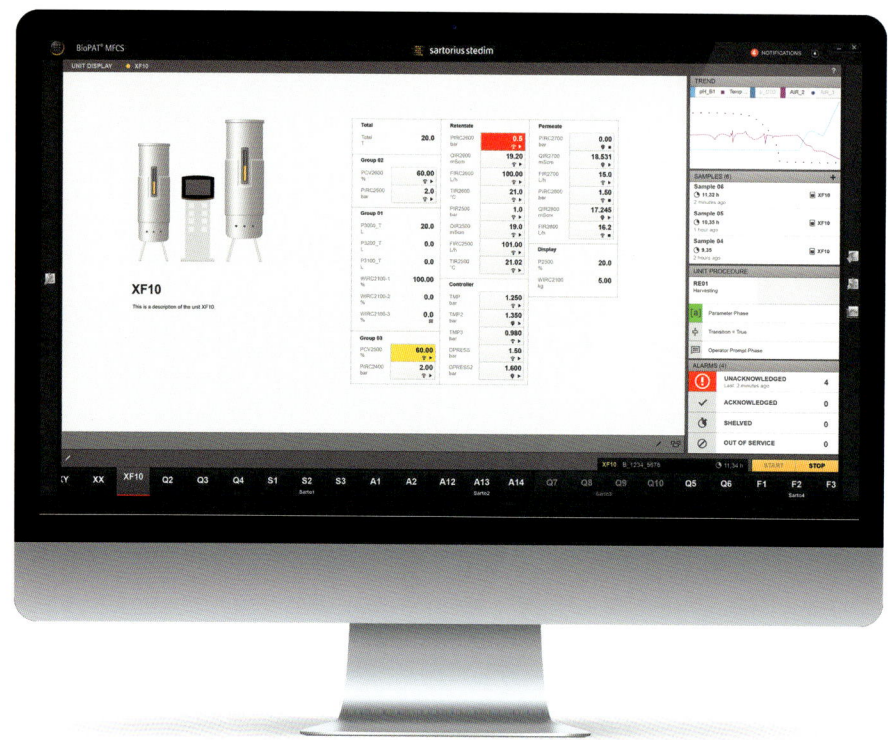

Interface & User Experience Design　　Spatial Communication　　Red Dot: Junior Award　　Designer Profiles　　Jury　　Index　　Red Dot – World of Design

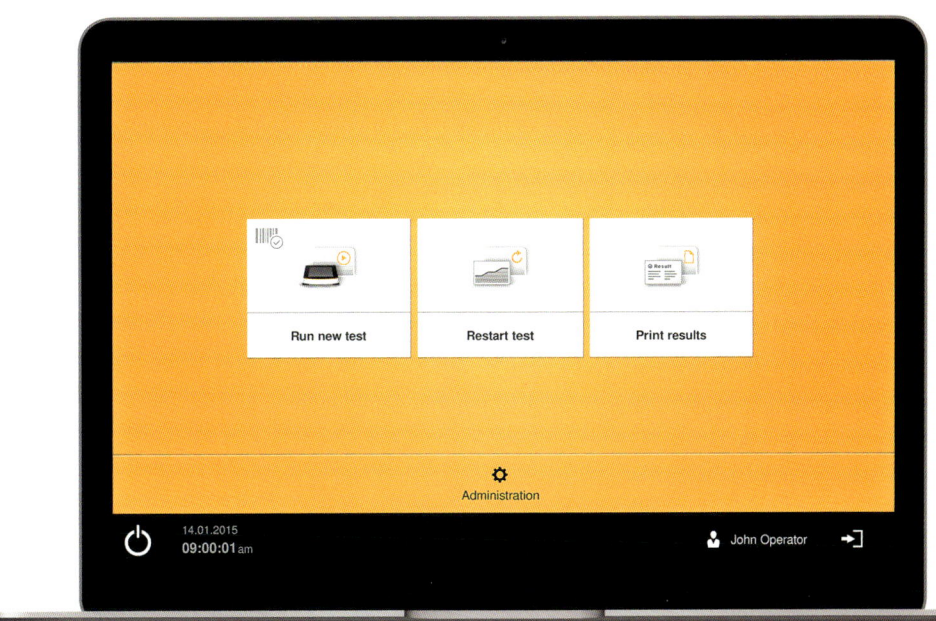

The Sartorius Group is an international partner of the biopharmaceutical industry and related research. For customers with high requirements on safety, efficiency and quality, it has developed a corporate user experience design that entirely focuses on user-friendliness and can be experienced in the areas of process visualisation, clear alerts, the interaction of hardware and software, user guidance, direct feedback and unmistakable design. The high quality of this sophisticated design extends to touch screens with 4.2", 7", 12" and 17", as well as software applications. For users, the cross-product uniform graphic implementation considerably simplifies operation to ensure efficient work.

Pathfinder
[Health Solutions]

Pathfinder is a simple but powerful application that gives clinical teams the ability to coordinate the care of chronic patients through every stage of treatment. It achieves this by automatically generating tasks based on the care plan for a specific patient and by alerting clinicians of deviations in vital signs recorded remotely by patients at home. Built on a clinically sound and flexible design system and open standards for storing clinical data, Pathfinder is easily configurable for different use cases across healthcare organisations.

Client
Better, Ljubljana, Slovenia

Design
Better, Ljubljana, Slovenia

Product Management
Tina V. Vaupotič

Design Direction
Samo Ačko

Design Team
Tadej Maligoj, Rok Benedik, Samo Ačko, Rok Pregelj, Barbara Hiti, Gregor Fras, Sai Pan, Jernej Tratnik, Ajda Bevc

→ Designer profile on page 514

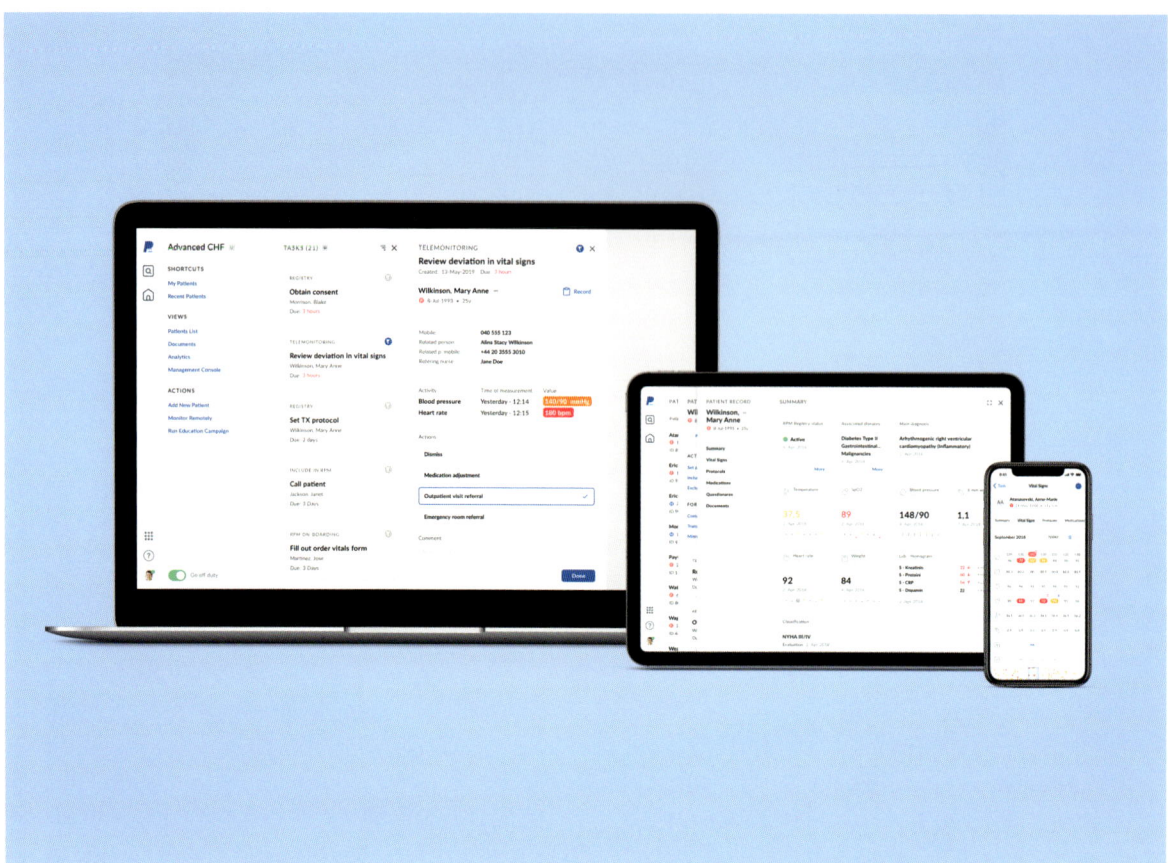

Proofit 1D

[Health Solutions]

Proofit 1D is a system that verifies whether the type and amount of medicine a pharmacist has put together for a patient is correct. It takes a photograph of the pharmaceutical packages and displays their fronts and backs side by side in a tiled screen layout. For better organisation, the medicine units are listed horizontally while the packaging units are listed vertically. Any object that proves difficult to automatically categorise is displayed at the top of the screen, so that users can immediately see whether it is something that requires further attention. In addition, items with incorrect dosages are marked in a yellow signal colour.

Client
FUJIFILM Corporation, Tokyo, Japan

Design
FUJIFILM Corporation, Tokyo, Japan

Aasted Smart Control

[User Interface Design]

Aasted Smart Control is a flexible user interface optimised for a wide range of monitor sizes and touch devices, featuring a unified operating concept for the different machine types in the chocolate industry. Presenting task-based functions and graphic charts visualising performance and efficiency in a clear colour code, the HMI is highly user friendly. Line overviews and dashboards allow continuous monitoring and control of all components in the production process. In addition, users can access contextual online help, FAQs and assisted workflows at any time.

Client
Aasted ApS, Farum, Denmark

Design
HMI Project GmbH, Würzburg, Germany

→ Clip online

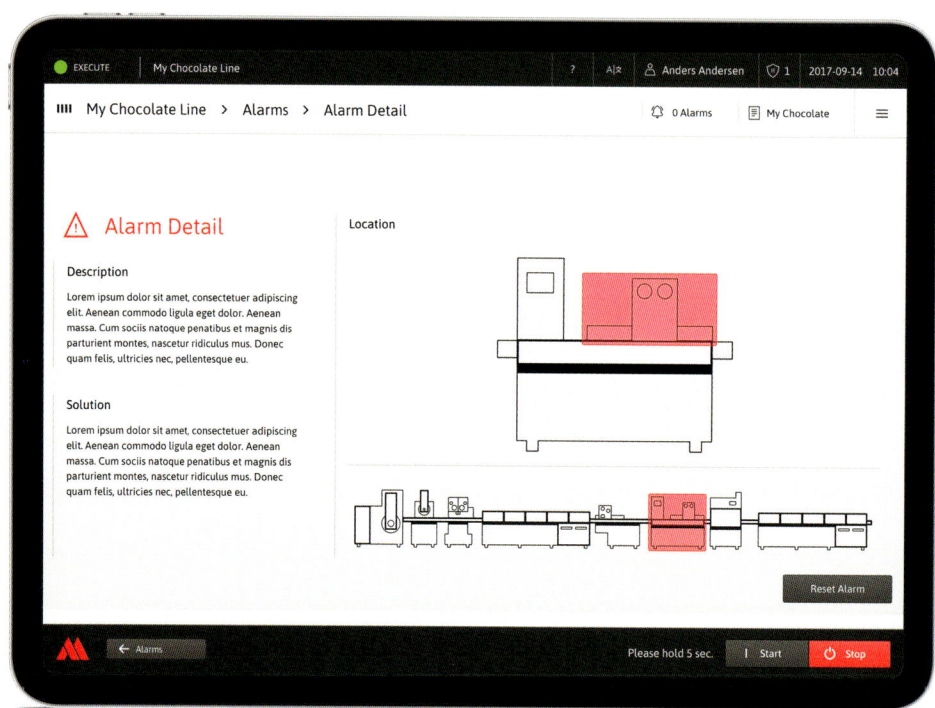

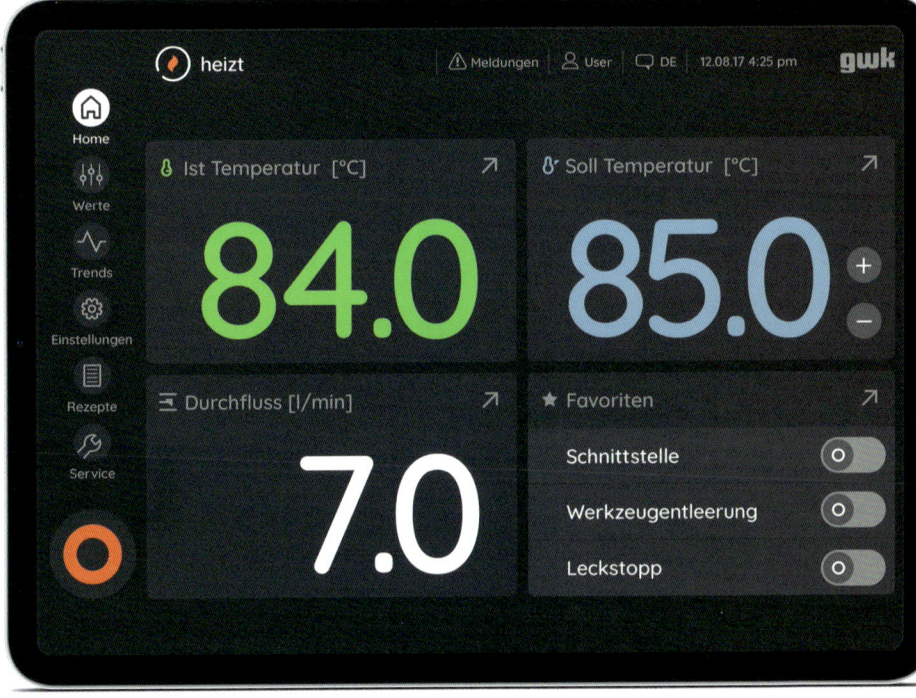

logotherm

[User Interface Design]

logotherm is a versatile interface used in industrial cooling and temperature control systems. It features a clear and intuitive user interface, an adaptive dashboard, and typographic information units that ensure quick orientation and ease of use. In addition to the clear design, its dynamic behaviour contributes to a positive user experience. The modular layout structure and the implementation with web technology guarantee consistent display principles on all output devices such as machine operating panels and mobile devices.

Client
gwk
Gesellschaft Wärme Kältetechnik mbH,
Meinerzhagen, Germany

Design
HMI Project GmbH, Würzburg, Germany

→ Clip online

Salvagnini Face

[User Interface Design,
Corporate HMI System]

Client
Salvagnini Group, Sarego (Vicenza), Italy

Design
NiEW Design, Modena, Italy

Digital Concept
Andrea Violante, Daniele De Cia,
Andrea Cattani, Michele Mariani

Graphic Design
Beatrice Cascio, Diego Lavecchia

→ Designer profile on page 554
→ Clip online

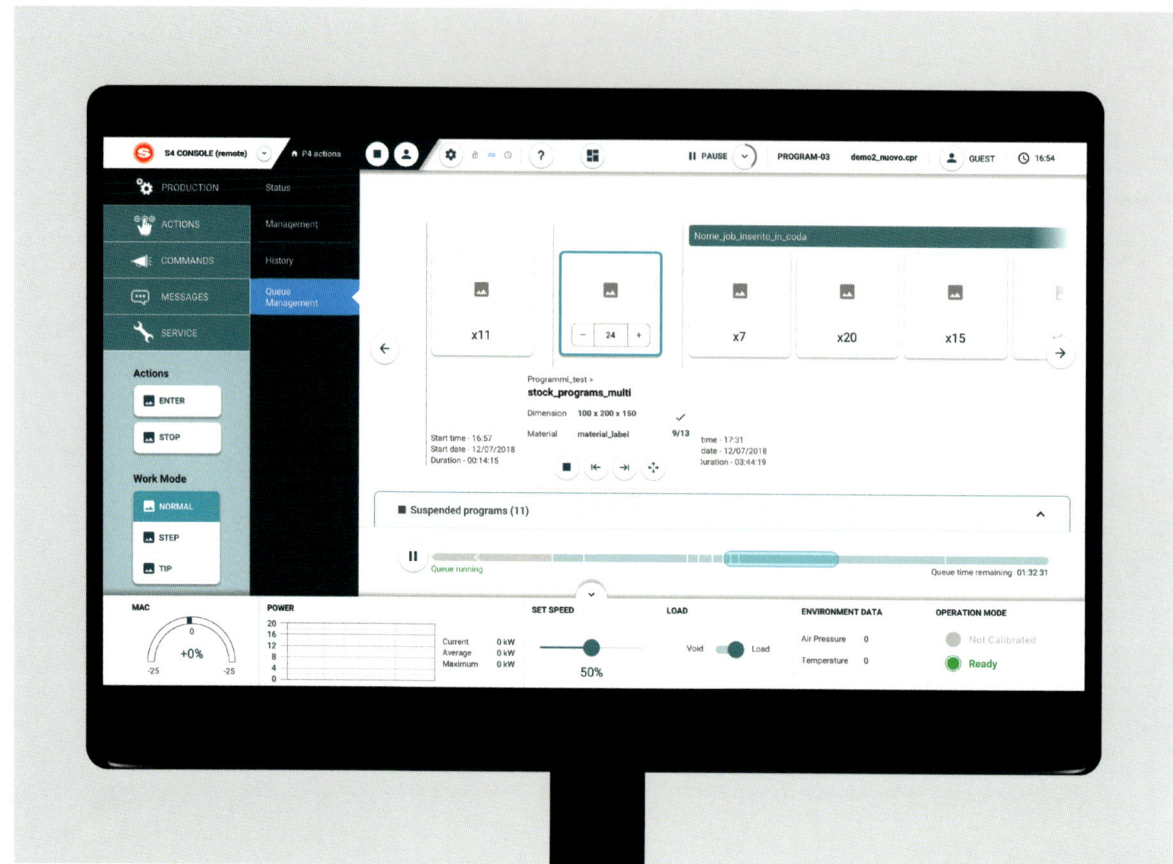

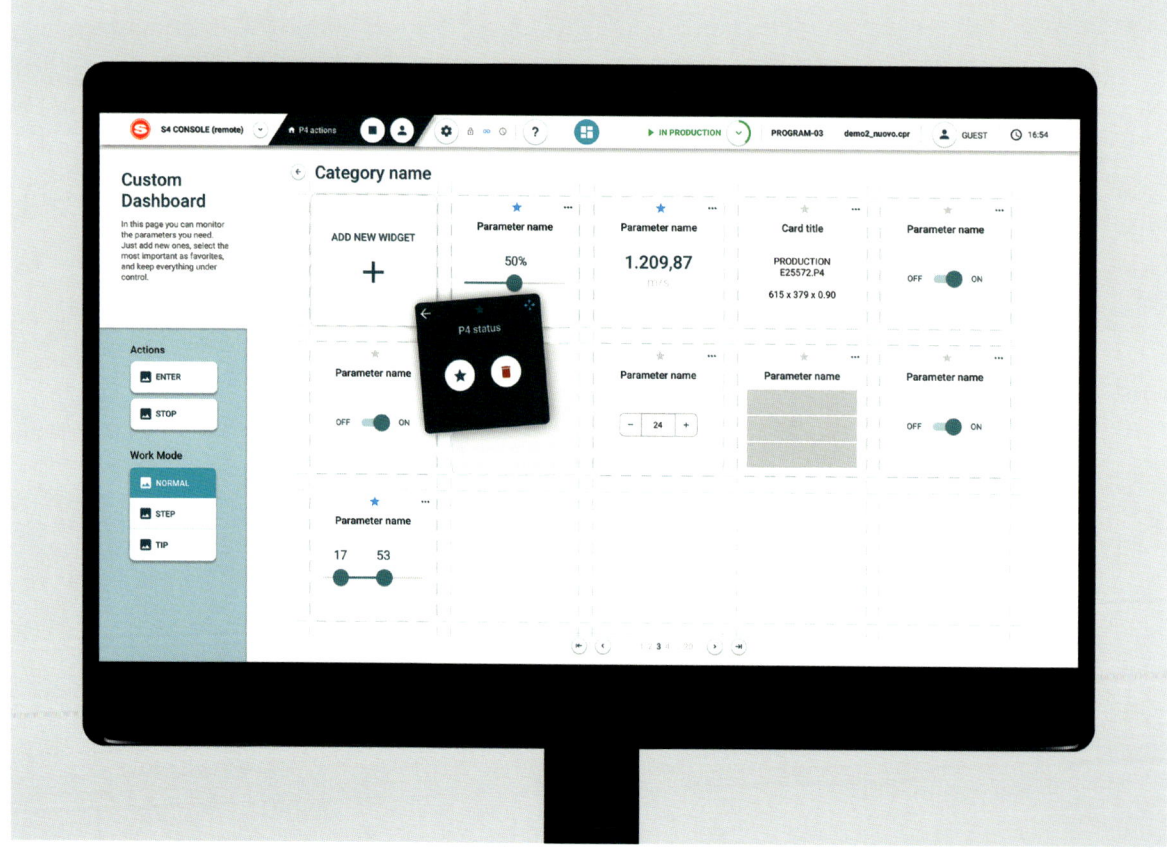

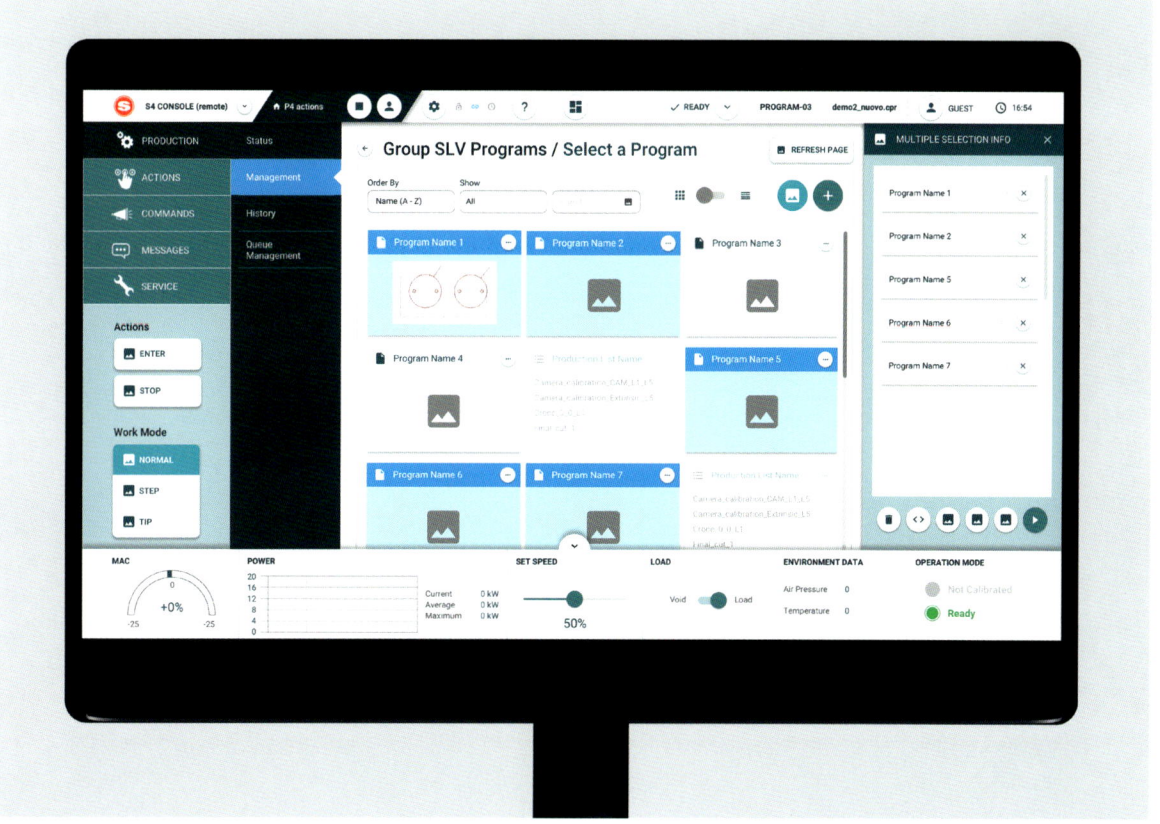

Face is the corporate machinery operating system of the Salvagnini Group, aimed at unifying all existing as well as future software suites for metal working machines. It merges different types of applications to create a comprehensive and consistent design system. Thanks to fail-proof guided paths, visual production overviews and a fully customisable dashboard, the system helps users be productive more quickly, manage strict deadlines more easily and recover from failures without external assistance. Distributed across different machines, the consistent and intuitive interface supports users in every phase of the production.

SCM Maestro Active

[User Interface Design,
Corporate HMI System]

Client
SCM Group S.p.A., Rimini, Italy

Design
NiEW Design, Modena, Italy

Digital Concept
Andrea Cattani, Andrea Violante,
Daniele De Cia

Art Direction
Silvia Ballerini

Graphic Design
Giorgio Pretto, Beatrice Cascio

→ Designer profile on page 554
→ Clip online

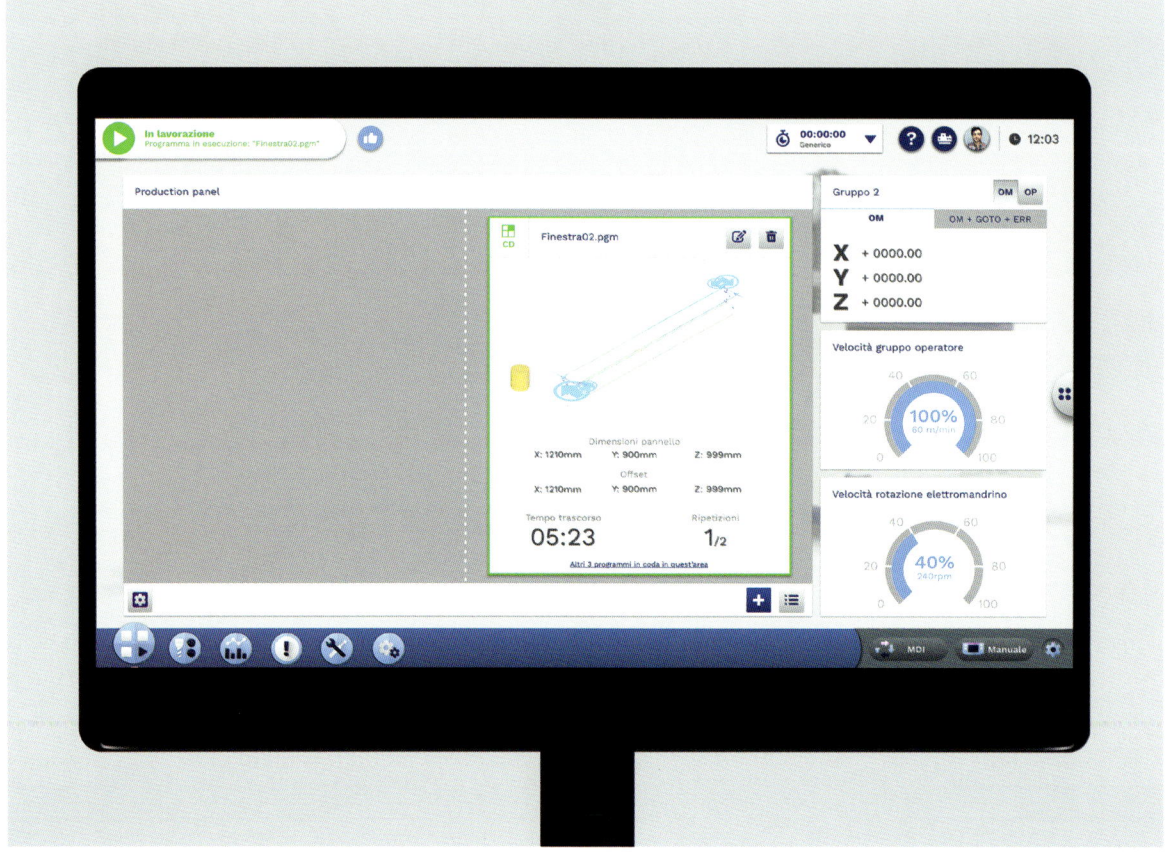

Interface & User Experience Design   Spatial Communication   Red Dot: Junior Award   Designer Profiles   Jury   Index   Red Dot – World of Design

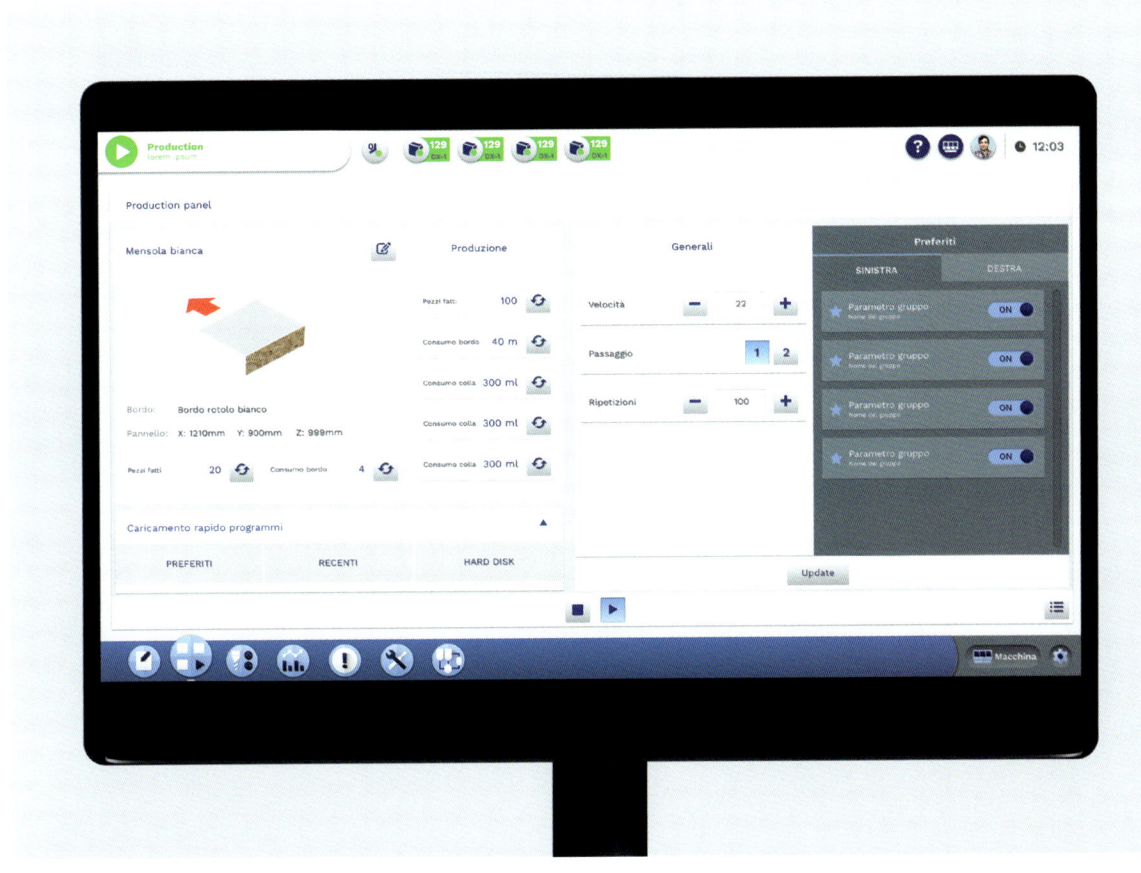

Maestro Active is the new operator interface of the SCM Group, featuring a uniform graphical interface for all SCM technologies. The challenge was to create a sophisticated and user-friendly design system that includes templates, components, illustrations, icons, guidelines and rules to support the SCM team in designing all applications of the software suite. Taking into account the needs of users, the design is based on methods from field research to concept development workshops, as well as prototyping and testing, in order to deliver a comprehensive design system platform.

KOCH easyControl

[User Interface Design]

Client
KOCH Pac-Systeme GmbH,
Pfalzgrafenweiler, Germany

Design
CaderaDesign GmbH,
Würzburg, Germany

Concept
Florian Fuchs

User Interface Design
Amelie Freund, Lucas Dittebrand

Programming
Georg Fischer, Mario Heigl

Industrial Design
Florian Labisch

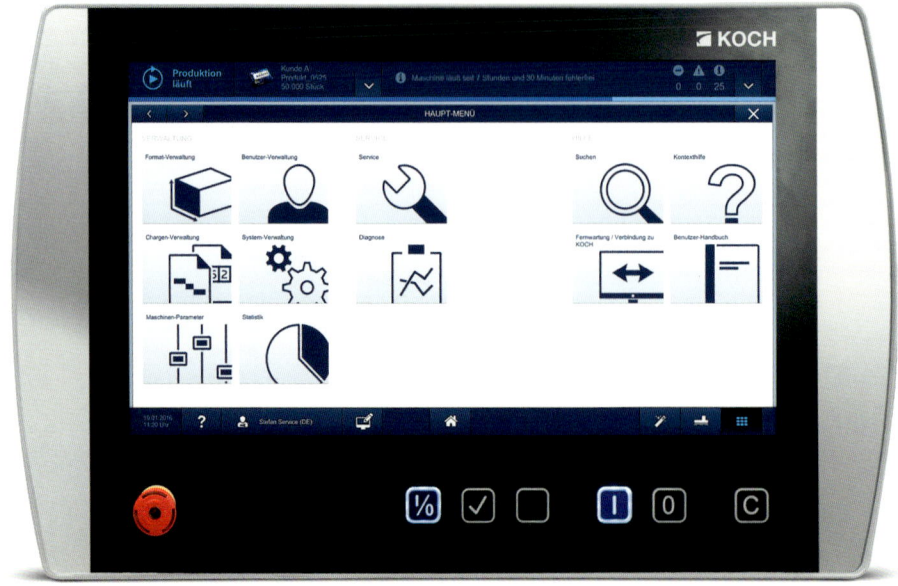

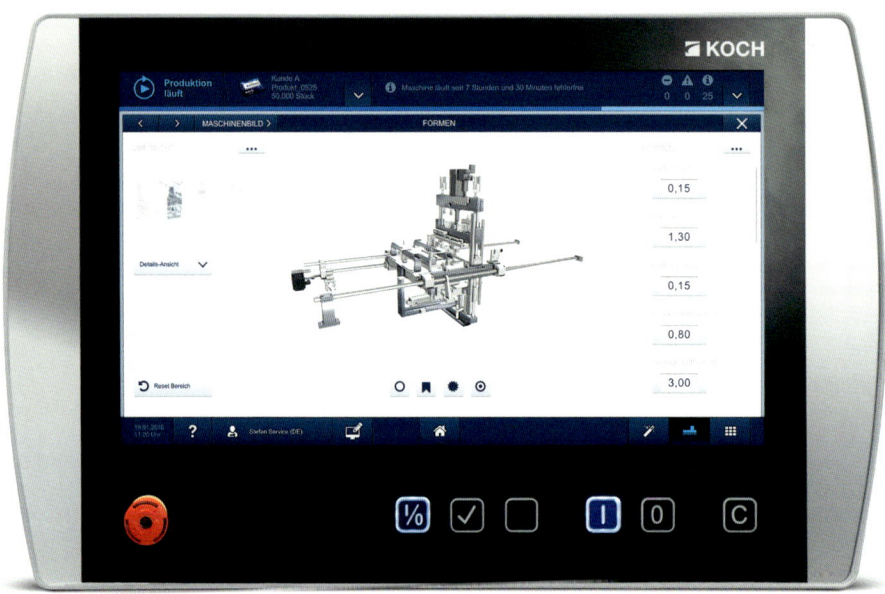

Interface & User Experience Design   Spatial Communication   Red Dot: Junior Award   Designer Profiles   Jury   Index   Red Dot – World of Design

The HMI by KOCH Pac Systems supports different types of users in the task of automatically packaging mass products. It features dashboards that are individually configurable depending on the user level. In addition, malfunctions in the packaging process can be quickly eliminated thanks to its comprehensive user and task orientation. Since the information volumes were reduced to the essentials, operation and control are simple and efficient. Hardware and software are closely synchronised and merge into a harmonious appearance, ensuring an excellent user experience throughout the entire operating process.

Prism

[User Interface Design, CAM App]

Prism is one of the first CAM applications for the iPad. It manages the entire cycle of machining – programming, simulation, post-processing and export to NC code. The real-time feedback of the 3D interface allows nearly anyone to understand CNC programming. Prism also opens a new era of smarter manufacturing by being a product to offer "recipes" for CNC machines – allowing machining experts to package and monetise their expertise, and thus making the machining know-how of the industry available to anyone. Prism is a fully integrated solution that modernises the machining process and reduces programming time by up to 94 per cent.

Client
Sandvik, Applied Manufacturing Technologies, Stockholm, Sweden

Design
Designit, Stockholm, Sweden

Interaction Design
Viktor Rosendahl, David Samuelson

Visual Design
Lucas Forsman Boothe

Web Design
Alecio Calixto

Design Direction
David Landgren

Project Management
Nina Wahlberg

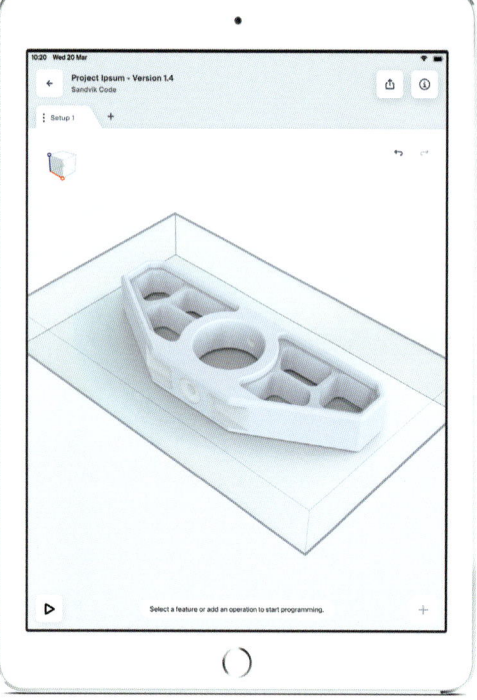

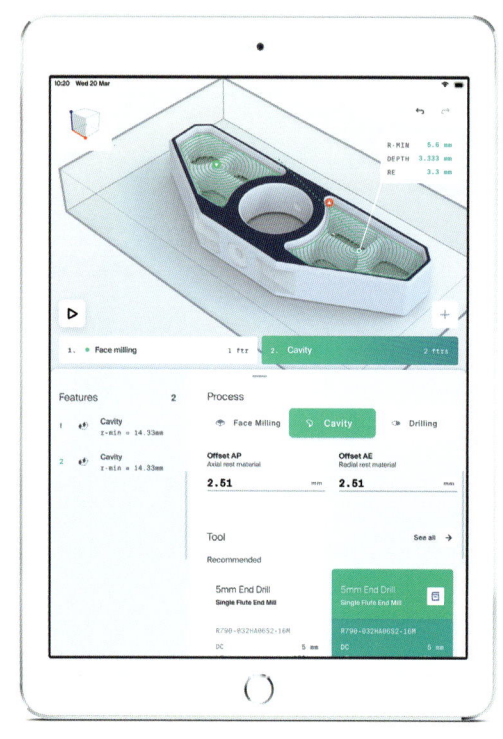
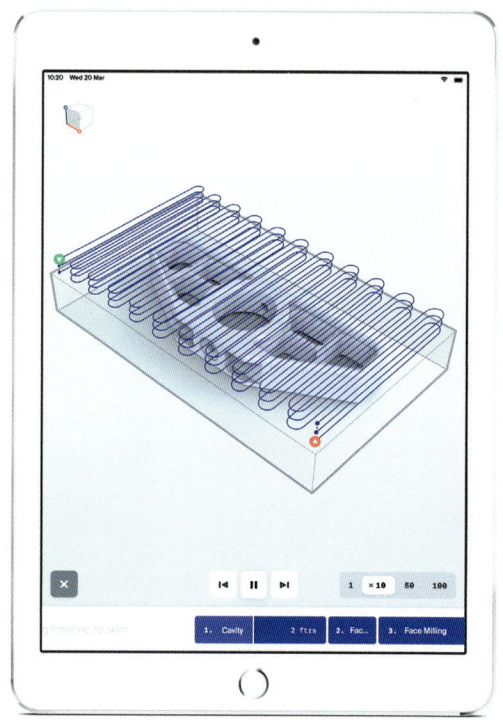

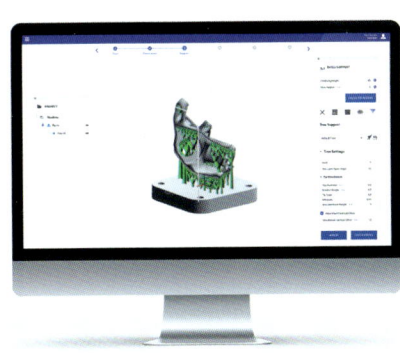

Additive.Designer®

[User Interface Design, Software Development]

The Additive.Designer is a versatile and customisable software solution for easy data preparation to handle complex components in additive manufacturing, providing a personalisable, intuitive user interface with a managed workflow. Two of the most important advantages of the software are cost reduction through error avoidance due to the good plannability of the build job and the resulting higher quality of the manufactured components. The data preparation process can take into account all factors from the selection of the machine to the post-processing of the component.

Client
CADS Additive GmbH, Perg, Austria

Design
CADS GmbH, Perg, Austria

Design Team
Verena Ehebruster, Melanie Marksteiner

Film Production
Bárbara González

CONiQ
[User Interface Design]

Client
Schenck Process Europe GmbH,
Darmstadt, Germany

Design
Custom Interactions GmbH,
Darmstadt, Germany
Schenck Process Europe GmbH,
Darmstadt, Germany

Product Management
Bernd Allenberg,
Schenck Process Europe GmbH

Marketing/Communication
Ann-Katrin Ripperger, Stefan Sauerwein,
Schenck Process Holding GmbH

User Interface Design
Benjamin Franz, Sascha Hiller,
Michaela Kauer-Franz, Marta Piqué,
Custom Interactions GmbH
Bernd Allenberg, Andreas Eggen,
Ulrich Rauchschwalbe,
Schenck Process Europe GmbH

→ Designer profile on page 519

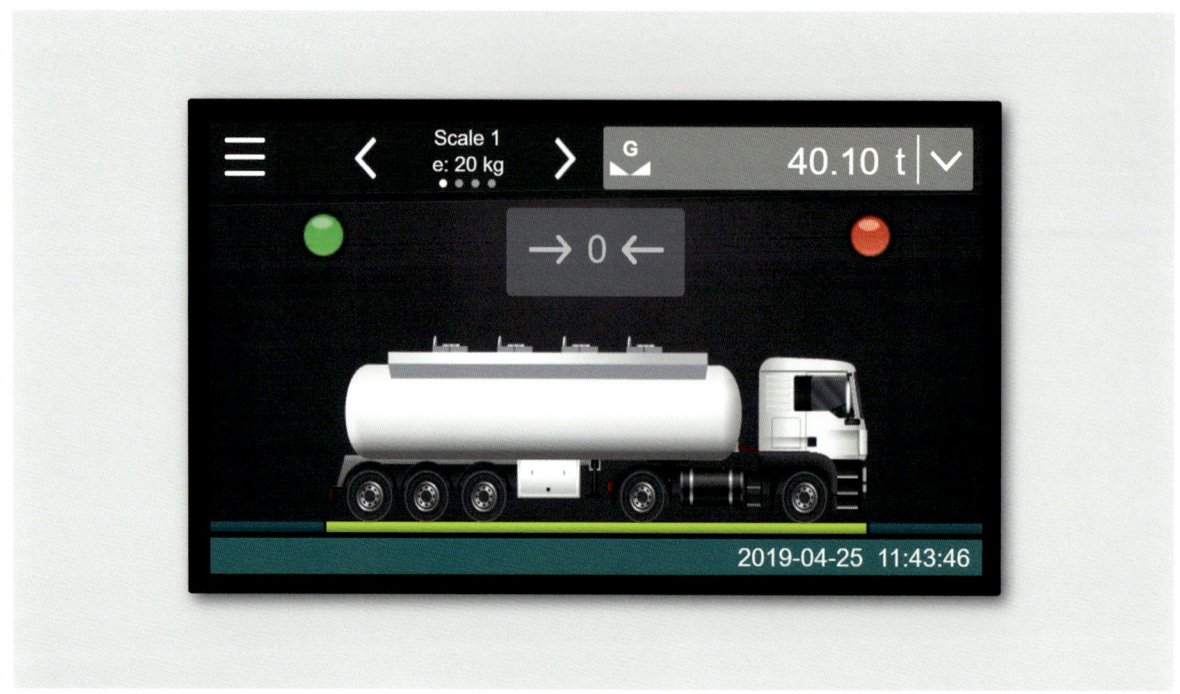

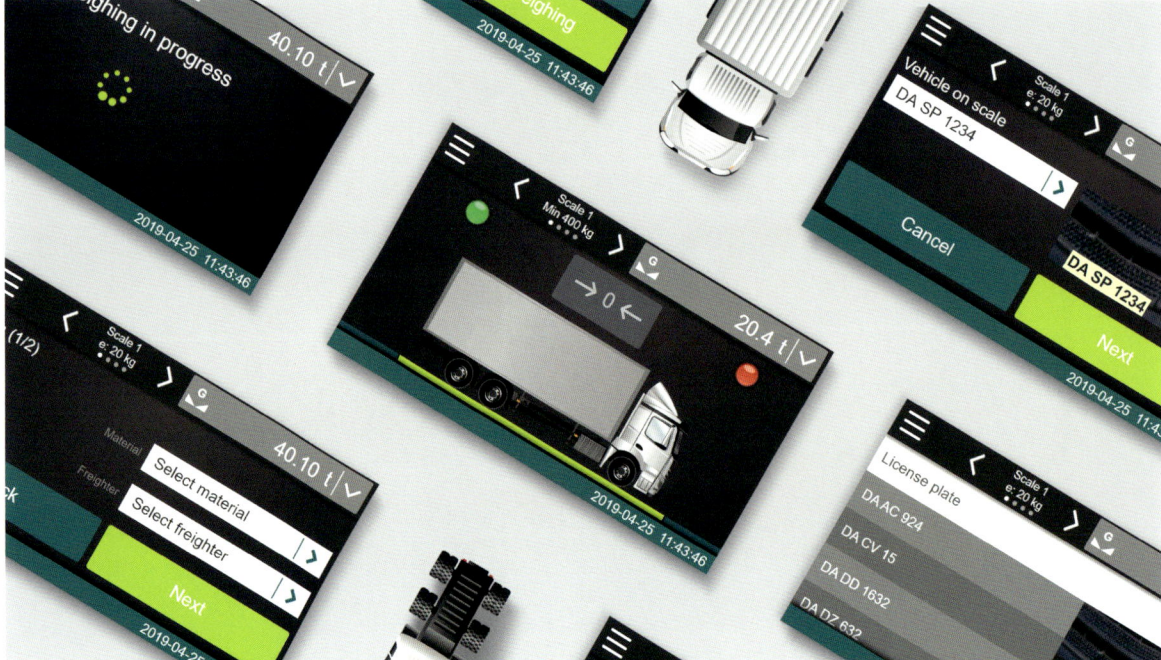

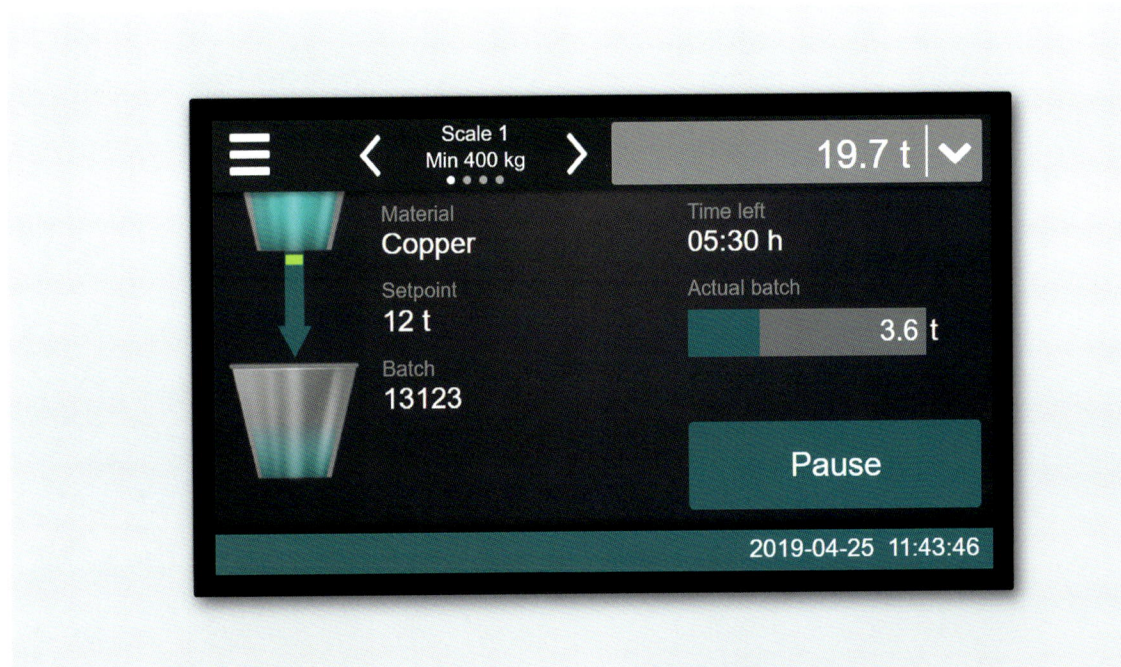

Schenck Process CONiQ is a weighing electronics for continuous and discontinuous measurement applications. The versatile device enables both simple and complex weighing applications. It is characterised by a unified interface and offers customised interaction styles for each application, allowing users to control a truck scale on a junkyard, a crane scale on a construction site or a loss-in-weight feeder in a production process, for example, all with one single device and specialised software. Its intuitive operation is supported by a colour scheme that clearly identifies buttons and selection fields. The dashboard can be configured for both experienced and inexperienced users.

SPATIAL COMMUNICATION

Red Dot: Grand Prix

BLOCBIRDS
[Exhibition Design]

The "BLOCBIRDS" exhibition is dedicated to the rich bird life in Europe with the thesis that we do not pay enough attention to it. Depicting these birds in an unusual manner, the exhibition challenges the visitors' perception. In a development lasting one and a half years, 25 colourful squares, each visualising a different bird, were generated from 25 realistic bird models. Each of these squares is an abstract graphic representation of the body shape and feathers of the respective bird. Through a different amount and variation of the selected colours, as well as their positioning, each square was given a specific appeal corresponding to the special characteristics of the bird. The installation of 25 × 25 cm single pictures, arranged as an impressive overall picture, is complemented by a corresponding stuffed bird exhibit. The exhibition sees itself as a tribute to the bird world and calls for action and bird protection.

Statement by the jury
This exhibition interprets birds in an impressively essential approach based on easily recognisable patterns. It is fascinating how visitors first perceive them as panels, which are then matched to the corresponding exhibits from memory. The meaningful patterns in their specific colour palette show that good design does not necessarily need to resort to novel technologies.

Interface & User Experience Design   Spatial Communication   Red Dot: Junior Award   Designer Profiles   Jury   Index   Red Dot – World of Design

reddot winner 2019
grand prix

Client
Studio 212 Fahrenheit,
Groningen, Netherlands

Design
Studio 212 Fahrenheit,
Groningen, Netherlands

→ Designer profile on page 566
→ Clip online

Red Dot: Best of the Best

Das Totale Tanz Theater
[Virtual Reality Dance Experience]

The virtual reality project "Das Totale Tanz Theater" (The Total Dance Theatre) was intended to reflect important works of the world-famous Bauhaus school. Taking place on the occasion of its founding anniversary, it was shown how the school has been influencing and shaping architecture, art, design and pedagogy until today. Inspired by the stage experiments of painter Oskar Schlemmer and the idea of the "Total Theatre" by Bauhaus founder Walter Gropius, a virtual world with costumed dance machines was conceived, which explores the relationship of man and machine in the digital age. Equipped with virtual reality headsets, four users simultaneously enter a huge virtual stage construction and, with their "dance machines", experience an interactive choreography across three levels. The movements of the dancers had been scanned via motion capturing and applied onto 3D models. The more than 2,500 resulting motion sequences were stored in a database and then reassembled into an interactive choreography by means of artificial intelligence. The interplay of man-made choreography, personal intervention and machine algorithms results in ever new forms of movement and dance.

Statement by the jury
This project provides a sophisticated virtual reality experience and uses it to express a leap forward towards creating a completely novel stage performance. It embodies a fantastic approach towards bringing a new dimension into the relation between humans and machines seamlessly tying in with the work of Oskar Schlemmer and the Bauhaus.

Client
Interactive Media Foundation gGmbH/
Filmtank GmbH, Berlin, Germany

Design
Artificial Rome GmbH, Berlin, Germany
Interactive Media Foundation gGmbH,
Berlin, Germany

Idea/Story
Diana Schniedermeier, Maya Puig

Virtual Reality Design
Maya Puig, Patrik de Jong,
Dirk Hoffmann

Executive Production
Diana Schniedermeier

Choreography
Richard Siegal

Composition
Lorenzo Bianchi-Hoesch

Sound Design
Victor Audouze

Art Direction
Dirk Hoffmann,
Nico Alexander Taniyama, Robert Werner

Technical Team
Torsten Sperling (Lead),
Sebastian Hein (Lead),
Dennis Timmermann, Hui-Yuan Tien

3D Design
Nico Alexander Taniyama (Lead),
Christian Rambow, Dana Würzburg

→ Designer profile on page 511

Red Dot: Best of the Best

007 ELEMENTS
[Exhibition Design, Cinematic Installation]

The objective of the "007 ELEMENTS" installation was to add an extended dimension to the world of film and at the same time develop a new typology for cinematic experience. This comprehensive concept was brought to life more than 3,000 metres above sea level at the peak of Gaislachkogl Mountain, high above the town of Sölden in Austria, where some of the key scenes in the film "Spectre" were shot and which are projected in a huge cinematic installation of more than 1,300 sqm. This cinematic installation guides visitors through a series of nine galleries and an outdoor plaza featuring stunning panoramas, dramatic soundscapes and interactive content. The spatial design was conceived as an integral element of the visitors' journey, aiming to add depth and authenticity to the experience. The conceptual approach is also a direct reference to the legacy of cinematography, forcing perspectives wherever possible in order to turn every visitor's point of view into the camera itself.

Statement by the jury
This cinematic installation creates a new value and conserves both the location and the moment of the recording permanently for people. The resulting vastness and structure enable a special kind of participation. The depicted space turns into a wonderful, unknown no man's land. This project creates an openness that transcends itself and thus embodies a new possibility in design.

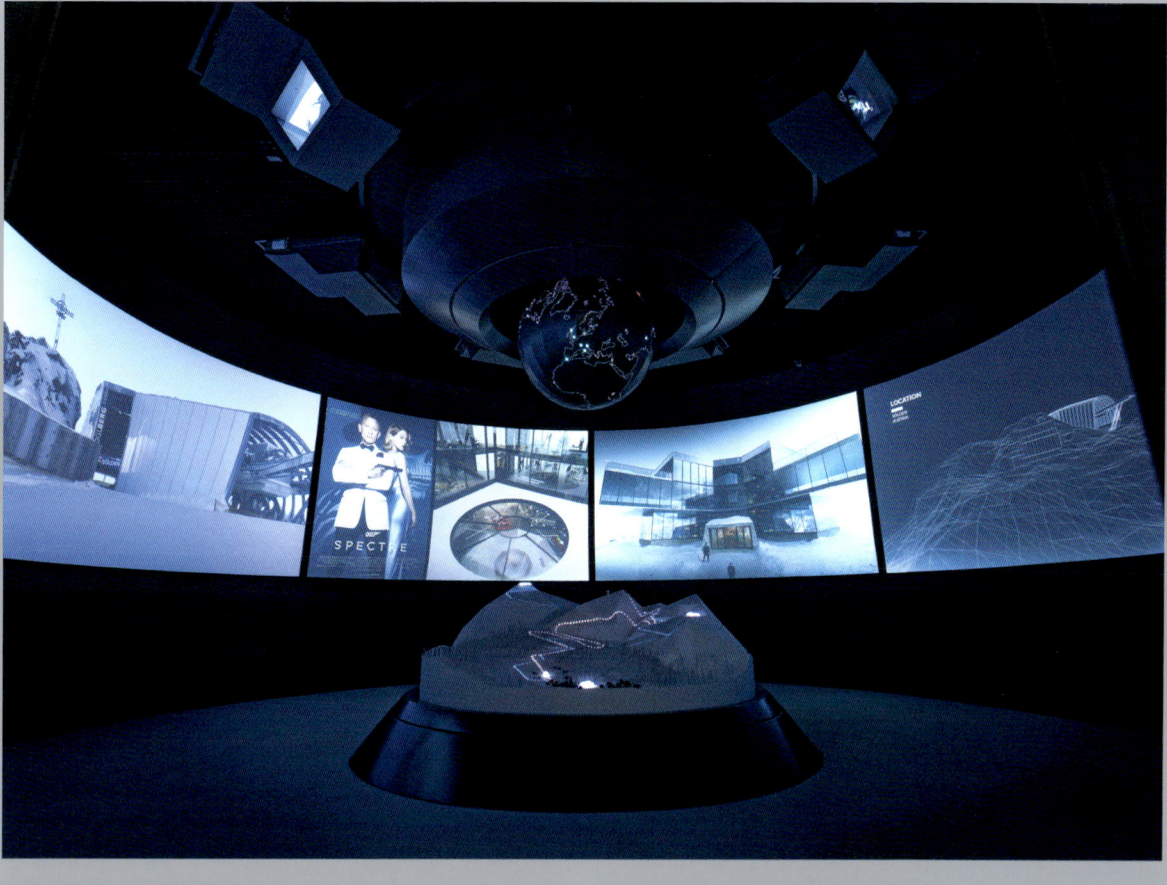

Client
Bergbahnen Sölden, Austria

Design
Optimist GmbH, Hamburg, Germany

Creative Direction
Neal Callow, EON,
London, United Kingdom

Architecture
Johann Obermoser,
Obermoser Arch-Omo, Innsbruck, Austria

→ Designer profile on page 556

Red Dot: Best of the Best

Constellations
[Live Performance]

Created to mark the inauguration of Frankfurt's new historical city centre, the light and media production "Constellations – A Symphony for the Frankfurt Altstadt" saw itself as a poetic homage to the contrasting and diverse metropolis. For the event, the live performance was impressively staged on the opening weekend which attracted around 280,000 visitors. A total of 110 drones equipped with LEDs performed a choreographic light show directly above the river Main, combined with specially composed music and spoken passages to pay homage to Frankfurt. The narrative of "Constellations" centred on prominent personalities and figures from the city, as well as historical milestones and landmarks. The sophisticated airborne choreography was particularly challenging as the stellar constellations, resulting from the position of the drones, had to be recognisable from as many different viewpoints as possible. The use of the latest technology helped create an iconographic performance that honoured Frankfurt's cosmopolitan approach in a series of poetic images.

Statement by the jury
"Constellations", a perfectly planned and orchestrated drone choreography shown in the Frankfurt sky, exemplarily demonstrated that spectacular events are also possible without air pollution. It was comparable to gigantic fireworks, but less loud. This new approach towards using drones enables innovations such as three-dimensional effects as well as conveying messages.

Client
Tourismus+Congress GmbH
Frankfurt am Main (TCF),
Frankfurt/Main, Germany

Design
Atelier Markgraph GmbH,
Frankfurt/Main, Germany

Implementation Partner
bright! GmbH, Maintal, Germany
SKYMAGIC, Singapore
Hoerfeld, Offenbach, Germany

Brand Partner
Lufthansa, Frankfurt/Main, Germany
Mainova, Frankfurt/Main, Germany
Verkehrsgesellschaft
Frankfurt am Main mbH (VGF),
Frankfurt/Main, Germany

→ Designer profile on page 545
→ Clip online

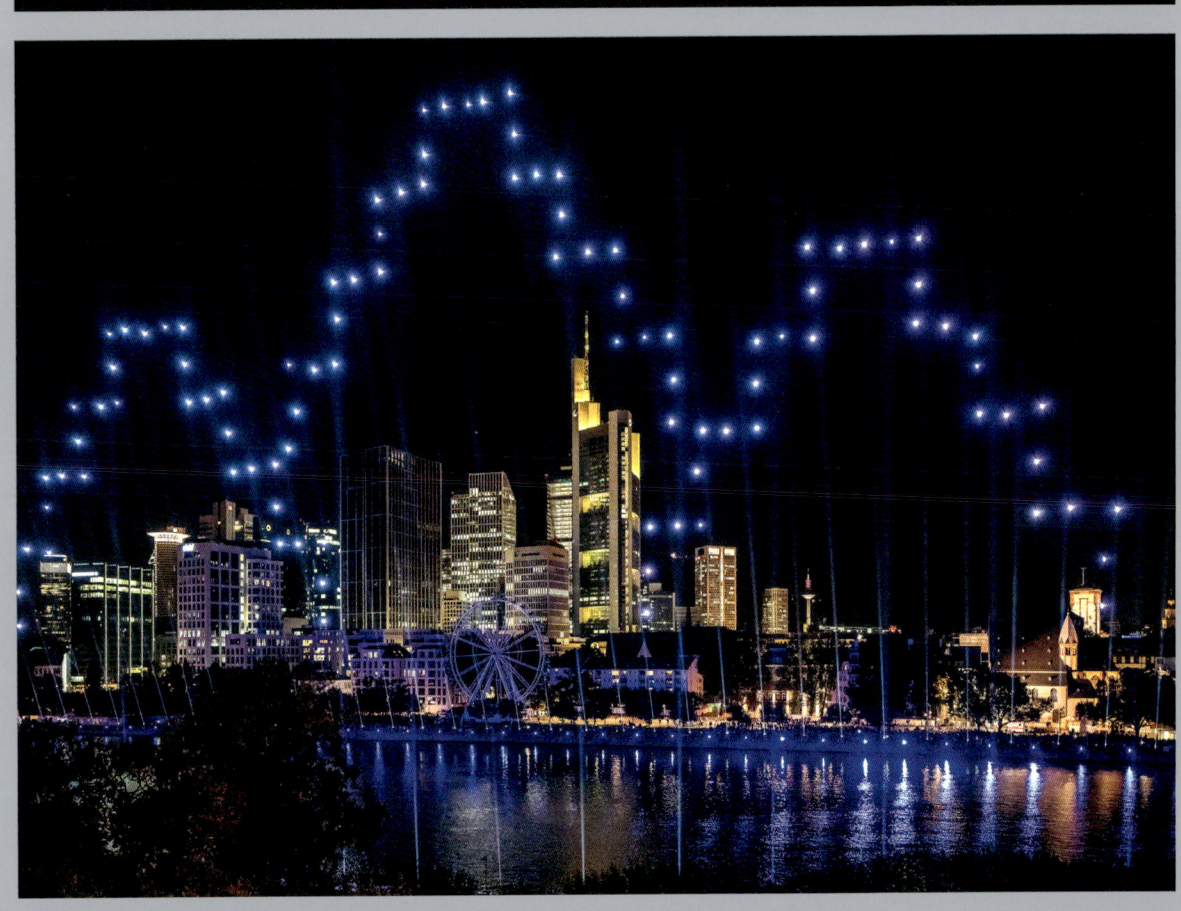

Red Dot: Best of the Best

The Macallan Visitor Experience
[Exhibition Design]

The home of one of the most famous single malt whiskies lies at the foot of the Scottish Highlands where a light-flooded distillery building has been embedded into the landscape. A visitor's route leads through the production hall (14,800 sqm), which is impressive in terms of both architecture and content. Sophistically designed information pillars, which act as key points along the tour, provide access to the history of the company, the processes within the distillery and the brand values. Each of these hands-on installations is positioned to directly link to the location it provides information on. They are made of high-quality materials and feature sophisticated kinetic models. The tour is complemented by three thematic pavilions that offer immersive experiences. All production stages and components leading to the whisky are presented in these walk-through installations. They explain the importance of wood for maturation in the oak barrel, the magic of blending, the composition of the whisky with its different colours, and last but not least the final product, the whisky itself.

Statement by the jury
This exhibition yields an impressive staging of the famous The Macallan whisky brand. The different types of whisky are effectively presented in tune with the surrounding architecture, the materials used and the lifestyle of its consumers. Visitors can experience everything in both a traditional and technological way and learn about the whisky's origins and different flavours. It tells a perfect story about the location.

Interface & User Experience Design | **Spatial Communication** | Red Dot: Junior Award | Designer Profiles | Jury | Index | Red Dot – World of Design

Client
The Edrington Group,
Glasgow, United Kingdom

Design
ATELIER BRÜCKNER, Stuttgart, Germany

Light Planning
Speirs + Major, London, United Kingdom

Media Planning
medienprojekt p2, Stuttgart, Germany

Media Design
TAMSCHICK MEDIA+SPACE,
Berlin, Germany

Kinetic Installation/Technical Implementation
MKT AG, Olching, Germany

Architecture
Rogers Stirk Harbour + Partners,
London, United Kingdom

Light Installation
Jason Bruges Studio,
London, United Kingdom

→ Designer profile on page 518

Pro Nemus

[Interactive Digital Experience]

This exhibition at the Pro Nemus Innovation Center features the future visions of the bioproducts by the Metsä Group. The aim is to provide an experiential cross-section of the life cycle of a forest and the impact of bioeconomics in a world that must increasingly rely on responsible, renewable raw materials. The exhibition is designed as a stage for interactive digital experiences and constructed out of ecological Finnish wood. The entire building was designed by architects to facilitate an immersive digital experience of how the physical is really integrated into the digital.

Client
Metsä Group, Espoo, Finland

Design
Great Apes/HiQ Finland, Helsinki, Finland
MKTG Finland, Helsinki, Finland

Production
Great Apes/HiQ Finland
MediaMonks, Hilversum, Netherlands

→ Designer profile on page 528

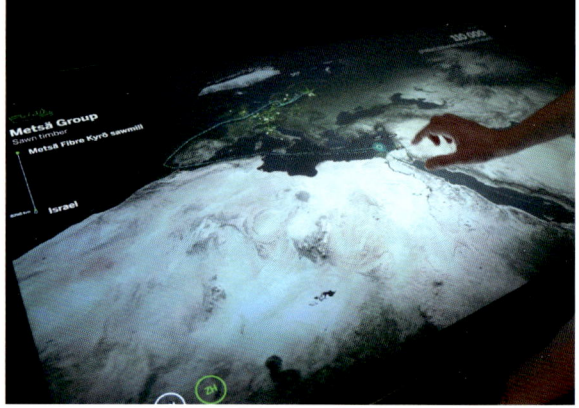

The Floating Island
[Public Installation]

The Floating Island is a temporary installation erected on the city's canal during the six-month exhibition period of the Bruges Triennial 2018. Stirring the medieval landscape of Bruges, the island-like structure added a new view to the city during the exhibition. Taking the shape of a floating, long freestyle white carpet, the island provided an experience as if walking on water. In the sense of intermittent spots of the linear pathway, it included a variety of spaces of different sizes and shapes where people could take a quiet break or get lost in meditation as they sat on a rope chair to watch the water quietly flow by.

Client
Triënnale Brugge, Bruges, Belgium

Design
OBBA, Seoul, South Korea
Dertien12, Bruges, Belgium

Design Team
Sojung Lee, Sangjoon Kwak, OBBA
Tom Gantois, Dertien12

Ocean Plastics Lab

[Exhibition Design]

Client
German Federal Ministry of Education and Research, Berlin, Germany

Design
familie redlich AG, Berlin, Germany

Project Management
Natalie Maaß-Stalp, Lisa Timmermann

Art Direction
Carsten Haar

Graphic Design
Nassar Allamaa

→ Clip online

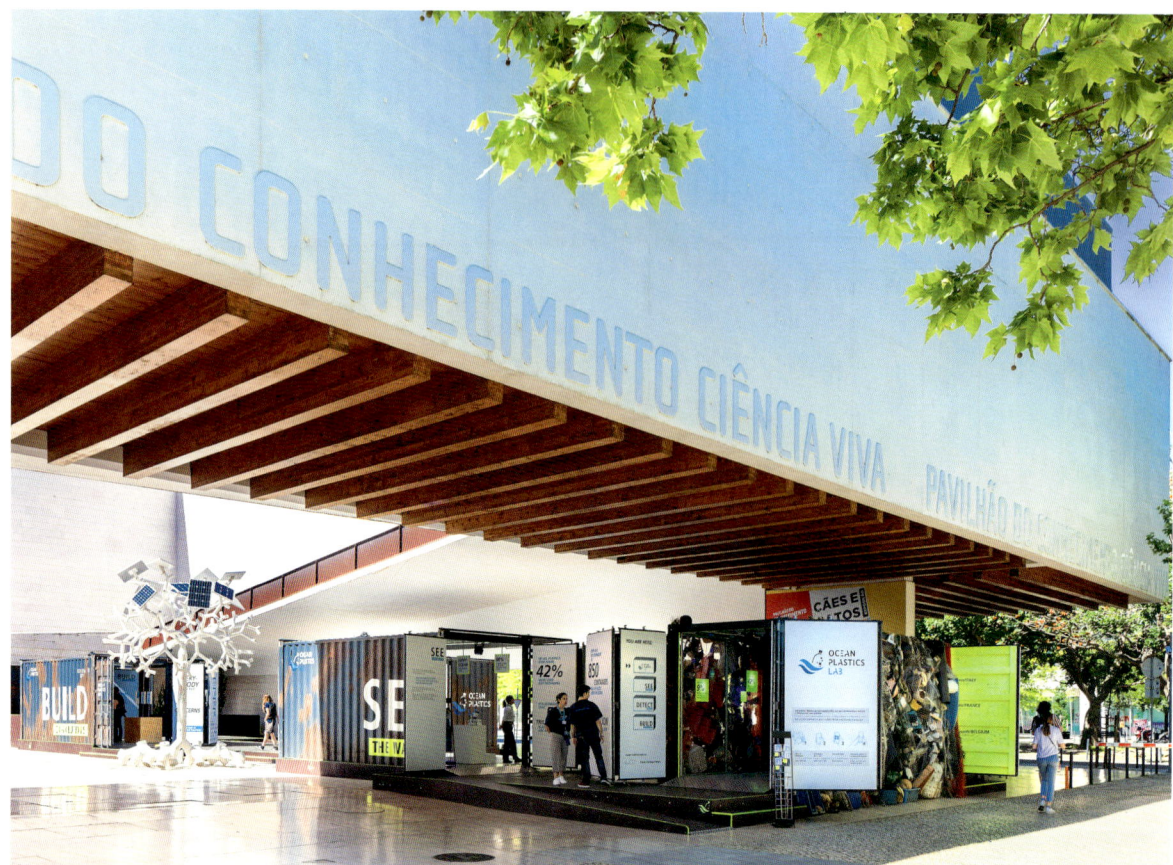

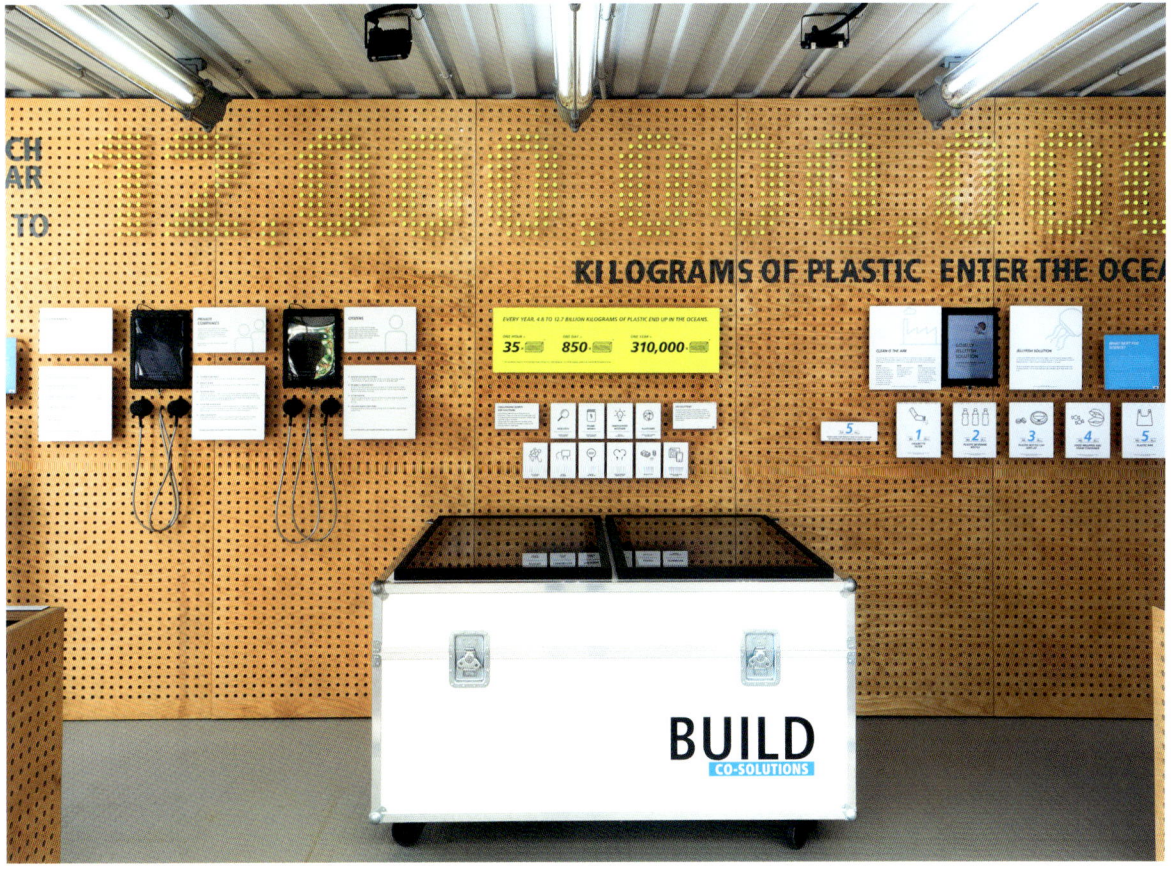

The International travelling exhibition Ocean Plastics Lab (OPL) documents the global flow of plastics and the pollution it causes. The aim of the exhibition is to visualise the issue, in particular since only little is known about the routes and impact of the waste. Therefore, five shipping containers show how science and research seek to understand and tackle the problem of plastics in the oceans. Interactive elements are also part of the didactic concept in order to convey emotions and get visitors involved. To achieve this, different perspectives are considered: those of children and teenagers, as well as those of decision-makers and experts. Each container focuses on a different topic to share scientific insights and information with people.

Highlight City Centre
[Public Installation]

This installation in the city centre of Karlsruhe, Germany, transforms public space into a stage. At the heart of the installation is a lamp that is a 10:1 scale model of a classic product from the region, aiming to stimulate dialogue with the venue. Materialised in adhesive film and chalk spray, the installation spotlight captivates the viewer. Several "table lights" draw attention to urban development issues and will travel through the city centre for two years to "highlight Karlsruhe's future". They are also the starting point of a campaign in which passers-by can share their impressions using the hashtag #spotonka on social media channels.

Client
Stadt Karlsruhe, Germany

Design
raumkontakt GmbH, Karlsruhe, Germany

Graphic Design/Realisation
Jürgen Lenhardt

All eyes on you
[Urban Installation]

"All eyes on you" was developed for the province of Groningen, Netherlands, considering the high number of major accidents occurring there. Designed as a golden camera pole with twenty fake cameras, this installation at the intersection of art and design intends to contribute to a change in behaviour among road users. Each camera has an eye that, based on a lenticular technique, "follows" the road users as they pass. Research shows that these drivers are very aware of their environment and adjust their behaviour. In addition, the urban installation has now become a benchmark in the landscape along the route, reminding people to take care of each other.

Client
Province of Groningen, Netherlands

Design
Studio 212 Fahrenheit,
Groningen, Netherlands

→ Designer profile on page 566

Sailing Castle

[Public Installation]

Client
Pingtung County Government,
Pingtung County, Taiwan

Design
Cheng-Tsung Feng Design Studio,
Nantou County, Taiwan

→ Clip online

As the first architectural installation at the Taiwan Lantern Festival, the Sailing Castle contrives a symbolic pavilion with wood constructions. Inspired by the view of many sailboats gathering in the harbour, as seen from the Donggang coast, the installation interpreted that view through white sails harmoniously intertwined among the structure, turning the pavilion into an enormous sculptural entity embodying that enchanting scenery. As a symbolic attraction, the installation thus evoked the image of fishermen and boats sailing off and making homeward voyages. The interaction among people and the Sailing Castle aimed at representing the prosperity of the local fishing industry and also the notions of communal unity, expectations and joy.

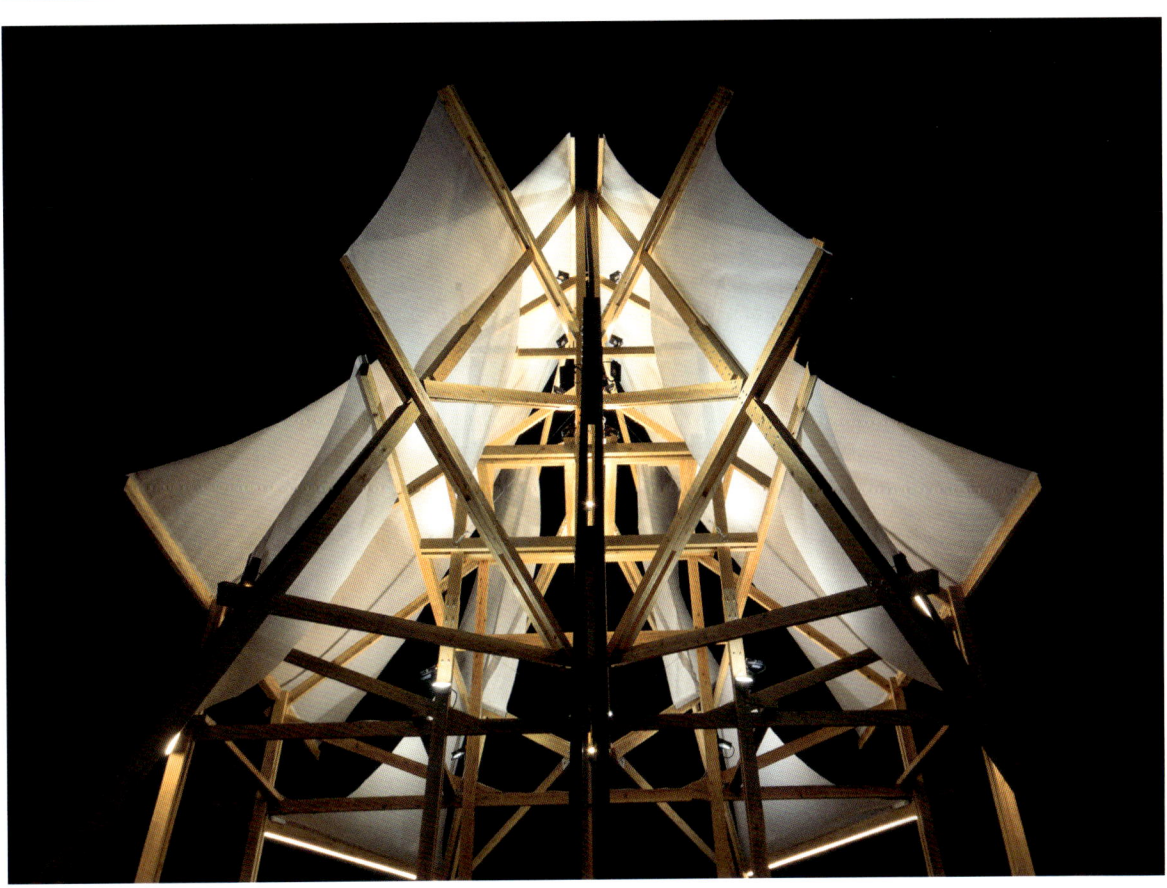

Penghu Arts Festival 2018 – The Rising Wind

[Event Design]

Penghu is an outlying island in Taiwan and a popular seaside tourist attraction, but only in the summer. The 2018 Penghu Arts Festival, under the theme "The Rising Wind", set out to change people's impression of the island through art and design. Promoting the winter beauty of Penghu, the festival featured local handmade art, food and travel, pictures of the locals in Penghu and international artists. In addition, there was a series of activities designed for people to explore the characteristics of Penghu's winter and thus to revitalise the local tourism economy. This was complemented by events such as land art and a workshop, as well as a three-day local trip.

Client
Penghu National Scenic Area Administration, Tourism Bureau, Penghu County, Taiwan

Design
Cheng-Tsung Feng Design Studio, Nantou County, Taiwan

Interface & User Experience Design | **Spatial Communication** | Red Dot: Junior Award | Designer Profiles | Jury | Index | Red Dot – World of Design

There is no such thing as a New Zealand typeface
[Exhibition Design]

Focusing on National 2, a typeface by Klim Type Foundry based in Wellington, New Zealand, this exhibition deals with the question of how identities are formed through symbols, imagery, beliefs and language. The exhibition interrogates the relationship between type and place, text and landscape, and thus ultimately identity. Across the exhibition title, a supergraphic was rendered along the gallery walls. The concept is complemented by 16 large-scale atmospheric photos with matching contours and shared horizons. Together they trace a fictitious visual journey from "the Valley of Darkness, up Mount Inaccessible to Farewell Spit".

Client
Klim Type Foundry,
Wellington, New Zealand

Design
Alt Group, Auckland, New Zealand
Klim Type Foundry,
Wellington, New Zealand

Creative Direction
Dean Poole, Alt Group
Kris Sowersby, Klim Type Foundry

Design Direction
Janson Chau, Alt Group

Graphic Design
Tim Gomez, Alt Group

Text
Mike Barrett, Alt Group

Photography
Alistair Guthrie, Auckland, New Zealand

Publishing & Print Media   Posters   Typography   Illustrations   Sound Design   Film & Animation   Online   Apps

PERGAMON
[Exhibition Design]

Since the Pergamon Museum in Berlin, Germany, is being renovated and will be partially closed during the building work, the original museum exhibits are on display in a temporary exhibition building where they are interwoven with the work of a contemporary artist. The 100-metre-long building contains 80 original items from Berlin's Museum of Greek and Roman Antiquities, staging them among spatial, light and moving image installations. The central piece is a 30-metre-high, 360-degree panorama in which artistic style, specialist knowledge and original exhibits merge together with the aim of enabling visitors to experience antiquity visually, acoustically and emotionally.

Client
Antikensammlung,
Staatliche Museen zu Berlin, Germany

Design
asisi, Berlin, Germany

Creative Direction
Yadegar Asisi, Mathias Thiel

Project Implementation
Ginny Lehmann

Art Direction
Sandra Knüpfer

Motion Design
Matthias Meye

Projection Mapping
Elias Asisi

Graphic Design
Dietmar Götzelmann, polyform,
Berlin, Germany

Production
Gerriets, Umkirch, Germany

Architecture
asisi, Berlin, Germany
spreeformat architekten, Berlin, Germany

Implementation Construction
spreeformat architekten, Berlin, Germany

The Great Tipsy

[Live Performance]

The Great Tipsy is a running repertory theatre show in Taiwan, in which five hotel rooms are converted into fantasy-style theatres with otherworldly settings. The audience can go through an immersive and interactive experience where reality is intertwined with fantasy, as the audience meets with real hotel guests from other countries while experiencing the show. One actor or actress in each room communicates with the audience up close as they saunter through the space. The hallway connecting the rooms is converted into a strip of theatre stage with lighting and sound installations.

Client
Surprise Lab., Taipei City, Taiwan
Home Hotel, Taipei City, Taiwan
King Kong Wave Production,
New Taipei City, Taiwan

Design
Surprise Lab., Taipei City, Taiwan
Home Hotel, Taipei City, Taiwan
King Kong Wave Production,
New Taipei City, Taiwan

→ Designer profile on page 567
→ Clip online

re.show

[Live Performance,
Dance Theatre Creation]

At the centre of this event on the occasion of the 15th anniversary of the agency "kontrastmoment" was the premiere of "re.show" – a dance theatre performance. Questioning the limits of digitisation and the concomitant demystification of everyday life, the project was designed as an experience that touches all of the senses. With the goal of reviving little magical moments, it appeals to human curiosity and spirituality. The performance was accompanied on all three days by the conference program "km: talk" with lectures on topics ranging from art and culture to society.

Client
kontrastmoment GmbH,
Munich, Germany

Design
kontrastmoment GmbH,
Munich, Germany

Concept
Andreas Waldenmaier

Choreography
Sanja Ristic

Music/Score
Alexander Naevecke

Creative Direction/Animation
Binh Le

Fashion Technology Design
Anja Dragan

Fashion Design
Layla De Mue

→ Designer profile on page 538
→ Clip online

Shanghai BFC Bona Cinema

[Interior Design]

The concept for this cinema visually conveys the idea that movies and light refraction are indispensable elements. The unique atmosphere with a natural feel is defined by a bold usage of pickled matte Rojo Alicante marble covering the entire ceiling, walls and lobby floor. Several rectangular marble plates overlap each other in different directions, adapting the form of light refraction. When visitors step into the lobby, they are welcomed by numerous rectangular copper metal 3D installations in the ceiling.

Client
Bona International Cineplex Investment and Management Co., Ltd., Beijing, China

Design
One Plus Partnership Limited, Hong Kong

→ Designer profile on page 555

Re:imagine Street ARt

[Urban Installation]

This campaign during Art Berlin, Germany, explored the possibilities of street art. The idea that street art interferes with its environment and teases observers was emphasised by extending the conceptual idea of the artworks through an additional layer in AR, thus transforming the role of the viewer from a passive consumer to an active participant. Five international artists unfolded their creativity in pop-up galleries, on walls and around monuments, with the artworks being enhanced through an AR app. Visitors were invited to walk through a spectacular installation and shape their own experience by interacting through augmented reality.

Client
Samsung Electronics,
Schwalbach am Taunus, Germany

Design
Cheil Germany GmbH,
Schwalbach am Taunus, Germany

→ Clip online

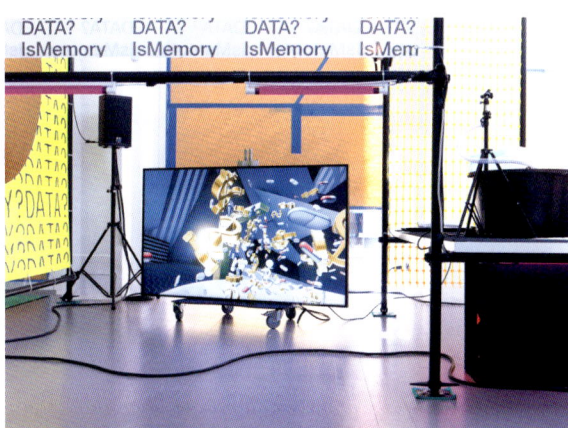

Hyper Fountain
[Virtual Reality Installation]

The Hyper Fountain is an immersive virtual reality installation uniting an HTC Vive with Leap Motion hand tracking. At the centre was the question of whether virtual experiences can recondition perception. Visitors were invited to stand at an ordinary plastic bucket and "wash" their hands in a thin water stream coming from a simple transparent hose. However, what they saw and felt in VR were distinct, creatively interpreted metaphors of water (e.g. glass fragments, rose petals or lava) that played with deeply rooted emotions in the human subconscious.

Client
Aloys F. Dornbracht GmbH & Co. KG,
Iserlohn, Germany

Design
Elastique. GmbH, Cologne, Germany

Creative Direction
Andreas Schimmelpfennig,
Betty Schimmelpfennig, Elastique. GmbH
Mike Meiré,
MEIRÉ UND MEIRÉ GmbH & Co. KG,
Cologne, Germany

Art Direction
Dmitry Zakharov, Elastique. GmbH
Hans von Bülow,
MEIRÉ UND MEIRÉ GmbH & Co. KG

Project Management
Christin Flosbach, Elastique. GmbH

Sprite – Drone Painter
[Live Performance]

To communicate the message that Sprite is a "refreshing" brand, the Drone Painter campaign demonstrated to viewers a creative use of drones. It gave them the opportunity to create their own mural on a specially designed website. Based on innovative software with an AI-based algorithm, the drone could be controlled without the need of human touch. The software analyses the wind speed and wind direction that enable the drone to fly safely and stably near the wall, allowing it to compose the individual elements of the mural and paint them layer by layer. The best painting was selected from the hundreds of murals made.

Client
The Coca-Cola Company, Kyiv, Ukraine

Design
Saatchi & Saatchi Ukraine, Kyiv, Ukraine

Creative Direction
Kosta Schneider

Art Direction
Illya Bondar, Vlad Moshenskiy

Text
Sergey Beloshitsky

Graphic Design
Ksenia Boldur, Dmytro Moloshnikov

Account Management
Marina Kondriyanenko, Olga Dovzhenko

Milan Design Week 2018 – Hidden Senses

[Exhibition Design]

Showcased at Milan Design Week 2018, this exhibition is about exploring new ways of interaction in people's daily households. Assuming that all the information we need blends into our daily behaviour and familiar objects, the minimal sensorial interfaces are aimed at bringing more comfort and calm into ordinary life. Comprising five case study rooms, the exhibition followed the concept of a journey with each room, gradually revealing conceptual interaction turned into examples of contextual application. Thus, step by step, visitors could experience how the hidden sensory method works through sound, visuals, tactility, products and space.

Client
Sony Corporation, Tokyo, Japan

Design
Sony Design, Tokyo, Japan

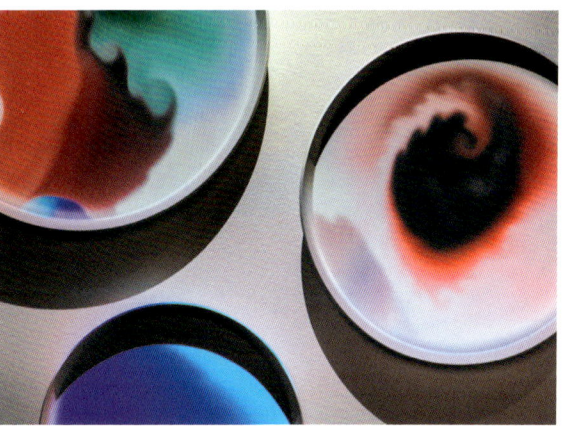

Roca One Day Design Challenge
[Event Design]

Client
Roca Sanitario, S.A, Barcelona, Spain

Design
Roca Sanitario, S.A, Barcelona, Spain

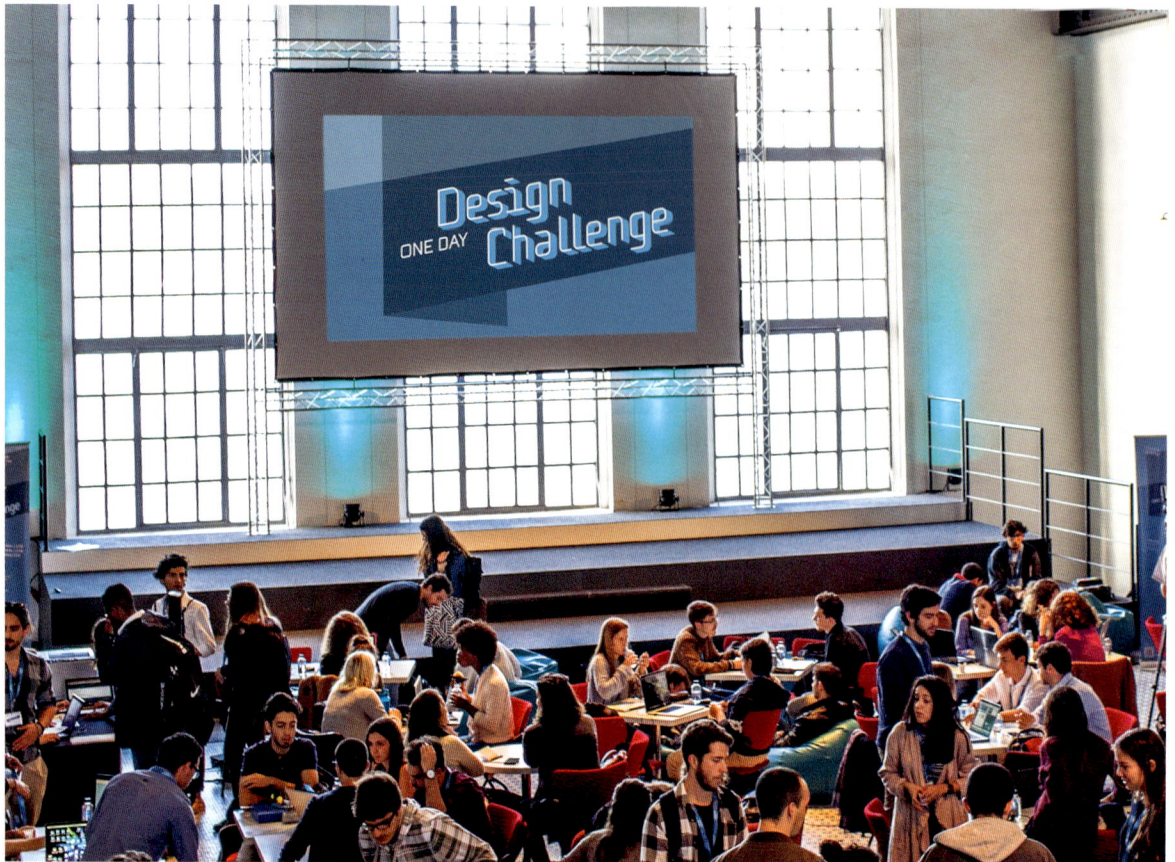

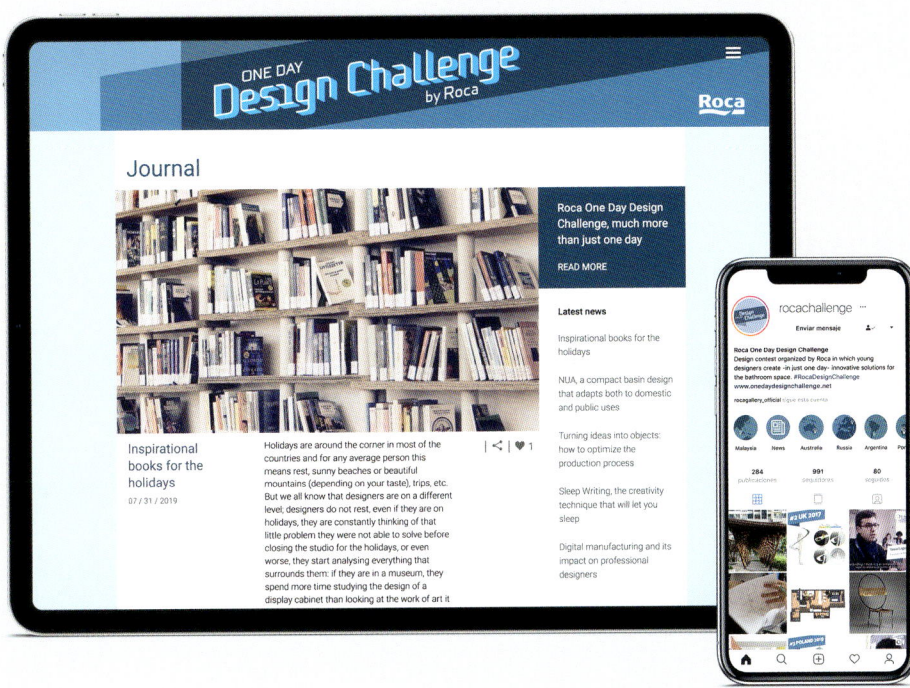

As a global communication campaign, the Roca One Day Design Challenge sets out to position the brand homogenously among young professionals and specifiers. It consists of a design contest aimed at promoting and giving visibility to young talent. Driven by the company Roca, the event challenges design and architecture students, as well as young professionals under the age of 30, to create original products related to the bathroom space in just one day. The competition gives four monetary awards, one of which is focused on sustainability. The projects are assessed by an internationally highly recognised jury. In 2020, the winners of the first prize of all editions will participate in a grand finale in Barcelona.

Hsinchu City Glass Art & Design Festival 2018 – Light Driving

[Exhibition Design]

Client
Hsinchu City Government,
Hsinchu City, Taiwan

Design
InFormat Design Curating,
Taipei City, Taiwan

Creative Direction
Yao-Pang Wang

Customer Advisory Service
Ying-Ying Weng

Project Management
Aaron Yang, Jue-Ning Chen, Li-Ching Liu

Spatial Design
Che-Wei Chang, Yi-Yang Peng

Graphic Design
Hao Zhuang, Tzu-Lin Liu, Yun-Da Chou

Marketing/Public Relations
Doris Hu

→ Clip online

This exhibition introduces the 2018 Hsinchu City Glass Art & Design Festival. As the Chinese city has been known for its glass industry since 1925, the exhibition showcases traditional craftsmanship as a drive for local creativity. By imagining glass as a "cultural container", the exhibition starts with a 143 cc glass cup, which is otherwise commonly seen in Taiwan food stalls. It explores themes of everyday life, including traditional pickled food, tea culture, temple snacks and souvenir savoury foods. The overall aim is to inspire a new understanding between glass and living aesthetics, urban marketing and cultural design.

Publishing & Print Media   Posters   Typography   Illustrations   Sound Design   Film & Animation   Online   Apps

WÜSTHOF Fair Stand Ambiente 2019
[Exhibition Design]

The brand presence of the knife manufacturer WÜSTHOF at the 2019 Ambiente fair in Frankfurt am Main, Germany, staged the idea of a perfectly executed cut under the motto of "Discover the Moment of Cutting". Four oversized upright blocks were spread throughout the entire exhibition stand and connected by obliquely cut edges to reference each other, while the inside surfaces showcased aesthetic macro shots of a freshly cut red cabbage. Thanks to the use of scientific photographs, the spatial cuts and motifs communicated an overall balanced appearance.

Client
WÜSTHOF GmbH, Solingen, Germany

Design
Milla & Partner, Stuttgart, Germany

Creative Direction
Sebastian Letz

Art Direction
Florian Holzer

Account Management
Kristin Becker

Architecture
Niklas Sternagel

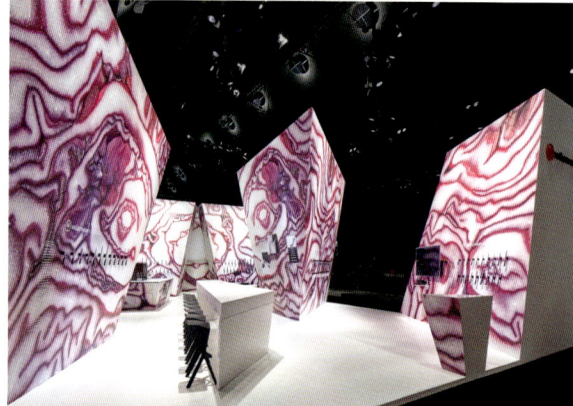
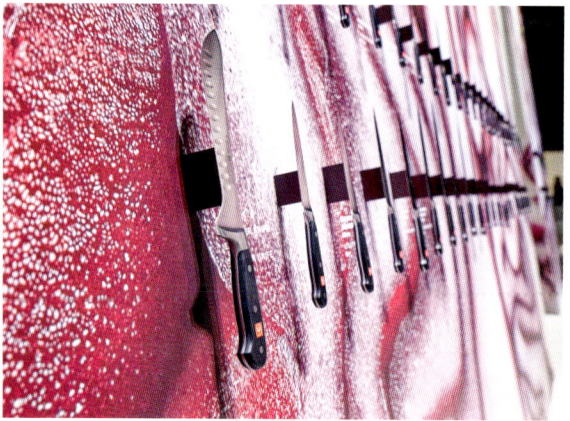

TRT Health Shop
[Orientation System, Signage Design]

This signage system for the Tongrentang Health (TRT Health) Shop interprets the store's atmosphere set between traditional Chinese medicine and modern healthcare products. The implementation aims to strengthen this contrast in a harmonious manner. Thus, it clearly designates the various shop areas with signs produced in copper that merge a Chinese character with its English translation. Realised as a smooth combination of craft and design, this makes for concise and intriguing signs. As the entire shop is conceived as an open space, the signs are hung from above on two thin copper sticks, instead of being placed on a stand in front of each area.

Client
Tongrentang Health, Beijing, China

Design
ToThree Design, Beijing, China

Design Team
Wu Sun, Rui Zhang, Yi Le, Peinan Zhang, Yuhan Li

Production Management
Xuihui Jiang

→ Designer profile on page 569

NFSQ

[Signage Design]

The implementation of the signage design for the company Nongfu Spring was guided by the idea of visualising the brand core values of "natural and healthy". Realised as a clear and humanised design, the guiding system has adopted a modern style that is inspired by the natural colours of the local YangShengTang park. Combining the notions of vitality and reality, the signs are integrated into their environment by using a variety of materials. The signage system thus provides information that helps visitors to know, understand and employ the space, while also enhancing and enriching the relationship between people and the various spaces.

Client
NFSQ, Hangzhou, China

Design
Box Brand Design Ltd., Hong Kong

Creative Direction
Joey Lo

Art Direction
Yvonne Chung

Graphic Design
Nate Zhang

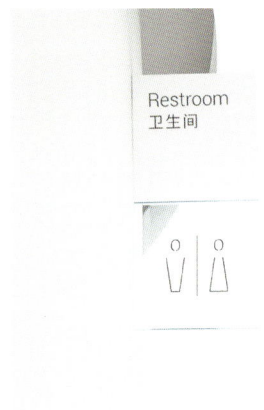
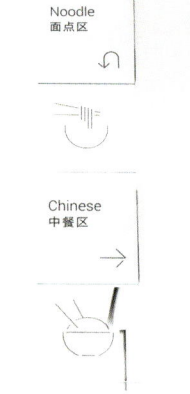
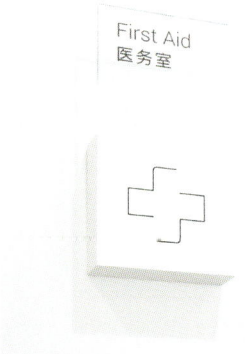

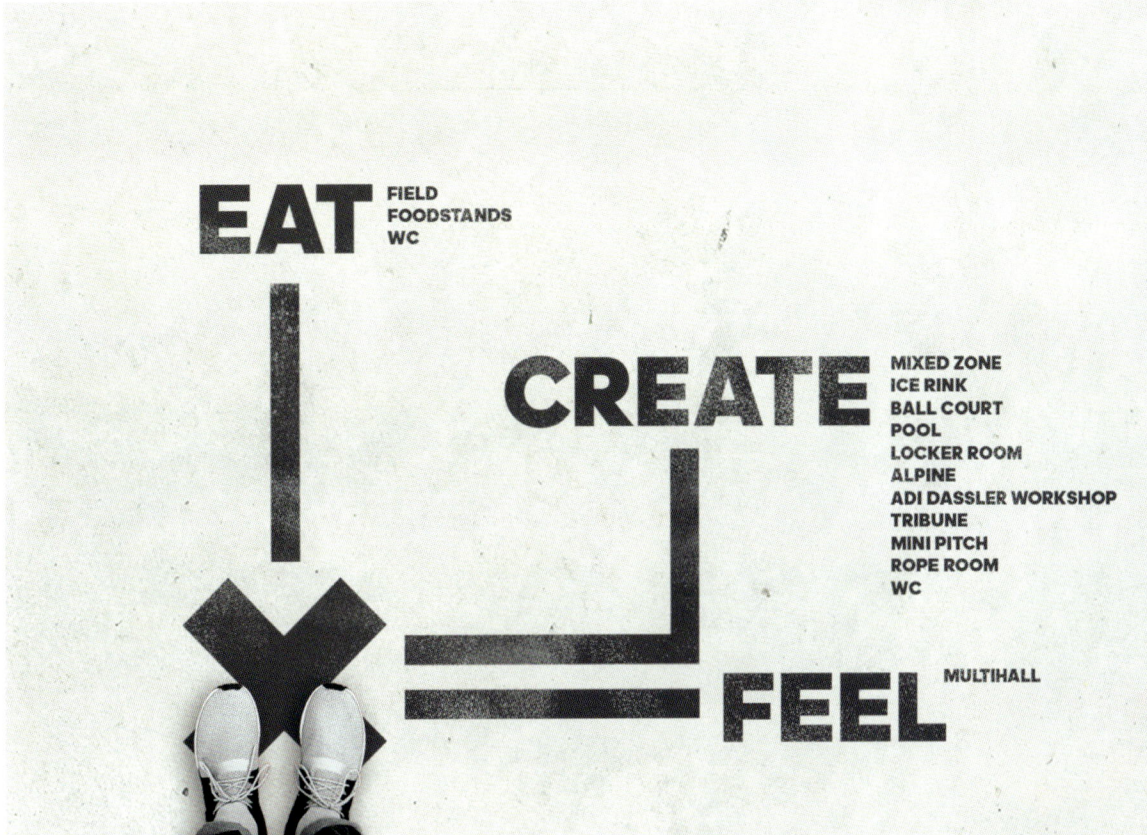

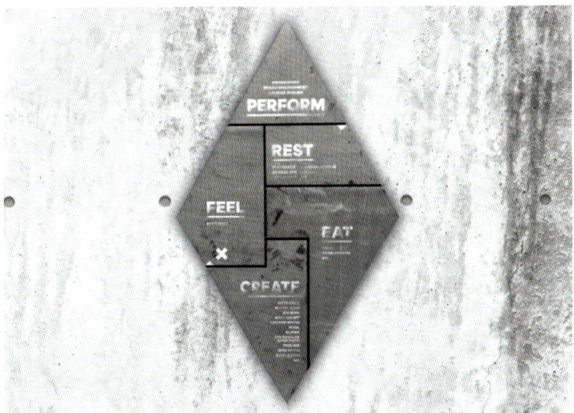

adidas HALFTIME
[Orientation System]

Created for the Halftime building, which is part of the adidas World of Sports, this orientation system combines graphic elements of game strategy and field marking with the architecture and materiality of the building to playfully guide visitors to their destinations. The central overview board picks up on the exterior shape of the building. The four information levels provide an overview, lead into the levels of the building and distinguish its rooms and spaces. The opulent glass surfaces of nine thematically designed meeting rooms are characterised by individual graphic elements.

Client
adidas AG, Herzogenaurach, Germany

Design
EIGA Design, Hamburg, Germany
COBE Architects, Copenhagen, Denmark

Creative Direction
Elisabeth Plass, Henning Otto,
EIGA Design

Art Direction
Maria Bessa, EIGA Design

Graphic Design
Barbara Madl, EIGA Design

Architecture
Ulrich Pohl, Yannik Courtin,
COBE Architects

Project Management
Ulrich Pohl, COBE Architects

Publishing & Print Media   Posters   Typography   Illustrations   Sound Design   Film & Animation   Online   Apps

The Future of Leadership (Salon) – Provoking a New Way of Thinking

[Event Design, Visual Identity]

The corporate design for the conference "The Future of Leadership (Salon)" in Düsseldorf, Germany, focuses on visualising openness towards thinking in new directions. It illustrates the idea of questioning everything that is known by integrating the familiar and well-known "ad absurdum" into the design. The logo is mirrored, the word "leadership" crossed out and the noble "Salon" placed in brackets. This idea is also continued in the motifs as conventional leadership maxims are caricatured in striking implementations. A black bar crosses out the motifs, while at the same time containing the communicative messages.

Client
Simon Consulting, Düsseldorf, Germany

Design
Grey Germany/KW43 BRANDDESIGN, Düsseldorf, Germany

Managing Director Creation
Rüdiger Goetz

Creative Direction
Jürgen Adolph

Creative Direction Digital
Tim Liedtke

Art Direction
Miriam Hugo, Marc Schäde

Art Direction Digital
Jacqueline Szurawicki

Copywriting
Michael Draheim

Account Management
Ramona Pander

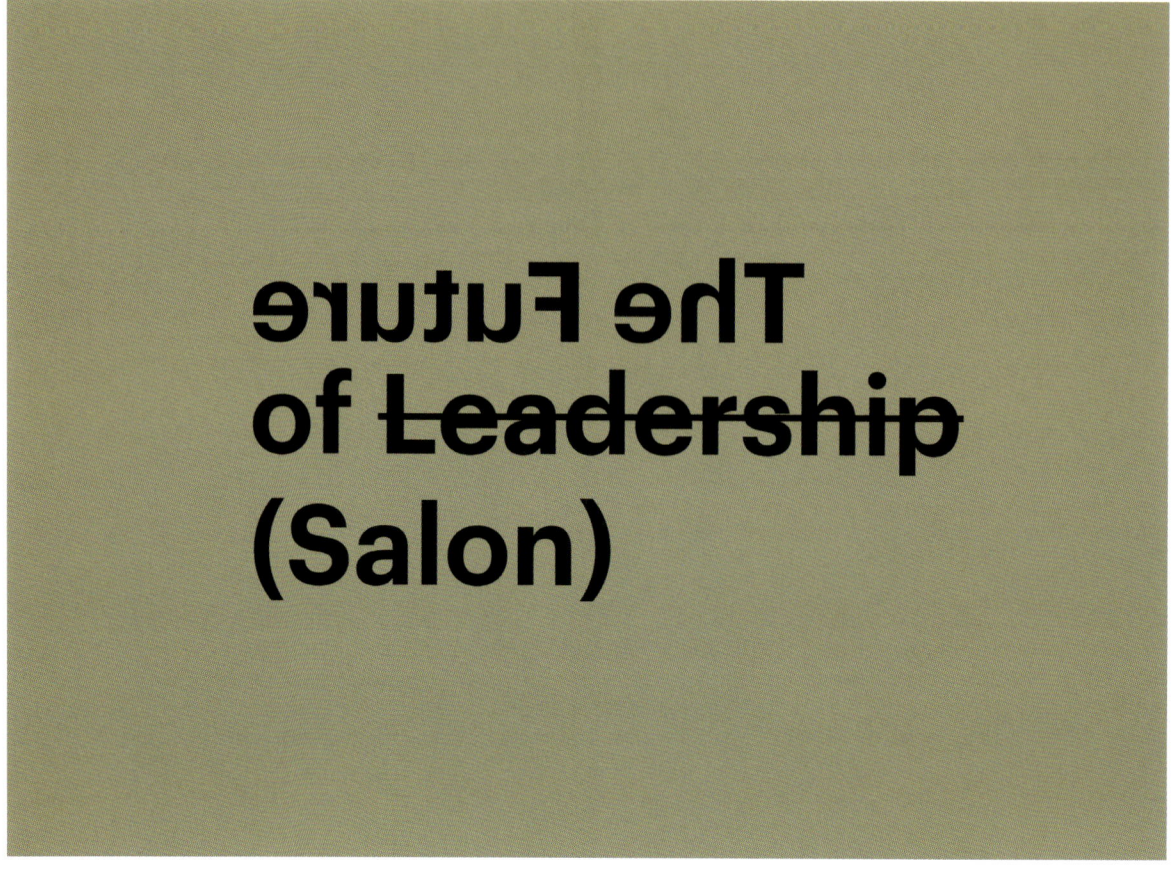

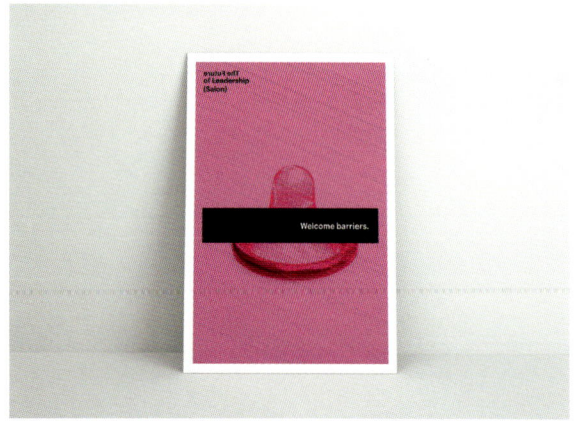

Spireworks

[Light Installation, Interactive Architectural Lighting App Design]

Spireworks is a building-scale interactive lighting installation with a corresponding app that allows users to control architectural lights in buildings in real time, using a range of different colours and animated graphics raising awareness for non-profit causes worldwide. The interface design and innovative interactions allow users to choose between iconic buildings in New York City. Visible from nearly 30 miles away, with the tap of a button, the public can see the building's colour change. Spireworks currently has access to the spire and podium of One World Trade Center, the spires of One Bryant Park and One Five One 42nd Street. More buildings are being added and the platform is beginning to expand its offerings.

Client
Spireworks, New York, USA

Design
L+R, New York/Barcelona, USA/Spain

Creative Direction
Alex Levin, Ryan Riegner

Account Management
Julia Keller

Graphic Design
Chris Martinié, Sharon Lee, Inyoung Kwon

Programming
Alex Queudot, Ivan Leider

Interaction Design
Mark Domino, Spireworks

→ Designer profile on page 539

FI-Forum

[Interactive Installation]

As a part of the FI-Forum by the company Finanz Informatik in Frankfurt am Main, Germany, this interactive installation visualises the process of digitisation by example of artificial intelligence, machine learning and big data. In the entrance area, the brand profile and the changed customer and work behaviour are explained by the phenomenon of the swarm principle. A digital signature in the form of an action-linked visualisation stages the topic with citations such as "The Internet does not sleep" on the sidewalls to accompany visitors into the expansive exhibition area.

Client
Finanz Informatik,
Frankfurt/Main, Germany

Design
beierarbeit GmbH, Bielefeld, Germany
Atelier Markgraph GmbH,
Frankfurt/Main, Germany

Publisher
Christoph Rutter, Finanz Informatik

Head of Marketing
Andreas Honsel, Finanz Informatik

Strategic Planning
Claudia Palermo, Finanz Informatik

Creative Direction
Christoph Beier, beierarbeit
Martin Schwember, Atelier Markgraph

Motion Design
Johannes Schmitz, APPARAT,
Hamburg, Germany

Programming
Oemer Enrique Erol, NSYNK,
Frankfurt/Main, Germany

→ Designer profile on page 545

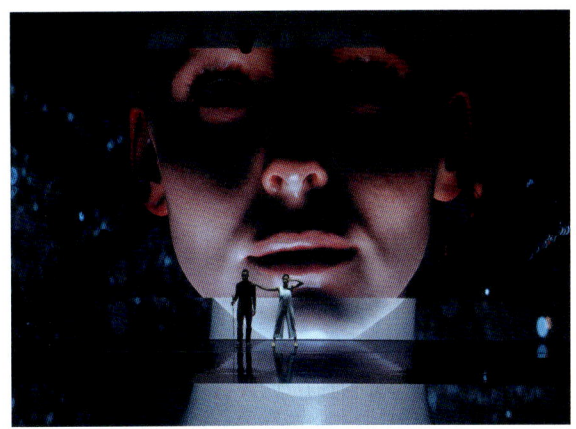

Technology Summit 2019 Opening Performance
[Live Performance]

Technology Summit is an event organised by the digital operator Turkcell. It is defined as an important platform where technological innovations, future theories, research and personal success stories are shared among the many attendees. The concept of the 2019 Live Performance focused on the event's own stories from the significant speeches of the past. This constituted the first part of the performance. The second part focused on social responsibility and technology. It discussed merging together through people's differences. During the third part, the LED panels opened up a new stage surface, and an interactive performance was created using scrim paper and motion tracking.

Client
TURKCELL Iletisim Hizmetleri A.S, Istanbul, Turkey

Design
BİŞEYLER New Media Works, Istanbul, Turkey

Creative Direction
B. Ece Okuyucu, Gökhan Okuyucu

Visual Creative Direction
Tiber Ergür

Choreography
Aslı Öztürk

Project Management
Alican Yılmaz

Music/Sound Design
Jacob Thomas Czech, Prozac Studio

Documentation
Ravv Studio

→ Clip online

Audi Dealer Meeting Marbella 2019

[Event Design]

Under the motto "Let's shake up the world", the Audi Dealer Meeting 2019 in Marbella, Spain, staged a "journey to other realms" with the aim of drawing attention to a new era of mobility. Therefore, a space shuttle was sent 18 times to distant worlds – each to a different, yet mutually complementing, future-oriented theme, including architecture, media, show elements and the costumes of the performers. In addition, the individual show elements were accompanied by a futuristic voice-over to complete the illusion. The show itself integrated innovation themes into the "space trip" by narrating them as existing missions.

Client
AUDI AG, Ingolstadt, Germany

Design
SCHMIDHUBER, Munich, Germany
MUTABOR, Hamburg, Germany

Concept/Architecture
SCHMIDHUBER

Concept/Communication
MUTABOR

Event Management
STAGG & FRIENDS, Düsseldorf, Germany

→ Clip online

Audi Lounge by BLUE NOTE Vol.11

[Event Design]

The aim of this marketing event was to communicate the brand image to a young generation. This idea was implemented through a strategy surpassing the limits of jazz, which has an elegant but somewhat dated image. An after-party with electronic dance music is meant to expand the influence of the Audi Lounge beyond the limits by featuring young and trendy artists. In order to visualise the slogan "Audi Lounge Vol.11, another Vol.1", the key visual featuring all over the venue is marked by vertical lines, which are not only reminiscent of the number 11 but are also a symbol of elevation, expansion and forward movement.

Client
Audi Korea, Seoul, South Korea

Design
PPW Korea, Seoul, South Korea

Head of Marketing
Changseok Son

Creative Direction
Yaesul Jo

Art Direction
Yeonjung Shin

Project Management
Wonhee Kang

→ Clip online

Audi Route B – Seoul Archive 2018

[Event Design]

This event centred on the goal of rendering an experience of the content and ideas of the "Route B" magazine. The private party with 400 selected guests took place in December 2018 in the "D Museum" in Seoul, South Korea. Just like in the magazine, the six featured themes of lifestyle and design, music, stay, dining, coffee and tea with dessert are spread throughout the exhibition space. In order to convey the magazine's ideas, the floor was painted like a road map and the AUDI A6 car was placed in the centre of the space. The city's atmosphere was staged by a fashion show under the motto "Night of the Seoul".

Client
Audi Korea, Seoul, South Korea

Design
COW Inspiration Group, Seoul, South Korea

Audi A4 Urban Culture Space

[Event Design]

Audi Urban Culture Space was a launching event for Audi A4 in 2018 in Seoul, South Korea, that included both a private party and a public exhibition. The venue took place in the old factory "Urban Source" located in the former industrial district of Seongsudong in Seoul. The event was accompanied by coherently designed invitations, brochures and space branding. The combination between a thousand vintage light bulbs and the cutting-edge lighting technology of the Audi A4 invited guests to appreciate the model in ever-shifting perspectives. A special partnership with local lifestyle brands highlighted the car's features.

Client
Audi Korea, Seoul, South Korea

Design
COW Inspiration Group,
Seoul, South Korea

RED DOT: JUNIOR AWARD

Red Dot: Junior Prize

A–B Magazine Issue No. 1 – Right of Asylum

A–B magazine is about the movement and migration of people and, against the backdrop of the current refugee crisis, explores the underlying forces of safety, security and refuge. In three chapters – "Contemplation" on our inner self and the universal desire to seek safety, "Refugee Crisis" on the refugees and their struggles around the world and "The Mundane" with a view on our regular asylum camps – the magazine aims at a better understanding of the asylum seekers. With a study of the history of migration, going back to Adam and Eve, as well as numerous impressive photographs and drawings by refugee children, the subject is examined from many different angles in words and images. The relevance of the topic is underlined by the orange colour that runs through the entire book and is also featured on the outside, in the form of a fluorescent zip pouch made from the characteristic ripstop nylon of refugee lifejackets.

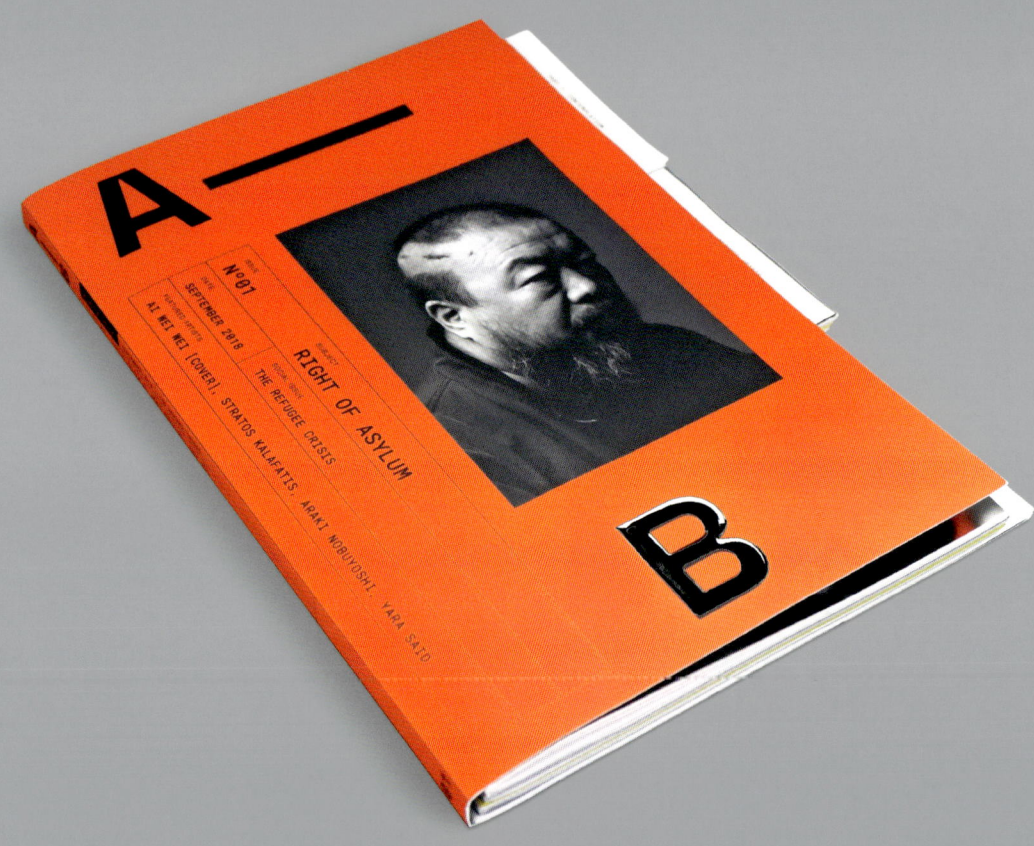

Interface & User Experience Design | Spatial Communication | **Red Dot: Junior Award** Publishing & Print Media | Designer Profiles | Jury | Index | Red Dot – World of Design

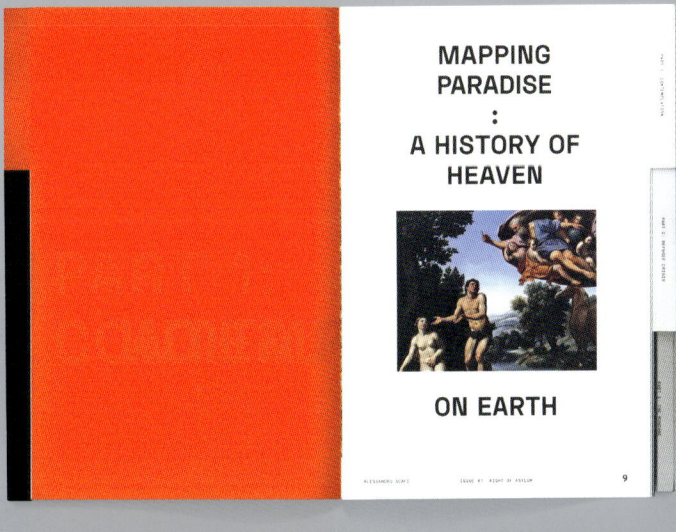

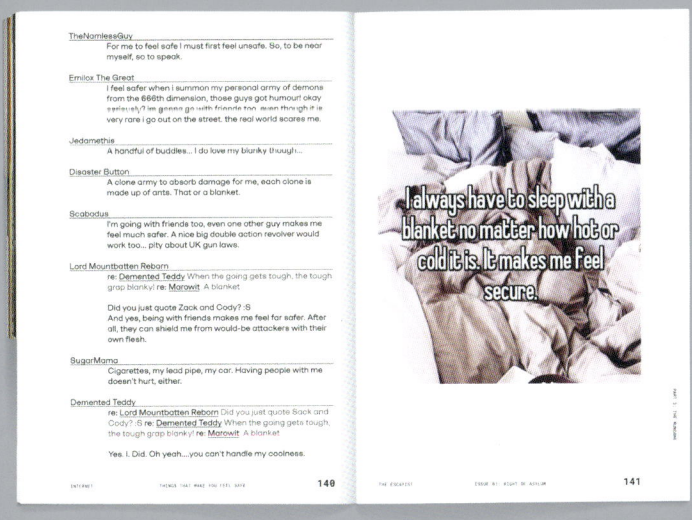

reddot winner 2019
junior prize

University
LASALLE College of the Arts, Singapore

Design
Edward Lau, LASALLE College of the Arts

→ Designer profile on page 540

Publishing & Print Media   Posters   Typography   Illustrations   Sound Design   Film & Animation   Online   Apps

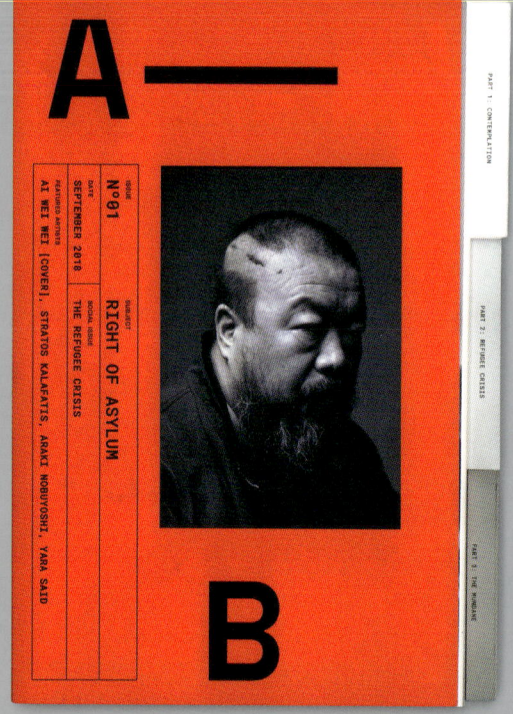

Red Dot: Junior Prize

"Safety – a Human Right?"

[Statement by the jury]

reddot winner 2019
junior prize

A magazine about the refugee crisis? Hasn't everything already been said, written and broadcast about this topic? Edward Lau also asked himself these exact questions when searching the right topic for his final project at LASALLE College of the Arts in Singapore. The very fact that this topic is extraordinarily widely reported on in the (social) media ultimately made it challenging for the young designer to find a new approach.

When he started creating his concept, he probably didn't yet realise the extent of the emotional reaction the A–B magazine would trigger. Tabs formally separate the three-part printed work, which lets the reader begin with the proverbial Adam and Eve and their banishment from paradise. The universal desire for safety and security, for a place to live without danger, a place to feel at home, has probably always been part of the human experience. The first section provides a glimpse of the situation from above, a kind of survey of this basic need – across national boundaries and without any judgement – and allows the reader to arrive at the conclusion that a sense of security is as existential to us as food and clothing.

In the second part, Edward Lau then pulls us right into the drama that unfurls day after day in many locations across the globe, namely the struggle to regain precisely this lost sense of safety and the sudden realisation that making the journey in puny rubber dinghies is just as dangerous as staying at home. The decision, made a million times over, to risk the lives of the entire family in order to maybe find a safe place to live … someday, somewhere. Using vivid photos – generally monochrome images combined with a bright orange – and an otherwise very restrained page design, this magazine compresses the refugee crisis in succinct and hard-hitting visuals. Overcrowded boats, corpses in the arms of helpers, but also children's drawings that show the desires of even the youngest refugees who cannot yet express these in words.

Finally, in the third section, we are released back into "our" world, which is so fundamentally different from the impressions we have just seen. What do we associate with a sense of security? A variety of quotes list many different aspects ranging from the blanket for sleeping to being with friends. Places, items or experiences that represent security in a very individual way. Sometimes it's mundane things that we are not consciously aware of but that translate into a feeling. This section also features an interview with Ai Weiwei, providing lots of food for thought.

This strong content-based concept combined with absolutely consistent execution – a balancing act between seeking attention and exercising restraint – shows just what design is able to achieve. It can literally force readers to sit up and pay attention and can open up new perspectives. For the former, Edward Lau chose a symbol that is likely to be synonymous with the refugee crisis for all time and no longer associated with a harmless boat trip: the first one hundred copies of the A–B magazine were packaged in hand-sewn life jackets. The bright orange is ultimately also the graphic element that links the three sections – one single cleverly chosen colour achieves the most emotionality possible. It also touched the emotions of the jury, which awarded this work with the Red Dot: Junior Prize 2019.

Red Dot: Best of the Best [Red Dot: Junior Prize nominee]

Sounds of Taiwan Cicada
[Special Publication]

Using various media, the project "Sounds of Taiwan Cicada" is based on nine different cicada species in Taiwan, as well as on the country's traditional toy of the bamboo cicada, which it transforms into a modern electronic version. For the visual design, the sound of real cicada chirps was analysed and categorised into three major frequencies, which were then translated into different colours and shapes by means of graphically abstracted patterns and illustrations. The packaging houses a handy electronic toy which, like the original cicada toy, is held on a string and gives off the typical sound of a cicada. An enclosed brochure and e-book describe the life cycle of the individual cicadas and provide a realistic insight into their appearance and life via photographs. A centrefold in the book, when spread open, includes on one side a detailed introduction to all nine species of cicadas and, on the other side, along a branch, visualises the different stages in the growth process of a cicada in a clear and easy-to-understand manner.

Statement by the jury
Merging packaging design and various media, this project is characterised by a high level of professionalism. The way in which readers are invited by the information booklet and e-book to learn about these nine cicadas, including through sound in photorealistic illustrations depicting their life cycles, is absolutely excellent. The entire visual appearance is deeply infused by high aesthetic standards, rich information and great attention to detail.

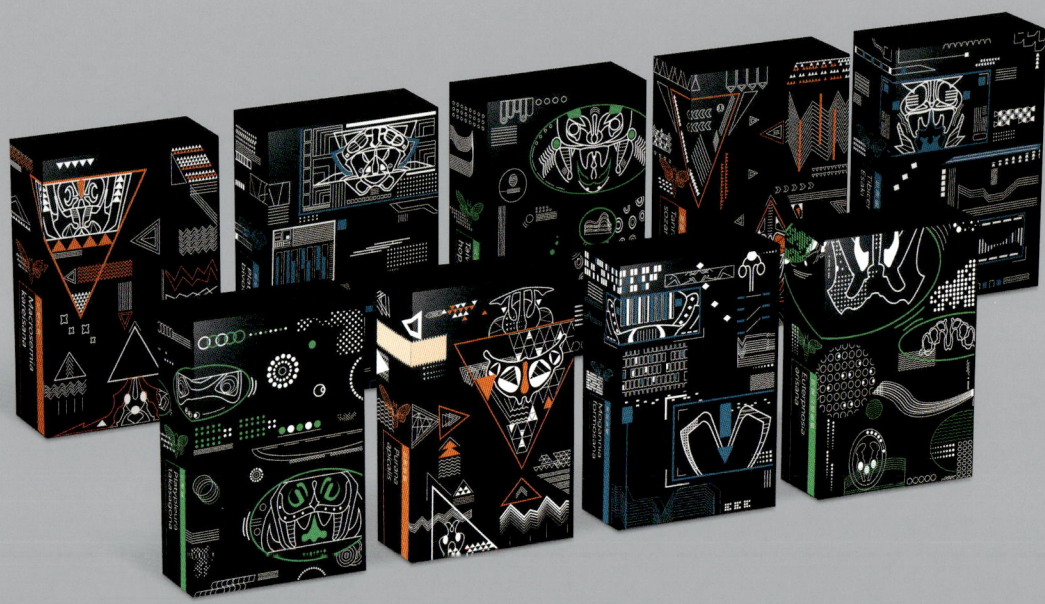

| Interface & User Experience Design | Spatial Communication | **Red Dot: Junior Award** Publishing & Print Media | Designer Profiles | Jury | Index | Red Dot – World of Design |

University
Shu-Te University, Kaohsiung, Taiwan

Supervising Professor
Cheng-Chang Chen

Design
Yu-Chih Lee, Kui-Shang Wong,
Chia-Hui Ting, Qiao-Ru Zeng,
Yu-Ping Tsai, Shu-Te University

→ Designer profile on page 541

Red Dot: Best of the Best

Empathy
[Poster Series]

The poster series "Empathy" focuses on the subject of empathy and thus on the ability to feel with other people and see things from their perspective, as well as to accept oneself just as others. The different illustrations aim to show ways how to counteract antagonism, hatred and discrimination. Against a grey background, each poster visualises a human gesture in simple strokes that can be recognised as a hug, mutual understanding or the feeling of tolerance. In addition to black and white, the only colour used is orange, which stands for the warmth and the energy that flows through hands and arms to support each other and to give one another courage and strength. The titles in combination with the Chinese characters "bao", "na" and "rong" get to the heart of the message of empathy in a simple and vivid manner.

Statement by the jury
This poster series convinces with a distinctive minimalist imagery that communicates the notions of empathy, security and tolerance. The underlying message of how to counteract discrimination and hatred is expressed in the reduced and subtly designed illustrations and complemented by simple word messages in a highly harmonious and convincing manner.

University
Asia University, Taichung, Taiwan

Supervising Professor
Ming-Lung Yu

Design
Po-Ya Yu, Asia University

→ Designer profile on page 573

Red Dot: Best of the Best

A-Ma Knows Best
[Editorial Illustration]

In a traditional Taiwanese family, the grandmother "A-Ma" represents the role of cultural inheritance and is considered a walking textbook of life experience and wisdom. Since the wisdom of the early ancestors has only been passed on orally, the publication "A-Ma Knows Best" records the knowledge of the grandmothers of the 1930s and 1940s in three highly detailed books covering the cultural history of "diet", "art" and "belief". The books are handbound and screen-printed to express the feeling of nostalgia. On the inside, the topics are connected by a wide variety of illustrations, materials and information on traditions and practices, providing a realistic insight into the history of these cultural assets. Picture stories, real objects and tactile elements, including different papers, thread stitching and a handmade wooden box, turn the topics into an experience that is also sensually tangible, inviting to a dialogue between generations.

Statement by the jury
This publication was preceded by substantive research into daily life in former times and the proverbial wisdom of grandmothers, as well as into past craftsmanship skills and techniques. The way the findings have been compiled in these three outstanding and lovingly handcrafted books not only reflects a high level of skill, it has also resulted in a highly aesthetic and harmonious expression in terms of the width and depth of this work.

| Interface & User Experience Design | Spatial Communication | Red Dot: Junior Award Illustrations | Designer Profiles | Jury | Index | Red Dot – World of Design |

University
China University of Technology,
Taipei City, Taiwan

Supervising Professor
Sheng-Chuan Chang, Chien-Yao Wang,
Chien-Hsun Chen

Design
Yun-Xuan Liu, Yu-Ru Liu, Yu-Han Chang,
Chih-Hao Wu, Department of Visual
Communication Design,
China University of Technology

→ Designer profile on page 544

Red Dot: Best of the Best

Hilight
[Navigation App for the Visually Impaired]

The Hilight app is designed to support blind and visually impaired people when on the go. According to a survey among blind people, the most difficult and dangerous navigation stages for them are crosswalks, traffic lights and vehicles. Using an artificial neural network, the app recognises these objects in real time and can, for example, read the numbers and destinations of busses. It announces the direction to the navigation objects using VoiceOver or TalkBack and indicates the distance to them via acoustic signals. The user interface has been tailored to the visually impaired in that it provides a colour-blind mode or a large font mode with words as used on road signs that are easy-to-understand in multiple languages. The app can be used without holding the phone in hand, since a pair of complementary glasses equipped with a camera can communicate with it via Bluetooth. The result is a tool that makes moving around the city in the daily life of visually impaired people easier and safer.

Statement by the jury
The Hilight app for visually impaired people is an absolutely outstanding project. The support that it offers acoustically or in large letters is not only thoughtfully researched and designed, it also makes the app easy and highly practical to use. In addition, it also impresses with its clear, consistent and user-friendly design that is tailored precisely to the needs of those affected.

Interface & User Experience Design · Spatial Communication · Red Dot: Junior Award Apps · Designer Profiles · Jury · Index · Red Dot – World of Design

University
British Higher School of Art & Design,
Moscow, Russia

Design
Artem Nekrasov, Vitaliy Korolev

Design Support
Sergey Galtsev, Pavel Popko,
Uliana Kovalenko, Ekaterina Zhokhova,
Anton Vdovichenko, Olga Moiseeva,
Yuliya Kritskaya, Michail Dubovik

→ Designer profile on page 549
→ Clip online

Mountain Pulses

[Book]

"Mountain Pulses" is inspired by the way traditional Chinese medicine looks at the human body. According to TCM, when an organism becomes ill, it expresses an energetic imbalance of the underlying elements. The book edition applies this idea to nature. With the intention of showing that human diseases and environmental disasters are interrelated, four diagnostic reports on mountains are introduced, each covering a different element. Inside, the books feature an exceptionally dense layout, which catches the reader's attention with an experimental framework of writing, images and graphic signs.

University
Ling Tung University, Taichung, Taiwan

Supervising Professor
Wei-Jen Huang, Yuen-Hsiu Yen

Design
Yi-Ting Liu, Yu-Chiao Chang, Yuan-Hsiang Chiu, Yi-Xiu Zheng, Ching-Wen Chuang, Ci-Yi Wang, Ling Tung University

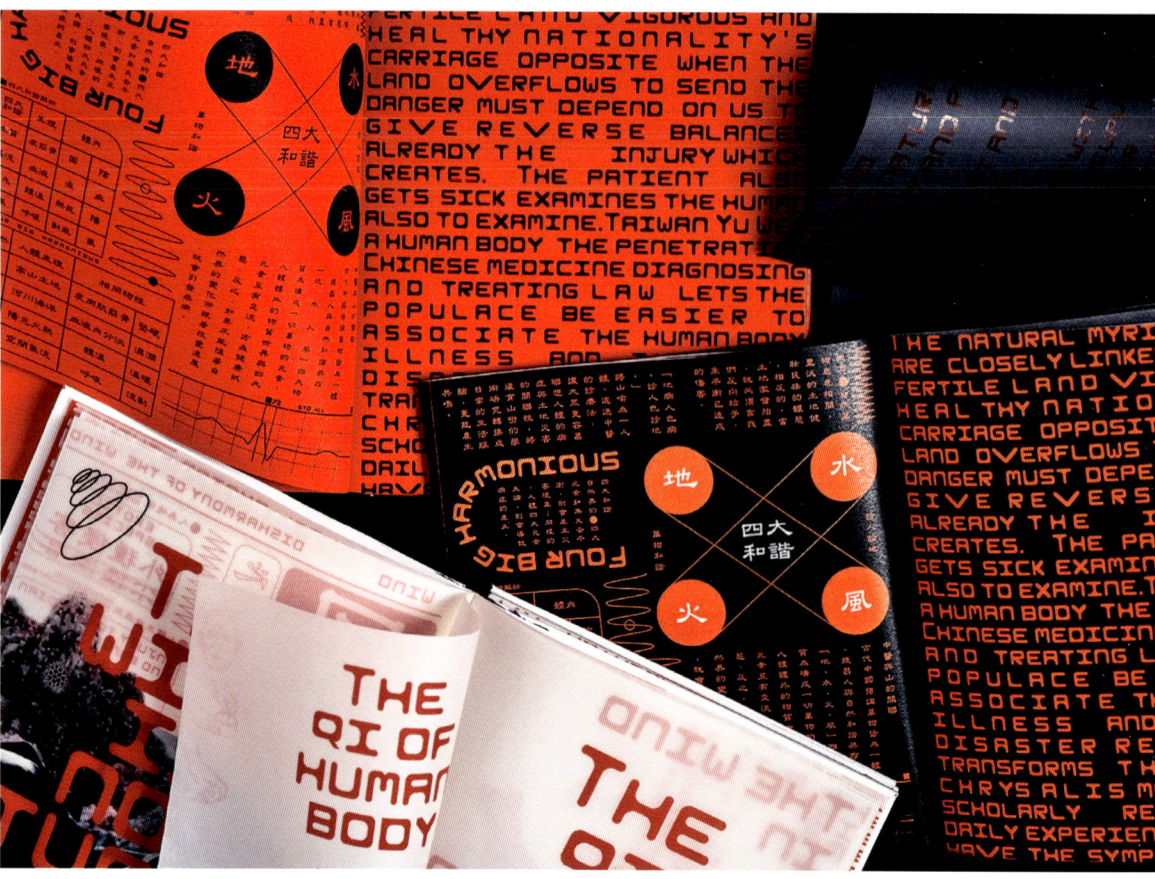

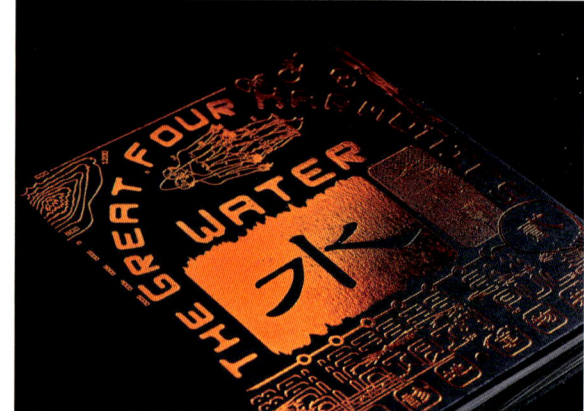

| Interface & User Experience Design | Spatial Communication | Red Dot: Junior Award Publishing & Print Media | Designer Profiles | Jury | Index | Red Dot – World of Design |

Signal in a Bottle
[Special Publication]

Putting a message in a bottle is a very old method of calling for help. The point of this project is that the message comes from the sea itself. Each of the three cylindrical "bottle books" reveals a current threat to the marine environment: oil pollution, rising temperatures and plastic waste. Like a scroll, the paper attached to the cylinder can be unrolled and read from both sides, while the colour scheme reflects the issue in question. In contrast to the detailed illustrations, the cover design attracts attention by means of reduction, focusing on a single meaningful number per object.

University
Shu-Te University, Kaohsiung, Taiwan

Supervising Professor
Cheng-Chang Chen

Design
Yi-Jung Hsiao, Wei-Hong Xue, Zhi-Yun Zheng, Ting-Yu Yao, Yi-Lun Li, Ren-Qi Jin, Shu-Te University

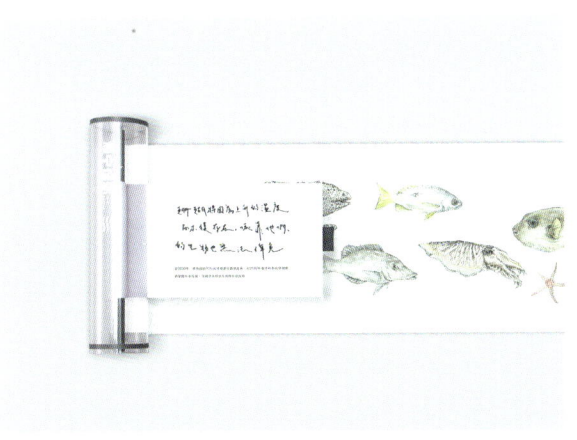

Publishing & Print Media | Posters | Typography | Illustrations | Sound Design | Film & Animation | Online | Apps

A to B Magazine – Factory Farming

A to B Magazine focuses on over-consumption related to food, fashion and technology. This issue deals with factory farming. Investigating different aspects of breeding, global warming and the views of activists and consumers, the publication provides readers with multi-faceted insights into the topic. The editorial design consistently employs blanks, a few striking text lines and large type. Through colour symbolism, the main concern of denouncing the slaughter of animals is brought to the fore. Red elements in the otherwise black-and-white layout stand for spilled blood and express the urgency of the situation.

University
LASALLE College of the Arts, Singapore

Design
Nora Jasmine Yee,
LASALLE College of the Arts

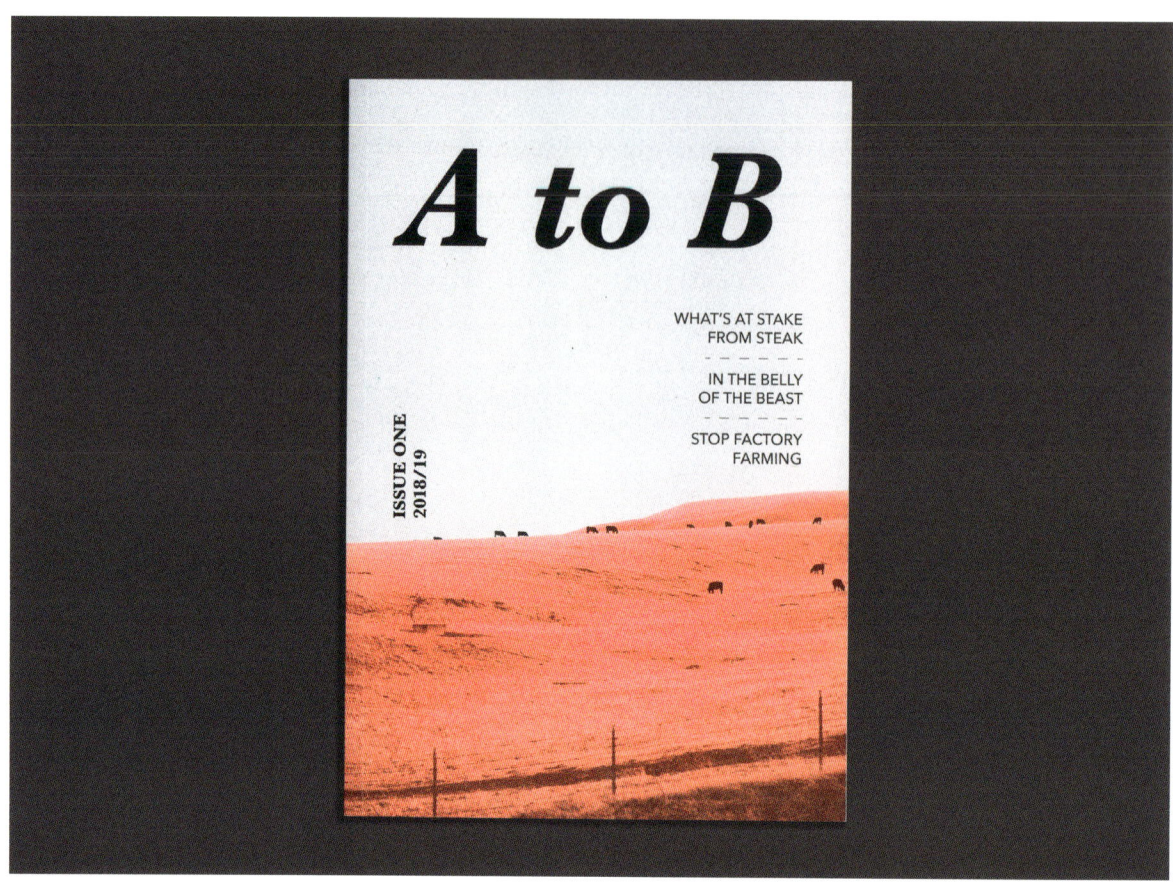
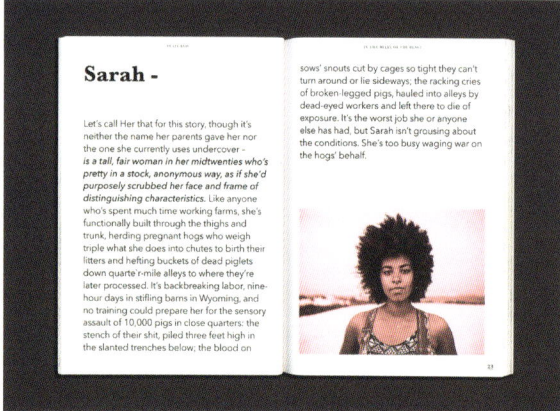

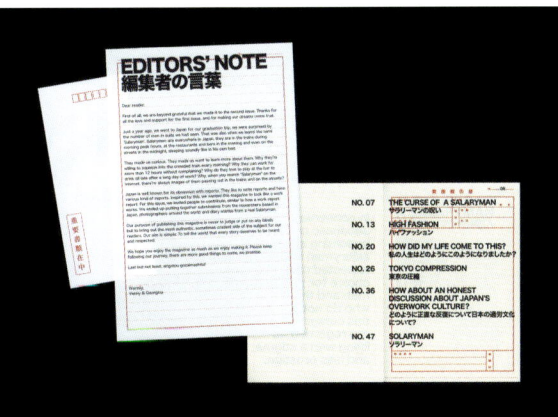
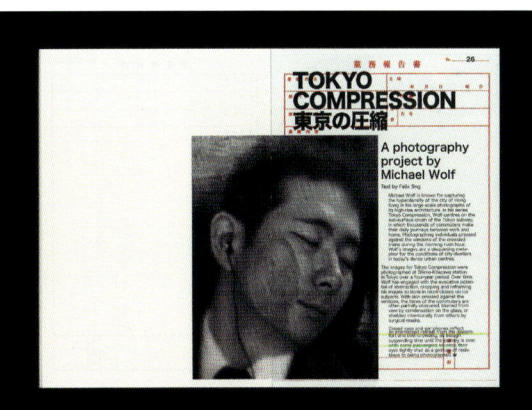
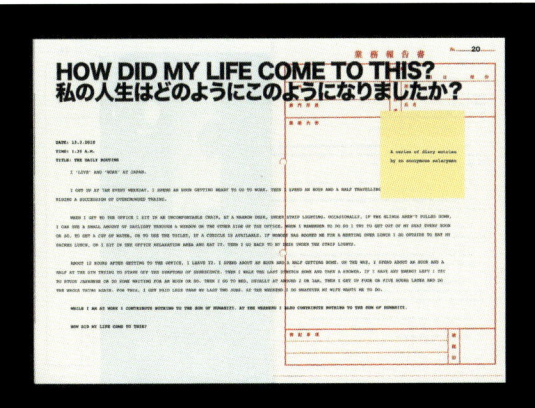

WORK Magazine – Salaryman

WORK is a biannual magazine featuring different work stories and working cultures. It aims to present the most authentic aspects of the chosen topic to the readers. This issue centres on Japanese office workers suffering from the extremely rigid work ethic in their country. The reader's attention is captivated by large black-and-white photos which communicate a sense of exhaustion and despair. Moreover, the text is presented in an unusually uniform, almost form-like manner, modelled on work reports that office workers in Japan often need to write for monitoring purposes.

University
LASALLE College of the Arts, Singapore

Design
Venny Chung Ping Siang,
LASALLE College of the Arts

Polychrom – Diversity is the Key

[Book]

This work seeks to promote diversity in German start-ups. The book is based on research showing that every third start-up has a designer as a founding member. However, only 14.6 per cent of all start-ups are currently founded by women. Showcasing the topic with fresh colours and dynamic forms, the cover reaches out to the reader. Inside, the layout conveys a sense of expertise through the skilful use of space and infographics. The printed edition is supplemented by a website and corresponding contributions on Instagram.

University
HAWK University of
Applied Sciences and Arts,
Faculty of Design,
Hildesheim, Germany

Design
Julia Schmidt, Katharina Lifke,
Sandra Bosse, Flora Taubner,
Faculty of Design, HAWK University of
Applied Sciences and Arts

Pre-Press
Tatjana Rabe

Project Management
Barbara Kotte

Interface & User Experience Design · Spatial Communication · Red Dot: Junior Award Publishing & Print Media · Designer Profiles · Jury · Index · Red Dot – World of Design

Designing Women
[Book]

This work explores the interaction between design and society with a focus on the depiction of women. The implementation underlines the versatility of the topic by presenting a tête-bêche bound book which can be read from both sides. Starting from one side, readers first encounter the chapter "Understanding Gender", from the other side the part "Designing Women". The chapters "Historical Context" and "Women Design" meet in the middle. Throughout the book, the layout plays with the interaction of black and white, emphasising that the contents are inextricably intertwined both artistically and thematically.

University
FH JOANNEUM – University of Applied Sciences, Graz, Austria

Supervising Professor
Daniel Perraudin

Design
Nina Botthof, Graz, Austria

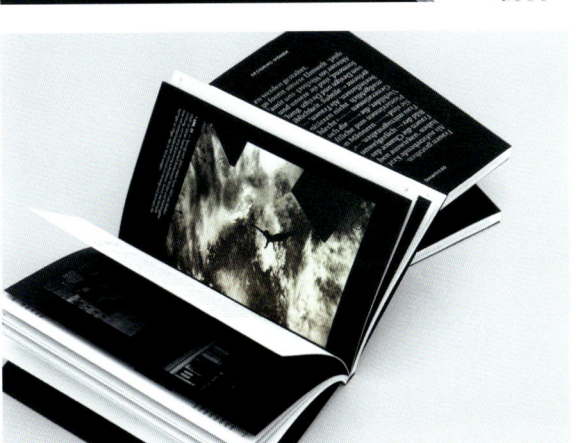

What A Mistake

[Book]

Dissatisfaction with one's own body and striving for perfection are currently widespread phenomena. "What A Mistake" seeks to encourage people to shed a positive light on their less popular peculiarities. The publication is based on an anonymous online survey on the topic "Which flaws do you love on yourself?" Reduced to the essentials, large-scale images and lettering address the curiosity of potential readers, play with positive and negative effects and convey the content in a humorous manner. Some of the concise motifs were also used for posters.

University
FH JOANNEUM – University of Applied Sciences, Graz, Austria

Design
Katharina Diem, Graz, Austria

again and again – The Power of Repetition in Visual Perception
[Book]

From architecture and music to profound structures of nature, repetitions surround, manipulate and stimulate us. This work analyses different aspects of repetition and seeks to create a link between psychology, art and design. Moreover, the book deals with practical questions. How does repetition come into effect at its best, and when should it be avoided? Understanding these relationships can help to create powerful designs. The editorial concept provides the content with a clear outline which pleases the eye with a well-measured amount of variation and illustrative examples.

University
FH JOANNEUM – University of Applied Sciences, Graz, Austria

Design
Katharina Saurer,
Rohrbach an der Lafnitz, Austria

366 days of love

[Calendar]

Featuring 340 different fonts, many illustrations and heart-warming words, the 366 sheets of this calendar revolve around the topic of love. In contrast to traditional tear-off calendars, this one offers not only a visual but also a tactile aspect, since the calendar contains instructions on how to fold the individual sheets into origami hearts. The playful concept has a double communicative function. After having read the date and the message of the day, users have the opportunity to share their affection with a beloved person by means of a paper object.

University
National Taichung University of Science and Technology, Taichung, Taiwan

Supervising Professor
Yi-Sheng Chiu

Design
Shu-Yun Cheng, Chia-Hsuan Yang, Chia-An Lin, Meng-Chu Hsu, National Taichung University of Science and Technology

Übernimmst du mal die Firma?

[Book]

Recent Studies have shown that family businesses in Germany and Austria provide about 60 per cent of all jobs. Many older entrepreneurs, however, do not have a successor. In order to open up new perspectives on the subject, the book "Übernimmst du mal die Firma?" (And You'll Take Over the Business?) sums up interviews with 25 founders, seniors and successors, who talk about their own experiences with succession. Using slightly blurred, newspaper-style images, the layout underlines the documentary value of the statements. By implementing the personal reports as a high-quality hardcover, the design expresses a special appreciation of the subject matter.

Client
Lars Schrage – buero fuer gestaltung, Friedeburg, Germany

Design
Lars Schrage – buero fuer gestaltung, Friedeburg, Germany

Editorial Work/Graphic Design
Lars Schrage

Publishing & Print Media | Posters | Typography | Illustrations | Sound Design | Film & Animation | Online | Apps

Windows of Oriental Elegance

[Special Publication]

Artfully crafted latticework in windows is characteristic of traditional Chinese architecture. However, these windows are gradually disappearing as old houses are increasingly replaced by prosaic modern buildings. "Windows of Oriental Elegance" aims to highlight the beauty of the traditional crafts by employing different media and offering tactile experiences. A book with movable and stamped-out elements presents different types of lattice windows, while a 3D desk calendar illustrates the spatial effect of the framework. Furthermore, a set of stamps invites users to design their own lattice patterns.

University
China University of Technology,
Taipei City, Taiwan

Supervising Professor
Shuo-Ting Wei, Chien-Hsun Chen

Design
Xinyi Jiang, Siting Xu, Hsinni Lo,
Department of Visual Communication
Design, China University of Technology

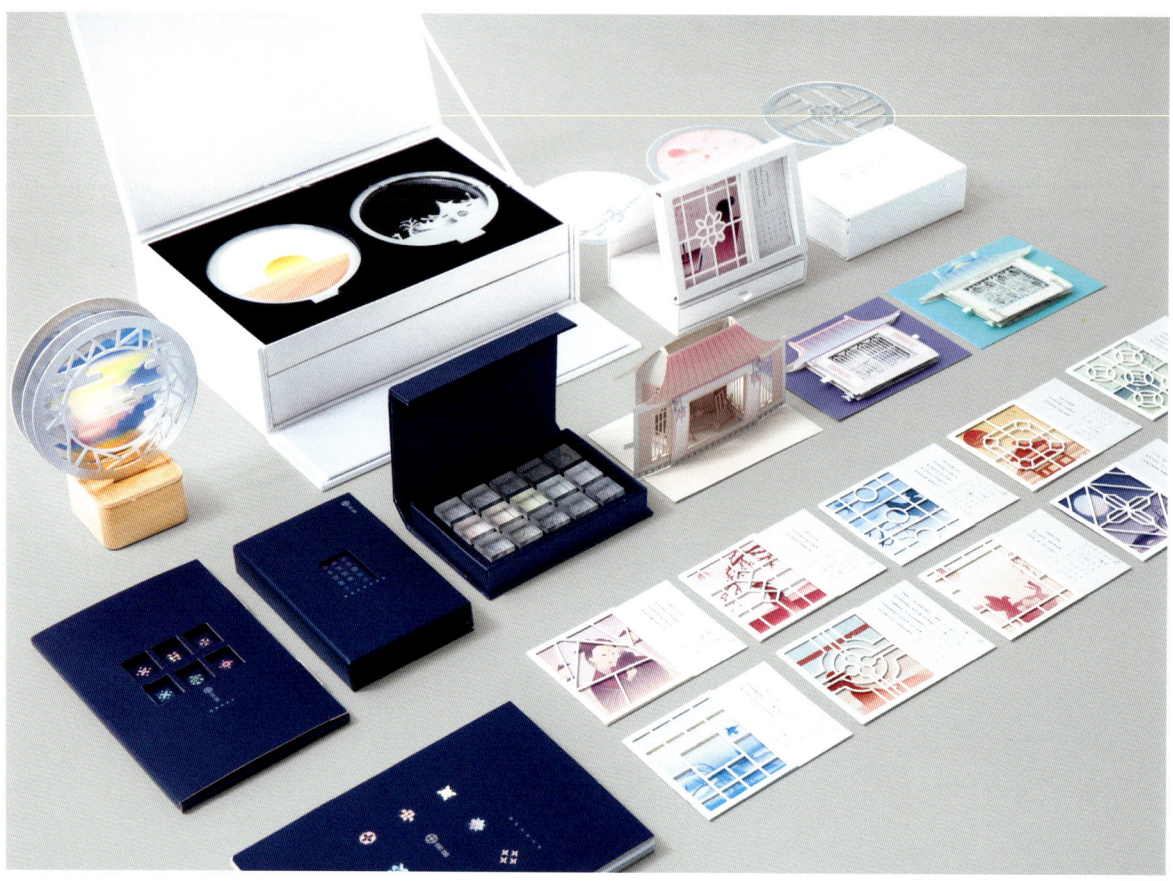

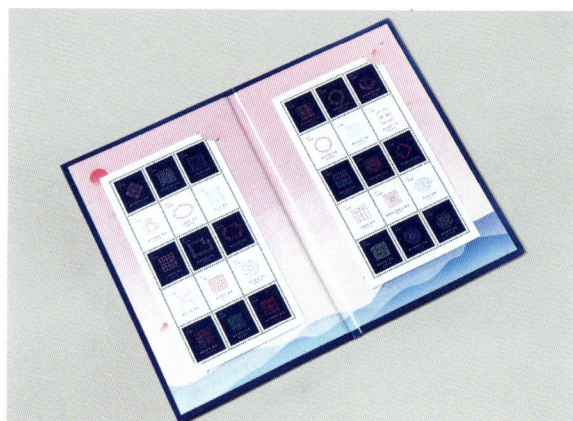
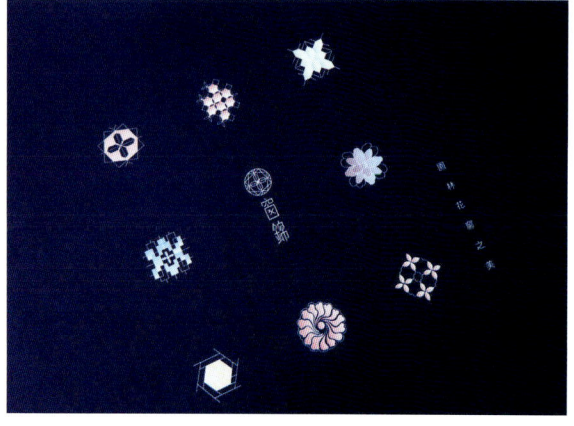
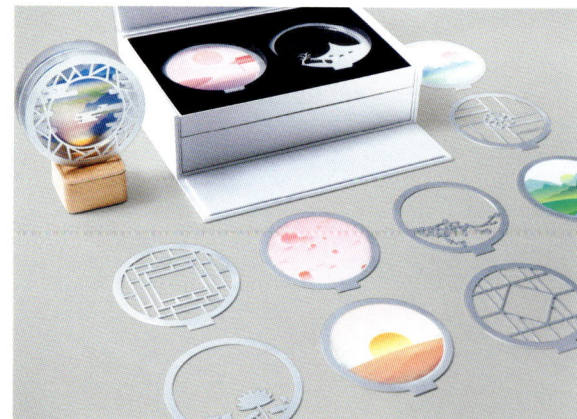

Telling the stories of the I Ching

[Special Publication]

Using a simple yet vivid imagery, this project introduces ten symbolic animals from an ancient Chinese divination text, the I Ching. The purpose of the creative visualisation is to make the traditional concepts accessible to a contemporary audience. The black-and-white pictures stand out by an unusually relaxed approach to reading the I Ching. The special publication is designed to be used for a simple divination game. Colour-coded fortune scrolls provide the necessary guidance, allowing even beginners to start divination without further assistance.

University
Cheng Shiu University, Kaohsiung, Taiwan

Supervising Professor
Yen-Lin Wu, Shou-Che Wu

Design
Ruo-Ya Juan, Cheng Shiu University

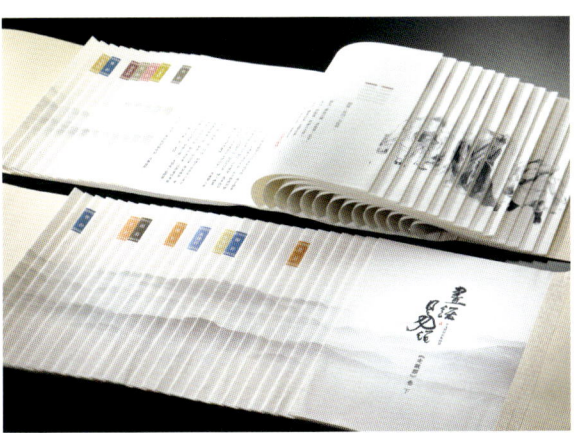

Sankt Poelten lebt!

[Book]

St Pölten, the capital of Lower Austria, is going to apply for the title of the European Capital of Culture 2024. Following a personal approach, the work "Sankt Poelten lebt!" (Sankt Poelten Is Alive!) presents an imaginative compendium for the title year. The design of the book is inspired by a philosophical concept by Gilles Deleuze and Félix Guattari – the rhizome. The term describes a root network which is dynamic, processual and anti-hierarchical. Accordingly, the common thread in the layout is formed by root-like graphics suggesting that the city is a living organism and emphasising the creative potential of various urban locations.

University
FH JOANNEUM – University of Applied Sciences, Graz, Austria

Design
Lisa Huber, Graz, Austria

→ Designer profile on page 532

EXPLORE – Exkursion Kolumbien

[Magazine]

This special magazine documents a student excursion to Colombia. The richly illustrated brochure introduces life at the partner university in Medellín as well as the multifaceted Colombian landscape and recalls a visit to a non-governmental organisation supporting coffee farmers. Printed on 100-gram uncoated paper and written in German and Spanish, the magazine expresses genuine respect and admiration for the South American country. The design of the cover sums up what the focus is on: discovering something new and taking responsibility for a common future.

University
HAWK University of
Applied Sciences and Arts,
Faculty of Design,
Hildesheim, Germany

Design
Dominik Wagenführ, Larissa Knaupp,
Cedric Fernandez Fernandez,
Sven Schröer, Alicia Wolpers,
Faculty of Design, HAWK University of
Applied Sciences and Arts

Project Management
Tatjana Rabe

Publishing & Print Media   Posters   Typography   Illustrations   Sound Design   Film & Animation   Online   Apps

Formosa – Rivers, Mountains, Birds
[Sightseeing Ticket Design]

This series of train tickets was developed for the Formosa Express, a popular tourist train in Taiwan. The tickets are designed to encourage passengers to go on further sightseeing trips. A total of 24 pictures of Taiwanese landscapes and wildlife is divided into three themes: rivers, mountains and birds. Placed side by side, the pictures embody a panorama of nature. Delicate colours and harmonious compositions create a visual language that is picturesque, stimulating and full of serenity. After the trip, the tickets make decorative souvenirs, which can be stored in specially designed luggage tags.

University
Southern Taiwan University of Science and Technology, Tainan, Taiwan

Supervising Professor
Rain Chen

Design
Jui-Hung Weng, Ya-Ling Wang, You-Ning Hou, Fang-Yu Cao, Department of Visual Communication Design, Southern Taiwan University of Science and Technology

Wen Wu Temple

[Special Publication]

The Wen Wu Temple of Sun Moon Lake is a well-known sight in Nantou County, Taiwan. On the occasion of the 50th anniversary of the temple, which was reconstructed in 1969, this multi-piece work celebrates the historical site. The bilingual book is written in Chinese and English, introducing foreign tourists to the architecture and the cultural significance of the temple. A striking feature is the format – when leafing through from front to back, the images are changing. The variable presentation harmonises with the content of the publication, which proceeds from the easy to more complicated aspects.

University
Chaoyang University of Technology, Taichung, Taiwan

Supervising Professor
Jay-Hui Lu

Design
Chun-Yi Lu, Jing-Wen Huang,
Wei-Ju Chen,
Chaoyang University of Technology

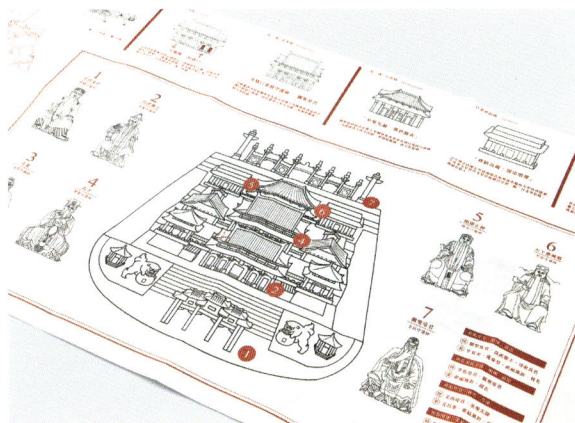

Lovething about BUG
[Magazine]

This quarterly magazine is dedicated to the topic of insect reproduction. Tearing open the transparent sleeve gives the impression of an insect hatching from a chrysalis. The content of each pack consists of three print editions dealing with one insect species. Since the illustrations use decorative patterns and graphic signs to depict the species, they subtly counteract insectophobia. Readers can also unfold the double-sided printed magazines and use the back as a poster. Thanks to their custom-made, poetic presentation, the booklets convey genuine enthusiasm for the biological subject.

University
Chaoyang University of Technology, Taichung, Taiwan

Supervising Professor
Kuei-To Wang

Design
Rung Chiang, Chia-Hui Feng, Chaoyang University of Technology

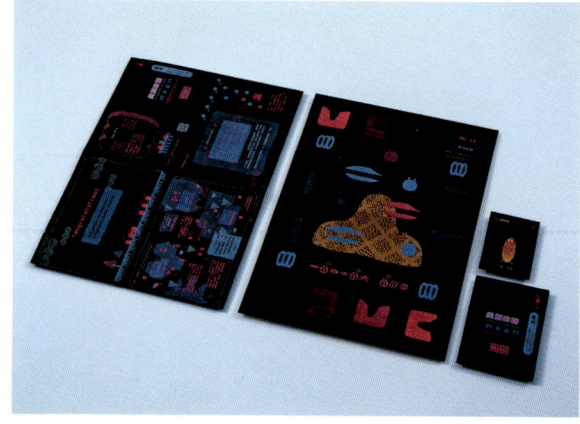

Sound of Nature – Landscape Sound Pop-up Cards

[Special Publication]

With a combination of visual and acoustic stimuli, "Sound of Nature" aims to point out the beauty of the environment, which is often forgotten in busy everyday life. Six lovingly designed pop-up cards depict Taiwanese landscapes: a valley, a forest, a sea cave, a city, a river and the sea. When unfolding a card, the integrated element appears as a spatial object, accompanied by corresponding ambient and animal sounds. The boxes show their content through punched-out holes, while the embossed lines in the slipcase hint at both contour lines and sound waves.

University
China University of Technology, Taipei City, Taiwan

Supervising Professor
Cheng-Ta Lee, Chien-Hsun Chen

Design
Chi Wang, Ya-Chu Chang, Xuan-Yu Huang, Yu-Hsiu Huang, Wei Lee, Department of Visual Communication Design, China University of Technology

Publishing & Print Media Posters Typography Illustrations Sound Design Film & Animation Online Apps

Taiwan Mineral Pigment
[Special Publication]

Many people are unaware that Taiwan produces numerous colourful minerals. This project aims to draw attention to local mineral resources by introducing a special paint made from mineral substances. The paint comes with specially designed plates which reflect the structure of the minerals through hexagonal or octagonal shapes. The accompanying book explains the characteristics of each stone, while lovingly implemented illustrations visualise the background of the minerals. By using a partly informal, painterly style, the imagery lends the publication a personal touch.

University
Shu-Te University, Kaohsiung, Taiwan

Supervising Professor
I-Tsen Liu

Design
Jin-Lun Zhuang, Yu-Xuan Li, Nian-En Liou, Jing-Wen Huang, Jia-Shen Chen, Hong-Jia Zhu, Shu-Te University

SCAD FASH – Pierre Cardin

[Invitation Card]

This elaborate invitation card has been designed for a Pierre Cardin show at the SCAD FASH Museum of Fashion and Film in Atlanta, Georgia. Inspired by a golden flowery dress, the design focuses on the pattern and features a conspicuous pop-up flower. The letters stand out due to foiling with gold colour on black paper. A matching gold-coloured sleeve lets the black insert shine through, displaying complex die-cut forms. All in all, the attention to detail in the card's finish effectively conveys the fashion designer's superior quality standards.

University
SCAD Savannah College of
Art and Design, Atlanta, Georgia, USA

Design
Hazel Hwang, SCAD

Dong Ba

[Book]

The Dong Ba symbols are a system of ancient pictographic glyphs. Still used by the Naxi people in southern China today, the script traces back to times before the Oracle bone script. This publication introduces stickers for chat software inspired by Dongba symbols. Like emojis, the simplified characters denote particular emotions or ideas in a concise manner. They are interpreted in a modern way in order to revive the traditional script. The handbook presents the whole sticker series and explains the background of the project in detail.

University
Shu-Te University, Kaohsiung, Taiwan

Supervising Professor
Yu-Lung Yang

Design
Shuai-Nan Chen, Rou-An Chen, Qi-Min Lin, Shu-Te University

Paper Lion
[Special Publication]

Lion Dance is a traditional Chinese dance in which performers move about in a lion costume to bring good luck and fortune. "Paper Lion" refers to this ancient custom by introducing innovative paper art. Each craft kit contains instructions on how to assemble the head of a paper lion from a few sheets of white paper. The nuanced design of the finished objects skilfully reflects the lines, the surfaces and the shapes of their three-dimensional models. Featuring white, natural material, the paper sculptures also emphasise the beauty and purity of the Lion Dance art.

Design
Yu Hsin-Tzu, New Taipei City, Taiwan
Chen Yu-Chun, Taoyuan, Taiwan
Li Tung-Lin, Taipei City, Taiwan

Abstract Inheritance
[Special Publication]

University
Shanghai Publishing and Printing College,
Shanghai, China

Supervising Professor
Fang Wu

Design
Xinyu Gan, Yejia Qian,
Shanghai Publishing and Printing College

→ Designer profile on page 572
→ Clip online

The pastoral poem is a genre of Chinese poetry which is characterised by images of nature and a peaceful spirit. This publication contains 24 pastoral poems by poets who lived more than a thousand years ago. The process of cultural inheritance is represented by three versions of each poem: a traditional Chinese version, which is printed on handmade bark paper with a retro-style font, a simplified Chinese version on rice paper with a specially designed font, and an English version on modern paper. The dwindling luxuriance of the pages effectively illustrates the point that something poetic may have been lost in translation.

Kaffee für alle?

[Book]

In the city of Graz – like in many other European cities – cafés have a special significance. They not only define the cityscape, but are also places to chill out, meeting points, working space and much more. "Kaffee für alle?" (Coffee for everybody) explores the coffeehouse in a cultural and social context. The content is presented to the readers in a clear, intuitively comprehensible form. The illustrations, limited to the colours of rusty red and white, appear as negative forms on the cover and as positive forms inside the book, complementing the text information with an emotional appeal.

University
FH JOANNEUM – University of Applied Sciences, Graz, Austria

Design
Johanna Kurz, Bad Vöslau, Austria

Weltsprachen – Sprachwelten

[Book]

The book "Weltsprachen – Sprachwelten" (Languages of the World – World of Languages) is divided into three segments, which are easy to distinguish thanks to a variation of uncoated and coated paper. Complementing the black-and-white layout, a series of photographs visualises the dynamics of language as flowing shapes. The core of the publication is dedicated to untranslatable words. These words cannot be translated by using just one term; instead, they need longer explanations in other languages in order to be comprehensible. The peculiar phenomenon is illustrated by a clearly arranged world map.

University
FH JOANNEUM – University of Applied Sciences, Graz, Austria

Design
Julia Baldauf, Graz, Austria

Publishing & Print Media   Posters   Typography   Illustrations   Sound Design   Film & Animation   Online   Apps

Thinking out of the Box
[Special Publication]

The contemporary format of this publication was designed for a young target group. The issues of the newspaper present different careers, seeking to guide readers through the current overload of information and help them find their place in society. In terms of design, the print edition catches the eye with an experimental all-over look in which colourful font and picture elements overlap and complement each other. Smartphones also play an important role in the concept – readers can scan embedded codes in the headlines to watch brief one-minute videos on selected topics.

University
Ling Tung University, Taichung, Taiwan

Supervising Professor
Wei-Jen Huang, Chien-Wen Chen

Design
Yi-Tzu Chan, Ting-Wei Liao, Tzu-Ning Hsu, Szu-Yu Chen, Ji-Cheng Luo, Kuo-Ming Tsou, Ling Tung University

Concrete Design

[Company Book]

Concrete Design Communications is a Toronto-based creative agency which fuses strategy and design. This design introduces the company through a premium book featuring an embossed black case. In order to underline the aesthetic quality of the projects, the book is designed with vellum and foiling. The agency's fresh take on brands, packaging and photography is reflected by a concise layout. For example, bright red graphics showing construction work are paired with black-and-white case studies, all in line with Concrete Design's motto: "We like to get our hands dirty."

University
SCAD Savannah College of
Art and Design, Atlanta, Georgia, USA

Design
Connie Lee, SCAD

Departure

[Exhibition Poster]

This work announces a graduation exhibition of design students in Kaohsiung. On the poster, a piece of sketch paper, torn off and discarded in the air, symbolises the end of student days. A distinctive feature which makes the motif stand out is its fine graphic nuances. They are the result of an elaborate printing process using two-tone printing and silver screen printing on the front, and white screen printing on the back. By showing the joy of experimentation, the poster also refers to the birth of ideas and the vigour of creative work in general.

University
Shu-Te University, Kaohsiung, Taiwan

Supervising Professor
Yu-Lung Yang

Design
Yu-Chao Wang, Shih-Ming Huang, Shu-Te University

Danger Is in Hidden Places

[Poster Series]

This poster series aims to draw attention to sexual assault and harassment. The posters visualise the delicate issue by employing reduced means. While a realistic representation makes up only a small part of each image, most of the space is occupied by a blurred zone, symbolising the fact that the victims are usually molested in secret. By not showing the injured body parts openly, the posters also refer to the victims' trauma. Viewers are encouraged to decode the meaning of missing details and to become aware of inner harm, which has a serious impact even though it is invisible.

University
Asia University, Taichung, Taiwan

Supervising Professor
Ming-Lung Yu

Design
Li-Ying Chen, Asia University

The Red Love

[Poster Series]

University
Shanghai Jiao Tong University,
Shanghai, China

Supervising Professor
Wei Wang

Design
Yih-Feng Weng, School of Design,
Shanghai Jiao Tong University

→ Designer profile on page 571

With a visual language that picks up on the red ribbon, the international symbol for AIDS and HIV, these posters seek to raise awareness of the devastating epidemic. Organic forms reflecting the shape and colour of the ribbon pique the viewer's curiosity and emerge as female body contours. The allusion to sexuality is complemented by a font detail. Tiny but prominently placed, the letter "I" is shaped like a condom. The posters thus promote the only current solution of how to protect oneself from the dangerous infection, including a wink of the eye.

Encroach on Culture

[Poster Series]

Zooming in on Japan's whaling culture, these works take a stand for whale conservation. The posters associate the image of a living whale with specialties like sake, sushi and oden. While the proportions in the pictures imply that the marine mammal is at the mercy of man, the truncated shapes of eating utensils invite viewers to fill the space outside the posters with their imagination. A red circle on white background, reminiscent of the Japanese flag, establishes a link between blood and the whaling nation Japan, aiming to fundamentally question this type of consumption.

University
Asia University, Taichung, Taiwan

Supervising Professor
Ming-Lung Yu

Design
Yu-Ci Ye, Asia University

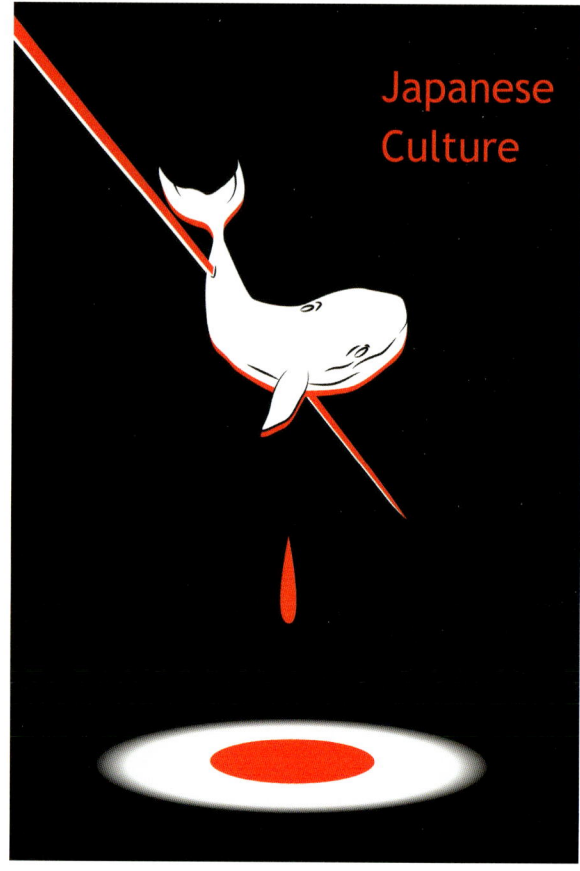

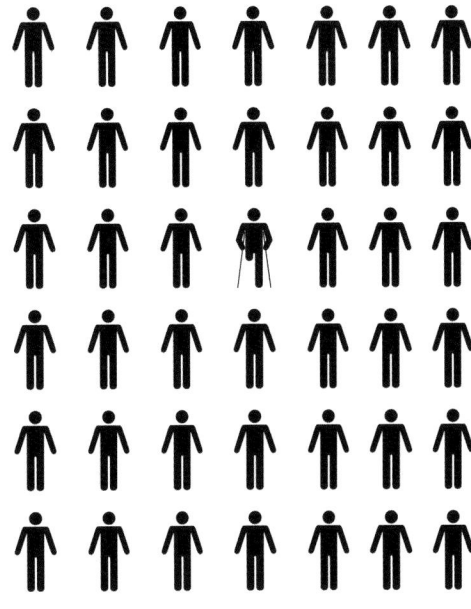

In My Eyes We Have No Difference

We Have No Difference
[Poster Series]

Many people with physical or mental impairments are hurt when being approached with excessive sympathy. Instead, they want to be treated with as much respect and appreciation as everyone else. This campaign promotes putting oneself in the position of those affected. At first glance, the schematic figures on the posters seem to be identical. Only a closer look reveals that one of the stick figures represents a disabled person. In a simple and precise manner, the posters thus communicate that a small divergence is irrelevant in view of many similarities.

University
Asia University, Taichung, Taiwan

Supervising Professor
Ming-Lung Yu

Design
Ding-Jyun Wang, Asia University

In My Eyes We Have No Difference

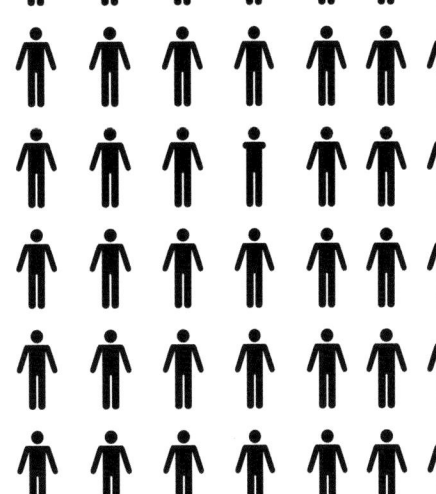

In My Eyes We Have No Difference

The Path to Charity

[Poster Series]

Using few graphical means, this poster project seeks to encourage people to stay on the ethically right path. The concise, vertical compositions are based on the Chinese characters for "benevolence", "compassion" and "kindness". The key design feature is the idea of the road as a direction which people give to their actions. Rough line textures and bold black-and-white contrasts lend emphasis to the images. The simple lines intersecting at certain points can be grasped intuitively, giving even those who do not speak Chinese the chance to understand the meaning of the posters.

University
Fuzhou University of International Studies and Trade, Fuzhou, China

Supervising Professor
Zi Zhi

Design
Jia-Qi Hong, Fuzhou University of International Studies and Trade

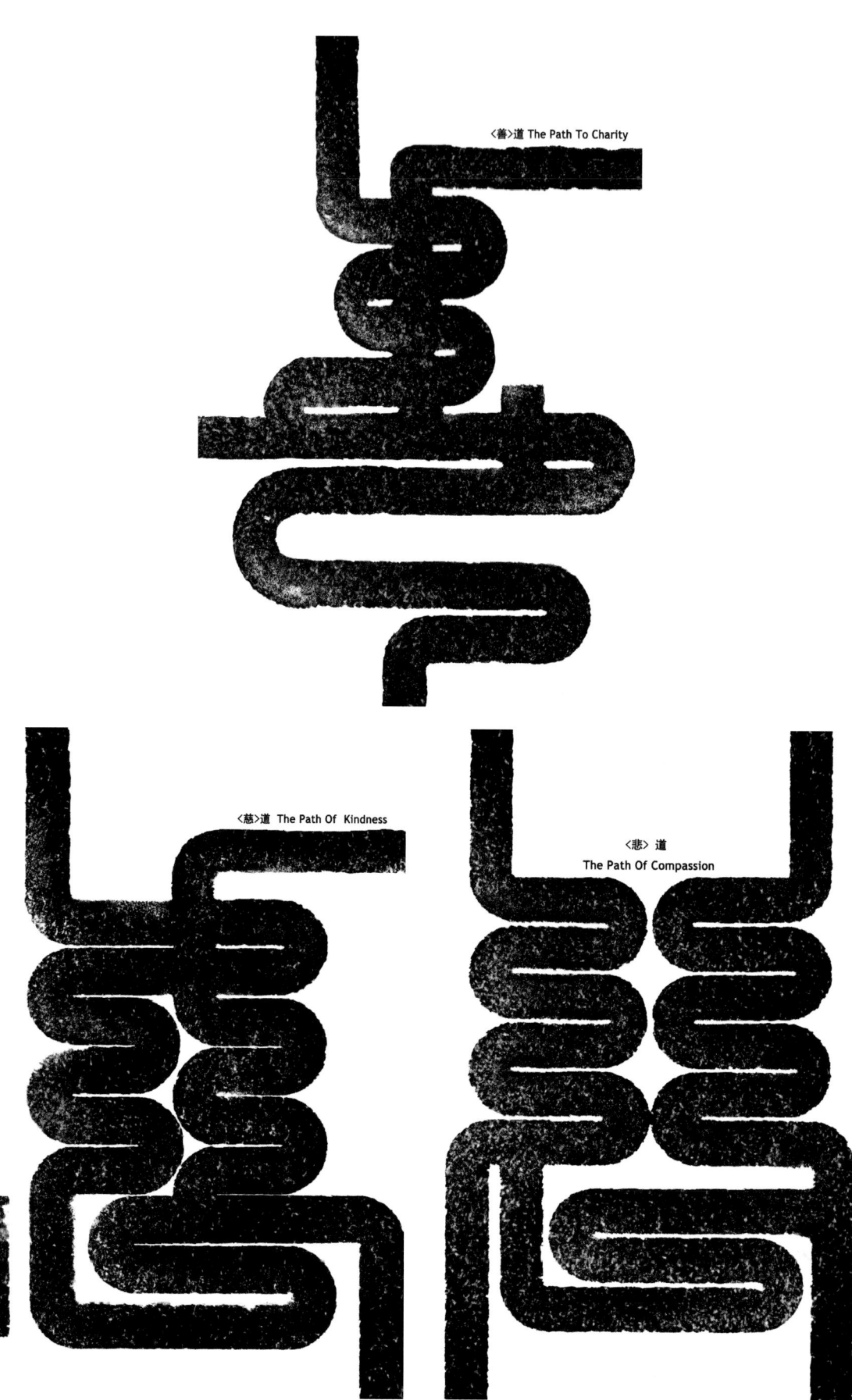

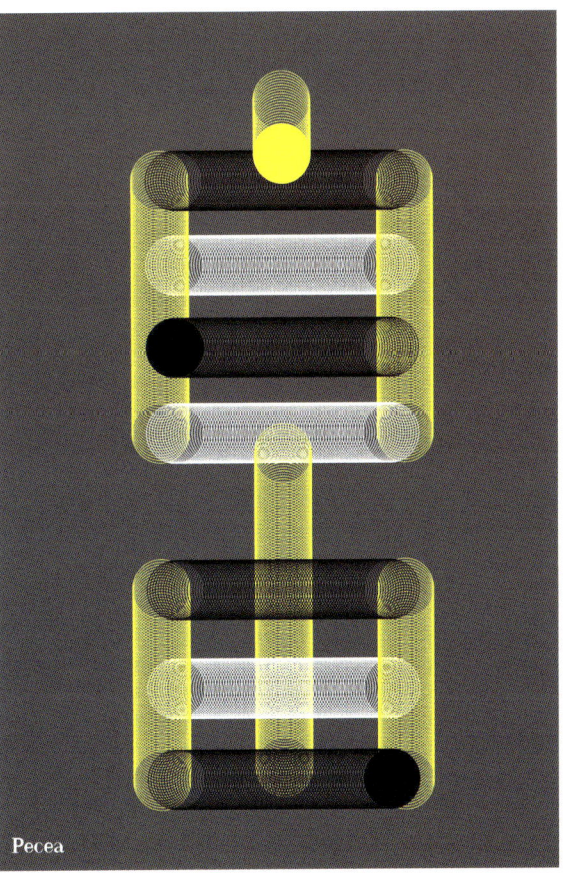

Peace

[Poster Series]

These posters are mainly composed of three groups of Chinese characters, meaning "peace", "equality" and "freedom". In view of the fact that life is often anything but peaceful, the project is intended to show an alternative. Each motif comprises interconnected circles as a symbol for individuals who are attached to each other. The harmonious forms spread a balanced mood. Since the spiral structure of the lines is reminiscent of springs, the posters also suggest another interpretation: just like elastic springs, people can withstand tension and remain resilient despite oppression.

University
Fuzhou University of
International Studies and Trade,
Fuzhou, China

Supervising Professor
Zi Zhi, Xi Cheng

Design
Yu-Yan Lin, Xue-Qin Lin, Min Hung,
Fuzhou University of
International Studies and Trade

Publishing & Print Media   Posters   Typography   Illustrations   Sound Design   Film & Animation   Online   Apps

Excessive Attention
[Poster Series]

University
Fuzhou University of
International Studies and Trade,
Fuzhou, China

Supervising Professor
Zi Zhi

Design
Xi-Xuan Hu, Xiao-Li Lin, Xiao-Jie Yin,
Fuzhou University of
International Studies and Trade

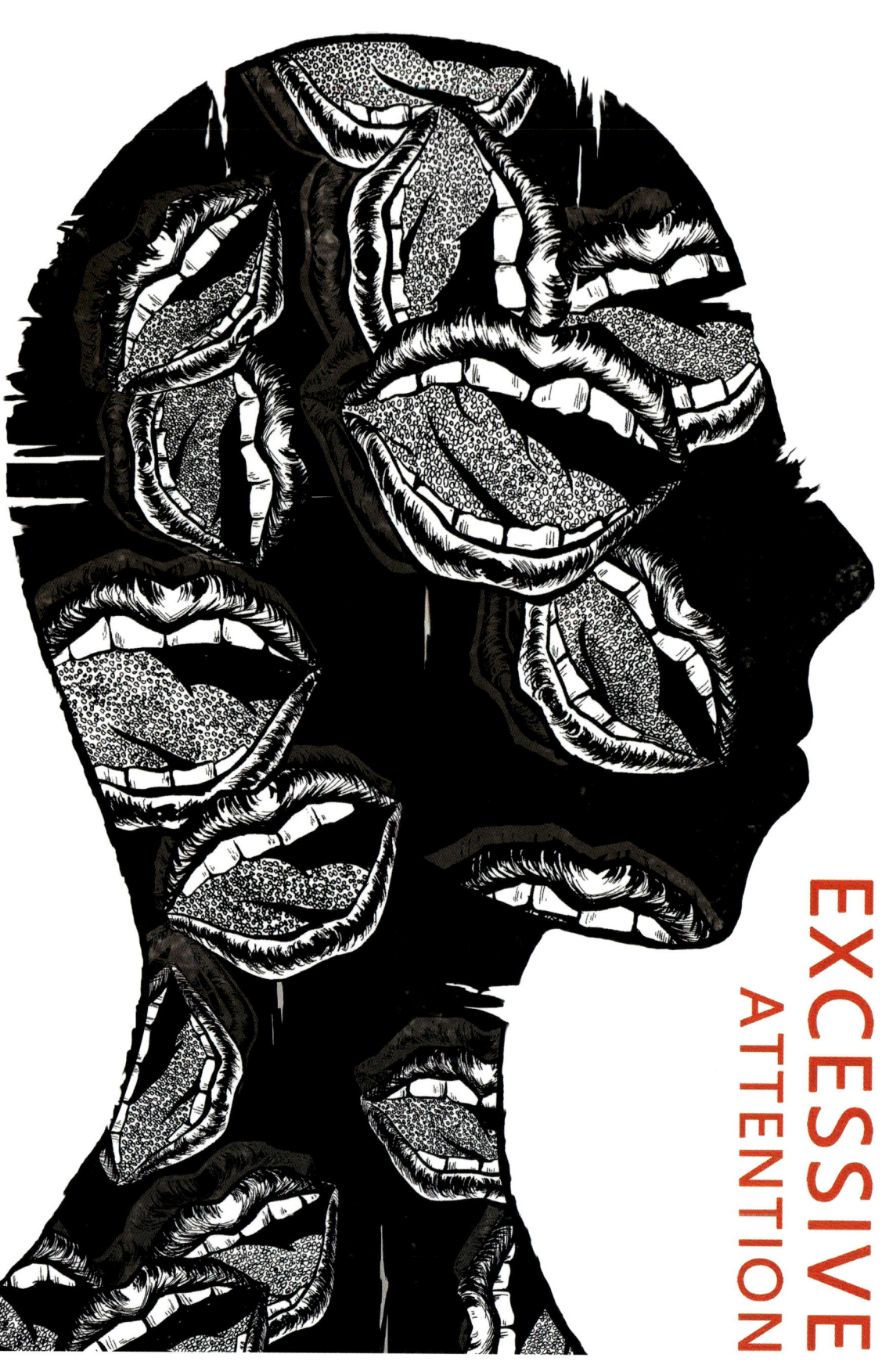

Interface & User Experience Design   Spatial Communication   Red Dot: Junior Award   Designer Profiles   Jury   Index   Red Dot – World of Design
Posters

EXCESSIVE ATTENTION

Excessive attention can damage relationships, as overly focused people do not consider whether the other party really needs their help or not. This project translates the issue into expressive images with surreal elements. The effect of constant observation and commenting, which occurs when attention is entirely focused on others, is visualised by a multitude of eyes and mouths within frayed heads. The agglomeration of motifs is designed to be both eye-catching and obtrusive. In this way, the posters seek to spread the message that we should give each other more space and freedom.

Shaping Human Cities

[Exhibition Design]

Employing innovative methods, "Shaping Human Cities" showcases ideas for a better quality of life in urban areas. The exhibition presents projects from eleven European cities as interactive minigolf courses. Nearby information boards and a gastronomic event convey the special features of the participating cities. Additional hands-on stations offer practical advice on how to improve the urban environment. By integrating visitors into all formats, the concept consistently pursues the goal of turning a visit to the exhibition into an informative and, at the same time, enjoyable experience.

University
FH JOANNEUM – University of Applied Sciences, Graz, Austria

Design
Tessa Kaczenski, Graz, Austria
Cara Mielzarek, Graz, Austria
Julia Prinz, Graz, Austria

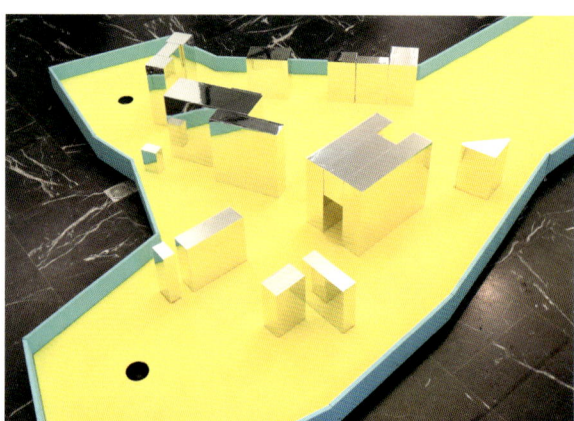

Lieblingsmakel
[Facade Design]

"Lieblingsmakel" (Favourite Blemish) is based on a social media survey on the question "What flaw do you love on yourself?" The aim of the project is to encourage people to not only accept their flaws but possibly even cherish them and to share them proudly with others. On the BIX media facade of the Graz Art Museum, the approach is continued in public. The online answers run alternating with minimalistic body images across the curvaceous facade. Thus staged effectively, the messages invite the spectators to follow the role models and treat themselves with similar benevolence.

University
FH JOANNEUM – University of Applied Sciences, Graz, Austria

Design
Katharina Diem, Graz, Austria

Film Production
Liz Kimquin Bahian, Graz, Austria

Programming
David Mischak, Graz, Austria

Photography
Johannes Diem, Feldbach, Austria

Project Management
Elisabeth Schlögl, Kunsthaus Graz, Austria

→ Clip online

Rooftop Kiters

[Documentary Short Film]

This short documentary focuses on a less popular side of Brazil, the slums of the favelas. Rather than emphasising the danger and uncertainty within these neighbourhoods, the film features playful, innocent young boys playing with their paper kites during school holidays. In expressive images and intense close-ups, the kite appears as a symbol for life in the favelas – drifting into any direction at any time or be cut off in a blink. At the same time, the kite delightfully gives joy to children who cannot afford other toys, distracts them from their problems and brings them together.

University
SCAD Savannah College of Art and Design, Savannah, Georgia, USA

Design
Daniel Paiva, SCAD

→ Clip online

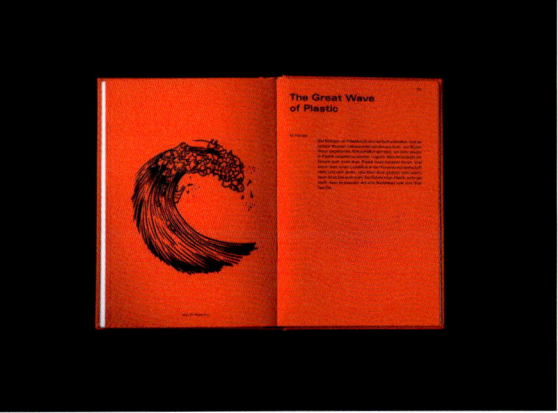

Views of China
[Hand-Drawn Animation]

This 2D animation, which was created during a six-month stay in China, is composed of eleven hand-drawn loops. The short film sums up the manifold impressions gained abroad. Blending smoothly into one another, the images provide insights into Chinese architecture, culture, religion, and engagement with nature. Through the loving implementation, drawn frame by frame, the animation reveals a great inner involvement. Viewers are taken onto an emotional rollercoaster ride, which holds much fascination but also recognises points of conflict.

University
FH JOANNEUM – University of Applied Sciences, Graz, Austria

Design
Christian Leban, Graz, Austria

Music/Sound Design
David Stockinger, Graz, Austria

→ Clip online

Publishing & Print Media Posters Typography Illustrations Sound Design Film & Animation Online Apps

Pitter Patter
[Short Film]

Without dialogue, this short film tells the story of a failed friendship between two high school girls. A guiding theme of the dark, blurred sequences is rain, which falls loudly, drowning words and hiding tears. The plot is marked by symbolic objects: crystals, glass and butterflies stand for illusions and fragility, while the mirror marks an invisible boundary between the protagonists. In a highly suggestive way, the atmospheric scenes focus on the mood of the characters, encouraging viewers to reconstruct and interpret the events for themselves.

University
Asia University, Taichung, Taiwan
National Taiwan University of Science and Technology, Taipei City, Taiwan

Design
Ching-Wei Liu, Asia University

Film Direction
Isara Chen

Camera
Wayne Lo

Sound Design
Blaire Ko

Visual Effect
Ian Chen

Film Editing
Hung-Yuan Hsu

→ Clip online

Cinematographer

[Documentary Short Film]

This short film introduces six cinematographers, trailblazers and up-and-comers, who share their insights into the politics of the position. Quiet interview sequences alternate with lively shots showing the work on the set. The statements of the professionals illustrate the difficulties women still face in the industry, yet point out that things are changing, not least because of the Me Too movement. By portraying the image designers in a decidedly human manner, the film helps the audience to empathise with them and listen to their concerns.

University
SCAD Savannah College of Art and Design, Savannah, Georgia, USA

Design
Demi Waldron, SCAD

→ Clip online

Ninety-Nine Days
[Computer Animation]

Client
Freya Yeh, Keelung City, Taiwan

Design
Freya Yeh, Keelung City, Taiwan

Music/Sound Design
Hsiao-Chin Lin, Szu-Yu Lin,
WinSound Studio, Taipei City, Taiwan

Score Mixing/Dubbing
Hsiao-Chin Lin, WinSound Studio

Voice Recording Engineering
Hsiao-Chin Lin, Szu-Yu Lin,
WinSound Studio

Voice Recording Studio
Fullight Music Recording Studio,
Taipei City, Taiwan

→ Clip online

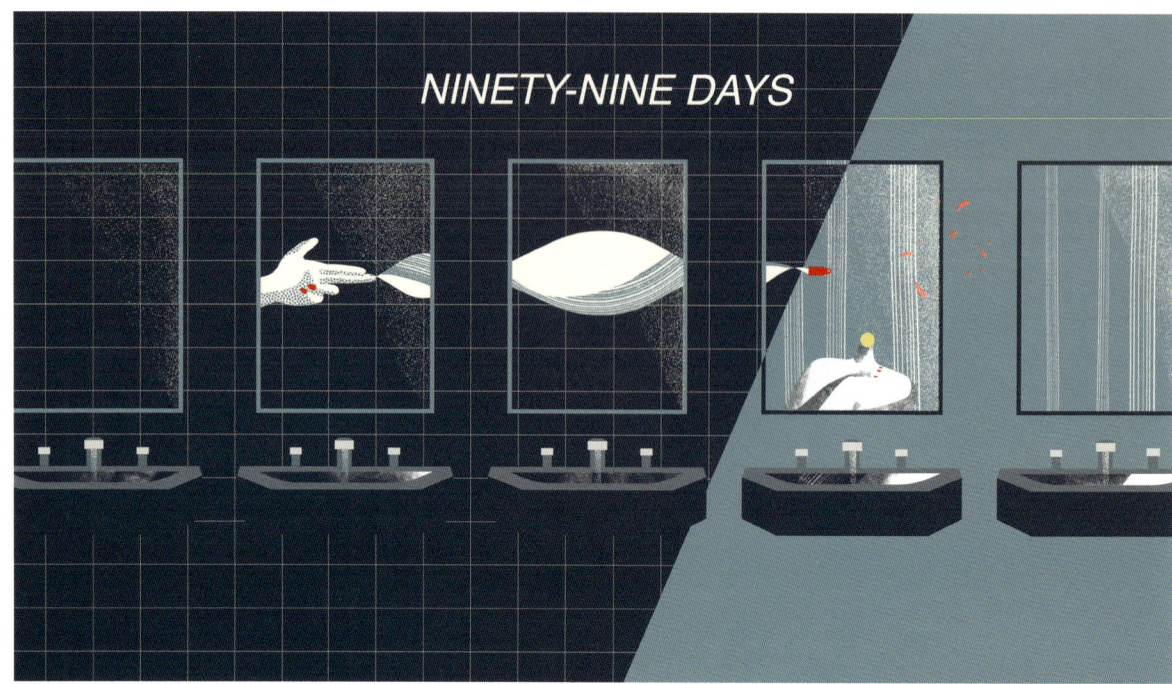

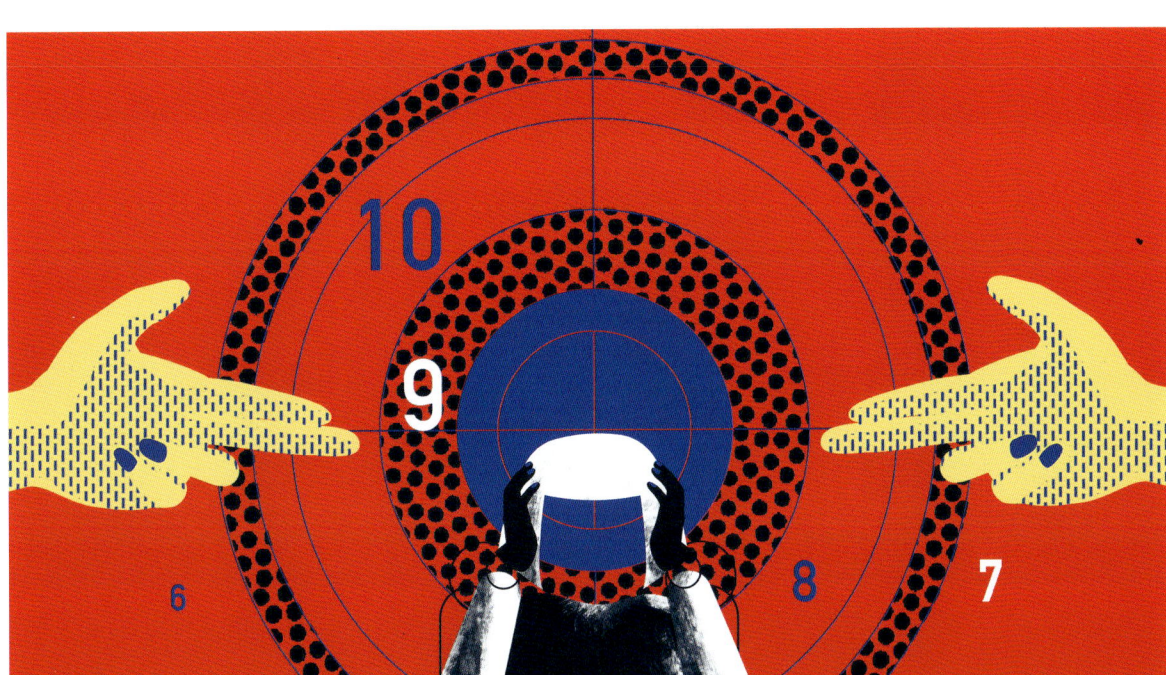

"Ninety-Nine Days" tells a personal story about coping with the experience of being a stranger. The short film begins with a shooting scene. It triggers dream-like sequences with a flood of acoustic and visual stimuli, in which balloons are the guiding elements. The way out of the chaos is finally indicated by a doorway. The symbolic threshold to the outside world can be crossed as soon as the protagonist embraces the unknown. Using simple graphic means, the animation succeeds in expressing complex psychological processes such as anxiety or the feeling of being overwhelmed in a poetic way.

Publishing & Print Media · Posters · Typography · Illustrations · Sound Design · Film & Animation · Online · Apps

The Assassination of Gianni Versace

[Title Sequence]

This title sequence is a redesign for an episode of the television series "American Crime Story". It deals with the case of fashion designer Gianni Versace, who was murdered by a serial killer in 1997. In order to create a visual link to the content, the sequence shows fleeting impressions of the fashion world, historical documents and Versace's glamorous lifestyle. The speed of the sequence, underscored by a hammering beat, is conceived to create tension typical of the genre. Featuring many dazzling colours, the blurred motifs reflect the aesthetics of the show and pique curiosity about the events.

University
SCAD Savannah College of Art and Design, Savannah, Georgia, USA

Design
Uladzimir Bahatyrevich, SCAD

→ Clip online

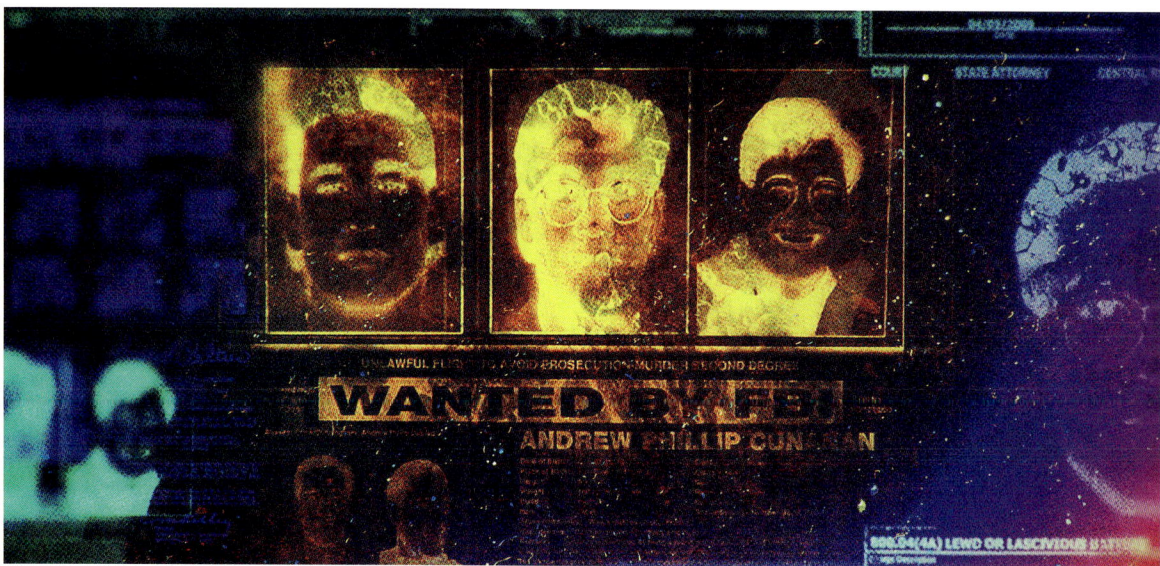

November

[Short Film]

"November" addresses the epidemic of depression, playing out single moments in the life of a depressed young woman. The protagonist, who works as a driver for a medical examiner's office, finds it hard to cope with the parallels of her personal and professional life. In the film, quiet tones and long shots capture a cloudy mood, while opposing character traits are used to show the perils of miscommunication. In order to make the viewer feel connected, the film is nearly exclusively shot with a hand-held camera and appeals to the audience with true-to-life images.

University
SCAD Savannah College of Art and Design, Savannah, Georgia, USA

Design
Maegan Mann, SCAD

→ Clip online

Publishing & Print Media   Posters   Typography   Illustrations   Sound Design   Film & Animation   Online   Apps

SPLENDOR
[Computer Animation]

Created on the occasion of a graduation exhibition at the Chaoyang University of Technology, this mixed media animation shows the range of projects involved. The image design combines film, hand-drawn animation, 3D animation and dynamic graphics in a surreal manner. At the end, the sequence culminates in a spectacular finale, implementing the idea of a wave which, after pulling back, strikes with full force. The burst of images clearly expresses that it is designed to leave a lasting impression on the audience.

University
Chaoyang University of Technology, Taichung, Taiwan

Supervising Professor
Kuo-Min Chuang

Design
Lin Tsai, Lu-Hong Chen, Zhi-Yu Xu, Jing-Wen Wang, Chen-Lin Hsieh, Yu-Qing Song, Bo-Wei Huang, Wen-Ying Fu,
Chaoyang University of Technology

→ Clip online

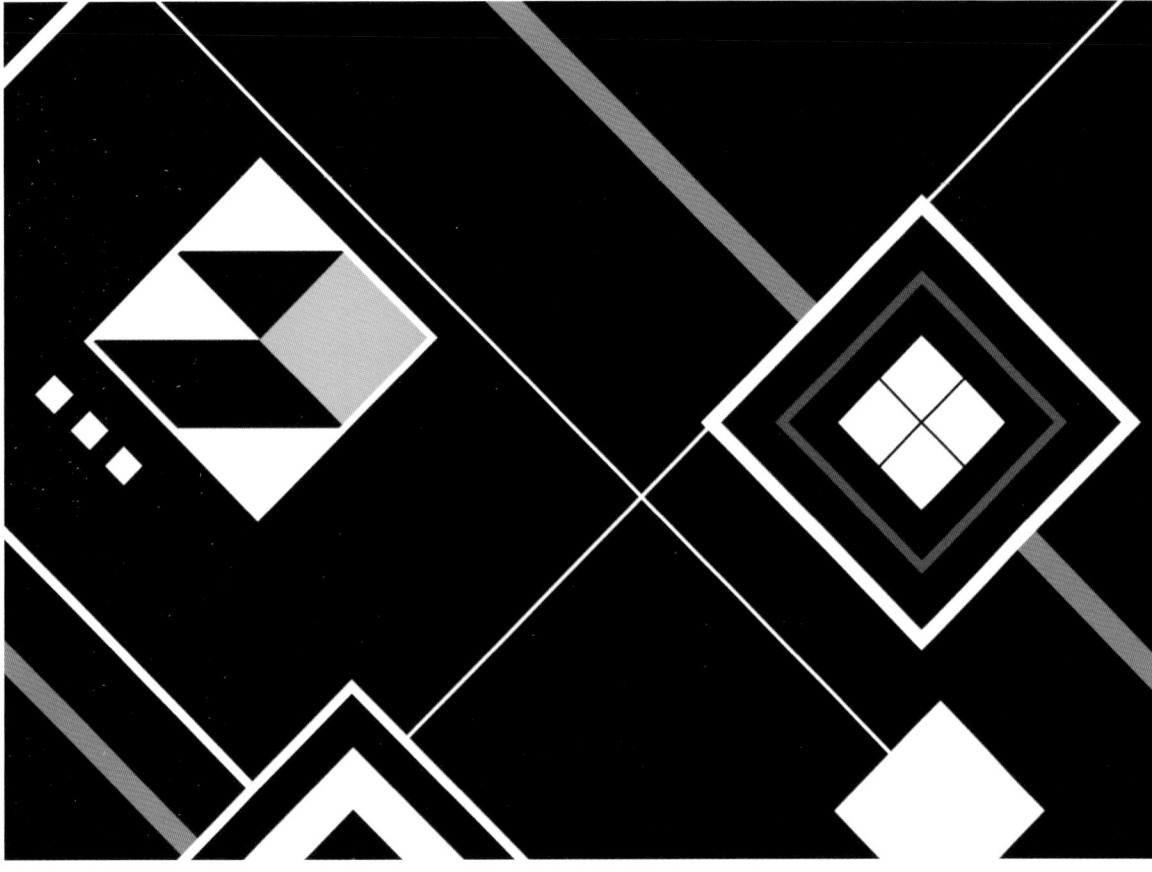

Seven Rooms

[Film Title Sequence]

"Seven Rooms" is a narrative by Otsuichi, a Japanese author. The story is about a little boy and his sister who find themselves trapped in a small concrete room. There are seven rooms in all, each containing a different prisoner – and everyone is to be massacred. In the intro, the plot is translated into a purely graphic concept. Lines and squares indicate the rooms. By flickering to the beat of electronic sounds, the abstract figures capture the attention of the viewers. Furthermore, the minimalist design radiates a disturbing cold atmosphere which anticipates the mood of the upcoming events.

University
SCAD Savannah College of Art and Design, Savannah, Georgia, USA

Design
Celia Hsu, SCAD

→ Clip online

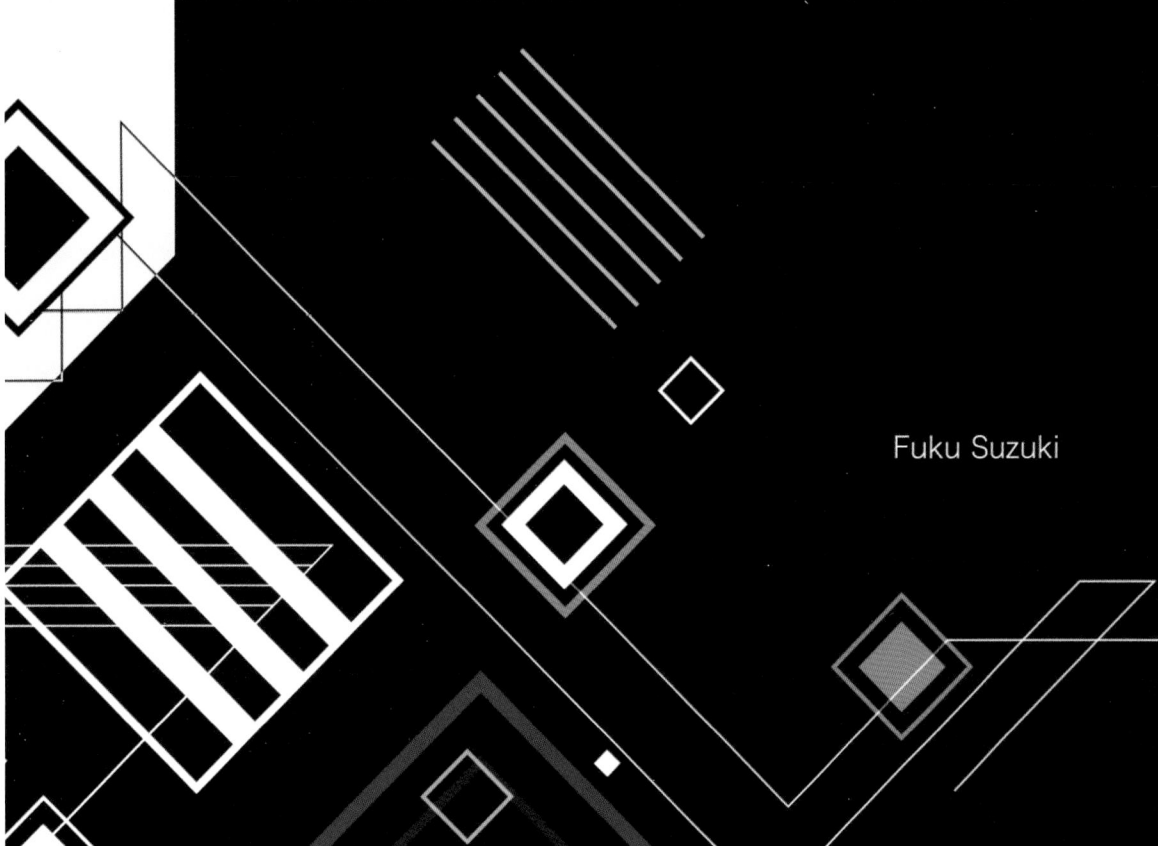

| Publishing & Print Media | Posters | Typography | Illustrations | Sound Design | Film & Animation | Online | Apps |

Expend

[Stop-Motion Animation]

"Expend" portrays the human tendency to exploit natural resources for petty desires. Without a sign of remorse, the protagonist of the film kills a stag. He uses the heart of the animal for a machine which generates electricity for his house. The energy, however, is consumed immediately, so the man sets off for the next raid. The medium of stop-motion chosen for this animation complements the viewer's emotions, communicating the stirring message with pictures that are tactile and tangible. The story is accentuated by a dense, atmospheric setting and corresponding sounds.

University
SCAD Savannah College of Art and Design, Savannah, Georgia, USA

Design
Bismark Fernandes, SCAD

→ Clip online

of Smaller Things
[Stop-Motion Animation]

The title of this animation refers to the novel "The God of Small Things" by Indian writer Arundhati Roy. "Small things", in this case, refers to moths. While Roy introduces the moth as a symbol of fear and unhappiness, it is also commonly associated with hidden desires. The film stages the insects in carefully choreographed close-ups, culminating in a finale in which a moth is drawn to the flame of a candle. The whirling movement of wings draws the viewer into the action and, in combination with piano runs, stimulates the imagination to further trace the meaning of the mystical animal.

University
SCAD Savannah College of Art and Design, Savannah, Georgia, USA

Design
Jim Downer, SCAD

→ Clip online

BLEND

[Pictogram System]

University
Ling Tung University, Taichung, Taiwan

Supervising Professor
Ding-Xian Yang, Wei-Jen Huang

Design
Lixuan Zheng, Yingjie Xu,
Ching-Chun Lan, Xuze Zhou, Yufan Chen,
Ling Tung University

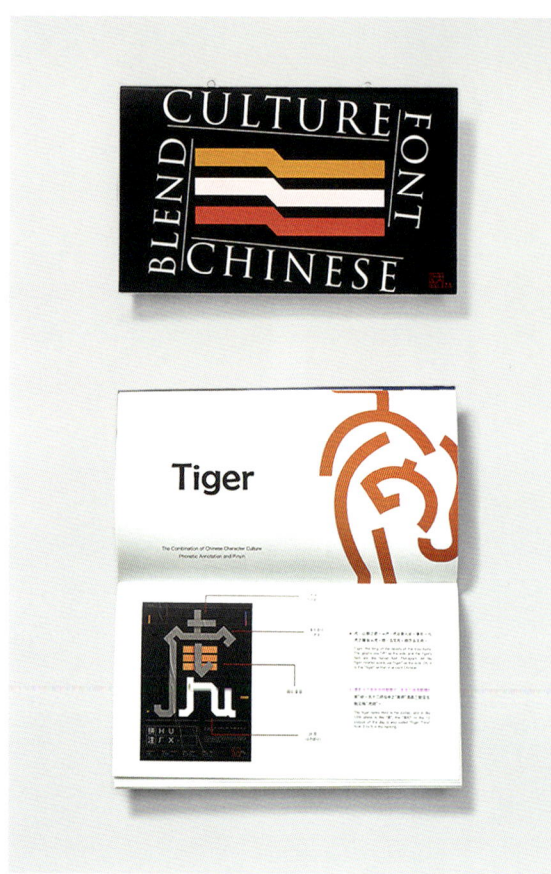

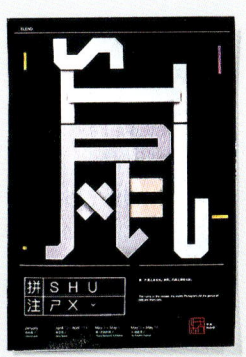 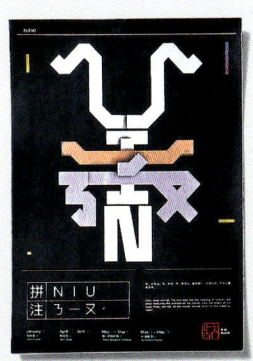 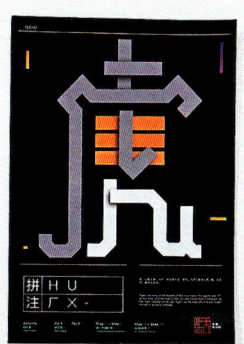
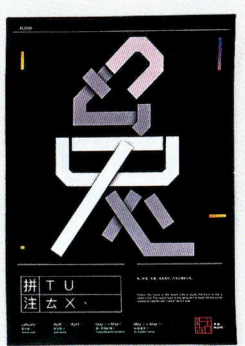  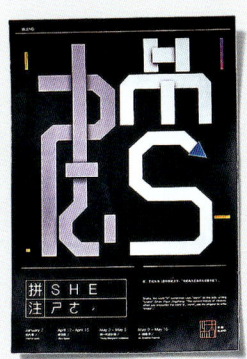
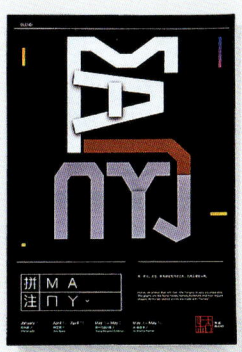 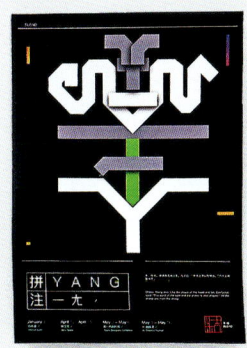 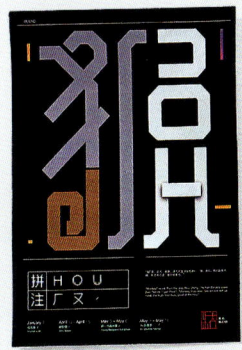
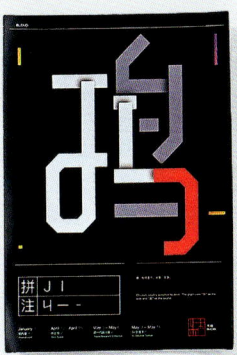 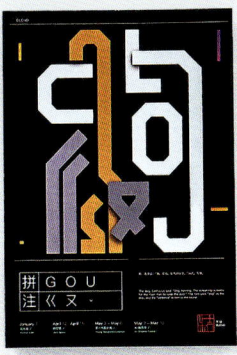 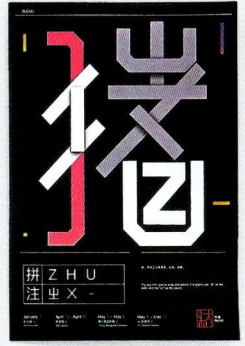

Chinese characters, used in both China and Taiwan, are transliterated into the Roman alphabet and Mandarin phonetic symbols respectively. BLEND takes the traditional Chinese zodiac signs, which are common to both cultures, as a framework. Each sign of the zodiac is characterised by a combination of the corresponding alphabetical and phonetic symbols. These 12 ideograms form the core of an educational tool which seeks to promote mutual understanding across the Taiwan Strait. With harmonious lines, the design conclusively embodies the overriding idea of being connected.

Four Tones Font

[Typeface]

University
Shanghai Publishing and Printing College,
Shanghai, China

Supervising Professor
Fang Wu

Design
Xinyu Gan,
Shanghai Publishing and Printing College

→ Clip online

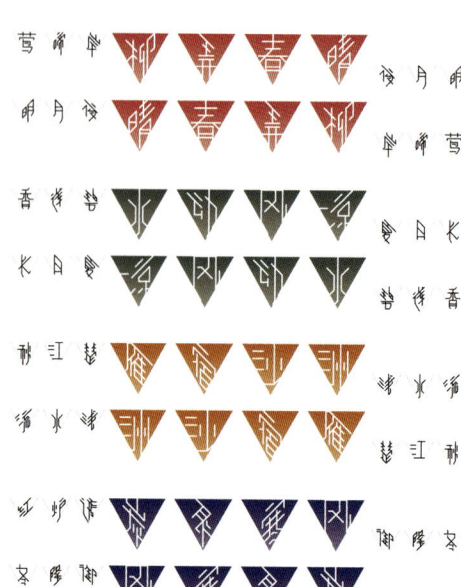

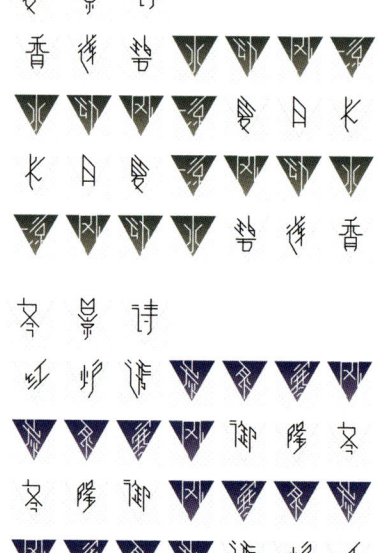

| Interface & User Experience Design | Spatial Communication | **Red Dot: Junior Award**
 Typography | Designer Profiles | Jury | Index | Red Dot – World of Design |

Chinese is a tonal language, which means that the way a syllable is pronounced can change its meaning. This typeface visualises the four tones of modern Mandarin – level tone, rising tone, low tone and falling tone. The font design is fundamentally inspired by the phonetic symbols of the four tones. When used for classical Chinese poetry, the expressive shapes of the font help readers understand the sound and rhythmic changes of a poem. Beyond practical benefit, the filigree characters exude an artistic charm.

Book Covers

This project redesigns the book covers of three international bestsellers by American author Robert Greene. In his books, the writer talks about power and universal rules to survive the design industry. Approaching the subject typographically, the covers display crossover graphics matching the author's bold, experimental style. The black-and-white palette and tight type create a strong contrast which illustrates the fearless statements of the books. In addition, carefully structured excerpts on the back covers provide readers with the opportunity to grasp the content at a glance.

University
SCAD Savannah College of Art and Design, Atlanta, Georgia, USA

Design
Leena Murdeshwar, SCAD

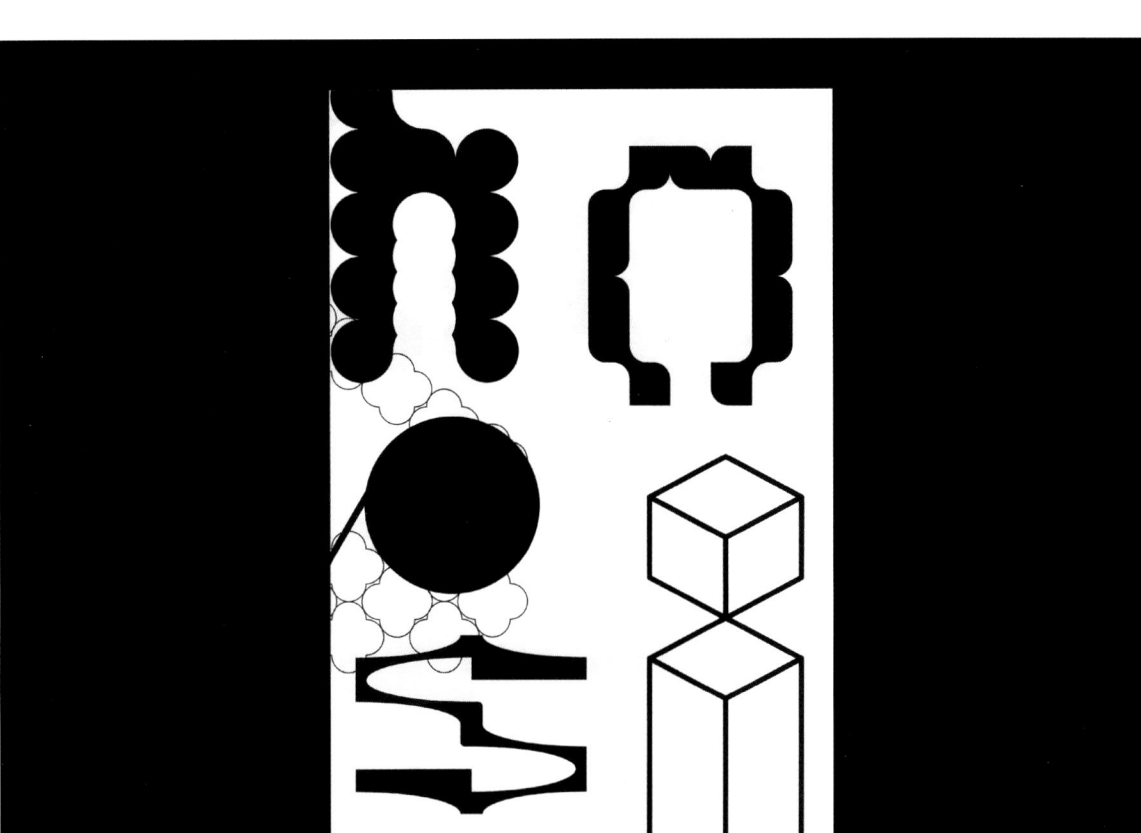

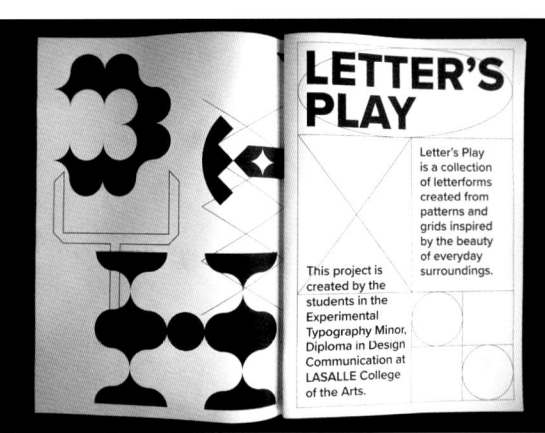
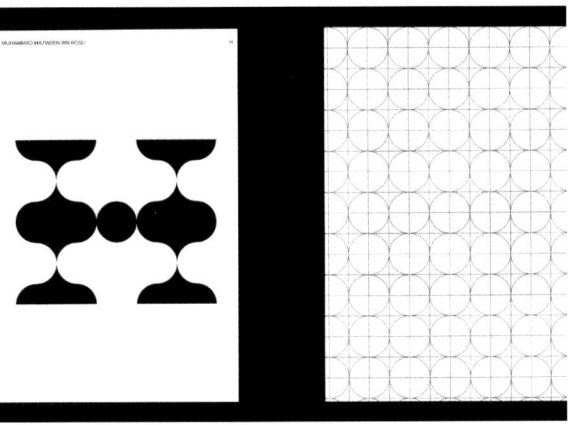
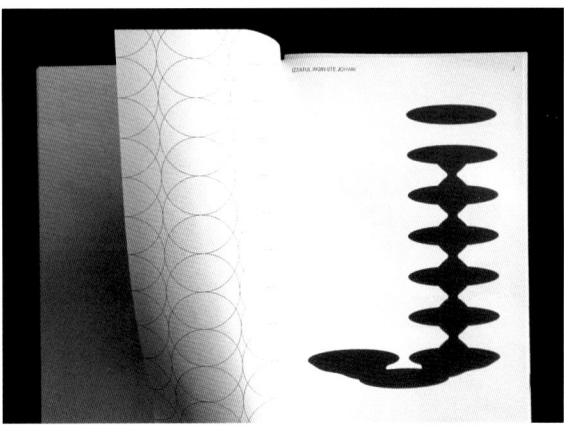

Letter's Play
[Letterforms]

The typography of Letter's Play is inspired by patterns and grids from everyday surroundings. Organically rounded forms are reminiscent of body parts or vases, while angular ones recall tools or industrial components. This design vocabulary cannot be unambiguously deciphered, but seeks to stimulate the viewer's imagination. Black-and-white contrasts and the interplay of positive and negative forms result in strong graphic effects. With simple means, the imaginative shapes thus succeed in maximising impact.

University
LASALLE College of the Arts, Singapore

Design
Venny Chung Ping Siang,
Nora Jasmine Yee,
LASALLE College of the Arts

CoMotion X 2019

[Cinematic Sounds]

CoMotion is a career conference hosted by motion media design students. The title sequence for CoMotion 2019 introduces the event by taking the audience on a journey through a thoroughly styled world. In a futuristic setting, a space capsule explores animated scenarios which stand for the past, present and future of the young designers and showcase common techniques and trends. The message that great creative potential is on its way is underscored with spheric music as well as energetic grooves. As the sound fades away, the capsule disappears into space, symbolising unlimited possibilities.

University
SCAD Savannah College of Art and Design, Savannah, Georgia, USA

Design
Ryan Sullivan, Ashton Faydenko, Chris Hopkins, SCAD

→ Clip online

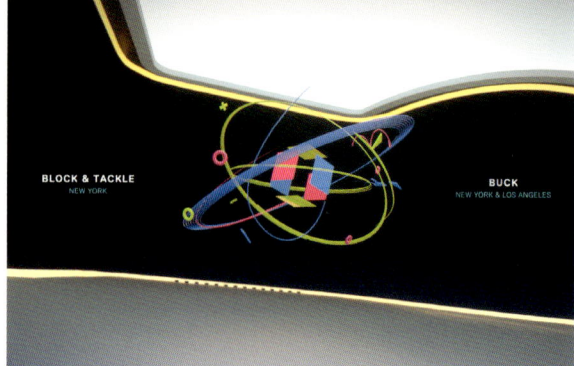
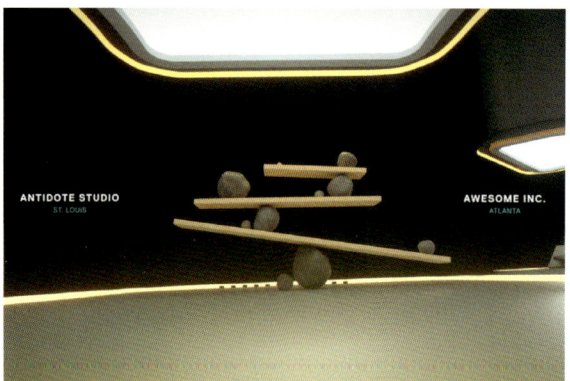

The Reframing of Being Forgotten

[Live Event Performance, Information Design]

This work introduces Sinawi, an ancient form of Korean folk music, which originally accompanied the dancing and singing of a shaman. While the audience is shown a video with an ensemble playing Sinawi, the improvised sounds are reflected in a special music score. In addition, a handkerchief, driven by a motor and fans, mimics the performance of a dancer. Through the finely tuned interaction of media, the information concept draws attention to the traditional music. It communicates the vigour of the sound in a modern and particularly lively manner.

University
Design Academy Eindhoven, Netherlands

Supervising Professor
Joost Grootens, Simon Davies, Gert Staal, Kim Bouvy, Koehorst in 't Veld

Design
Suk Go, Daejeon, South Korea

Musical Advice
So-Yeon Kim, Samuel Vriezen

Technical Advice
ANOIZ, Seoul, South Korea

→ Clip online

Flyer

[Mobile App, Website]

When living in a city, it is easy to feel lost. Flyer helps by connecting citizens with non-profit organisations and other people in their local community. On the platform, users can search for organisations, engage in discussions and volunteer for charitable activities. Presenting users with weekly mixes of events based on their interests, organisations are able to post events on the Flyer website. Appealing imagery and a functional interface underline the project's ambition to not only inform users but to help them play a useful role in society.

University
SCAD Savannah College of Art and Design, Savannah, Georgia, USA

Design
Ka-Hyun Lee, Graeme Smith, Aby Iberkleid, Oscar Kwong, SCAD

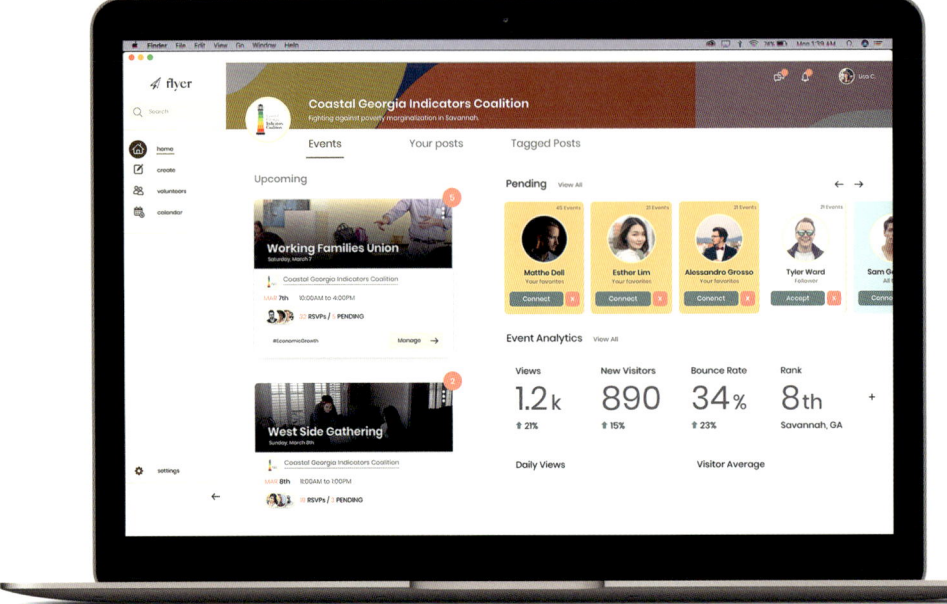

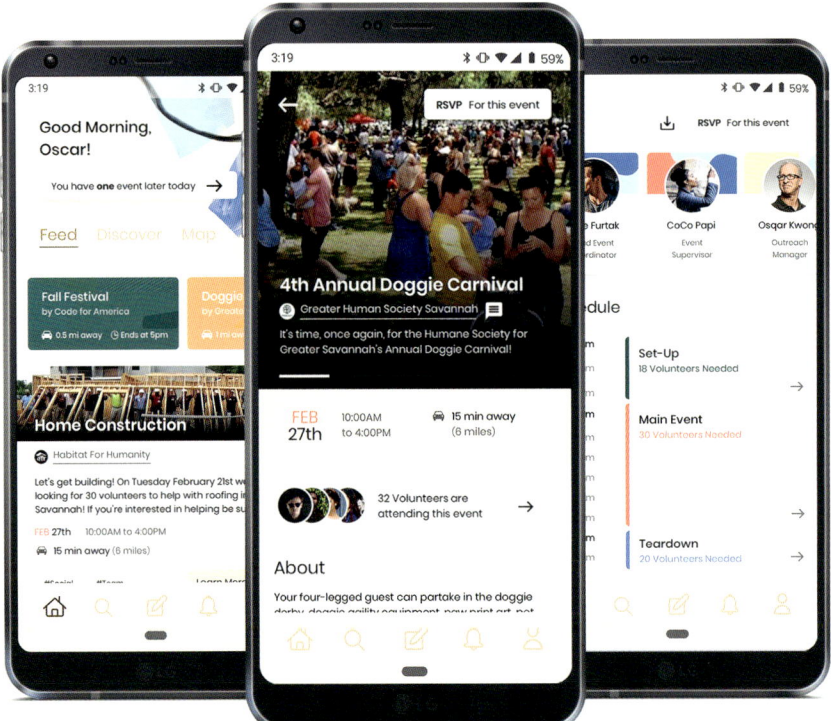

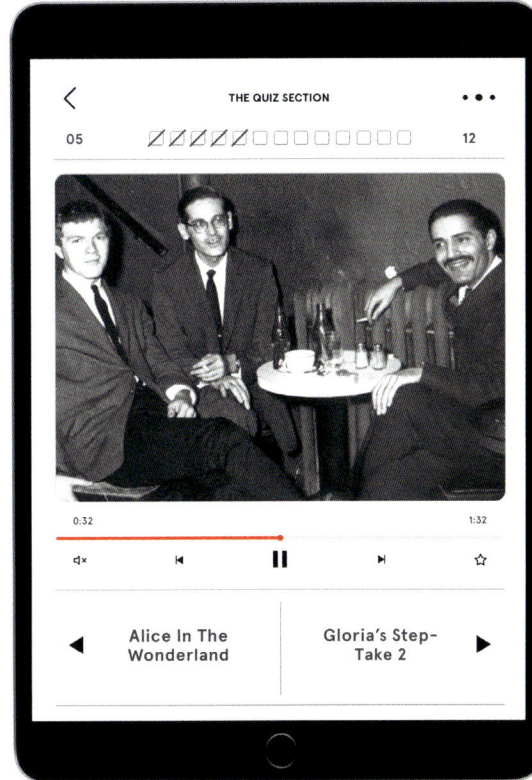

Bolsters

[Social Networking]

In view of an ageing society, Bolsters aims to connect people in different life stages through shared interests. The reciprocal digital platform works according to the principle of hobby matching and skill exchange. Two users from different age groups can share their knowledge about specific topics and run an isolated group page to invite more users to participate. With an easily accessible interface and catchy icons, the platform simplifies the communication process, improves networking efficiency and lowers barriers for elderly people to handle digital devices.

University
Pratt Institute, New York, USA

Design
Huei-Tai Chen, Pratt Institute

Seoulist

[Travel App]

University
Hansung University, Seoul, South Korea

Design
Sunghee Lee, Seoul, South Korea

→ Clip online

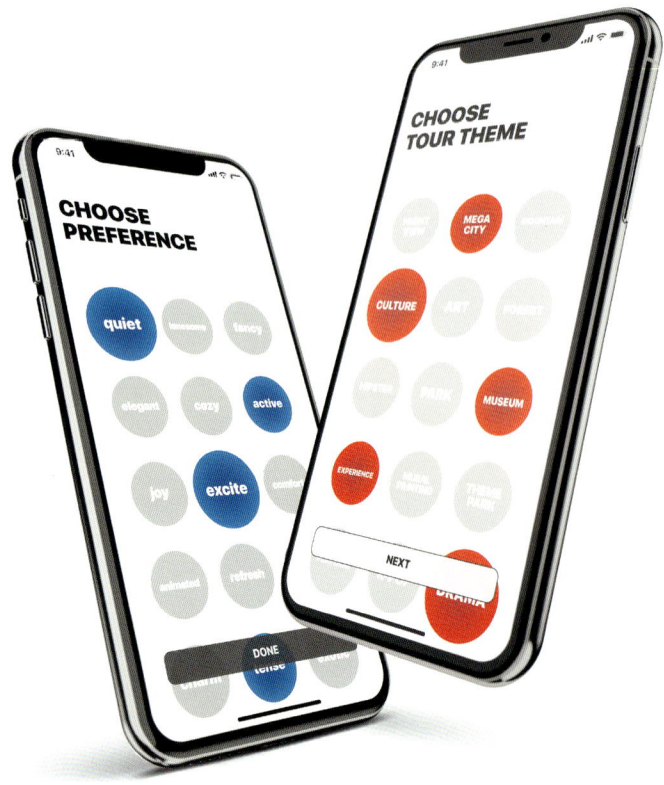

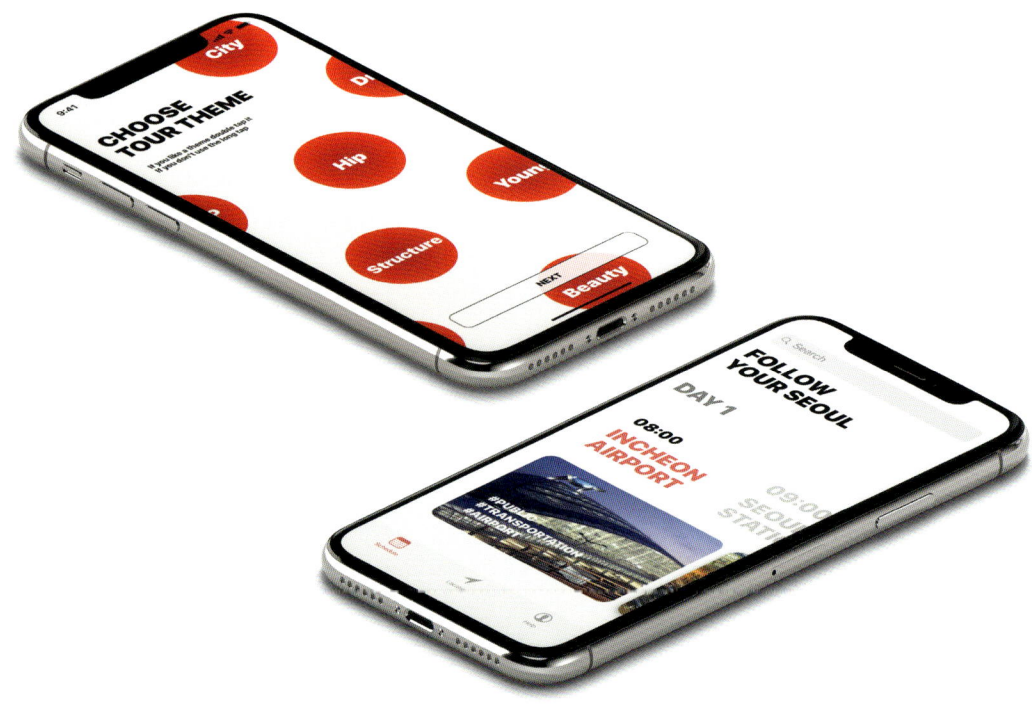

Interface & User Experience Design   Spatial Communication   Red Dot: Junior Award Apps   Designer Profiles   Jury   Index   Red Dot – World of Design

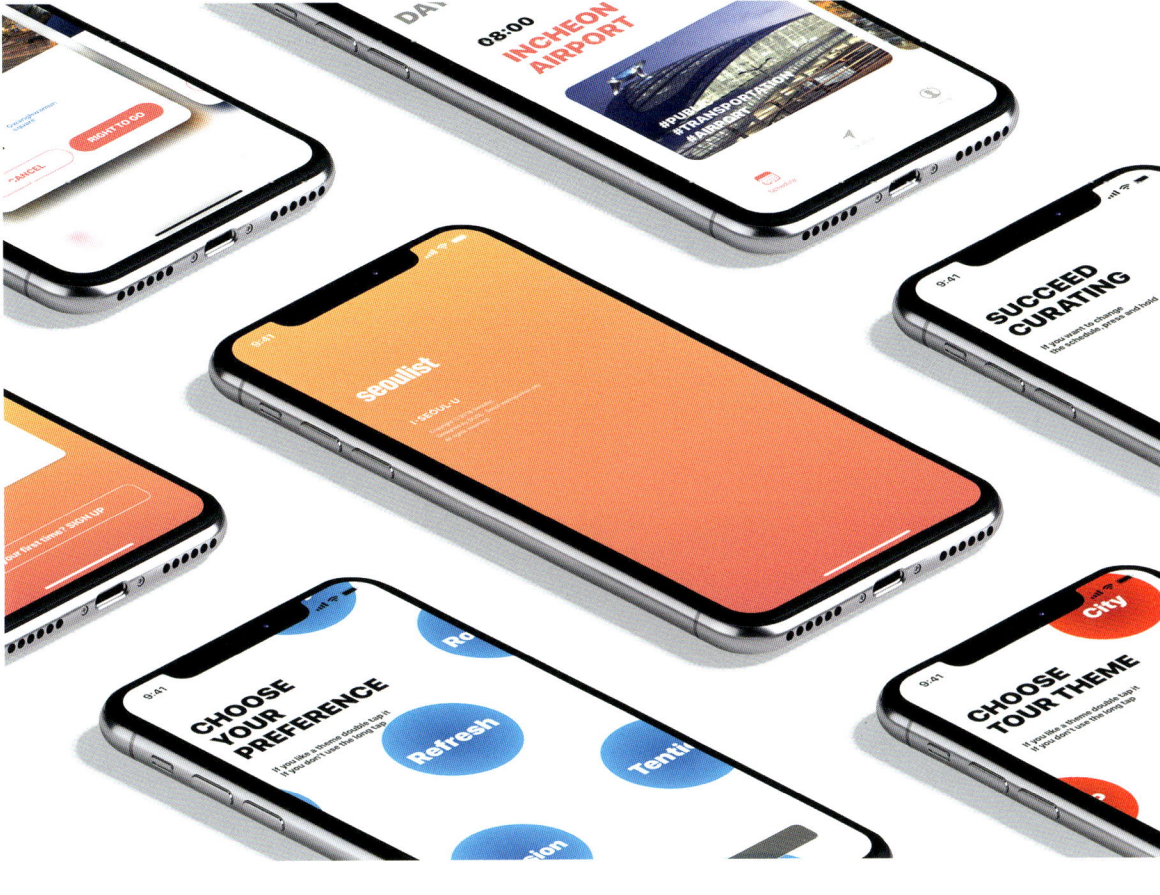

This travel app aims to help foreign tourists customise their trip to Seoul. The application allows travellers to select attractions in the megacity from a variety of topics and proposes a guided tour on this basis. After the tour, users can review their pictures and evaluate personal data, such as the time spent at an exhibition, in public transport or walking. The layout of the application is tailored to meet operating situations on the go by offering easy one-hand use. In addition, it facilitates navigation with a clear contrast of colours and shapes.

  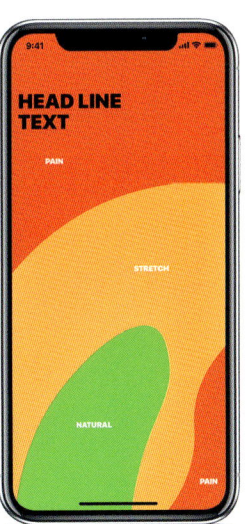 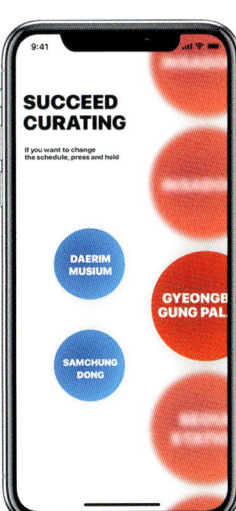

Felo

[Childhood Companion AI Robot with Associated App]

Felo is an AI companion designed to improve the interpersonal skills of children in a controlled, positive environment. The key areas targeted are physical activity, responsibility and empathy. Via the associated app, parents are able to set schedules and daily events for their child. The robot models these settings by, for example, getting "sleepy" at a given time, and serves as a guide for the child. In turn, the robot's feedback is encouraging if the child responds to its needs. Through the use of add-ons, Felo can also foster outdoor activities.

University
SCAD Savannah College of Art and Design, Savannah, Georgia, USA

Design
Mackinzi Blank, Daniel Benedict, Meshal Almazyad, Samantha Klein, SCAD

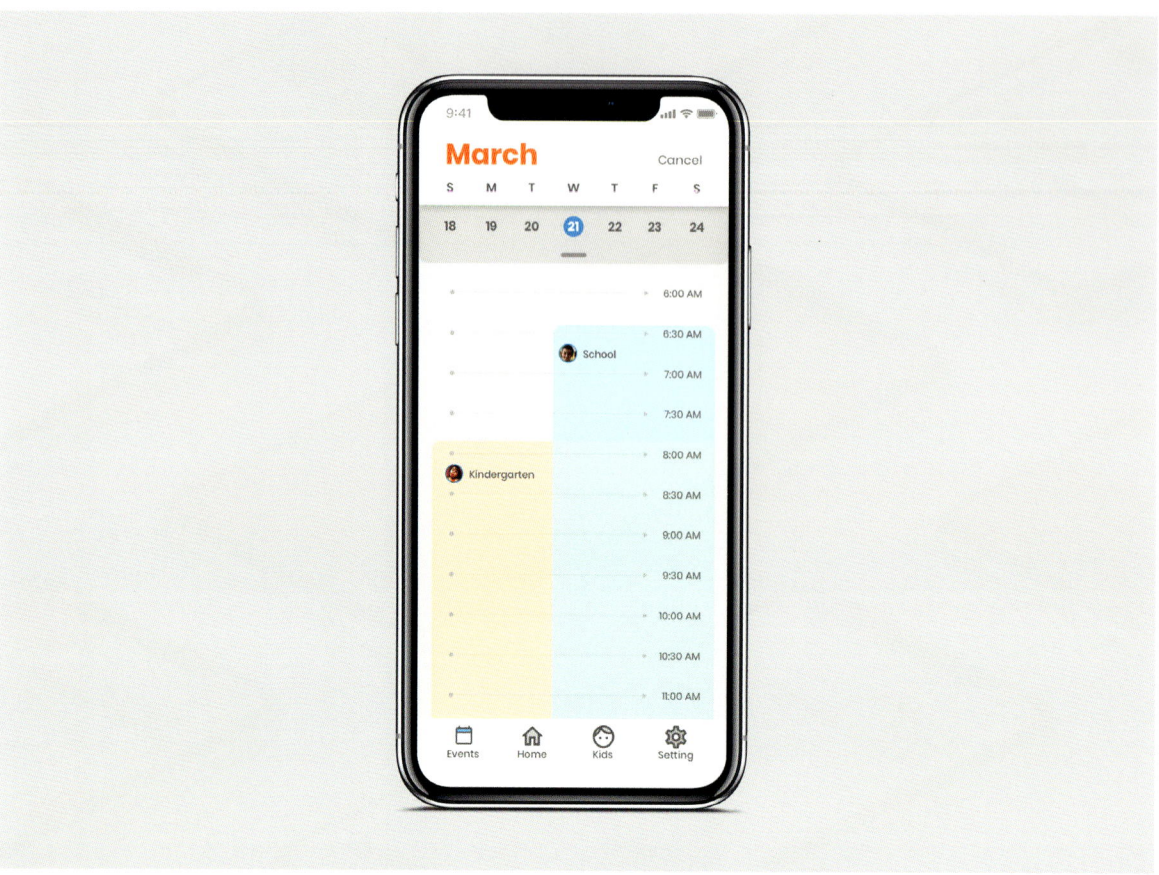
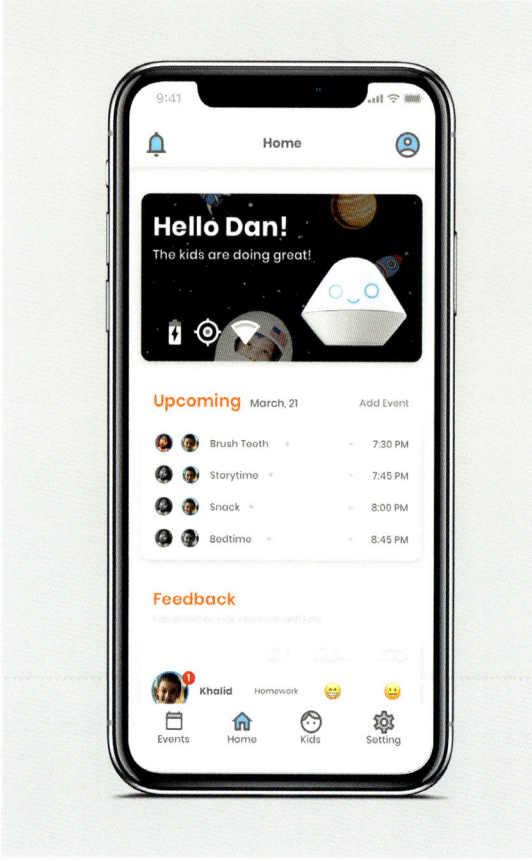
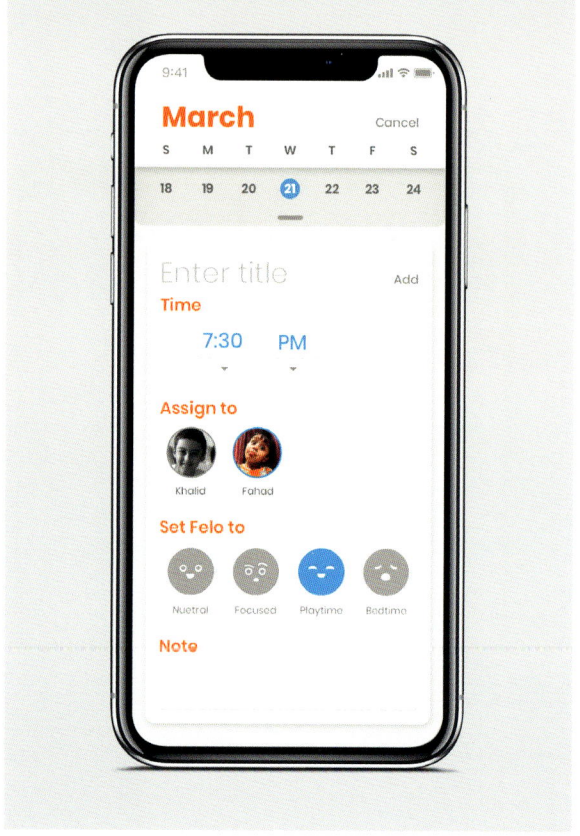

| Interface & User Experience Design | Spatial Communication | Red Dot: Junior Award Apps | Designer Profiles | Jury | Index | Red Dot – World of Design |

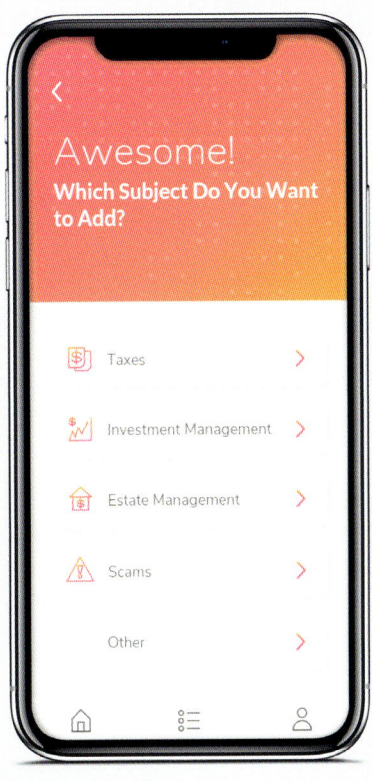

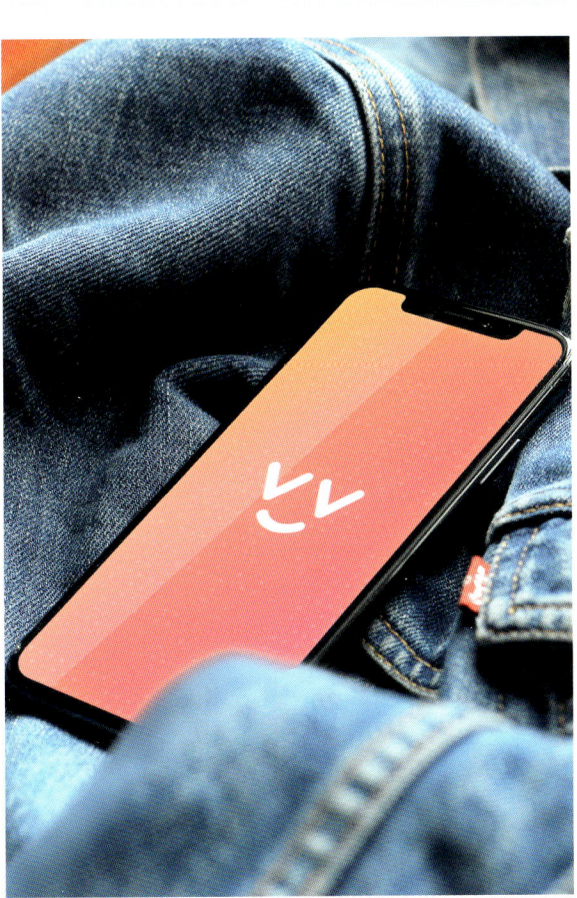

Savvi
[Educational Networking App]

Savvi is designed to connect learners in need of life management skills with experienced instructors. By linking users to human support rather than offering automated solutions, the app enables a learning experience tailored to individual needs. In turn, it rewards benevolent instructors by allowing them to offer services without committing full-time dedication. Supported by digital as well as physical interaction, a convenient structure and a clear visual language, the application helps users to perform skilled tasks themselves instead of having them done by someone else.

University
SCAD Savannah College of Art and Design, Savannah, Georgia, USA

Design
Lidia De Oleo, Maya Zimmer, Nathasya Effendy, Steven Ou, Ryan Stifler, SCAD

Publishing & Print Media | Posters | Typography | Illustrations | Sound Design | Film & Animation | Online | Apps

Amuzi

[Recycling Rewards System for Cities, User Interface Design]

University
Art Center College of Design, Pasadena, USA

Supervising Professor
Brian Boyle, Krystina Castella

Design
George Zixuan Weng, Connie Yoo, Cynthia Shen, Art Center College of Design

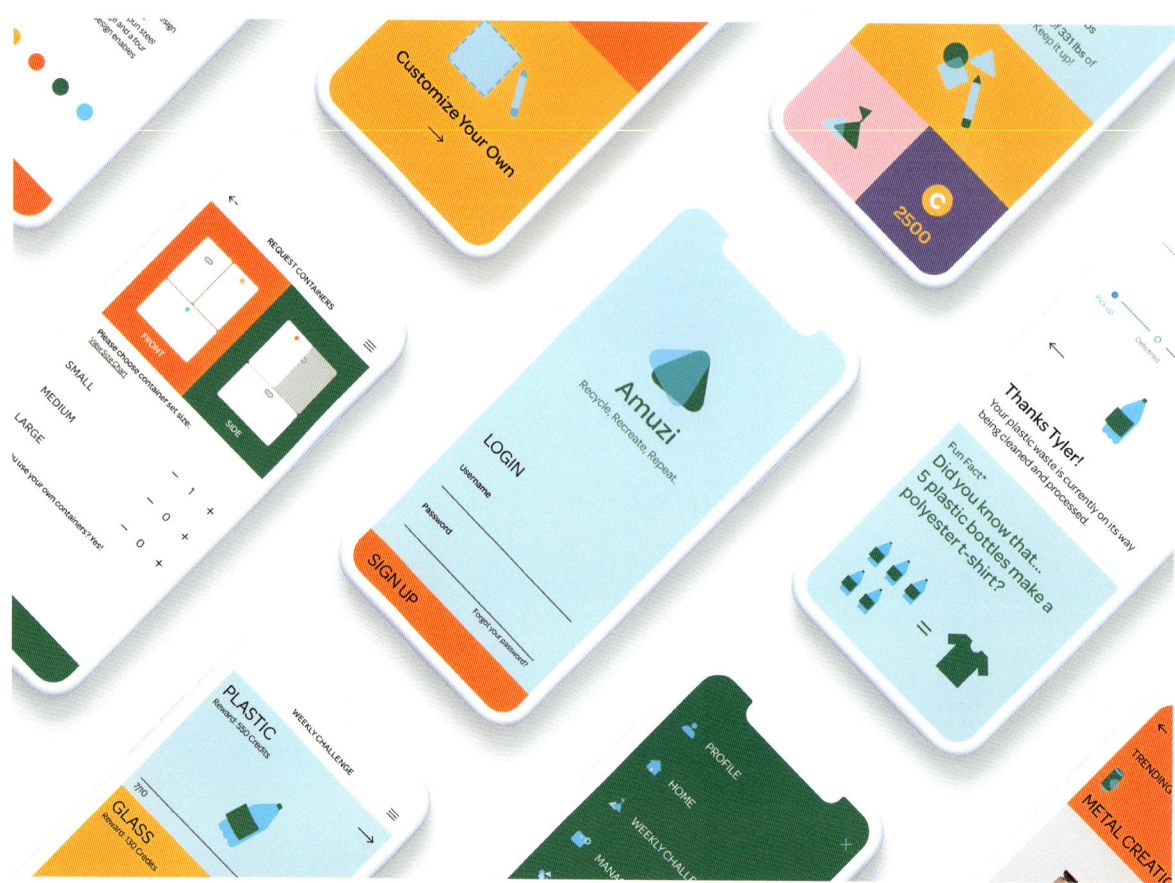

Amuzi is an integrated system designed to help cities solve existing problems in waste management. The system cooperates with mass production companies, waste haulers and processing manufacturers to keep the wastes on track. Users can request containers or view where their waste is going after collection. To motivate them, the platform also provides them with physical rewards and gameplay. As a one-place solution, the system comes with a fresh graphic appeal, highlighting the mutual benefits of the recycling process for both users and the environment.

The Cleaner

[Poster Illustration]

This poster series uses an ironic tone to draw the public's attention to the problem of littering. Each poster merges a photo of a cleaning utensil with graphic textures to form a new visual entity. Thus, the images represent marine animals removing dirt like a vacuum cleaner, a mop or a rubbish bin. In paradoxical beauty, the large-format motifs communicate their message at a glance. They clearly refer to the issue of pollutants and plastics ending up and accumulating in the bodies of animals, which leads to the question: who is producing this waste, and why?

University
Ling Tung University, Taichung, Taiwan

Supervising Professor
Tyng-Chau Hwang, Ching-Wei Liu

Design
Yu-Rung Lin, Yu-Mei Chen, Huan-Hsuan Lee, Yu-Heng Chen, Ling Tung University

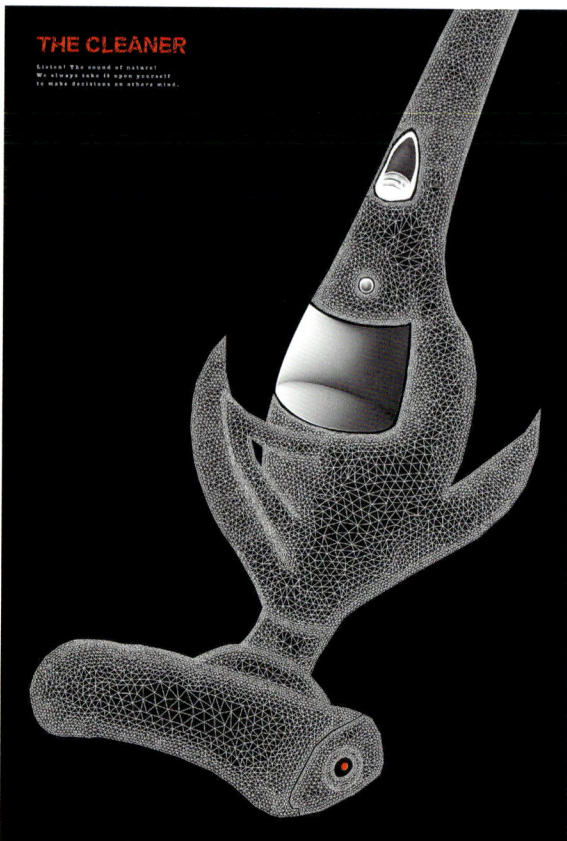
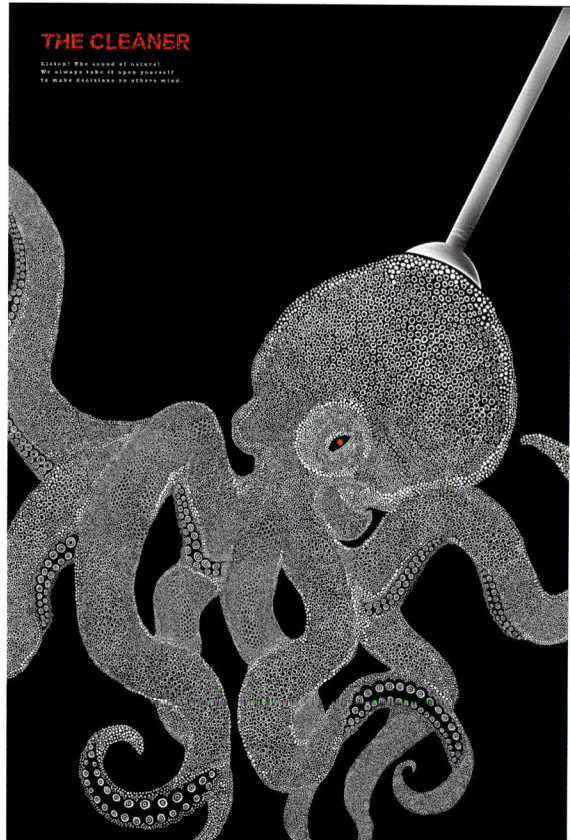
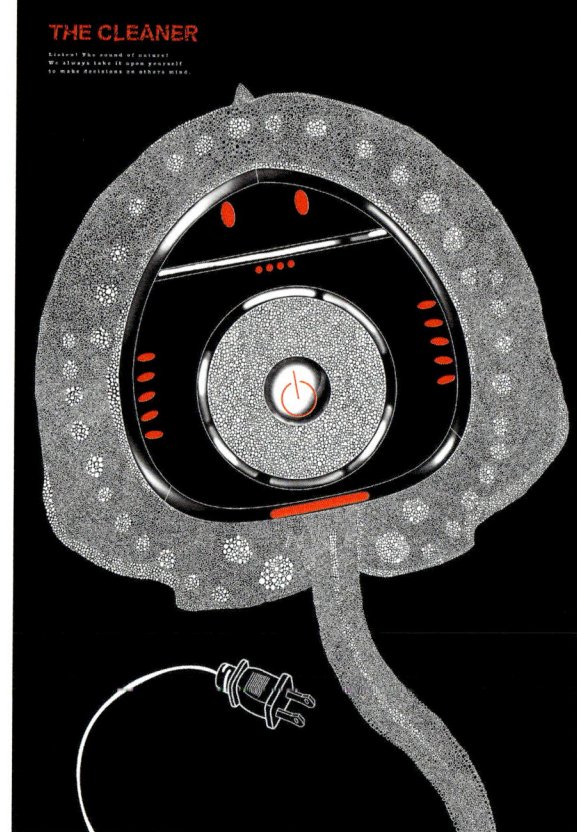

Life
[Poster Illustration]

In an allegorical way, this poster series visualises the damage done to the environment by human activity. Two species of monsters, which stand for the consequences of human destruction, seek to remind the audience to have a certain awe for nature. The negative forms on a black background unfold a dramatic effect, triggering the imagination how the mutated creatures might have come into being. Apart from that, the expressive motifs offer the thrill of identifying every single disgusting detail.

University
Fuzhou University of
International Studies and Trade,
Fuzhou, China

Supervising Professor
Zi Zhi, Xi Cheng

Design
Guo-Da Lin, Feng Luo, Kai-Qiang Hou,
Fuzhou University of
International Studies and Trade

→ Designer profile on page 574

The Walk
[Picture Book]

The illustrated book depicts the story of a little girl and her guardian who go on a walk into an imaginary world. Less a book than a panorama one-shot movie, the characters' journey presents the themes of growth, life circulation and bravery. On each spread, creatures appear huge in comparison to the human figures. The reversal of proportions underlines the symbolic content of the narrative, generates a sense of tension and conveys the child's amazement. By creating a dreamy mood with soft colours, the illustrations leave plenty of room for the reader's own associations.

University
SCAD Savannah College of Art and Design, Atlanta, Georgia, USA

Design
Hannah Li, SCAD

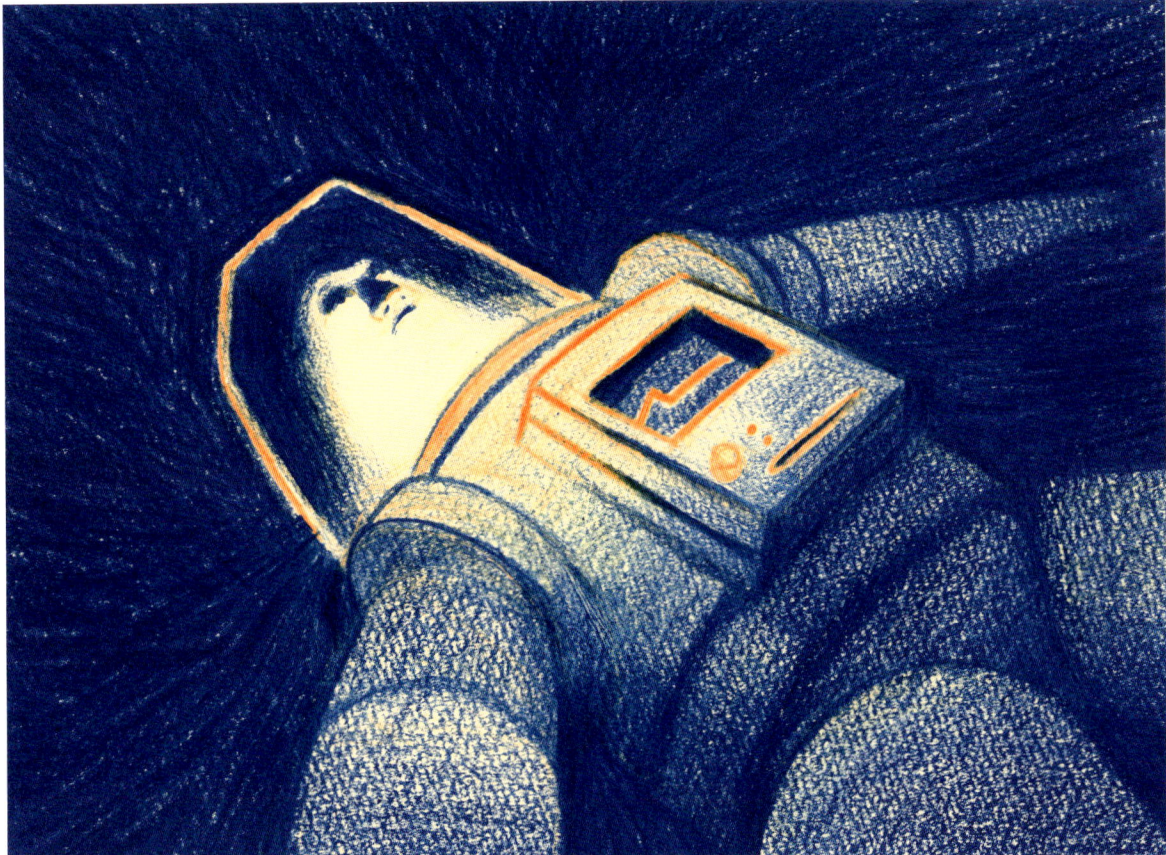

The Illustrated Man
[Book Illustration]

"The Illustrated Man" is a collection of short stories by Ray Bradbury. Bradbury's tales are considered a milestone in science fiction, as they emotively depict the fate of those who are slaves to technology. These illustrations focus on three stories considered emblematic of the work as a whole. The underlying psychology of the characters is highlighted by effective use of positive and negative space. In addition, a minimal colour palette and a strong sense of light and shadow contribute to conveying the poetic atmosphere of the stories.

University
SCAD Savannah College of
Art and Design, Savannah, Georgia, USA

Design
Mackenzie Quick, SCAD

Publishing & Print Media   Posters   Typography   Illustrations   Sound Design   Film & Animation   Online   Apps

Atypical Daily

[Editorial Illustration]

This project denounces destructive behaviour in modern societies. The issues addressed are partly related to media consumption, such as gaming addiction and hacking, but also include phenomena like social disregard and emotional blackmail. A critical attitude is expressed through distorted images in a colourful comic style. The illustrations are designed to be hung on the wall, encouraging viewers to discover more and more daunting subtleties and serving as a motivation to reconsider one's own behaviour.

University
Ling Tung University, Taichung, Taiwan

Supervising Professor
Ching-Wei Liu

Design
Ying-Hua Shih, Meng-Xuan Li, Zi-Qi Liu, Li-Xin Wang, Wun-Jie Chen, Ling Tung University

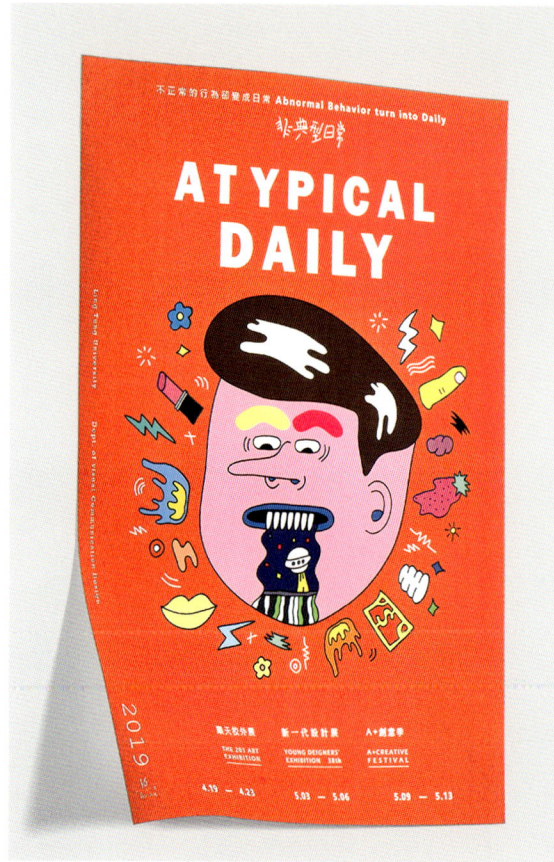

Lecheng Temple

[Poster Illustration]

The Lecheng Temple is a 200-year-old site in Taichung. Introducing images of traditional Taiwanese gods, these posters focus on the spiritual background of the temple. Each poster presents one deity, which is shown in a frontal view and thus directly addresses the public. Since the motifs are embedded in dynamic lettering, the static posture of the figures is harmoniously balanced. Thanks to some grotesquely exaggerated features, the pictures also have an entertaining effect. The unique imagery serves to make the religious content more accessible, especially to young people.

University
Ling Tung University, Taichung, Taiwan

Supervising Professor
Szu-Ming Sung, Ching-Wei Liu

Design
Chia-Hui Su, Qian-Han Lin, Min-Yin Liao, Yi-Xuan Lin, Ling Tung University

Prison Education

[Educational Illustration]

Taichung Prison has established a special rehabilitation programme in which inmates produce lacquerware. This series of illustrations takes the unusual workshop as a starting point to depict numerous scenes of life in prison. Stylistically, the work is limited to simply drawn figures which remain anonymous in a discreet manner. At the same time, soft colours and the round shapes of the characters unfold a childlike charm. In this way, the illustrations express a compassionate attitude and appeal to the public to look at the prisoners without prejudice.

University
Ling Tung University, Taichung, Taiwan

Design
I-Ching Chiang, Yee-Teng Chan, Yu-Tzu Lee, Ci-Zhen Xu, Yu-Ying Yan, Ling Tung University

Pick for Luck

[Educational Illustration]

The lunar calendar plays an important role in oriental culture. It is based on the idea that the forces of the moon do not only cause the tides but also have a huge impact on our daily life. The booklet "Pick for luck" shows which days in the lunar cycle are best for certain activities. A series of illustrations helps users to have a better understanding of the calendar by explaining difficult terms through dialogues between grandmothers and grandchildren. In a humorous way, the pictures convey the message that the tradition of the lunar calendar is still of great use and deserves more attention.

University
National Taichung University of Science and Technology, Taichung, Taiwan

Design
Mei-Xiu Guo, Chia-Yu Liu, Fang-Yi Lin, National Taichung University of Science and Technology

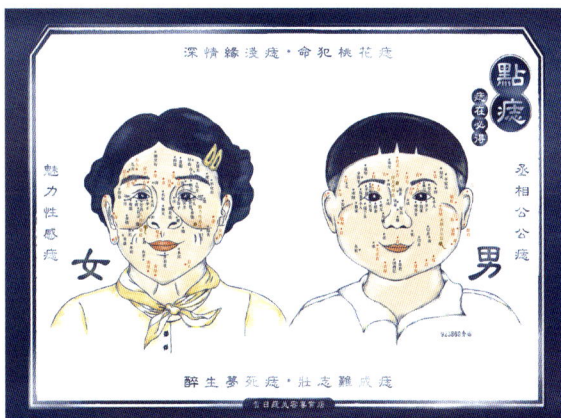

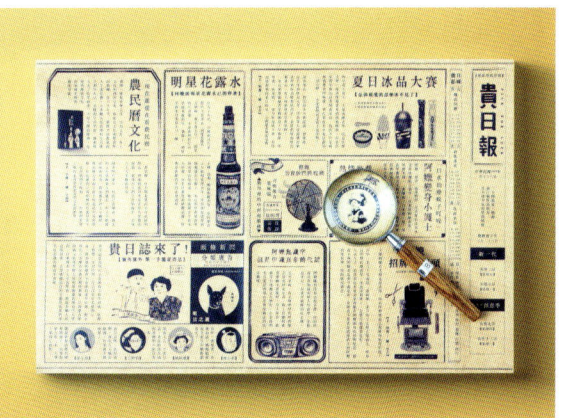

Taiwan National Park League

[Editorial Illustration]

With the aim of promoting the special ecosystems of Taiwan's national parks, this visual identity has been created for travel guides and area maps. Regional features are depicted in detail and with harmoniously embedded lettering. The colour scheme plays an important role in this concept. Each national park is marked by colours that reflect the character of the landscape. The skilful combination of two soft tones is the key to communicating the beauty of nature and, what is more, to presenting it in a coherent way.

University
Shu-Te University, Kaohsiung, Taiwan

Supervising Professor
Yu-Lung Yang

Design
Cheng-Chun Lee, Jing-Yan Liu, Yi-Rong Que, Shu-Te University

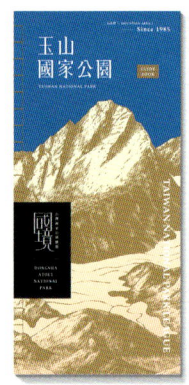

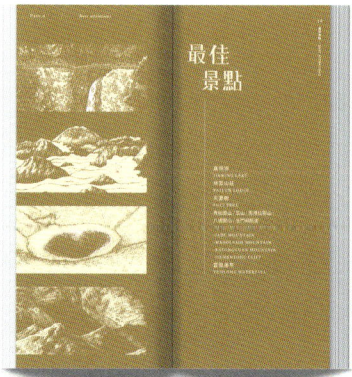

The Best Metro Station in China 2018–2019

[Advertising Illustration]

The search for the best metro station in China is a large-scale national campaign, co-sponsored by design magazines and the Shanghai Creative Design Workers Association. The key visual for the event uses a selected city's landmark buildings and integrates the architectural forms in a geometric, nested composition. The metropolitan theme is interpreted in a distinctive black-and-white scheme, offset by yellow accents. By showing ingenious railway constructions, the illustrations highlight the connecting function of rail transit in urban areas.

Client
The Best Metro Station Committee, Shanghai Academy of Fine Arts (SAFA), Shanghai, China

Design
Lin Zhiyun, Chen Bolan, Chen Zhigang, Bai Yan

Art Direction/Graphic Design
Lin Zhiyun

Digital Concept
Chen Bolan

Project Management
Chen Zhigang

Editorial Work
Bai Yan

→ Designer profile on page 542

Forest Stand

[Poster Illustration, Character Design]

"Forest Stand" deals with reckless meat consumption, visualising the topic in the form of posters, action figures and complementary accessories. Five elderly animals represent endangered species in Taiwan. At first glance, the scenarios look like a nostalgic toy world. But they quickly reveal a dark core, as the animals turn out to be market vendors selling meat specialties. It is through this pinch of black humour that the characters get the message across – consumers are supposed to stop the macabre sellout and change their eating habits.

University
Cheng Shiu University, Kaohsiung, Taiwan

Supervising Professor
Yueh-Hsing Lai, Hsien-Bii Su,
Chin-Lang Chang, Shou-Che Wu

Design
Yu-Xuan Chen, Chia-Chun Hsieh,
Yi-Hua Ding, Cian-Mu Li,
Guang-Qin Lin, Man-Hsuan Chang,
Cheng Shiu University

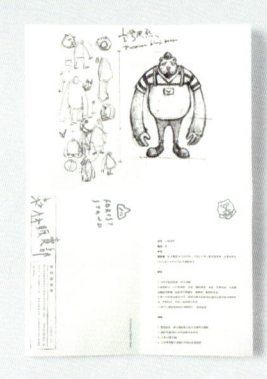

Organ Healthcare

[Editorial Illustration]

This guide to a healthy diet with Taiwanese fruits and vegetables is based on the traditional Chinese concept of the Five Elements. Posters and brochures present the organs associated with the five basic elements: heart, liver, spleen, lungs and kidneys. Since each motif is provided with a special colour, viewers can immediately recognise which food is beneficial for a particular body function. By showing the organs as miniature worlds with helpful nutrient spirits inside, the design of the illustrations appeals to the audience to take a closer look at the pictures.

University
Shu-Te University, Kaohsiung, Taiwan

Supervising Professor
Hui-Lin Chiu

Design
An-Chiao Hsiao, Jia-Fu Lin, Yi-Xuan Chen, Jie-Ling Tsai, Yi-Ning Su, Shu-Te University

Taiwanese Food Museum

[Poster Illustration]

This work seeks to convey that cultural diversity is fruitfully reflected in Taiwanese cuisine. An illustration of handmade flair awakens curiosity for Taiwan's constantly evolving food culture. The lines of the motifs are inspired by the decoration of ancient tableware, yet deconstructed to reflect the inventive character of the dishes. In terms of colour, the design focuses on coral pink, effectively contrasted by green. By using screen printing technique, in which ink is applied layer by layer, the illustration also refers to the stacked creations of classical Taiwanese cuisine.

University
Ling Tung University, Taichung, Taiwan

Supervising Professor
Chung-Yuan Kuo, Izen Tu

Design
Xiao-Fan Lao, Hsiao-Wen Huang, Hsuan-Hsuan Li, Wen-Hsuan Chiu, Jae-Oh Park, Ling Tung University

Rainbow Island
[Packaging Illustration]

This rice dish packaging focuses on Taiwan's indigenous peoples. In order to recall the local rice dish culture and the heritage of the native peoples, the packaging illustrations depict various rural scenes, from harvesting and fishing to music and dance. The overall theme is an indigenous festival, which, of course, is accompanied by delicious food. The abundance of motifs is designed to attract the consumer's attention. Since the illustrations are implemented as simple line drawings and incorporate lettering, they also function as a link to modern life.

University
Cheng Shiu University, Kaohsiung, Taiwan

Supervising Professor
Yu-Jin Lin, Yueh-Hsing Lai, Shou-Che Wu

Design
Rou-Wei Wu, Hsuan-Tse Kao, Pei-Xuan Zhang, Tzu-Ting Lin, Cheng Shiu University

Publishing & Print Media   Posters   Typography   Illustrations   Sound Design   Film & Animation   Online   Apps

Yi-Mo-Yien

[Packaging Illustration]

Yi-Mo-Yien is a brand of cosmetics which features classical Chinese rouge and the ways to put it on. The packaging illustration tells stories about the manufacturing of rouge with humorous details about beauty care in ancient China. While the graphics are characterised by a modern, reduced style, the colours are typical shades of the Tang Dynasty, dating back more than 1,000 years. By blending the stylistic elements, the illustrations emphasise the value of the established and bridge the gap between life in the past and today's lifestyle.

University
China University of Technology,
Taipei City, Taiwan

Supervising Professor
Shuo-Ting Wei, Chien-Hsun Chen

Design
Yian Chen, Chun-Ming Lin, Xin-Ling Hong, Wei-Shan Ruei, Department of Visual Communication Design,
China University of Technology

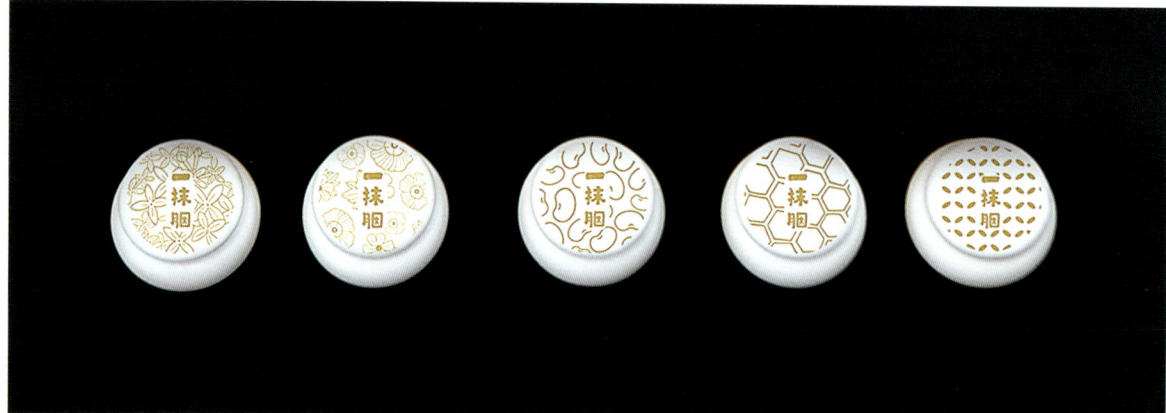

Purr

[Packaging Illustration]

This illustration series uses ten different cat types to decorate cat food packaging. A closer look reveals that each cat wears sunglasses, enhancing the brand recognition with a humorous detail. The cute style of the motifs reaches out to cat owners who love to cuddle with their pets. Soft colours, standing out against the black background of the packaging, present the product in a pleasant manner. In addition, the harmonious combination of a simple motif with a dense, ornamental pattern enhances the appeal of the packaging.

University
China University of Technology, Taipei City, Taiwan

Supervising Professor
Cheng-Ta Lee, Chien-Hsun Chen

Design
Yibay Lin, Xinyi Chou, Houhsin Lee, Department of Visual Communication Design, China University of Technology

DESIGNER PROFILES

ADITO Software GmbH
Tobias Feldmann, Florian Graf, Markus Escher, Robert Loipfinger
— We create a platform for all your challenges.

Red Dot
→ Interface & User Experience Design: page 324

The design and development department forms the basis for the sustainable success of ADITO Software GmbH and provides individual departments with a toolbox they can use to create customised products for their customers. Over the past two years, the team has been fine-tuning a new UX design that is visually appealing, but above all offers effective functionality. In order to create the greatest possible efficiencies at the customer, the design and development team was guided above all by the needs of the end users when it came to implementing the design and technology.

How can designers be ahead of their time?
By going through the world with open eyes and an open mind, by constantly questioning their own work and by not considering anything as a given.

What do you need in order to be creative?
The most important thing is peace and time. Only then does one have enough headspace and can attain a state of mind in which one can completely let go. That is how one gets into the right mood to be able to make full use of one's own creative potential.

What do you particularly like about your award-winning work?
The interplay of forms and colours, as well as the deliberate reduction to the essentials.

Artificial Rome
Dirk Hoffmann, Patrik de Jong
— We create immersive experiences in digital worlds.

Red Dot: Best of the Best
→ Spatial Communication: page 368–369

Red Dot
→ Interface & User Experience Design: page 261

Artificial Rome is an independent digital studio with offices in Berlin and Hamburg that operates as a crossover agency for commercial and cultural projects at the interface between art and technology. Together with partners from the arts, culture, politics and the sciences, as well as agencies and business, the studio develops state-of-the-art digital experiences and has received numerous awards in competitions such as at ADC 2019 (five Gold awards and Grand Prix Digital).

How can designers be ahead of their time?
By having the courage to try the unknown and by being willing to experiment.

What opportunities and threats has digitalisation produced in the world of design?
Technology on the one hand allows us to create immersive digital worlds. On the other hand, we have to be careful not to become subordinate to the demands of the new technologies, but to remain free and intelligent.

What do you need in order to be creative?
Ideas or visual concepts are the result of movement. Communication is an important form of that.

What do you particularly like about your award-winning work?
The fact that it translates the concepts of Oskar Schlemmer and Walter Gropius to the present day.

banda.agency
— Design – it's about effectiveness, not just about design.

Red Dot: Best of the Best
→ Film & Animation: page 140–141

Red Dot
→ Film & Animation: page 161

Banda Agency is an independent creative agency based in Kyiv. Founded in 2011 by Pavel Vrzhesch (creative director), Egor Petrov (head of art) and Yaroslav Serdiuk (strategy director), the studio was recognised as the most creative and effective agency in Ukraine in the years 2012 to 2015. In 2016, branding and design became strong separate agency directions and the team undertook many successful projects for clients from industries such as real estate, culture and retail in the Ukraine and San Francisco, as well as for the Eurovision Song Contest 2017.

What makes somebody a good designer?
A good designer is someone who understands the real design task and solves it in the most effective way. Not the one who just sees the job of creating a design and creates it.

What are the main challenges you have to overcome in your work life?
The main challenge which we take on in the process of work is to make the best of the possible options, and even when we are at a dead end, not to agree to "let it go at that", but to achieve the perfect result for us and the client.

Beetroot Design Group
— We blend colours, shapes, sounds and ideas to build brands, have fun and inspire.

Red Dot: Best of the Best
→ Posters: page 72-73

Red Dot
→ Illustrations: page 114
→ Illustrations: page 115
→ Illustrations: page 126
→ Film & Animation: page 142

Beetroot is a multi-award-winning communication design team and think tank that consists of specialists with a wide and diverse set of skills in the creative field. It provides exciting design solutions to a worldwide clientele including some of the most established brands in the world. Although specialising in communication design, Beetroot often generates and develops a variety of concepts and projects including information campaigns, exhibitions, product/industrial design, interior design, sound design, installations, performance design and art.

How can designers be ahead of their time?
You have to be in a constant state of observing and learning.

How do you convince non-designers of the relevance of good design?
You don't. It is a collective process that takes time.

To which aspect did you pay special attention when designing your award-winning work?
To shaking off the expected design treatments of the past.

What was the first thought that came to your mind when you heard about your award?
Yay, Berlin!

Better
Samo Ačko, Tadej Maligoj,
Rok Pregelj, Ajda Bevc,
Barbara Hiti, Jernej Tratnik,
Rok Benedik, Gregor Fras,
Sai Pan
— Never settle for good enough.

Red Dot
→ Interface & User Experience Design: page 350

Better's internal design studio is deeply involved in designing next-generation healthcare solutions. Its main goal is to improve the user experience for medical personnel working with electronic health records, medication management and chronic disease management applications and design a robust, scalable and clinically sound design system for clinical application building. The studio is led by Samo Ačko, award-winning design director with a varied background in news, brand, information, type and digital design, and co-led by Tadej Maligoj, award-winning senior UX designer and architect.

How can designers be ahead of their time?
Our universal advice: look outside of your field, stay well informed of the advances of others. Not just technology, everything is relevant. Design serves as connective tissue, but to connect, you have to know the subject matter.

What opportunities and threats has digitalisation produced in the world of design?
Digital tools and mediums need to be mastered to be effective, just like any others. The wonderful thing about digitisation is that it is still somewhat in its infancy, which brings seemingly endless opportunities in figuring new things out. The risks are in embracing the endlessness without accounting for the limits of real life.

Blackmagic Design
Denny Trieu, Alex Diaz, Alex Creedy, James O'Shea, Mathieu Henrijean, Matt Dowling, Alana Manning, Marcio Lima, Mio Hu, Rodrigo Reichert
— Styles come and go. Good Design is a language, not a style.
(Massimo Vignelli)

Red Dot: Best of the Best
→ Interface & User Experience Design: page 252-253

Red Dot
→ Interface & User Experience Design: page 344-345

The Blackmagic Design User Interface Team works out of Melbourne with team members from Australia, Belgium, Brazil, China, Columbia, Ireland, New Zealand and South Korea. It has been designing products for the TV and film industry for the last seven years and won numerous design awards worldwide with the goal of designing awesome products and having fun while doing it.

What opportunities and threats has digitalisation produced in the world of design?
The spread of digitalisation into almost every aspect of life is creating more opportunities for designers to solve interesting and complex problems that impact people lives. That is genuinely exciting. The main risk is that as a society we are eliminating boredom. Daydreaming on a train has been replaced with mindless consumption of a scrolling feed. This is detrimental to the creative habit.

What do you need in order to be creative?
An inquisitive mind, a sense of humour and a genuine appreciation of craft.

What design developments are currently influencing your work?
The users of our products are moving away from specialisation. They want to capture film, edit a cut and mix the audio. They are using our products in ways that nobody anticipated, which is forcing us to rethink our workflows between products.

Bronce Estudio
Miguel Ayesa, Javier Aznárez, Alicia Puebla, Germán Úcar
— What time is love?

Red Dot
→ Publishing & Print Media: page 28-29

Bronce is an interdisciplinary team dedicated to graphic design and communication strategy, located in Pamplona and Saragossa, Spain. It places the greatest value on people, in the belief that a continuous flow of dialogue is essential to the smooth running of any project in which a message has to be conveyed through words and pictures. Loving books, part of its work is designing and developing projects for institutions, museums, galleries and publishing houses. This work takes place in the context of reading and writing, of making and shaping text, of designing and publishing books. In the team, communication strategy consultants and designers come together, exploring ways to connect brands and business models to people.

How can designers be ahead of their time?
When we think about the future and the global acceleration in which we live, we think it is a good idea to be a pioneer in something. The importance of the designer may now lie not in walking ahead, but in identifying, understanding and selecting what may be immediately future-proof.

What do you particularly like about your award-winning work?
It is both a design project but also a content creation one. All the text and images for the book were created in the studio. We have enjoyed the history investigation. Offering a promotional product with this content and a different shape compared to the usual promotional marketing for clients, has been very interesting.

Bruce B.
— Think before you make.

Red Dot: Best of the Best
→ Publishing & Print Media: page 18-19

In 2001 birth as virtual founder and instigator of the Bruce B. corporate communication GmbH.

How can designers be ahead of their time?
By keeping your ears to the ground.

How do you convince non-designers of the relevance of good design?
By consulting their senses.

What do you need in order to be creative?
A purpose.

To which aspect did you pay special attention when designing your award-winning work?
To celebrating the connection between form and content.

What was the first thought that came to your mind when you heard about your award?
It is going to be difficult to top that.

What else would you like to learn in the future?
How to improve.

ATELIER BRÜCKNER
— Form follows content.

Red Dot: Best of the Best
→ Spatial Communication: page 374-375

ATELIER BRÜCKNER is an interdisciplinary design practice for architecture, exhibition design and scenography which designs, plans and devises museums, museum exhibitions, visitor centres, EXPO pavilions and brand experiences worldwide. In the office in Stuttgart, an international team of, currently, 120 specialists in 12 design disciplines works on completing projects, taking them through all phases of the planning process. With more than 150 projects completed worldwide, the company is among the world's leading design practices for innovative exhibition design and scenography.

How can designers be ahead of their time?
For us it is not about being ahead of our time, but about creating a piece, a "Gesamtkunstwerk" which is in itself unique. Our work will only last for a limited time, so that gives us the possibility to try out, to fail, to succeed and sometimes to be ahead for a short time.

What opportunities and threats has digitalisation produced in the world of design?
For us digital media is just another tool alongside all the other disciplines we employ. It remains to be seen if the digital world will begin to substitute reality, but we believe in the real, in the physical experience in space and in the authentic object.

How do you convince non-designers of the relevance of good design?
Design plays a major role in our world. Non-designers can probably feel and appreciate the difference good design makes even if they are not directly aware of it, because good design is so often invisible.

Custom Interactions
Dr. Benjamin Franz,
Dr. Michaela Kauer-Franz,
Marta Piqué, Sascha Hiller
— Everybody's time is valuable – with 3DUX® to an inspiring interface.

Red Dot
→ Interface & User Experience Design: page 362-363

Dr. Benjamin Franz studied engineering and explored the topic of man-machine in his thesis. He is a co-founder of Custom Interactions and the 3DUX approach, and lectures on digitalisation-related matters at various events.
Dr. Michaela Kauer-Franz studied psychology and obtained her doctorate for a thesis on the acceptance of technology, then went on to co-found Custom Interactions and the 3DUX approach. As a UX researcher her experience is invaluable in her role as a lecturer at TU Darmstadt and in her position on various usability standards bodies.
Marta Piqué studied design in Barcelona and has since worked as a multidisciplinary designer, conceptualising appealing and creative solutions for different environments at Custom Interactions.
Sascha Hiller studied interactive media design and specialised in usability and user experience in the realm of interface design during a master's degree. With this focal background, he takes on the role of design lead at Custom Interactions.

How can designers be ahead of their time?
Designers should pay attention to technical and research-oriented topics in order to identify potential future scenarios. They should furthermore not only interact with users and customers purely on the factual and solution-based level, but also on the level of needs.

How do you convince non-designers of the relevance of good design?
By showing and allowing them to experience it.

Agnė Dautartaitė-Krutulė
— Daily: 5 grams curiosity + 2 grams trust + 7 grams passion + 3 grams freedom + 4 grams sensitivity

Red Dot: Best of the Best
→ Publishing & Print Media: page 10–11

Agnė Dautartaitė-Krutulė is a book designer who works on individual projects and is not tied to a particular publisher. She lectures on book art disciplines at the Vilnius Academy of Arts in the Graphic Art Department. She is also one of the organisers of the "6 pt" book design conference and faces a challenge – to keep it going until the tenth edition.

How can designers be ahead of their time?
Honesty and the ability to retreat from safe, well-known methods may lead to the outstanding ideas of today.

How do you convince non-designers of the relevance of good design?
There is a golden rule – to capture a person's interest. Then they will make the decision by themselves. In my view, aesthetics don't need to be convincing, but the hidden inner values of design need to be explained, especially to those who come from different fields. Intelligence depends on our ability to understand.

What do you need in order to be creative?
I'm a book designer while my inspirations come from architecture and jazz. There are moments of insight and understanding when the people I love are bored. Sometimes inspiration comes from a challenge, sometimes from love and freedom.

denkwerk
Tassilo Morino, Monika Tran, Prabhu Kandavelu, Sammy Haddad, Christoph Wesseling, Laurent Mondoloni, Marie Wehrhahn

Red Dot
→ Online: page 176

denkwerk is a pioneering digital agency that creates value for brands by creating value for people. The studio partners with daring clients to shape the next generation of digital products and meaningful experiences. It embraces a human-centred, creativity-driven approach to make brands stand out by providing value for user. The teams work using an agile process designed to deliver better results faster and directly collaborate with a client's team to define a common goal they are all committed to achieving. denkwerk provides a broad spectrum of digital solutions across all disciplines and has in-depth technical expertise.

How do you convince non-designers of the relevance of good design?
Truly good design becomes almost imperceptible. It is like a really well-designed chair on which one can sit comfortably for a long time. Good design helps us to cope better with our day and to enjoy it more. Bad design tends to be noticed more quickly, because it is irritating.

What do you need in order to be creative?
Inspiration is very important to us. At denkwerk we get it through our closeness to the latest technologies and our experiments in areas such as AI or AR.

What design developments are currently influencing your work?
We are currently researching and developing a lot in the area of artificial intelligence. Here too it is exciting to create the interface between AI and humans.

Deutsche Bahn, DB Fernverkehr/forwerts
Christian Bischoping, Caroline Sturm, Julian Schwarz, Sebastian Baldauf
— Users are your employers – so you'd better do a damned good job to satisfy them.

Red Dot
→ Interface & User Experience Design: page 286-287

In 2018, the digital design office forwerts and DB Fernverkehr set up a design team to relaunch the ICE Portal. Guided by DB UX lead Caroline Sturm and forwerts creative director Julian Schwarz, the interconnected teams worked miracles to reimagine the system. Caroline Sturm was the first to campaign for UX standards at Deutsche Bahn and established them in the enterprise system. Her close cooperation with product owner Christian Bischoping, who contributed his expertise in entertainment systems gained from prior work, enabled a strong link between design and development which was crucial for the success of the project.
Julian Schwarz is a founder and partner of forwerts, an agency that specialises in innovative UX designs. Prior to forwerts, he was involved in the development of the car2go mobility service and acted as a creative director at Deutsche Bahn to establish a user-centred understanding of design across the company. Sebastian Baldauf helped to lead the team and create the design.

What opportunities and threats has digitalisation produced in the world of design?
The biggest risk with everything is apathy – but we prefer to spend our time thinking about the opportunities digitalisation presents.

How do you convince non-designers of the relevance of good design?
For us, it's all about the people using our products and their needs. If you provide users with informative and easily accessible content without distractions, without them needing to question themselves – then you've got a design that works, looks and feels right.

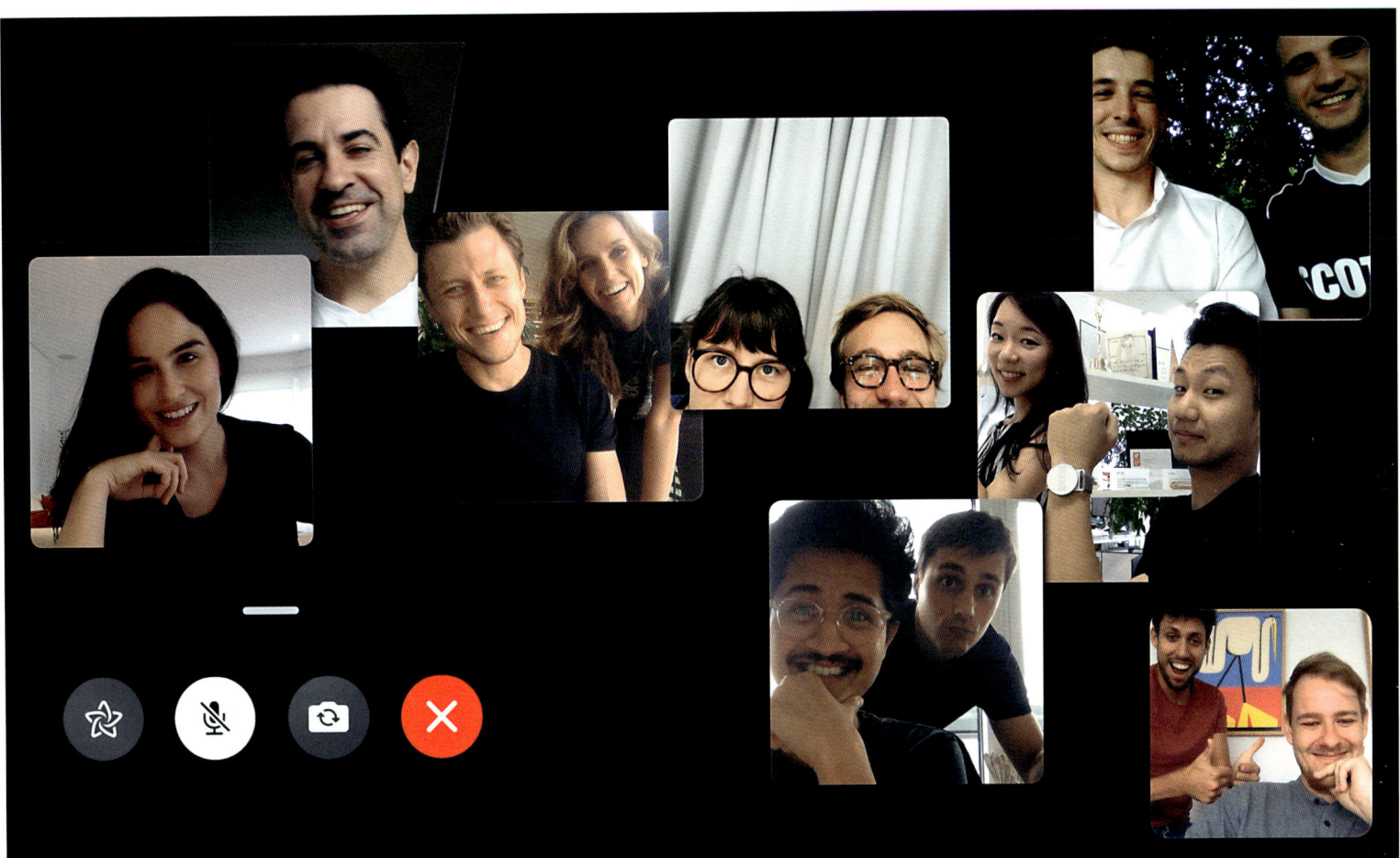

Dot Incorporation, Serviceplan Innovation, Hyperinteractive, Standardabweichung, Moby Digg
— 1 + 1 > 2

Red Dot: Grand Prix
→ Online: page 170-171

Red Dot
→ Interface & User Experience Design: page 268

Dot Translate came into being through the close collaboration between different partners: Dot Incorporation, leader in innovative tactile solutions for the blind and visually impaired, Serviceplan Innovation, the innovation department of Europe's biggest independent communication agency Serviceplan, Hyperinteractive, a digital development studio based in Hamburg, the creative coding studio Standardabweichung and the digital design studio Moby Digg, both based in Munich.

How can designers be ahead of their time?
Don't care about trends.

How do you convince non-designers of the relevance of good design?
Create design that's relevant to them.

What do you need in order to be creative?
Time, either a lot or very little.

To which aspect did you pay special attention when designing your award-winning work?
Collaboration.

What do you particularly like about your award-winning work?
The reactions of people experiencing it.

Publishing & Print Media   Posters   Typography   Illustrations   Sound Design   Film & Animation   Online   Apps

Eat, Sleep + Design
Frank Gräfe, Daniel Reiss

Red Dot
→ Illustrations: page 118-119
→ Film & Animation: page 144-145

Eat, Sleep + Design was founded in 2004 by Frank Gräfe and Daniel Reiss. We design and illustrate really well!

How can designers be ahead of their time?
"Time is always with you, wherever you go. You carry it in you. And it carries you. It sees and hears everything you do and say." (Dark, season 2)

How do you convince non-designers of the relevance of good design?
By enjoying our work.

What do you need in order to be creative?
Time, peace and a good mood.

To which aspect did you pay special attention when designing your award-winning work?
To melding image and sound into a single unit.

What do you particularly like about your award-winning work?
The freedom and the trust that Upon You Records give us.

FRUM
Myungjin Kim
— Imagination composer.

Red Dot
→ Film & Animation: page 154-155
→ Online: page 200-201

FRUM is a creative consulting group that brings new value to corporate marketing activities by providing tangible solutions based on professional expertise and innovative creativity in combination with up-to-date technology. It provides consulting services by discovering clients' hidden insights based on its experience of the entire business process. The group then develops a concrete solution in a team headed by the corporate brand manager and business consultants and backed by professionals such as creative directors.

How can designers be ahead of their time?
Designers have to start by examining the fundamental problems in depth and should be more flexible and open-minded in their response to a continuously changing world.

What opportunities and threats has digitalisation produced in the world of design?
The areas in which designers can become more influential are changing due to digitalisation. Their significance rises and, from time to time, disappears. Sometimes, it even extends into other career fields. Many conventional designers perceive digitalisation as a crisis. However, designers have expertise that is relevant to many different fields and can bring great insight to diverse issues. Hence, we perceive digitalisation as an opportunity rather than a threat.

What do you need in order to be creative?
In order to establish a creative strategy, we require clear insight so we can define the problem and consider business and brand in advance.

Shenzhen Future Life Product Planning Design Co., Ltd./ Communication University of Zhejiang
Chao Yang
— A good designer is someone who constantly goes beyond himself.

Red Dot: Best of the Best
→ Posters: page 70–71

Chao Yang, currently associate professor at the Communication University of Zhejiang, has won over 150 influential design awards in competitions around the world, including the Red Dot Award and iF Design Award in Germany, the A' Design Award and Competition in Italy (Gold Award), as well as the International Design Awards in the USA (Gold Award). He has also served as jury member for many important international design competitions, including the A' Design Award and Competition in Italy, the 3rd International Poster Contest by Graphic Stories Cyprus and the 6th International Socio-Political Poster Biennale in Poland.

How can designers be ahead of their time?
Designers keep their own avant-garde thinking on design through experimental and exploratory design practices in their work.

What or who has most influenced your career as a designer?
China's traditional culture and philosophy has influenced me. With five thousand years of history, Chinese traditional culture and philosophy give me unlimited creative inspiration and wisdom. In addition, the German Bauhaus design philosophy, Swiss design style, etc. have also influenced my design career.

Gagarin
— Interactive storytelling.

Red Dot: Best of the Best
→ Interface & User Experience Design: page 246-247

Red Dot
→ Illustrations: page 109
→ Interface & User Experience Design: page 256

Gagarin has been making a name for itself in the field of interactive experience design. Its client base consists mostly of corporations and institutions intent on crafting a media message and creating an interesting experience for visitors. Gagarin strives to present exhibits as attractive and user-friendly, all the while keeping in mind the creation of an experience that is as meaningful and memorable as possible. The team of creative artists, designers, animators, programmers, producers, film and sound specialists has years of experience in the design and production of interactive media, working with a multitude of media, interfaces, devices and technologies.

How can designers be ahead of their time?
By not anxiously following trends but rather empathetically caring for those who will inhabit the future.

How do you convince non-designers of the relevance of good design?
By exposing them to it.

What do you need in order to be creative?
At Gagarin we always try to find ways to think way outside the box, to turn everything around and try to see things from a variety of perspectives. It's all done so we can get closer to the core and find a fresh, critical way of seeing. A good storyline is also essential to come up with successful creative ideas.

Great Apes/HiQ Finland
Niko Sipilä
— No design ever comes out as good as you first picture it, yet sometimes better.

Red Dot: Best of the Best
→ Interface & User Experience Design: page 248-249

Red Dot
→ Online: page 191
→ Spatial Communication: page 376

Niko Sipilä is head of design at HiQ Finland and has been creative director of the agency Great Apes since 2008, an agency that he co-founded and which was acquired by HiQ International in 2016. Before that, Niko Sipilä worked at Satama Interactive, The Uncles, kliQue plus (part of the BBDO Network) and co-founded Eightball Media. He has already received more than 80 national and global design awards with works featured in numerous publications around the world.

What or who has most influenced your career as a designer?
In general, I would say the Internet just because it literally has everything – good and bad. Also, I am more grateful for truly bad design than great design because it often teaches you more.

What do you need in order to be creative?
A solid brief and enough time to disregard or refine the initial impulses of how to execute it.

To which aspect did you pay special attention when designing your award-winning work?
The variety of interaction methods and types that the project included was a big part of it. We had a huge variety of touchscreen sizes, projections, VRs, etc. So, keeping the ease of use through all installations with recurring interactive elements was crucial.

hesign
Jianping He
— A book is not only for information – it must become an artistic collector's item.

Red Dot: Grand Prix
→ Publishing & Print Media: page 6-7

Jianping He, born in China, now lives in Berlin, working as a graphic designer, professor and publisher. He studied graphic design at the China Academy of Art in Hangzhou (1991–1994), fine arts at the Berlin University of the Arts (1997–2001) and received his PhD in cultural history from the FU Berlin in 2011. He has been teaching at Berlin University of the Arts, works as a guest professor at Hong Kong Polytechnic University and China Academy of Art, and as the PhD student supervisor of China Academy of Art. In 2002, he established his own design studio and publishing house, hesign, based in Berlin with the other branch in Hangzhou since 2008. His works have won awards around the world, and he acts as an international juror in competitions such as 100 Best Posters of the Year – Germany, Austria, Switzerland. He is also a member of the Alliance Graphique Internationale (AGI).

How do you convince non-designers of the relevance of good design?
If it is a really good design, I don't have to convince them. They have already judged and understood it.

What design developments are currently influencing your work?
The development of motion graphics has influenced my thinking, no longer leaving me satisfied with traditional graphic design.

What else would you like to learn in the future?
To explore design that can interact with people.

HOLYDESIGN
Fan Cao, Hongrui Shen
— Diversity opens up our horizons and gives us insights into local culture.

Red Dot: Best of the Best
→ Posters: page 68-69

HOLYDESIGN is a visual design and art studio based in Shanghai, China, focusing on design-driven branding and cultural projects including visual identity, product packaging, space design, motion and more. By shaping brand and product images, it provides innovative visual solutions for local and global clients. HOLYDESIGN also creates a wide range of independent projects, including exhibitions, lectures, publications and events, to incorporate the influence of design into contemporary visual culture and communications.

What opportunities and threats has digitalisation produced in the world of design?
We can solve problems more effectively with new media, but the basis of design has not changed.

How do you convince non-designers of the relevance of good design?
Good design is not defined by the designers. There are multiple interpretations in terms of function and form.

To which aspect did you pay special attention when designing your award-winning work?
We were trying to integrate the opening up of horizons with an insight into local culture.

What do you particularly like about your award-winning work?
Back to basics is what we admire in our work.

Huawei UCD Center
Shaolei Wang, Chang Tang,
Ren Li, Yuanfeng Chu
— To create a gorgeous link between
AI and business.

Red Dot: Best of the Best
→ Interface & User Experience Design: page 254-255

Red Dot
→ Interface & User Experience Design: page 323
→ Interface & User Experience Design: page 334
→ Interface & User Experience Design: page 335

Founded in 2005, the Huawei UCD Center gathers talent from multiple disciplines including psychology, design, art, and computer technology. With the help of research into user experience, human-computer interaction and user interface technologies, the UCD Center is dedicated to improving the usability and overall experience of key products such as the network O&M, consumer devices, the cloud and AI.

How do you convince non-designers of the relevance of good design?
Visualise user stories to make it easy for users of non-design backgrounds to understand the value of the experience.

What or who has most influenced your career as a designer?
The habit of reading, and famous designers such as Kenya Hara. He has taught us a lot about design thinking and processes.

What do you particularly like about your award-winning work?
The design proposition is the basis of the whole design, which is "how to allow users to gradually trust AI".

What was the first thought that came to your mind when you heard about your award?
To say "woohoo" ... and share the news with our buddies.

Lisa Huber

Red Dot: Junior Award
→ Publishing & Print Media: page 436

Lisa Huber works as a designer and independent artist in illustration, interior design, trade fair and exhibition design, conceptual and graphic design. After graduating from the New Design University in St. Pölten, Austria, she worked in interior design before focusing on conceptual design and studying exhibition design. This is where she discovered her passion for illustration and graphic design and her interest in exploring the tension that exists between how we present and perceive ourselves.

How did you discover your passion for design?
I noticed early on that I have developed a highly individual way of viewing the world. Through my work I have found a way to communicate.

What would you like to design one day?
I would like to focus on social projects in future not only to convey beautiful things, but also contents that may be able to make the world a little bit better.

Which part of the design process do you particularly enjoy?
The moment when something joins up with the next thing, when the concept suddenly becomes completely logical.

How do you approach new design projects?
I gather inspiration, speak to lots of different people about my project and try to approach the task at hand in an abstract way.

Hufax Arts/FJCU
Fa-Hsiang Hu
— We create, design, and imagine.

Red Dot
→ Typography: page 102

Fa-Hsiang Hu is an assistant professor at the Department of Applied Arts at Fu Jen Catholic University (FJCU), director of the Taiwan Graphic Design Association, director of GDA-ROC Association, director of Taiwan Poster Design Association and executive creative director of Hufax Arts. His works have been recognised by the Taiwan Visual Design Award and numerous awards from leading design organisations worldwide, including D&AD Awards, London International Awards, Red Dot Award, New York Type Directors Club, Communication Arts Award of Excellence, Golden Pin Design Award, Hong Kong Designers Association Global Design Awards or International Design Awards.

What opportunities and threats has digitalisation produced in the world of design?
The convenience and diversification of digitalisation do make designers' work easier and also encourage them to try something new. However, digital art creation also causes many designers to rely too much on the technology and results in their work and ideas becoming too mechanical and systematic.

How do you convince non-designers of the relevance of good design?
We need to understand the way non-designers think, to use visual language that they can understand and to interpret the relevance of their habits and customs.

Sergio Ingravalle
— The most exciting of journeys lies within us.

Red Dot
→ Illustrations: page 120-121

Sergio Ingravalle decided to pursue illustration after a long trip from Sydney to Beijing in 2011, which he undertook as part of his communication design dissertation when completing his studies at the University of Applied Sciences Düsseldorf. In the beginning, he produced graphics for Esprit and Marc O'Polo before portraits and illustrations of sportsmen attracted the attention of clients such as Coca-Cola, adidas, Marvel and FC Bayern Munich. The personal "Mindshot" illustration project led to collaboration with the German federal government on illustrations for the anniversary edition of the Basic Law for the Federal Republic of Germany. Sergio Ingravalle also lectures at founder events and educational institutions.

How can designers be ahead of their time?
By seeing as much as possible, but at the same time not allowing oneself to be influenced too much by what one has seen. In the end, what is strongest sleeps within us.

What do you need in order to be creative?
At the moment, it's a place in my favourite café in the old town of Bielefeld, lots of loose A4 pieces of paper and instrumental music, mainly from film or video game soundtracks.

What was the first thought that came to your mind when you heard about your award?
"That's impossible!" was my first reaction. When I was a student I looked up to the award-winning projects, so I was delighted.

Interactive Pioneers
— First, we invent castles in the air, then we build them.

Red Dot: Best of the Best
→ Online: page 174-175

Interactive Pioneers is an award-winning digital agency from Aachen, Germany, that has been putting consultancy, design and development at the service of ambitious businesses to enable them to achieve digital added value through user experiences. The agency brings its concepts and designs to life, makes emotions visible and moves processes into the digital world. Interactive Pioneers was founded by Carlo Matic in 1997 and has since produced more than 1,000 interactive solutions for web, mobile, desktop and POS applications ranging from apps and websites to games and user interfaces for self-driving cars.

How can designers be ahead of their time?
A great deal of intercultural input, constant experimentation and new combinations lead to innovations.

What opportunities and threats has digitalisation produced in the world of design?
Connectivity has created many new possibilities that were unthinkable in the past. Thanks to automation we are able to simplify UX design, intelligent systems with more data allow us to come up with completely new ideas. The greatest risk posed by this plethora of technical possibilities is that we could forget the person in front of the machine when we are designing.

To which aspect did you pay special attention when designing your award-winning work?
To our core values, to a reduction to the essentials and always to the user.

Publishing & Print Media   Posters   Typography   Illustrations   Sound Design   Film & Animation   Online   Apps

iPrefer/Moët Hennessy Taiwan
— Modern Taiwanese Cuisine – Fuel on our philosophy to mix.

Red Dot
→ Film & Animation: page 159

iPrefer was founded in 2003 and started out as a digital production company that offers clients efficient marketing strategies, giving target audiences brand-new choices. Its role is to solve problems with creativity and to create more happiness through beautiful things.
Moët Hennessy Taiwan, established in October 2001, represents the wine and spirits division of the LVMH group and distributes a number of leading premium brands, including Hennessy, Glenmorangie, Moët & Chandon, Dom Pérignon and Veuve Clicquot.

How can designers be ahead of their time?
Listen to and understand consumers' needs and come up with practical and needed solutions.

How do you convince non-designers of the relevance of good design?
Create brand contents and pleasant brand experiences which can offer them benefits.

To which aspect did you pay special attention when designing your award-winning work?
Whether the information conveyed by the brand is clearly and correctly received.

What do you particularly like about your award-winning work?
That it connects with local culture and integrates the brand successfully into local life.

jangled nerves/Klangerfinder
Ingo Zirngibl,
Prof. Florian Käppler
– Stay curious and listen!

Red Dot: Best of the Best
→ Sound Design: page 132-133

Ingo Zirngibl, born in 1965, studied architecture at University of Stuttgart and at Robert Gordon University Aberdeen. Since 1998, he has been managing partner of jangled nerves and, from 2006 to 2009, he held a lectureship at Stuttgart Media University. Professor Florian Käppler is a composer and founder of Klangerfinder, the Stuttgart-based studio for audio communication. Working as a sound strategist, composer and acoustic scenographer, he has initiated many award-winning projects in the stress field connecting brands and music, media and space, art and economics, science and technology. He is the founder and head of the interdisciplinary music design programme at the State University of Music in Trossingen, established in cooperation with Furtwangen University.

How can designers be ahead of their time?
Be fast. Be smart. Keep your curiosity.

What opportunities and threats has digitalisation produced in the world of design?
The risk to fail and the chance to succeed.

How do you convince non-designers of the relevance of good design?
By listening to their needs.

What or who has most influenced your career as a designer?
People – because we are part of them. Nature – because we are part of it.

kontrastmoment
Andreas Waldenmaier
— If you always do what you've always done, you always get what you've always gotten.

Red Dot
→ Spatial Communication: page 388

Andreas Waldenmaier is managing director and owner of kontrastmoment, an independent studio with 60 specialists from a wide range of different disciplines and countries. The company carries out projects in research, communication, event, advertising and operations concepts, design development and series production design with a focus on automotive interfaces.
Andreas Waldenmaier studied liberal arts in Stuttgart and visual design at the HfG Schwäbisch Gmünd, then worked at various studios in Schwäbisch Gmünd, Heidenheim, Munich and London until he was employed by the design studio design:thesis where he became managing director in 2000. He has taught interface design at the Stuttgart State Academy of Art and Design and, in 2002, founded the kontrastmoment studio in Munich, which has supported all the development stages of BMW's in-car communication and entertainment system iDrive for all brands, markets and languages worldwide.

How can designers be ahead of their time?
By allowing themselves to be constantly surprised, by staying curious and by always questioning themselves and their work.

How do you convince non-designers of the relevance of good design?
Designers are the interpreters between very diverse disciplines, needs and technologies. Design is the advocate of the user and lifts the product to another level. Design is an investment and not a cost.

L+R
Alex Levin, Ryan Riegner
– Strategy + Aesthetics.

Red Dot
→ Spatial Communication: page 403

L+R is an international strategy consulting, design and technology firm established in New York in 2012. Its team is also based in Los Angeles, Barcelona and Milan, and its focus is on delivering tangible value for its clients by unlocking innovation. Strategy applies critical analysis to problem solving over the long term; aesthetics is the rewarding emotional perception of harmony. Together, strategy and aesthetics guide the work of the team across branding, design, and software development.

How can designers be ahead of their time?
By continuously building their creative confidence. Designers have a natural instinct for creating what they feel the world needs. With uninhibited confidence, they can seamlessly tap into a state of inspiration – allowing them to find ideas, concepts and lateral thoughts throughout their day-to-day. This state of creative confidence allows a designer to distil the complexities of our world into a harmonious moment.

To which aspect did you pay special attention when designing your award-winning work?
The seamless digital experience. The work is not simply an app nor is it simply a beautiful spatial communication design. It is the only public touchpoint for the most famous skyline in the world. Users are encouraged to look up, play and interact with the interactive architectural lighting in a one-of-a-kind, creative and powerful experience.

Edward Lau
— Gratitude, hard work and humility will take you a long way.

Red Dot: Junior Prize
→ Publishing & Print Media: page 412-415

Edward Hao Jun Lau holds a diploma in communication design from LASALLE College of the Arts in Singapore where he recently graduated. He has a keen interest in branding and editorial work.

How did you discover your passion for design?
I discovered my passion for design when I took my first Photoshop class. Having had no previous contact with design whatsoever, my first feeble attempts at what I remember as a photo manipulation exercise sowed the seeds for my decision to study this full time.

Where do you have your best ideas?
I have the best ideas usually during bus rides, especially when I'm daydreaming. It's like my brain is unconsciously making sense of all the information, influences and visuals I have ever seen and putting them all together for whatever project I'm working on.

Which part of the design process do you particularly enjoy?
The beginning, when nothing has been set in stone and no ideas have been thrown out yet, especially if the brief is particularly interesting. The idea of being able to create and do something new has always excited me.

What message does your award-winning work convey?
The message of the project is to tell people that the need to feel safe is universal and human. We all have our own ways of trying to feel that. Through the presentation of different aspects of asylum, the magazine hopes to get readers to empathise with the plight of refugees all around the world.

Yu-Chih Lee, Kui-Shang Wong, Chia-Hui Ting, Qiao-Ru Zeng, Yu-Ping Tsai
— Be unexpected and extraordinary.

Red Dot: Junior Award
Best of the Best
→ Publishing & Print Media: page 416-417

Yu-Chih Lee, Kui-Shang Wong, Chia-Hui Ting, Qiao-Ru Zeng and Yu-Ping Tsai are a design team studying visual communication design at Shu-Te University, Taiwan. They want to be able to communicate the client's needs and create packaging in a mix of Chinese traditional culture and modern fashion elements. Each new brief creates a new challenge.

What would you like to design one day?
To keep up with the world's new creations and things, we will focus on how to improve quality of life. We are all part of society and have our own souls and dreams with different perspectives.

What goals have you set yourself for your career going forward?
Beginning our career and gaining more experience are our short-term goal. Our long-term goal is to keep learning new things, to move beyond branding and start our own businesses. To build our own brands.

How do you approach new design projects?
First of all, we have to understand who to design for and then think about the design method.

What message does your award-winning work convey?
By using the charm of the cicada to attract the public's attention, our aim is to make them want to know more about the cicada and to appeal to everyone to preserve the environment.

Lin Zhiyun
— Find the right question.

Red Dot: Junior Award
→ Illustrations: page 501

Lin Zhiyun is a graphic designer, illustrator and cultural curator. Since the beginning of 2019, he has served as design director of Chengzhi Creative Strategy and has played a key role in the development of the company's experimental printing project. In 2017, he started his master's programme at Shanghai University. To date, he has led the visual design for more than 90 cultural activities, including Urban Transformation Through Art – Shanghai International Art City Forum, Best Metro Station in China 2018–2019, Shanghai New Year Model Competition and Shanghai Curators Lab. His works have been selected for more than 70 domestic and foreign exhibitions and competitions, including the Mexico International Poster Biennial, Taiwan International Creative Design Award and China Illustration Biennale 2017–2018.

What would you like to design one day?
Science books. Or a regional biennale.

What goals have you set yourself for your career going forward?
To contribute to the promotion of cultural undertakings.

Where do you have your best ideas?
My father's study. I read a lot of books there.

What message does your award-winning work convey?
Expressing old themes in new ways.

Little Voice
Dmytro Izotov,
Vladimir Khokhlov
— Explore the problem in depth.
Relentlessly iterate. Don't stop until
it resonates.

Red Dot
→ Interface & User Experience Design: page 282

Dmytro Izotov and Vladimir Khokhlov have honed their craftsmanship at companies like Microsoft, Nokia, Philips, Skype and Sony. They first worked together on various high-profile user interface design transformations at Skype and have a portfolio of 13 patents. It was their passion for the craft, how technology works and what makes people tick, that propelled them to set up their own design agency, Little Voice, in 2018. It helps businesses differentiate their connected products, retain and attract customers, and de-risk their product delivery through clear and powerful user interface designs. With offices in London and Kyiv, the clients include Konica Minolta, Leica Camera and Michelin.

How can designers be ahead of their time?
By looking beyond design. They need to understand and form opinions about how today's culture, socio-economic drivers and technological and business trends will impact human behaviour and vice versa, and therefore what the world will look like in the future.

What or who has most influenced your career as a designer?
We were fortunate to work for people such as Yutaka Hasegawa at Sony Creative Center and Jim Palmer, then at Skype. They showed us how to unlock the potential of design and see at first hand the impact a well-designed product can have on the business and the world at large. This has inspired us to help our clients harness the transformative power of well-designed technology.

Yun-Xuan Liu, Yu-Ru Liu, Yu-Han Chang, Chih-Hao Wu
— If you want to have good ideas, you must first live hard and concentrate.

Red Dot: Junior Award
Best of the Best
→ Illustrations: page 420-421

Yun-Xuan Liu, Yu-Ru Liu, Yu-Han Chang and Chih-Hao Wu are students of communication design. In their award-winning project, they have portrayed the tradition and meaning of an "A-Ma", a grandma of great wisdom and many memories. In the past, in the land of Formosa (Taiwan), most A-Mas didn't have the chance to obtain a higher level of education. They could, however, rely on the wisdom of their ancestors to master life. The creative team has therefore assembled this expertise in editing, illustration or silk-screen printing.

How did you discover your passion for design?
For us, ordinary life is the starting point of our passion for design. When we try to activate our five senses to observe, feel and experience daily life, even the most ordinary details can be transformed and reveal themselves as an entirely new universe.

What goals have you set yourself for your career going forward?
We look forward to turning our faith in our country and culture into seeds that germinate and grow continuously in the minds of our audiences.

How do you approach new design projects?
Taiwan is a country with many ethnic groups and a rich history and culture. We hope to use the creative methods we have learned to record Taiwanese daily life more extensively, to communicate it and create empathy across generations, ethnic groups and cultures.

Atelier Markgraph
Stefan Weil
— Understand. Transform. Connect. Fascinate.

Red Dot: Best of the Best
→ Spatial Communication: page 372–373

Red Dot
→ Spatial Communication: page 404

Stefan Weil started at Meiré und Meiré at the end of the 1980s as a graphic designer. After short spells at Tassilo von Grolman and Saatchi and Saatchi, he joined Leo Burnett as creative director. At the turn of the millennium, he moved to Atelier Markgraph, one of the innovators for cultural and corporate spatial experiences: spatial communication, exhibition design and scenography. Since 2005, he has been a member of the board and, since 2016, the co-owner of Atelier Markgraph. Stefan Weil is also a member of the ADC, D&AD, the German Design Council and DDC.

How can designers be ahead of their time?
With intuition, by being alert and staying curious. Through futurology, reflection and analysis.

How do you convince non-designers of the relevance of good design?
Beauty captivates and is a distinguishing feature. Good design is user-oriented and facilitates use of the product. An impressive design gives people pleasure and the product an identity.

What do you need in order to be creative?
Time. Space for intuitive processes. Freedom.

What design developments are currently influencing your work?
The increasing influence of virtual worlds on real, spatial environments. Phantasies and dreams as a source of the new.

Merry Go Round
— Keep filming fun.

Red Dot
→ Film & Animation: page 160

Merry Go Round is a group of partners who are passionate about visual storytelling. They began collaborating in Taipei in 2007. Their documentary "Go Grandriders" set new documentary box office records in Taiwan and Hong Kong. Their commercial works include Gong Yoo's ZenFone 4 Asia-Pacific TV commercial, and they have filmed works in collaboration with G.E.M. and Jay Chou. In 2017, Merry Go Round served as video marketing consultant and visual director to the Taipei 2017 Universiade and bore responsibility for planning and arranging marketing strategies and publicity for the entire sporting event.

To which aspect did you pay special attention when designing your award-winning work?
What we tried to emphasise the most was creative expression and integrity throughout the whole series. Every person's specific function was meant to have their own consistent logic to ensure that each video is separate, independent and creates a different impression if viewed together with the other ones. This makes it possible for the personified worldview of "Mi Family" to be continuously expanded.

What was the first thought that came to your mind when you heard about your award?
This is the first time we have entered an international award based on advertising work, and we are delighted to have won the Red Dot. We were incredibly excited when we heard that we had won this award.

METER Group, University of Tokyo, Serviceplan Innovation, Nick Frank, Moby Digg
— 1 + 1 > 2

Red Dot: Best of the Best
→ Publishing & Print Media: page 12–13

"Made in Fukushima" came to life through the close collaboration of different partners: METER Group, a leader in innovative solutions for environmental and agricultural sciences, the Department of Global Agricultural Sciences at the University of Tokyo, Serviceplan Innovation, the innovation department of Europe's biggest independent communication agency Serviceplan, renowned photographer Nick Frank and the digital design studio Moby Digg, both based in Munich.

How can designers be ahead of their time?
Don't care about trends.

What opportunities and threats has digitalisation produced in the world of design?
Opportunities: unlimited possibilities. Threats: unlimited possibilities.

How do you convince non-designers of the relevance of good design?
Create a design that's relevant to them.

What do you need in order to be creative?
Time, either a lot or very little.

What do you particularly like about your award-winning work?
The reactions of people experiencing it.

MIUI Design Team
Lu Haixu, Zhang Hanyi, Lu Zhenzhou, Ma Jinglu, Chen Qiaozhuo, Li Feilong
— Details tell stories.

Red Dot
→ Sound Design: page 135
→ Interface & User Experience Design: page 298

The MIUI Design Team is a digital innovation group based in Beijing. It is responsible for the user experience design of the Xiaomi smartphone system. In just nine years, it has developed into a comprehensive design team consisting of more than 50 specialists in both visual and audio design. It keeps exploring ways for people to interact with all type of devices in a meaningful manner.

How can designers be ahead of their time?
Keep learning about new technology and think about the unexposed pain points they may bring in future.

To which aspect did you pay special attention when designing your award-winning work?
People have complex feelings about mobile phones. The devices offer efficiency and convenience but interrupt people's private time. Solving this contradiction is the original intention behind the design of this product.

What do you particularly like about your award-winning work?
24-hour notifications: a series of light-hint natural sounds that change over time.

What else would you like to learn in the future?
Artificial intelligence and speech semantic recognition.

Olga Moiseeva, Yuliya Kritskaya, Michail Dubovik, Pavel Popko, Artem Nekrasov, Uliana Kovalenko, Vitaliy Korolev, Sergey Galtsev, Ekaterina Zhokhova

— To make the world more comfortable for everyone.

Red Dot: Junior Award
Best of the Best
→ Apps: page 422–423

Artem Nekrasov and Vitaliy Korolev are students at the British Higher School of Art & Design. They are specialised in user experience/ user interface design, web design, development or automation. Uliana Kovalenko and Ekaterina Zhokhova are industrial designers and worked on the design of the glasses. Olga Moiseeva, Yuliya Kritskaya, Michail Dubovik are from Moscow Film School and worked on the film. Pavel Popko helped test the concept of the application.

What goals have you set yourself for your career going forward?
Working on projects and design concepts for things that people really need.

How do you approach new design projects?
Systematically. First of all, it is necessary to define the purpose of the project, to answer the questions "for whom are we developing this project?" and "why are we doing this project?" Next, you need to analyse your competitors, highlight the strengths of the project (its killer features), then define the functionality for MVP, build a quick prototype and test it on users.

What message does your award-winning work convey?
To draw public attention to the problems of accessibility for disabled people. Many solutions in the digital environment help them in everyday life. At the same time, after a survey, we have identified many problems that still need to be solved. One of these problems – the ability of blind and visually impaired people to move around the city – we tried to partially solve within the Hilight project.

Monotype

Charles Nix, Jan Hendrik Weber, Alexander Roth, Juan Villanueva, Steve Matteson, Jim Ford, Terrance Weinzierl, Tom Rickner — Mr. Nix loves you. When he's not with you, his heart aches – and so he makes type.

Red Dot: Best of the Best
→ Typography: page 92–93

Monotype empowers creative minds to build and express authentic brands through design, technology and expertise. The Monotype Library of typefaces consists of 14,000 battle-tested designs that offer varying fit, form and function for global brands. It supports companies with their visual communications and gives brands a recognisable global voice.

Charles Nix, a type director at Monotype, is one of eight designers of Helvetica Now. He has designed a number of popular typefaces in the Monotype library, including Walbaum and Hope Sans, which received a Certificate of Typographic Excellence in the 22nd Annual TDC Typeface Design Competition. Moreover, he has designed hundreds of books and has taught at the Center for Advanced Design in Malaysia, at the Parsons School of Design in New York as well as on dozens of courses.

How can designers be ahead of their time?
By being very much in the present. One needs to be aware, to be curious and to be analytical.

What opportunities and threats has digitalisation produced in the world of design?
Design has been digital for decades now, but we're still weighing what does and doesn't work. And that's good. It points to a degree of care. The chief risk is that we lose touch with the methods and benefits – the intelligence – of pre-digital design. The opportunities are vast. We work faster, have more powerful tools and artificial intelligence that encourage us to expand our vision.

Must
Evgeny Muravjev, Alexey Sekachov
— Only small teams of passionate people can make breathtaking products.

Red Dot
→ Apps: page 219

Must is a social app for movie and box set fans, established in 2016 by Evgeny Muravjev. He is the founder and CEO of Must and has a wide-ranging background in product design and design management.
Alexey Sekachov, a lead product designer focused on interaction design and mobile interfaces, has been working with Must since 2016.

How do you convince non-designers of the relevance of good design?
As humans, we were born to strive for beauty. People stare at a breathtaking sunset without even knowing why they can't take their eyes off it. All attempts at persuasion and arguments should be aimed at this inner sense of beauty.

What or who has most influenced your career as a designer?
Steve Jobs. A person who combined a vision with a thorough understanding of human nature and a love of beautiful things.

What design developments are currently influencing your work?
Fashion, especially streetwear brands. They're shaping a language for a whole generation and connect people the way music and movies used to do.

What do you particularly like about your award-winning work?
How the user interface stays in the background, making content the centrepiece.

MUTABOR
Moritz Carstens, Lasse Lemster, Sven Ritterhoff, Simon Büßem, Jan Hellmerichs
— Our leitmotif for Bahlsen: No cookies. No progress.

Red Dot: Best of the Best
→ Typography: page 94–95

In 1993, MUTABOR was published as a design magazine by the two communication designers Johannes Plass and Heinrich Paravicini. In 1998, they both founded an agency of the same name in Hamburg. Today, more than 140 creatives work together in five business units (Identity, Strategy, Experience, Architecture and Technology). With over 500 awards, MUTABOR – as the "Leading House for Design and Transformation" – takes brands and companies such as VW, Audi and Vodafone to the next level.

How can designers be ahead of their time?
With cookies.

What do you need in order to be creative?
Cookies.

To which aspect did you pay special attention when designing your award-winning work?
To cookies.

What do you particularly like about your award-winning work?
The cookies.

What was the first thought that came to your mind when you heard about your award?
We need cookies.

newtype imageworks
Jinwook Kim, Kiyoon Park, Yongmin Joh, Inwoong Kim
— newtype imageworks – digital convergence.

Red Dot
→ Interface & User Experience Design: page 336

newtype imageworks is a creative design consultancy, established in Seoul in 2008 with a wide range of references such as digital media, branding, graphic, video, publishing and exhibition design. The team focuses on flexible communication, accountability and high-quality creativity. Based on these experiences, it provides a new integrated media solution that meets customer needs. newtype imageworks works for clients such as Facebook, Samsung, Naver, LG Electronics, AIA Korea, SAMOO Architects & Engineers and the Hyundai Motor Company.

How do you convince non-designers of the relevance of good design?
We talk to them as easily and intuitively as possible. It's like getting a kindergartener to understand our design.

What design developments are currently influencing your work?
Understanding and interpretation of space. That includes both real and digital space.

What do you particularly like about your award-winning work?
That it balances visual aesthetics with information composition.

What else would you like to learn in the future?
Architecture and psychology. After all, all attention is connected to people.

NiEW Design
Daniele De Cia,
Giancarlo Gamberini,
Andrea Ceci, Valentina Marzola,
Giorgio Pretto, Beatrice Cascio,
Andrea Cattani, Andrea Violante
— Design for strategy.

Red Dot
→ Interface & User Experience Design: page 354–355
→ Interface & User Experience Design: page 356–357

NiEW Design is a strategic consultancy company, based in Modena, Italy, right in the heart of the "Packaging Valley". The studio is focused on digital design and innovation in manufacturing, applying design thinking to solutions that develop the way in which leading companies create value. Globally, it designs tailor-made solutions for HMI, MES, ERP technology and IoT platforms.

How can designers be ahead of their time?
Designers should be ahead of their time by their very nature, since their job is to imagine and create things that do not exist yet.

To which aspect did you pay special attention when designing your award-winning work?
Great attention has been paid to creating a culture of design among our customers. Along with design consultancy, some design lessons and some organisational suggestions were provided. The result of the entire project was a different approach to innovation, thanks to a user-centred process that now includes qualitative field research, conceptual co-design and prototype validation. The main beneficiaries of this evolution were the product managers.

One Plus Partnership Limited
Virginia Lung, Ajax Law
— Theme-driven design.

Red Dot
→ Spatial Communication: page 389

Established in 2004 by directors Ajax Law and Virginia Lung, One Plus Partnership Limited designs a variety of projects, including more than 60 cinemas and other venues such as restaurants, retail stores, club houses and sales offices, also working on branding and product design projects. Over the past 15 years, One Plus has been awarded 597 international interior design awards from the USA, Germany, Italy, the UK, The Netherlands, Japan, Korea, Singapore, Taiwan and China.

How do you convince non-designers of the relevance of good design?
It is not an easy task. We think that everyone has their own preferences. If someone does not like your work, you cannot force him to. Luckily, clients who contact us about work, probably only ask us after having seen our previous projects and because they like our style in general. But still, sometimes it may be hard for a non-designer to visualise our design, so they will rely heavily on visuals.

What or who has most influenced your career as a designer?
We are influenced by our competitors. We consider them as external stimuli that interact with us and always push us to move forward. When we see their work, it triggers us to think of ways to develop something different and even better.

What do you need in order to be creative?
Curiosity is definitely the key as is the determination to innovate and not to repeat ourselves.

Optimist
Tino Schaedler
— I don't know where I'm going from here, but I promise it won't be boring.
(David Bowie)

Red Dot: Best of the Best
→ Spatial Communication: page 370–371

Tino Schaedler is an established production designer, art director and architect. Named one of Lürzer's "Best Digital Artists", his multidisciplinary approach and progressive vision have established him as a leader in the field exploring the intersection of film, music, architecture and design. With film credits including "Charlie and the Chocolate Factory" and "Harry Potter", blending spatial design, sound, material and digital innovation, Tino Schaedler has produced works for Nike, Google, BMW, Daft Punk, Kanye West and Lady Gaga. Recently, his interdisciplinary expertise to translate multifaceted brands into meaningful experiences was cemented with the opening of the world's first James Bond museum "007 ELEMENTS" at the peak of Gaislachkogl Mountain, high above the town of Sölden in Austria.

How can designers be ahead of their time?
The most important skill for me is to stay open and curious. I try to take in as much as possible – to pull inspiration from unrelated fields or from looking at the past. I try to find new perspectives to analyse, to question. Then I let design intuition do the rest in order to add a unique and relevant angle.

How do you convince non-designers of the relevance of good design?
To corrupt the saying "actions are stronger than words" for my argument: I guess the best way to do this is to create amazing designs that people respond to. I prefer to convince people through experiences rather than talking about them.

Otium
Damiano Fraccaro
— Soli omnium otiosi sunt qui sapientiae vacant, soli vivunt.

Red Dot: Best of the Best
→ Publishing & Print Media: page 8–9

Otium is a multidisciplinary communication studio based in northeast Italy. Thanks to the wealth of different competences within the studio, Otium is able to tackle complex projects for a variety of clients, from cultural institutions to commercial businesses. Otium provides strategic thinking, graphic design, photography, videomaking, web development, publishing and installations.
Damiano Fraccaro, graphic designer and art director, joined the studio in 2012, after obtaining his master's degree in communication design at the IUAV University of Venice. He is also active in the didactic field at IUAV and received prestigious industrial design awards in competitions such as an Honorable Mention at the Premio Compasso d'Oro ADI and Gold at the European Design Awards.

What design developments are currently influencing your work?
I am fascinated by new relationships of meaning created by digital devices. I am also interested in generative design, moving graphics and any typographic-led projects.

What do you particularly like about your award-winning work?
The biggest satisfaction for me is to observe people's reactions when they interact with the book for the first time. Being an unusual format, it generates quite a lot of astonished looks!

What was the first thought that came to your mind when you heard about your award?
Shock! And immediately after, I secretly hoped I didn't have to speak in public – I always find it slightly awkward.

Overman
Seung Eun Jang
— Anyone can have ideas.
It's making them a reality that counts.

Red Dot
→ Online: page 183

As a creative director and a brand communicator with 24 years of experience, Seung Eun Jang has won awards at Cannes Lions and the New York Festivals. She tries to merge down-to-earth strategies that get to the core of the business with what she calls "up-to-the-universe" imagination – to think outside the box, to address problems. In 2015, she set up Overman in a bid to break with the conventions of existing agencies. Overman has built a reputation for maximising its clientele's business performance with optimal solutions. As a result, the studio received awards in prestigious competitions such as the Effie Awards and the Agency of the Year Awards.

What opportunities and threats has digitalisation produced in the world of design?
Take David Hockney for example. In the process of creating his "multiple points of view", he had the help of digital photography and Photoshop. From Polaroids to cameras and digital cameras, his tools evolved as did his "Moving Focus" and large multi-canvas paintings. As such, whether digitalisation is progress or regression depends on the hands and skills of the designer.

What do you particularly like about your award-winning work?
Since children may not be so comfortable with verbal language, we used visual language, which I believe was authentic and had a truthful resonance.

Quinsay Design
Tong Yi
— Open-minded design thinking helps designers work better.

Red Dot: Grand Prix
→ Typography: page 90–91

Tong Yi, graphic and product designer, works as an art director at Quinsay Design. The open-minded design agency has been challenging the design industry with its signature experimental approach and its vision in innovation.

How can designers be ahead of their time?
By thinking deeply about history and modern society.

What opportunities and threats has digitalisation produced in the world of design?
Looking forward, there is no threat. Digitalisation will rather bring about changes such as improved efficiency, greater expression and more possibilities.

What or who has most influenced your career as a designer?
Literature and history which give us ideas for potential design concepts.

What design developments are currently influencing your work?
New production processes and technologies.

What do you particularly like about your award-winning work?
The fact that the design uses multiple materials.

Publishing & Print Media Posters Typography Illustrations Sound Design Film & Animation Online Apps

SAM CHUV
Numa Luraschi, Aliénor Held, Aris Zenone, Pierre Dubois, Jessica Scheurer
— Making things simpler, smarter and more fun.

Red Dot: Best of the Best
→ Publishing & Print Media: page 14–15

Founded in 1984, the SAM is a multimedia agency based within the University Hospital of Lausanne. Its mission is to meet the needs of the hospital and university in terms of audiovisual communication, training and research. Working within the hospital walls means that it collaborates very closely with various clients and teams ranging from nurses, professors and students to human resources professionals, cooks and architects. The agency provides a variety of services with a team of 22 creatives who are passionate about providing top-quality, human-centred design.

What opportunities and threats has digitalisation produced in the world of design?
The opportunity offered by digitalisation is the capacity for sharing, interaction, transmission and feedback, which are endless and immediate. But these can never replace the finesse and beauty of a physical object.

How do you convince non-designers of the relevance of good design?
Fortunately, the graphic and typographic culture is strong in Switzerland.

What do you need in order to be creative?
Happiness and endorphins!

To which aspect did you pay special attention when designing your award-winning work?
The typographic details and the simplicity of the finished object.

SAP
Sven Schwerin-Wenzel,
Lydia Tallau, Alexander Schräder,
Irene Schick
— Our sports products are role-based, adaptive, coherent, simple and delightful.

Red Dot
→ Apps: page 224
→ Interface & User Experience Design: page 300
→ Interface & User Experience Design: page 301

Sven Schwerin-Wenzel has held global SAP positions for more than 20 years and works as design thinker for the sports and entertainment industry at SAP.
Lydia Tallau is design lead of visual and interaction design for SAP Sports One and also senior user experience designer in which role she applies previous experience she gained working on other SAP software.
Alexander Schräder has been with SAP since 2015 and has worked on numerous designs for SAP Sports One for mobile end-to-end scenarios.
Irene Schick has worked on conceptual and visual design of user interfaces in several agencies and companies prior to joining the SAP Sports and Entertainment design team.

What or who has most influenced your career as a designer?
Design thinking has taught us empathy for our customers. This approach has most influenced our careers as designers in bringing together what is desirable from a human point of view with what is technologically feasible and economically viable.

What design developments are currently influencing your work?
With the rise and advance of AI and machine learning, solutions are getting more intelligent, smart and efficient.

What else would you like to learn in the future?
How we can help the world to run better and improve people's lives even more through our technology and solutions.

Shih Chien University, Department of Communications Design
— The female strength of visual design and animation.

Red Dot
→ Film & Animation: page 146

The visual design team of the Department of Communications Design was formed by female alumni of Shih Chien University, Taiwan, thereby representing the new female face of visual design and animation. This year, it created the visual design for the 53rd Golden Bell Awards, the biggest television award in Taiwan. It celebrates TV direction, screenplay, scriptwriting, storytelling and creativity each year.

How can designers be ahead of their time?
A good designer observes both the past and the future closely. Be sensitive to what has happened and what might happen, so you're always prepared.

What opportunities and threats has digitalisation produced in the world of design?
Nowadays, the threat of digitalisation is that it allows people too much freedom, so nothing is really secured. However, it also offers thousands of intriguing methods to achieve a goal; and your idea is never unrealistic since innovation happens every day.

To which aspect did you pay special attention when designing your award-winning work?
We paid a lot of attention to visual communication – how to deliver the concept of "television" and "colour bar" in a fun and enjoyable way. The colour bar plays a key role in our design; it not only represents the past and future of television, but also the dynamic, complex humanity of our culture.

Shinhan Financial Group, Platform Marketing Team, Media4th & Company
Woo Kyoung Ahn,
Choong Heon Choi,
Ki Boum Kim, Eun Hye Yoo,
Min Kwan Park
— Digital Transformation:
A new mobile experience for
next-generation customers.

Red Dot
→ Interface & User Experience Design: page 293

In 2017, Shinhan Financial Group, the largest financial company in South Korea, established the Platform Marketing Team. Thus, customers can see the financial information from across the group without needing to install numerous different applications. The team, led by Woo Kyoung Ahn, wanted to make it easier for customers to use banking, credit card, investment and insurance services. Media4th & Company, specialised in UI/UX, was established in South Korea in 1996 and designs web services including those for the finance sector.

How do you convince non-designers of the relevance of good design?
From a service perspective, good design leads to service activation, a goal we want to achieve by making the service convenient for users to use. So, by showing the design of a service that many people use, and by explaining its features, we can demonstrate the excellence of the design.

To which aspect did you pay special attention when designing your award-winning work?
Plenty of communication was needed in order to develop a new UI/UX and we gave a lot of thought to combining each individual financial service with a coherent UI. We therefore tried to allow customers to experience various functions and the contents of different financial services in a single application.

SimpleInfo Design
Chih-Chyi Chang
— Make profits while transforming our society.

Red Dot: Best of the Best
→ Online: page 172–173

SimpleInfo Design was founded in Taipei, Taiwan, in 2015 and is a design team covering multiple sectors that include graphic design, motion design, website design, social media design and YouTube channels. It has already received a number of prestigious awards in international competitions such as the Red Dot Award, iF Design Award and Good Design Award.

How do you convince non-designers of the relevance of good design?
A good design itself is already convincing. Our job is to ensure it is seen by more people. We focus on design and on how to market our work and deliver it to the right audience.

What or who has most influenced your career as a designer?
The Sunflower Student Movement in Taiwan. It was the largest "civil disobedience" movement since the 1980s, triggered by the attempt of Taiwan's Legislative Yuan to forcefully pass an agreement, the Cross-Strait Service Trade Agreement (CSSTA) with China, which violated procedural justice. This incident illustrated the pursuit of democracy and freedom by Taiwan's population. During the movement, the positive impact of digital tools for society when used to pass on information deeply influenced us. For this reason, we entered the field of information design, hoping to pass on detailed information to more people in a friendly and creative way; and by changing how information is delivered through design, we hope to bring about improvements in society.

STRICHPUNKT
Jeannette Kohnle,
Jochen Theurer,
Linda Beiermeister,
Bianca Bunsas, Leonie Werner
— The future belongs to the brave.

Red Dot: Best of the Best
→ Publishing & Print Media: page 16–17

With its more than 135 employees, STRICHPUNKT is one of the leading design and branding agencies in the German-speaking countries. It was founded in 1996 and is still an independent agency whose specialists in brand, experience, culture and business design service clients such as Audi, Deutsche Post DHL Group, Otto Group, Porsche or Trumpf as well as Asian brands like Weltmeister and Deli from their offices in Stuttgart, Berlin and Shanghai.

What opportunities and threats has digitalisation produced in the world of design?
As a dimension of design what matters is to think about and link the different design disciplines creatively, conceptually and above all completely freely. That's when you achieve truly holistic brand experiences that move and excite people. In this respect, digitalisation is therefore an enormous opportunity for the design world, but perhaps also a threat if one does not use it and does not design in a considered, deliberate, self-aware way.

What do you need in order to be creative?
Very little. Creative ping-pong, lifeblood, free thinking, kindred spirits, those who are of a different opinion. And concentration.

To which aspect did you pay special attention when designing your award-winning work?
With regard to the Bosch Megatrend Report it was important to us to deliberately permit complexity and make it comprehensible instead of simplifying everything and thereby taking away its magic. It was intended as a Wimmelbook for the mind.

Studio 212 Fahrenheit
Albert Buring, Paul Mulder
— Just do it.
(Nike)

Red Dot: Grand Prix
→ Spatial Communication: page 366–367

Red Dot
→ Illustrations: page 110
→ Spatial Communication: page 381

Studio 212 Fahrenheit is a Dutch design studio which was founded by Albert Buring and Paul Mulder. They both graduated from the Minerva Art Academy in Groningen and have a strong belief in the power of narrative, distinctive design for spaces, installations, products and art. Studio 212 Fahrenheit creates specific designs for governments, agencies, brands and museums. It is Groningen-based but works internationally.

How do you convince non-designers of the relevance of good design?
Good design should speak for itself.

What or who has most influenced your career as a designer?
Multiple things have; other artists and designers, museum visits and nature.

What do you need in order to be creative?
Free space in our heads and time to develop.

What do you particularly like about your award-winning work?
"BLOCBIRDS" was our first non-commissioned work. And to see it win an award is a big deal for us.

What was the first thought that came to your mind when you heard about your award?
We were overwhelmed with pride. It's a great honour and a privilege to be part of this.

Surprise Lab./Home Hotel/ King Kong Wave

Red Dot
→ Spatial Communication: page 387

Surprise Lab. is a company that focuses on experience design and tickling people's senses. It has executed projects such as "Dining In The Dark" and "table for ONE". In 2019, "The Great Tipsy", a 90-minute immersive experience, was launched.
Home Hotel bases its architectural design on the concept of "home", creating a space that is welcoming, full of warmth and with all the comforts of home. In 2018 and 2019, it was listed in the Michelin Guide Taipei. Home Hotel organises events such as "13 Rooms Festival" in which 13 artists are invited to transform hotel rooms with their own art medium.
King Kong Wave is a production company focusing on interdisciplinary art and immersive theatre. In 2018, King Kong Wave realised projects such as "How I Eat Faust – Tang Sanzang", "Imaginary Fish" at the Taipei Free Art Fair and was nominated for the Taishin Arts Award for "Human Party" and the space project "Return to Life".

How can designers be ahead of their time?
Observe, think and act. Observe the world, society and the people in it and ask what problems our society is facing.

How do you convince non-designers of the relevance of good design?
Their feelings convince them, not us. Our job is to design a process which can resonate with our audience.

What was the first thought that came to your mind when you heard about your award?
The teammates aiming for the same goal.

TCS Interactive
Aditya Sareen, Scott Daniels, Tim Peters, Michelle Taylor, Sujesh Jastee, Fumie Piontkowski, Kayvan Mojtahedzadeh, Blake T. Bennett, Howard Schargel, Haley Price, Steven Touart, Michael J. Ricker
— Delivering award-winning iconic digital experiences.

Red Dot: Best of the Best
→ Interface & User Experience Design: page 250–251

TCS Interactive is a leader in the digital customer experience space. With a human-first approach, the company applies design, engineering, business strategy and subject matter expertise to deliver award-winning iconic digital experiences for its clients.

How can designers be ahead of their time?
By going out and meeting people who are pushing the limits of good design and leveraging new technologies. Ask a lot of questions. Listen more than you speak. Pay attention to what's happening in the world and be on the lookout for problems that need solving.

What opportunities and threats has digitalisation produced in the world of design?
Digitalisation enables us to leverage new technologies to gain efficiencies and scale – but doing more and faster doesn't necessarily lead to great design. Good human-centred design requires understanding – and until technologies like AI evolve a bit more, we need to do the work required to gain that understanding.

To which aspect did you pay special attention when designing your award-winning work?
Our focus was on building a location-specific, fan-based experience that promoted the NYC Marathon through an activity that encourages fitness. The trick there was to make sure we were creating an inclusive experience that could be equally enjoyed by runners, wheelers (wheelchair athletes) and spectators who were attending the event.

ToThree Design
— To realise the humanistic value of design through environmental visual systems.

Red Dot
→ Spatial Communication: page 399

ToThree is a design studio that specialises in environmental visual system design for architecture and urban environments. The name is based on the book "To Three" by Emery Studio. "To" is a pun, which not only reveals the essence of graphic design in environmental information: two-(to)dimensional, but also indicates the trend of the future and the studio's ultimate goal: to make the design three-dimensional. By making the graphic signage design three-dimensional, the team creates live visual communication, intriguing spaces with boundless imagination. With diverse professional backgrounds and extensive experience, the studio has completed many award-winning projects such as the Tianjin Art Museum, Luna Lake or the Rolling Dragon installation.

What opportunities and threats has digitalisation produced in the world of design?
On the one hand, digitalisation frees designers from repetitive work and enables them to create with a brand-new perception; on the other hand, it can be misleading. Designers have to be careful not to be carried away by the technology and must always be aware of the core of each design.

What or who has most influenced your career as a designer?
Otl Aicher. Because as a designer, no matter what the outside environment or atmosphere was, he could always stay impartial and ensure his creativity was not affected.

Tubik Studio
Marina Yalanska, Sergii Valiukh, Aleksandr Petulko,
Ksenia Lashko, Denys Koloskov, Vladyslav Taran, Polina Taran
— Everything has beauty. Design finds the best way to reveal it to the world.

Red Dot
→ Online: page 205

Tubik is a team of bright creatives from various disciplines: UI/UX design for web and mobile, graphic and motion design, product development, digital art, project management and copywriting. The company was founded in 2013, beginning with outsourced UI and UX design and expanding its range of services year by year. Today, Tubik is a full-stack award-winning digital agency with all the specialists required to produce effective creative processes from scratch, ranging from concept and branding to complex information architecture and high usability of websites and applications, effective landing pages and videos for marketing goals.

How can designers be ahead of their time?
To be proactive and innovative enough in the design sphere, it's important for a designer not to be afraid of bold decisions that are poised on the edge between a colossal success and a complete flop. And if the latter happens, you have to analyse it, draw your conclusions and keep going.

What opportunities and threats has digitalisation produced in the world of design?
The main threat is standardisation. Designs are becoming super similar. New designers sometimes find it challenging to establish their own original style or technique, as everybody around them is using the same tools. On the other hand, these conditions, in fact, push the limits and that opens up enormous opportunities for creative self-realisation.

Yih-Feng Weng
— Don't forget what you yearned to be and what you used to be as time goes by.

Red Dot: Junior Award
→ Posters: page 454–455

Yih-Feng Weng, born in Malaysia and raised in Taiwan, developed a passion for the arts and, in 2014, went back to Malaysia to study art in high school where he also became president of the graduation art exhibition. In 2016, he graduated as the top student, received the excellence award in arts in the UEC examinations and was among the top five art students in Malaysia in that year. Currently, he is majoring in visual communication design at Shanghai Jiao Tong University.

What would you like to design one day?
I would like to design a famous social media "check-in place" so that I can be tagged in people's posts.

Where do you have your best ideas?
I usually have the best ideas in the bathroom and on the subway, because those are usually the places where I am most often idle.

What message does your award-winning work convey?
My award-winning work focuses on conveying the concept of AIDS prevention. I use the red ribbon to depict the adult body in an exaggerated and indirect way to make a deeper impression to the public, hoping to draw attention to the problem of AIDS and AIDS prevention.

Publishing & Print Media   Posters   Typography   Illustrations   Sound Design   Film & Animation   Online   Apps

Fang Wu, Xinyu Gan, Yejia Qian
— What I cannot create, I do not understand.

Red Dot: Junior Award
→ Publishing & Print Media: page 446

Xinyu Gan and Yejia Qian are studying visual communication design at Shanghai Publishing and Printing College. In their third year at college, they started preparing their award-winning projects, Abstract Inheritance and Four Tones Font, under the guidance and inspiration of associate professor Fang Wu. As a team, they were honoured, among others, with the Benny Award (Best of Category) of the 69th Premier Print Awards by Printing Industries of America (PIA), and the Shortlist Award of the 19th Platinum Originality International University Students Graphic Design Competition.

What would you like to design one day?
An eternal font design as evidence of a spark of thought.

What goals have you set yourself for your career going forward?
To become an independent designer with style. To try to take our design to another level and raise the standard.

Where do you have your best ideas?
In the online world where there are thousands of sparks of inspiration.

How do you approach new design projects?
Observe, analyse, understand.

What message does your award-winning work convey?
To combine tradition with modernity, to convey abstract ideas through specific design.

Po-Ya Yu
— Believe your efforts will eventually pay off.

Red Dot: Junior Award
Best of the Best
→ Posters: page 418–419

Po-Ya Yu is a student in the Department of Visual Communication Design at Asia University.

How did you discover your passion for design?
I started to work in the field of design when I was in college. For me, design is conveying my ideas as entities to others. If someone understands my design, I feel happy. That gives me motivation to create.

What goals have you set yourself for your career going forward?
There are no clear goals yet, but I want to try out more different design areas.

Which part of the design process do you particularly enjoy?
Discussions with others, because through discussion I can discover things I hadn't noticed before and can modify the things that are bad.

How do you approach new design projects?
By collecting information and using it as a source of inspiration.

What message does your award-winning work convey?
This series of works is based on empathy and uses three Chinese characters, "bao", "na" and "rong". They are combined with images to show the main concept, so that the person looking at the images can discern the power of mutual tolerance and acceptance.

Zi Zhi, Feng Luo, Guo-Da Lin, Kai-Qiang Hou, Xi Cheng
— Express life and ideas with design.

Red Dot: Junior Award
→ Illustrations: page 493

The team members are students from the Department of Visual Communication Design, Academy of Arts and Design, Fuzhou University of International Studies and Trade where great value is attached to the development of design disciplines and to training applied art talents of innovative spirit and entrepreneurial ability.

How did you discover your passion for design?
When observing all kinds of things in life.

What goals have you set yourself for your career going forward?
To become an excellent designer.

How do you approach new design projects?
With research and communication.

What message does your award-winning work convey?
That humans need to revere nature.

ZJY (Beijing)
Tourism and Culture

Jianhua Wu, Zhenyu Yang, Bin Zhang, Linyi Luo, Bin Qiu, Wenchao Han, Wenjie Zhang, Zhichao Zhao

— Being creative is not a hobby, it is a way of life.

Red Dot
→ Apps: page 215

The design team of ZJY applies modern media perspectives to an artistic expression of ancient and modern China and other countries in order to revive traditional and regional folk culture. By integrating online interactive experiences with offline entities and combining consumer experiences with commercial forms, the team incorporates the concept of the brand into daily activities, creating a label with a varied cultural and historical background and providing users with an immersive tour experience.

How can designers be ahead of their time?
Through a multifaceted approach that takes in all perspectives, through ownership awareness and integrated design.

How do you convince non-designers of the relevance of good design?
With empathy, on the operational front, through ownership awareness.

What or who has most influenced your career as a designer?
Xianghong Chen, who built the ideal city with his pen and with utopia in mind.

What do you particularly like about your award-winning work?
The use of black technology and fashion art to transfer ancient oriental culture to the modern world.

What else would you like to learn in the future?
How to create greater value for society.

JURY

Publishing & Print Media Posters Typography Illustrations Sound Design Film & Animation Online Apps

01 | 02

Renne Angelvuo
Finland

01 | 02 THE SEVENTH CUP
Corporate identity and packaging design concept for a single packaging series and a premium gift box for Finnish client THE SEVENTH CUP, a premium tea company collecting high-quality tea from carefully selected small farms. The logo was designed based on the company name, the number seven and a teacup. Tea leaf embossings and delicate colours combined with soft haptic packaging materials reflect the product's high quality.

Renne Angelvuo studied advertising, marketing and design at the Institute of Marketing in Helsinki and followed this up with an arts degree from the Free Art School Helsinki. Since 1980, he has been working as an art director in advertising and design. In 1994, he launched the company PRIORITY Advertising & Design, and in 2004 set up Win Win Branding, which is today called Win Win Design. Renne Angelvuo has years of expertise in packaging design, industrial design, branding and packaging innovations. His clients include many big Finnish and international brands such as Nokia, MySQL, Nestlé, Metsä Tissue, UPM-Kymmene and Saarioinen. He was president of the European Packaging Design Association from 2015 to 2018 and is still a member of the board.

What do you enjoy most about your profession?
It is always the unknown that challenges your creativity. The more passion and love you put into a project, the more you can achieve. I have been lucky to work on big and small packaging and brand design projects which have been rewarding. That's the driver that keeps you trying hard for every project.

How will packaging be designed in ten years' time?
Food packaging and FMCG will change tremendously. Urbanisation is speeding up people's move into the cities. Our planet's food production will experience a revolution through vertical farming and new nutrition and protein resources. Climate change and the change in food production will also affect the packaging industry as customers demand increasingly sustainable materials and production techniques.

01

Prof. Masayo Ave
Japan / Germany

01 "Square, Circle, Triangle"
by Bruno Munari
Book design for Japanese editions
published by Heibonsha, Japan, 2010.

Professor Masayo Ave is the founder of the design studio Masayo-Ave creation and SED.Lab, Sensory Experience Design Laboratory, in Berlin. The Japanese designer merges culture and disciplines and brings to bear her expertise in her sensory-based innovative design works and also in the field of design education. A graduate in architecture from Hosei University in Japan, her design career began in Milan in the early 1990s. Taking a sensorial and imaginative approach to basic design principles, her focus on material exploration and experimental design development brought her critical fame and numerous international design awards. In the early 2000s, Masayo Ave also became involved in the field of design education and was appointed a professor at the Berlin University of the Arts, the Estonian Academy of Arts and recently at Berlin International University of Applied Sciences.

How has the design profession changed over the past five years thanks to developments in technology?
The latest developments in printing technology open up so many new options for enriching human sensory experiences in design.

What or who has most influenced your career as a designer? Why?
Bruno Munari and Oscar Niemeyer, because these masters show us how to invent joy in order to discover future.

Good communication design is …
… a holistic sensory experience.

01 | 02

Špela Čadež
Slovenia

01 | 02 Orange Is the New Black – Unraveled
Slovenia/United Kingdom/Singapore, 2017

Špela Čadež, born in 1977, graduated in graphic design in Ljubljana, Slovenia, in 2002. She continued her studies at the Academy of Media Arts Cologne, Germany, and has been working as an independent animation director and producer since 2008. Her films have been screened worldwide. "Boles" (2013) has received 50 awards, distinctions and nominations including a Grand Prix at the DOK Leipzig and the Best Debut Award at the Hiroshima International Animation Festival. Špela Čadež' latest film "Nighthawk" (2016) has to date received 23 awards and distinctions including the Grand Prix at the Holland Animation Film Festival (HAFF) and Animafest Zagreb. It has been screened at international festivals such as the Sundance Film Festival, Clermont-Ferrand International Short Film Festival and Annecy International Animation Film Festival.

How do you come up with new ideas?
I am guided by the content and topic, and then have lots of ideas.

What challenges does animation as a discipline bring with it?
Animation combines a number of different areas such as film, design and sound. In order to produce a good animation, you need to invest a lot of time.

What characterises well-designed sound projects?
If you don't just hear but also feel the sound.

To what do you pay attention when assessing the submissions?
The project needs to be based on a good idea that has been executed in a consistent way.

01

Eric Chang
Taiwan

01 Taiwan Life Insurance – After School Care Programme
Selective mutism is a rare form of speech disorder in Taiwan. The issue of the rural-urban gap still exists; many children grow up in low-income families and lack education resources. Consequently, Taiwan Life Insurance launched an After School Care Programme which sends teachers to remote areas to take care of children who desperately need help. The campaign encourages people to pay more attention to children in rural areas in Taiwan.

Eric Chang holds a master's degree from the University of Wisconsin–Madison and currently teaches at National Chengchi University, Taiwan. Specialised in marketing, direct marketing, customer relationship management (CRM) and digital marketing, he is an expert with in-depth knowledge of the theory and application of integrated and digital marketing. He joined McCann Worldgroup Taiwan as CEO in 2018, providing clients with services such as digital marketing strategies and digital media planning, CRM strategy consulting and communications planning. Before taking on this role, he worked for Ogilvy for more than 20 years and served as vice president of business development for OgilvyOne in the Asia-Pacific region.

What are the biggest challenges in the field of online communication at present?
Too much focus on technology usage and too little on creativity enhancement.

What are the three characteristics of a well-designed app?
Users want to keep it, use it and continue using it on their mobile devices.

What defines successful marketing?
Proven results from marketing campaigns and it does not matter whether those results are positive or negative.

Designers and companies should enter the Red Dot Award …
… because winning a Red Dot is the recognition that your work exceeds the global design standard.

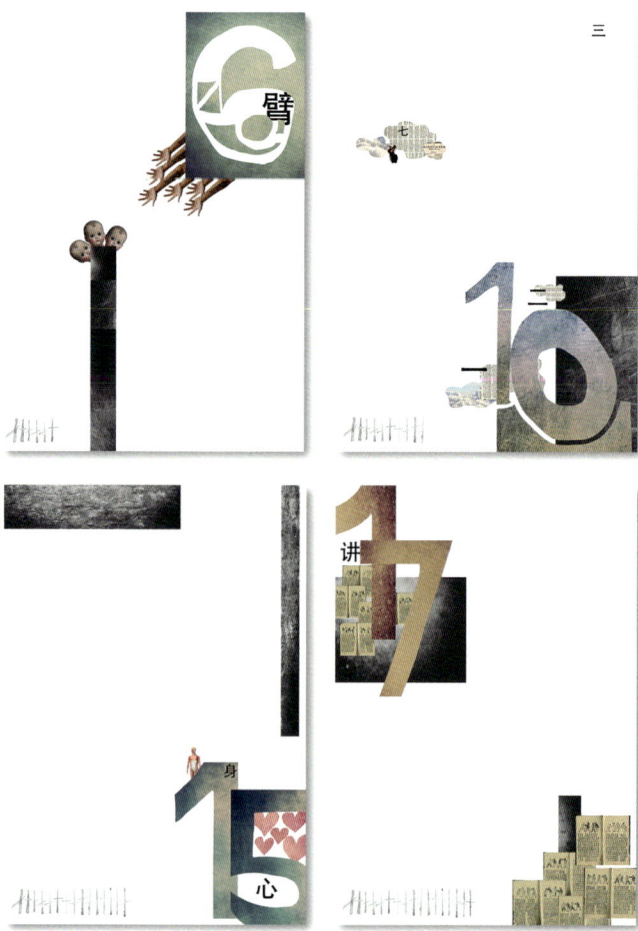

01

Kelley Cheng
Singapore

01 Posters for the Kelley Cheng 20-year retrospective
A series of 20 posters that play on the numbers in Chinese while, at the same time, chronicling the 20-year design journey of its creator, Kelley Cheng in an abstract way. In celebration of her two decades in the design industry, this series of posters was created especially for her retrospective exhibition at the National Design Centre, Singapore in 2019.

A leading designer in Singapore, Kelley Cheng is an architectural graduate turned polymath whose activities range from magazine editor, public speaker and art gallery owner to designer. She runs her own publishing and design consultancy, The Press Room, a multidisciplinary studio designing everything from books, brands, graphics, documentaries to spaces, stages and film sets. Her projects include the Youth Olympic Games, the Singapore Pavilion at the World Expo 2012, Yeosu, Korea, the National Gallery Singapore and the President's Design Award 2013 and 2016. In collaboration with Studio Milou, The Press Room won the President's Design Award 2015 for the National Gallery Singapore brand design. Kelley Cheng serves as adjunct lecturer in interior architecture at LASALLE College of the Arts, Singapore, and as an advisory board member for the Singapore Polytechnic, School of Design. In 2009, she was celebrated as one of the "Great Women of Our Time" and in 2010 as one of the "50 Most Inspirational Women" in Singapore.

Which aspect of your work do you most enjoy?
The creative process itself. Once I get to the execution, the idea starts to crystallise and you begin to tweak the design. Often the outcome is quite different to the initial sketch. That is why there is a bit of art in every design.

What characterises well-designed apps?
Apps have become a big part of our daily life so we primarily want them to be useful. Then we look for easy navigation, simplicity of access and use, cybersecurity, and, last but not least, visual aesthetics.

01 | 02

Prof. Michel de Boer
Netherlands

**01 | 02 I. M. Pei Foundation and
I. M. Pei Award – Visual Identity**
Developed to promote art and culture on a global scale, the visual identity of the I. M. Pei Foundation and I. M. Pei Award is inspired by the distinct geometric quality of I. M. Pei's unique approach to modernist architecture. This contemporary visual identity references the core values of his architectural works. The systematic visual aim was to communicate the renowned architect's philosophy: "Let the light create the design."

Professor Michel de Boer studied at the Academy of Fine Arts and Higher Technologies in Rotterdam. In 1989, he became creative managing partner at Studio Dumbar. In 2011, he started his independent design company, MdB Associates, with associated offices in Germany, Korea and Hong Kong. In 2014, he opened his new office De Boer Wang Studio in Shanghai. With more than 30 years of experience, Michel de Boer has worked for clients such as Apple, Allianz, Shell, Nike, Jaguar and Mercedes-Benz. In 2005, he became visiting professor at the Istituto Universitario di Architettura in Venice, Italy. He runs an educational bachelor's programme in branding, identity and public space at the SIVA DeTao School of Design and is professor at Tongji University, College of Design and Innovation, for a master's programme. He is a member of the Alliance Graphique Internationale (AGI) and of D&AD in the UK.

How do you approach new design projects?
Not trusting my own expertise. Routine is another word for it. It can make you lazy and therefore predictable. To be uncertain is the best thing for a designer. It allows you to elevate the conceptual mindset.

How do you forge a link between brand and design?
By defining a matching strategy and translating this into an applicable design with a strong systematic approach.

What is the most exciting part of your work as a jury member?
To be pleasantly surprised by a specific and genuine piece of work that creates that wow effect.

Publishing & Print Media | Posters | Typography | Illustrations | Sound Design | Film & Animation | Online | Apps

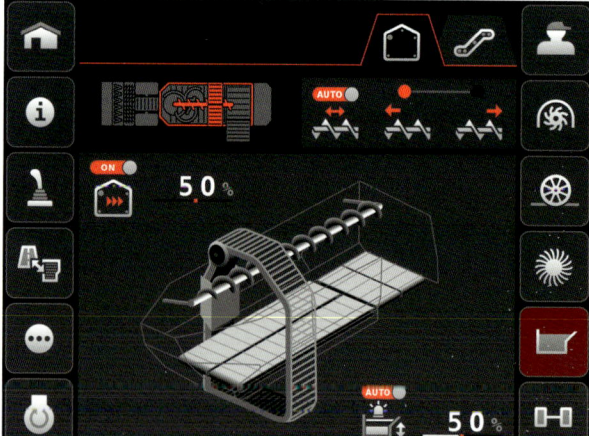

01 | 02

Andrea Finke-Anlauff
Germany

01 | 02 Interface of a Beet Harvester
For Grimme, an interface system was developed which can be applied to all machine types. The workflow is divided into logical steps. Each part of the machine dealing with a certain step during the workflow is accessed by tapping on the easily accessible right-hand side of the screen where it is also illustrated as an icon. The interface visualisation of this enormous beet harvester is limited to 480 x 640 pixels and 264 colours due to the universal ISOBUS standard and has to work without text.

Andrea Finke-Anlauff studied product and graphic design in Braunschweig (Germany), Barcelona and Helsinki, and graduated from the Braunschweig University of Arts with a diploma. Already during her degree course, she worked for various departments of Nokia in Great Britain, Japan and Finland, and signed a consultancy agreement with Nokia in 1992. In 1994, she founded the company mangodesign, which specialises in product design and interaction design, and which has been able to secure numerous awards and patents ever since. In 2003, Andrea Finke-Anlauff co-founded the design manufacturer mangoobjects, which specialises in small-scale series and individual product presentations. She has taught user interface and user experience design at various art schools and universities. She lectures at design events and has acted as a jury member for several international design awards.

What role does the digital world play in your everyday life?
It is impossible to imagine my professional or private life without it, but it also makes me increasingly aware of and appreciate the straightforward, analogue side of life – which I now enjoy even more.

What are the biggest developments in UX Design at present?
The projection of contents into physical surroundings using VR and AR. This is still very much at the development stage, but has already been used in an exciting way in app development.

01 | 02

Gustavo Greco
Brazil

01 | 02 Design against Poverty Wheel
In this social project by Greco Design, children create logos pro bono for the favela's entrepreneurs.

Gustavo Greco is the founder and creative director of Greco Design. He is professor of the brand management postgraduate course at PUC Minas and also director of ABEDESIGN, the Brazilian Association of Design Companies. Moreover, he acts as a juror in the D&AD Awards, Cannes Lions, Prémios Lusos, FIAP, 10th Brazilian Graphic Design Biennial, El Ojo de Iberoamérica and iF concept award. Gustavo Greco received awards from e.g. the Cannes Lions, D&AD Awards, Red Dot Award, iF Design Award, El Ojo de Iberoamérica, London International Awards, Bienal Iberoamericana de Diseño and HOW International Design Awards.

What is the most enriching aspect of your work?
One major characteristic is that we are changing a lot, all the time. I am restless, and this is reflected in my team and keeps us from getting too comfortable. We like new ideas and are always trying new ways of experimenting with new things.

How important is teamwork for the design process?
It is fundamental. Working in a team brings together the repertoire and experiences of each individual member. The greater the number of viewpoints considered during the creative process, the richer the resulting design will be.

What role do illustrations play in the field of design?
Illustrations are the most powerful communication element in a design project. They are what make us understand best. An image really is worth more than a thousand words.

Publishing & Print Media   Posters   Typography   Illustrations   Sound Design   Film & Animation   Online   Apps

01 | 02

Rainer Hirt
Germany

Rainer Hirt was born in Überlingen, Germany, in 1979 and studied communication design at the University of Applied Sciences in Konstanz, Germany. He founded the corporate sound information portal www.audio-branding.de in 2003, a resource well known to experts in the field. After his studies, he also co-founded audity, an agency specialised in audio branding and audio interaction. Rainer Hirt is also supervisor of various research projects at several universities, as well as co-founder of the Audio Branding Academy, the first independent institute for acoustic brand communication.

01 Brand Sound of Tyrol
Tyrol is characterised by the harmony of contrasts: nature and culture, tradition and innovation, constancy and renewal, regionalism and internationalism, tranquillity and movement, homesickness and wanderlust. They are all differing poles that make Tyrol a preferred place of rejuvenation.

02 Tirol, der Kraft-Klang-Ort
Tyrol's soundscape: tradition and modernity, familiar and unexpected, dynamic and calm, highs and lows, loud and soft, echo and reverberation, question and answer all come together in sound branding in an acoustic overall theme: "Tirol, der Kraft-Klang-Ort" (Tyrol, the Place of Power and Sound).

How has the profession of sound designer changed over the past ten years thanks to developments in technology?
Sound designers today face the challenge of having to think not only about auditory design, but also about "digital viability". They therefore also have to get to grips with software development issues.

What are the criteria you use to assess acoustic projects?
Sound follows function: design concept, practical implementation, degree of innovation.

How has the quality of the submissions in the "Sound Design" category developed in recent years?
There has been an exciting development in the conceptual approaches and in implementation. A very high standard of conceptual and strategic quality is noticeable particularly in the areas of audio branding/brand sound projects.

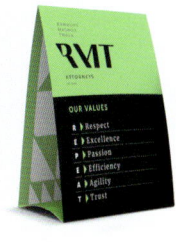

01 | 02

Thebe Ikalafeng
South Africa

01 RMT
Corporate identity for Ramushu Mashile Twala Attorneys.

02 African Business
The African Business magazine reports on "Africa's Best Brands" and how they entrench their positions in Africa. Brand Africa founder and Brand Leadership chairman Thebe Ikalafeng gives a perspective on the latest Brand Africa 100.

Thebe Ikalafeng is a leading global African brand and reputation architect, advisor and author. He has worked on over 100 local and global brands across Africa. He is the founder of the Brand Leadership Group, a non-executive director of Cartrack Holdings, Mercantile Bank Holdings, World Wide Fund for Nature and South African Tourism. Thebe Ikalafeng holds BSc and MBA degrees from the Marquette University (USA), and followed the executive education programmes at Wits Business School and Harvard Business School. He has been to every country in Africa.

What is the most enriching aspect of your work?
Africa has traditionally engaged with brands as a consumer rather than a creator. I'm inspired to be part of the journey to recreate that narrative – to build excellent "Made in Africa" brands and to tell that story in an authentic African narrative and compete globally. I started "Brand Africa 100 – Africa's Best Brands" in 2011 specifically to track how African brands are competing against global brands and to see which "Made in Africa" brands are redefining the landscape. A rewarding journey so far.

How important is "being different" for market success?
Great brands are built on having a clear and relevant proposition, authenticity and, most importantly, competitive differentiation. The challenge is to differentiate or die.

What are the latest trends in corporate design?
Simplicity. Fewer graphics, less colour and less complication.

01

Hjalti Karlsson
USA

01 Reykjavík Art Museum
The Reykjavík Art Museum is the preeminent art museum in Iceland, with three locations across the capital, each focusing on different decades and artists. The new identity and design system for the museum needed to speak to both local and international audiences.

Hjalti Karlsson founded the award-winning design studio karlssonwilker inc. with partner Jan Wilker in 2000. Karlsson has launched a number of notable creative projects over the course of his career, including work for MINI/BMW, Bloomberg Businessweek, Nintendo, Swatch, Museum of the Moving Image, Vitra and Reykjavík Art Museum. He is a recipient of the Torsten and Wanja Söderberg Prize and has been featured in numerous publications. Karlsson has served on design juries internationally, also in the position of chairman of the design jury at the Clio Awards and for Red Dot Design Award. He lectures regularly around the globe and is a member of AGI (Alliance Graphique Internationale). Karlsson was born and raised in Reykjavík, Iceland and studied at Parsons School of Design.

What do you enjoy most about your profession?
We specialise in museum branding and wayfinding, but I love it when our office has a variety of projects going on.

How do you come up with new ideas?
When we start on a new project, my partner and I discuss the project with our senior designer, Connor Muething, and then all of us start sketching and coming up with rough ideas. It is a very collaborative process.

How important is typography in brand design and corporate design?
Very important. I see so many similar typography solutions these days that I'm pleasantly surprised and happy whenever I see something that is a little bit different or new.

01 | 02

Akira Kobayashi
Germany

01 | 02 Tazugane Gothic
Tazugane Gothic is the first Japanese typeface by Monotype. The project is a fusion of my abilities and those of Adrian Frutiger. It is a Japanese typeface that goes well with Neue Frutiger. Art Director: Akira Kobayashi, Designers: Kazuhiro Yamada, Ryota Doi.

Akira Kobayashi, born in 1960, started his career as a type designer at Sha-Ken Co., Ltd. in 1983. In 1989, he studied calligraphy and typography in London. On his return to Japan in 1990, he joined Jiyu-Kobo. From 1993 to 1997, he worked for TypeBank, where he designed a Latin alphabet to match the digital Japanese fonts of the foundry. Afterwards, he became a freelance type designer and won numerous international awards. In 2001, he moved to Germany to assume his current position as type director at Monotype GmbH (formerly Linotype). Akira Kobayashi has also collaborated with the two pre-eminent designers Adrian Frutiger and Hermann Zapf to modernise their earlier type designs. He is a frequent speaker at international type conferences and a juror in international design competitions.

Who or what inspires you?
I am particularly interested in information in the public sector, for instance, the shape of letters on street signs, information boards and hand-painted signs. Their shapes are highly stylised so that beauty/aesthetics and efficiency can coexist.

How important is the choice of typography for the success of a company?
The typeface is the visible "voice" of companies. It conveys their mentality or way of thinking, whether loudly or in a whisper.

Good typography ...
... is like good cutlery or a good cup. One can use them without thinking too much about them, but they are nonetheless completely functional.

Publishing & Print Media   Posters   Typography   Illustrations   Sound Design   Film & Animation   Online   Apps

01 | 02

Prof. Shu-Chang Kung
Taiwan

**01 | 02 Harvest Blessings Pavilion –
2018 Taichung World Flora Exposition**
The poster design represents Taiwanese agriculture and food – rice, fruit, mushrooms and tea. The Harvest Blessings Pavilion hosted many events and exhibitions about Taiwanese agriculture and food.

Professor Shu-Chang Kung studied architecture and design at the Harvard Graduate School of Design and in 1997 established AURA Architects & Associates in Taipei. He is currently professor at the Graduate Institute of Architecture at National Chiao Tung University, Taiwan, and chairman of the board for the Chinese Society of Interior Designers (CSID). His work has received many international awards. Shu-Chang Kung has served as Taiwan's representative at the Hong Kong & Shenzhen Bi-City Biennale of Urbanism/Architecture and at the Next-Gene 20 of the 11th International Architecture Biennale in Venice, both in 2008. He was also the chief curator of the "Taipei Pavilion" at the Hong Kong and Shenzhen Bi-City Biennale of Urbanism/Architecture in 2011–2012 and of the the "Harvest Blessings Pavilion" at the 2018 Taichung World Flora Expo.

What is your design philosophy?
I think design must be based on an essence of human sensibility that responds to our critical environmental challenges and our future way of life.

To what do you pay attention when assessing the submissions?
A good spatial design should express the spirit of the brand with a series of consistent and moving elements.

What advice would you like to pass on to the next generation of designers?
The most important challenge is to retain the essence of human sensibility and interaction. What we want to create is a design that can really move people!

01 | 02

Prof. Laurent Lacour
Germany

01 | 02 Hager Group – Corporate Design
Hager Group is a leading supplier of solutions and services for electrical installations in residential, commercial and industrial buildings. The range of solutions and services extends from energy distribution to cable management and from security systems to building automation.

Professor Laurent Lacour studied visual communication and art at the University of Art and Design in Offenbach, Germany. He is managing partner of the design studio hauser lacour that carries out extensive and award-winning works. These include branding and corporate design projects, among others for Siemens, Swiss Re, Munich Re, De Gruyter Wissenschaftsverlag, Fraport AG and Deutsche Börse Group. Its portfolio also includes projects for clients from the cultural sector, such as Kölner Philharmonie, Museum für Moderne Kunst in Frankfurt or Max-Planck-Institut Florenz. Laurent Lacour has taught at the universities of Zürich, Basel, Karlsruhe and Darmstadt. In 2011, he took up a full professorship at the design department of the University of Applied Sciences in Düsseldorf.

What was your first project as a designer?
After I completed my degree, Ruedi Baur and I developed the corporate design for a German insurance company called Bayerische Rückversicherung. We were following in illustrious footsteps, because the previous communication design had been developed by Otl Aicher and the customer had very fixed, preconceived ideas about the philosophy and value of communication design.

How does one attract attention with the help of design?
By telling good stories and presenting a role model of an extensive holistic approach and by applying both of these to brands and people.

Why are print products still relevant?
The feel of the material, the complexity of the medium and the resulting ability to surprise are still unachievable in the digital context.

01

Johnason Lo
Taiwan

01 Taiwan Golden Melody Awards
The Golden Melody Awards in its 30th year was celebrated with a gathering of legendary and new generation artists.

Johnason Lo is the founder and creative director of JL DESIGN, the first motion design studio in Taiwan, which became a hybrid creative agency as the nature of the projects began to change. Apart from rebranding global channels such as Al Jazeera, Syfy, HBO Asia, FOX Classics Japan, Disney Channel Taiwan and CCTV-9 Documentary Channel, JL DESIGN has worked on films, digital platforms and events. Johnason Lo was one of the three curators for the 2015 Creative Expo Taiwan. Having won awards at PromaxBDA, iF Design Award, Red Dot Award and having featured in international magazines, he has also been regularly invited to speak at international forums such as TEDxTaipei, KL Design Week, Taiwan National Art Exhibition and PromaxBDA Asia Awards.

In your opinion, what characterises a good animation?
Good storytelling is essential because we are not moved by technicality or the art direction alone, but by the story that it wants to tell.

What is the most important aspect when designing digital realities?
At the end of the day, it has to be about humanity. Somehow it has to be human-centred and designed to be fully immersive.

What developments do you expect to see in film and animation over the next five years?
I expect that the experience will become real-time and truly immersive for all of our senses.

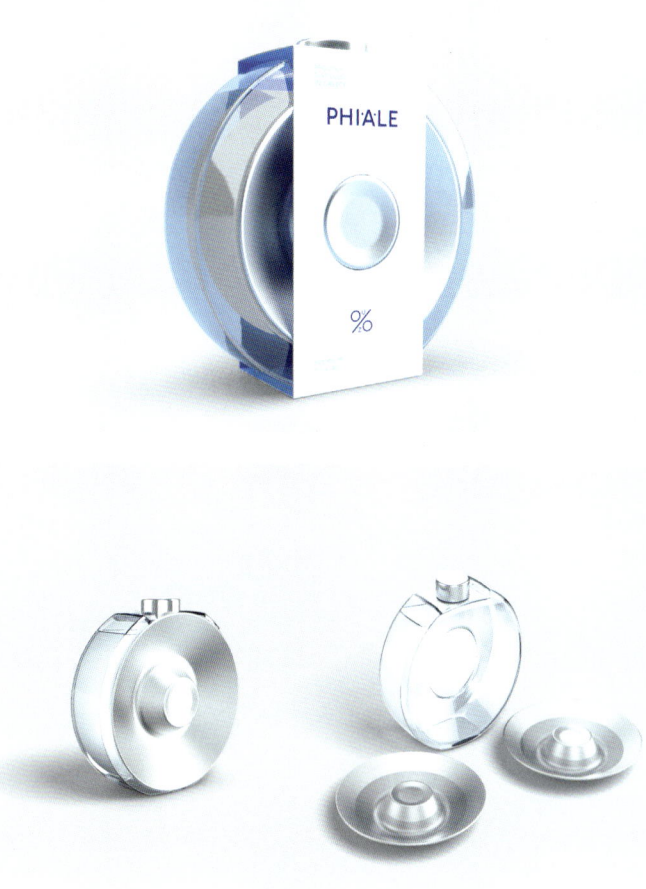

01 | 02

Uwe Melichar
Germany

01 | 02 Phiale
Conceptual development for the brand and packaging of Phiale, a premium ouzo. The idea behind the project is based on the drinking culture of ancient Greece around 500 BC with vessels such as libation bowls.

Uwe Melichar, born in 1968, studied communication design at the Muthesius University in Kiel and has worked at the brand agency FACTOR since 1995. In 1999, he became a managing partner. As head of the packaging division, he has realised projects for adidas, Bosch, C&A, Gardena, Omron and Miele. Together with his team, Uwe Melichar develops packaging and communication design for clients in Japan, Russia, China, the USA and various European countries. He is also a lecturer at several universities, such as the University of Augsburg, is a member of the Type Directors Club New York, and president of the European Brand & Packaging Design Association.

What is your strategy for always being able to come up with new solutions?
Not looking to the right or the left to see what the competition is doing, but to look inwards, forwards and sometimes even into the past at the brand and product history.

What is the biggest challenge in packaging design?
Achieving a balance between protecting the product, communication, appeal and minimal environmental impact.

How will packaging be designed in future?
Packaging will, in the future, manage with the minimal possible use of resources. Sustainability is the driver so that packaging of the future will be geared towards the principles of the circular economy. Simplicity and clarity will be the strongest drivers for design.

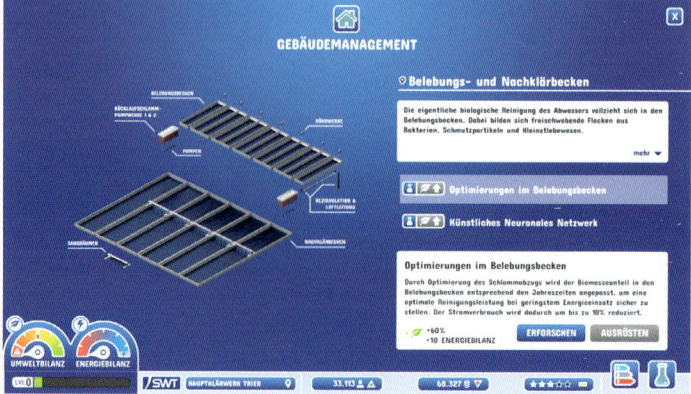

01 | 02

Prof. Dr. Christof Rezk-Salama
Germany

01 | 02 SWT Stadtwerke Trier
Serious game for a sewage treatment plant: school children learn how to build a modern sewage plant which is energy self-sufficient and ecologically beneficial.

Professor Dr. Christof Rezk-Salama studied computer science at the Friedrich-Alexander University in Erlangen/Nuremberg, Germany, and subsequently obtained his PhD with honours. After working as a design engineer at Siemens Medical, he completed his postdoctoral research qualification at the University of Siegen in 2009 with a focus on computer graphics and data visualisation. In 2012, he accepted a professorship for game technology at the University of Applied Sciences in Trier, Germany. Since 2019, he has been co-founder of Skilltree, a company specialised in transferring game technology to industrial applications.

Where does your fascination with game design stem from?
Well-made games make it possible to involve people more in the solution of conflicts than a novel or film can.

What do you enjoy most about your profession?
In the academic world, I enjoy the freedom to follow the area of interest that most fascinates me. In my company, I am stimulated by the challenge of making complex relationships, involving totally different specialist areas, understandable in an entertaining way.

Which user interface/user experience trends have great potential for the future and why?
The enormous value but also the risks of artificial intelligence have been a matter of intense debate for a number of years. I believe the use of artificial intelligence to have great potential if we can use machines as analytical supports in the service of humankind rather than misusing them as replacements for human creativity.

01

Jean Jacques Schaffner
Switzerland

01 Alphanumerix_Mono
Advertising poster for a new font named "Alphanumerix_Mono", based on a 33-element module.

Jean Jacques Schaffner, born in Basel, Switzerland, in 1954, studied graphic design at Basel Art School. This was followed by further training as a photographer and as a TV music director as well as study stays in Paris, London, San Francisco and at the University of Utah. In 1976, he founded Schaffner & Conzelmann Designersfactory in Basel, a full-service communication and design agency and one of the most renowned agencies in Switzerland. Its client portfolio comprises all segments of the economy, public and cultural institutions as well as NGOs. From 2000 to 2003, Jean Jacques Schaffner was president of the European Packaging Design Association. He has also been a member of many design juries.

Is there a project you are especially proud of?
I am and always have been proud of projects that meet high design expectations despite commercial constraints and that manage to combine duty and freedom.

How do you come up with new ideas?
The best ideas always come when I don't think about a project too much. The key is to get to know the facts and then to let go. Most of the time, more ideas surface than one needs and then one is spoilt for choice.

What are the characteristics of good retail design?
In order to be able to assess good retail design, it is critical to analyse the specified task. There is a difference if the design is for a discounter, a chic boutique or a shopping mall. Innovation and inventiveness are possible everywhere.

Publishing & Print Media Posters Typography Illustrations Sound Design Film & Animation Online Apps

01 | 02

Niels Schrader
Netherlands

01 | 02 #What is Design?
"#What is Design?" is a spatial installation of typographic murals on display from 12 April to 29 September 2019 at Droog Amsterdam. It presents Mieke Gerritzen's design manifesto in the form of large-scale slogans and examines the dissolution of the design discipline. The walls create a multilayered visual mapping sourced from the manifesto and online platforms like Google and Twitter. It overwhelms its audience by generating an immersive Facebook wall that again feeds a new publishing cycle of endless visitor selfies and retweets.

Niels Schrader is a concept-driven information designer with a fascination for numbers and data. He is the founder of the Amsterdam-based design studio Mind Design, and member of both, the Alliance Graphique Internationale (AGI) and the advisory panel for the Creative Industries Fund NL. He graduated with a degree in communication design from the University of Applied Sciences in Düsseldorf and completed his academic studies with the master's programme in design at the Sandberg Institute in Amsterdam. In addition to his design practice, Niels Schrader has lectured at various academies and universities in and outside of Europe. Together with Roosje Klap, he is head of the graphic design department and Non-Linear Narrative master's programme at the Royal Academy of Art in The Hague.

How has the design profession changed thanks to developments in technology?
Increasing digitalisation means that the designed products are also less likely to be physical objects. Inevitably, this results in designers increasingly paying less attention to the design of artifacts and more to the design of processes.

How do you attract attention online?
Through media skills and unconventional communication strategies. The emergence of social media has meant that the Internet has split into a wide range of environments for ever smaller special interest groups. Today, a particular communications concept is not enough. More important is the correct mix of platform, message, frequency and timing.

01

Bettina Schulz
Germany

01 novum – World of Graphic Design
The anniversary edition with six cover versions by Hansje van Halem, Fons Hickmann, Mirko Ilić, Q, Holger Windfuhr, Yarza Twins.

Bettina Schulz, born in 1974 in Munich, was editor in chief of the international trade magazine novum World of Graphic Design from 2001 until 2019. She had been a member of the editorial team since 1994 and had also worked as a freelance journalist and copywriter for various international trade magazines and customers in industry. She is a member of a number of juries for international design competitions (e.g. the European Design Awards, Designpreis der Stadt München, Best of Content Marketing, Global Illustration Award, DesignEuropa Awards, IIIDawards). She is furthermore a founding member of the Creative Paper Conference and set up her own copywriting and editorial agency in Munich in July 2019.

Which developments in the realm of print do you find particularly noteworthy at present?
The variety of the printing industry and their refinements are in the process of being rediscovered. Old techniques are being applied once more and are being reinterpreted. Approachable, authentic communication is easier to achieve with print which appeals to more than just the visual sense.

How can an annual report impress you?
If it makes the most of the opportunity to convey the company philosophy credibly and gets the receiver on its side emotionally by means of storytelling. Documenting economic success must be combined with the communication of values in order to paint a full picture of a company.

01 | 02

Sylvia Vitale Rotta
France

01 La vache qui rit
The packaging design for the organic cheese of the French brand "La vache qui rit" (The Laughing Cow) by Bel was guided by iconicity, simplicity, naturalness and proximity.

02 Volvic
The packaging design for the new eight-litre bottle of Volvic, the natural mineral water, follows an approach that is iconic, consumer-friendly and ever more responsible. In collaboration with the Danone Research Packaging Center, Team Créatif imagined a 100 per cent R-PET bottle with a paper label that is easy to carry and has a lighter cap. Engraved handles at the base make the bottle easier to use and compress for recycling.

Sylvia Vitale Rotta, born in Tanzania, studied at the London School of Arts. Together with Nick Craig she founded Team Creatif in 1986. Today, it is a group of four agencies, which include branding & packaging, retail, market services, and a production & digital platform. Team Creatif has become a reference for branding and packaging identity on the international market, working in 52 countries worldwide with 250 employees. In 2008, Sylvia Vitale Rotta was appointed president of the first design jury at Eurobest and, in 2009, acted as president of the design category at Cannes Lions. In 2013, she was part of the jury at Dubai Lynx. She has given classes at Parisian schools such as Istec and Estacom, Intuit Lab and has also participated in the TedxParis conference. In 2017, she received a knighthood from the French Ministry of Foreign Affairs which is awarded in recognition of an exceptional design career spanning more than 30 years.

Which part of the design process do you particularly enjoy?
The ideation part where the ideas are actually found, then the execution of the idea where every single detail counts.

Why are print products still popular?
Because of the sensation people get when they touch or stroke the paper and sometimes even because of the smell.

Which innovations are you noticing in the realm of print at present?
The incredible choice of inks, with their colours and brightness ranging from metallic to pearl to deep matt hues and their infinite textures.

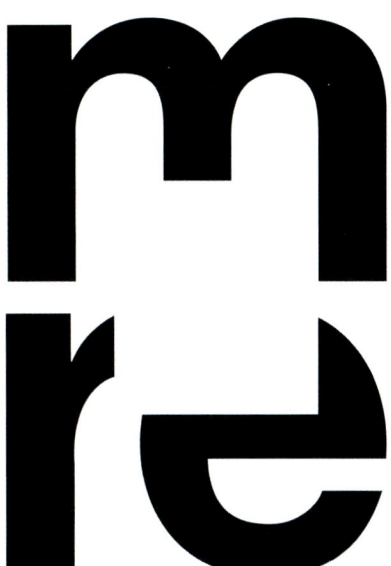
01

Thilo von Debschitz
Germany

01 Museum Reinhard Ernst
Logotype for the Museum Reinhard Ernst, a new museum of abstract art that is being constructed in Wiesbaden and should open in 2022.

Thilo von Debschitz studied communication design at the RheinMain University of Applied Sciences in Germany. After positions as an art director in various companies, he founded the Q design agency in Wiesbaden in 1997 together with Laurenz Nielbock. The agency has since won numerous international awards. In addition to his agency work, Thilo von Debschitz writes books with a focus on the visual arts. He attracted great attention with the rediscovery of the infographics pioneer Fritz Kahn and the publication of a monograph dedicated to him. Thilo von Debschitz has taught at the RheinMain University of Applied Sciences and at the IMK, the Institute of Marketing and Communication in Wiesbaden. Today, he is also a regular guest speaker at conferences on the topic of design.

Do you prefer to play safe or to experiment? Why?
Both are important and both are possible; it depends on the assignment and the willingness of the customer to take risks. A safe option which is acceptable to one customer may be completely out of the question for another.

Which part of the design process do you particularly enjoy?
Once the content input of a task has largely been completed and the first concepts are ready, suddenly a whole lot of doors start opening up. That is always a special moment.

To what do you pay particular attention when assessing publications?
The triad of ideas for content, creative energy and excellent implementation.

Publishing & Print Media   Posters   Typography   Illustrations   Sound Design   Film & Animation   Online   Apps

01

Holger Windfuhr
Germany

01 Newspaper Cover
Three different carnival mask designs were printed on the cover of a broadsheet newspaper special section in a split run. All of them to be cut out, pasted on thicker paper and worn. Illustrations: Tim McDonagh.

Born and raised in the United States, Holger Windfuhr studied psychology at the University of Michigan and graphic design at the U5 Academy in Munich. In 2010, he completed the Kellogg-WHU Executive MBA Programme. He began his career as a member of the development team at "Focus" magazine and then moved to the German edition of "Forbes". After co-founding the digital consulting agency "The Media Machine" in New York, he joined "Money" magazine at Time Inc. and then "House & Garden" at Condé Nast. Returning to Germany, he redesigned "impulse" at Gruner+Jahr. From 2000 to 2016, he was the creative head of the German business magazine "WirtschaftsWoche" and guided the visual aesthetics of the brand. Since 2017 Holger Windfuhr has been the art director of the German newspaper "Frankfurter Allgemeine Zeitung", since September 2018 also of "Frankfurter Allgemeine Woche". He is a member of the Art Directors Club and has won numerous design awards.

How can a publication impress you at first glance?
With an original take on the topic – without "overselling" it. Or by visually approaching the topic from different, unusual angles that add depth to the topic. Surprise me!

How does typography contribute to a publication?
By making it easy to read, for one. The choice of font should also subtly support the content and subconsciously deliver an emotional component.

Good communication design ...
... appeals to the brain and to the heart.

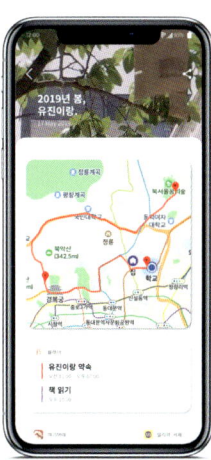

01

Prof. Dr. Seung Hun Yoo
South Korea

01 LG Cloud Archiving Service
User experience design by Seung Hun Yoo and Sumin Ahn. Users' data on application usage, multimedia files, timeline events and file sharing with co-workers are automatically curated on the company supporting data space just one touch away from the lock screen.

Professor Dr. Seung Hun Yoo is the founder of the CO:UX Design Lab at the School of Art & Design, Korea University. He holds a master's degree in design and a PhD in industrial engineering. He has worked at Samsung Mobile among others and designed many of the company's flagship mobile handsets. After seven years of working as UX Director at Samsung's Korea headquarters and at design offices in the USA, he began working at Korea University in cognitive UX design research studies and education in 2012. His CO:UX Design Lab performs UX design based on users' cognitive behaviour research. Seung Hun Yoo and his team are currently conducting cross-disciplinary UX design projects such as transparent UX display design, medical UX design and next-generation wearable devices.

Are there design principles that you always adhere to?
My design research field encompasses both design-based approaches and theoretical methods based on cognitive engineering. A beautiful artefact design, which is grounded in a solid understanding of the way in which users process the information, is what I always highlight in real design projects.

Which developments in user experience design have the greatest potential for the future? Why?
AI applied design has lots of potential for users and designers, but the field is not limited to the visual dimension. AI both challenges and expands the role of designers. With AI, we are at the portal of a new era of design.

Index Designers

0–9

2YOLK
www.2yolk-branding.com
Vol. 2: 84
Vol. 1: 98, 99, 163

A

ABCdesign
www.abcdesign.ru
Vol. 2: 20

ADITO Software GmbH
www.adito.de
Vol. 2: 324, 510

ÅF Sound & Vibration
www.afconsult.com/
soundandvibration
Vol. 2: 134

Alt Group
www.altgroup.net
Vol. 2: 37, 385
Vol. 1: 457

amoeba
www.amoeba.co.kr
Vol. 2: 220–221

anschlaege.de
www.anschlaege.de
Vol. 2: 21

Ansichtssache GmbH & Co. KG
www.ansichtssache.de
Vol. 2: 52
Vol. 1: 297

Art Light Design Consultants, Inc.
www.artlight.com.tw
Vol. 2: 56

Artificial Rome GmbH
www.artificialrome.com
Vol. 2: 261, 368–369, 511

asisi
www.asisi.de
Vol. 2: 386

B

Uladzimir Bahatyrevich
SCAD Savannah College of
Art and Design
www.scad.edu
www.vlad.us.com
Vol. 2: 470

Bai Yan
Vol. 2: 501

Baidu Online Network Technology
(Beijing) Co., Ltd.
www.baidu.com
Vol. 2: 296–297

Julia Baldauf
www.juliabaldauf.at
Vol. 2: 449

Didac Ballester
www.didacballester.com
Vol. 2: 196

banda.agency
www.banda.agency
Vol. 2: 140–141, 161, 512
Vol. 1: 84–85, 88–89, 156, 166, 545

Bär Tiger Wolf GmbH
www.baertigerwolf.de
Vol. 2: 148

BASIC®
www.basicagency.com
Vol. 2: 186–187

Beetroot Design Group
www.beetroot.gr
Vol. 2: 72–73, 114, 115, 126, 142, 513
Vol. 1: 86–87, 288, 546

beierarbeit GmbH
www.beierarbeit.de
Vol. 2: 99, 129, 404

Berry Creative
www.berrycreative.fi
Vol. 2: 54–55, 123

Better
www.better.care
Vol. 2: 350, 514

BİŞEYLER New Media Works
www.biseyler.com.tr
Vol. 2: 405

Blackmagic Design
www.blackmagicdesign.com
Vol. 2: 252–253, 344–345, 515

Mackinzi Blank, Daniel Benedict, Meshal Almazyad, Samantha Klein
SCAD Savannah College of
Art and Design
www.scad.edu
Vol. 2: 488

BLCH Ltd.
www.blch.co
Vol. 2: 65

BOND
www.bond-agency.com
Vol. 2: 123

Bonfire Labs
www.bonfirelabs.com
Vol. 2: 158

Born05
www.born05.com
Vol. 2: 198, 284

Nina Botthof
www.nina-b.at
Vol. 2: 429

Box Brand Design Ltd.
www.boxbranddesign.com
Vol. 2: 400
Vol. 1: 353

Branders Group AG
www.branders.ch
Vol. 2: 23

brandneo GmbH
www.brandneo.de
Vol. 2: 325

Bronce Estudio
http://broncestudio.com
Vol. 2: 28–29, 516

BROTLOS Verlag
www.brotlos-verlag.de
Vol. 2: 122

Bruce B.
corporate communication GmbH
www.bruce-b.com
Vol. 2: 18–19, 517

ATELIER BRÜCKNER
www.atelier-brueckner.com
Vol. 2: 374–375, 518

bueroparallel GmbH
www.bueroparallel.de
Vol. 2: 182

Büro Grotesk
www.buero-grotesk.de
Vol. 2: 192

C

CaderaDesign GmbH
www.caderadesign.de
Vol. 2: 358–359

CADS GmbH
www.cads.at
Vol. 2: 361

Henrik Callerstrand Design
www.callerstrand.com
Vol. 2: 24

Cee Cee Creative
www.ceeceecreative.com
Vol. 2: 33

Yi-Tzu Chan, Ting-Wei Liao,
Tzu-Ning Hsu, Szu-Yu Chen,
Ji-Cheng Luo, Kuo-Ming Tsou
Ling Tung University
www.ltu.edu.tw
Vol. 2: 450

Cheetah Mobile
www.cmcm.com
Vol. 2: 278

Cheil Germany GmbH
www.cheil.de
Vol. 2: 152–153, 214, 390
Vol. 1: 269

Chen Bolan
Vol. 2: 501

Huei-Tai Chen
Pratt Institute
www.pratt.edu
Vol. 2: 485

Li-Ying Chen
Asia University
www.asia.edu.tw
Vol. 2: 453

Shuai-Nan Chen,
Rou-An Chen, Qi-Min Lin
Department of Visual
Communication Design
Shu-Te University
www.vcd.stu.edu.tw
Vol. 2: 444

Yian Chen, Chun-Ming Lin,
Xin-Ling Hong, Wei-Shan Ruei
Department of Visual
Communication Design
China University of Technology
www.cute.edu.tw
Vol. 2: 506

Chen Yu-Chun
www.behance.net/
gallery/78389939/-Paper-Lion
Vol. 2: 445

Yu-Xuan Chen, Chia-Chun Hsieh,
Yi-Hua Ding, Cian-Mu Li,
Guang-Qin Lin, Man-Hsuan Chang
Cheng Shiu University
www.csu.edu.tw
Vol. 2: 502

Chen Zhigang
Vol. 2: 501

Shu-Yun Cheng, Chia-Hsuan Yang,
Chia-An Lin, Meng-Chu Hsu
National Taichung University
of Science and Technology
www.nutc.edu.tw
Vol. 2: 432

I-Ching Chiang, Yee-Teng Chan,
Yu-Tzu Lee, Ci-Zhen Xu,
Yu-Ying Yan
Ling Tung University
www.ltu.edu.tw
Vol. 2: 498

Rung Chiang, Chia-Hui Feng
Chaoyang University of Technology
www.cyut.edu.tw
Vol. 2: 440

China Mobile (Hangzhou)
Information Technology
www.chinamobileltd.com
Vol. 2: 320

CLEVER°FRANKE
www.cleverfranke.com
Vol. 2: 204, 275, 305

clicksgefühle GmbH & Co KG
www.clicksgefühle.at
Vol. 2: 210

COBE Architects
www.cobe.dk
Vol. 2: 401

COBE GmbH
www.cobeisfresh.com
Vol. 2: 294, 302

Communication University
of Zhejiang
www.zjicm.edu.cn
Vol. 2: 70–71, 112, 113, 526

Publishing & Print Media   Posters   Typography   Illustrations   Sound Design   Film & Animation   Online   Apps

Index Designers

COW Inspiration Group
www.cowgroup.co.kr
Vol. 2: 408, 409

Creative ZOO A/S
www.czoo.dk
Vol. 2: 46

Custom Interactions GmbH
www.custom-interactions.com
Vol. 2: 362–363, 519

cyclos design GmbH
www.cyclos-design.de
Vol. 2: 197
Vol. 1: 192

D
Dallas Sthlm AB
www.dallas.se
Vol. 2: 166

Daresay
www.daresay.co
Vol. 2: 235, 271

Das Buro
Branding Agency
www.dasburo.nl
Vol. 2: 85

Agnė Dautartaitė-Krutulė
www.typography.lt
Vol. 2: 10–11, 520

dayy GmbH
www.dayy.de
Vol. 2: 242

DBstudio
www.dbstudio.cc
Vol. 2: 22

Lidia De Oleo, Maya Zimmer,
Nathasya Effendy,
Steven Ou, Ryan Stifler
SCAD Savannah College of
Art and Design
www.scad.edu
Vol. 2: 489

DeepL GmbH
www.deepl.com
Vol. 2: 188–189, 266–267

Demodern GmbH
www.demodern.com
Vol. 2: 340

denkwerk
www.denkwerk.com
Vol. 2: 176, 188–189, 266–267, 521

Dentsu Taiwan Inc.
www.dentsu.com.tw
Vol. 2: 76–77

Depart./Tokyu Agency Inc.
www.tokyu-agc.co.jp
Vol. 2: 78, 143

Depot branding agency
www.depotwpf.com
Vol. 2: 83
Vol. 1: 97, 148–149, 311, 313, 433, 558

Dept
www.deptagency.com
Vol. 2: 260

Dertien12
www.dertien12.be
Vol. 2: 377

Design3 GmbH
www.design3.de
Vol. 2: 285

designaffairs GmbH
www.designaffairs.com
Vol. 2: 280–281

Designfever
www.designfever.com
Vol. 2: 156, 190

Designit
www.designit.com
Vol. 2: 360

Deutsche Bahn
DB Fernverkehr AG
www.deutschebahn.com
Vol. 2: 286–287, 522

Deutsche Bank AG
www.deutsche-bank.de
Vol. 2: 290–291

Deutsche Telekom AG
www.telekom.com
Vol. 2: 330–331

Katharina Diem
www.katharinadiem.com
Vol. 2: 430, 463

digital broking GmbH
www.meinmvp.de
Vol. 2: 326

Qi Dong
Xi'an Jiaotong University
www.xjtu.edu.cn
Vol. 2: 57

Dot Incorporation
www.dotincorp.com
Vol. 2: 170–171, 268, 523

Jim Downer
SCAD Savannah College of
Art and Design
www.scad.edu
Vol. 2: 475

DR Design
www.drdesign.org
Vol. 2: 97

E
Eat, Sleep + Design
www.eatsleepanddesign.com
Vol. 2: 118–119, 144–145, 524

ECARX DESIGN
www.ecarx.com.cn
Vol. 2: 308

EIGA Design
www.eiga.de
Vol. 2: 401
Vol. 1: 171, 238

Elastique. GmbH
www.elastique.de
Vol. 2: 257, 391

Ergosign GmbH
www.ergosign.de
Vol. 2: 347

F
Facit Research GmbH & Co. KG
www.facit-group.com
Vol. 2: 49

Bojana Fajmut
www.linkedin.com/in/
bojana-fajmut-49796824
Vol. 2: 39

familie redlich AG
www.familie-redlich.de
Vol. 2: 378–379

Cheng-Tsung Feng Design Studio
www.chengtsung.com
Vol. 2: 382–383, 384

Bismark Fernandes
SCAD Savannah College of
Art and Design
www.scad.edu
www.bismarkfernandes.com
Vol. 2: 474

Filmstyler Pictures GmbH
www.filmstyler.com
Vol. 2: 167

Finnair Oyj
www.finnair.com
Vol. 2: 288

FJCU
Fu Jen Catholic University
www.fju.edu.tw
Vol. 2: 102, 533
Vol. 1: 134–135, 571

Flatfy OÜ
www.flatfy.com
Vol. 2: 229, 270

forwerts interactive GmbH
www.forwerts.com
Vol. 2: 286–287, 522

Freshheads
www.freshheads.com
Vol. 2: 211, 228

FRUM
www.frum.co.kr
Vol. 2: 154–155, 200–201, 525

Fuenfwerken Design AG
www.fuenfwerken.com
Vol. 2: 339
Vol. 1: 155, 162, 478–479

FUJIFILM Corporation
http://design.fujifilm.com
Vol. 2: 351

Shenzhen Future Life Product
Planning Design Co., Ltd.
www.c-idea.com
Vol. 2: 70–71, 526

G
Gagarin
www.gagarin.is
Vol. 2: 109, 246–247, 256, 527

Xinyu Gan
Shanghai Publishing and
Printing College
www.sppc.edu.cn
Vol. 2: 478–479

Xinyu Gan, Yejia Qian
Shanghai Publishing and
Printing College
www.sppc.edu.cn
Vol. 2: 446–447, 572

GENERATIONDESIGN GmbH
www.generationdesign.de
Vol. 2: 234

GIANTSTEP
www.giantstep.co.kr
Vol. 2: 154–155

Gláma•Kim
www.glamakim.is
Vol. 2: 109, 256

Suk Go
www.sook.today
Vol. 2: 483

Google
https://store.google.com
Vol. 2: 186–187

Grass Jelly Studio
www.grassjelly.tv
Vol. 2: 147

Great Apes/HiQ Finland
www.greatapes.fi
Vol. 2: 191, 248–249, 376, 528

Grey Germany/KW43
BRANDDESIGN
www.grey.com/germany
Vol. 2: 75, 82, 86, 402
Vol. 1: 6–17, 157, 169, 577

Mei-Xiu Guo, Chia-Yu Liu,
Fang-Yi Lin
National Taichung University
of Science and Technology
www.nutc.edu.tw
Vol. 2: 499

H
Haier Innovation Design Center
www.haier.com
Vol. 2: 310, 311, 315

Haselwanter Grafik_und Design
www.haselwanter.cc
Vol. 2: 53

Hegii Co., Ltd.
www.hegii.com
Vol. 2: 96

Index Designers

Heine Warnecke Design GmbH
www.heinewarnecke.com
Vol. 2: 38
Vol. 1: 328–329

Helmig Bergerhausen
www.helmigbergerhausen.de
Vol. 2: 265

Herren der Schöpfung
www.herrenderschoepfung.com
Vol. 2: 199

hesign International GmbH
www.hesign.com
Vol. 2: 6–7, 529

HID Human
Interface Design GmbH
www.human-interface.de
Vol. 2: 348–349

HMI Project GmbH
www.hmi-project.com
Vol. 2: 352, 353

Hochschule Mainz
University of Applied Sciences
www.hs-mainz.de
Vol. 2: 101

HOLYDESIGN
www.holydesign.cn
Vol. 2: 68–69, 530

Home Hotel
www.homehotel.com.tw
Vol. 2: 387, 567

Jia-Qi Hong
Fuzhou University of
International Studies and Trade
www.fzfu.com
Vol. 2: 458

hongdesign Ltd.
www.hongdesign.com
Vol. 2: 127

An-Chiao Hsiao, Jia-Fu Lin,
Yi-Xuan Chen, Jie-Ling Tsai,
Yi-Ning Su
Department of Visual
Communication Design
Shu-Te University
www.vcd.stu.edu.tw
Vol. 2: 503

Yi-Jung Hsiao, Wei-Hong Xue,
Zhi-Yun Zheng, Ting-Yu Yao,
Yi-Lun Li, Ren-Qi Jin
Department of Visual
Communication Design
Shu-Te University
www.vcd.stu.edu.tw
Vol. 2: 425

Celia Hsu
SCAD Savannah College of
Art and Design
www.scad.edu
www.seesawpig.com
Vol. 2: 473

Xi-Xuan Hu, Xiao-Li Lin,
Xiao-Jie Yin
Fuzhou University of
International Studies and Trade
www.fzfu.com
Vol. 2: 460–461

Huawei Technologies Co., Ltd.
www.huawei.com
Vol. 2: 254–255, 323, 334, 335, 531

Hubei Fine Arts Publishing House
www.guanshanjue.com
Vol. 2: 59

Lisa Huber
www.behance.net/lisa_huber1b67e
Vol. 2: 436, 532

Hufax Arts
www.hufax.com.tw
Vol. 2: 102, 533
Vol. 1: 134–135, 571

Hazel Hwang
SCAD Savannah College of
Art and Design
www.scad.edu
Vol. 2: 443

I

IBM Studios
www.ibm.com/design
Vol. 2: 327

Jeykhun Imanov Studio
www.jis.az
Vol. 2: 195

inDare Design Strategy Limited
www.indare.love
Vol. 2: 103

InFormat Design Curating
www.informat-design.com.tw
Vol. 2: 396–397

Sergio Ingravalle
www.maivisto.de
Vol. 2: 120–121, 534

Inition Inc.
UX Design Studio
www.inition.kr
Vol. 2: 272–273

INNOCEAN
Worldwide Europe GmbH
www.innocean.eu
Vol. 2: 199

innogy SE
www.innogy.com
Vol. 2: 241, 289

innovation mecom GmbH
www.innovationmecom.de
Vol. 2: 306–307

Interactive Media
Foundation gGmbH
www.interactivemedia-
foundation.com
www.dastotaletanztheater.com
Vol. 2: 261, 368–369

Interactive Pioneers
www.interactive-pioneers.de
Vol. 2: 174–175, 535

intive GmbH
www.intive.com
Vol. 2: 313

IP Deutschland GmbH
www.ip.de
Vol. 2: 49

iPrefer Digital Integrated
Marketing Co., Ltd.
www.iprefer.com.tw
Vol. 2: 159, 536

Isobar iProspect SA
www.isobar.com
Vol. 2: 150

J

JAC-Gestaltung
www.jac-gestaltung.de
Vol. 2: 34

jäger&jäger
www.jaegerundjaeger.de
Vol. 2: 42, 203

jangled nerves gmbh
www.janglednerves.com
Vol. 2: 132–133, 537

Xinyi Jiang, Siting Xu, Hsinni Lo
Department of Visual
Communication Design
China University of Technology
www.cute.edu.tw
Vol. 2: 434

Jiangxi Normal University
www.jxnu.edu.cn
Vol. 2: 74

Jingdezhen Ceramic Institute
Vol. 2: 113

Ruo-Ya Juan
Cheng Shiu University
www.csu.edu.tw
Vol. 2: 435

K

Tessa Kaczenski
Vol. 2: 462

King Kong Wave Production
www.facebook.com/kingkongwave
Vol. 2: 387, 567

Kitcast Inc.
www.kitcast.tv
Vol. 2: 328

Klangerfinder GmbH & Co KG
www.klangerfinder.de
Vol. 2: 132–133, 136, 537

Klim Type Foundry
www.klim.co.nz
Vol. 2: 385

kontrastmoment GmbH
www.kontrastmoment.de
Vol. 2: 388, 538

Johanna Kurz
www.kurzjohanna.at
Vol. 2: 448

Kuudes Kerros
www.kuudes.com
Vol. 2: 26
Vol. 1: 348

KW43 BRANDDESIGN
www.kw43.de
Vol. 2: 75, 82, 86, 402
Vol. 1: 6–17, 157, 169, 577

Kyowon
Wells Design Lab
www.kyowonwells.com
Vol. 2: 309

L

L+R
www.levinriegner.com
Vol. 2: 403, 539

Landor Hamburg
www.landor.com
Vol. 2: 87, 128, 194
Vol. 1: 170

Xiao-Fan Lao, Hsiao-Wen Huang,
Hsuan-Hsuan Li, Wen-Hsuan Chiu,
Jae-Oh Park
Ling Tung University
www.ltu.edu.tw
Vol. 2: 504

Edward Lau
LASALLE College of the Arts
www.lasalle.edu.sg
Vol. 2: 412–415, 540

Christian Leban
www.christianleban.com
Vol. 2: 465

Cheng-Chun Lee,
Jing-Yan Liu, Yi-Rong Que
Department of Visual
Communication Design
Shu-Te University
www.vcd.stu.edu.tw
Vol. 2: 500

Connie Lee
SCAD Savannah College of
Art and Design
www.scad.edu
Vol. 2: 451

Ka-Hyun Lee, Graeme Smith,
Aby Iberkleid, Oscar Kwong
SCAD Savannah College of
Art and Design
www.scad.edu
Vol. 2: 484

Sunghee Lee
Vol. 2: 486–487

Publishing & Print Media   Posters   Typography   Illustrations   Sound Design   Film & Animation   Online   Apps

Index Designers

Yu-Chih Lee, Kui-Shang Wong,
Chia-Hui Ting, Qiao-Ru Zeng,
Yu-Ping Tsai
Department of Visual
Communication Design
Shu-Te University
www.vcd.stu.edu.tw
Vol. 2: 416–417, 541
Vol. 1: 516

Leopard Mobile
www.cmcm.com
Vol. 2: 279

Maria Leutner
www.marialeutner.com
Vol. 2: 47

LG Electronics Inc.
www.lg.com
Vol. 2: 264, 299, 304, 312, 333

LG Uplus
www.uplus.co.kr
Vol. 2: 217, 220–221, 222–223

Chaosheng Li
Zhejiang Gongshang University
www.zjgsu.edu.cn
Vol. 2: 81

Hannah Li
SCAD Savannah College of
Art and Design
www.scad.edu
www.hannahliart.com
Vol. 2: 494

Li Tung-Lin
www.behance.net/
gallery/78389939/-Paper-Lion
Vol. 2: 445

Guo-Da Lin, Feng Luo,
Kai-Qiang Hou
Fuzhou University of
International Studies and Trade
www.fzfu.com
Vol. 2: 493, 574

Yibay Lin, Xinyi Chou, Houhsin Lee
Department of Visual
Communication Design
China University of Technology
www.cute.edu.tw
Vol. 2: 507

Yu-Ju Lin
National Taipei University
of Business
www.ntub.edu.tw
Vol. 2: 104–105
Vol. 1: 468–469

Yu-Rung Lin, Yu-Mei Chen,
Huan-Hsuan Lee, Yu-Heng Chen
Ling Tung University
www.ltu.edu.tw
Vol. 2: 492

Yu-Yan Lin, Xue-Qin Lin, Min Hung
Fuzhou University of
International Studies and Trade
www.fzfu.com
Vol. 2: 459

Lin Zhiyun
www.behance.net/spider_lin37f5
Vol. 2: 501, 542

Little Voice (BYOD & DIY) Ltd.
www.littlevoice.io
Vol. 2: 282, 543

Ching-Wei Liu
Asia University
www.asia.edu.tw
Vol. 2: 466

Yi-Ting Liu, Yu-Chiao Chang,
Yuan-Hsiang Chiu, Yi-Xiu Zheng,
Ching-Wen Chuang, Ci-Yi Wang
Ling Tung University
www.ltu.edu.tw
Vol. 2: 424

Yun-Xuan Liu, Yu-Ru Liu,
Yu-Han Chang, Chih-Hao Wu
Department of Visual
Communication Design
China University of Technology
www.cute.edu.tw
Vol. 2: 420–421, 544

Logitech
www.logitech.com
Vol. 2: 157, 158

Lollypop Design Studio
www.lollypop.design
Vol. 2: 314

Chun-Yi Lu, Jing-Wen Huang,
Wei-Ju Chen
Chaoyang University of Technology
www.cyut.edu.tw
Vol. 2: 439

Luxlotusliner
www.luxlotusliner.de
Vol. 2: 124–125, 164–165

M

m.Doc GmbH
www.mdoc.one
Vol. 2: 178–179

m.i.r. media
www.mir.de
Vol. 2: 202

Make Architects
www.makearchitects.com
Vol. 2: 32

Maegan Mann
SCAD Savannah College of
Art and Design
www.scad.edu
www.maeganmann.com
Vol. 2: 471

ManvsMachine
www.mvsm.com
Vol. 2: 157

Atelier Markgraph GmbH
www.markgraph.de
Vol. 2: 372–373, 404, 545

Media4th & Company, Inc.
www.media4thncompany.co.kr
Vol. 2: 293, 563

Merry Go Round Inc.
www.mgrstudio.net
Vol. 2: 160, 546

MetaDesign Beijing
www.metadesign.com
Vol. 2: 137

METER Group Inc.
www.metergroup.com
Vol. 2: 12–13, 547

MHP Management- und
IT-Beratung GmbH
www.mhp.com
Vol. 2: 322

Cara Mielzarek
www.caramielzarek.eu
Vol. 2: 462

Milkinside
www.dribbble.com/glebich
Vol. 2: 240

Milla & Partner
www.milla.de
Vol. 2: 398

minigram
Studio für Markendesign GmbH
www.minigram.de
Vol. 2: 36

MIUI Design Team
Beijing Xiaomi
Mobile Software Co., Ltd.
www.mi.com
Vol. 2: 135, 298, 548

MKTG Finland
www.mktg.fi
Vol. 2: 248–249, 376

Moët Hennessy Taiwan
Jas Hennessy (Far East) Ltd.,
Taiwan Branch
www.lvmh.com
Vol. 2: 159, 536

Olga Moiseeva, Yuliya Kritskaya,
Michail Dubovik, Pavel Popko,
Artem Nekrasov, Uliana Kovalenko,
Vitaliy Korolev, Sergey Galtsev,
Ekaterina Zhokhova
British Higher School of
Art & Design
www.britishdesign.ru
Vol. 2: 422–423, 549

Monotype
www.monotype.com
Vol. 2: 92–93, 550

muehlhausmoers corporate
communications gmbh
www.muehlhausmoers.com
Vol. 2: 61

Leena Murdeshwar
SCAD Savannah College of
Art and Design
www.scad.edu
www.leenamurdeshwar.com
Vol. 2: 480

Must App Corp.
www.mustapp.com
Vol. 2: 219, 551

MUTABOR
www.mutabor.de
Vol. 2: 50, 94–95, 180, 406, 552
Vol. 1: 193, 228, 464

Designstudio Mathilda Mutant
www.instagram.com/
mathildamutant
Vol. 2: 100

N

Artem Nekrasov, Vitaliy Korolev
British Higher School of
Art & Design
www.britishdesign.ru
Vol. 2: 422–423, 549

New Cat Orange
www.new-cat-orange.de
Vol. 2: 48

newtype Imageworks, Inc.
www.newtype.design
Vol. 2: 336–337, 553

NiEW Design
www.niew.it
Vol. 2: 354–355, 356–357, 554

nodesign
www.nodesign.com
Vol. 2: 51

O

OBBA
www.o-bba.com
Vol. 2: 377

One Plus Partnership Limited
www.onepluspartnership.com
Vol. 2: 389, 555

Opera Software AS
www.opera.com
Vol. 2: 262–263

Optimist GmbH
www.optimistinc.com
Vol. 2: 370–371, 556

Orchid Creation
www.orchidcreation.com
Vol. 2: 108

Otium
www.otium.tv
Vol. 2: 8–9, 557

OUTERMEDIA GmbH
www.outermedia.de
Vol. 2: 206

Index Designers

Overman
www.overman.kr
Vol. 2: 183, 558

Overtone
www.overtone.dk
Vol. 2: 97

P

Daniel Paiva
SCAD Savannah College of
Art and Design
www.scad.edu
Vol. 2: 464

Gabor Palotai Design
www.gaborpalotai.com
Vol. 2: 117

PAO Sberbank of Russia
www.sberbank.ru
Vol. 2: 243

Philips Design
www.philips.com
Vol. 2: 230, 233

Phoenix Design
www.phoenixdesign.com
Vol. 2: 232

Plan.Net Group
www.serviceplan.com
Vol. 2: 225
Vol. 1: 90–91, 591

POLARWERK GmbH
www.polarwerk.de
Vol. 2: 25
Vol. 1: 225

Possible Moscow
www.possiblegroup.ru
Vol. 2: 177, 185
Vol. 1: 250–251, 439, 592

PPW Korea
www.ppwkorea.com
Vol. 2: 407
Vol. 1: 140

Julia Prinz
Vol. 2: 462

Proximity
BBDO Russia Group
https://bbdogroup.ru
Vol. 2: 292

Marcell Puskás
www.behance.net/puskaas
Vol. 2: 45

Q

Mackenzie Quick
SCAD Savannah College of
Art and Design
www.scad.edu
Vol. 2: 495

Quinsay Design
www.quinsaydesign.com
Vol. 2: 90–91, 559

R

raumHOCH GmbH
www.raumhoch.de
Vol. 2: 339

raumkontakt GmbH
www.raumkontakt.de
Vol. 2: 43, 380
Vol. 1: 212–213, 595

Reaktor Oy
www.reaktor.com
Vol. 2: 288

Resoluut
www.resoluut.com
Vol. 2: 239, 295

Right Brain
www.rightbrain.co.kr
Vol. 2: 217, 222–223

Roca Sanitario, S.A
www.roca.es
Vol. 2: 394–395
Vol. 1: 266–267

RT
www.rt.com
https://romanovs100.com
Vol. 2: 258–259

S

S12 GmbH
www.s12.de
Vol. 2: 136

Saatchi & Saatchi Ukraine
www.saatchi.com.ua
Vol. 2: 392

SAM CHUV
www.sam-chuv.ch
Vol. 2: 14–15, 560

Samsung Electronics
www.samsung.com
Vol. 2: 343

Samsung SDS
CX Innovation Team
www.samsungsds.com
Vol. 2: 226, 321, 342

SAP SE
User Experience Design for
Sports and Entertainment
www.sap.com
Vol. 2: 224, 300, 301, 561

Katharina Saurer
www.katharinasaurer.com
Vol. 2: 431

Schenck Process Europe GmbH
www.schenckprocess.com
Vol. 2: 362–363

Hanns Schmid Grafikdesign
www.hannsschmid.ch
Vol. 2: 80

SCHMIDHUBER
www.schmidhuber.de
Vol. 2: 406

Julia Schmidt, Katharina Lifke,
Sandra Bosse, Flora Taubner
Faculty of Design
HAWK University of
Applied Sciences and Arts
www.hawk.de
Vol. 2: 428

Lars Schrage – buero fuer
gestaltung
www.schragelars.eu
Vol. 2: 433

Serious Business
www.serious.business
Vol. 2: 151

SERVICEPLAN GERMANY
www.serviceplan.com
Vol. 2: 12–13, 162, 163, 170–171,
227, 268, 523, 547
Vol. 1: 248–249, 252–253, 254, 257,
261, 265, 270, 364, 598, 599

Serviceplan Group
www.serviceplan.com
Vol. 2: 60

Shih Chien University
Department of Communications
Design
www.usc.edu.tw
Vol. 2: 146, 562

Ying-Hua Shih, Meng-Xuan Li,
Zi-Qi Liu, Li-Xin Wang,
Wun-Jie Chen
Ling Tung University
www.ltu.edu.tw
Vol. 2: 496

Shinhan Financial Group
www.shinhangroup.com
Vol. 2: 293, 563

Venny Chung Ping Siang
LASALLE College of the Arts
www.lasalle.edu.sg
Vol. 2: 427

Venny Chung Ping Siang,
Nora Jasmine Yee
LASALLE College of the Arts
www.lasalle.edu.sg
Vol. 2: 481

Siemens AG
www.siemens.com
Vol. 2: 274

Signify Design Team
www.signify.com
Vol. 2: 231

Simple GmbH
www.simple.de
Vol. 2: 346

SimpleInfo Design
www.simpleinfo.cc
Vol. 2: 172–173, 564

Skelter Labs
www.skelterlabs.com
Vol. 2: 318–319, 332

SMAL GmbH
www.smal.de
Vol. 2: 236–237

Soda studio
www.sodastudio.nl
Vol. 2: 239, 295

Qun Song
www.yingtaihang.com
Vol. 2: 57

Catrin Sonnabend
www.catrinsonnabend.de
Vol. 2: 47

Sony Design
www.sony.net/design
Vol. 2: 393

Starship Technologies Oy
www.starship.co
Vol. 2: 269

STRICHPUNKT
www.sp.design
Vol. 2: 16–17, 565
Vol. 1: 218–219, 222–223,
230–231, 603, 604

Studio 212 Fahrenheit
www.212f.nl
Vol. 2: 110, 366–367, 381, 566

Studio Dumbar
Dept
www.studiodumbar.com
www.deptagency.com
Vol. 2: 98
Vol. 1: 128

studio NUR
www.studionur.com
Vol. 2: 116

Chia-Hui Su, Qian-Han Lin,
Min-Yin Liao, Yi-Xuan Lin
Ling Tung University
www.ltu.edu.tw
Vol. 2: 497

Ryan Sullivan, Ashton Faydenko,
Chris Hopkins
SCAD Savannah College of
Art and Design
www.scad.edu
Vol. 2: 482

Sunmi Design Center
www.sunmi.com
Vol. 2: 329

Surprise Lab.
www.surpriselab.com.tw
Vol. 2: 387, 567

T

TASS Russian News Agency
www.tass.ru
Vol. 2: 207, 208, 209

TCS Interactive
www.tcs.com/interactive
Vol. 2: 250–251, 568

Index Designers

The Techno Creatives
www.technocreatives.com
Vol. 2: 338, 341

Telekom Design
www.telekom.com
Vol. 2: 303

Tencent Music
Entertainment Group
Music User eXperience
Design Center
www.tencentmusic.com
Vol. 2: 216

Tencent Technology
(Shenzhen) Co., Ltd.
www.tencent.com
Vol. 2: 218, 238

TM
www.tm-studio.co.uk
Vol. 2: 44, 79

TOFU Studio
www.tofu.pl
Vol. 2: 41

ToThree Design
www.tothree.cn
Vol. 2: 399, 569

Tower 5
www.tower5.de
Vol. 2: 193

Trimarca AG
www.trimarca.ch
Vol. 2: 64

Lin Tsai, Lu-Hong Chen, Zhi-Yu Xu,
Jing-Wen Wang, Chen-Lin Hsieh,
Yu-Qing Song, Bo-Wei Huang,
Wen-Ying Fu
Chaoyang University of Technology
www.cyut.edu.tw
Vol. 2: 472
Vol. 1: 494–495, 611

Tubik Studio
www.tubikstudio.com
Vol. 2: 205, 570

TutkovBudkov
www.tutkovbudkov.com
Vol. 2: 30–31, 184

U
UDIT GmbH
www.udit.de
Vol. 2: 241, 289

ui/deation GmbH & Co. KG
www.uideation.com
Vol. 2: 346

UNGESTRICHEN
Büro für Kommunikationsdesign
www.ungestrichen.com
Vol. 2: 35

upside relationship
marketing GmbH
www.upside.de
Vol. 2: 330–331

User Interface Design GmbH
www.uid.com
Vol. 2: 313

V
Michaela Vargas Coronado
www.vargas-coronado.com
Vol. 2: 40
Vol. 1: 296, 613

The Visual Truth
www.visualtruth.tv
Vol. 2: 149

Vodafone Group Services GmbH
www.vodafone.com
Vol. 2: 236–237

Oliver Wurm &
Andreas Volleritsch Gbr
www.dasgrundgesetz.de
Vol. 2: 27

Botond Vörös
www.botondvoros.com
Vol. 2: 111

Vorwerk International & Co. KmG
www.thermomix.com
Vol. 2: 313

Julia Vukovic
www.juliavukovic.com
Vol. 2: 47

W
Dominik Wagenführ,
Larissa Knaupp,
Cedric Fernandez Fernandez,
Sven Schröer, Alicia Wolpers
Faculty of Design
HAWK University of
Applied Sciences and Arts
www.hawk.de
Vol. 2: 437

Demi Waldron
SCAD Savannah College of
Art and Design
www.scad.edu
www.demiwaldron.com
Vol. 2: 467

Chi Wang, Ya-Chu Chang,
Xuan-Yu Huang, Yu-Hsiu Huang,
Wei Lee
Department of Visual
Communication Design
China University of Technology
www.cute.edu.tw
Vol. 2: 441

Ding-Jyun Wang
Asia University
www.asia.edu.tw
Vol. 2: 457

Yu-Chao Wang, Shih-Ming Huang
Department of Visual
Communication Design
Shu-Te University
www.vcd.stu.edu.tw
Vol. 2: 452

WAYS GmbH
www.ways.de
Vol. 2: 325

Weis Communications GmbH
www.weis-communications.de
Vol. 2: 62–63

George Zixuan Weng, Connie Yoo,
Cynthia Shen
Art Center College of Design
www.artcenter.edu
Vol. 2: 490–491

Jui-Hung Weng, Ya-Ling Wang,
You-Ning Hou, Fang-Yu Cao
Department of Visual
Communication Design
Southern Taiwan University
of Science and Technology
www.stust.edu.tw
Vol. 2: 438

Yih-Feng Weng
School of Design
Shanghai Jiao Tong University
www.sjtu.edu.cn
Vol. 2: 454–455, 571

why do birds
www.whydobirds.de
Vol. 2: 137

Fang Wu, Xinyu Gan, Yejia Qian
Shanghai Publishing and
Printing College
www.sppc.edu.cn
Vol. 2: 446–447, 572

Rou-Wei Wu, Hsuan-Tse Kao,
Pei-Xuan Zhang, Tzu-Ting Lin
Cheng Shiu University
www.csu.edu.tw
Vol. 2: 505

Oliver Wurm &
Andreas Volleritsch Gbr
www.dasgrundgesetz.de
Vol. 2: 27

wysiwyg*
www.wysiwyg.de
Vol. 2: 265

X
Beijing Xiaomi
Mobile Software Co., Ltd.
www.mi.com
Vol. 2: 135, 276–277, 283, 298, 316, 317, 548

Y
Y.STUDIO
www.yuziji.studio
Vol. 2: 58
Vol. 1: 94

Yu-Ci Ye
Asia University
www.asia.edu.tw
Vol. 2: 456

Nora Jasmine Yee
LASALLE College of the Arts
www.lasalle.edu.sg
Vol. 2: 426

Freya Yeh
www.freyayeh.com
Vol. 2: 468–469

Mo-Li Yeh
Lunghwa University of Science
and Technology
www.lhu.edu.tw
Vol. 2: 104–105
Vol. 1: 468–469

Shenzhen Yimu
Technology Co., Ltd.
www.yimu.info
www.ecomo.io
Vol. 2: 181

Yu Hsin-Tzu
www.behance.net/
gallery/78389939/-Paper-Lion
Vol. 2: 445

Po-Ya Yu
Asia University
www.asia.edu.tw
Vol. 2: 418–419, 573

Z
Lixuan Zheng, Yingjie Xu,
Ching-Chun Lan,
Xuze Zhou, Yufan Chen
Ling Tung University
www.ltu.edu.tw
Vol. 2: 476–477

Zi Zhi, Feng Luo, Guo-Da Lin,
Kai-Qiang Hou, Xi Cheng
Fuzhou University of
International Studies and Trade
www.fzfu.com
Vol. 2: 493, 574

Jin-Lun Zhuang, Yu-Xuan Li,
Nian-En Liu, Jing-Wen Huang,
Jia-Shen Chen, Hong-Jia Zhu
Department of Visual
Communication Design
Shu-Te University
www.vcd.stu.edu.tw
Vol. 2: 442
Vol. 1: 519

zigzag GmbH
www.zigzag.is
Vol. 2: 274

ZJY (Beijing)
Tourism and Culture Co., Ltd.
www.zjart.net.cn
Vol. 2: 215, 575

ZWEIPRO
www.zweipro.de
Vol. 2: 192

Index Clients/Universities

0–9

26th Warsaw International
Poster Biennale
www.warsawposterbiennale.com
Vol. 2: 74

A

Aasted ApS
www.aasted.eu
Vol. 2: 352

adidas AG
www.adidas-group.com
Vol. 2: 401

ADITO Software GmbH
www.adito.de
Vol. 2: 324

Airbus
www.airbus.com
Vol. 2: 240

Albert Heijn
www.ah.nl
Vol. 2: 295
Vol. 1: 317

Alliance Graphique Internationale
www.a-g-i.org
Vol. 2: 6–7

alsecco GmbH
www.alsecco.de
Vol. 2: 42

Anheuser-Busch InBev Germany
www.becks.de
Vol. 2: 227

Antikensammlung
Staatliche Museen zu Berlin
www.smb.museum
Vol. 2: 386

ARD Design and Presentation
www.ard-design.de
Vol. 2: 124–125, 164–165

Art Center College of Design
www.artcenter.edu
Vol. 2: 490–491
Vol. 1: 492–493

Art Light Design Consultants, Inc.
www.artlight.com.tw
Vol. 2: 56

Asia University
www.asia.edu.tw
Vol. 2: 418–419, 453, 456, 457, 466
Vol. 1: 490–491, 508, 522, 523, 524, 530–531

AUDI AG
www.audi.de
Vol. 2: 406
Vol. 1: 464

Audi Korea
www.audi.co.kr
Vol. 2: 407, 408, 409
Vol. 1: 140

B

B'in Music International Limited
www.bin-music.com
Vol. 2: 147

Bahlsen GmbH & Co. KG
www.bahlsen.de
Vol. 2: 94–95
Vol. 1: 193

Baidu Online Network Technology
(Beijing) Co., Ltd.
www.baidu.com
Vol. 2: 296–297
Vol. 1: 32–35

Beetroot Design Group
www.beetroot.gr
Vol. 2: 115
Vol. 1: 288

Beijing Institute of
Fashion Technology
www.bift.edu.cn
Vol. 2: 22

Bergbahnen Sölden
www.soelden.com
Vol. 2: 370–371

Better
www.better.care
Vol. 2: 350

Beyond Digital Business e. K.
Vol. 2: 241, 289

BF Coach GmbH & Co. KG
www.bf-coach.de
Vol. 2: 225
Vol. 1: 90–91

Blackmagic Design
www.blackmagicdesign.com
Vol. 2: 252–253, 344–345

BMW Group
www.bmw.com
Vol. 2: 163

Bolichwerke KG
Lichttechnische Fabrik
www.bolichwerke.de
Vol. 2: 43

Bona International Cineplex
Investment and
Management Co., Ltd.
Vol. 2: 389

Robert Bosch GmbH
www.bosch.com
Vol. 2: 16–17

Brain Magazine
www.brain.com.tw
Vol. 2: 76–77

British Higher School of
Art & Design
www.britishdesign.ru
Vol. 2: 422–423

BROTLOS Verlag
www.brotlos-verlag.de
Vol. 2: 122

Bruce B.
corporate communication GmbH
www.bruce-b.com
Vol. 2: 18–19

Budapest Giftbook
www.facebook.com/
budapestgiftbook
Vol. 2: 111

Bühnen und Orchester der
Stadt Bielefeld
Rudolf-Oetker-Halle/
Konzerthaus Bielefeld
www.rudolf-oetker-halle.de
Vol. 2: 99

C

CADS Additive GmbH
www.cads.at
Vol. 2: 361

Carrefour China
www.carrefour.com.cn
Vol. 2: 238

Città di Castelfranco Veneto
www.comune.
castelfrancoveneto.tv.it
Vol. 2: 8–9

Chaoyang University of Technology
www.cyut.edu.tw
Vol. 2: 439, 440, 472
Vol. 1: 494–495, 500, 511, 528–529

Cheetah Mobile
www.cmcm.com
Vol. 2: 278

Jun-Liang Chen
FREEiMAGE DESIGN
Vol. 2: 104–105
Vol. 1: 468–469

Cheng Shiu University
www.csu.edu.tw
Vol. 2: 435, 502, 505
Vol. 1: 501

China Mobile (Hangzhou)
Information Technology
www.chinamobileltd.com
Vol. 2: 320

China University of Technology
www.cute.edu.tw
Vol. 2: 420–421, 434, 441, 506, 507
Vol. 1: 503, 506–507, 514, 517, 527, 534–535

CHUV
Lausanne University Hospital
www.chuv.ch
Vol. 2: 14–15

Clariant International Ltd.
www.clariant.com
Vol. 2: 339
Vol. 1: 228

Clas Ohlson
www.clasohlson.com
Vol. 2: 235, 271

Closer
www.facebook.com/closerkiev
Vol. 2: 140–141
Vol. 1: 88–89

The Coca-Cola Company
www.coca-cola.ua
Vol. 2: 392

Communication University
of Zhejiang
www.zjicm.edu.cn
Vol. 2: 70–71

Continental AG
www.continental-corporation.com
Vol. 2: 151

COPRO Sales & Services GmbH
www.copro-gruppe.de
Vol. 2: 33

Coronado Design
www.vargas-coronado.com
Vol. 2: 40

Costes Restaurant
www.costes.hu
Vol. 2: 116

D

Daimler AG
smart
www.daimler.com
Vol. 2: 340

DB Privat- und
Firmenkundenbank AG
Digital Factory
www.deutsche-bank.de
Vol. 2: 290–291

DeepL GmbH
www.deepl.com
Vol. 2: 188–189, 266–267

Dematic GmbH
www.dematic.com
Vol. 2: 346

Dentsply Sirona
Deutschland GmbH
www.dentsplysirona.com
Vol. 2: 347

Dentsu Aegis Network
www.dentsuaegisnetwork.com
Vol. 2: 150

Design Academy Eindhoven
www.designacademy.nl
Vol. 2: 483

Deutsche Bahn
DB Fernverkehr AG
www.deutschebahn.com
Vol. 2: 286–287

Deutsche Telekom AG
www.telekom.com
Vol. 2: 303, 330–331
Vol. 1: 28–31

Publishing & Print Media Posters Typography Illustrations Sound Design Film & Animation Online Apps

Index Clients / Universities

Ding Ding Co., Ltd.
www.facebook.com/DingDingYYXL
Vol. 2: 102

DKMS gemeinnützige GmbH
www.dkms.de
Vol. 2: 176

Aloys F. Dornbracht GmbH & Co. KG
www.dornbracht.com
Vol. 2: 257, 391

Dot Incorporation
www.dotincorp.com
Vol. 2: 170–171, 268

Dott
www.ridedott.com
Vol. 2: 239

DR – The Danish Broadcasting
Corporation
www.dr.dk
Vol. 2: 97

E
ECARX Co., Ltd.
www.ecarx.com.cn
Vol. 2: 308

The Edrington Group
www.edrington.com
Vol. 2: 374–375

Social Municipality of Eleusis
www.aisxylia.gr
Vol. 2: 84
Vol. 1: 163

Ergon Food
www.ergonfoods.com
Vol. 2: 114

Expormim
www.expormim.com
Vol. 2: 196

Exterion Media Netherlands
www.exterionmedia.com
Vol. 2: 98

F
Farmrise
www.climate.com/climate-farmrise
Vol. 2: 314

FAW-Volkswagen
www.faw-vw.com
Vol. 2: 137

Fedrigoni UK
www.fedrigoni.co.uk
Vol. 2: 44, 79

FH JOANNEUM
University of Applied Sciences
www.fh-joanneum.at
Vol. 2: 429, 430, 431, 436, 448,
449, 462, 463, 465
Vol. 1: 512

Finanz Informatik
www.f-i.de
Vol. 2: 129, 404

Finnair Oyj
www.finnair.com
Vol. 2: 288

FishAct e.V.
www.2048.fishact.org
Vol. 2: 180

Fisher & Paykel
www.fisherpaykel.com
Vol. 2: 37
Vol. 1: 457

Flatfy OÜ
www.flatfy.com
Vol. 2: 229, 270

Frankfurter Allgemeine
Zeitung GmbH
www.faz.net
Vol. 2: 47

Fresenius Medical Care GmbH
Deutschland
www.freseniusmedicalcare.com
Vol. 2: 48

Fritz-Effekt
Unternehmerberatung GmbH
www.leadership-audit.de
Vol. 2: 325

FUJIFILM Corporation
www.fujifilm.com
Vol. 2: 351

Fuzhou University of
International Studies and Trade
www.fzfu.com
Vol. 2: 458, 459, 460–461, 493

G
Gamesa Gearbox
www.gamesagearbox.com
Vol. 2: 28–29

Generali Deutschland AG
www.generali.de
Vol. 2: 87, 128, 194
Vol. 1: 170

German Federal Ministry of
Education and Research
www.bmbf.de
Vol. 2: 378–379

Fotografie Brigida González
www.brigidagonzalez.de
Vol. 2: 203

Google
https://store.google.com
Vol. 2: 186–187

Great Apes/HiQ Finland
www.greatapes.fi
Vol. 2: 191

Grön Ungdom
www.gronungdom.se
Vol. 2: 24

Province of Groningen
www.provinciegroningen.nl
Vol. 2: 381

Wuhan Guanshanjue
Culture Media Co., Ltd.
www.guanshanjue.com
Vol. 2: 59

Gürzenich Orchester Köln
www.guerzenich-orchester.de
Vol. 2: 51

Gutenberg-Museum
www.gutenberg-museum.de
Vol. 2: 100, 101

gwk Gesellschaft Wärme
Kältetechnik mbH
www.gwk.com
Vol. 2: 353

Gymnasieskolernes Lærerforening
www.gymnasieskolen.dk
Vol. 2: 46

H
Haier Group
www.haier.com
Vol. 2: 310, 311, 315

Hamburger Hochbahn AG
www.hochbahn.de
Vol. 2: 285

Hansung University
www.hansung.ac.kr
Vol. 2: 486–487

Haufe Akademie GmbH & Co. KG
www.haufe-akademie.de
Vol. 2: 148

HAWK University of
Applied Sciences and Arts
Faculty of Design
www.hawk.de
Vol. 2: 428, 437

Hegii Co., Ltd.
www.hegii.com
Vol. 2: 96

HEIWA Paper Co., Ltd.
www.heiwapaper.co.jp
Vol. 2: 78, 143

Hochschule Mainz
Fachbereich Gestaltung
www.hs-mainz.de
www.theworldswritingsystems.org
Vol. 2: 265

Home Hotel
www.homehotel.com.tw
Vol. 2: 387

Hsinchu City Government
www.hccg.gov.tw
Vol. 2: 396–397
Vol. 1: 437

Huawei Technologies Co., Ltd.
www.huawei.com
Vol. 2: 254–255, 323, 334, 335

Hyundai Motor Europe
Technical Center GmbH
www.hmetc.com
Vol. 2: 306–307

I
i.d.a.-Dachverband e.V.
Dachverband
deutschsprachiger Lesben-/
Frauenarchive, -bibliotheken
und -dokumentationsstellen
www.ida-dachverband.de
Vol. 2: 206

IBM Cloud
www.ibm.com/cloud
Vol. 2: 327

Icelandic Museum of
Natural History
www.nmsi.is
Vol. 2: 246–247

inDare Design Strategy Limited
www.indare.love
Vol. 2: 103

Sergio Ingravalle
www.maivisto.de
Vol. 2: 120–121

Interactive Media
Foundation gGmbH
Filmtank GmbH
www.interactivemedia-
foundation.com
www.dastotaletanztheater.com
Vol. 2: 261, 368–369

Interactive Pioneers
www.interactive-pioneers.de
Vol. 2: 174–175

Invitro
www.invitro.ru
Vol. 2: 177

IP Deutschland GmbH
www.ip.de
Vol. 2: 49

J
Jiangsu Folk Literature and
Art Association Creation Base
Vol. 2: 68–69

K
Stadt Karlsruhe
www.karlsruhe.de
Vol. 2: 380

Kerber Verlag
www.kerberverlag.com
Vol. 2: 21

Index Clients / Universities

Verlag Kettler
www.verlag-kettler.de
Vol. 2: 34

Kia Motors Europe GmbH
www.kia.com
Vol. 2: 199

King Kong Wave Production
www.facebook.com/kingkongwave
Vol. 2: 387

Kitcast Inc.
www.kitcast.tv
Vol. 2: 328

Klim Type Foundry
www.klim.co.nz
Vol. 2: 385

KLM Royal Dutch Airlines
www.klm.com
Vol. 2: 198, 284

KOCH Pac-Systeme GmbH
www.koch-pac-systeme.com
Vol. 2: 358–359

Koelnmesse
www.koelnmesse.com
Vol. 2: 342

De Koninklijke Nederlandsche
Wielren Unie (KNWU)
www.knwu.nl
Vol. 2: 305

kontrastmoment GmbH
www.kontrastmoment.de
Vol. 2: 388

Koorbiënnale
www.koorbiennale.nl
Vol. 2: 85

KOSTAL Industrie Elektrik GmbH
www.kostal-industrie-elektrik.com
Vol. 2: 234

KRELL Automotive
www.krellautomotive.com
Vol. 2: 154–155, 200–201

Kyowon
Wells Design Lab
www.kyowonwells.com
Vol. 2: 309

L

Landestheater Detmold GmbH
www.landestheater-detmold.de
Vol. 2: 202

LASALLE College of the Arts
www.lasalle.edu.sg
Vol. 2: 412–415, 426, 427, 481

The Legacy Museum
https://museumandmemorial.eji.org
Vol. 2: 108

Leica Camera AG
www.leica-camera.com
Vol. 2: 282

Leopard Mobile
www.cmcm.com
Vol. 2: 279

Sylvia Lerch Material & Produktion
www.sylvialerch.de
Vol. 2: 52

LG Electronics Inc.
www.lg.com
Vol. 2: 264, 299, 304, 312, 333
Vol. 1: 454–455

LG Uplus
www.uplus.co.kr
Vol. 2: 217, 220–221, 222–223

Ling Tung University
www.ltu.edu.tw
Vol. 2: 424, 450, 476–477, 492, 496, 497, 498, 504
Vol. 1: 488–489, 532, 533

Lions at Work – conmoto
www.conmoto.com
Vol. 2: 35

Lithuanian Artists' Association
www.ldsajunga.lt
Vol. 2: 10–11

Local bendi
www.yingtaihang.com
Vol. 2: 57

Logitech
www.logitech.com
Vol. 2: 157, 158

M

m.Doc GmbH
www.mdoc.one
Vol. 2: 178–179

M.Y. inženiring d.o.o.
www.wine-advent-calendar.com
Vol. 2: 39

MAGENWIRTH Technologies GmbH
www.magura.com
Vol. 2: 25

Make Architects
www.makearchitects.com
Vol. 2: 32

Media Evolution
Southern Sweden AB
www.mediaevolution.se
Vol. 2: 134

METER Group Inc.
www.metergroup.com
Vol. 2: 12–13

Metsä Group
www.metsagroup.com
Vol. 2: 248–249, 376

MJR Melanie JeanRichard
Mediterrane Blumen
www.melaniejeanrichard.ch
Vol. 2: 23

Moët Hennessy Taiwan
Jas Hennessy (Far East) Ltd.,
Taiwan Branch
www.lvmh.com
Vol. 2: 159

Monotype
www.monotype.com
Vol. 2: 92–93

muehlhausmoers corporate
communications gmbh
www.muehlhausmoers.com
Vol. 2: 61

Museum of Failure, Inc.
www.museumoffailure.com
Vol. 2: 82
Vol. 1: 157

Must App Corp.
www.mustapp.com
Vol. 2: 219

N

The National Museum in Gdańsk
www.mng.gda.pl
Vol. 2: 41

National Taichung University
of Science and Technology
www.nutc.edu.tw
Vol. 2: 432, 499
Vol. 1: 438

National Taiwan University
of Science and Technology
www.ntust.edu.tw
Vol. 2: 466
Vol. 1: 509, 515, 520, 521

NAVER Business Platform Corp.
www.ncloud.com
Vol. 2: 336–337

New York Road Runners
www.nyrr.org
Vol. 2: 250–251

NFSQ
www.yst.com.cn
Vol. 2: 400

O

OLX
www.olx.ua
Vol. 2: 161

Opera Software AS
www.opera.com
Vol. 2: 262–263

Osterrath GmbH & Co. KG
www.osterrath.de
Vol. 2: 86

Österreichisches Staatsarchiv
www.oesta.gv.at
Vol. 2: 210

P

PAL – U-Werk Karoline GmbH
www.pal-tv.de
Vol. 2: 50

Gabor Palotai Design
www.gaborpalotai.com
Vol. 2: 117

PAO Sberbank of Russia
www.sberbank.ru
Vol. 2: 243

PASHA Insurance OJSC
www.pasha-insurance.az
Vol. 2: 195

Penghu National Scenic
Area Administration
Tourism Bureau
www.penghu-nsa.gov.tw
Vol. 2: 384

PENNY-Markt GmbH
www.penny.de
Vol. 2: 162

Philips
www.philips.com
Vol. 2: 230, 233
Vol. 1: 36–39

pics4peace e.V.
www.pics4peace.de
Vol. 2: 182

Pilzgarten GmbH
www.pilzgarten.de
Vol. 2: 38

Pingtung County Government
www.pthg.gov.tw
Vol. 2: 382–383

Pohjolan Voima
www.pohjolanvoima.fi
Vol. 2: 26

Dr. Ing. h.c. F. Porsche AG
www.porsche.com
Vol. 2: 136
Vol. 1: 237

The Post of Finland
www.posti.fi
Vol. 2: 54–55

Pratt Institute
www.pratt.edu
Vol. 2: 485

Puma Hong Kong Ltd.
www.puma.com
Vol. 2: 65

Marcell Puskás
www.behance.net/puskaas
Vol. 2: 45

Index Clients / Universities

Q
Quinsay
www.quinsaydesign.com
Vol. 2: 90–91

R
Taiwan RE-THINK Environmental
Education Association
www.rethinktw.org
Vol. 2: 172–173

Reggeborgh Investment &
Management GmbH
www.reggeborgh.de
Vol. 2: 36

RKW Architektur +
Rhode Kellermann
Wawrowsky GmbH
www.rkw.plus
Vol. 2: 192

Roca Sanitario, S.A
www.roca.es
Vol. 2: 394–395
Vol. 1: 266–267

RT
www.rt.com
Vol. 2: 258–259

Mediengruppe RTL
Deutschland GmbH
www.mediengruppe-rtl.de
Vol. 2: 167

S
Salvagnini Group
www.salvagninigroup.com
Vol. 2: 354–355

Samsung C&T
Everland Resort
www.samsungcnt.com
Vol. 2: 226

Samsung Electronics
www.samsung.com
Vol. 2: 127, 152–153, 156, 190, 214,
343, 390
Vol. 1: 269

Samsung SDS
www.samsungsds.com
Vol. 2: 321

Jingdezhen Sanbao
Ceramic Institute
Vol. 2: 112

Sandvik
Applied Manufacturing
Technologies
www.home.sandvik
Vol. 2: 360

SAP SE
www.sap.com
Vol. 2: 224, 300, 301

SARAM – Stiftung für
Menschenrechte in Nordkorea
www.saram-nk.org
Vol. 2: 75
Vol. 1: 169

Sartorius Corporate
Administration GmbH
www.sartorius.com
Vol. 2: 348–349

Save the children
www.sc.or.kr
Vol. 2: 183

SCAD Savannah College of
Art and Design
www.scad.edu
Vol. 2: 443, 451, 464, 467, 470, 471,
473, 474, 475, 480, 482, 484, 488,
489, 494, 495
Vol. 1: 486–487, 502

Pius Schäfler AG
www.piusschaefler.ch
Vol. 2: 64

Stahlstich & Prägedruck
Martin Schall GmbH
www.schall-drucktechnik.de
Vol. 2: 52

Schenck Process Europe GmbH
www.schenckprocess.com
Vol. 2: 362–363

Hanns Schmid Publishers
www.hannsschmid.ch
Vol. 2: 80

SCHOTT AG
www.schott.com
Vol. 2: 193

Lars Schrage – buero fuer
gestaltung
www.schragelars.eu
Vol. 2: 433

SCM Group S.p.A.
www.scmgroup.com
Vol. 2: 356–357

SCP Grey Sweden
www.grey.com/sweden
Vol. 2: 341

Self Club
www.selfclub.ru
Vol. 2: 83
Vol. 1: 148–149

Serviceplan Group
www.serviceplan.com
Vol. 2: 60

SETTV
www.settv.com.tw
Vol. 2: 146

Shanghai Jiao Tong University
www.sjtu.edu.cn
Vol. 2: 454–455

Shanghai Publishing and
Printing College
www.sppc.edu.cn
Vol. 2: 446–447, 478–479

Shinhan Financial Group
www.shinhangroup.com
Vol. 2: 293

Shu-Te University
www.stu.edu.tw
Vol. 2: 416–417, 425, 442, 444,
452, 500, 503
Vol. 1: 516, 519

Siemens AG
www.siemens.com
Vol. 2: 274

Signify
www.signify.com
Vol. 2: 231

Simon Consulting
www.futureofleadership.salon
Vol. 2: 402

Sinotea Co., Ltd.
Vol. 2: 58

SK Networks Co., Ltd.
www.sknetworks.co.kr
Vol. 2: 272–273

skantherm GmbH & Co. KG
www.skantherm.de
Vol. 2: 197

Skelter Labs
www.skelterlabs.com
Vol. 2: 318–319, 332

Skillbox
www.skillbox.ru
Vol. 2: 185

Smartum
www.smartum.fi
Vol. 2: 123

Sony
www.playstation.com
Vol. 2: 184

Sony Corporation
www.sony.net
Vol. 2: 393

Southern Taiwan University
of Science and Technology
www.stust.edu.tw
Vol. 2: 438

Spireworks
www.spireworks.org
Vol. 2: 403

StadtPalais – Museum for Stuttgart
www.stadtpalais-stuttgart.de
Vol. 2: 132–133

Starship Technologies Oy
www.starship.co
Vol. 2: 269

Stedelijk Museum Breda
www.stedelijkmuseumbreda.nl
Vol. 2: 211

STIEBEL ELTRON GmbH & Co. KG
www.stiebel-eltron.com
Vol. 2: 232

Studio 212 Fahrenheit
www.212f.nl
Vol. 2: 110, 366–367

Shanghai Sunmi
Technology Co., Ltd.
www.sunmi.com
Vol. 2: 329

Surprise Lab.
www.surpriselab.com.tw
Vol. 2: 387

Sveriges Television AB
Kunskapskanalen
www.kunskapskanalen.se
Vol. 2: 166

T
TASS Russian News Agency
www.tass.ru
Vol. 2: 207, 208, 209

Tencent Music
Entertainment Group
Music User eXperience
Design Center
www.tencentmusic.com
http://moo.qq.com
Vol. 2: 216

Tencent Technology
(Shenzhen) Co., Ltd.
www.tencent.com
Vol. 2: 218

The Best Metro Station Committee
Shanghai Academy of
Fine Arts (SAFA)
www.arts.shu.edu.cn
Vol. 2: 501

Thessaloniki Film Festival
www.filmfestival.gr
Vol. 2: 72–73, 142
Vol. 1: 86–87

Thingvellir National Park
www.thingvellir.is
Vol. 2: 109, 256

Tongrentang Health
www.tongrentang.com
Vol. 2: 399

Tourismus+Congress GmbH
Frankfurt am Main (TCF)
www.frankfurt-tourismus.de
Vol. 2: 372–373

Tretyakov Gallery
www.tretyakovgallery.ru
Vol. 2: 20

Triënnale Brugge
www.triennalebrugge.be
Vol. 2: 377

Tubik Studio
www.tubikstudio.com
Vol. 2: 205

TURKCELL Iletisim Hizmetleri A.S.
www.turkcell.com.tr
Vol. 2: 405

Index Clients / Universities

U

Upon You Records
www.uponyou-records.com
Vol. 2: 118–119, 144–145

URALCHEM Group
www.uralchem.com
Vol. 2: 30–31

V

Van Gogh Museum
www.vangoghmuseum.nl
Vol. 2: 260

Verein zur Förderung
akzeptierender Jugendarbeit
www.vaja-bremen.de
Vol. 2: 149

VHV Allgemeine Versicherung AG
www.vhv.de
Vol. 2: 326

Visa International
www.visa.com
Vol. 2: 292

Vodafone Group Services GmbH
www.vodafone.com
Vol. 2: 236–237

Vodafone Kabel
Deutschland GmbH
https://kabel.vodafone.de
Vol. 2: 302

Volkswagen AG
www.volkswagenag.com
Vol. 2: 322
Vol. 1: 264

Volkswagen China
www.vw.com.cn
Vol. 2: 137

Oliver Wurm &
Andreas Volleritsch Gbr
www.dasgrundgesetz.de
Vol. 2: 27

Volvo Car Germany GmbH
www.volvocars.com
Vol. 2: 242

Volvo Group Connected Solutions
www.volvogroup.com
Vol. 2: 338

Vorwerk International & Co. KmG
www.thermomix.com
Vol. 2: 313

W

Wacom Europe GmbH
www.wacom.com
Vol. 2: 126
Vol. 1: 64–65

Warner Music Group
www.wmg.com
Vol. 2: 204, 275

Weis Communications GmbH
www.weis-communications.de
Vol. 2: 62–63

Wirecard Issuing
Technologies GmbH
www.beboon.com
Vol. 2: 294

Wirtschaftskammer Vorarlberg
Sparte Tourismus +
Freizeitwirtschaft
www.wkv.at
Vol. 2: 53

Beijing Wtown
www.wtown.com
Vol. 2: 215

Oliver Wurm &
Andreas Volleritsch Gbr
www.dasgrundgesetz.de
Vol. 2: 27

WÜSTHOF GmbH
www.wuesthof.com
Vol. 2: 398

X

Xiaomi Corporation
www.mi.com
Vol. 2: 160

Beijing Xiaomi
Mobile Software Co., Ltd.
www.mi.com
Vol. 2: 135, 276–277, 283, 298, 316, 317

Y

Freya Yeh
www.freyayeh.com
Vol. 2: 468–469

Shenzhen Yimu
Technology Co., Ltd.
www.yimu.info
www.ecomo.io
Vol. 2: 181

YoungOnes
www.youngones.works
Vol. 2: 228

Shanghai Yue Restaurant
Vol. 2: 113

Z

Carl Zeiss AG
www.zeiss.com
Vol. 2: 280–281

Zhejiang Gongshang University
www.zjgsu.edu.cn
Vol. 2: 81

Red Dot Design Award
The worldwide platform for evaluating good design

With its origins dating back to 1955 and being led by Professor Dr. Peter Zec since 1991, the Red Dot Award offers a platform for evaluating the quality of design. In order to cope with the diversity in this field, Red Dot is hosting three different competitions, each of which is organised annually and divided into further categories. Manufacturers and designers can submit their industrial products to the Red Dot Award: Product Design, while visions and prototypes are in the spotlight of the Red Dot Award: Design Concept. And the Red Dot Award: Brands & Communication Design is open for brands as well as for creative works and projects. In 2019, designers, manufacturers, brands, agencies and companies from more than 70 countries submitted over 18,000 projects from a varied range of industries. Only entries which convinced the Red Dot Juries were awarded with the internationally coveted Red Dot seal for good design quality.

In search of good design
Design is a worldwide business with transnational relationships. Consequently, it has to be evaluated from a global point of view and with a comprehensive expertise. This is why Red Dot annually appoints designers, professors and specialised journalists from around the world to form the juries. With their special know-how, cultural background and experience, the experts can take the specifics of the projects' origin and target markets into account when evaluating them. Furthermore, the adjudication follows a canon of strict criteria and each entry is tested, discussed and evaluated individually and on its own merits, since the submissions do not compete with each other.

reddot design museum

Red Dot Jury 2019

Design promotion at an international level
"Qualifying by selecting and presenting" – following this leitmotif, Red Dot presents the projects which were selected by the juries, among others, in the Red Dot Design Museums, online and in publications, thus imparting a broad public the value of good design. This way, companies and designers as well as consumers become qualified. As an evaluation platform for state-of-the-art design accomplishments, the Red Dot Award identifies the most prominent trends worldwide and provides orientation in a market that is becoming increasingly complex. Furthermore, it also creates and advances differentiation as Red Dot awarded projects rank among the best in their respective field.

Red Dot Award: Brands & Communication Design
With more than 25 years of experience, the Red Dot Award: Brands & Communication Design finds the best achievements from 54 participating countries today. The competition is geared to designers, agencies and companies from around the world, and since 2019 also to brands. This is why the competition breaks down into the "Brands" section, in which companies are invited to submit their holistic brand communication, and into the "Communication Design" section, in which all participants can enter individual projects. Emerging creatives are also encouraged to prove their design quality and put their achievements to the test. As part of the Red Dot Award: Brands & Communication Design, the Red Dot: Junior Award is intended for trainees, students and young professionals, who have graduated within the last two years. They run the chance to be awarded with the Red Dot: Junior Prize. It goes to the best work submitted by a young designer and is endowed with a prize money of 10,000 euros.

In search of design quality and creative achievement
From automotive to medical & healthcare sector to telecommunication and from advertising campaigns to fair stands to online projects, in 2019 there were 36 industries available for participating in the "Brands" section and 17 categories for entering the "Communication Design" section. To recognise the international nature and diversity of the projects entered, the jury was equally diverse, with 24 experts from different specialist areas and countries. Over several days, they evaluated the brands and projects individually and on site, taking various evaluation criteria into account. In the field of "Communication Design", these include originality and creativity, design quality and innovation as well as comprehensibility and emotional significance. When assessing the brands, the experts pay attention to vision and brand values, design and brand communication as well as brand identity and differentiation. The intensive scrutiny and critical exchange between the jury members allow for a well-founded final decision. Only brands and works which convince with their overall design quality and creative achievement receive an award.

Celebrating design excellence
The grand finale for the Red Dot Award: Brands & Communication Design takes place in Berlin, where the laureates are duly honoured at the award ceremony. The Red Dot Gala unites the international design scene at the Konzerthaus Berlin in Germany's capital. The festivities continue at the Designers' Night where the design scene celebrates the successes of the year and enjoys the winners' exhibition.

Publishing & Print Media   Posters   Typography   Illustrations   Sound Design   Film & Animation   Online   Apps

Red Dot Design Museum Essen

Communication design in Essen: exhibition of award-winning works

Red Dot Design Museums
Fascinating exhibition forums at three venues worldwide

Every year, design experts from all over the world evaluate the entries of the Red Dot Award and ultimately decide which earn the Red Dot seal of quality and thus their deserved place in the Red Dot Design Museums. The best products, brands, communication works and design concepts are presented to an international audience in the museums in Essen, Germany, in Singapore and in Xiamen, China.

Unparalleled exploratorium for good design
Being the first of all Red Dot Design Museums, the venue in Essen is both the home of the Red Dot Award and the largest exhibition of contemporary design worldwide. Approximately 2,000 international, Red Dot awarded products are presented in the former boiler house of the Zollverein Coal Mine Industrial Complex. In order to meet the requirements of a presentation forum, it was redesigned by high-profile British architect Lord Norman Foster. The museum's unique atmosphere is created by the contrast between the old and the new, between historical industrial architecture and latest product culture. As part of the UNESCO World Heritage Site, the Red Dot Design Museum Essen attracts a lot of attention. Throughout the exhibition year, 150,000 international guests experience Red Dot awarded products. Furthermore, the top achievements of the international communication design scene are showcased during a multi-week special exhibition with the latest prize-winning works, thus completing the insight into the current developments of the creative industry.

Red Dot Design Museum Singapore

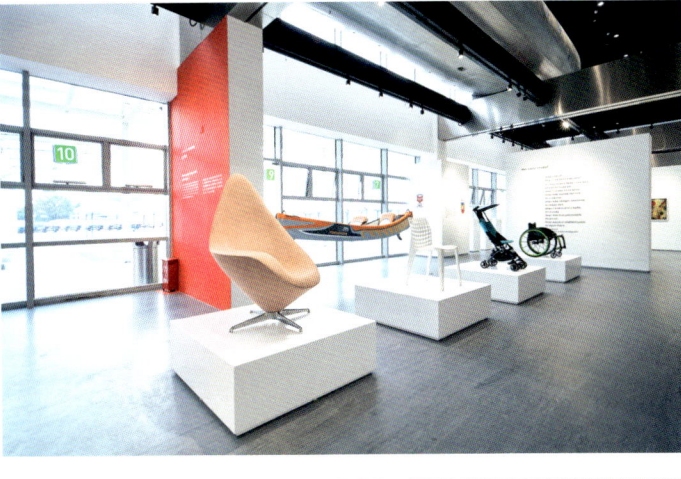

Red Dot Design Museum Xiamen

Creative hotspot at Marina Bay

The Red Dot Design Museum Singapore provides another exclusive venue for the design scene and its creative works. It is located at the Marina Bay Waterfront Promenade, one of the city's most prestigious addresses. Being the home of the Red Dot Award: Design Concept, the museum presents the concepts and prototypes that received a prize in this competition. Thus, it provides an inspiring insight into the future of our world of products and design. The Red Dot Design Museum Singapore was the first contemporary design museum in Asia and is considered to be one of the top design museums. With its visionary orientation, it also showcases a selection of the Red Dot awarded products and communication designs, attracting around 110,000 visitors every year.

New exhibition venue in South China

In 2018, a new Red Dot Design Museum opened its doors in Terminal 2 of Xiamen Gaoqi Airport. Thus, the exhibition space is located in the centre of the action of one of China's most promising design-oriented and economic regions. Xiamen is both a popular tourism destination as well as a much-frequented trade fair and congress metropolis. Since 2012, the city of Xiamen and Red Dot are in a close relationship. Among others, selected award-winners are presented to the more than 300,000 visitors of the Xiamen International Design Week in a huge exhibition every year. The opening of the Red Dot Design Museum Xiamen intensifies Red Dot's engagement in China, where the awareness of good design is continuously increasing. The new Red Dot Design Museum serves as a platform for communicating about design and business, thus further boosting international cooperations.

Its exhibitions aim to provide companies, designers and the broad public with background knowledge about design and its potential as a business factor.

Design inspiration around the globe

Whether in Essen, Singapore, Xiamen or in special and travelling exhibitions around the globe – enabling visitors to experience good design quality at first hand is the purpose of Red Dot's exhibitions. That is why touching and testing many of the exhibited products, brands, communication works and design concepts is allowed, thus making the Red Dot Design Museums unparalleled design exploratoriums and sources of inspiration.

Publishing & Print Media   Posters   Typography   Illustrations   Sound Design   Film & Animation   Online   Apps

Red Dot Services

Red Dot Services
Winner shop and edition

Red Dot Winner Shop
If you want to stay up to date with the latest developments in product and communication design, then there is no better way than to review the Red Dot yearbooks and other reference works on the subject. The easiest way to find and order these and other Red Dot communication materials, such as winner's certificates, stickers, acrylic holders, etc., is through www.myreddot.de. The winner shop allows those interested in design to browse at their leisure and to order both the volumes of the Red Dot Design Yearbook 2019/2020 and the International Yearbook Brands & Communication Design 2019/2020, as well as previous years' editions and other reference books. Moreover, beautiful coffee-table books on design and further Red Dot products that also make good presents, such as the annual Design Diary, can be ordered directly and around the clock without having to visit a retail store.

Red Dot Edition
The yearbooks on the Red Dot Design Award document the latest developments and trends in the industry. For many years now, they have been widely regarded as international reference works for outstanding design. The on-site publishing house, Red Dot Edition, is a specialist publisher dedicated entirely to the topic of design. So far, a total of around 200 titles have been published by Red Dot Edition. In addition to the yearbooks on the competition, the publisher's range includes sociological and economic analyses on the topic of design, compilations of the industry's Who's Who and the annual bestseller, the Design Diary.

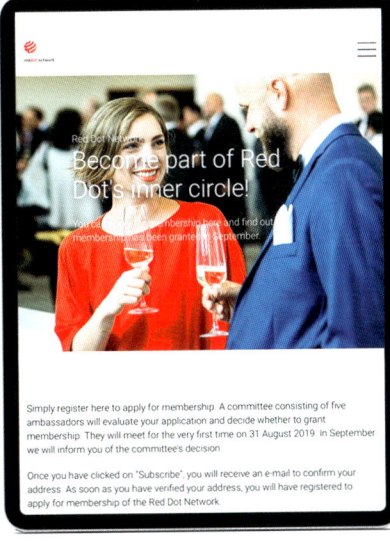
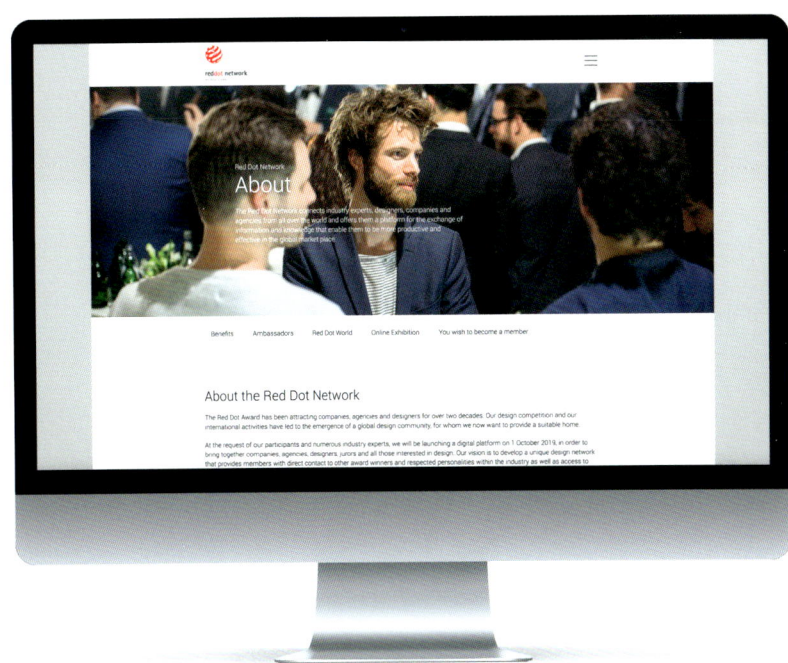

A digital network for the global design community

Red Dot Network

The Red Dot Network is a new digital design platform that has been bringing together companies, agencies, designers, jury members and design enthusiasts from across the world since 1 October 2019. Network members can make contact directly with other award-winners or leading lights in the field and are able to take advantage of numerous exclusive services.

Among these, for example, is access to the Red Dot Winners from 2011 to 2019 of the Red Dot Awards and the opportunity to gain insights into selected research and lectures. In addition, members receive benefits when participating in the Red Dot competition, gain free entry to the Red Dot Design Museums in Essen, Singapore and Xiamen, enjoy preferential treatment when booking tickets for events organised by Red Dot, and can also purchase Red Dot Edition publications at a discount.

reddot edition

Editor
Peter Zec

Project supervision
Vito Oražem

Project and editorial management
Sophie Angerer

Editorial work
Kirsten Müller (supervision), Essen, Germany
Mareike Ahlborn, Essen, Germany
Bettina Derksen, Simmern, Germany
Karin Kirch, Essen, Germany
Bettina Laustroer, Wuppertal, Germany
Astrid Ruta, Essen, Germany
Marie-Christine Sassenberg, Essen, Germany
Regina Schier, Essen, Germany
Martina Stein, Otterberg, Germany
Corinna Ten-Cate, Wetter, Germany

"Red Dot: Agency of the Year"
Dr. Stefanie Roenneke, Bochum, Germany

Statement "Red Dot: Junior Prize"
Bettina Schulz, Munich, Germany

Translation
Heike Bors-Eberlein, Tokyo, Japan
Stanislaw Eberlein, Tokyo, Japan
Bill Kings, Wuppertal, Germany
Kocarek GmbH, Essen, Germany
Tara Russell, Dublin, Ireland
Regina Schier, Essen, Germany
Philippa Watts, Exeter, Great Britain

Proofreading
Klaus Dimmler (supervision), Essen, Germany
Mareike Ahlborn, Essen, Germany
Jörg Arnke, Essen, Germany
Dawn Michelle d'Atri, Kirchhundem, Germany
Bill Kings, Wuppertal, Germany
Karin Kirch, Essen, Germany
Regina Schier, Essen, Germany
SPRACHENWERFT GmbH, Hamburg, Germany
Philippa Watts, Exeter, Great Britain

Project assistance
Claudia Auerswald, Jess Chen, Birthe Herder,
René Klügling, Anja Lakomski, Jiyoun Lee,
Yen-Ming Lin, Judith Lindner, Louisa Mücher,
Lena Poteralla, Tobias Schmidt, Yiming Zeng,
Romina Zimmer

Layout
Lockstoff Design GmbH, Meerbusch, Germany
Nicole Slink (supervision)
Christina Jörres
Alica Kern
Katja Kleefeld
Alexandra Korschefsky
Alina Laase
Thorsten Renken
Saskia Rühmkorf

Cover/Chapter openers
Typography
Murmure, Paris, France (design & art direction)
Jérémy Landes, Studio Triple, Paris, France (type design)

Implementation
Lockstoff Design GmbH, Meerbusch, Germany

Photographs
Masaharu Hatta, Vol.1, page 586
Franziska Kranz, Vol.1, page 576
Anna Staneviciene, Vol.2, page 520

Jury photographs
eventfotograf.in (Schuchrat Kurbanov,
Alex Muchnik), Essen, Germany

Company photographs

Production
gelb+, Düsseldorf, Germany
Bernd Reinkens

Lithography
gelb+, Düsseldorf, Germany
Bernd Reinkens (supervision)
Wurzel Medien GmbH, Düsseldorf, Germany
Jonas Mühlenweg

Printing
Dr. Cantz'sche Druckerei Medien GmbH,
Esslingen, Germany

Bookbindery
Conzella Verlagsbuchbinderei, Pfarrkirchen, Germany

International Yearbook Brands & Communication Design 2019/2020
ISBN: 978-3-89939-218-0

© 2019/2020 Red Dot GmbH & Co. KG

The competition "Red Dot Award: Brands & Communication Design" is the continuation of the "Red Dot Award: Communication Design" and "German Prize for Communication Design". The "International Yearbook Brands & Communication Design" is the continuation of the "International Yearbook Communication Design" and "red dot communication design yearbook".

All rights reserved, especially those of translation. No liability is accepted for the completeness of the information.

Publisher + worldwide distribution
Red Dot GmbH & Co. KG
Gelsenkirchener Str. 181
45309 Essen, Germany
Book publisher ID no. 13674 (Börsenverein Frankfurt)

Red Dot Edition
Design Publisher
Sabine Wöll
Phone +49 201 81418 22
Fax +49 201 81418 195
E-mail edition@red-dot.de
www.red-dot-edition.com

Bibliographic information published by the Deutsche Nationalbibliothek
The Deutsche Nationalbibliothek lists this publication in the Deutsche Nationalbibliografie; detailed bibliographic data are available in the Internet at http://dnb.ddb.de